SCOTT FORESMAN

READING STREET

COMMON CORE 

Program Authors

Peter Afflerbach
Camille Blachowicz
Candy Dawson Boyd
Elena Izquierdo
Connie Juel
Edward Kame'enui
Donald Leu
Jeanne R. Paratore
P. David Pearson
Sam Sebesta
Deborah Simmons
Susan Watts Taffe
Alfred Tatum
Sharon Vaughn
Karen Kring Wixson

Glenview, Illinois

Boston, Massachusetts

Chandler, Arizona

Upper Saddle River, New Jersey

We dedicate Reading Street to
Peter Jovanovich.

His wisdom, courage,
and passion for education
are an inspiration to us all.

The Acknowledgments page appears in the back of the book immediately following the Oral Vocabulary section and constitutes an extension of this copyright page.

PEARSON

ISBN-13: 978-0-328-72526-7
ISBN-10: 0-328-72526-9
1 2 3 4 5 6 7 8 9 10 V064 16 15 14 13 12

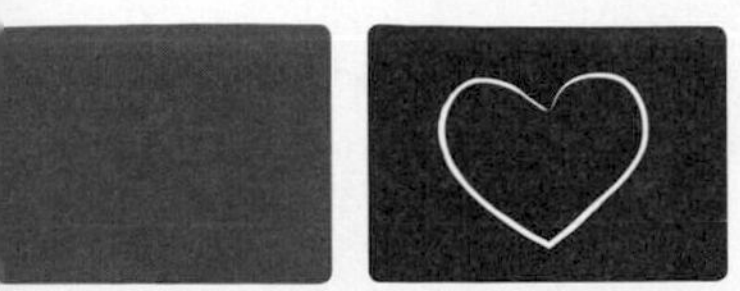

Program Authors

Peter Afflerbach, Ph.D.
Professor; Department of Curriculum and Instruction, University of Maryland; College Park, Maryland
Areas of Expertise: Common Core State Standards English Language Arts Work Team, Assessment, and Comprehension

Camille L. Z. Blachowicz, Ph.D.
Professor; National College of Education, National-Louis University; Skokie, Illinois
Areas of Expertise: Vocabulary and Comprehension

Candy Dawson Boyd, Ph.D.
Professor, School of Education; Saint Mary's College; Moraga, California
Areas of Expertise: Children's Literature and Professional Development

Elena Izquierdo, Ph.D.
Associate Professor, University of Texas at El Paso
Area of Expertise: English Language Learners

Connie Juel, Ph.D.
Professor of Education; Stanford University; Stanford, California
Areas of Expertise: Phonics, Oral Vocabulary, and Intervention

Edward J. Kame'enui, Ph.D.
Dean-Knight Professor of Education and Director, Institute for the Development of Educational Achievement, and the Center on Teaching and Learning; College of Education; University of Oregon
Areas of Expertise: Assessment, Intervention, and Progress Monitoring

Donald J. Leu, Ph.D.
John and Maria Neag Endowed Chair in Literacy and Technology Board of Directors, International Reading Association; University of Connecticut; Storrs, Connecticut
Areas of Expertise: Comprehension, Technology, and New Literacies

Jeanne R. Paratore, Ed.D.
Professor of Literacy, Language, and Cultural Studies; Boston University School of Education; Boston, Massachusetts
Areas of Expertise: Intervention and Small Group Instruction

P. David Pearson, Ph.D.
Professor of Language, Literacy and Culture, and Human Development; Graduate School of Education; University of California; Berkeley, California
Areas of Expertise: Common Core State Standards English Language Arts Work Team, Comprehension

Sam L. Sebesta, Ph.D.
Professor Emeritus; Curriculum and Instruction College of Education, University of Washington; Seattle, Washington
Areas of Expertise: Children's Literature, Reader Response, and Motivation

Deborah Simmons, Ph.D.
Professor in the Department of Educational Psychology, College of Education and Human Development, Texas A&M University
Areas of Expertise: Literacy Development, Phonics, and Intervention

Susan Watts Taffe, Ph.D.
Associate Professor and Program Coordinator, Literacy and Second Language Studies, School of Education; University of Cincinnati; Cincinnati, Ohio
Areas of Expertise: Vocabulary, Comprehension, and New Literacies

Alfred Tatum, Ph.D.
Associate Professor and Director, UIC Reading Clinic, University of Illinois at Chicago
Areas of Expertise: Adolescent Literacy, Reader Response, and Motivation

Sharon Vaughn, Ph.D.
H. E. Hartfelder/The Southland Corporation Regents Professor; University of Texas; Austin, Texas
Areas of Expertise: Literacy Development, Intervention, Professional Development, English Language Learners, Vocabulary, and Small Group Instruction

Karen Kring Wixson, Ph.D.
Dean of Education, University of North Carolina, Greensboro
Areas of Expertise: Common Core State Standards English Language Arts Work Team, Assessment, Small Group Instruction

Consulting Authors

Jeff Anderson, M.Ed.
Author and National Literacy Staff Developer

Jim Cummins, Ph.D.
Professor; Department of Curriculum, Teaching and Learning; University of Toronto

Tahira A. DuPree Chase, Ed.D.
Director of Curriculum and Instruction, Mt. Vernon City School District, New York

Lily Wong Fillmore, Ph.D.
Professor Emerita; Graduate School of Education, University of California, Berkeley

Georgia Earnest Garcia, Ph.D.
Professor; Language and Literacy Division, Department of Curriculum and Instruction, University of Illinois at Urbana-Champaign

George A. Gonzalez, Ph.D.
Professor (Retired); School of Education, University of Texas-Pan American, Edinburg

Adria Klein, Ph.D.
Professor Emeritus; School of Education, California State University, San Bernadino

Lesley Maxwell, M.S., CCC-SLP
Director of Clinical Education, Clinical Associate Professor; Department of Communication Sciences and Disorders, MGH Institute of Health Professions

Valerie Ooka Pang, Ph.D.
Professor; School of Teacher Education, San Diego State University

Sally M. Reis, Ph.D.
Board of Trustees Distinguished Professor; Department of Educational Psychology, University of Connecticut

Jon Scieszka, M.F.A.
Children's Book Author and Founder of GUYS READ, First National Ambassador for Young People's Literature 2008

Grant Wiggins, Ed.D.
President of Authentic Education, coauthor of *Understanding by Design*

Nurture the love of reading.

Help students learn to read *and* love to read. *Reading Street Common Core* supports reading, writing, and language development. Amazing literature on amazing devices inspires students in a whole new way.

Literature students love

The best literary and informational text

On devices they crave!

Whiteboards, tablets, computers, mobile devices

Build a foundation for reading.

Reading Street Common Core helps students develop foundational skills for reading more complex text. Common Core experts helped design the plan. Classroom results prove it works.

Early Reading Success

Reading Street students outperformed their peers by 15 percentile points, even though they started below the comparison students.

Kindergarten GRADE Total Score

50
48
46
44
42
40
38
Baseline
End of Year
Comparison
Reading Street

Greater Reading Enjoyment Later

Fourth-grade *Reading Street* students had more positive attitudes toward reading.

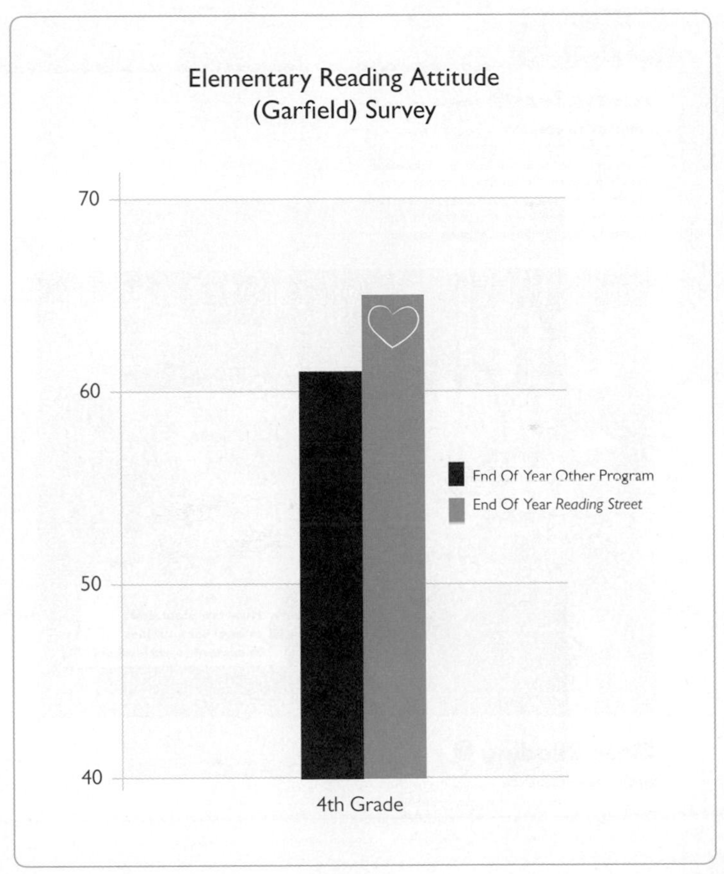

"The texts children read provide them with a foundation not just for what they're going to read, but also for what they're going to write and talk about."

Jeanne R. Paratore, Ed.D.
Program Author

Grow student capacity.

Reading Street Common Core builds students' capacity to read complex texts. Zoom in on elements critical to the Common Core State Standards.

Text-Based Comprehension

Modeling, analysis, and guided practice prepare students for more demanding text.

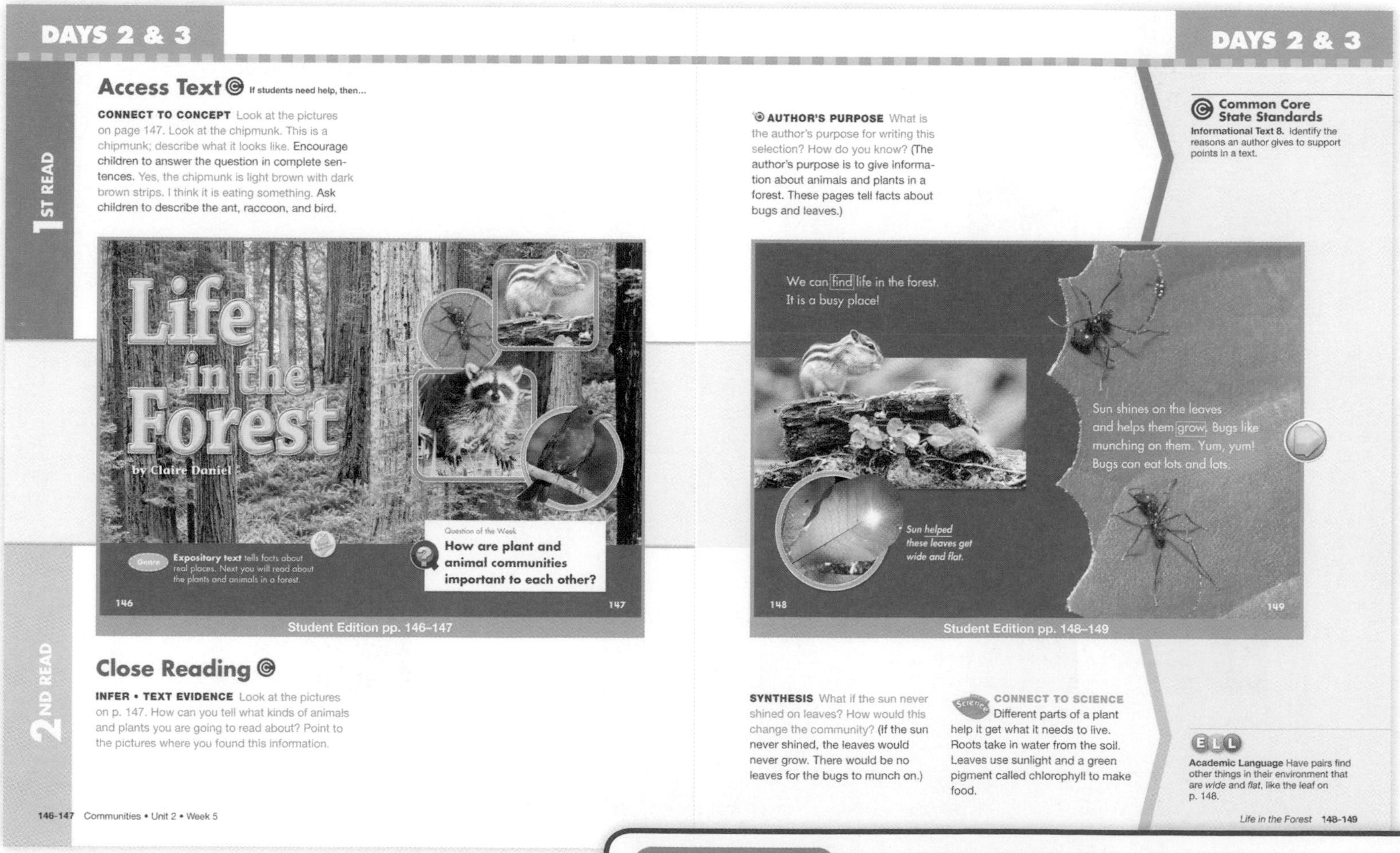

DAYS 2 & 3

1ST READ

Access Text — If students need help, then...

CONNECT TO CONCEPT Look at the pictures on page 147. Look at the chipmunk. This is a chipmunk; describe what it looks like. Encourage children to answer the question in complete sentences. Yes, the chipmunk is light brown with dark brown strips. I think it is eating something. Ask children to describe the ant, raccoon, and bird.

Life in the Forest
by Claire Daniel

Expository text tells facts about real places. Next you will read about the plants and animals in a forest.

Question of the Week
How are plant and animal communities important to each other?

146 147

Student Edition pp. 146–147

2ND READ

Close Reading

INFER • TEXT EVIDENCE Look at the pictures on p. 147. How can you tell what kinds of animals and plants you are going to read about? Point to the pictures where you found this information.

146-147 Communities • Unit 2 • Week 5

DAYS 2 & 3

AUTHOR'S PURPOSE What is the author's purpose for writing this selection? How do you know? (The author's purpose is to give information about animals and plants in a forest. These pages tell facts about bugs and leaves.)

Common Core State Standards
Informational Text 8. Identify the reasons an author gives to support points in a text.

We can find life in the forest.
It is a busy place!

Sun shines on the leaves and helps them grow. Bugs like munching on them. Yum, yum! Bugs can eat lots and lots.

Sun helped these leaves get wide and flat.

148 149

Student Edition pp. 148–149

SYNTHESIS What if the sun never shined on leaves? How would this change the community? (If the sun never shined, the leaves would never grow. There would be no leaves for the bugs to munch on.)

CONNECT TO SCIENCE Different parts of a plant help it get what it needs to live. Roots take in water from the soil. Leaves use sunlight and a green pigment called chlorophyll to make food.

ELL
Academic Language Have pairs find other things in their environment that are *wide* and *flat*, like the leaf on p. 148.

Life in the Forest 148-149

Read for Understanding Routine

Routines provide weekly opportunities to develop deep understanding and build higher-order thinking skills through Close Reading.

Routine — Read for Understanding

Deepen understanding by reading the selection multiple times.

1. **First Read**—use the **Access Text** notes to help children clarify understanding.
2. **Second Read**—use the **Close Reading** notes to help children draw knowledge from the text.

Content Knowledge

Weekly and unit instruction is built around science and social studies concepts. These concepts connect every piece of literature, vocabulary, and writing, allowing students to develop deep knowledge.

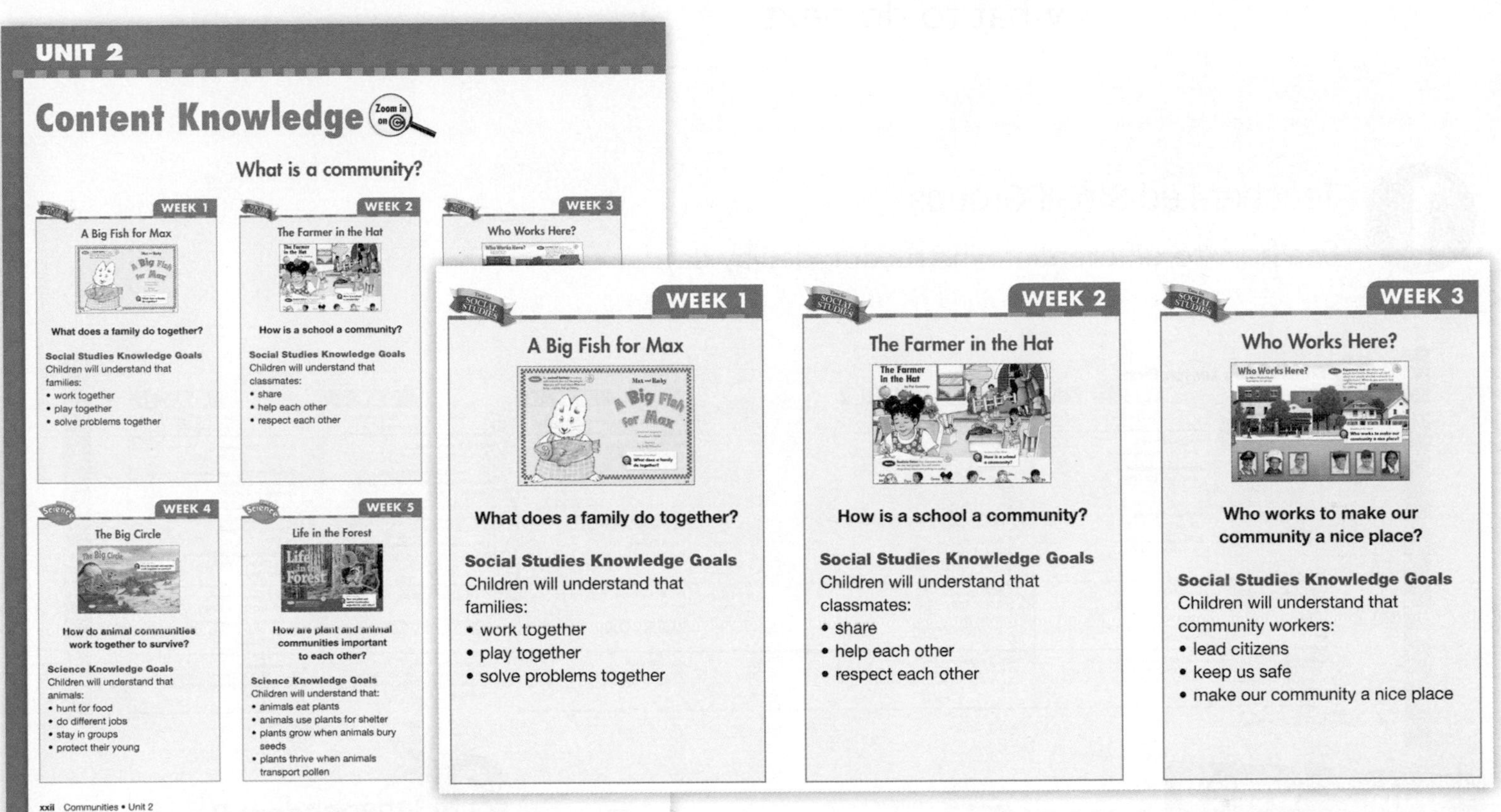

UNIT 2

Content Knowledge

What is a community?

WEEK 1 — A Big Fish for Max

What does a family do together?

Social Studies Knowledge Goals
Children will understand that families:
- work together
- play together
- solve problems together

WEEK 2 — The Farmer in the Hat

How is a school a community?

Social Studies Knowledge Goals
Children will understand that classmates:
- share
- help each other
- respect each other

WEEK 3 — Who Works Here?

Who works to make our community a nice place?

Social Studies Knowledge Goals
Children will understand that community workers:
- lead citizens
- keep us safe
- make our community a nice place

WEEK 4 — The Big Circle

How do animal communities work together to survive?

Science Knowledge Goals
Children will understand that animals:
- hunt for food
- do different jobs
- stay in groups
- protect their young

WEEK 5 — Life in the Forest

How are plant and animal communities important to each other?

Science Knowledge Goals
Children will understand that:
- animals eat plants
- animals use plants for shelter
- plants grow when animals bury seeds
- plants thrive when animals transport pollen

xxii Communities • Unit 2

Writing

Varied writing tasks help students write to inform or explain.

DAILY	WEEKLY	UNIT
• 10-minute mini-lessons on writing traits and craft allow students to write in response to their reading • Quick Write routine for writing on demand	• Different writing product each week • Writing mini-lessons and organizational models • Mentor text to exemplify good traits	• One- or two-week Writing Workshops • Writing process lessons

Inspire confidence.

"What do I do in group time?" Follow the simple 3-step plan. *Reading Street Common Core* provides a road map to help you teach with confidence. You'll know exactly where to go and what to do next.

1 Teacher-Led Small Groups

See how to differentiate instruction day by day.

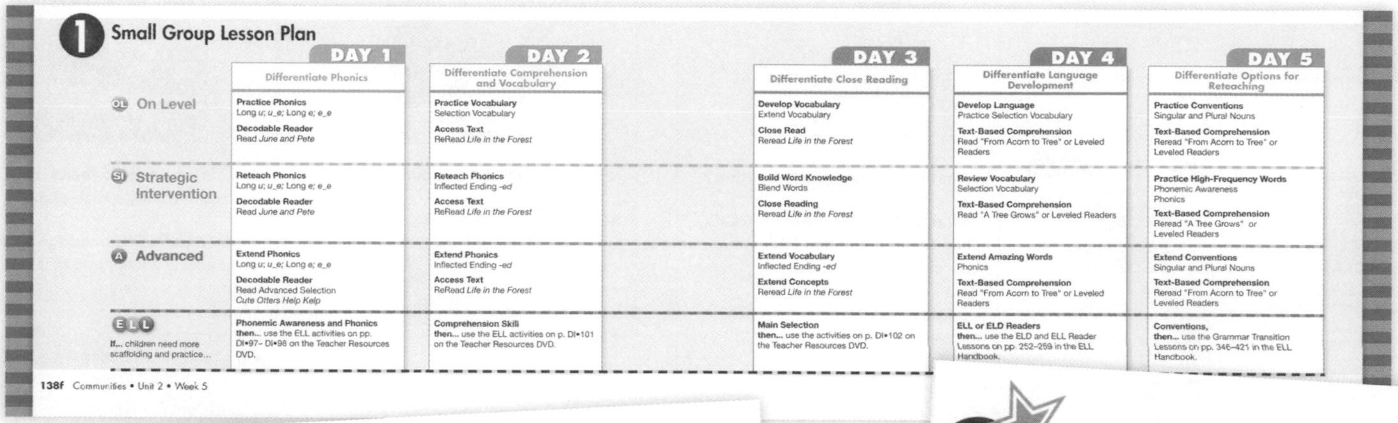

1 Small Group Lesson Plan

	DAY 1 Differentiate Phonics	DAY 2 Differentiate Comprehension and Vocabulary	DAY 3 Differentiate Close Reading	DAY 4 Differentiate Language Development	DAY 5 Differentiate Options for Reteaching
OL On Level	**Practice Phonics** Long *u*; *u_e*; Long *e*; *e_e* **Decodable Reader** Read *June and Pete*	**Practice Vocabulary** Selection Vocabulary **Access Text** ReRead *Life in the Forest*	**Develop Vocabulary** Extend Vocabulary **Close Read** Reread *Life in the Forest*	**Develop Language** Practice Selection Vocabulary **Text-Based Comprehension** Read "From Acorn to Tree" or Leveled Readers	**Practice Conventions** Singular and Plural Nouns **Text-Based Comprehension** Reread "From Acorn to Tree" or Leveled Readers
SI Strategic Intervention	**Reteach Phonics** Long *u*; *u_e*; Long *e*; *e_e* **Decodable Reader** Read *June and Pete*	**Reteach Phonics** Inflected Ending *-ed* **Access Text** ReRead *Life in the Forest*	**Build Word Knowledge** Blend Words **Close Reading** Reread *Life in the Forest*	**Review Vocabulary** Selection Vocabulary **Text-Based Comprehension** Read "A Tree Grows" or Leveled Readers	**Practice High-Frequency Words** Phonemic Awareness Phonics **Text-Based Comprehension** Reread "A Tree Grows" or Leveled Readers
A Advanced	**Extend Phonics** Long *u*; *u_e*; Long *e*; *e_e* **Decodable Reader** Read Advanced Selection *Cute Otters Help Kelp*	**Extend Phonics** Inflected Ending *-ed* **Access Text** ReRead *Life in the Forest*	**Extend Vocabulary** Inflected Ending *-ed* **Extend Concepts** Reread *Life in the Forest*	**Extend Amazing Words** Phonics **Text-Based Comprehension** Read "From Acorn to Tree" or Leveled Readers	**Extend Conventions** Singular and Plural Nouns **Text-Based Comprehension** Reread "From Acorn to Tree" or Leveled Readers
ELL **If...** children need more scaffolding and practice...	**Phonemic Awareness and Phonics** **then...** use the ELL activities on pp. DI•97– DI•98 on the Teacher Resources DVD.	**Comprehension Skill** **then...** use the ELL activities on p. DI•101 on the Teacher Resources DVD.	**Main Selection** **then...** use the activities on p. DI•102 on the Teacher Resources DVD.	**ELL or ELD Readers** **then...** use the ELD and ELL Reader Lessons on pp. 252–259 in the ELL Handbook.	**Conventions,** **then...** use the Grammar Transition Lessons on pp. 346–421 in the ELL Handbook.

138f Communities • Unit 2 • Week 5

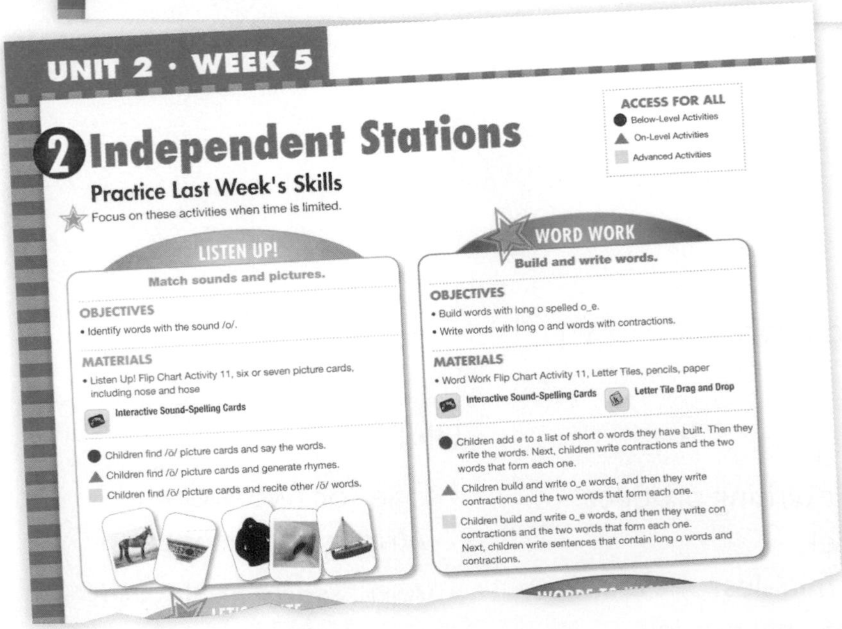

UNIT 2 · WEEK 5

2 Independent Stations

Practice Last Week's Skills

Focus on these activities when time is limited.

ACCESS FOR ALL
- ● Below-Level Activities
- ▲ On-Level Activities
- ■ Advanced Activities

LISTEN UP!

Match sounds and pictures.

OBJECTIVES
- Identify words with the sound /o/.

MATERIALS
- Listen Up! Flip Chart Activity 11, six or seven picture cards, including nose and hose

Interactive Sound-Spelling Cards

- ● Children find /ō/ picture cards and say the words.
- ▲ Children find /ō/ picture cards and generate rhymes.
- ■ Children find /ō/ picture cards and recite other /ō/ words.

WORD WORK

Build and write words.

OBJECTIVES
- Build words with long o spelled o_e.
- Write words with long o and words with contractions.

MATERIALS
- Word Work Flip Chart Activity 11, Letter Tiles, pencils, paper

Interactive Sound-Spelling Cards Letter Tile Drag and Drop

- ● Children add e to a list of short o words they have built. Then they write the words. Next, children write contractions and the two words that form each one.
- ▲ Children build and write o_e words, and then they write contractions and the two words that form each one.
- ■ Children build and write o_e words, and then they write con contractions and the two words that form each one. Next, children write sentences that contain long o words and contractions.

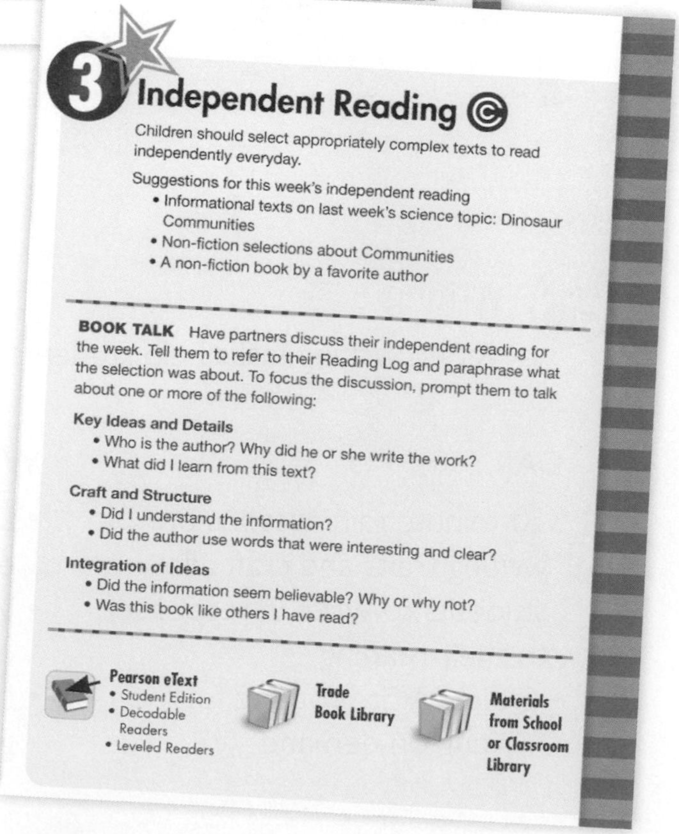

3 Independent Reading

Children should select appropriately complex texts to read independently everyday.

Suggestions for this week's independent reading
- Informational texts on last week's science topic: Dinosaur Communities
- Non-fiction selections about Communities
- A non-fiction book by a favorite author

BOOK TALK Have partners discuss their independent reading for the week. Tell them to refer to their Reading Log and paraphrase what the selection was about. To focus the discussion, prompt them to talk about one or more of the following:

Key Ideas and Details
- Who is the author? Why did he or she write the work?
- What did I learn from this text?

Craft and Structure
- Did I understand the information?
- Did the author use words that were interesting and clear?

Integration of Ideas
- Did the information seem believable? Why or why not?
- Was this book like others I have read?

Pearson eText
- Student Edition
- Decodable Readers
- Leveled Readers

Trade Book Library

Materials from School or Classroom Library

2 Independent Practice Stations

Level activities and provide focus when time is limited.

3 Independent Reading

Suggest concept-related reading and partner activities.

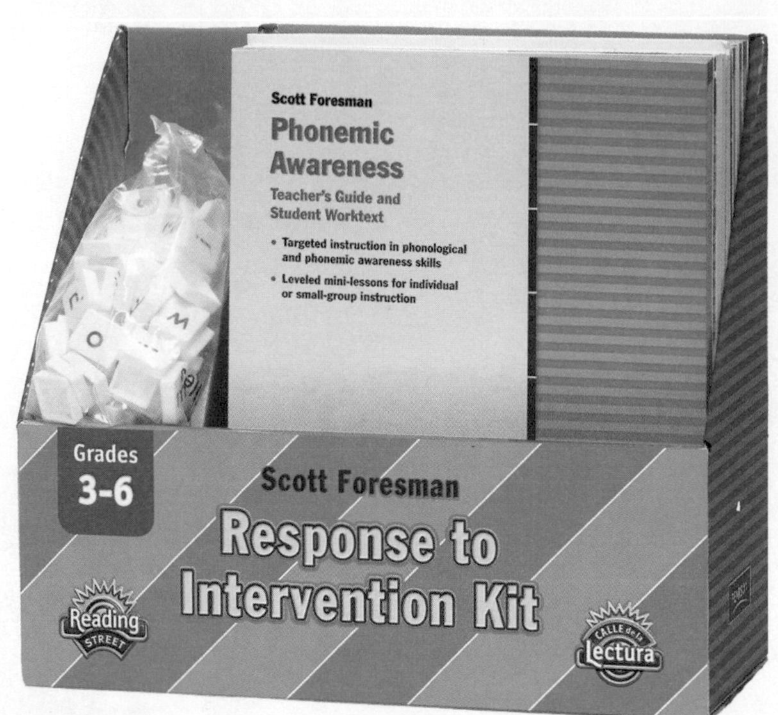

Response to Intervention Kit

Tier 2 RTI Kit provides a targeted focus and leveled mini-lessons for individuals and small groups.

Intensive Intervention

My Sidewalks Intensive Intervention

Conceptually related to *Reading Street, My Sidewalks* provides 30 weeks of instruction for struggling readers.

"What we need to do is to increase the support strategies to help students cope with complex text."

P. David Pearson
Program Author

TABLE OF CONTENTS

YOU ARE HERE

UNIT 6 Traditions

UNIT 1 Exploration

TABLE OF CONTENTS

UNIT 2
Working Together

UNIT 3
Creative Ideas

UNIT 4 Our Changing World

UNIT 5 Responsibility

eStreet Interactive
www.ReadingStreet.com

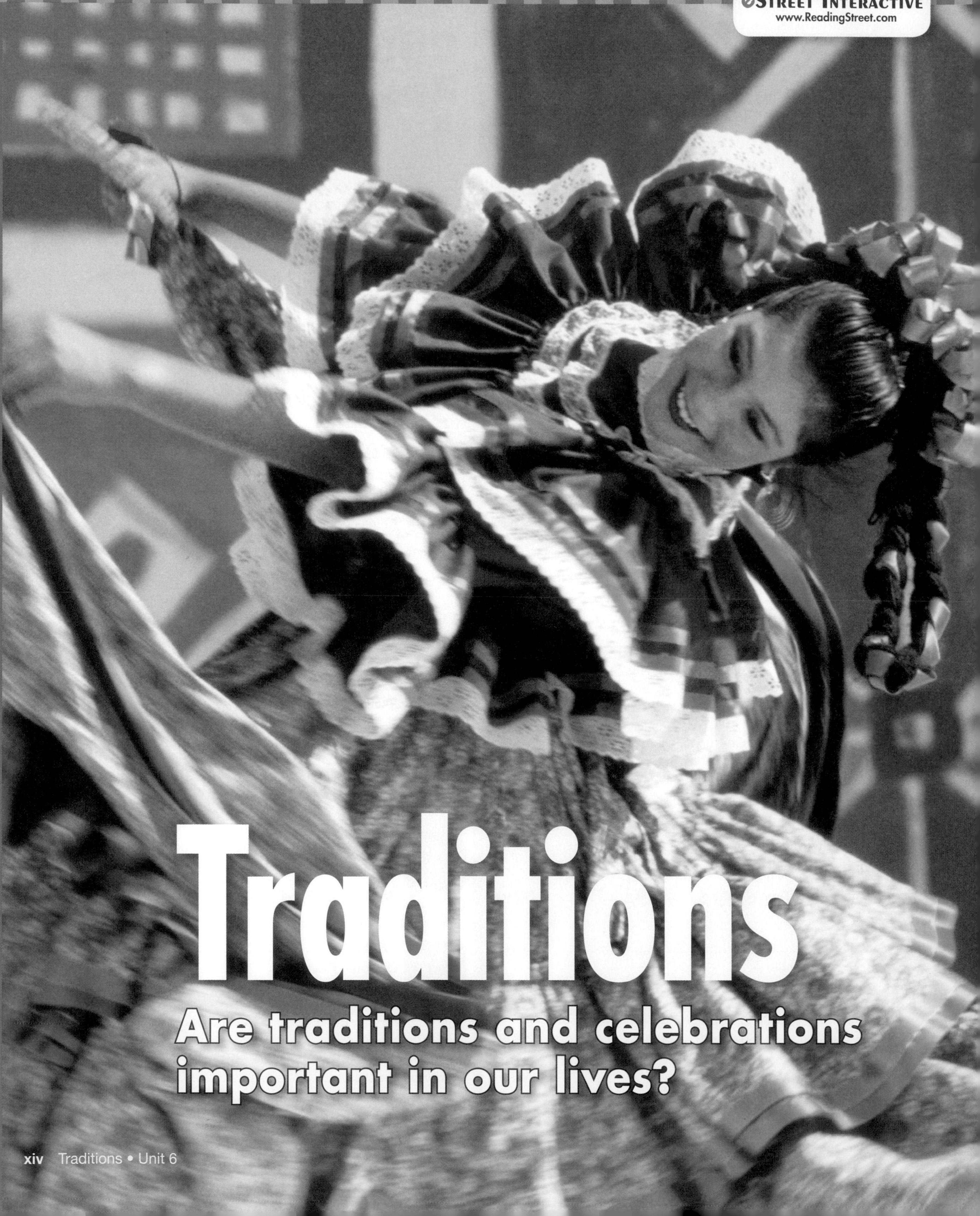

Traditions

Are traditions and celebrations important in our lives?

Just Like Josh Gibson

REALISTIC FICTION

Why are sports traditions important in our country?

Paired Selection
How Baseball Began
EXPOSITORY TEXT

Red, White, and Blue: The Story of the American Flag

INFORMATIONAL TEXT

What traditions and celebrations involve our country's flag?

Paired Selection
"You're a Grand Old Flag"
POETRY

A Birthday Basket for Tía

REALISTIC FICTION

Why are family celebrations special?

Paired Selection
Family Traditions: Birthdays
21ST CENTURY SKILLS

Cowboys

INFORMATIONAL TEXT

What can we learn about cowboy traditions?

Paired Selection
Cowboy Gear
INFORMATIONAL TEXT

Grace for President

REALISTIC FICTION

How are different traditions celebrated and shared?

Paired Selection
Home Sweet Home
INFORMATIONAL TEXT

Skills Overview

Key
- **T** Tested Skill
- Target Skill

		WEEK 1	WEEK 2	WEEK 3
		Just Like Josh Gibson Realistic Fiction, pp. 368–381 **How Baseball Began** Expository Text, pp. 386–389	**Red, White, and Blue: The Story of the American Flag** Informational Text, pp. 400–417 **"You're a Grand Old Flag"** Poetry, pp. 422–423	**A Birthday Basket for Tía** Realistic Fiction, pp. 434–447 **Family Traditions: Birthdays** 21st Century Skills, pp. 452–455
Build Content Knowledge	Integrate Science and Social Studies	American Heroes; Cultural Traditions; Geography: Maps; History of Baseball	 American Revolution; American Heroes; Thirteen Colonies/States; U.S. Symbols, Holidays; Geography	 Cultural Traditions; Celebrations; Birthdays
	Weekly Question	*Why are sports traditions important in our country?*	*What traditions and celebrations involve our country's flag?*	*Why are family celebrations special?*
	Knowledge Goals	Children will understand that sports are: • an important tradition in our culture • enjoyed by players and spectators • played by both boys and girls	Children will understand some of the traditions that honor the flag, including: • the Pledge of Allegiance • the National Anthem • the Fourth of July	Children will understand that family celebrations: • involve cultural traditions • include certain activities • include special foods
Get Ready to Read	Phonics	**T** Inflected Endings **Review** Plurals	**T** Abbreviations **Review** Contractions	**T** Final Syllables *-tion, -ture, -ion* **Review** Final Syllable *-le*
	Spelling	Inflected Endings	Abbreviations	Final Syllables *-tion, -ture*
Read and Comprehend	Selection Vocabulary	**T** *bases, cheers, field, plate, sailed, threw*	**T** *America, birthday, flag, freedom, nicknames, stars, stripes*	**T** *aunt, bank, basket, collects, favorite, present*
	Comprehension	**T** **Skill** Compare and Contrast **Strategy** Monitor and Clarify **Review Skill** Draw Conclusions	**T** **Skill** Author's Purpose **Strategy** Summarize **Review Skill** Fact and Opinion	**T** **Skill** Draw Conclusions **Strategy** Questioning **Review Skill** Cause and Effect
	Vocabulary	Homophones	Multiple-Meaning Words	Words from Other Languages
	Fluency	Accuracy and Appropriate Rate	Accuracy	Appropriate Phrasing
Language Arts	Writing	Realistic Fiction Trait: Organization	Descriptive Poem or Song Trait: Voice	Invitation Letter Trait: Sentences
	Conventions	**T** Using Capital Letters	**T** Quotation Marks	**T** Prepositions and Prepositional Phrases
	Listening and Speaking	Use Clear and Specific Vocabulary	Evaluate Advertisements	Listen to a Description
	Research Skills	Globe	Chart	Interview and Natural Sources

 WEEK 4	 WEEK 5	 WEEK 6
Cowboys Informational Text, pp. 466–487 **Cowboy Gear** Informational Text, pp. 492–493	**Grace for President** Realistic Fiction, pp. 504–519 **Home Sweet Home** Informational Text, pp. 524–527	**Optional Review**
 American West; Cowboys; U.S. Growth; Transportation; Geography	 Elections; Democracy; Slogans	 Traditions
What can we learn about cowboy traditions?	*How are different traditions celebrated and shared?*	*Are traditions and celebrations important in our lives?*
Children will understand that cowboys: • worked hard • had difficult working conditions • wore protective clothing	Children will understand that traditions can be: • shared and celebrated at special events • brought from other lands • learned at home and at school	Connect the Question of the Week to the Big Question
T Suffixes *-ness, -less, -able, -ible* **Review** Final Syllables *-tion, -ture, -ion*	**T** Prefixes *mis-, mid-, micro-, non-* **Review** Suffixes *-ness, -les, -able, -ible*	**Review** Unit 6 Phonics Skills
Suffixes *-ness, -less*	Prefixes *mis-, mid-*	**Review** Unit 6 Spelling Patterns
T *campfire, cattle, cowboy, galloped, herd, railroad, trails*	**T** *assembly, election, microphone, rallies, slogan, speeches*	**Review** Unit 6 Selection Vocabulary
T **Skill** Sequence **Strategy** Text Structure **Review Skill** Main Idea and Details	**T** **Skill** Facts and Details **Strategy** Predict and Set Purpose **Review Skill** Compare and Contrast	**Review** Unit 6 Target Comprehension Skills and Strategies
Unfamiliar Words	Multiple-Meaning Words	**Review** Unit 6 Target Vocabulary Skills
Accuracy and Appropriate Rate	Appropriate Phrasing	**Review** Unit 6 Fluency Skills
Compare-and-Contrast Text Trait: Focus/Ideas	Persuasive Statement Trait: Word Choice	Quick Write for Fluency
T Commas	**T** Commas in Compound Sentences	**Review** Unit 6 Conventions
Media Literacy: Identify Written Conventions	Listen for Speaker's Purpose	
Schedule	Interview and Natural Sources	

Assessment

5 Steps to Success on Reading Street

RIGHT IN YOUR TEACHER'S EDITION

Step 1

Begin the Year

The Assessment Handbook provides ideas and support to begin the school year and beyond.

The Baseline Group Test helps identify where children are. Use the Baseline Test results to make initial grouping decisions and to differentiate instruction based on ability levels.

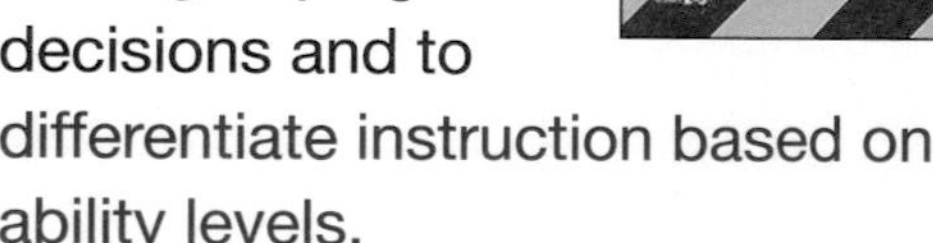

Online Assessment
Save time by using digital assessments. All Reading Street assessments are available on ExamView and in SuccessTracker.

Step 2

Every Day

During the day, use these tools to monitor student progress.

- **Corrective Feedback** provides point of use support.

Corrective feedback | **If...** students are unable to answer the comprehension questions, **then...** use the Reteach lesson in *First Stop*.

- **Monitor Progress** boxes each day check phonics, selection words, retelling, fluency, and oral vocabulary.

Don't Wait Until Friday
MONITOR PROGRESS Check Retelling
If... students have difficulty retelling,
then... use the Retelling Cards/Story Sort to scaffold their retellings.

Step 3

Every Week

- **Weekly Assessments** on Day 5 check phonics, high-frequency words, and comprehension.

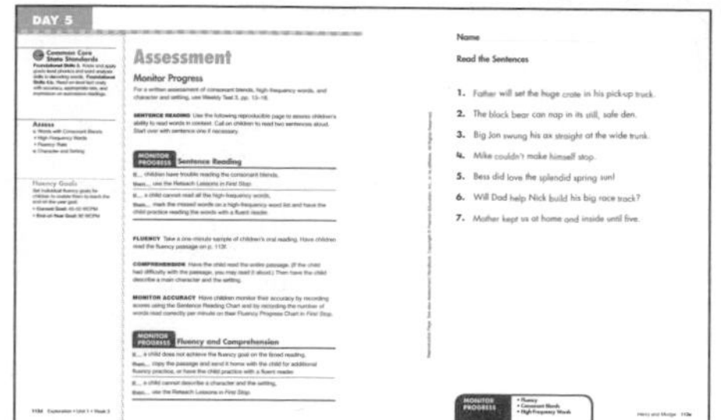

- **Weekly Tests** assess target skills for the week.

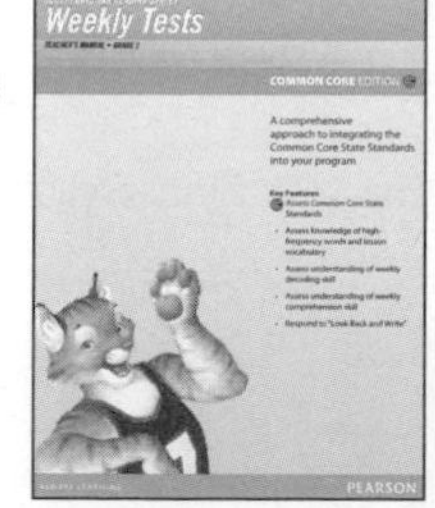

- **Fresh Reads** assesses fluency and comprehension as children read a new passage.

- **Reading Street Sleuth** assesses children's ability to find clues in text through close reading.

Step 4

Every Unit

- **Unit Benchmark Tests** assess mastery of unit skills: comprehension, vocabulary, conventions, and writing.
- **Unit Benchmark Tests** provide professional development and support with performance-based assessment.

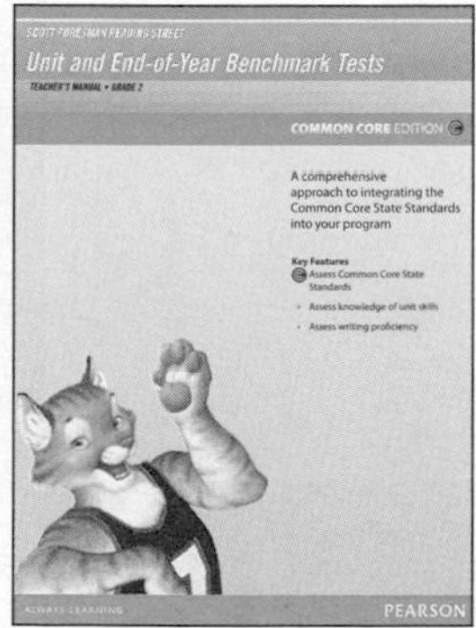

- **Performance-Based Assessments** assess children's ability to demonstrate text-based comprehension and application of higher-order thinking skills.

Step 5

End the Year

- **End-of-Year Benchmark Test** measures student mastery of skills covered in all six units with options for performance-based assessment.

5 Steps to Success on Reading Street

1. Begin the Year
2. Every Day
3. Every Week
4. Every Unit
5. End the Year

Digital Assessment

SuccessTracker™

eStreet Interactive
www.ReadingStreet.com

Implementing eStreet Interactive

Power up your classroom and put time back on your side!

eSTREET INTERACTIVE
www.ReadingStreet.com

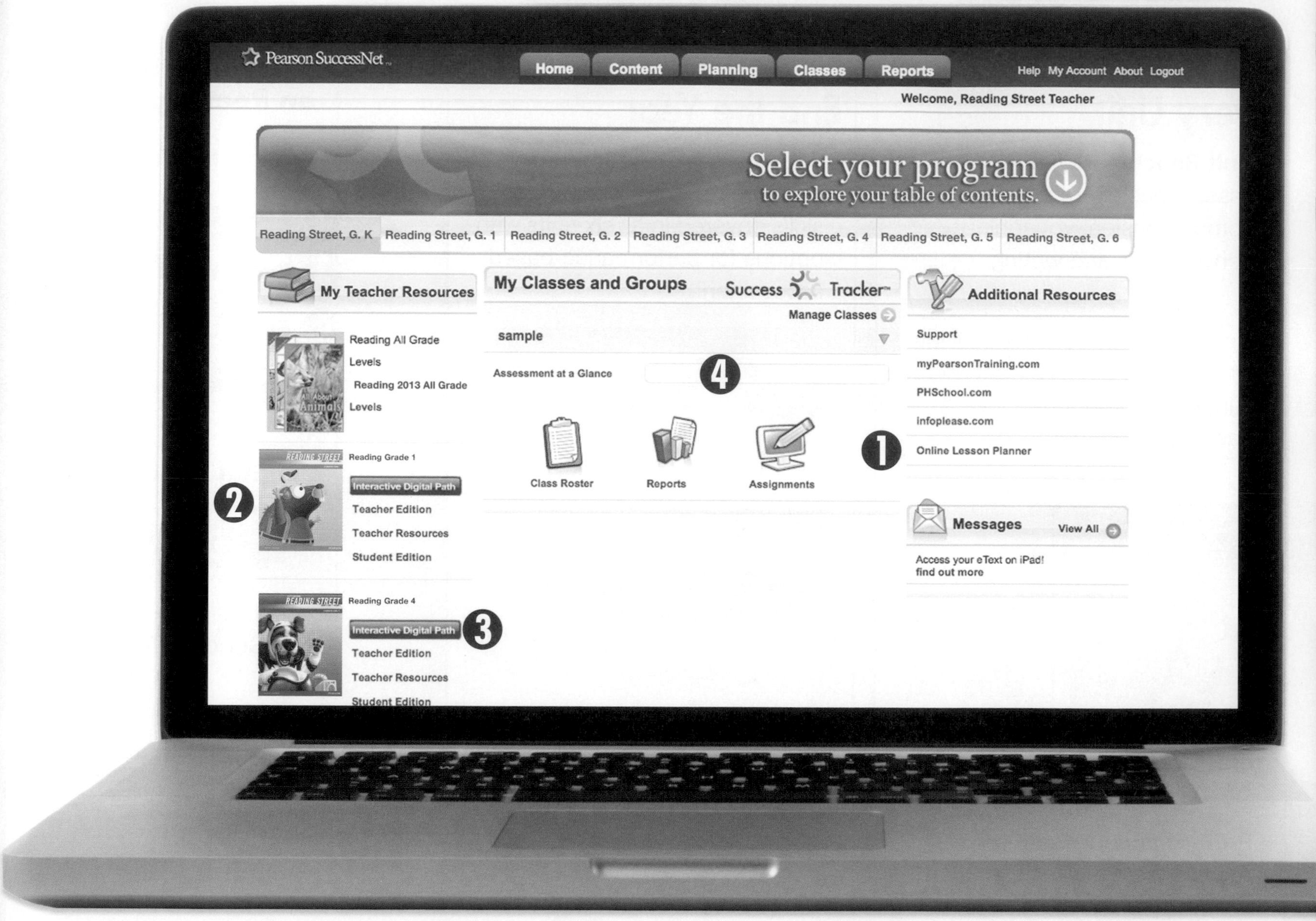

Pearson SuccessNet

Home | Content | Planning | Classes | Reports

Help My Account About Logout

Welcome, Reading Street Teacher

Select your program
to explore your table of contents.

Reading Street, G. K | Reading Street, G. 1 | Reading Street, G. 2 | Reading Street, G. 3 | Reading Street, G. 4 | Reading Street, G. 5 | Reading Street, G. 6

My Teacher Resources

Reading All Grade Levels
Reading 2013 All Grade Levels

Reading Grade 1
2 Interactive Digital Path
Teacher Edition
Teacher Resources
Student Edition

Reading Grade 4
Interactive Digital Path 3
Teacher Edition
Teacher Resources
Student Edition

My Classes and Groups
Success Tracker™
Manage Classes
sample
Assessment at a Glance 4
Class Roster
Reports
Assignments

Additional Resources
Support
myPearsonTraining.com
PHSchool.com
infoplease.com
1 Online Lesson Planner

Messages View All
Access your eText on iPad!
find out more

Additional Digital Support

AudioText CD
Sing with Me CD
Background Building CD
Teacher Resources DVD

Plan

Customize your daily plan by clicking, dragging, and posting!

- Online Lesson Planner
- Online Teacher's Edition

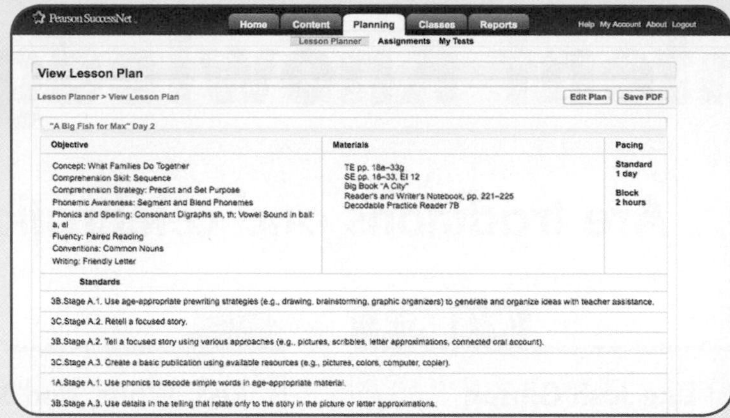

Online Lesson Planner

Teach

Engage through interactive media!

- Concept Talk Videos
- Interactive Sing with Me Big Book
- Interactive Sound-Spelling Cards
- Letter Tile Drag and Drop
- Envision It! Animations
- Grammar Jammer

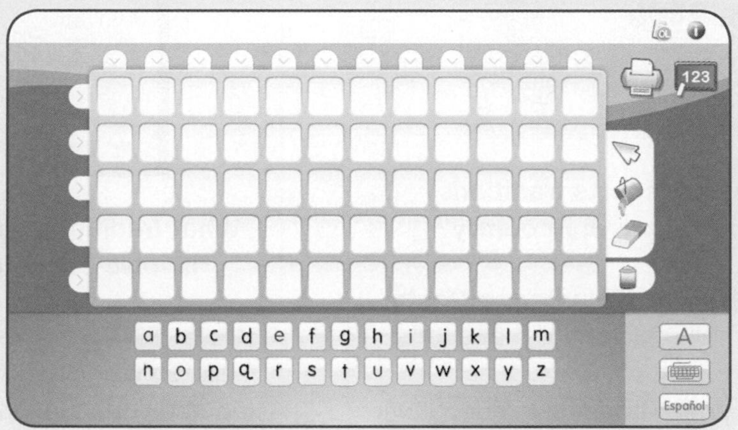

Letter Tile Drag and Drop

Practice

Motivate through personalized practice activities!

- Story Sort
- Pearson eText
- Journal
- Vocabulary Activities
- Leveled Reader Database

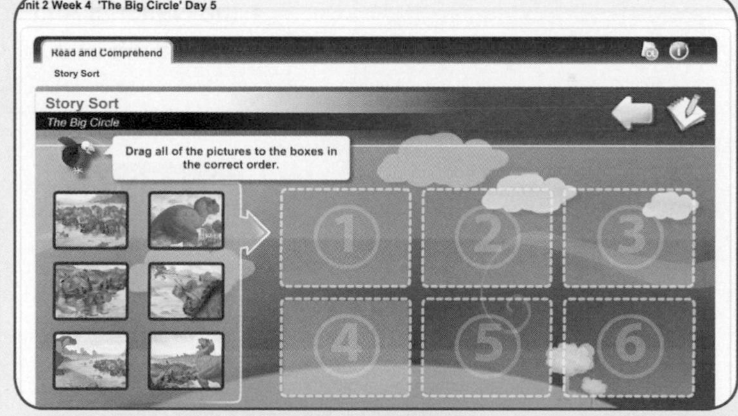

Story Sort

Manage and Assess

Respond to individual needs!

- Monitor Student Progress
- Assign
- Prescribe
- Remediate

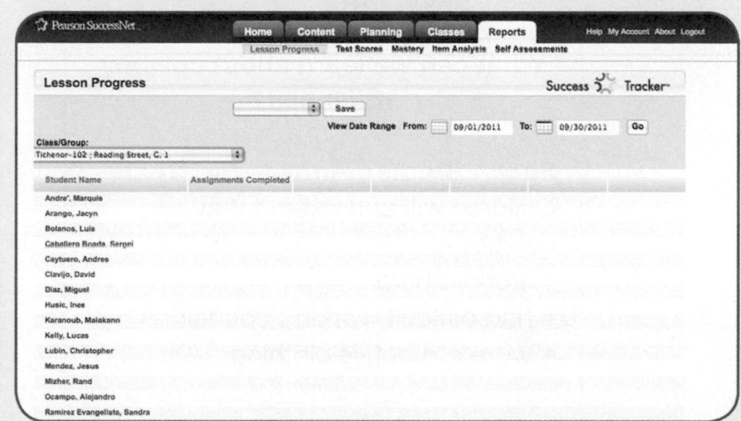

Class Management

Content Knowledge

Are traditions and celebrations important in our lives?

WEEK 1

Just Like Josh Gibson

Why are sports traditions important in our country?

Social Studies Knowledge Goals
Children will understand that sports are:

- an important tradition in our culture
- enjoyed by players and spectators
- played by both boys and girls

WEEK 2

Red, White, and Blue: The Story of the American Flag

What traditions and celebrations involve our country's flag?

Social Studies Knowledge Goals
Children will understand some of the traditions that honor the flag, including:

- the Pledge of Allegiance
- the National Anthem
- the Fourth of July

WEEK 3

A Birthday Basket for Tía

Why are family celebrations special?

Social Studies Knowledge Goals
Children will understand that family celebrations:

- involve cultural traditions
- include certain activities
- include special foods

WEEK 4

Cowboys

What can we learn about cowboy traditions?

Social Studies Knowledge Goals
Children will understand that cowboys:

- worked hard
- had difficult working conditions
- wore protective clothing

WEEK 5

Grace for President

How are different traditions celebrated and shared?

Social Studies Knowledge Goals
Children will understand that traditions can be:

- shared and celebrated at special events
- brought from other lands
- learned at home and at school

Tennessee Common Core Edition 

This Week's Target Skills and Strategies

Target Skills and Strategies	Common Core State Standards for English Language Arts	Tennessee CUs and GLEs
Phonics and Spelling **Skill:** Inflected Endings	**CCSS Foundational Skills 3.** Know and apply grade-level phonics and word analysis skills in decoding words. **(Also CCSS Language 2.)**	**TN CU 0201.1.11** Apply phonics generalizations in order to decode words.
Text-Based Comprehension **Skill:** Compare and Contrast	**CCSS Informational Text 1.** Ask and answer such questions as *who*, *what*, *where*, *when*, *why*, and *how* to demonstrate understanding of key details in a text.	**TN CU 0201.8.6** Derive meaning while reading by employing strategies.
Strategy: Monitor and Clarify	**CCSS Informational Text 1.** Ask and answer such questions as *who*, *what*, *where*, *when*, *why*, and *how* to demonstrate understanding of key details in a text.	**TN CU 0201.8.6** Derive meaning while reading by employing strategies.
Vocabulary **Skill:** Homophones **Strategy:** Context Clues	**CCSS Language 4.a.** Use sentence-level context as a clue to the meaning of a word or phrase.	Reviews Grade K **TN CU 0001.1.8** Use context clues to identify vocabulary in text.
Fluency **Skill:** Accuracy and Appropriate Rate	**CCSS Foundational Skills 4.b.** Read on-level text orally with accuracy, appropriate rate, and expression on successive readings.	**TN CU 0201.8.9** Read orally with fluency and accuracy, using appropriate pacing and expression.
Listening and Speaking Express Ideas and Establish Tone	**CCSS Speaking/Listening 6.** Produce complete sentences when appropriate to task and situation in order to provide requested detail or clarification. **(Also CCSS Speaking/ Listening 3., CCSS Language 3.a.)**	**TN CU 0201.2.6** Speak clearly, properly, and politely; recognize the difference between formal and informal language. **(Also TN GLE 0201.1.1)**
Six-Trait Writing **Trait of the Week:** Organization	**CCSS Writing 3.** Write narratives in which they recount a well-elaborated event or short sequence of events, include details to describe actions, thoughts, and feelings, use temporal words to signal event order, and provide a sense of closure.	**TN CU 0201.3.7** Arrange events in a logical and sequential order when writing. **(Also TN CU 0201.3.2, TN CU 0201.3.8)**
Writing Realistic Fiction	**CCSS Writing 3.** Write narratives in which they recount a well-elaborated event or short sequence of events, include details to describe actions, thoughts, and feelings, use temporal words to signal event order, and provide a sense of closure.	**TN CU 0201.3.7** Arrange events in a logical and sequential order when writing. **(Also TN CU 0201.3.2, TN CU 0201.3.8)**
Conventions **Skill:** Using Capital Letters	**CCSS Language 2.** Demonstrate command of the conventions of standard English capitalization, punctuation, and spelling when writing. **(Also CCSS Language 2.a.)**	**TN GLE 0201.1.1** Demonstrate control of basic English usage, mechanics, spelling, and sentence structure.

Access for All to Differentiate Instruction

Reading Street Sleuth

Josh Gibson, Homerun King
pp. 68–69

Follow the path to close reading using the Super Sleuth tips:

- Look for Clues
- Ask Questions
- Make Your Case
- Prove it!

This Week's Optional Tennessee Readers Provide Informational Text

Concept Literacy

CCSS Informational Text 1.; TN CU 0201.8.6

Below Level

CCSS Informational Text 1.; TN CU 0201.8.6

On Level

CCSS Informational Text 1.; TN CU 0201.8.6

Advanced

CCSS Informational Text 1.; TN CU 0201.8.6

ELL

CCSS Literature 2., CCSS Literature 3.; TN CU 0201.8.1, TN CU 0201.8.10

ELD

CCSS Literature 2., CCSS Literature 3.; TN CU 0201.8.1, TN CU 0201.8.10

ISBN-13: 978-0-328-73472-6 ISBN-10: 0-328-73472-1

Assessment

Tennessee Assessment Resources for Common Core Test Success

Tennessee Daily Formative Assessment in Your Teacher's Edition

Baseline Group Tests

CCSS Weekly Tests, pp. 151–156

CCSS Fresh Reads, pp. 151–156

Unit 6 CCSS Benchmark Test

CCSS Success Tracker, ExamView, and Online Lesson Planner

RTI

Response to Intervention Kits Increase Instruction and Progress Monitoring

Intensive Intervention *My Sidewalks* Level B, Unit 6, pp. 162–177

Writing, Grammar, and Spelling

Six-Trait Writing

- Focus/Ideas
- Organization/Paragraphs
  Trait of the Week
  CCSS Writing 3.
  TN CU 0201.3.7
- Voice
- Word Choice
- Sentences
- Conventions

Resources for Six-Trait Writing, Grammar, and Spelling

Reader's and Writer's Notebook
- Practice Reading
- Practice Spelling
- Practice Grammar
- Practice Writing

Writing Rubrics and Anchor Papers

Digital Resources
- Online Journal
- Online Writing Transparencies
- Grammar Jammer

Teacher Resources DVD-ROM
- Reader's and Writer's Notebook
- Let's Practice It!
- Graphic Organizers
- Writing Transparencies

Grade 2 Skills Trace

Skills and Strategies	Looking Back	This Week's Selection	Looking Ahead
Phonics and Spelling **Skill:** Inflected Endings	**Unit 1** 117a, 118, 118a, 118b–118c, 120c, 140c–140d, 144d, 144e–144f, 148c	362a, 362–363, 363a, 363c–363d, 366c, 382c, 382d, 386d, 386e–386f, 390c, 391e	**Unit 6** 422c, 492d
Text-Based Comprehension **Skill:** Compare and Contrast	**Unit 2** 319a–319b, 320h, 324–325 **Unit 3** 423a, 424h, 426–427	364a, 364–365, 368a, 372–373, 378–379, 381a, 383a, 388–389, 391b, 391f	**Unit 6** 454–455, 512–513, 520h
Strategy: Monitor and Clarify	**Unit 1** 26h, 30–31, 38–39 **Unit 4** 158a, 158–159, 162a, 164–165	364a, 364–365, 368a, 372–373, 376–377, 378–379, 380–381, 383a, 386–387, 388–389	Grade 3 **Units 2, 4, 5**
Vocabulary **Skill:** Homophones **Strategy:** Context Clues	**Unit 4** 26g, 26–27, 32–33, 42g, 52–53	366g, 366–367, 376–377, 381a, 390–391	Grade 3 **Units 3, 5**
Fluency **Skill:** Accuracy and Appropriate Rate	**Unit 4** 42f, 51b, 53a **Unit 5** 248f, 253b, 255a, 255d	382f, 389a, 391a, 391d	**Unit 6** 488f, 493b, 495a, 495d
Listening and Speaking Express Ideas and Establish Tone	Skill not previously taught	389e	Skill not subsequently taught
Six-Trait Writing **Trait of the Week:** Organization	**Unit 4** 41d–41e, 44–45, 45a **Unit 5** 227c–227d, 247d–247e	365c–365d, 381d–381e, 384–385, 385a, 389c–389d	Grade 3 **Units 1, 2, 4, 5, 6**
Writing Realistic Fiction	**Unit 1** 87d–87e, 103c–103d, 106–107, 111c–111d **Unit 3** 457d–457e, 496c–496d, 472–473, 477c, 477d **Unit 5** 227c–227d9i, 247d–247e, 250–251, 253d–253e	365c–365d, 381d–381e, 384–385, 385a, 389c–389d, 391h–391i	Grade 3 **Unit 1**
Conventions **Skill:** Using Capital Letters	Grade 1 **Unit 2**	365b, 381c, 384a, 384–385, 389b, 391g	Grade 3 **Unit 6**

Tennessee Science and Social Studies Standards Taught During the Reading Lesson

TN GLE 0207.12.2 Realize that things fall toward the ground unless something holds them up.
TN 2.1.01.b Recognize communities have customs and cultures that differ.
TN 2.5.02.b Use vocabulary related to chronology, including past, present and future.

Teaching the Common Core State Standards This Week

The Common Core State Standards for English Language Arts are divided into strands for **Reading** (including **Foundational Skills**), **Writing**, **Speaking and Listening**, and **Language**. The chart below shows some of the content you will teach this week, strand by strand. Turn to this week's 5-Day Planner on pages 360d–360e to see how this content is taught each day.

Reading Strand

- **Phonics:** Inflected Endings
- **Text-Based Comprehension:** Compare and Contrast; Monitor and Clarify
- **Fluency:** Accuracy and Appropriate Rate
- **Literary Text:** Speaker/Narrator
- **Genre:** Main Selection: Realistic Fiction; Paired Selection: Expository Text

Writing Strand

- **Writing Mini-Lesson:** Realistic Fiction
- **Trait:** Organization
- **Look Back and Write:** Text Evidence

Common Core State Standards for English Language Arts

Speaking and Listening Strand

- **Content Knowledge:** Build Oral Language
- **Listening and Speaking:** Use Vocabulary to Express Ideas and Establish Tone
- **Research and Inquiry**

Language Strand

- **Oral Vocabulary: Amazing Words** *athlete*, *challenge*, *effort*, *dainty*, *disguise*, *champion*, *professional*, *shortstop*
- **Vocabulary:** Homophones; Context Clues
- **Selection Vocabulary:** *bases*, *cheers*, *field*, *plate*, *sailed*, *threw*
- **Academic Vocabulary:** *inflected endings, compare, contrast, characters, setting, realistic fiction, foreshadowing, monitor, clarify, globe, draw conclusions, expository text, time-order transition words, graphic sources*
- **Conventions:** Using Capital Letters
- **Spelling:** Inflected Endings

Text-Based Comprehension

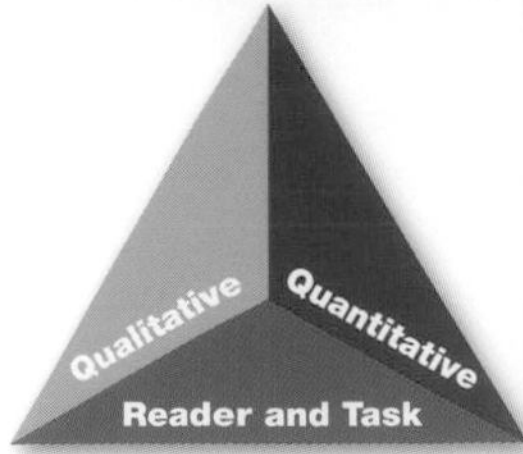

Text Complexity Measures

Use the rubric to familiarize yourself with the text complexity of ***Just Like Josh Gibson***.

Bridge to Complex Knowledge

Quantitative Measures	**Lexile**	950L
	Average Sentence Length	15.76
	Word Frequency	3.60

Qualitative Measures	**Levels of Meaning**	understand realistic fiction; figurative language: hyperbole
	Structure	flash-back; explicit structure
	Language Conventionality and Clarity	clear language; some antiquated language
	Theme and Knowledge Demands	a basic knowledge of baseball; common experiences; simple theme; singular perspective

Reader and Task Suggestions

FORMATIVE ASSESSMENT Based on assessment results, use the **Reader and Task Suggestions** in Access Main Selection to scaffold the selection or support independence for children as they read ***Just Like Josh Gibson***.

READER AND TASK SUGGESTIONS	
Preparing to Read the Text	**Leveled Tasks**
• Review strategies for understanding homophones. Refer to the vocabulary skill lesson on p. 366g. • Point out the author's use of flashback at the beginning of this selection. • Remind children that as they encounter unfamiliar words, they may need to read more slowly to better understand the text.	• **Structure** If children have difficulty understanding flashback, have them identify where the story changes and how they determined the shift to present day. • **Levels of Meaning • Analyze** If children find hyperbole confusing, help them identify examples and discuss the meanings of the exaggerations.

Recommended Placement Several of the quantitative measures suggest this text may be outside the Grade 2–3 text complexity band. Scaffolded support for the longer sentences will help children stretch to be successful accessing this content.

Focus on Common Core State Standards

Main Selection, pp. 368–381

Paired Selection, pp. 386–389

Text-Based Comprehension

Compare and Contrast
CCSS Informational Text 1.

Monitor and Clarify
CCSS Informational Text 1.

Fluency

Accuracy and Appropriate Rate
CCSS Foundational Skills 4.b.

Writing and Conventions

Trait: Organization
CCSS Writing 3.

Writing Mini-Lesson: Realistic Fiction
CCSS Writing 3.

Conventions: Using Capital Letters
CCSS Language 2., CCSS Language 2.a.

Oral Vocabulary

Amazing Words

athlete	challenge
effort	dainty
disguise	champion
professional	shortstop

CCSS Language 6.

Vocabulary

Skill: Homophones
CCSS Language 4.a.

Strategy: Context Clues
CCSS Language 4.a.

bases	cheers	field
plate	sailed	threw

Phonics and Spelling

Inflected Endings
CCSS Foundational Skills 3., CCSS Language 2.

tried	trying	planned
planning	liked	liking
skipped	skipping	heavier
heaviest	lighter	lightest

Listening and Speaking

Use Vocabulary to Express Ideas and Establish Tone
CCSS Speaking/Listening 6., CCSS Language 3.a.

Preview Your Week

Why are sports traditions important in our country?

Main Selection, pp. 368–381

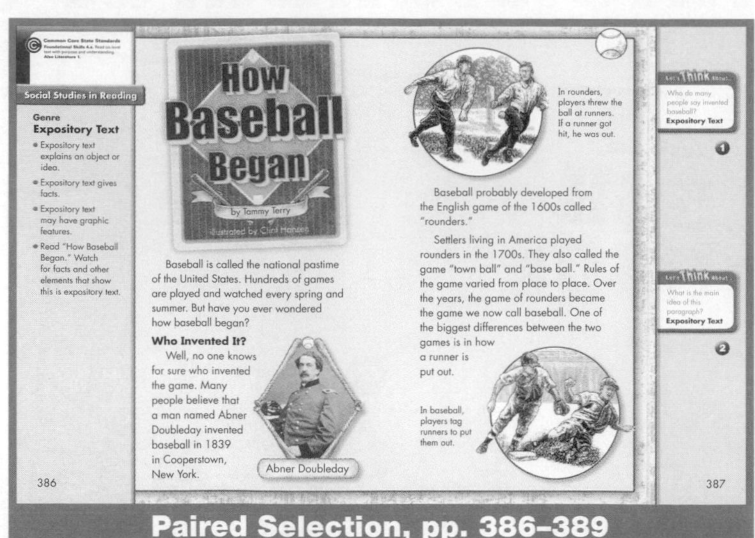

Paired Selection, pp. 386–389

Genre: Realistic Fiction

- **Phonics:** Inflected Endings
- **Text-Based Comprehension:** Compare and Contrast
- **Vocabulary:** Homophones

Social Studies in Reading

Genre: Expository Text

Build Content Knowledge

KNOWLEDGE GOALS

Children will understand that sports are:

- an important tradition in our culture
- enjoyed by players and spectators
- played by both boys and girls

THIS WEEK'S CONCEPT MAP

Develop a concept-related graphic organizer like the one below over the course of this week.

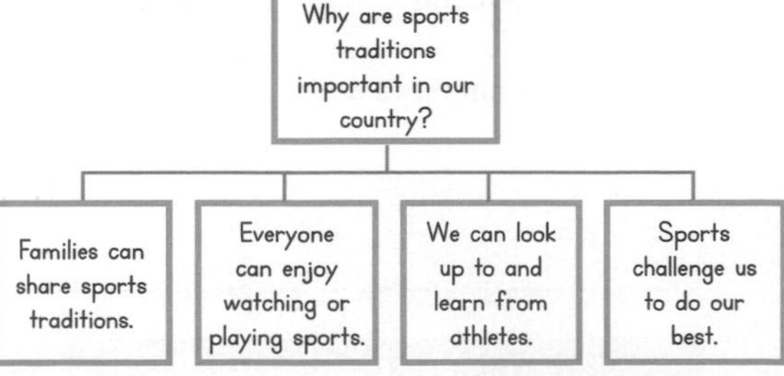

BUILD ORAL VOCABULARY

This week, children will acquire the following academic vocabulary/domain-specific words.

Amazing Words

athlete	challenge
effort	dainty
disguise	champion
professional	shortstop

OPTIONAL CONCEPT-BASED READING Use the Digital Path to access readers offering different levels of text complexity.

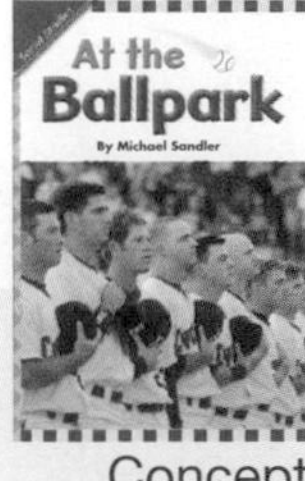

Concept Literacy

Below Level

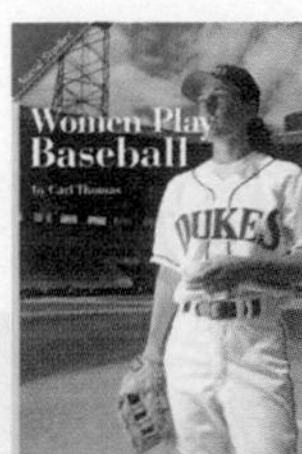

On Level

Advanced

ELL

ELD

This Week's Digital Resources

eStreet Interactive
www.ReadingStreet.com

Get Ready to Read

Background Building Audio CD This audio CD provides valuable background information about what it was like for women to play professional baseball many years ago to help children read and comprehend the weekly texts.

Concept Talk Video Use this video on the Digital Path to build momentum and introduce the weekly concept of sports traditions.

Interactive Sing with Me Big Book "An Athlete's Challenge," sung to the tune of "On Top of Old Smokey," introduces the Amazing Words with a catchy, concept-related song.

Interactive Sound-Spelling Cards With these interactive cards on the Digital Path, children see an image, hear the image name, and see the spelling patterns of words with inflected endings.

Pearson eText Use the eText for the Decodable Readers on the Leveled Reader Database for phonics and fluency support.

Letter Tile Drag and Drop Using this interactive tool on Pearson SuccessNet, children click and spell words to enhance their phonics skills.

Read and Comprehend

Envision It! Animations Use this colorful animation on the Digital Path to explain the target comprehension skill, Compare and Contrast.

Pearson eText Read the eText of the main selection, *Just Like Josh Gibson*, and the paired selection, "How Baseball Began," with audio support on Pearson SuccessNet.

Story Sort Use the Story Sort Activity on the Digital Path after reading *Just Like Josh Gibson* to involve children in summarizing.

Journal: Word Bank Use the Word Bank on the Digital Path to have children write sentences using this week's selection words.

Vocabulary Activities A variety of interactive vocabulary activities on the Digital Path help children practice concept-related words.

Language Arts

Grammar Jammer Choose a whimsical animation on the Digital Path to provide an engaging grammar lesson that will capture children's attention.

Pearson eText Find the Student Edition eText of the Let's Write It! and Let's Learn It! pages with audio support on Pearson SuccessNet.

Additional Resources

Teacher Resources DVD-ROM Use the following resources on the TR DVD or on Pearson SuccessNet throughout the week:

- Amazing Word Cards
- Reader's and Writer's Notebook
- Writing Transparencies
- Daily Fix-It Transparencies
- Scoring Rubrics
- Grammar Transparencies
- Research Transparencies
- Let's Practice It!
- Graphic Organizers
- Vocabulary Cards
- Vocabulary Transparencies

This Week's Skills

Phonics/Spelling
Inflected Endings

Comprehension
Compare and Contrast
Monitor and Clarify

Language
Vocabulary: Homophones
Conventions: Using Capital Letters

Fluency
Accuracy and Appropriate Rate

Writing
Realistic Fiction

5-Day Planner

DAY 1

Get Ready to Read

Content Knowledge 360j
Oral Vocabulary: *athlete, challenge, effort*

Phonics/Spelling 362a
Inflected Endings
Spelling Pretest
READ Decodable Reader 26A
Reread for Fluency

Monitor Progress
Check Word Reading

Read and Comprehend

Text-Based Comprehension 364a
Compare and Contrast
Monitor and Clarify

Selection Vocabulary 365a
Selection Words: *bases, cheers, field, plate, sailed, threw*

Language Arts

Conventions 365b
Using Capital Letters

Writing 365c
Realistic Fiction

Research and Inquiry 365e
Identify and Focus Topic

DAY 2

Get Ready to Read

Content Knowledge 366a
Oral Vocabulary: *dainty*

Phonics/Spelling 366c
Inflected Endings
Review Plurals
Spelling: Inflected Endings

Read and Comprehend

Selection Vocabulary 366e
Review Selection Words: *bases, cheers, field, plate, sailed, threw*
Skill: Homophones
Reread for Fluency

Monitor Progress
Check Selection Words/ High-Frequency Words

Text-Based Comprehension 367a
READ *Just Like Josh Gibson*—1st Read

Literary Text 381b
Speaker/Narrator

Language Arts

Conventions 381c
Using Capital Letters

Writing 381d
Realistic Fiction

Handwriting 381f
Cursive *U, V, W, Y*/Letter and Word Spacing

Research and Inquiry 381g
Research Skill: Globe

DAY 3

Get Ready to Read

Content Knowledge 382a
Oral Vocabulary: *disguise*

Phonics/Spelling 382c
Build Words
Fluent Word Reading
Decode and Read
Spelling: Dictation

Read and Comprehend

Fluency 382f
Accuracy and Appropriate Rate

Selection Vocabulary 382g
Selection Words: *bases, cheers, field, plate, sailed, threw*
Homophones

Text-Based Comprehension 382h
READ *Just Like Josh Gibson*—2nd Read
Monitor Progress Check Retelling

Language Arts

Conventions 384a
Using Capital Letters

Writing 384–385
Realistic Fiction

Research and Inquiry 385b
Gather and Record Information

DAY 4

Get Ready to Read

Content Knowledge 386a
Oral Vocabulary: *champion, professional, shortstop*

Phonics/Spelling 386c
Review Vowel Patterns *aw, au, au(gh), al*
Spiral Review Fluent Word Reading
READ Decodable Reader 26C
Spelling: Inflected Endings

Read and Comprehend

Social Studies in Reading 386h
READ "How Baseball Began" Paired Reading

Fluency 389a
Accuracy and Appropriate Rate
Monitor Progress Fluency Check

Language Arts

Conventions 389b
Using Capital Letters

Writing 389c
Realistic Fiction

Listening and Speaking 389e
Use Clear and Specific Vocabulary

Research and Inquiry 389f
Synthesize

DAY 5

Get Ready to Read

Content Knowledge 390a
Review Oral Vocabulary
Monitor Progress
Check Oral Vocabulary

Phonics/Spelling 390c
Review Inflected Endings
Spelling Test

Read and Comprehend

Vocabulary 390–391
Fluency 391a
Listening and Speaking 391a

Text-Based Comprehension 391b
Review Compare and Contrast

Vocabulary 391b
Review Selection Words: *bases, cheers, field, plate, sailed, threw*

Genre 391c
Review Expository Text

Assessment 391d
Monitor Progress
Sentence Reading; Fluency and Comprehension

Language Arts

Conventions 391g
Review Using Capital Letters

Writing 391h
Realistic Fiction

Research and Inquiry 391j
Communicate

Wrap Up Your Week! 391k

Access for All

What do I do in group time?

It's as easy as 1-2-3!

1 TEACHER-LED SMALL GROUPS → 2 INDEPENDENT PRACTICE STATIONS → 3 INDEPENDENT READING

Small Group Time

Bridge to Common Core

SKILL DEVELOPMENT
- Inflected Endings
- Homophones
- Compare and Contrast
- Monitor and Clarify

DEEP UNDERSTANDING

This Week's Knowledge Goals

Children will understand that sports are:
- an important tradition in our culture
- enjoyed by players and spectators
- played by both boys and girls

1 Small Group Lesson Plan

	DAY 1 Differentiate Phonics	DAY 2 Differentiate Comprehension
OL On-Level pp. SG•2–SG•6	**Practice Phonics** Additional Words with Inflected Endings **Decodable Reader** Read *The Nicest Surprise*	**Build Word Knowledge** Practice Selection Vocabulary **Access Text** Read *Just Like Josh Gibson*
SI Strategic Intervention pp. SG•7–SG•11	**Reteach Phonics** Blend Words with Inflected Endings **Decodable Reader** Read *The Nicest Surprise*	**Build Word Knowledge** Reteach Selection Vocabulary **Access Text** Read *Just Like Josh Gibson*
A Advanced pp. SG•12–SG•17	**Extend Phonics** More Words with Inflected Endings **Advanced Selection** Read "Babe Didrikson"	**Build Word Knowledge** Extend Selection Vocabulary **Access Text** Read *Just Like Josh Gibson*
Independent Inquiry Project	Introduce	Investigate
ELL **If...** children need more scaffolding and practice with...	**Phonics** **then...** use the Phonics Transition Lessons on pages 213–309 in the *ELL Handbook.*	**Comprehension Skill** **then...** use the ELL activities on p. DI•17 in the Teacher Resources section on SuccessNet.

Reading Street Sleuth

- Provides access to grade-level text for all children
- Focuses on finding clues in text through close reading
- Builds capacity for complex text

Build Text-Based Comprehension

Zoom in on

Just Like Josh Gibson

Optional Leveled Readers

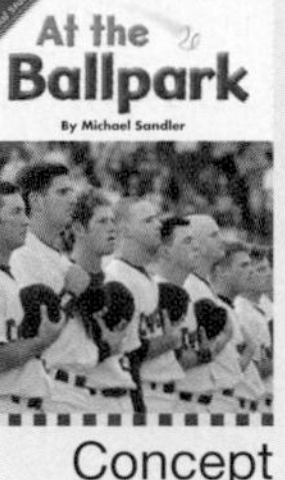

Concept Literacy

Below Level

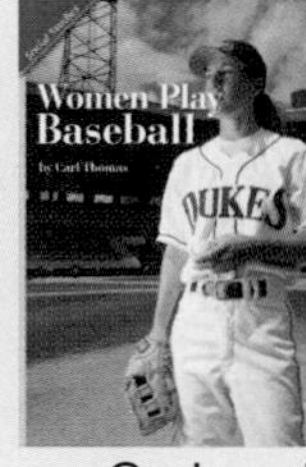

On Level

Advanced

ELL

ELD

DAY 3 Differentiate Close Reading	DAY 4 Differentiate Vocabulary	DAY 5 Differentiate Reteaching
Reread to Develop Vocabulary **Close Reading** Reread *Just Like Josh Gibson*	**Build Word Knowledge** Develop Language Using Amazing Words **Text-Based Comprehension** Read *Reading Street Sleuth,* pp. 68–69, or Leveled Readers	**Practice** Using Capital Letters **Text-Based Comprehension** Reread *Reading Street Sleuth,* pp. 68–69, or Leveled Readers
Reread to Develop Vocabulary **Close Reading** Reread *Just Like Josh Gibson*	**Build Word Knowledge** Review/Discuss Amazing Words **Text-Based Comprehension** Read *Reading Street Sleuth,* pp. 68–69, or Leveled Readers	**Review** Using Capital Letters **Text-Based Comprehension** Reread *Reading Street Sleuth,* pp. 68–69, or Leveled Readers
Reread to Develop Vocabulary **Close Reading** Reread *Just Like Josh Gibson* Investigate	**Build Word Knowledge** Extend Amazing Words and Selection Vocabulary **Text-Based Comprehension** Read *Reading Street Sleuth,* pp. 68–69, or Leveled Readers Organize	**Extend** Using Capital Letters **Text-Based Comprehension** Reread *Reading Street Sleuth,* pp. 68–69, or Leveled Readers Communicate
Main Selection **then...** use the activities on p. DI•18 in the Teacher Resources section on SuccessNet.	**Amazing Words** **then...** use the routine on pp. xxxvi–xxxvii in the *ELL Handbook.*	**Conventions and Writing** **then...** use the Grammar Transition Lessons on pp. 310–385 in the *ELL Handbook.*

2 Independent Stations

Practice Last Week's Skills

 Focus on these activities when time is limited.

ACCESS FOR ALL
- ● Below-Level Activities
- ▲ On-Level Activities
- ■ Advanced Activities

WORD WISE

Spell words.

OBJECTIVES
- Spell words with the vowel patterns *aw, au, au(gh),* and *al.*

MATERIALS
- *Word Wise* Flip Chart, Letter Tiles, paper, pencils, crayons

 **Interactive Sound-Spelling Cards**  **Letter Tile Drag and Drop**

● Children spell *draw, auto, caught,* and *talk* with Letter Tiles. They say and write the words, circling the vowel patterns. They draw and label a picture of each word.

▲ Children write *cause, August, chalk, thaw, taught,* and *caught* in the correct column of a four-column chart. They then add one new word to each column.

■ Children write *applause, awkward, squawked, audience, vault,* and *naughty* in the correct column of a four-column chart. They write a new word for each pattern and use six words in a poem.

WORD WORK

Identify vowels.

OBJECTIVES
- Identify, use, and pronounce words with the vowel patterns *aw, au, au(gh),* and *al.*

MATERIALS
- *Word Work* Flip Chart; Sound-Spelling Cards: 56–58, 106; Teacher-made word cards: *awful, audio, taught, talk, drawn, auto, caught, walk, saucer, paw, pause, chalk;* paper; pencils; crayons

 **Modeled Pronunciation Audio CD**  **Interactive Sound-Spelling Cards**

● Children say the Sound-Spelling Card words. They find word cards *audio, taught,* and *talk.* They say and draw the words.

▲ Children say the Sound-Spelling Card words. They find word cards for each pattern and say and write the words. They find another set of cards for each pattern.

■ Children find two word cards for each pattern and say and write the words. They write riddles using the words and add new words to the list.

 LET'S WRITE!

Write fiction.

OBJECTIVES
- Write a piece of humorous fiction.
- Vary sentences by using different beginnings and by combining sentences.

MATERIALS
- *Let's Write!* Flip Chart, paper, pencils

 **Grammar Jammer**

● Children write a funny story about something gone wrong, as in a large dog wrecking a house. They write at least two sentences to tell this humorous, made-up story.

▲ Children write a humorous story about something gone terribly wrong. They vary sentence beginnings and length.

■ Children plan and write a humorous story about something gone harmlessly, if terribly wrong. They vary sentence length and combine short sentences.

WORDS TO KNOW

Use suffixes.

OBJECTIVES
- Identify and use suffixes to determine a word's meaning.

MATERIALS
- *Words to Know* Flip Chart; Teacher-made word cards: *blame, help, doubt, cheer, care;* dictionaries; paper; pencils

 **Vocabulary Activities**

● Children write *helpless.* They use the suffix to guess its meaning. They write *seedless, endless,* and *beautiful.* They use dictionaries to guess and check the meanings.

▲ Children write *joyful, actor, colorful,* and *painless.* They use dictionaries to guess and check the meanings. They write sentences using each word.

■ Children read word cards and add *-ful* and *-less* to make new words. They guess and check the meanings. They choose three words and write sentences for each.

READ FOR MEANING

Use text-based comprehension tools.

OBJECTIVES

- Identify the main idea in a story.

MATERIALS

- *Read for Meaning* Flip Chart, 2.5.5 Leveled Readers, paper, pencils

 **Pearson eText**
- Leveled eReaders

 **Envision It! Animations**

● Children read *Andrew's Mistake* and write a sentence or two telling the main idea.

▲ Children read *Freda the Signmaker* and write a sentence telling the main idea. They write a paragraph telling what they liked best, underlining their main idea.

■ Children read *Marty's Summer Job* and record the main idea. They write a paragraph telling how they would continue the story, underlining their main idea.

GET FLUENT

Practice fluent reading.

OBJECTIVES

- Read aloud with appropriate phrasing.

MATERIALS

- *Get Fluent* Flip Chart, 2.5.5 Leveled Readers

 **Pearson eText**
- Leveled Readers

● Children work with a partner to take turns reading from *Andrew's Mistake.* They note punctuation for proper phrasing.

▲ Children work with a partner to take turns reading from *Freda the Signmaker.* They note punctuation for proper phrasing.

■ Children work with a partner to take turns reading from *Marty's Summer Job.* They note punctuation for proper phrasing.

Manage the Stations

Use these management tools to set up and organize your Practice Stations:

Practice Station Flip Charts

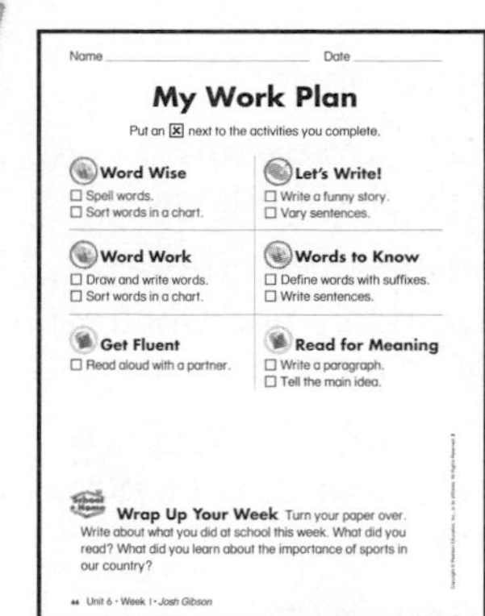
Name Date

My Work Plan

Put an ☒ next to the activities you complete.

Word Wise	Let's Write!
☐ Spell words. ☐ Sort words in a chart.	☐ Write a funny story. ☐ Vary sentences.
Word Work	**Words to Know**
☐ Draw and write words. ☐ Sort words in a chart.	☐ Define words with suffixes. ☐ Write sentences.
Get Fluent	**Read for Meaning**
☐ Read aloud with a partner.	☐ Write a paragraph. ☐ Tell the main idea.

Wrap Up Your Week Turn your paper over. Write about what you did at school this week. What did you read? What did you learn about the importance of sports in our country?

Unit 6 • Week 1 • Josh Gibson

Classroom Management Handbook for Differentiated Instruction Practice Stations, p. 44

3 Independent Reading

Children should select appropriately complex texts to read and write about independently every day before, during, and after school.

Suggestions for this week's independent reading:
- Fictional texts on last week's social studies topic: How can we be responsible when we make a mistake?
- Fiction selections about how we can be responsible when we make a mistake
- Fiction book by a favorite author

BOOK TALK Have partners discuss their independent reading for the week. Tell them to refer to their Reading Log and paraphrase what the selection was about. To focus the discussion, prompt them to talk about one or more of the following:

Key Ideas and Details
- Did I understand the main idea and why events happened?
- What did I learn from this text?
- How do the characters interact with each other?

Craft and Structure
- What happens first, next, and last?
- Did the events flow smoothly, or were they confusing?

Integration of Ideas
- Did the story seem believable? Why or why not?
- Was this book like others I have read?

 **Pearson eText**
- Student Edition
- Decodable Readers
- Leveled Readers

 **Trade Book Library**

 **Materials from School or Classroom Library**

DAY 1 at a Glance

Content Knowledge
Oral Vocabulary

Phonics/Spelling
Inflected Endings

Text-Based Comprehension
Compare and Contrast
Monitor and Clarify

Selection Vocabulary
bases, cheers, field, plate, sailed, threw

Conventions
Using Capital Letters

Writing
Realistic Fiction

Research and Inquiry
Identify and Focus Topic

Materials
- Student Edition
- Sing with Me Big Book
- Sound-Spelling Cards
- Decodable Reader 26A
- Reader's and Writer's Notebook

Bridge to Common Core

INTEGRATION OF KNOWLEDGE/IDEAS
This week children read, write, and talk about sports traditions.

Texts This Week
- "An Athlete's Challenge"
- "What Makes a Ball Bounce?"
- "The Princesses Have a Ball"
- "Tigers Over Lions"
- *Just Like Josh Gibson*
- "Yankee Doodle Shortstop"
- "How Baseball Began"

Social Studies Knowledge Goals
Children will understand that sports are
- an important tradition in our culture
- enjoyed by players and spectators
- played by both boys and girls

Street Rhymes!

Do you like baseball? I do too!
Its my favorite thing to do!
Like Gibson who could really hit,
I practice and play quite a bit.
It's no secret I have a dream
To someday join a big league team.

- To introduce this week's concept, read aloud the poem several times and ask children to join you.

Content Knowledge

Sports Traditions

CONCEPT TALK To help children gain knowledge and understanding, tell them that this week they will talk, sing, read, and write about sports traditions. Write the Question of the Week, *Why are sports traditions important in our country?,* and track the print as you read it.

Build Oral Language

TALK ABOUT SPORTS TRADITIONS Have children turn to pages 360–361 in their Student Edition. Read the title and look at photos. Use these questions to guide discussion and create the "Why are sports traditions important in our country?" concept map.

- What is the man teaching the boy in the picture on page 360? (He's teaching the boy to dribble, or to play basketball.) Let's add *Families can share sports traditions* to our concept map.
- Look at page 361. Why might the girls want the female athlete to sign a ball for them? (They are her fans and look up to her as an athlete and can learn from her.) Let's add this idea to our map.
- Look at the picture of the boys holding their Special Olympics medals. How might sports be important to these athletes? (Sports challenge them; sports help them feel proud of their accomplishments.) Let's add *Sports challenge us to do our best* to our map.

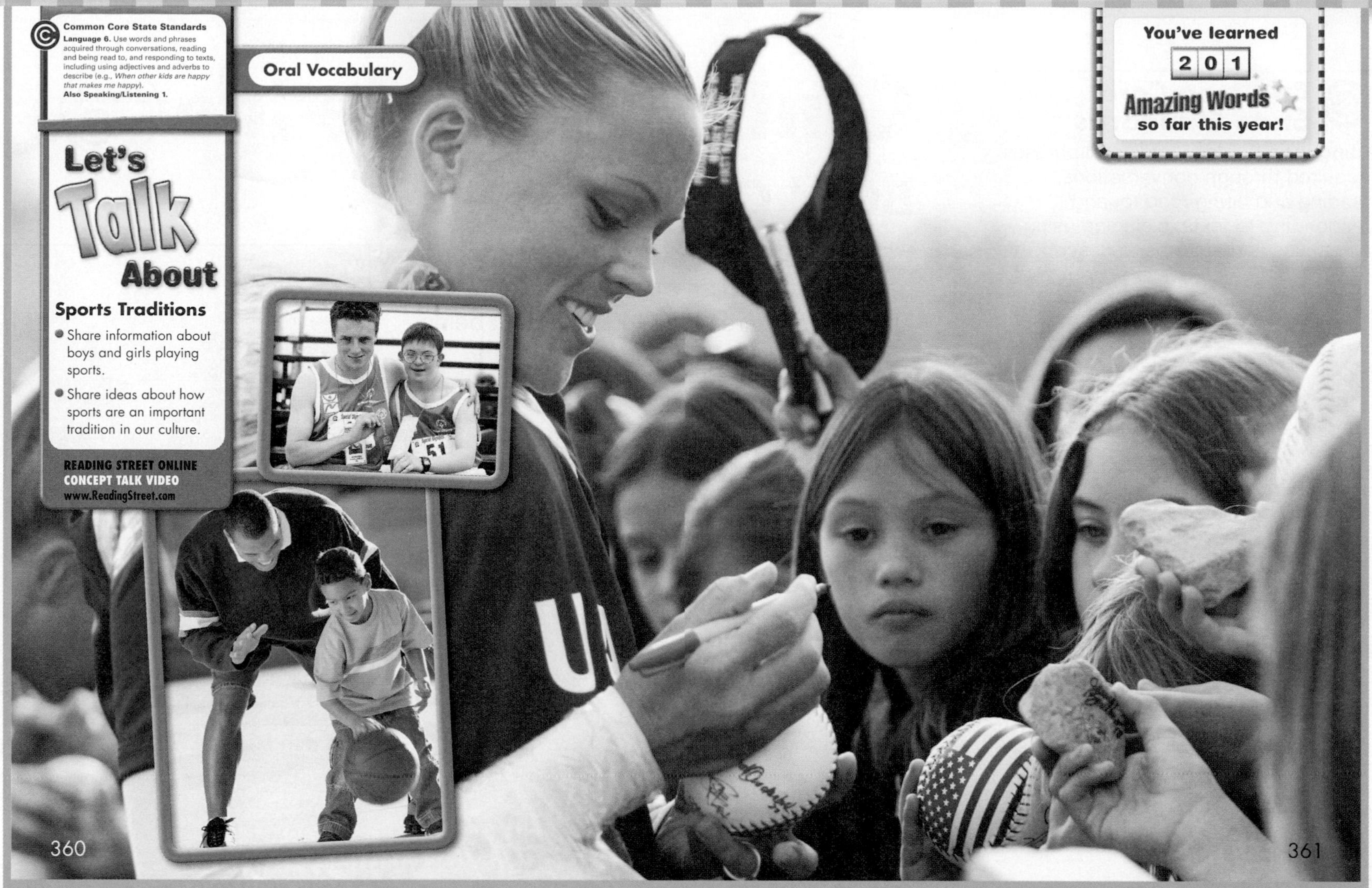

Common Core State Standards
Language 6. Use words and phrases acquired through conversations, reading and being read to, and responding to texts, including using adjectives and adverbs to describe (e.g., *When other kids are happy that makes me happy*).
Also Speaking/Listening 1.
Oral Vocabulary
Let's Talk About
Sports Traditions
Share information about boys and girls playing sports.
Share ideas about how sports are an important tradition in our culture.
READING STREET ONLINE
CONCEPT TALK VIDEO
www.ReadingStreet.com
You've learned
2 0 1
Amazing Words
so far this year!
360
361
Student Edition, pp. 360–361

CONNECT TO READING Explain that this week, children will read about a girl who loved to play baseball. Let's add *Everyone can enjoy watching or playing sports* to our map.

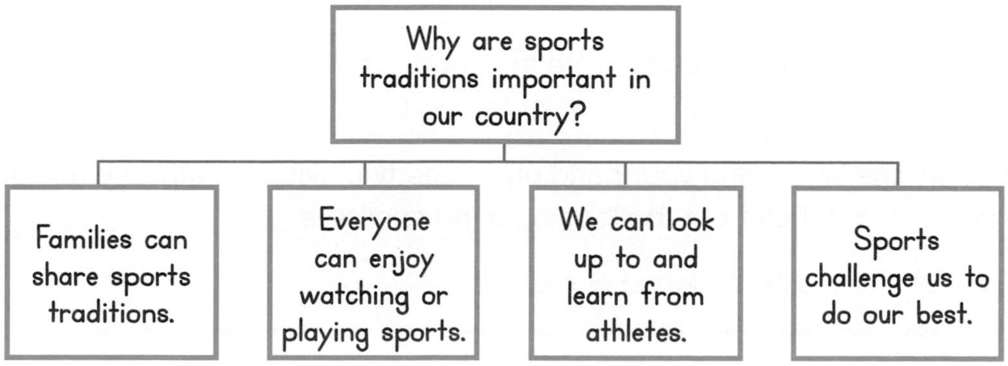

Why are sports traditions important in our country?
Families can share sports traditions.
Everyone can enjoy watching or playing sports.
We can look up to and learn from athletes.
Sports challenge us to do our best.

eStreet Interactive
www.ReadingStreet.com
- **Pearson eText**
  - Student Edition
- **Big Question Video**
- **Concept Talk Video**

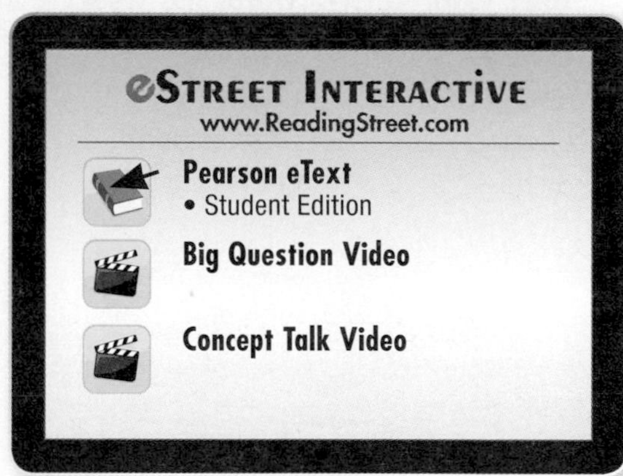

ELL

Preteach Concepts Use the Day 1 instruction on ELL Poster 26 to assess and build background knowledge, develop concepts, and build oral vocabulary.

ELL Support Additional support is provided in the *ELL Handbook* and in the ELL Support Lessons on the *Teacher Resources DVD-ROM.*

Common Core State Standards

Language 6. Use words and phrases acquired through conversations, reading and being read to, and responding to texts, including using adjectives and adverbs to describe (e.g., *When other kids are happy that makes me happy*).

Content Knowledge

Build Oral Vocabulary

INTRODUCE AMAZING WORDS Display page 26 of the *Sing with Me* Big Book. Tell children they are going to sing about being an athlete. Ask children to listen for the Amazing Words *athlete, challenge,* and *effort* as you sing. Sing the song again and have children join you.

Sing with Me Big Book, p. 26

Amazing Words

You've learned 2 0 1 words so far.

You'll learn 0 0 8 words this week!

athlete	disguise
challenge	champion
effort	professional
dainty	shortstop

Amazing Words Robust Vocabulary Routine

1. **Introduce the Word** Relate the word *athlete* to the song. *Athletes* work hard to help their team. Supply a child-friendly definition. An *athlete* is somebody who uses skills and abilities to play sports. Have children say the word.

2. **Demonstrate** Provide examples to show meaning. The basketball players were skilled *athletes.* The fastest *athletes* competed in the race.

3. **Apply** Have children demonstrate their understanding. Act out how an *athlete* would play one of your favorite sports.

4. **Display the Word** Run your hand under the two syllables *ath-lete* as you read the word. Point out the long *e* sound spelled *e_e.*

See p. OV•1 to teach *challenge* and *effort.*

Routines Flip Chart

AMAZING WORDS AT WORK Have children look at the picture on p. 26.

- I see that one *athlete* holds a bat in this picture. One *athlete* wears a mitt. What kind of sport might an *athlete* play with a bat and a mitt? Use *athlete* in your answer. (An athlete might play baseball with a bat and a mitt.)
- What *challenge* might a baseball player face in a game? Use *challenge* in your answer. (Possible response: A baseball player might face the challenge of hitting the ball and getting on base.)
- Why must everyone on a team make his or her best *effort* to compete? (Possible response: Everyone must make his or her best effort to compete because it takes everyone on the team to win.)

APPLY AMAZING WORDS Have children demonstrate their understanding of the Amazing Words by completing these sentences orally.

He used great **effort** to move the _______.

Kim's **challenge** was to _______.

The **athlete's** _______ are very strong.

Corrective feedback	**If...** children have difficulty using the Amazing Words, **then...** remind them of the definitions and provide opportunities for children to use the words in sentences.

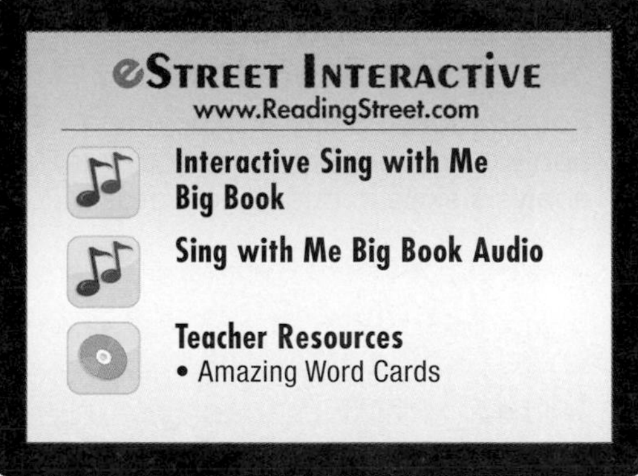

Access for All

Sentence Production If children omit the final *s* sound of the possessive, then say the sentences, stressing the sound, and have children repeat the sentences with you.

Cognates The word *athlete* may have a cognate in children's home languages. Invite Spanish speakers to identify the cognate *atleta.* Point out how this prior knowledge can help children learn new words.

Common Core State Standards

Foundational Skills 3. Know and apply grade-level phonics and word analysis skills in decoding words.

Skills Trace

 **Inflected Endings**

Introduce U6W1D1

Practice U6W1D2; U6W1D3; U6W1D4

Reteach/Review U6W1D5; U6W2D4

Assess/Test Weekly Test U6W1 Benchmark Test U6

KEY: U=Unit W=Week D=Day

Access for All

SI Strategic Intervention

Syllables Explain to children that adding *-s* to verbs does not change the number of syllables they say. Adding *-es, -ing, -er,* and *-est* will add a spoken syllable. Tell children that they will need to read *-ed* as its own syllable or as the sound /t/ or /d/ at the end of the base word.

Vocabulary Support

You may wish to explain the meaning of these words.

spicier having more spices, or seasonings

chatted talked

Phonics

Teach/Model

Inflected Endings

CONNECT Write *smaller* and *hurried.* Point out to children that they have already studied words like these. Ask them what they know about these words. (The endings *-er* and *-ed* were added to base words. The spelling of the base word *hurry* changed when *-ed* was added.)

Sound-Spelling Card 130

USE SOUND-SPELLING CARDS Display Card 130. Point to *-ies.* In this word, the *y* at the end of *cry* was changed to *i* before *-es* was added. Have children say *cry, cries* as you point to *cries.* Repeat with Cards 124, 139, 127, and 128, reviewing adding *-es* to words ending in *s, x, z, sh,* and *ch,* doubling the final consonant when a word ends in a single vowel and consonant, and dropping a final *e.*

Sound-Spelling Card 124

MODEL Write *drop.* This word is *drop.* Beneath, write *dropped.* The word *dropped* has the ending *-ed.* The final *p* was doubled. Run your finger along *dropped,* reading the base word and ending: *drop, /t/, dropped.* Follow this procedure to model *kiss, kisses; joke, joking;* and *try, tried.*

Write *spicier.* This word looks hard to read, but I see the spelling pattern *-ier* at the end. This pattern gives me a clue that the base word ends in *y.* The *y* was changed to *i* before adding the ending *-er.* I read one part at a time. Then I read the parts together: *spi, ci, er—spicier.*

GROUP PRACTICE Have children read all the words with you. Then write the words below. Have children identify the base word and ending. Have them read each part and then read the parts together.

smarter	**skated**	**judging**	**dries**	**happiest**
running	**walks**	**driving**	**bigger**	**chatted**

Sound-Spelling Card 127

REVIEW What do you know about reading base words with endings? (If a word has an ending look closely at the base word, because it may have a spelling change. Read the base word and then the ending.)

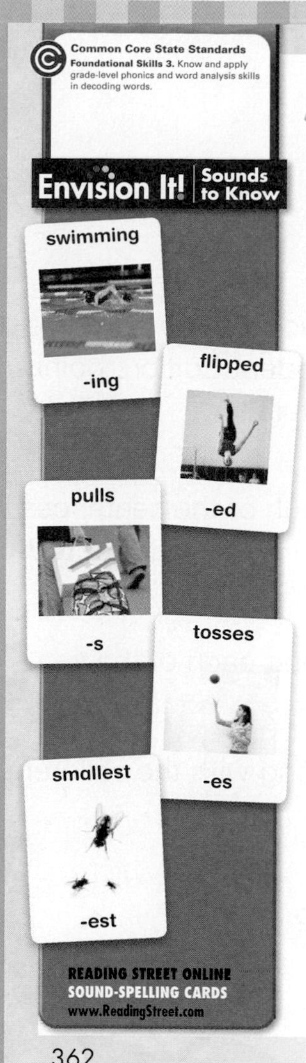

Phonics

Inflected Endings

Words I Can Blend

tapping
stopped
silliest
rides
ranches

Sentences I Can Read

1. Did Katie hear tapping on the window?
2. We stopped telling him the silliest jokes.
3. Who rides on those ranches near you?

362

The happiest persons never stop learning. Is your goal riding your bike faster? Or would you like to know how a person bakes the nicest cakes and cookies? Some people are finding out how to sing the prettiest songs. Others wish to find out about swimming longer distances. Keep looking for things that you find interesting. If you stay interested in finding out about yourself and the world around you, you will never be bored.

You've learned

Inflected Endings

363

Student Edition, pp. 362–363

Guide Practice

BLEND WORDS Have children turn to page 362 in their Student Edition. Look at the pictures on this page. I see pictures of a person swimming, a person who has flipped, a person who pulls a tote carrier, a person who tosses a ball, and the smallest of three flies. Each word has a base word and an ending. In *swimming,* the base word is *swim,* and the ending is *-ing.* In *flipped,* the base word is *flip,* and the ending is *-ed.* In *pulls,* the base word is *pull,* and the ending is *-s.* In *tosses,* the base word is *toss,* and the ending is *-es.* In *smallest,* the base word is *small,* and the ending is *-est.*

GROUP PRACTICE For each word in "Words I Can Blend," ask children to say each word part. Make sure they identify the base word and the ending. Then have children read the whole word.

Corrective feedback	**If...** children have difficulty decoding a word, **then...** model sound-by-sound blending or the word parts strategy for decodable words.

Inflected Endings Many languages do not use inflected endings. Familiarize children with their meanings as well as the appropriate situations for their use.

Pronunciation Children of various language backgrounds many not hear the difference between *-ing* and *-in,* so they may say *readin* and *sleepin* instead of *reading* and *sleeping.* Say verbs, such as *walk* and *eat,* and have children say the present participle form of the verb.

Common Core State Standards

Foundational Skills 3. Know and apply grade-level phonics and word analysis skills in decoding words. **Language 2.** Demonstrate command of the conventions of standard English capitalization, punctuation, and spelling when writing.

Academic Vocabulary

inflected ending a letter or group of letters added to a base word that changes the word's tense, voice, number, etc.

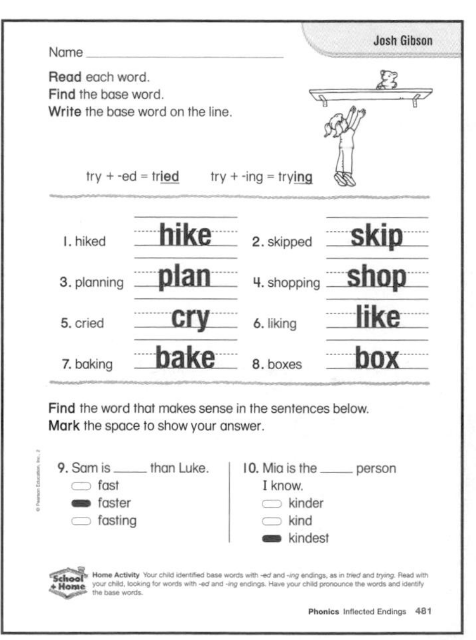
Name ______ Josh Gibson

Read each word.
Find the base word.
Write the base word on the line.

try + -ed = tr**ied**   try + -ing = try**ing**

1. hiked	hike	2. skipped	skip
3. planning	plan	4. shopping	shop
5. cried	cry	6. liking	like
7. baking	bake	8. boxes	box

Find the word that makes sense in the sentences below.
Mark the space to show your answer.

9. Sam is ____ than Luke.
- fast
- faster
- fasting

10. Mia is the ____ person I know.
- kinder
- kind
- kindest

School + Home **Home Activity** Your child identified base words with -*ed* and -*ing* endings, as in *tried* and *trying*. Read with your child, looking for words with -*ed* and -*ing* endings. Have your child pronounce the words and identify the base words.

Phonics Inflected Endings 481

Reader's and Writer's Notebook, p. 481

Phonics

Apply

DECODE WORDS IN ISOLATION After children can successfully combine the word parts to read the words on page 362 in their Student Edition, point to words in random order and ask children to read them naturally.

DECODE WORDS IN CONTEXT Have children read each of the sentences on page 362. Have them identify words in the sentences that have **inflected endings.**

Team Talk Pair children and have them take turns reading each of the sentences aloud. Have them identify any spelling changes.

Chorally read the "I Can Read!" passage on page 363 along with the children. Then have them read the passage aloud to themselves.

ON THEIR OWN Use *Reader's and Writer's Notebook,* p. 481.

Inflected Endings

FORMATIVE ASSESSMENT Write the following words and have the class read them. Notice which words children miss during the group reading. Call on individuals to read some of the words.

tried	reaches	bouncing	jogging	funnier	**Spiral Review**
phoned	luckier	stringiest	graphs	laughing ←	Row 2 reviews consonant patterns *ph, gh, ck, ng.*
chopped	stretches	shiniest	thinking	whispers ←	Row 3 reviews consonant digraphs.

If... children cannot read base words and endings at this point,

then... use the Small Group Time Strategic Intervention lesson, p. SG•7, to reteach inflected endings. Continue to monitor children's progress using other instructional opportunities during the week. See the Skills Trace on p. 362a.

Spelling Pretest

Inflected Endings

DICTATE SPELLING WORDS Dictate spelling words. Have children write words. If needed, break the words into meaningful word parts, clarify pronunciations, and give a definition for each word. Have children check their pretests and correct misspelled words.

1. tried	I **tried** to cook breakfast by myself.
2. trying	I'm **trying** to eat healthy snacks.
3. planned	We **planned** to visit Grandma next week.
4. planning	Our class is **planning** to have a party.
5. liked	My sister **liked** my new haircut.
6. liking	Everyone is **liking** the fruit salad.
7. skipped	I **skipped** one problem on the test.
8. skipping	Jeff and I like **skipping** rocks on the pond.
9. heavier	That big cat is **heavier** than the small dog.
10. heaviest	Ben wears his **heaviest** coat in the snow.
11. lighter	A feather is **lighter** than a big flower.
12. lightest	Sam carries the **lightest** bag of groceries.

ON THEIR OWN Use Let's Practice It!, p. 295 on the *Teacher Resources DVD-ROM.*

Access for All

Advanced

Extend Spelling Allow children who spell words correctly to spell more difficult words such as *earns, knitting, circles, distinguishing,* and *crumbled.*

Phonics/Spelling Generalization

Each spelling word ends in one of the inflected endings.

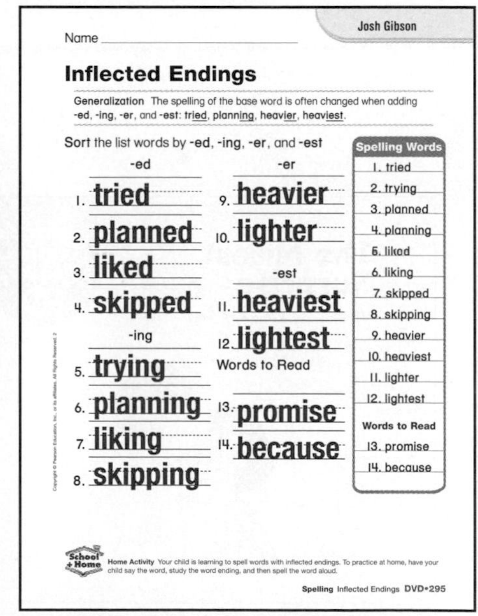

Name Josh Gibson

Inflected Endings

Generalization The spelling of the base word is often changed when adding -ed, -ing, -er, and -est: tried, planning, heavier, heaviest.

Sort the list words by -ed, -ing, -er, and -est

-ed
1. tried
2. planned
3. liked
4. skipped

-ing
5. trying
6. planning
7. liking
8. skipping

-er
9. heavier
10. lighter

-est
11. heaviest
12. lightest

Words to Read
13. promise
14. because

Spelling Words
1. tried
2. trying
3. planned
4. planning
5. liked
6. liking
7. skipped
8. skipping
9. heavier
10. heaviest
11. lighter
12. lightest

Words to Read
13. promise
14. because

School + Home Home Activity Your child is learning to spell words with inflected endings. To practice at home, have your child say the word, study the word ending, and then spell the word aloud.

Spelling Inflected Endings DVD•295

Let's Practice It! TR DVD•295

Day 1 SMALL GROUP TIME • Differentiate Phonics, p. SG•1

OL On-Level
- **Practice Phonics** Additional Words with Inflected Endings
- **Read** Decodable Reader *The Nicest Surprise*

SI Strategic Intervention
- **Reteach Phonics** Blend Words with Inflected Endings
- **Read** Decodable Reader *The Nicest Surprise*

A Advanced
- **Extend Phonics** More Words with Inflected Endings
- **Read** Advanced Selection for Words with Inflected Endings
- **Introduce** Inquiry Project

If... children need more scaffolding and practice with **Phonics,** **then...** use the Phonics Transition Lessons on pages 213–309 in the *ELL Handbook.*

Common Core State Standards

Foundational Skills 3. Know and apply grade-level phonics and word analysis skills in decoding words. **Foundational Skills 4.** Read with sufficient accuracy and fluency to support comprehension.

Decodable Reader 26A

If children need help, then...

Read *The Nicest Surprise*

DECODE WORDS IN ISOLATION Have children turn to page 181 in *Decodable Practice Readers* 2.2 and decode each word.

READ HIGH-FREQUENCY WORDS Have children identify and read the high-frequency words *trip, surprise, returns, keep,* and *flowers* on the first page.

PREVIEW DECODABLE READER Have children read the title and preview the story. Tell them they will read words with endings *-s, -ed, -ing, -er,* and *-est.*

DECODE WORDS IN CONTEXT Pair children for reading and listen carefully as they decode. One child begins. Children read the entire story, switching readers after each page. Partners reread the story. This time the other child begins.

Decodable Practice Reader 26A

The Nicest Surprise

Written by Renee McLean

Inflected Endings *-s, -ed, -ing, -er, -est*

longest	planning	biggest	returns	tried
excited	helped	prettiest	tied	flowers
nicer	soaps	pointed	thinking	cleaned
cooking	making	likes	hopped	going
waved	faster	cried	rushed	peeking
called	closed	opened	nicest	coming
hugged				

High-Frequency Words

trip	surprise	returns
keep	flowers	

181

Decodable Practice Reader 26A

Mom was on the longest trip.
Ben and Jake are planning the biggest surprise for when she returns.
They have tried to keep it a secret.
They are so excited!

182

Dad helped Ben gather the prettiest flowers in the garden.
Ben tied the bundle.
He set his flowers on the table.

183

Jake put nicer soaps in Mom's bathroom.
"Maybe she will enjoy a bubble bath," Jake pointed out.
"That is good thinking," Ben said.

184

Jake and Ben cleaned while Dad was cooking.
"Dad is a good cook," Jake said.
"I hope he is making what Mom likes."
Jake went to talk to Dad.

185

Dad, Ben, and Jake hopped in the car.
They were going to pick up Mom!
She waved faster at them.
"It's Mom!" Jake and Ben cried.

186

They rushed home.
"No peeking!" Ben called.
Mom closed her eyes as Ben and Jake led her inside.
Then she opened her eyes wide.

187

"This is the nicest surprise!
When I go away, I like coming home the best!" Mom cried.
Ben and Jake hugged her tightly.

188

Corrective feedback

If... children have difficulty decoding a word,
then... refer them to the Sound-Spelling Cards to identify the sounds in a decodable word; prompt them to blend the word. If the word has an inflected ending, have them identify all the word parts and read them together to say the word.

- What is the new word?
- Is the new word a word you know?
- Does it make sense in the story?

CHECK DECODING AND COMPREHENSION Have children retell the story to include characters, setting, and events. Then have children find words that include inflected endings in the story. For each word, have children identify any spelling change. Children should supply the following words:

-s: *returns, flowers, soaps, likes, eyes*

-ed: *tried, excited, helped, tied, pointed, cleaned, hopped, waved, cried, rushed, called, closed, opened, hugged*

-ing: *planning, thinking, cooking, making, going, peeking, coming*

-er: *nicer, faster*

-est: *longest, biggest, prettiest, nicest*

Reread for Fluency

REREAD DECODABLE READER Have children reread Decodable Practice Reader 26A to develop automaticity reading words with inflected endings.

Routine Oral Rereading

1. **Read** Have children read the entire book orally.
2. **Reread** To achieve optimal fluency, children should reread the text three or four times.
3. **Corrective Feedback** Listen as children read. Provide corrective feedback regarding their fluency and decoding.

Routines Flip Chart

Inflected Endings

Beginning Before reading, guide children on a picture walk of *The Nicest Surprise.* Connect the pictures to the words *tied, cleaned, waved, closed,* and *hugged.* Explain that the ending *-ed* shows the action happened in the past. Have children echo the word and model the action.

Intermediate After reading, have children page through *The Nicest Surprise* using the pictures to retell the story. Encourage them to use words with inflected endings. Record the words and have children identify the ending of each word.

Advanced Create a four-column chart with the headings "No change," "Double the consonant," "Drop *e,*" and "Change *y* to *i.*" Have partners categorize words with inflected endings on the first three pages of *The Nicest Surprise* by writing the words under the correct heading. Have them identify the base words.

Text-Based Comprehension

Compare and Contrast

Monitor and Clarify

Common Core State Standards

Informational Text 1. Ask and answer such questions as *who, what, where, when, why,* and *how* to demonstrate understanding of key details in a text.

Skills Trace

Compare and Contrast

Introduce U2W5D1; U3W3D1; U6W1D1

Practice U2W5D2; U2W5D3; U2W5D4; U3W3D2; U3W3D3; U3W3D4; U6W1D2; U6W1D3; U6W1D4

Reteach/Review U1W4D3; U2W4D3; U2W5D5; U3W3D5; U6W1D5; U6W5D3

Assess/Test Weekly Tests U2W5; U3W3; U6W1
Benchmark Test U2

KEY: U=Unit W=Week D=Day

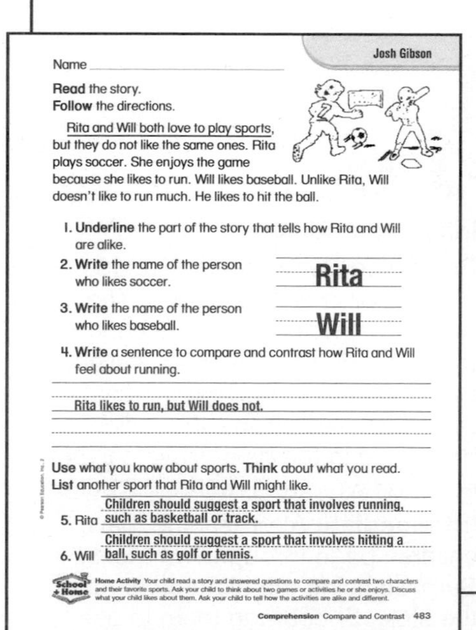

Name ______

Josh Gibson

Read the story.
Follow the directions.

Rita and Will both love to play sports, but they do not like the same ones. Rita plays soccer. She enjoys the game because she likes to run. Will likes baseball. Unlike Rita, Will doesn't like to run much. He likes to hit the ball.

1. **Underline** the part of the story that tells how Rita and Will are alike.
2. **Write** the name of the person who likes soccer. **Rita**
3. **Write** the name of the person who likes baseball. **Will**
4. **Write** a sentence to compare and contrast how Rita and Will feel about running.
   Rita likes to run, but Will does not.

Use what you know about sports. **Think** about what you read. **List** another sport that Rita and Will might like.

5. Rita Children should suggest a sport that involves running, such as basketball or track.
6. Will Children should suggest a sport that involves hitting a ball, such as golf or tennis.

Home Activity Your child read a story and answered questions to compare and contrast two characters and their favorite sports. Ask your child to think about two games or activities he or she enjoys. Discuss what your child likes about them. Ask your child to tell how the activities are alike and different.

Comprehension Compare and Contrast 483

Reader's and Writer's Notebook, pp. 483 and 491

READ Remind children of the weekly concept—Sports Traditions. Have children follow along as you read "What Makes a Ball Bounce?" on page 365.

Think Aloud **MODEL A CLOSE READ** Demonstrate close reading for children. Have children follow along as you reread the first two sentences of "What Makes a Ball Bounce?" The first sentence compares a baseball and a tennis ball by saying they look almost the same. The second sentence explains one way they look alike: they are both round. When I see the words *same* and *both,* I know that they are clues that the balls are being compared.

INTRODUCE Have children read p. 364. Explain that the skill of compare and contrast and the strategy of monitor and clarify are tools they can use to deepen their understanding. Review the bulleted items and explanations on p. 364. Then have children use a graphic organizer like the one shown to **compare** and **contrast** a baseball and a tennis ball.

IDENTIFY TEXT EVIDENCE Have children reread "What Makes a Ball Bounce?" using the callouts as guides. Then ask volunteers to respond to the callouts, citing specific examples from the text to support their answers.

APPLY Use *Reader's and Writer's Notebook,* pp. 483 and 491 for additional practice with comparing and contrasting. Children may also turn to pp. EI•5 and EI•21 to review the skill and strategy if necessary.

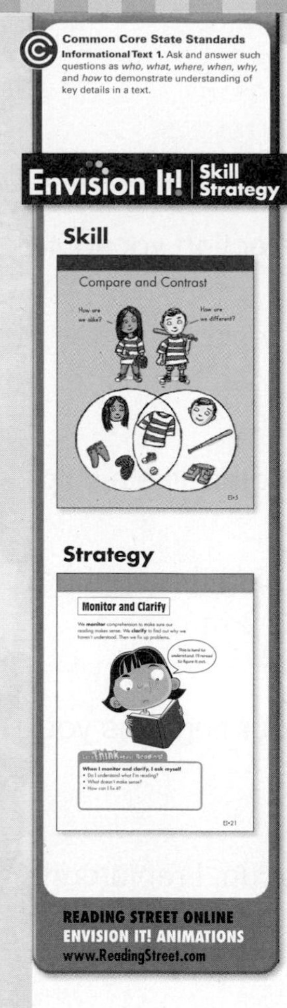

Comprehension Skill

Compare and Contrast

- When you compare, you tell how things are alike. When you contrast, you tell how things are different.
- *Like, also, both,* and *unlike* are clue words.
- Use what you learned about compare and contrast to fill in a diagram like the one below as you read "What Makes a Ball Bounce?"

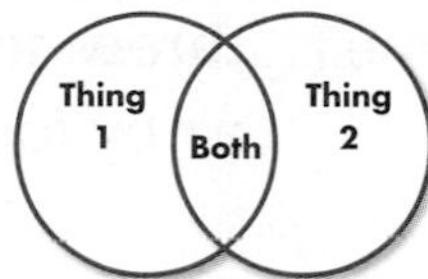

Comprehension Strategy

Monitor and Clarify

Active readers ask themselves questions during and after reading. If you are not sure of the exact answer to the question, you can go back and read again. Look for clue words or sentences to help you find the answer.

364

What Makes a Ball Bounce?

A baseball and a tennis ball look almost the same. They are both round. They are about the same size. They also have seams on the outside.

What would happen if you used a tennis ball to play baseball or a baseball to play tennis? The answer is in the bounce.

A tennis ball has much more bounce than a baseball. If you drop a tennis ball and a baseball from the same height, the tennis ball will go higher.

A tennis ball is made of rubber and is filled with air. Rubber and air help balls bounce. Unlike tennis balls, baseballs have a little rubber, but not much, and are solid inside.

It is a good thing that baseballs don't bounce as high as tennis balls. A tennis ball hit with a bat might bounce right out of the park!

Skill This paragraph tells how baseballs and tennis balls are alike. What clue words are used to compare?

Strategy Are you confused? Ask yourself, *What are some differences?* Read the article again, and look for clue words to find the answer.

Your Turn!

Need a Review? See the *Envision It! Handbook* for additional help with compare and contrast and monitor and clarify.

Let's Think About...

Ready to Try It? As you read *Just Like Josh Gibson,* use what you learned to understand the text.

365

Student Edition, pp. 364–365

Model Fluent Reading

ACCURACY AND APPROPRIATE RATE Have children listen as you read paragraph 1 of "What Makes a Ball Bounce?" and model how to read without mistakes at an appropriate rate.

Routine Paired Reading

1. **Reread** To achieve optimal fluency, children should reread the text three or four times with appropriate phrasing.
2. **Corrective Feedback** Listen as children read. Provide corrective feedback regarding their fluency and decoding.

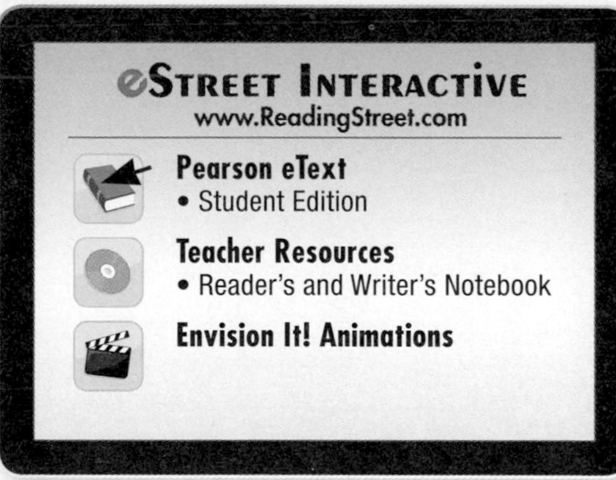

Skills/Strategies

Skill The clue words are *same* and *both.*

Strategy A tennis ball is made of rubber and filled with air, to help it bounce. A baseball has just a little rubber and is solid. The word *unlike* is a clue to the contrast.

Academic Vocabulary 

compare to show how things are alike

contrast to show how things are different

Common Core State Standards

Language 2. Demonstrate command of the conventions of standard English capitalization, punctuation, and spelling when writing. **Language 2.a.** Capitalize holidays, product names, and geographic names.

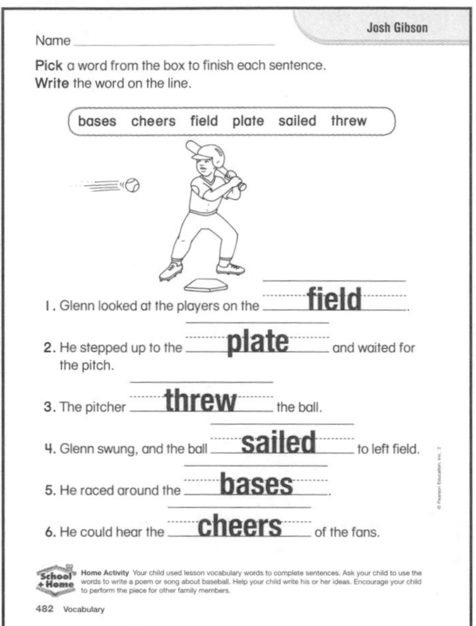

Josh Gibson

Name ______________

Pick a word from the box to finish each sentence.
Write the word on the line.

bases cheers field plate sailed threw

1. Glenn looked at the players on the **field**.
2. He stepped up to the **plate** and waited for the pitch.
3. The pitcher **threw** the ball.
4. Glenn swung, and the ball **sailed** to left field.
5. He raced around the **bases**.
6. He could hear the **cheers** of the fans.

School + Home **Home Activity** Your child used lesson vocabulary words to complete sentences. Ask your child to use the words to write a poem or song about baseball. Help your child write his or her ideas. Encourage your child to perform the piece for other family members.

482 Vocabulary

Reader's and Writer's Notebook, p. 482

Selection Vocabulary

Use the following routine to introduce this week's tested selection vocabulary.

bases places that are stations or goals in certain games, such as baseball

cheers happy or encouraging shouts

field a place of land used for some special purpose

plate a hard rubber slab that a baseball player stands beside to bat

sailed moved smoothly like a ship with sails

threw sent something through the air by force of your arm

SEE IT/SAY IT Write *bases.* Scan across the word with your finger as you say it: ba-ses.

HEAR IT Use the word in a sentence. After hitting a home run, I ran around the bases.

DEFINE IT Elicit definitions from children. How would you tell another child what *bases* are? Clarify or give a definition when necessary. Yes, *bases* are "stations in some games, such as baseball." Restate the word in child-friendly terms. In baseball, you run around the bases.

Team Talk What sports use bases? Turn to your partner and talk about this. Be prepared to explain your answer. Allow children time to discuss. Ask for examples. Rephrase their examples for usage when necessary or to correct misunderstandings.

MAKE CONNECTIONS Have children discuss the word. When do you stand on the bases in baseball? Turn and talk to your partner about this. Then be prepared to share. Have children share. Rephrase their ideas for usage when necessary or to correct misunderstandings.

RECORD Have children write the word and meaning.

Continue this routine to introduce the remaining words in this manner.

ON THEIR OWN Use *Reader's and Writer's Notebook,* p. 482.

Corrective feedback | **If...** children are having difficulty understanding, **then...** review the definitions in small groups.

Conventions

Using Capital Letters

MAKE CONNECTIONS Write the following sentence on the board. *Dr. Weaver's office was closed on Monday because it was Columbus Day.* Look at the sentence. What words are capitalized? Explain that there are rules we must follow with capital letters.

TEACH Explain that names of months, days of the week, titles for people, and holidays begin with a capital letter. *January, Tuesday, Mrs. Rossi,* and *Labor Day* all begin with capital letters.

MODEL Display Grammar Transparency 26. Read the definition aloud. Model identifying the capitalized word or words in each example. Then read the directions and model number 1.

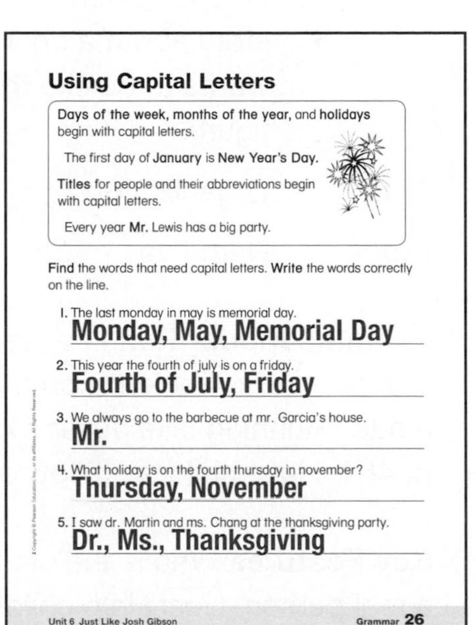

Using Capital Letters

Days of the week, months of the year, and **holidays** begin with capital letters.

The first day of **January** is **New Year's Day.**

Titles for people and their abbreviations begin with capital letters.

Every year **Mr.** Lewis has a big party.

Find the words that need capital letters. **Write** the words correctly on the line.

1. The last monday in may is memorial day. **Monday, May, Memorial Day**
2. This year the fourth of july is on a friday. **Fourth of July, Friday**
3. We always go to the barbecue at mr. Garcia's house. **Mr.**
4. What holiday is on the fourth thursday in november? **Thursday, November**
5. I saw dr. Martin and ms. Chang at the thanksgiving party. **Dr., Ms., Thanksgiving**

Unit 6 Just Like Josh Gibson — Grammar 26

Grammar Transparency 26 TR DVD

GUIDE PRACTICE Continue with items 2–5, having children identify words that need capital letters and write them correctly.

APPLY Have the class answer these questions orally in complete sentences. Have them identify the words in their sentences that need a capital letter.

1. **What is today's date?**
2. **What is your favorite day of the week?**
3. **What is our principal's name?**

Team Talk Pair children and have them answer the following questions: What is your birthday month? What is your favorite holiday? Then have them identify which words in their answers require capital letters.

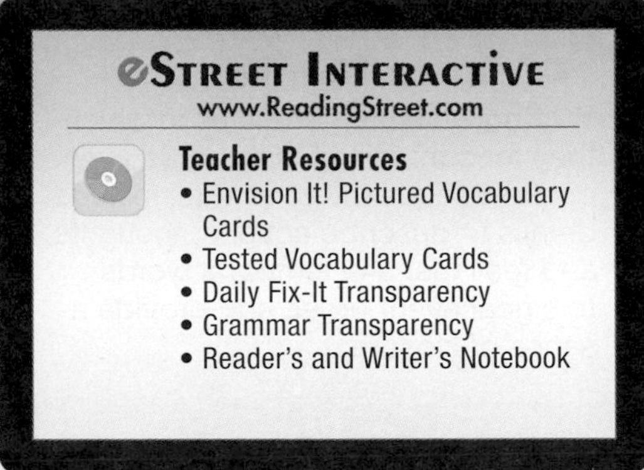

Access for All

Word Production Help children remember words that require capital letters by having them say the names of months, days of the week, holidays, and titles.

Daily Fix-It

1. i want to be an atlete.
   I want to be an athlete.
2. they're watching ken play
   They're watching Ken play.

Discuss the Daily Fix-It corrections with children. Review capitalization, punctuation, and consonant digraph *th.*

Conventions Support In languages such as Spanish, French, and Portuguese, the days and months are not usually capitalized. Provide additional practice with this English spelling convention.

Options for Conventions Support To provide children with practice with capitalization, use the grammar lessons on pp. 312–313 in the *ELL Handbook.*

Common Core State Standards

Writing 3. Write narratives in which they recount a well-elaborated event or short sequence of events, include details to describe actions, thoughts, and feelings, use temporal words to signal event order, and provide a sense of closure.

Bridge to Common Core

TEXT TYPES AND PURPOSES

This week children write a realistic story about a character who wants to be like a sports hero.

Narrative Writing

Through reading and discussion, children will gain a deeper understanding of sports traditions. They will use the knowledge from the texts to write and support realistic fiction narratives.

Throughout the week, children will improve the range and content of their writing through daily mini-lessons.

5-Day Plan

DAY 1	Read Like a Writer
DAY 2	Sequence
DAY 3	Writer's Craft: Sequence
DAY 4	Revise: Adding Words and Phrases
DAY 5	Proofread

Academic Vocabulary

characters people or animals who take part in the events of a story

setting where and when a story takes place

Writing

Zoom in on

Realistic Fiction

Mini-Lesson Read Like a Writer

- **Introduce** This week you will write realistic fiction. Realistic fiction is a story that is made up, but it is like real life. You can imagine this kind of story really happening.

Prompt Think about one of your favorite sports heroes. Now write a story about a character who wants to be like that sports figure.

Trait Organization

Mode Narrative

Name Josh Gibson

Writing • Realistic Story

Running Like Jesse Owens

Rayshaun took his place on the track for the next running event, the 100-meter dash. He thought about his hero, Jesse Owens, who also ran track in high school. Over 80 years ago, Owens tied the world record for the 100-meter dash several times with a time of 9.4 seconds. Rayshaun's best time was 9.8. Could he tie Owen's record today?

The starting gun went off! The runners raced down the track. Rayshaun tried to do his best.

When Rayshaun crossed the finish line, the clock showed 9.7 seconds. Rayshaun had taken a tenth of a second off of his time. He was even closer to Owen's record!

Key Features of a Realistic Story
- Characters and setting seem real.
- Characters do things that could really happen.
- The story has a beginning, middle, and end.

484 Writing Realistic Story

Reader's and Writer's Notebook, p. 484

- **Examine Model Text** Let's listen to a realistic story. Track the print as you read aloud "Running Like Jesse Owens" on *Reader's and Writer's Notebook,* p. 484. Have children follow along.

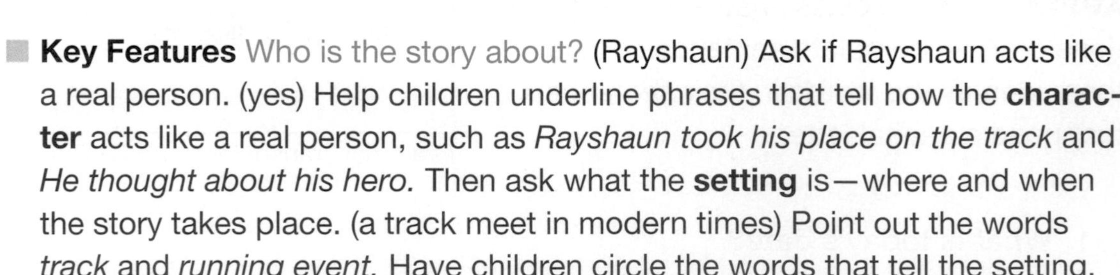

- **Key Features** Who is the story about? (Rayshaun) Ask if Rayshaun acts like a real person. (yes) Help children underline phrases that tell how the **character** acts like a real person, such as *Rayshaun took his place on the track* and *He thought about his hero.* Then ask what the **setting** is—where and when the story takes place. (a track meet in modern times) Point out the words *track* and *running event.* Have children circle the words that tell the setting.

This story has a character who is like a real person. The setting is like a real place, too. The writer tells about events that could really happen at a track.

The story has a beginning as Rayshaun takes his place on the track and thinks about his hero, Jesse Owens. In the middle, Rayshaun runs the race. At the end, Rayshaun crosses the finish line and compares his time to Owens' time. Have children number from 1 to 3 the beginning, middle, and end of the story.

Review Key Features

Review key features of realistic fiction with children. You may want to post these key features in the classroom to allow children to refer to them as they work on their stories.

Key Features of Realistic Fiction

- characters and setting seem real
- characters do things that could really happen

Connect to Familiar Texts

Use examples from *Bad Dog, Dodger!* (Unit 5) or another realistic story familiar to children. In *Bad Dog, Dodger!* the main characters are a boy and his new puppy. There are realistic events at the beginning (Sam works to show he is responsible), the middle (Sam gets a puppy and trains it to behave), and the end (Dodger behaves during Sam's ball game). The settings, a home and a ball field, are realistic places for a boy and dog.

Routine Quick Write for Fluency

Team Talk

1. **Talk** Read these questions aloud, and have children respond.
   Where are different kinds of sports played?
   Who are some athletes who play these sports?
2. **Write** Have children write short sentences to answer the questions. Make sure sentences and proper nouns begin with a capital letter.
3. **Share** Partners can read their answers to one another and identity words with capital letters.

Routines Flip Chart

Write Guy *by Jeff Anderson*

Organization

Organization is a trait of good writing, but let's not be so concerned with form that we forget about meaning. A child may develop a good way to communicate ideas that does not precisely follow the format we expect. There isn't only one way to reach the goal. And there isn't just one way to organize your writing. Reward creativity and help children see what other writers do in mentor texts.

Common Core State Standards

Speaking/Listening 1. Participate in collaborative conversations with diverse partners about grade 2 topics and texts with peers and adults in small and larger groups.

21st Century Skills

Internet Guy *Don Leu*

Weekly Inquiry Project

STEP 1	Identify and Focus Topic
STEP 2	Research Skill
STEP 3	Gather and Record Information
STEP 4	Synthesize
STEP 5	Communicate

Research and Inquiry

Step 1 Identify and Focus Topic

TEACH Display and review the concept map that explores this week's question: *Why are sports traditions important in our country?* What ideas about sports traditions would you like to learn more about? Ask children to share their interests. Help them identify ways that sports traditions help athletes.

Think Aloud **MODEL** I want to know how sports traditions help athletes. First, I will think about traditions that athletes might use. Then I am going to look for information about athletes to find out if they use those sports traditions.

GUIDE PRACTICE Give children time to think about questions they have relating to how sports traditions help athletes. Record children's questions in a chart.

Topic: Sports Traditions Help Athletes

Question	Answer
How do athletes learn the sport?	

Wrap Up Your Day!

✔ **Phonics: Inflected Endings** Write *smiled* and *clapping.* Have children read the words and identify the base word and ending in each.

✔ **Spelling: Inflected Endings** Have children add *-ed* and *-ing* to *plan* and *try.* Have children add *-er* and *-est* to *light* and *heavy.*

✔ **Content Knowledge** Have children recall what happened in the *Sing with Me* song "An Athlete's Challenge." Why is being part of a team an important tradition? (Possible response: It is important to learn the skills of the sport, to learn to work with others, and to develop team spirit.)

✔ **Homework** Send home this week's Family Times Newsletter from Let's Practice It!, pp. 291–292 on the *Teacher Resources DVD-ROM.*

Name

Family Times

You are your child's first and best teacher!

This week we're

Reading Just Like Josh Gibson

Talking About Why sports are important in our country

Learning About Inflected Endings
Compare and Contrast

1

Let's Practice It!
TR DVD•291–292

Tell children that tomorrow they will read about a girl who liked to play baseball, an American sports tradition.

DAY 2 at a Glance

Content Knowledge
Oral Vocabulary

Phonics/Spelling
Inflected Endings

Selection Vocabulary
bases, cheers, field, plate, sailed, threw
Homophones

Text-Based Comprehension
Compare and Contrast
Monitor and Clarify

Conventions
Using Capital Letters

Writing
Realistic Fiction
Writing Trait: Organization

Handwriting
Cursive *U, V, W, Y*/Letter and Word Spacing

Research and Inquiry
Research Skill: Globe

Materials

- Student Edition
- Sing with Me Big Book
- Read Aloud Anthology
- Reader's and Writer's Notebook
- Sound-Spelling Cards

Common Core State Standards

Speaking/Listening 2. Recount or describe key ideas or details from a text read aloud or information presented orally or through other media. **Language 6.** Use words and phrases acquired through conversations, reading and being read to, and responding to texts, including using adjectives and adverbs to describe (e.g., *When other kids are happy that makes me happy*).

Content Knowledge

Sports Traditions

EXPAND THE CONCEPT To reinforce concepts and to focus children's attention, have children sing "An Athlete's Challenge" from the *Sing with Me* Big Book. What does the song say about how athletes work together? (They play together on a team.)

Build Oral Language

INTRODUCE AMAZING WORDS Have children read the title "The Princesses Have a Ball." Identify the author. Explain that in the story, the author uses some Amazing Words. Read the story and have children listen for the word *dainty.*

"The Princesses Have a Ball"

TALK ABOUT SENTENCES AND WORDS Reread this sentence from the story.

But they didn't dance, as a point of pride, and their dainty step was a healthy stride.

- Have children repeat the sentence with you. What does *their dainty step was a healthy stride* mean? (They walked with long steps rather than with tiny, graceful steps.)
- What does *dainty* mean? ("small, graceful")
- **Team Talk** What other words could we use in place of *dainty?* Have children share their suggestions.
- After children have tried other words, ask: Why do you think the author chose the word *dainty?* (In the phrase *dainty step,* it implies a certain grace and it contrasts nicely with a "healthy stride.")
- **Team Talk** Turn to your partner and say the sentence again using your own words rather than *dainty step* and *healthy stride.*

Build Oral Vocabulary

Amazing Words — Robust Vocabulary Routine

1. **Introduce the Word** Relate the word *dainty* to the story. The princesses do not have a *dainty* way of walking. Supply a child-friendly definition. *Dainty* means "delicate and pretty." Have children say the word.
2. **Demonstrate** Provide examples to show meaning. The dress has a *dainty* lace collar. Those small, white flowers are very *dainty*.
3. **Apply** Have children demonstrate their understanding. Name a word that means the opposite of *dainty*. Show me what it would look like to have a *dainty* way of walking.
4. **Display the Word** Run your hand under the two syllables *dain-ty* as you read the word. Point out the long *a* sound spelled *ai*.

Routines Flip Chart

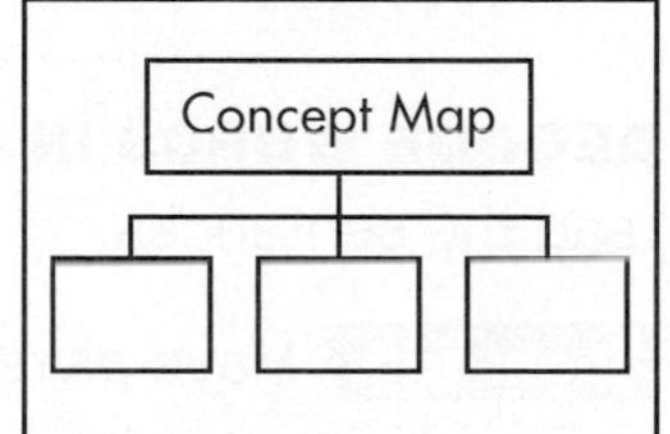

ADD TO THE CONCEPT MAP Discuss how sports traditions are important and how people can enjoy watching and playing sports.

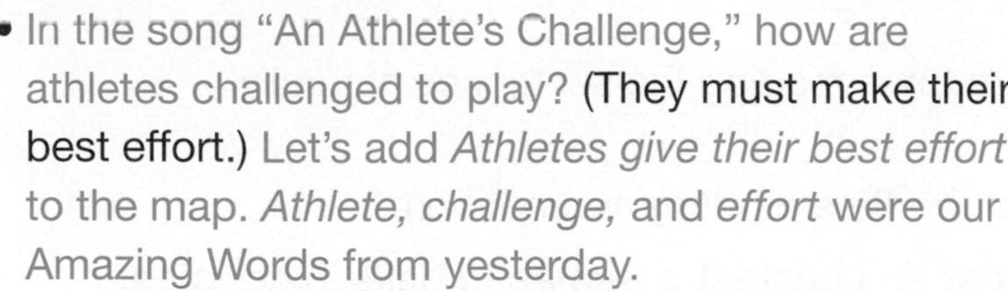

- In the song "An Athlete's Challenge," how are athletes challenged to play? (They must make their best effort.) Let's add *Athletes give their best effort* to the map. *Athlete, challenge,* and *effort* were our Amazing Words from yesterday.
- In "The Princesses Have a Ball," why do the princesses play basketball in secret? (They think their father would not want girls to play sports.) What happens after the king sees his daughters playing ball? (The girls play whenever they want and their father is the referee.) Let's add *Girls and boys can play sports* and *Families play games together* to the map.

Amazing Words

athlete	disguise
challenge	champion
effort	professional
dainty	shortstop

Reinforce Vocabulary Use the Day 2 instruction on ELL Poster 26 to reinforce the meanings of selection vocabulary.

Access Content Help children recognize the meanings of the words *athlete* and *team* by showing them photos of individual athletes and teams.

Common Core State Standards

Foundational Skills 3. Know and apply grade-level phonics and word analysis skills in decoding words. **Language 2.** Demonstrate command of the conventions of standard English capitalization, punctuation, and spelling when writing. **Also Language 2.d.**

Phonics

Review Plurals

Inflected Endings

REVIEW SOUND-SPELLINGS Review spelling patterns of plurals using Sound-Spelling Cards 139, 140, 141, and 142 and base words with inflected endings using Sound-Spelling Cards 121, 122, 123, 124, 125, 126, 127, 128, 129, and 130.

DECODE WORDS IN ISOLATION Display these words. Have the class combine meaningful word parts to read the words. Then point to the words in random order and ask children to read them quickly.

fried	**mixes**	**driving**
pauses	**trimming**	**happiest**
taller	**bunnies**	**dresses**

Corrective feedback | Model combining word parts to read the words and then ask children to combine and read them with you.

DECODE WORDS IN CONTEXT Display these sentences. Have the class read the sentences.

Team Talk Have pairs take turns reading the sentences naturally.

The **puppies snapped** at the **flies circling** around them.

Jan **chooses** the **sweetest** and **juiciest peaches** to bake in her **pies.**

The **mothers cheered** and **clapped** when their **babies tried** to walk.

Spelling

Inflected Endings

GUIDE PRACTICE Tell children that you will break the spelling words into meaningful word parts. They should say the parts of each word aloud as they write them. Check the spelling of each word before saying the next word. Have children use resources such as a dictionary to find correct spellings.

1.	tried	**tried**	**7.**	skipped	**skipped**
2.	try ing	**trying**	**8.**	skipp ing	**skipping**
3.	planned	**planned**	**9.**	heavi er	**heavier**
4.	plann ing	**planning**	**10.**	heavi est	**heaviest**
5.	liked	**liked**	**11.**	light er	**lighter**
6.	lik ing	**liking**	**12.**	light est	**lightest**

ON THEIR OWN Use *Reader's and Writer's Notebook,* p. 485.

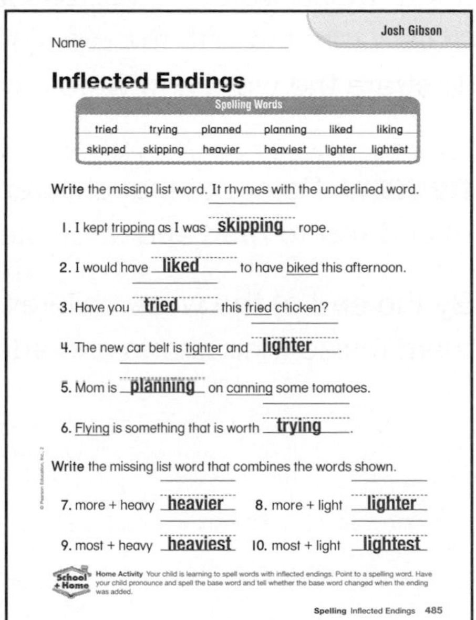

Name ______________ Josh Gibson

Inflected Endings

Spelling Words					
tried	trying	planned	planning	liked	liking
skipped	skipping	heavier	heaviest	lighter	lightest

Write the missing list word. It rhymes with the underlined word.

1. I kept tripping as I was **skipping** rope.
2. I would have **liked** to have biked this afternoon.
3. Have you **tried** this fried chicken?
4. The new car belt is tighter and **lighter**.
5. Mom is **planning** on canning some tomatoes.
6. Flying is something that is worth **trying**.

Write the missing list word that combines the words shown.

7. more + heavy **heavier** 8. more + light **lighter**

9. most + heavy **heaviest** 10. most + light **lightest**

School + Home **Home Activity** Your child is learning to spell words with inflected endings. Point to a spelling word. Have your child pronounce and spell the base word and tell whether the base word changed when the ending was added.

Spelling Inflected Endings 485

Reader's and Writer's Notebook, p. 485

Access for All

SI Strategic Intervention

Support Spelling Review that the ending *-ed* can have the sounds /d/ as in *tried,* /t/ as in *liked,* and /ə/ /d/ as in *hunted,* but the spelling pattern is always *-ed.* Write the spelling words ending in *-ed* and chorally read them. Have children say the sound of *-ed.*

Pronunciation Some languages, including Cantonese, Korean, and Mandarin, do not have a sound for *d.* Children may benefit from additional attention to the articulation of the sound of /d/ in words such as *tried.* Focus on tongue and lip position as well as jaw tension.

Common Core State Standards

Language 4.e. Use glossaries and beginning dictionaries, both print and digital, to determine or clarify the meaning of words and phrases. **Language 6.** Use words and phrases acquired through conversations, reading and being read to, and responding to texts, including using adjectives and adverbs to describe (e.g., *When other kids are happy that makes me happy*).

Selection Vocabulary

ACTIVATE PRIOR KNOWLEDGE Create a picture and caption chart as shown below.

Word	Definition	Picture	Caption
field	a piece of land used for some special purpose		A baseball field
cheers			
threw			
sailed			
plate			
bases			

Read each word to children and have them discuss what they already know about these words. Guide children in using a dictionary to find the definition of *field* that fits with the topic of baseball. Then have them draw a picture to illustrate the word and write a caption for the picture.

REVIEW Point out that children can use their knowledge of the endings *-s* and *-ed* to read and understand *cheers* and *sailed.*

By the end of the week children should know the selection vocabulary. Have them revise their charts and add definitions.

Check Selection Vocabulary/ High-Frequency Words

FORMATIVE ASSESSMENT Write the following words and have the class read them. Listen for children who miss words during the reading. Call on those children to read some of the words individually.

sailed	**field**	**threw**	**bases**	**Spiral Review** Rows 3 and 4 review previously taught high-frequency words.
plate	**cheers**			
shoe	**watch**	**guess**	**science**	←
village	**pretty**			←

If... children cannot read these words,

then... use the Small Group Time Strategic Intervention lesson, p. SG•8, to reteach the words. Monitor children's fluency with these words during reading and provide additional practice.

Access for All

SI Strategic Intervention

Act It Out Using paper cutouts to represent home plate and bases, set up a modified baseball field in the room. Have children act out a batter, pitcher, and base runner. As children pantomime the actions of a baseball game, pretend you are a radio announcer detailing the events using the selection words. Encourage the children watching to cheer. Then let children take turns being the announcer.

ELL

Visual Support English learners will benefit from additional visual support to understand selection vocabulary. Use the pictures in *Just Like Josh Gibson* to scaffold understanding. For example, use the words *field, bases, plate,* and *sailed* as you point to the picture on pages 374–375. Pantomime the motions for the words *cheers* and *threw.*

Multilingual Vocabulary Lists Children can apply knowledge of their home languages to acquire new English vocabulary by using the Multilingual Vocabulary Lists (*ELL Handbook,* pages 429–440).

Common Core State Standards

Language 4.a. Use sentence-level context as a clue to the meaning of a word or phrase.

Selection Vocabulary

bases places that are stations or goals in certain games, such as baseball

cheers happy or encouraging shouts

field a piece of land used for a special purpose

plate a hard rubber slab that a baseball player stands beside to bat

sailed moved smoothly like a ship with sails

threw sent something through the air by force of your arm

Academic Vocabulary

homophone word that has exactly the same sound as another word but has a different spelling and meaning

context clues words and sentences around a word that can help a reader understand the word's meaning

Bridge to Common Core

VOCABULARY ACQUISITION AND USE

When children interact with this week's selection vocabulary, they are learning grade-appropriate domain-specific words that they will encounter in school and beyond. Teaching the strategy of using context clues to determine the meaning of a homophone will help children gain independence in reading when they encounter homophones in other contexts.

Vocabulary Skill

Homophones

READ Have children read "Tigers Over Lions" on p. 367. Use the vocabulary skill and strategy as tools to build comprehension.

TEACH Explain that **homophones** are words that sound alike but have different spellings and different meanings. Discuss how readers can use **context clues**—the words and sentences around a word—to decide which homophone is being used in a particular sentence. Refer children to Words! on p. W•7 in the Student Edition for additional practice. Then read "Tigers Over Lions" on page 367 with children.

Think Aloud Write on the board: *The ballplayer threw the ball to third base.* Circle the word *threw,* and below it write *through.* The word *threw* means "made something move in the air." It is a homophone of the word *through,* as in "I walked through the park." I can tell that the first sentence uses the word *threw* meaning "made something move in the air" because a baseball player makes the ball move in the air.

GUIDE PRACTICE Have children write a sentence with the word *threw* and a sentence with the word *through*. Ask them to identify the context clues that show which meaning is used in each sentence.

ON THEIR OWN Have children reread "Tigers Over Lions" on page 367. Have them identify other homophones and use the context to determine their meanings. Then have them use context to determine the meanings of the other Words to Know. For additional practice, use *Reader's and Writer's Notebook,* p. 486.

Name ______ Josh Gibson

Find a word that is a homophone in each sentence. **Write** the word and its homophone on the line below.

1. Did you know that today is my birthday?
   know, no
2. We have eight members in the band.
   eight, ate
3. Look who just walked through that door!
   through, threw
4. For the costume party, Mark dressed up as a knight.
   knight, night

Read the pair of sentences. **Write** the correct word from the box on the line.

pair/pear

5. a. I need a new **pair** of shoes.
   b. My favorite fruit to eat is a **pear**.

School + Home Home Activity Your child learned about words that sound the same but are spelled differently. Have your child look for homophones in some of his or her favorite storybooks.

486 Vocabulary

Reader's and Writer's Notebook, p. 486

Vocabulary Strategy for

Homophones

Context Clues Homophones are words that sound alike but have different spellings and meanings. For example, *know* and *no* are homophones. So are *ate* and *eight*. Use context clues to help you determine a word's relevant meaning.

1. When you read a word that has a homophone, look at the words around it.
2. Use the context clues to determine the meaning of the homophone.

As you read "Tigers Over Lions," look for words that are homophones. On a separate sheet, write each word and its homophone. Define both words.

Words to Write Reread "Tigers Over Lions." Write one page about an exciting game you have played. Use words from the *Words to Know* list in your writing.

366

Tigers Over Lions

The fifth-place Terryville Tigers played the sixth-place Lincoln Lions last night. The game promised to be an even contest. Tiger pitcher Mike Petrov has won nine games so far. Lions pitcher Kurt Geiger has won 10. Both teams have good hitters. But Petrov had a great night. He threw a perfect game. Geiger was perfect too. Well . . . almost. For eight and one-half innings, Petrov and Geiger did not give up a hit. Batter after batter went down swinging, popped up, or flied out.

In the bottom of the ninth, the Tigers' last batter was Darrell Swann. He looked at a ball and took two strikes. Then Geiger threw a ball hard and outside, and Swann hit it. The ball sailed into the far corner of right field. Swann raced around the bases. He slid across home plate just before the tag. The umpire yelled "Safe!" The cheers of the crowd said it all. The Tigers won the game 1–0.

Your Turn!

Need a Review? For more help with using context clues to help you determine the meanings of homophones, see *Words!* on p. W•12.

Let's Think About...

Ready to Try It? Read *Just Like Josh Gibson* on pp. 368–381.

367

Student Edition, pp. 366–367

Reread for Fluency

Have children reread paragraph 2 of "Tigers Over Lions."

Routine Paired Reading

1. **Reread** To achieve optimal fluency, have partners reread the text three or four times.
2. **Corrective Feedback** Listen as children read. Provide corrective feedback regarding their fluency and decoding.

Routines Flip Chart

eStreet Interactive
www.ReadingStreet.com

Pearson eText
- Student Edition

Teacher Resources
- Envision It! Pictured Vocabulary Cards
- Tested Vocabulary Cards
- Reader's and Writer's Notebook

Zoom in on 

Text-Based Comprehension

Introduce Main Selection

Student Edition, pp. 368–369

GENRE **Realistic fiction** is a made-up story that could happen in real life. As they read *Just Like Josh Gibson,* ask children to look for events that indicate this story could happen in real life.

PREVIEW AND PREDICT Have children identify the title of the story, the author, and the illustrator. Remind them that **foreshadowing** suggests something that will happen later in the story. Help children preview the first paragraph on page 372 and use foreshadowing to predict what will happen.

PURPOSE By analyzing *Just Like Josh Gibson,* children learn about sports traditions.

MONITOR AND CLARIFY During reading, good readers **monitor** their understanding. If something is confusing, they **clarify** by using fix-up strategies. Have children turn to page EI•21 in their Student Edition.

Look at this picture. The child realizes that she does not understand what she is reading. What fix-up strategy is she going to use? As I read *Just Like Josh Gibson,* I will monitor my understanding. I will clarify by rereading and looking at the pictures.

Student Edition, p. EI•21

Common Core State Standards

Literature 1. Ask and answer such questions as *who, what, where, when, why,* and *how* to demonstrate understanding of key details in a text. **Literature 7.** Use information gained from the illustrations and words in a print or digital text to demonstrate understanding of its characters, setting, or plot.

Bridge to Common Core

CRAFT AND STRUCTURE

As children preview the selection and predict what it is about, they are determining how the purpose is connected to the content and style of realistic fiction. This sets the stage for children to see how different parts of realistic narratives are connected to each other and the whole.

Academic Vocabulary 

realistic fiction made-up story that could happen in real life

foreshadowing the use of hints or clues about what will happen later in a story

monitor a comprehension strategy by which readers actively think about understanding their reading and know when they understand and when they do not

clarify use appropriate strategies to make sense of difficult words, ideas, or passages

Strategy Response Log

Monitor and Clarify Have children use p. RR32 in their *Reader's and Writer's Notebook* to review and use the strategy of monitor and clarify and to discuss fix-up strategies.

Access Main Selection

READER AND TASK SUGGESTIONS	
Preparing to Read the Text	**Leveled Tasks**
• Review strategies for understanding homophones. Refer to the vocabulary skill lesson on p. 366g. • Point out the author's use of flashback at the beginning of this selection. • Remind children that as they encounter unfamiliar words, they may need to read more slowly to better understand the text.	• **Structure** If children have difficulty understanding flashback, have them identify where the story changes and how they determined the shift to present day. • **Levels of Meaning • Analyze** If children find hyperbole confusing, help them identify examples and discuss the meanings of the exaggerations.

See Text Complexity Measures for *Just Like Josh Gibson* on the tab at the beginning of the week.

READ Tell children that today they will read *Just Like Josh Gibson* for the first time. Use the Read for Understanding routine.

Routine Read for Understanding

Deepen understanding by reading the selection multiple times.

1. **First Read**—If children need support, use the **Access Text** notes to help them clarify understanding.
2. **Second Read**—Use the **Close Reading** notes to help children draw knowledge from the text.

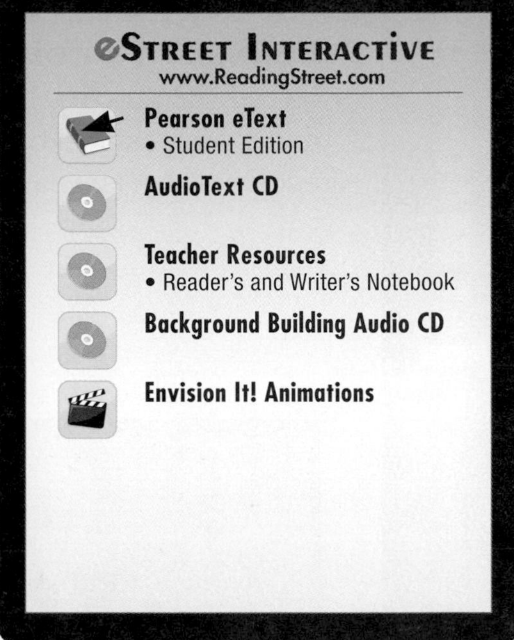

Preview Main Selection Ask children what they already know about playing baseball, using the picture on pp. 370–371 as a prompt. Then do a picture walk of the selection so children can talk about how people learn, practice, and play baseball.

1ST READ

Access Text If children need help, then...

CONNECT TO CONCEPT Look at the picture on pages 368 and 369. Who is in the picture? (a girl and a professional baseball player) Describe what each of them is wearing. Encourage children to answer in complete sentences. What tradition is this girl enjoying? (The girl is enjoying the tradition of playing baseball.)

Student Edition, pp. 368–369

2ND READ

Close Reading

INFERENCE • TEXT EVIDENCE Who do you think is the shadowy baseball player behind the girl? How is the girl like that baseball player? Use clues from the picture and title to answer the questions. (He's Josh Gibson. The girl wants to be as good at baseball as he was. She is holding a bat. She has the same batting stance.)

Time for Social Studies

CONNECT TO SOCIAL STUDIES In the early 1900s, few women competed in sports. Today girls and women play most sports.

Team Talk Have children discuss with a partner some sports they have watched girls or women compete in.

USE DECODING Have children check their reading of new words using these questions:

- Did I blend the sounds to read the word?
- Did I put the new word in the sentence to make sure it made sense?
- Did I look for word parts to help me understand the word?

Common Core State Standards

Literature 1. Ask and answer such questions as *who, what, where, when, why,* and *how* to demonstrate understanding of key details in a text. **Foundational Skills 3.** Know and apply grade-level phonics and word analysis skills in decoding words. **Also Foundational Skills 4.c.**

Let's Think About...
What do you already know about baseball?
Background Knowledge

1

Grandmama says there's nothing like baseball.
The story goes. . . .

370

Josh Gibson once hit a baseball in Pittsburgh so hard that it didn't come down.

The next day he was playing in Philadelphia, and the ball dropped out of the sky, right into a fielder's glove. The umpire pointed at Josh and said, "You're out yesterday in Pittsburgh!"

Let's Think About...
Could the story of Josh Gibson's hit really have happened?
Questioning

2

371

Student Edition, pp. 370–371

Let's Think About...

1 BACKGROUND KNOWLEDGE Remind children to use their background knowledge to help them understand what they read. Discuss what they know about baseball.

2 QUESTIONING Explain that good readers ask many questions as they read. Children should ask whether a ball really could be in hit in one city and come down in another one many miles away. Children recognize that the description is an exaggeration.

Access Text If children need help, then...

COMPARE AND CONTRAST • REREAD CHALLENGING TEXT How is playing baseball the same and different for a girl and a boy at the time this story takes place? Have children reread pages 372 and 373 to help them find the answer to the question. (Both girls and boys played baseball, but only boys could play on teams.)

REVIEW SELECTION VOCABULARY Have children locate the selection word *sailed* on page 372. What does *sailed away* describe? (It describes the ball flying smoothly through the air.)

Student Edition, pp. 372–373

Let's Think About...

3 MONITOR AND CLARIFY Help children use picture and text clues to determine that a Louisville slugger is a baseball bat.

4 MONITOR AND CLARIFY Have children reread to find the answer "girls in the forties didn't play baseball."

5 QUESTIONING The boys know that Grandmama plays as well or better than they do, but she can't be on the team because she is a girl.

COMPARE AND CONTRAST How are Grandmama and her cousin Danny alike? How are they different? (They both like to play baseball. Danny imagines he's playing for the Dodgers, but Grandmama imagine she's Josh Gibson, playing for the Grays.)

REVIEW SELECTION VOCABULARY Have children locate the selection word *plate* on page 374. What is the *plate* that Grandmama steps up to? (It is the hard rubber slab that marks the batter's place in a baseball game.)

Common Core State Standards

Literature 1. Ask and answer such questions as *who, what, where, when, why,* and *how* to demonstrate understanding of key details in a text. **Literature 4.** Describe how words and phrases (e.g., regular beats, alliteration, rhymes, repeated lines) supply rhythm and meaning in a story, poem, or song. **Also Language 4.**

Student Edition, pp. 374–375

Close Reading

INFERENCE • TEXT EVIDENCE Why do you think the author repeats the phrase *sailed away* in the last sentence on page 372? (To show that the girl could hit the ball high and far and that like the ball the days passed by quickly and are now gone.)

INFERENCE • TEXT EVIDENCE Why do you think the author repeats the words *too bad she's a girl?* Use clues in the text to support your answer. (The author wanted to emphasize that despite her skill, Grandmama was kept from playing on a team because she was a girl.)

1ST READ

Access Text If children need help, then...

REVIEW HOMOPHONES Homophones are words that sound the same but are spelled differently and have different meanings. What is the meaning of *eight* on page 376? (eight in number) What is the meaning of *ate?* Have children use *eight* and *ate* correctly in sentences.

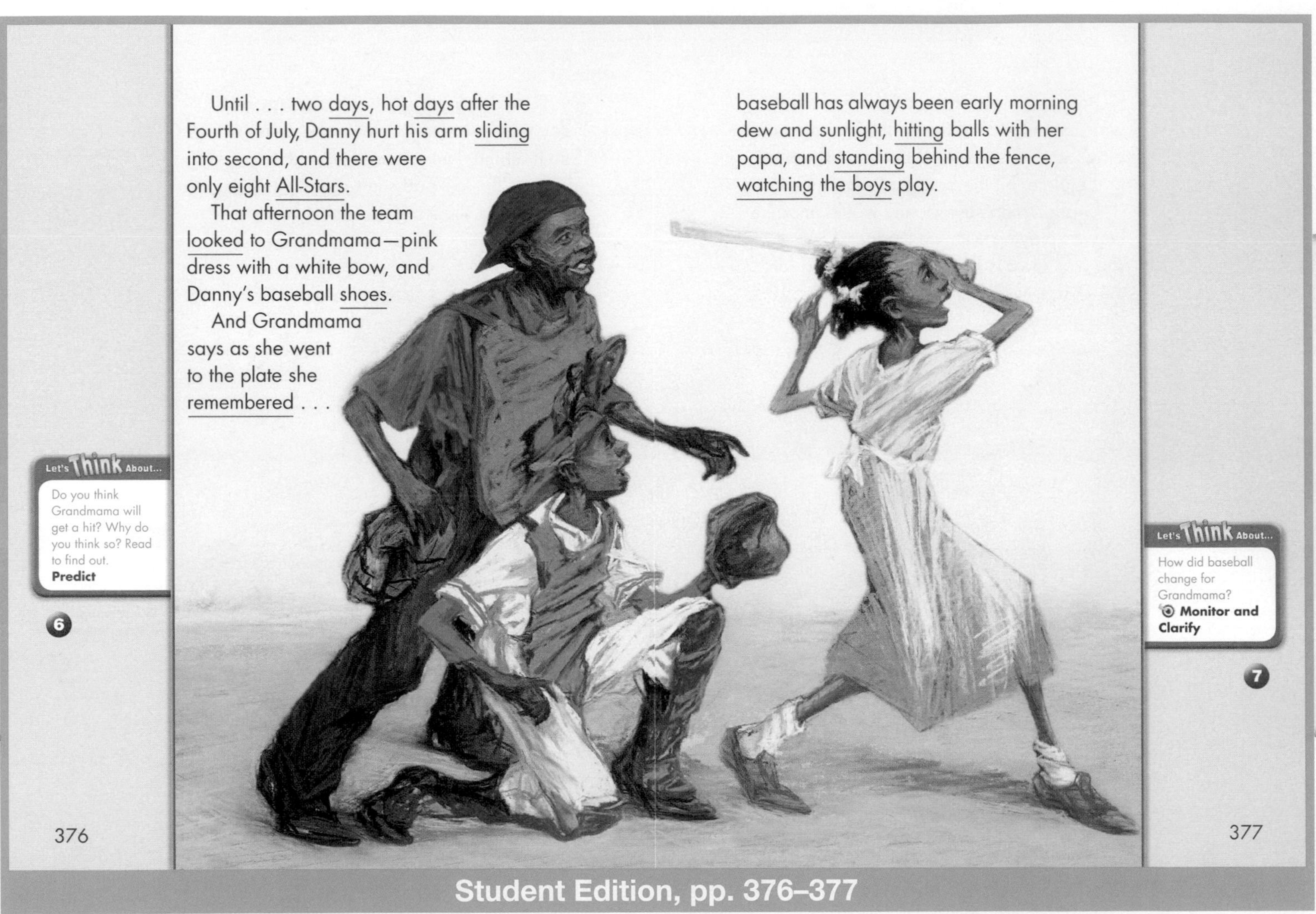

Student Edition, pp. 376–377

2ND READ

Close Reading

ANALYSIS • TEXT EVIDENCE Why did the boys look to Grandmama on that July day? Use clues in the text and your background knowledge to answer the question. (They wanted Grandmama to play in Danny's place so the team would have nine players and could play the game.)

Let's Think About...

6 **PREDICT** Encourage children to make their own predictions and to read on to confirm predictions.

7 **MONITOR AND CLARIFY** Baseball changed for Grandmama because she actually played in a game and added that memory to her other baseball memories.

COMPARE AND CONTRAST How are Grandmama and Josh Gibson alike? How are they different? (They both are great baseball players. People tell stories about them. But Josh Gibson is famous and Grandmama is not. Josh Gibson is a grown man, and Grandmama is a little girl in the story.)

Common Core State Standards

Literature 1. Ask and answer such questions as *who, what, where, when, why,* and *how* to demonstrate understanding of key details in a text.

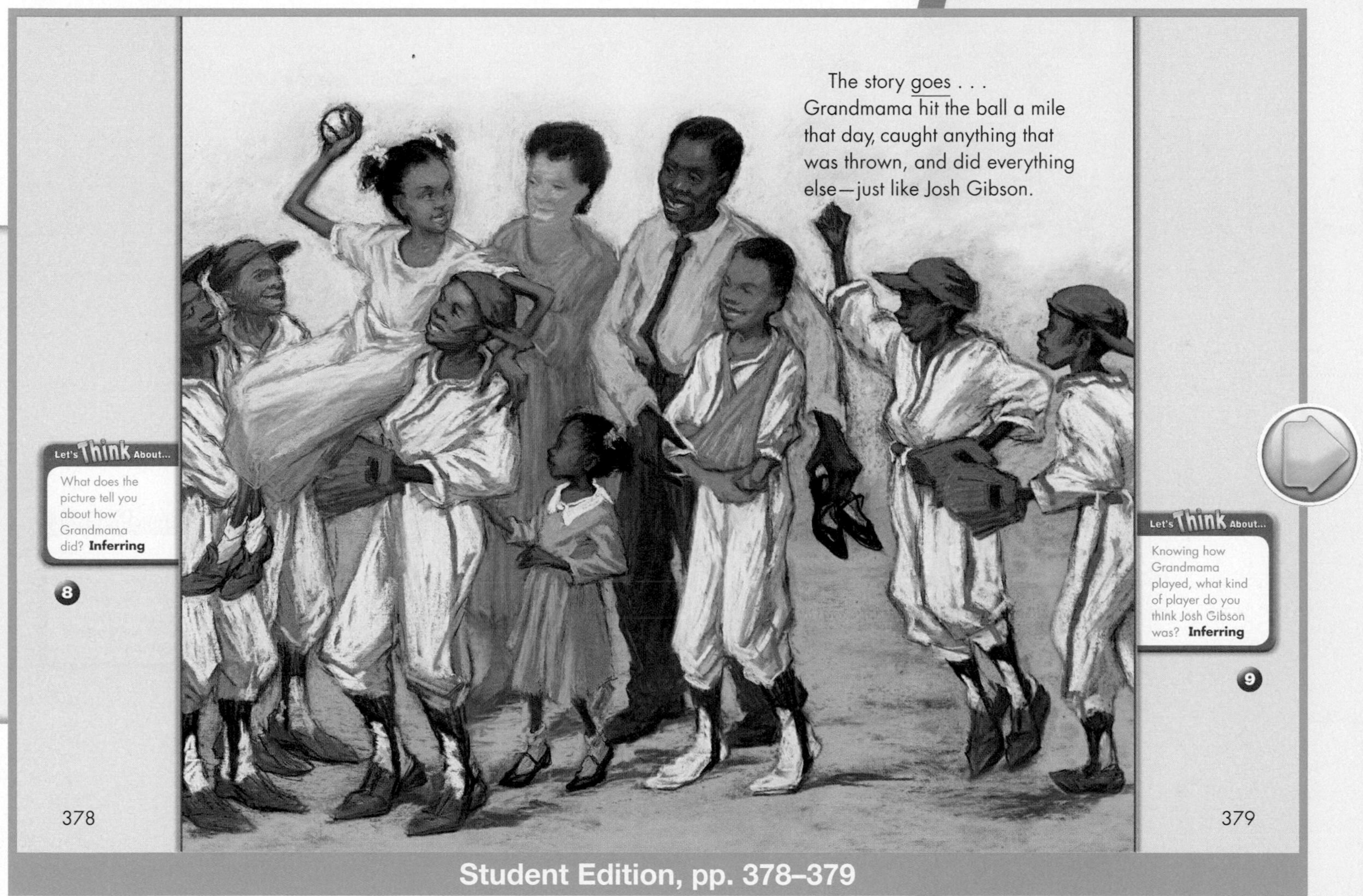

Student Edition, pp. 378–379

8 INFERRING The picture shows the boys smiling and carrying Grandmama. I think Grandmama must have been the best player that day.

9 INFERRING The text says Grandmama played very well that day and that she played just like Josh Gibson, so Josh Gibson must have been a very good player too who could hit, catch, and do everything else.

1ST READ

Access Text ⓒ If children need help, then...

CROSS-TEXT EVALUATION

Use a Strategy to Self-Check How did the story "The Princesses Have a Ball" from the *Read Aloud Anthology* help you understand this selection? How did girls in both stories participate in sports traditions?

Continue to DAY 2
Text-Based Comprehension
p. 381a

Student Edition, pp. 380–381

2ND READ

Let's Think About...

10 MONITOR AND CLARIFY Grandmama is teaching her granddaughter about baseball and how she loved it especially when she heard people cheering for her.

Close Reading ⓒ

SYNTHESIS • TEXT EVIDENCE Using what you learned in this selection, tell how participation in sports is important to people. Have children cite examples from the text.

Continue to DAY 3
Think Critically
p. 382–383

Text-Based Comprehension

Check Understanding

Have children discuss each question with a partner. Ask several pairs to share their responses.

- ☑ **Realistic Fiction** What events in this story could happen in real life? What is one event that could not? (Grandmama could play well and hear the cheers in the big game. Josh Gibson could not hit the ball in Pittsburgh and have it come down in Philadelphia.)
- ☑ **Confirm Predictions** How did you use the foreshadowing on page 372 to predict what would happen in the story? (I used the foreshadowing to predict that Grandmama's papa would teach Grandmama to hit home runs.)
- ☑ **Author's Purpose** Why do you think the author wrote this story? (The author wanted to share a story about a little girl who loved baseball and was very good at it but was unable to play on a team because she was a girl.)
- ☑ **Draw Conclusions** How do you think Grandmama feels about baseball today? How do you know? (Grandmama still loves baseball today. She tells her granddaughter "there's nothing like baseball," and she still has her ball and mitt from the big game.)
- ☑ **Connect Text to Self** Josh Gibson is Grandmama's hero. Who is your hero? Why? How might Grandmama be a hero to her granddaughter? (Her granddaughter looks up to her for not giving up and for being brave enough to play in a boys' baseball game.)

Common Core State Standards

Literature 1. Ask and answer such questions as *who, what, where, when, why,* and *how* to demonstrate understanding of key details in a text. **Literature 3.** Describe how characters in a story respond to major events and challenges. **Literature 7.** Use information gained from the illustrations and words in a print or digital text to demonstrate understanding of its characters, setting, or plot.

Support Discussion Ask *yes* or *no* questions to start children's responses. For example: *Does Grandmama still love baseball today?* (Yes) Extend language opportunities for children by asking follow-up questions, such as: *Why? What does Grandmama say about baseball?*

Day 2 SMALL GROUP TIME • Differentiate Comprehension, p. SG•1

OL On-Level	SI Strategic Intervention	A Advanced
• **Practice** Selection Vocabulary • **Read** *Just Like Josh Gibson*	• **Reteach** Selection Vocabulary • **Read** *Just Like Josh Gibson*	• **Extend** Selection Vocabulary • **Read** *Just Like Josh Gibson* • **Investigate** Inquiry Project

ELL

If... children need more scaffolding and practice with the **Comprehension Skill,**
then... use the ELL activities on p. DI•17 in the Teacher Resources section on SuccessNet.

Common Core State Standards

Literature 1. Ask and answer such questions as *who, what, where, when, why,* and *how* to demonstrate understanding of key details in a text. **Language 2.** Demonstrate command of the conventions of standard English capitalization, punctuation, and spelling when writing. **Language 2.a.** Capitalize holidays, product names, and geographic names.

Literary Text

Speaker/Narrator

IDENTIFY THE NARRATOR Explain to children that the speaker or narrator of a story is the person who is telling about the events. Use "The Princesses Have a Ball" to identify the narrator of a literary selection.

- Who are the characters in "The Princesses Have a Ball"? (The king, the princesses, and Jack are the characters.)
- How could you tell if one of the characters in the story was the narrator? (The character would use the word *I* when describing the events.)
- Who is the narrator of "The Princesses Have a Ball"? (someone who is not a character in the story)

GUIDE PRACTICE Explain that the class will now identify the narrator of *Just Like Josh Gibson.* Display Graphic Organizer 26 and write the heads shown below. Ask children to tell what you should write in each column.

Characters Who Might Be the Narrator	Details from the Story	Narrator
Josh Gibson	Josh Gibson is talked about, but he does not speak.	Grandmama's granddaughter
Grandmama	The story is about Grandmama, but she doesn't tell the story.	
Grandmama's granddaughter	Grandmama's granddaughter is a character, and she tells the story. She uses the words *I* and *me.*	
a person not in the story	This story is told using *I* and *me,* so the narrator must be someone in the story.	

Graphic Organizer 26

ON THEIR OWN Divide the class into small groups and assign each group a previously read story from the Student Edition. Have them identify the narrator of the selection and share their information with the class.

Conventions

Using Capital Letters

TEACH Write *December, Sunday,* and *Dr. J. M. Jackson* on the board. Point to each word as you read it. Ask children to identify the types of words that begin with capital letters. (months, days, names and titles) The title and initials in people's names are capitalized and have periods after them. Write the following abbreviations on the board: *Dec. Sun.* The abbreviations for days and months begin with a capital letter and have periods after them too. What do these abbreviations mean? (December, Sunday)

GUIDE PRACTICE Write the following sentences on the board. Explain that words that come from proper nouns, such as *American,* are capitalized. Tell children that titles of books, poems, songs, and the first word in a quotation also begin with a capital letter. Have children capitalize as needed.

1. The umpire said, "you're out!"	**(You're)**
2. dr. m. l. King Jr. Day is monday.	**(Dr. M. L., Monday)**
3. My favorite book is charlotte's web.	**(Charlotte's Web)**
4. I can speak the korean language.	**(Korean)**

APPLY Have the class orally answer each question using complete sentences. Have children identify the words that need a capital letter.

1. What day of the week is it today?
2. What is your favorite song?
3. In what month were you born?

ON THEIR OWN Use *Reader's and Writer's Notebook,* p. 487.

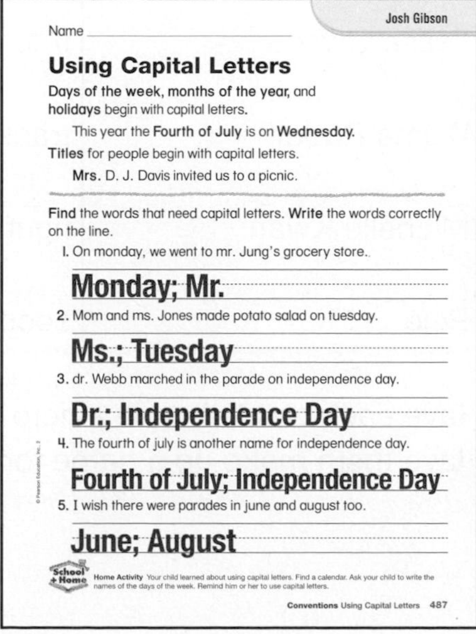
Josh Gibson

Name ______

Using Capital Letters

Days of the week, months of the year, and **holidays** begin with capital letters.

This year the **Fourth of July** is on **Wednesday.**

Titles for people begin with capital letters.

Mrs. D. J. Davis invited us to a picnic.

Find the words that need capital letters. **Write** the words correctly on the line.

1. On monday, we went to mr. Jung's grocery store.
Monday; Mr.
2. Mom and ms. Jones made potato salad on tuesday.
Ms.; Tuesday
3. dr. Webb marched in the parade on independence day.
Dr.; Independence Day
4. The fourth of july is another name for independence day.
Fourth of July; Independence Day
5. I wish there were parades in june and august too.
June; August

School + Home **Home Activity** Your child learned about using capital letters. Find a calendar. Ask your child to write the names of the days of the week. Remind him or her to use capital letters.

Conventions Using Capital Letters 487

Reader's and Writer's Notebook, p. 487

Access for All

Support Conventions If children have difficulty identifying words that are capitalized, point out examples around the classroom (e.g., calendars, names on doors and bulletin boards, daily schedules).

Daily Fix-It

3. The croud cheers for me.
The crowd cheers for me.

4. I raned Around the basis.
I ran around the bases.

Discuss the Daily Fix-It corrections with children. Review diphthongs *ow* and *ou,* homophones *basis* and *bases,* irregular past-tense verbs, capitalization, and the correct spelling of *cheers.*

Conventions Support Children who are literate in nonalphabetic languages such as Chinese and Japanese may not be familiar with the English conventions of capitalization. Allow them extra practice in mastering this skill.

Common Core State Standards

Writing 3. Write narratives in which they recount a well-elaborated event or short sequence of events, include details to describe actions, thoughts, and feelings, use temporal words to signal event order, and provide a sense of closure.

Writing

Realistic Fiction

Writing Trait: Organization

INTRODUCE THE PROMPT Review with children the key features of a realistic story. Point out that "Running Like Jesse Owens" is a realistic story. Assure them that they can make up a brief story with characters who seem real and a setting that is like a real place. Explain that today children will plan their own story with events that could really happen. It will be a story with a beginning, a middle, and an end. Read aloud the writing prompt.

Writing Prompt

Think about one of your favorite sports heroes. Now write a story about a character who wants to be like that sports figure.

GENERATE STORY IDEAS

To plan a new story, think of athletes who are heroes. Let's make a chart of those athletes, the sports they play, and a characteristic that makes them a hero. Display a three-column chart. I'll start with Josh Gibson, the hero of the girl in the story *Just Like Josh Gibson.*

Guide children in completing the chart. Possible ideas are shown. Record the responses, and keep the chart available so that children can plan and draft their stories.

Hero	Sport	Characteristic
Josh Gibson	baseball	good batter
Jesse Owens	track	fast runner and Olympic medalist
Wilma Rudolf	track	fast runner and Olympic medalist
Michelle Kwan	figure skater	graceful skater and Olympic medalist
Pelé	soccer	a top scorer

Have each child choose a hero for a new story. Circulate to guide children. Have them make up a name for a child who will be their main character.

Mini-Lesson Sequence

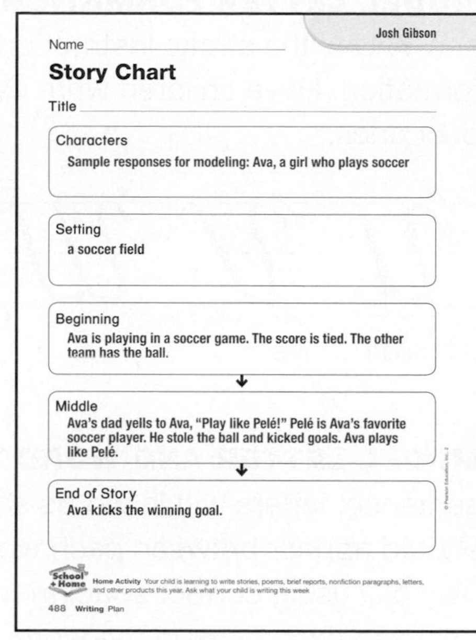

Name Josh Gibson

Story Chart

Title

Characters
Sample responses for modeling: Ava, a girl who plays soccer

Setting
a soccer field

Beginning
Ava is playing in a soccer game. The score is tied. The other team has the ball.

Middle
Ava's dad yells to Ava, "Play like Pelé!" Pelé is Ava's favorite soccer player. He stole the ball and kicked goals. Ava plays like Pelé.

End of Story
Ava kicks the winning goal.

School + Home Home Activity Your child is learning to write stories, poems, brief reports, nonfiction paragraphs, letters, and other products this year. Ask what your child is writing this week.

488 Writing Plan

Reader's and Writer's Notebook, p. 488

- **Introduce** Use *Reader's and Writer's Notebook,* p. 488 to model story planning. I have chosen Pelé as my hero. He played professional soccer in the past. Now I will write my story using a chart. I don't need a title yet, but my character will be Ava, a girl who plays soccer. I'll write the name in the Characters box. In the Setting box, I'll write *a soccer field.* Now I will plan what happens in the beginning, middle, and end of my story.

- **Model** At the beginning, Ava is playing in a soccer game. The score is tied. The other team has the ball. I'll write that in the Beginning box. In the middle of the story, I plan that Ava's dad yells to her to play like Pelé. Pelé is Ava's hero. He stole balls and kicked goals. Ava will do the same thing. I'll write that in the Middle box. At the end, Ava will kick the winning goal. I'll write that idea in the End box. Now plan your story. Circulate to guide and assist children.

Routine Quick Write for Fluency

Team Talk

1. **Talk** Have partners take three minutes to name their sports hero and tell the events in their story.
2. **Write** Each child briefly writes about the events at the beginning, middle, and end of the planned story. Remind them to include information about the sports hero.
3. **Share** Each child reads the story ideas to the partner.

Routines Flip Chart

Access for All

A Advanced

Researching a Hero Encourage children to find three facts about their chosen sports hero that support the stated characteristic. Have them include the facts in their stories.

Support Prewriting

Beginning Children can draw story events, label them, and share with a partner, possibly one who speaks the same home language.

Intermediate Have children draw pictures or write phrases to express story event ideas. Have them describe the story plan to other children.

Advanced Have children draw pictures or write short sentences in their story charts. As they share the plan with partners, children can clarify and add ideas.

Common Core State Standards

Writing 7. Participate in shared research and writing projects (e.g., read a number of books on a single topic to produce a report; record science observations). **Speaking/ Listening 1.** Participate in collaborative conversations with diverse partners about grade 2 topics and texts with peers and adults in small and larger groups.

Handwriting

Cursive *U, V, W, Y/Letter and Word Spacing*

MODEL LETTER FORMATION Display capital cursive letters: *U, V, W,* and *Y*. Use the stroke instructions pictured below to model proper letter formation. Have children write each letter several times and circle their best ones.

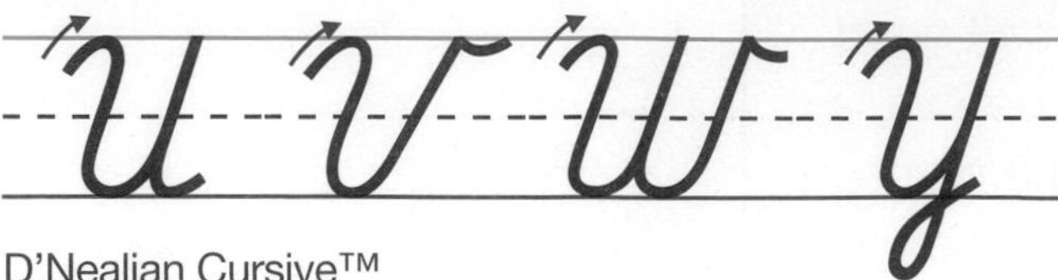

D'Nealian Cursive™

MODEL LETTER AND WORD SPACING Explain that when we write a sentence, letters within words should be evenly spaced, and extra space should appear between each word in the sentence. Write the sentence *Kids play ball* using correct spacing. When I write each word, I use even spaces between each letter in the word. When I begin a new word, I leave a larger space between the words. Write *Kids play ball* again, with uniform spacing between all the letters and between words. The spaces between words should not be the same as the spaces between letters. Write *Kids play ball* a third time, with varying amounts of space between each word. The spaces between words should not be big in some places and small in others. By correctly spacing letters and words, I make it easier for others to read what I write. Ask children which of the three writing examples is easiest to read and have them explain why.

GUIDE PRACTICE Write the following sentence, using the same spacing within words and between words.

Yes, Vic is helping Will.

Team Talk Have children work in pairs to discuss what is wrong with the sentence and how to fix it. Then have them write the sentence correctly, leaving appropriate margins for readability.

Research and Inquiry

Step 2 Research Skill: Globe

TEACH Review with children that a **globe** represents Earth as an astronaut would see it from space. Remind them that a globe is round because Earth is round. Review that a globe helps identify parts of the world. Explain that globes use different colors to show the various features of Earth, such as oceans and continents.

Think Aloud **MODEL** In *Just Like Josh Gibson,* Josh Gibson was Grandmama's hero. My baseball hero is Roberto Clemente. He was born in Puerto Rico and played for the Pittsburgh Pirates. A globe can help me gather information about Puerto Rico. First, I have to locate Puerto Rico. It is southeast of the United States. Puerto Rico is part of a string of islands. The Atlantic Ocean and Caribbean Sea border Puerto Rico. I see a star that shows a city called San Juan. I know that the star means that San Juan is the capital city.

GUIDE PRACTICE Have children work in small groups. Tell each group to choose one country on the globe. Have them gather information about the country they chose. Then have the groups tell two facts they gather about the country from looking at the globe, such as nearby countries, closest bodies of water, major rivers or mountain ranges, and capital cities.

Academic Vocabulary

globe a spherical model of Earth that uses colors to show locations, such as continents and water

Bridge to Common Core

RESEARCH TO BUILD AND PRESENT KNOWLEDGE

Children will gather evidence from texts and other sources to use in answering questions for their research projects. They will also

- learn to use a globe as a source of information

Wrap Up Your Day!

✔ **Content Knowledge** Monitor children's use of oral vocabulary as they respond. Ask: Would you describe Grandmama as dainty? Why or why not? (No, she was strong and athletic.) What challenge did Grandmama face? (She had to get the boys to accept her and give her a chance to play.)

Preview DAY 3

Tell children that tomorrow they will reread *Just Like Josh Gibson.*

DAY 3 at a Glance

Content Knowledge
Oral Vocabulary

Phonics/Spelling
Inflected Endings

Fluency
Accuracy and Appropriate Rate

Selection Vocabulary
bases, cheers, field, plate, sailed, threw
Homophones

Text-Based Comprehension
Review Draw Conclusions

Conventions
Using Capital Letters

Writing
Realistic Fiction

Research and Inquiry
Gather and Record Information

Materials

- Student Edition
- Sing with Me Big Book
- Read Aloud Anthology
- Reader's and Writer's Notebook
- Decodable Reader 26B
- Retelling Cards

Common Core State Standards

Speaking/Listening 2. Recount or describe key ideas or details from a text read aloud or information presented orally or through other media. **Language 6.** Use words and phrases acquired through conversations, reading and being read to, and responding to texts, including using adjectives and adverbs to describe (e.g., *When other kids are happy that makes me happy*).

Content Knowledge

Sports Traditions

EXPAND THE CONCEPT To reinforce concepts and to focus children's attention, have children sing "An Athlete's Challenge" from the *Sing with Me* Big Book. How do athletes feel about winning a game? (Each win is a dream.)

Build Oral Language

LISTEN FOR AMAZING WORDS Read the title and identify the author of the *Read Aloud Anthology* story "The Princesses Have a Ball." Read the story and have children listen for the word *disguise.* Have them also think about the princesses' participation in sports.

- Who discovered what the girls were doing? What clues did he use to figure out the girls were playing sports? (Jack, a cobbler or shoemaker, discovered that the princesses were playing sports when he examined their shoes.)

"The Princesses Have a Ball"

TALK ABOUT SENTENCES AND WORDS
Write the following sentence from "The Princesses Have a Ball" on sentence strips or on the board.

One believed disguise would reveal the truth, but the girls caught on and threw out that sleuth!

- Ask children to read it with you as you track the print.
- Point to and read *One believed disguise would reveal the truth.* What does this mean? (The detective thought that by changing how he looked he could spy on others and find out what they were doing.) Why does the author use the word *disguise?* (He is using it as an opposite to revealing truth by suggesting that hiding how one looks can help one find the truth.) What other words could the author have used?
- Now point to and read … *but the girls caught on and threw out the sleuth!* What does *sleuth* mean? ("detective" or "spy") Why do you think the author chose the word *sleuth?* (It a good replacement word for *detective;* it rhymes with *truth.*)

- **Team Talk** Now have children work with a partner to replace key words in the sentence with simpler words or synonyms. Use the following sentence frame.

  One believed _______ would _______ the truth, but the girls caught on and threw out that _______!

Build Oral Vocabulary

Amazing Words — Robust Vocabulary Routine

1. **Introduce the Word** Relate the word *disguise* to the book. The twelve princesses *disguise* their beds to make it look like they are sleeping. Supply a child-friendly definition. When you change your appearance so you won't be recognized, you *disguise* yourself. Have children say the word.
2. **Demonstrate** Provide examples to show meaning. The spy wore a *disguise* so she wouldn't be recognized. She wore a wig and a beard to *disguise* herself.
3. **Apply** Have children demonstrate their understanding. Tell about a time when you have seen someone in *disguise.*
4. **Display the Word** Run your hand under the two syllables *dis-guise* as you read the word.

Routines Flip Chart

ADD TO THE CONCEPT MAP Use these questions to discuss the importance of sports traditions as you add to the concept map.

Concept Map

- In *Just Like Josh Gibson,* who taught Grandmama to play baseball? (her papa) Let's add *Parents teach children to play sports* to the map. Why does Grandmama love baseball? (She is good at it; it helps her remember playing with her papa; she loves hearing the cheers.) Let's add *Players love to hear people cheer for them* to our map.
- We know that Grandmama looks up to Josh Gibson. Let's add information about admiring players and wanting to be like them to our map.
- What do the boys say about Grandmama as a baseball player? (She is just as good at playing baseball as the boys are.) Let's add *Girls and boys can play sports equally well* to the map.

Amazing Words

athlete	disguise
challenge	champion
effort	professional
dainty	shortstop

Access for All

 **Advanced**

Amazing Words Challenge children who demonstrate an understanding of *disguise* to use it in sentences as a noun and as a verb.

Expand Vocabulary Use the Day 3 instruction on ELL Poster 26 to expand children's use of English vocabulary to communicate about lesson concepts.

Common Core State Standards

Foundational Skills 3. Know and apply grade-level phonics and word analysis skills in decoding words.

Phonics

Build Words

MODEL WORD BUILDING Write *Base Word, -s or -es, -ed, -ing, -er,* and *-est* as headings on a six-column chart. Now we are going to build words with endings. Write *pet* in the first column. I am going to see which endings I can add to *pet* to make new words. *Pet* is a one-syllable word that ends in a consonant. I can add the ending *-s.* Model writing and reading *pets.* I can add the ending *-ed,* but since *pet* is a one-syllable word that ends in a consonant, I need to double the consonant. Write and read *petting.* Since *pet* is a verb or a noun, not an adjective, adding the endings *-er* and *-est* do not make words.

GUIDE PRACTICE Have children read the words and write the new words under the appropriate heading. Monitor children's work.

Base Word	*-s* or *-es*	*-ed*	*-ing*	*-er*	*-est*
pet	pets	petted	petting	X	X
cry	cries	cried	crying	X	X
silly	X	X	X	sillier	silliest
brave	braves	braved	braving	braver	bravest
mess	messes	messed	messing	X	X
slow	slows	slowed	slowing	slower	slowest

Corrective feedback For corrective feedback, model the correct spelling and have children tell how the spelling changed.

Fluent Word Reading

MODEL Write *dancing.* I recognize the meaningful word parts *danc* and *ing.* I put the base word and ending together to read the word *dancing.*

GUIDE PRACTICE Write the words below. Look for word parts you know. When I point to the word, we'll read it together. Allow one second per word part previewing time for the first reading.

closed	closes	trimming	prettier	prettiest	hurrying

ON THEIR OWN Have children read the list above three or four times, until they can read one word per second.

Decode and Read

DECODE WORDS IN ISOLATION Have children turn to page 189 in *Decodable Practice Readers* 2.2 and find the first list of words. Each word in this list has an ending. Let's read these words. Be sure that children correctly read each word part.

Next, have children read the high-frequency words.

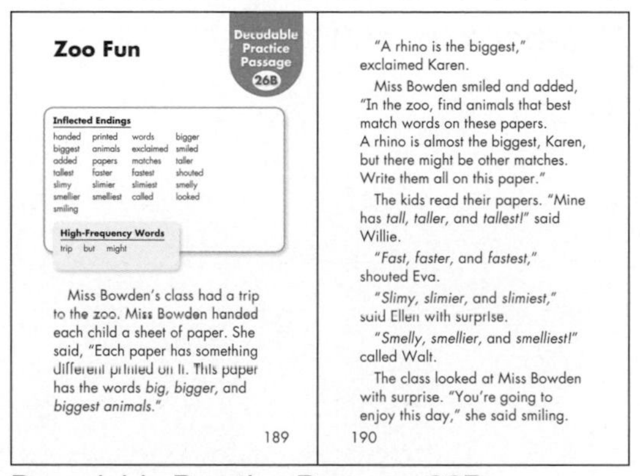

Zoo Fun

Decodable Practice Passage 26B

Inflected Endings

handed	printed	words	bigger
biggest	animals	exclaimed	smiled
added	papers	matches	taller
tallest	faster	fastest	shouted
slimy	slimier	slimiest	smelly
smellier	smelliest	called	looked
smiling			

High-Frequency Words

trip but might

Miss Bowden's class had a trip to the zoo. Miss Bowden handed each child a sheet of paper. She said, "Each paper has something different printed on it. This paper has the words *big, bigger,* and *biggest animals.*"

189

"A rhino is the biggest," exclaimed Karen.

Miss Bowden smiled and added, "In the zoo, find animals that best match words on these papers. A rhino is almost the biggest, Karen, but there might be other matches. Write them all on this paper."

The kids read their papers. "Mine has *tall, taller,* and *tallest!*" said Willie.

"*Fast, faster,* and *fastest,*" shouted Eva.

"*Slimy, slimier,* and *slimiest,*" said Ellen with surprise.

"*Smelly, smellier,* and *smelliest!*" called Walt.

The class looked at Miss Bowden with surprise. "You're going to enjoy this day," she said smiling.

190

Decodable Practice Passage 26B

DECODE WORDS IN CONTEXT Chorally read the story along with children. Have children identify words in the story that have endings and tell how the base words change.

Team Talk Pair children and have them take turns reading the story aloud to each other. Monitor children as they read to check for proper pronunciation and appropriate pacing.

Access for All

SI Strategic Intervention

Sort Words Write words from various columns of the word-building activity on self-stick notes and distribute them. Have children tape the words in the appropriate column and tell the spelling change. Have children chorally read the words.

A Advanced

Build Words Have children compile a list of words that accept all endings, such as *thin, wet, dry, empty, clean,* and *busy.*

Visual Support As you read words from the word-building chart, use facial expressions or body motions to reinforce meaning. For example, point to *pet* and say it. Then pretend to pet a cat with your hands while saying *pet*. Repeat and have children join in.

Common Core State Standards

Language 2. Demonstrate command of the conventions of standard English capitalization, punctuation, and spelling when writing. **Foundational Skills 4.b.** Read on-level text orally with accuracy, appropriate rate, and expression on successive readings.

Spelling Words

Inflected Endings

1. tried	7. skipped
2. trying	8. skipping
3. planned	9. heavier
4. planning	10. heaviest
5. liked	11. lighter
6. liking	12. lightest

High-Frequency Words

13. promise **14. because**

Spelling

Inflected Endings

SPELL HIGH-FREQUENCY WORDS Add the word *because* to the Word Wall. Write *promise* and *because* and point them out on the Word Wall. Have children say and spell the words with you and then without you.

DICTATION Have children write these sentences. Say each sentence. Then repeat it slowly, one word at a time.

1. **I'll keep trying because I made a promise.**
2. **He liked planning the hiking trip.**
3. **Sam tried on the heaviest coat from the rack.**

PROOFREAD AND CORRECT Write each sentence, spelling words one at a time. Have children circle and rewrite any misspelled words.

ON THEIR OWN Use *Reader's and Writer's Notebook,* p. 490.

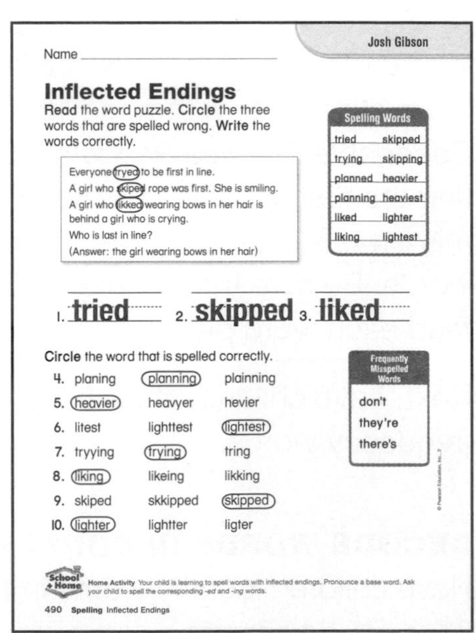

Josh Gibson

Name ________________

Inflected Endings

Read the word puzzle. **Circle** the three words that are spelled wrong. **Write** the words correctly.

Everyone fryed to be first in line.
A girl who skiped rope was first. She is smiling.
A girl who likked wearing bows in her hair is behind a girl who is crying.
Who is last in line?
(Answer: the girl wearing bows in her hair)

Spelling Words	
tried	skipped
trying	skipping
planned	heavier
planning	heaviest
liked	lighter
liking	lightest

1. tried 2. skipped 3. liked

Circle the word that is spelled correctly.

4.	planing	(planning)	plainning
5.	(heavier)	heavyer	hevier
6.	litest	lighttest	(lightest)
7.	tryying	(trying)	tring
8.	(liking)	likeing	likking
9.	skiped	skkipped	(skipped)
10.	(lighter)	lightter	ligter

Frequently Misspelled Words
don't
they're
there's

School + Home **Home Activity** Your child is learning to spell words with inflected endings. Pronounce a base word. Ask your child to spell the corresponding *-ed* and *-ing* words.

490 **Spelling** Inflected Endings

Reader's and Writer's Notebook, p. 490

If... children need more scaffolding and practice with reading the **Main Selection,**
then... use the ELL activities on p. DI•18 in the Teacher Resources section on SuccessNet.

Day 3 SMALL GROUP TIME • Differentiate Close Reading, p. SG•1

OL On-Level
- **Reread** to Develop Vocabulary
- **Reread** *Just Like Josh Gibson*

SI Strategic Intervention
- **Reread** to Develop Vocabulary
- **Reread** *Just Like Josh Gibson*

A Advanced
- **Reread** to Develop Vocabulary
- **Reread** *Just Like Josh Gibson*
- **Investigate** Inquiry Project

Fluency

Accuracy and Appropriate Rate

MODEL FLUENT READING Have children turn to Student Edition pp. 370–371. Follow along as I read these pages. I will try to read with no mistakes. I want to read just the way I speak.

GUIDE PRACTICE Have children read the pages with you. Then have them reread the pages as a group without you until they read with no hesitation and no mistakes. Continue in the same way with pp. 372–373.

Corrective feedback	**If...** children have difficulty reading at a good pace, **then...** prompt: • Are you reading too fast? • Are you reading too slow? • Try to read the sentences at a rate so people can follow along.

Reread for Fluency

Routine Choral Reading

1. **Select a Passage** For *Just Like Josh Gibson,* use pp. 374–375.
2. **Model** First, have children track the print as you read.
3. **Guide Practice** Then have children read along with you.
4. **Corrective Feedback** Have the class read aloud without you. Monitor progress and provide feedback. For optimal fluency, children should reread three to four times.

Routines Flip Chart

CHECK COMPREHENSION Have children compare and contrast what Grandmama and Danny imagine during baseball practice.

Access for All

Rate If children are reading too slowly, have them select their own passages from stories previously read. Then have them practice reading their passages aloud with partners before they read for you.

Options for Oral Rereading

Use *Just Like Josh Gibson* or the Day 1 Decodable Reader.

Common Core State Standards

Language 5. Demonstrate understanding of word relationships and nuances in word meanings.

Access for All

 Strategic Intervention

Homophones If children are having difficulty using two homophones in one sentence, have them write a sentence for each homophone. Then have partners discuss how the context of the sentence helps them figure out the meaning of the homophone.

Selection Vocabulary

bases places that are stations or goals in certain games, such as baseball

cheers happy or encouraging shouts

field a piece of land used for a special purpose

plate a hard rubber slab that a baseball player stands beside to bat

sailed moved smoothly like a ship with sails

threw sent something through the air by force of your arm

Vocabulary

Selection Vocabulary

REVIEW SELECTION WORDS Display and review the selection words *field, cheers, threw, sailed, plate,* and *bases.* Have children read the words aloud.

Team Talk Have children work in pairs to write and illustrate a sentence using two of the selection words. For example, they could use *field* and *cheers.* (The crowd cheers when the players run on the field.)

Homophones

REVIEW HOMOPHONES Remind children that homophones are words that sound alike but have different spellings and meanings. Point out that the selection word *threw* is a homophone. Write *threw* and *through.* Explain that *threw* means "sent something through the air by force of your arm," and *through* means "from one side to the other." Tell children that they can usually determine the relevant meaning of a homophone by using context clues.

GUIDE PRACTICE Write *won* and *one.* These words are homophones. This word is *won—w, o, n.* It means "to have done the best." A sentence using this word is *Our team won the baseball game.* This word is *one—o, n, e.* It means "less than two." A sentence is *I can find only one shoe.*

Write the following words with homophones.

two	**theirs**	**here**	**clothes**
hair	**meat**	**sun**	**road**

Read each word in the list. Have children tell what the word means and use it in a sentence. Then have them spell and define a homophone for the word. Tell them to use it in a sentence. Supply a prompt as necessary.

two, to, too	**theirs, there's**	**here, hear**	**clothes, close**
hair, hare	**meat, meet**	**sun, son**	**road, rode**

Team Talk Have children work in pairs to think of more homophones. Challenge them to write one sentence that uses each set of homophones, such as, *I want to buy a pair of pears.*

Text-Based Comprehension

Read Main Selection

REVIEW DRAW CONCLUSIONS Remind children that as they read, they should **draw conclusions,** or think about facts and details and decide something about them. Thinking about the information we read, and using what we already know, can help us to figure out characters, events, and ideas the author has included in the story. Have children turn to page 376 of their Student Edition. How many players did the All-stars have without Danny? How many players does the All-Stars team need to play? (eight; nine) For additional practice with drawing conclusions, use Let's Practice It!, p. 294 on the *Teacher Resources DVD-ROM.*

Josh Gibson

Name ____________

Read the story. **Ask** yourself **what is happening. Answer** each question.

Today was the big day! Jason couldn't wait for his mom and dad to get home from the store. They had promised him a bike for his birthday. Jason's older brother Tim said he would teach Jason how to ride. The van drove into the driveway. Jason's mom and dad had big smiles on their faces.

1. Who is Jason? **a boy**
2. Where is he? **at home**
3. What special day is it? **Jason's birthday**
4. How is he feeling? **happy, excited**
5. Write a sentence that tells why you think Jason's mom and dad were smiling.

They had a bike for Jason in the van; they knew Jason was happy about his new present.

School + Home **Home Activity** Your child read a story and drew conclusions from the information in the story. Read a story to your child. Stop occasionally to ask your child questions about what is happening in the story and how the characters feel about what is happening.

DVD•294 **Comprehension** Draw Conclusions Review

Copyright © Pearson Education, Inc., or its affiliates. All Rights Reserved. 2

Let's Practice It! TR DVD•294

GENRE: REALISTIC FICTION Remind children that realistic fiction is a made-up story that could happen in real life. Have children recall facts from *Just Like Josh Gibson* that indicate this story could happen in real life. (It has characters, a plot, and a setting that come from real life.)

READ Return to pages 368–381 and use the **2nd Read/Close Reading Notes** to reread *Just Like Josh Gibson.*

Routine — Read for Understanding

Deepen understanding by reading the selection multiple times.

1. **First Read**—If children need support, use the **Access Text** notes to help them clarify understanding.
2. **Second Read**—Use the **Close Reading** notes to help children draw knowledge from the text.

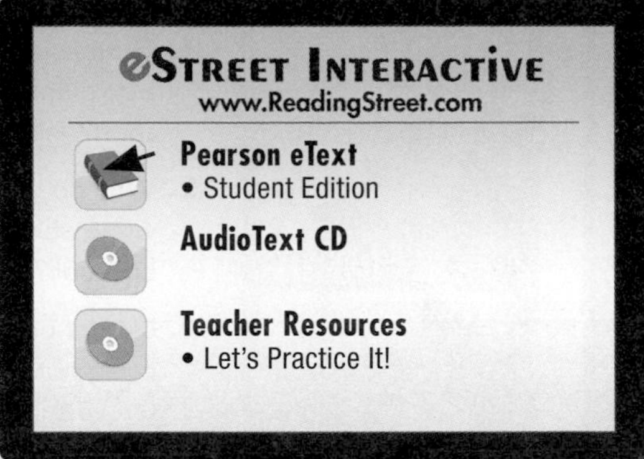

Academic Vocabulary

draw conclusions to think about facts and details and decide something about them

Think Critically

1. Grandmama liked playing baseball. Do you play baseball or another sport? Tell about it. Text to Self
2. Why do you think the author wrote about Grandmama and baseball? Think Like an Author
3. Look at page 373. Grandmama could not play baseball on the Maple Grove All-Stars because she was a girl. How is that different from girls' sports today? Compare and Contrast
4. Think of a question about Grandmama playing baseball. Reread to find the answer. What clues helped you answer the question? Monitor and Clarify
5. **Look Back and Write** Look back at page 379. How can a girl play baseball just like Josh Gibson? Provide evidence to support your answer.
Key Ideas and Details • Text Evidence

382

Meet the Author

Angela Johnson

Angela Johnson has written many great stories. Childhood memories of her father's baseball games inspired *Just Like Josh Gibson*. She says, "I remember the smell of the glove oil, the sound the bats made as the players tapped them on home plate, and the hot dogs I couldn't get enough of. Baseball is a wonderful memory for me. I wanted to write a book about it being a memory for another little girl."

Ms. Johnson recently won an important award to help her continue to write her wonderful stories.

Read two more books by Angela Johnson.

Violet's Music

Do Like Kyla

Reading Log
Use the *Reader's and Writer's Notebook* to record your independent reading.

383

Student Edition, pp. 382–383

Common Core State Standards

Literature 1. Ask and answer such questions as *who, what, where, when, why,* and *how* to demonstrate understanding of key details in a text. **Also Literature 7. and Writing 3.**

Bridge to Common Core

KEY IDEAS AND DETAILS

By reading the text multiple times, children will make logical inferences from the text and cite textual evidence when writing or discussing the knowledge they have gained.

Use the Think Critically page to ensure a thorough understanding of *Just Like Josh Gibson.*

Think Critically

1. **TEXT TO SELF** If children do play baseball or another sport, they should give details about their play.
2. **THINK LIKE AN AUTHOR** The author wanted to entertain us with a story about a girl who achieved something unusual in her day.
3. **COMPARE AND CONTRAST** In the past, girls were not supposed to play baseball with the boys. Today girls can play almost any sport, including baseball.
4. **MONITOR AND CLARIFY** Children might say that they asked how Grandmama got to be so good at baseball. They could reread to find out that her father threw balls to her even when she was very little.
5. **LOOK BACK AND WRITE • TEXT EVIDENCE** For writing fluency, assign a five-minute time limit. As children finish, encourage them to reread their response and proofread for errors.

Scoring Rubric Look Back and Write

TOP-SCORE RESPONSE A top-score response uses details from the text and the pictures to tell how a girl could play baseball like Josh Gibson.

A top-score response might include:
When Danny hurt his arm sliding into second, the team let Grandmama play. She had practiced hitting baseballs with her father when she was little. So she was able to hit the ball hard, catch anything that was thrown, and do everything else that Josh Gibson could do.

Retell

Have children work in pairs, retelling the story to one another. Remind children that their partners should include the characters, setting, and events from the beginning, middle, and end of the story. Have children use the retelling strip in the Student Edition or the Story Sort to retell the selection. Monitor children's retellings.

Scoring Rubric Narrative Retelling

	4	3	2	1
Connections	Makes connections and generalizes beyond the text	Makes connections to other events, stories, or experiences	Makes a limited connection to another event, story, or experience	Makes no connection to another event, story, or experience
Author's Purpose	Elaborates on author's purpose	Tells author's purpose with some clarity	Makes some connection to author's purpose	Makes no connection to author's purpose
Characters	Describes the main character(s) and any character development	Identifies the main character(s) and gives some information about them	Inaccurately identifies some characters or gives little information about them	Inaccurately identifies the characters or gives no information about them
Setting	Describes the time and location	Identifies the time and location	Omits details of time or location	Is unable to identify time or location
Plot	Describes the events in sequence using rich detail	Tells the plot with some errors in sequence that do not affect meaning	Tells parts of plot with gaps that affect meaning	Retelling has no sense of story

Don't Wait Until Friday **MONITOR PROGRESS** Check Retelling

If... children have difficulty retelling the selection,

then... use Story Sequence Graphic Organizer 23 and the Retelling Cards/ Story Sort to scaffold their retelling.

Strategy Response Log

Monitor and Clarify Have children revisit the text and identify places where they had difficulty with comprehension. Have them use p. RR32 in their *Reader's and Writer's Notebook* to explain a fix-up strategy they used that helped them clarify their understanding.

Plan to Assess Retelling

- ☑ **This Week** Assess Strategic Intervention children.
- ☐ **Week 2** Advanced
- ☐ **Week 3** Strategic Intervention
- ☐ **Week 4** On-Level
- ☐ **Week 5** Strategic Intervention
- ☐ **Week 6** Assess any children you have not yet checked during this unit.

Meet the Author

Read aloud page 383 as children follow along. Ask children what an author does. Discuss what it means to say that childhood memories "inspired" Angela Johnson to write.

Read Independently

Have children enter their independent reading into their Reading Logs.

Common Core State Standards

Language 2.a. Capitalize holidays, product names, and geographic names. **Writing 3.** Write narratives in which they recount a well-elaborated event or short sequence of events, include details to describe actions, thoughts, and feelings, use temporal words to signal event order, and provide a sense of closure.

Daily Fix-It

5. I thruw the ball to left feild.
   I threw the ball to left field.
6. the crowd cheerd for him.
   The crowd cheered for him.

Discuss the Daily Fix-It corrections with children. Review sentence capitalization, the *ie* spelling pattern for long *e,* the *ew* spelling pattern for /ü/, and the *-ed* ending.

Conventions

Using Capital Letters

REVIEW Remind children that days, months, holidays, titles of books, poems, and songs begin with capital letters. Point out that initials and titles in people's names, geographic names, and abbreviations of days and months are capitalized and end with a period. Mention that some adjectives, such as *Indian* or *Mexican,* begin with capital letters too.

GUIDE PRACTICE Write these words and abbreviations on the board.

dr m tallchief, united states, feb, tues, dec, mr

Which words and titles should begin with a capital letter? Which should end with a period?

Team Talk Have partners work together to correct the examples on the board. Have them discuss what word each abbreviation stands for.

APPLY Have children say a sentence that includes one of the following proper nouns.

Thursday
Dr. Witt
Italian meatballs

ON THEIR OWN Use Let's Practice It!, p. 297 on the *Teacher Resources DVD-ROM.*

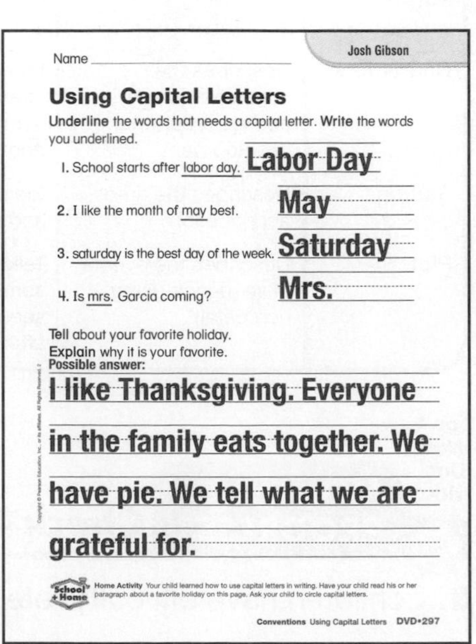

Name ______ Josh Gibson

Using Capital Letters

Underline the words that needs a capital letter. **Write** the words you underlined.

1. School starts after labor day. **Labor Day**
2. I like the month of may best. **May**
3. saturday is the best day of the week. **Saturday**
4. Is mrs. Garcia coming? **Mrs.**

Tell about your favorite holiday. **Explain** why it is your favorite.
Possible answer:
I like Thanksgiving. Everyone in the family eats together. We have pie. We tell what we are grateful for.

Home Activity Your child learned how to use capital letters in writing. Have your child read his or her paragraph about a favorite holiday on this page. Ask your child to circle capital letters.

Conventions Using Capital Letters DVD•297

Let's Practice It! TR DVD•297

Common Core State Standards
Writing 3. Write narratives in which they recount a well-elaborated event or short sequence of events, include details to describe actions, thoughts, and feelings, use temporal words to signal event order, and provide a sense of closure.
Also Language 2., 2.a.

Let's Write It!

Key Features of Realistic Fiction
- characters and the setting seem real
- characters do things that could really happen

READING STREET ONLINE
GRAMMAR JAMMER
www.ReadingStreet.com

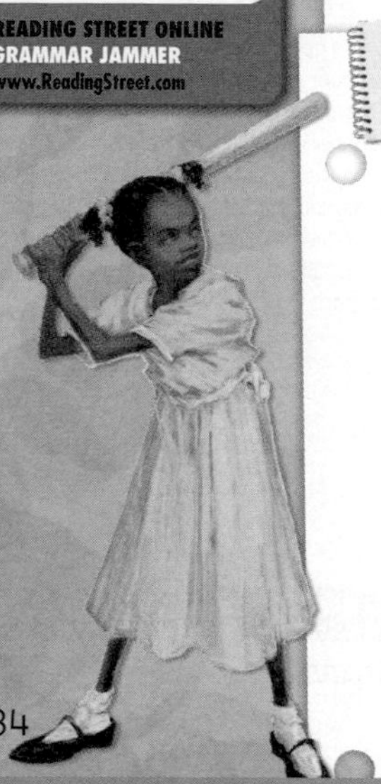

Narrative

Realistic Fiction

Realistic fiction tells about made-up events that could really happen. The student model on the next page is an example of realistic fiction.

Writing Prompt Think about one of your favorite sports heroes. Now write a story about a character who wants to be like that sports figure.

Writer's Checklist

Remember, you should ...
- ✓ include events that could really happen.
- ✓ include a strong ending.
- ✓ use capital letters correctly.

384

Student Model

The Walter Payton Fan

Grandma told Mark about Walter Payton. Payton played football years ago. Mark read a book about him.

Ever since then, Mark wanted to be a good runner like Walter Payton.

Last Thanksgiving, Mark played football with his brothers. He scored the winning touchdown.

Now Grandma smiles and calls Mark "Mr. Payton."

Genre Realistic fiction has events that could really happen.

The writer has **capitalized** the name of a holiday.

Writing Trait Organization The writer included an interesting ending.

Conventions

Using Capital Letters

Days of the week, **months,** and **holidays** begin with capital letters. **Titles** for people begin with capital letters. **Mr.** Lee played ball on the **Fourth of July**.

385

Student Edition, pp. 384–385

Let's Write It!

WRITE REALISTIC FICTION Use pp. 384–385 in the Student Edition. Read aloud the Key Features of Realistic Fiction and the definition of realistic fiction. Read aloud the Writing Prompt and discuss the Writer's Checklist.

REVIEW THE STUDENT MODEL Read "The Walter Payton Fan" on p. 385 aloud. Point out the story's realistic characters and events. Help children recognize the beginning, middle, and ending. Read aloud and briefly discuss the side notes about genre, the writing trait, and capitalization.

Scoring Rubric

TOP-SCORE RESPONSE Help children understand that a top-score response has a beginning, a middle, and an interesting ending, and uses appropriate capitalization. For a complete rubric see Writing Rubric 26 from the *Teacher Resources DVD-ROM.*

CONNECT TO CONVENTIONS Read the Conventions note about capital letters. Point out *Grandma, Thanksgiving,* and *Mr. Payton* in the model story.

eSTREET INTERACTIVE
www.ReadingStreet.com

Pearson eText
- Student Edition

Teacher Resources
- Let's Practice It!
- Daily Fix-It Transparency
- Scoring Rubric

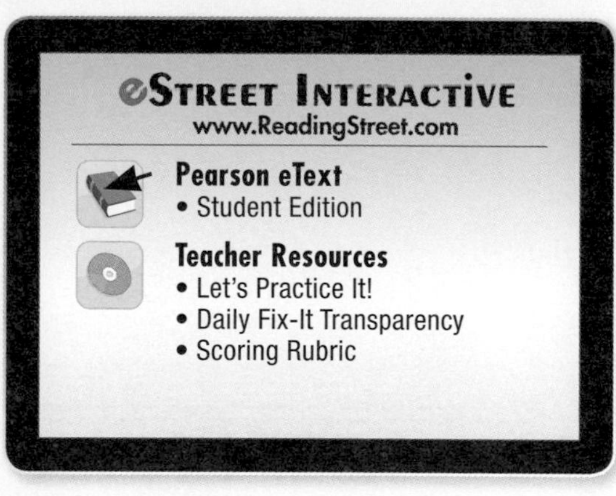

Common Core State Standards

Writing 3. Write narratives in which they recount a well-elaborated event or short sequence of events, include details to describe actions, thoughts, and feelings, use temporal words to signal event order, and provide a sense of closure. **Writing 7.** Participate in shared research and writing projects (e.g., read a number of books on a single topic to produce a report; record science observations). **Writing 8.** Recall information from experiences or gather information from provided sources to answer a question.

Writing

Zoom in on

Realistic Fiction

Mini-Lesson Writer's Craft: Sequence

- **Introduce** Use your story chart from yesterday and Writing Transparency 26A to model writing the beginning, middle, and end of a story. Yesterday I wrote these ideas in my chart to help me tell my story in order: in the beginning, Ava is playing in a soccer game, the score is tied, and the other team has the ball. In the middle of the story, Dad yells to Ava to play like Pelé. At the end, I wrote Ava kicks the winning goal. I think that is an exciting ending, but when I wrote my story I added details to make it even better. Read aloud the draft on the transparency to show the beginning, middle, and end of the story.

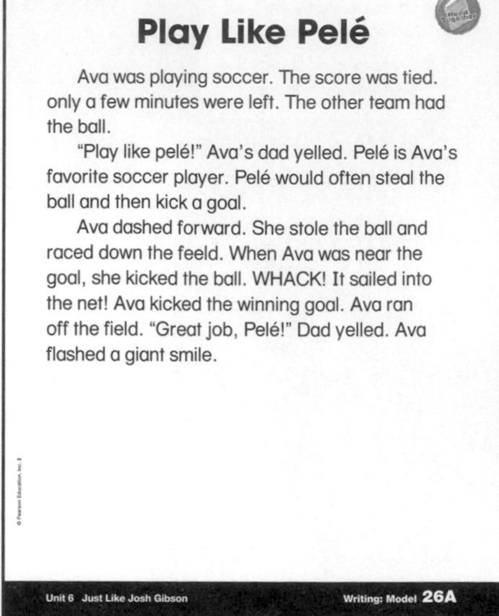

Play Like Pelé

Ava was playing soccer. The score was tied. only a few minutes were left. The other team had the ball.

"Play like pelé!" Ava's dad yelled. Pelé is Ava's favorite soccer player. Pelé would often steal the ball and then kick a goal.

Ava dashed forward. She stole the ball and raced down the feeld. When Ava was near the goal, she kicked the ball. WHACK! It sailed into the net! Ava kicked the winning goal. Ava ran off the field. "Great job, Pelé!" Dad yelled. Ava flashed a giant smile.

Unit 6 Just Like Josh Gibson — Writing: Model 26A

Writing Transparency 26A TR DVD

- Explain how children can use their sequence chart to draft a story to show the beginning, middle, and end. Remind them that the goal is to write their ideas on paper. They can edit later to correct the words.

GUIDE WRITING Now it is time to write your story. Tell what your character does to be like a sports hero. Have children use their story charts. Help them expand on the ideas in their sequence charts. Then guide children as they draft the story.

Routine Quick Write for Fluency

Team Talk

1. **Talk** Have partners take one minute to talk about what they do that is like a sports hero.
2. **Write** Each child writes a sentence about how he or she is like his or her sports hero.
3. **Share** Partners point out the capital letters in the others' sentences.

Routines Flip Chart

Research and Inquiry

Step 3 Gather and Record Information

TEACH Tell children that today they will gather information about ways sports traditions help athletes. Their goal is to find sources that will help them answer their questions and record the answers.

Think Aloud **MODEL** Display the list of questions that the class created on Day 1. We have our list of questions. I'm interested in finding out how athletes learn the sport. There are many athletes. Each may learn a different way. I can read about the lives of famous athletes to find out how different athletes learned their sport. The best place to look will be in books, such as biographies, that tell the life story of well-known athletes. Model using one of the sources to locate information about an athlete learning a sport by playing with other people. Record it in the chart.

GUIDE PRACTICE Have partners use a relevant source to research a chart question. You may wish to provide a number of books about athletes to use as sources. Record answers children find. Tell children that tomorrow they will review their topic to make sure their question was answered.

Topic: Sports Traditions Help Athletes

Question	Answer
How do athletes learn the sport?	They play the sport with other people.

Access for All

A Advanced

Use a Globe As children research players, have them note the country of birth. If a player was born in another country, have the child find it on the globe and show the class where the country is.

Wrap Up Your Day!

✔ **Compare and Contrast** How are the sports of baseball and basketball alike and different?

✔ **Monitor and Clarify** Have children tell why it is important to ask questions about the selection as they read.

Tell children that tomorrow they will read how baseball began.

DAY 4 at a Glance

Content Knowledge
Oral Vocabulary

Phonics
Review Vowel Patterns *aw, au, au(gh), al*

High-Frequency Words
Review

Spelling
Inflected Endings

Social Studies in Reading
Expository Text

Fluency
Accuracy and Appropriate Rate

Conventions
Using Capital Letters

Writing
Realistic Fiction: Revise

Listening and Speaking
Use Clear and Specific Vocabulary

Research and Inquiry
Synthesize

Materials

- Student Edition
- Sing with Me Big Book
- Read Aloud Anthology
- Decodable Reader 26C
- Reader's and Writer's Notebook

Common Core State Standards

Speaking/Listening 2. Recount or describe key ideas or details from a text read aloud or information presented orally or through other media. **Language 6.** Use words and phrases acquired through conversations, reading and being read to, and responding to texts, including using adjectives and adverbs to describe (e.g., *When other kids are happy that makes me happy*).

Content Knowledge

Sports Traditions

EXPAND THE CONCEPT To reinforce concepts and to focus children's attention, have children sing "An Athlete's Challenge" from the *Sing with Me* Big Book. What do athletes love to hear? (They love to hear cheers.) When might people cheer during a game?

Build Oral Language

REVIEW GENRE: REALISTIC FICTION
Have children tell the key features of realistic fiction: it tells about made-up people and events, but the characters and events seem real. The setting of a realistic story seems real. Explain that today you will read about a girl who wants to be a great baseball player in "Yankee Doodle Shortstop" by Helen J. Hinterberg.

"Yankee Doodle Shortstop"

MONITOR LISTENING COMPREHENSION
Recall the challenges Grandmama faced as a girl who was not allowed to play on a boys' team. Have children listen to "Yankee Doodle Shortstop."

Team Talk **TALK ABOUT SPORTS TRADITIONS** Read aloud the seventh paragraph of page 144 of "Yankee Doodle Shortstop." Display it on a white-board if possible, and track the print as you read.

- Have pairs of children generate questions for each other about what they think the pressure of playing sports are after reading this paragraph.
- Add words generated in the discussion to the concept map.

Build Oral Vocabulary

Amazing Words — Robust Vocabulary Routine

1. **Introduce the Word** Relate the word *champion* to the book. Meg's mother was a *champion* at baseball. Supply a child-friendly definition. A *champion* is the winner of a game or competition. Have children say the word.
2. **Demonstrate** Provide examples to show meaning. The *champions* had ten wins and no losses. This year our team beat last year's *champion.*
3. **Apply** Have children demonstrate their understanding. Do you know any *champions?* Describe them.
4. **Display the Word** Run your hand under the three syllables *cham-pi-on* as you read the word.

See p. OV•1 to teach *professional* and *shortstop.*

Routines Flip Chart

ADD TO THE CONCEPT MAP Discuss how sports can be an important tradition.

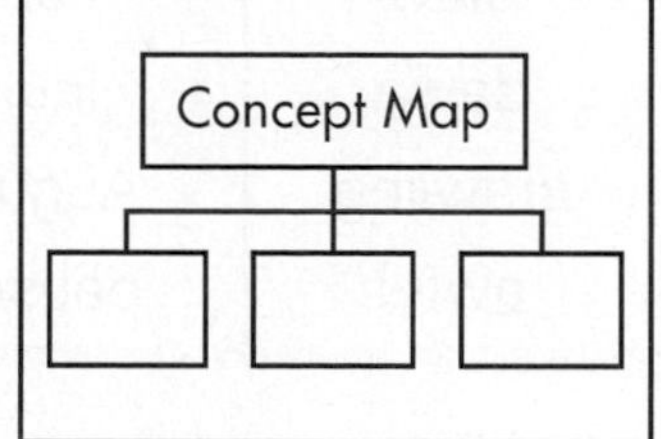

- In "Yankee Doodle Shortstop," what is Meg's mom known for? (She is a baseball champion.) What memories do Meg's parents share with her? (their memories of playing sports) Where can we add this idea to our concept map?
- How do Meg's coach and her father help her become a better player? (The coach believes in her natural talent; her father suggests singing a song while she plays.) Where can we add this information to our concept map?

Amazing Words

athlete	disguise
challenge	champion
effort	professional
dainty	shortstop

Reinforce Vocabulary Use the Day 4 instruction on ELL Poster 26 to extend and enrich language.

Preview Comprehension Use ELL Poster 26 before reading the story to discuss what a baseball diamond looks like and where a shortstop plays. If needed, explain that the children on the poster are playing kickball, not baseball.

Access Content To help children better understand the title of the story and the song it is based on, play or sing "Yankee Doodle" and discuss the lyrics before reading the story.

Common Core State Standards

Foundational Skills 3. Know and apply grade-level phonics and word analysis skills in decoding words. **Foundational Skills 3.b.** Know spelling-sound correspondences for additional common vowel teams. **Foundational Skills 3.f.** Recognize and read grade-appropriate irregularly spelled words.

Josh Gibson

Name ____________

saw auto caught chalk

Circle the word for each picture. **Write** the word on the line.

1. talk took — talk
2. hook hawk — hawk
3. lawn lane — lawn
4. small smell — small
5. face faucet — faucet
6. tote taught — taught

Pick a word from the box to finish each sentence. **Write** the word on the line.

daughter launch

7. Anna and her daughter are late.

8. They will miss the launch.

Home Activity Your child reviewed words with the vowel sound in *fall*, spelled *aw* as in *saw*, *au* as in *auto*, *augh* as in *caught*, and *al* as in *chalk*. Ask your child to name words that rhyme with some of the lesson words above. Help your child write humorous sentences using pairs of rhyming words.

Phonics Vowels *aw, au, augh, al* Review DVD•293

Let's Practice It! TR DVD•293

Phonics

Review Vowel Patterns *aw, au, au(gh), al*

REVIEW VOWEL PATTERNS To review last week's phonics skill, write *paw, cause, daughter,* and *small.* You studied words like these last week. What do you know about the sound you hear when a word has the spelling pattern *aw, au, augh,* or *al?* (The vowel sound is /ȯ/.) What letters spell the sound /ȯ/ in *paw?* *(aw)* Continue with the remaining words.

Corrective feedback	If children are unable to answer the questions about vowel patterns *aw, au, au(gh),* and *al,* refer them to Sound-Spelling Cards 58, 56, 57, and 106.

GUIDE PRACTICE Write *aw, au, augh* and *al* as heads in a four-column chart. When I write a word, read it in your head. Decide which spelling the sound /ȯ/ has in the word and tell me in which column the word belongs. Write: *claw, caught, chalk, dawn, haul, fault, daughter, crawling, false, naughty, August, awful, always, taught, walnut, pauses.* As children respond, write each word in the appropriate column. Then have children read the columns.

aw	*au*	*augh*	*al*
claw	haul	caught	chalk
dawn	fault	daughter	false
crawling	August	naughty	always
awful	pauses	taught	walnut

ON THEIR OWN Use Let's Practice It!, p. 293 on the *Teacher Resources DVD–ROM.*

Fluent Word Reading

Spiral Review

READ WORDS IN ISOLATION Display these words. Tell children that they can blend or chunk some words on this list and others are Word Wall words.

Have children read the list three or four times until they can read at the rate of two to three seconds per word.

rock	**watch**	**shoe**	**rings**	**tries**
pretty	**show**	**which**	**guess**	**matches**
gophers	**rough**	**science**	**along**	**black**
while	**driving**	**studied**	**village**	**phone**

Corrective feedback
Word Reading

If... children have difficulty reading whole words,
then... have them use sound-by-sound blending or combine word parts for decodable words or have them say and spell high-frequency words.

If... children cannot read fluently at a rate of two to three seconds per word,
then... have pairs practice the list until they can read it fluently.

READ WORDS IN CONTEXT Display these sentences. Call on individuals to read a sentence. Then randomly point to review words and have children read them. To help you monitor word reading, high-frequency words are underlined and decodable words are italicized.

Can you <u>guess</u> *which rock* we *studied* in <u>science</u> class?

The *phone rings while* they <u>watch</u> a *show* about *gophers*.

The family is *driving along* a *rough* road to get to the <u>village</u>.

Ling *tries* on the <u>pretty</u> *black* <u>shoe</u> *that matches* her dress.

Corrective feedback
Sentence Reading

If... children are unable to read an underlined high-frequency word,
then... read the word for them and spell it, having them echo you.

If... children have difficulty reading an italicized decodable word,
then... guide them in blending or combining word parts.

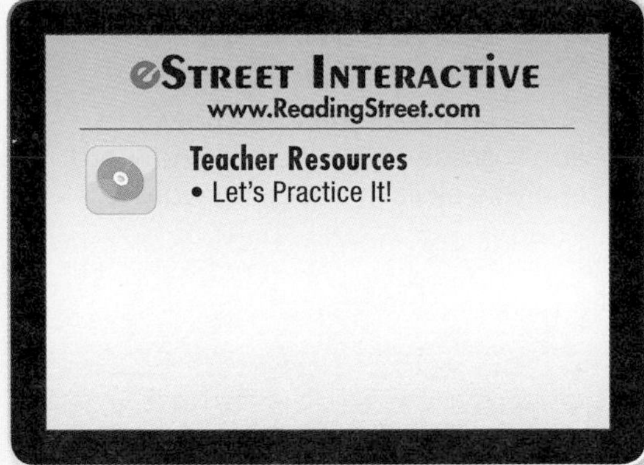

Access for All

 Strategic Intervention

Inflected Endings For children having difficulty reading words with inflected endings, have them write the rules for adding inflected endings (add *-s,* add *-es,* add *-ed,* add *-ing,* double the last consonant, drop the final *e,* change *y* to *i*) on separate index cards. Point to words with inflected endings and have children show the rule card that matches each word before reading the word.

Spiral Review

These activities review

- your previously taught high-frequency words *guess, pretty, science, watch, village, shoe.*
- inflected endings.
- consonant patterns *ph, gh, ck, ng.*
- consonant digraphs.

Fluent Word Reading Have children listen to a more fluent reader model the words or have pairs read the words together.

Common Core State Standards

Foundational Skills 3. Know and apply grade-level phonics and word analysis skills in decoding words.

Decodable Reader 26C

If children need help, then...

Read *The Happiest King*

DECODE WORDS IN ISOLATION Have children turn to page 191 in *Decodable Practice Readers* 2.2 and decode each word.

READ HIGH-FREQUENCY WORDS Have children identify and read the high-frequency words *king, but, ever,* and *afraid* on the first page.

PREVIEW Have children read the title and preview the story. Tell them they will read words with inflected endings.

DECODE WORDS IN CONTEXT Pair children for reading and listen carefully as they decode. One child begins. Children read the entire story, switching readers after each page. Partners reread the story. This time the other child begins.

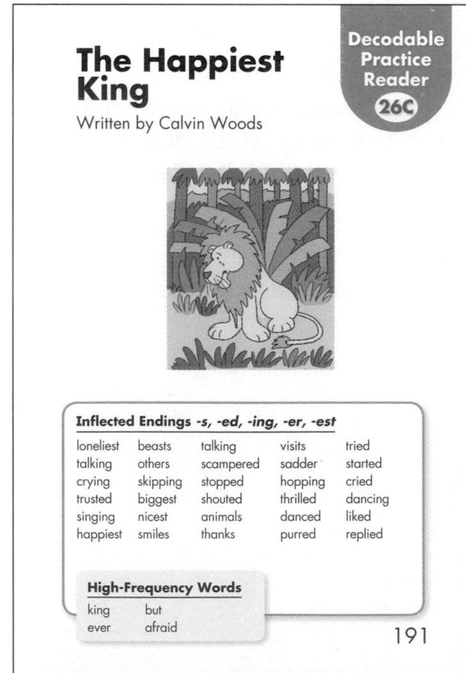

The Happiest King

Written by Calvin Woods

Decodable Practice Reader 26C

Inflected Endings *-s, -ed, -ing, -er, -est*

loneliest	beasts	talking	visits	tried
talking	others	scampered	sadder	started
crying	skipping	stopped	hopping	cried
trusted	biggest	shouted	thrilled	dancing
singing	nicest	animals	danced	liked
happiest	smiles	thanks	purred	replied

High-Frequency Words

king	but
ever	afraid

191

Decodable Practice Reader 26C

Lonny was the loneliest.
He is king of this jungle,
but other beasts don't like
talking with him.
Nobody ever visits.

192

Lonny tried talking to others,
but most just scampered off.
Lonny got sadder and sadder.
He started crying.

193

Bonny Bunny came skipping by.
She saw Lonny crying.
Bonny felt afraid.
Then she stopped to think.
Why did the king cry?

194

Bonny started hopping toward Lonny.
"Hello!" she cried.
Lonny trusted Bonny.
He told Bonny how he felt.

195

"Let's throw the biggest party!"
shouted Bonny.
She was thrilled to help.
"We can plan dancing and singing.
They will see that you are the nicest."

196

That's what Bonny and Lonny did.
All those animals came.
They danced and sang.
Everyone liked talking with Lonny.
All of them had fun.

197

Lonny is the happiest king.
Now he smiles and smiles.
"Thanks so much, Bonny!"
Lonny purred.
"Anything to help," she replied.

198

Corrective feedback

If... children have difficulty decoding a word,
then... refer them to the Sound-Spelling Cards to identify sounds in a decodable word; prompt them to blend the word. If the word has an inflected ending, have them identify all the word parts and read them together to say the word.

- What is the new word?
- Is the new word a word you know?
- Does it make sense in the story?

CHECK DECODING AND COMPREHENSION Have children retell the story to include characters, setting, and events. Then have children find words that include verb endings *-s, -ed,* and *-ing;* and comparative endings *-er* and *-est* in the story. For each word, have children identify any spelling change. Children should supply the following words:

-s: *beasts, visits, others, animals, smiles*

-ed: *tried, scampered, started, stopped, cried, trusted, shouted, thrilled, danced, liked, purred, replied*

-ing: *talking, crying, skipping, hopping, dancing, singing*

-er: *sadder*

-est: *loneliest, biggest, nicest, happiest*

Reread for Fluency

REREAD DECODABLE READER Have children reread Decodable Practice Reader 26C to develop automaticity reading words with inflected endings.

Routine Oral Rereading

1. **Read** Have children read the entire book orally.
2. **Reread** To achieve optimal fluency, children should reread the text three or four times.
3. **Corrective Feedback** Listen as children read. Provide corrective feedback regarding their fluency and decoding.

Routines Flip Chart

Leveled Support

Beginning Write these words from *The Happiest King: started, stopped, trusted, shouted, thrilled, danced.* Circle the base word and underline *-ed* in each word. Say each word aloud, clapping to show the syllables. Repeat and have children join in. State that sometimes the ending *-ed* forms its own syllable. Then say the words again. Have children stand if they hear a word that has two syllables.

Intermediate After reading, have children find words with inflected endings in *The Happiest King* and say them aloud. Then have children use each word in a sentence. For example: *I like talking to my friends.*

Advanced After reading, have children find words from the story in which the spelling changed when the ending was added, such as *loneliest, tried, sadder,* and *stopped.* Have them write the base words and use the words in sentences.

Common Core State Standards

Language 2. Demonstrate command of the conventions of standard English capitalization, punctuation, and spelling when writing.

Spelling

Inflected Endings

PARTNER REVIEW Supply pairs of children with index cards on which the spelling words have been written. Have one child read a word while the other writes it. Then have children switch roles. Have them use the cards to check their spelling and correct any misspelled words.

ON THEIR OWN Use Let's Practice It!, p. 296 on the *Teacher Resources DVD-ROM.*

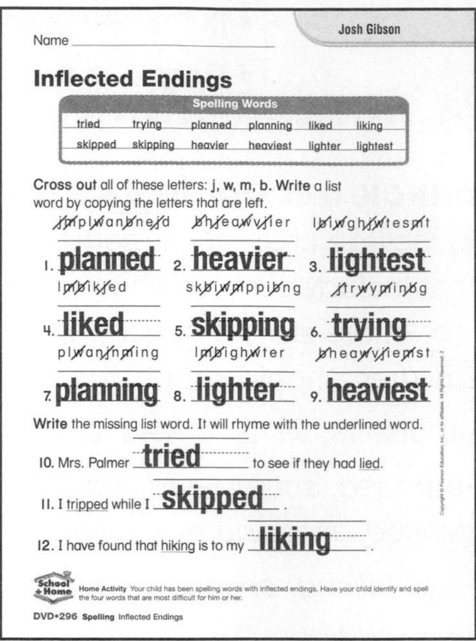

Name ________________ Josh Gibson

Inflected Endings

Spelling Words					
tried	trying	planned	planning	liked	liking
skipped	skipping	heavier	heaviest	lighter	lightest

Cross out all of these letters: **j, w, m, b. Write** a list word by copying the letters that are left.

jmplwanbnejd — 1. planned
bhjeawvjier — 2. heavier
lbiwghjwtesmt — 3. lightest
lmbikjed — 4. liked
skbiwmppibng — 5. skipping
jtrwyminbg — 6. trying
plwanjnming — 7. planning
lmbighwter — 8. lighter
bheawvjiemst — 9. heaviest

Write the missing list word. It will rhyme with the underlined word.

10. Mrs. Palmer tried to see if they had lied.
11. I tripped while I skipped.
12. I have found that hiking is to my liking.

School + Home **Home Activity** Your child has been spelling words with inflected endings. Have your child identify and spell the four words that are most difficult for him or her.

DVD•296 **Spelling** Inflected Endings

Let's Practice It! TR DVD•296

If... children need more scaffolding and practice with **Amazing Words, then...** use the routine on pp. xxxvi—xxxvii in the *ELL Handbook.*

Day 4 SMALL GROUP TIME • Differentiate Vocabulary, p. SG•1

OL On-Level	SI Strategic Intervention	A Advanced
• **Develop** Language Using Amazing Words • **Read** *Reading Street Sleuth,* pp. 68–69	• **Review/Discuss** Amazing Words • **Read** *Reading Street Sleuth,* pp. 68–69	• **Extend** Amazing Words and Selection Vocabulary • **Read** *Reading Street Sleuth,* pp. 68–69 • **Organize** Inquiry Project

Social Studies in Reading

Expository Text

ACTIVATE PRIOR KNOWLEDGE Ask children to think about the story *Just Like Josh Gibson.* Ask them what they read about baseball in that story. (Players hit the ball, throw, and run around the bases. Josh Gibson was a great African American hitter. Long ago girls were not allowed to play baseball.)

PREVIEW AND PREDICT Have children turn to page 386 in their Student Edition. Read the title and the author's name of the selection. Have children look through the selection, read the subheads, and tell what they see in the illustrations. (people playing baseball, baseball graphs, and globes) Ask children to predict whether "How Baseball Began" tells a story or gives information. (gives information)

READ AN EXPOSITORY TEXT Tell children that they will read **expository text.** Review the key features of expository text: it explains an object or idea, it gives facts, and it may include graphics.

Genre

LET'S THINK ABOUT... As children read "How Baseball Began," use Let's Think About in the Student Edition to help them focus on the features and structure of expository text.

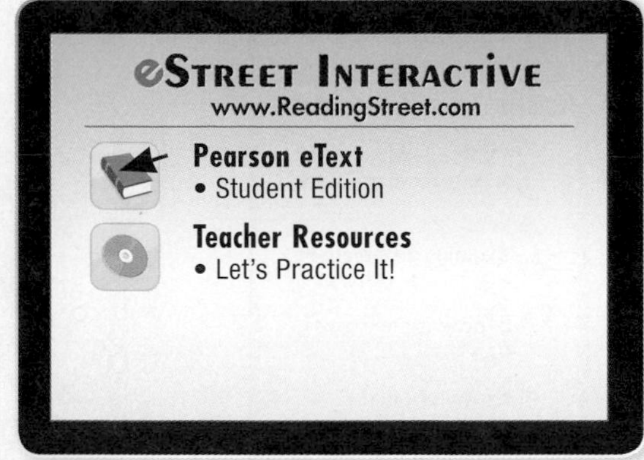

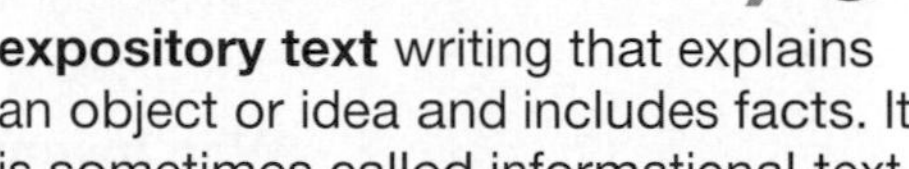

Academic Vocabulary

expository text writing that explains an object or idea and includes facts. It is sometimes called informational text.

Common Core State Standards
Foundational Skills 4.a. Read on-level text with purpose and understanding. **Also Literature 1.**

Social Studies in Reading

Genre
Expository Text

- Expository text explains an object or idea.
- Expository text gives facts.
- Expository text may have graphic features.
- Read "How Baseball Began." Watch for facts and other elements that show this is expository text.

How Baseball Began

by Tammy Terry

illustrated by Clint Hansen

Baseball is called the national pastime of the United States. Hundreds of games are played and watched every spring and summer. But have you ever wondered how baseball began?

Who Invented It?

Well, no one knows for sure who invented the game. Many people believe that a man named Abner Doubleday invented baseball in 1839 in Cooperstown, New York.

Abner Doubleday

386

In rounders, players threw the ball at runners. If a runner got hit, he was out.

Baseball probably developed from the English game of the 1600s called "rounders."

Settlers living in America played rounders in the 1700s. They also called the game "town ball" and "base ball." Rules of the game varied from place to place. Over the years, the game of rounders became the game we now call baseball. One of the biggest differences between the two games is in how a runner is put out.

In baseball, players tag runners to put them out.

Let's Think About...
Who do many people say invented baseball?
Expository Text

1

Let's Think About...
What is the main idea of this paragraph?
Expository Text

2

387

Student Edition, pp. 386–387

Common Core State Standards

Informational Text 1. Ask and answer such questions as *who, what, where, when, why,* and *how* to demonstrate understanding of key details in a text. **Informational Text 8.** Describe how reasons support specific points the author makes in a text.

Access Text

Think Aloud

MONITOR AND CLARIFY Explain that good readers monitor their reading. If they don't understand something, they ask questions and look for answers by rereading or reading on. When I read that one of the biggest differences between baseball and rounders is how a runner is put out, I asked myself, "What *is* the difference?" Then I looked for clues in the text and saw that the captions next to the illustrations answered my question.

LET'S THINK ABOUT... features of expository text.

1. Many people believe Abner Doubleday invented baseball, but no one knows for sure.
2. Baseball probably developed from the English game called rounders.

Players and Teams

The first official baseball game was played in Hoboken, New Jersey, on June 19, 1846. The New York Nine beat the Knickerbockers 23–1. More people became fans of the sport as more games were played.

In 1869, the Cincinnati Red Stockings became the first baseball team to get paid to play baseball. They won every game they played that year. Support for baseball continued to grow. More professional teams were formed. In 1876, eight teams joined to form the National League. The American League began in 1900 with eight teams.

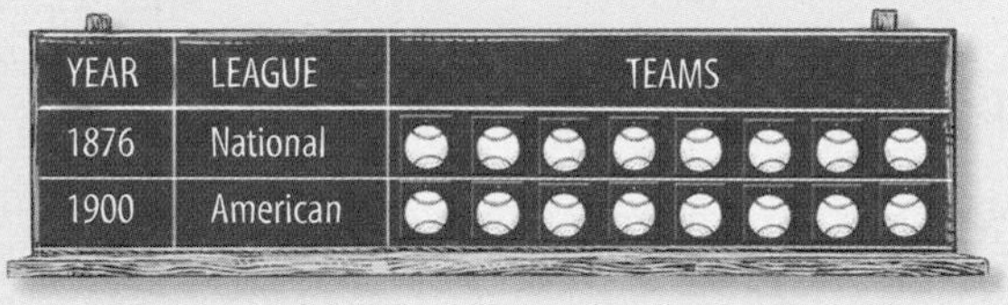

YEAR	LEAGUE	TEAMS
1876	National	
1900	American	

Let's Think About...

What information can you learn about the two leagues from these charts? **Expository Text**

3

Today, sixteen teams play in the National League. There are fourteen teams in the American League.

YEAR	LEAGUE	TEAMS
2009	National	
2009	American	

They play in cities across the United States **(1)** and Canada **(2)**. Each year, millions of people go to baseball games, watch the games on TV, and read about the teams in newspapers. The sport has spread throughout the world, and baseball is now played in countries such as Japan **(3)**, Italy **(4)**, and South Africa **(5)**.

Let's Think About...

Reading Across Texts Use what you read in this article to figure out how long after the "invention" of baseball by Abner Doubleday it was that Grandmama played baseball.

Writing Across Texts Make a time line to show the important dates in baseball history. Be sure to include the time when Grandmama played.

388 389

Student Edition, pp. 388–389

FACTS AND DETAILS What reasons does the author give to support the claim that baseball may have developed from rounders? (The games were similar. Some people called rounders "base ball.")

LET'S THINK ABOUT... features of expository text.

3 You can learn how many teams were in the National League in 1876, in the American League in 1900, and in both leagues in 2009.

Reading and Writing Across Texts

Have children locate the sentence in "How Baseball Began" that tells when Doubleday "invented" baseball—1839. Help them compare that date to the 1940s—more than 100 years later—when Grandmama played. Tell children to draw a line and mark off 1700, 1800, 1900, and 2000. Then have them skim the article for important dates.

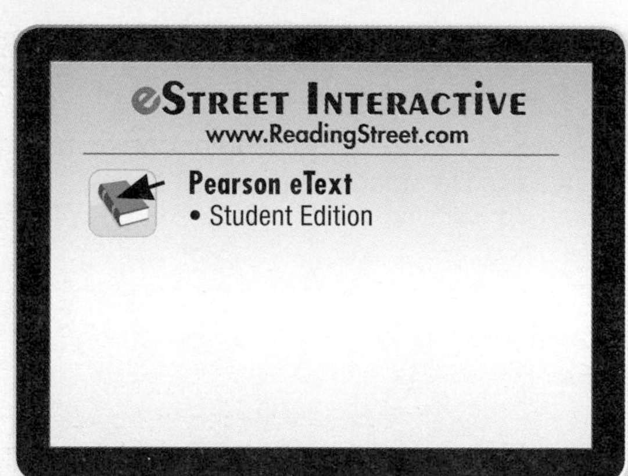

Social Studies Vocabulary

national having to do with a nation, or country

settlers people who move from one area to a new area to live

Common Core State Standards

Foundational Skills 4.b. Read on-level text orally with accuracy, appropriate rate, and expression on successive readings. **Language 2.a.** Capitalize holidays, product names, and geographic names.

Access for All

 Advanced

Rate If children already read at 90 words correct per minute, have them read more challenging text.

Fluency Assessment Plan

Do a formal fluency assessment with eight to ten children every week. Assess four or five children on Day 4 and four or five children on Day 5. Use the reproducible fluency passage, Teacher's Edition, p. 391f.

Options for Oral Rereading

Use *Just Like Josh Gibson* or one of this week's Decodable Practice Readers.

Fluency

Accuracy and Appropriate Rate

- Have children turn to pp. 376–377 in *Just Like Josh Gibson.*
- Have children follow along as you read the pages accurately and at an appropriate rate.
- Have the class read the pages with you and then reread the pages as a group until they read with no hesitation and no mistakes. To provide additional fluency practice, pair nonfluent readers with fluent readers.

Routine Paired Reading

1. **Select a Passage** For *Just Like Josh Gibson* use pp. 378–381.
2. **Model** First, have children track the print as you read.
3. **Guide Practice** Then have children read along with you.
4. **On Their Own** For optimal fluency, have partners reread three or four times.

Routines Flip Chart

MONITOR PROGRESS Fluency Check

As children reread with a partner, monitor their progress toward their individual fluency goals. Current Goal: 80–90 words correct per minute. End-of-Year-Goal: 90 words correct per minute.

If... children cannot read fluently at a rate of 80–90 words correct per minute,
then... have children practice with text at their independent level.

Conventions

Using Capital Letters

TEST PRACTICE Use *Reader's and Writer's Notebook,* p. 492 to help children understand identifying words and titles that should be capitalized in test items. Recall that names of days, months, and holidays, as well as initials and titles, begin with capital letters. Remind children that titles of songs, books, and poems are also capitalized. Model identifying words that should be capitalized by writing this sentence on the board, reading it aloud, and underlining the capitalized words.

<u>Mr.</u> <u>See</u> read his favorite book, <u>Frindle</u>, to our class <u>Monday</u>.

Then read the *Reader's and Writer's Notebook,* p. 492 directions. Guide children as they mark the answer for number 1.

ON THEIR OWN Use *Reader's and Writer's Notebook,* p. 492.

APPLY After children mark the answers to numbers 1–6, review the correct choices aloud, and have children read each sentence aloud and point out words that begin with capital letters.

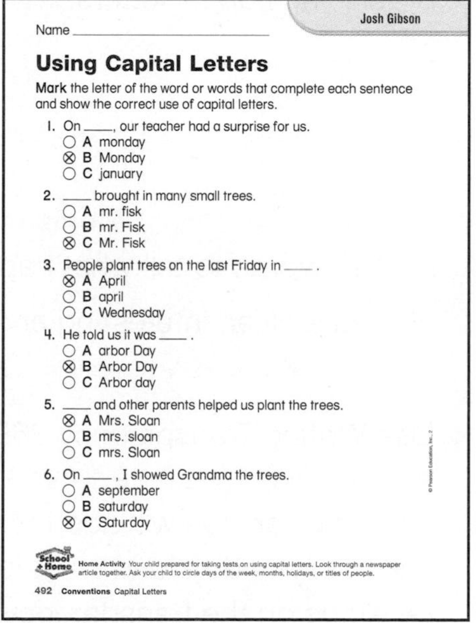

Name ____________ Josh Gibson

Using Capital Letters

Mark the letter of the word or words that complete each sentence and show the correct use of capital letters.

1. On ____, our teacher had a surprise for us.
   - ○ A monday
   - ⊗ B Monday
   - ○ C january
2. ____ brought in many small trees.
   - ○ A mr. fisk
   - ○ B mr. Fisk
   - ⊗ C Mr. Fisk
3. People plant trees on the last Friday in ____ .
   - ⊗ A April
   - ○ B april
   - ○ C Wednesday
4. He told us it was ____ .
   - ○ A arbor Day
   - ⊗ B Arbor Day
   - ○ C Arbor day
5. ____ and other parents helped us plant the trees.
   - ⊗ A Mrs. Sloan
   - ○ B mrs. sloan
   - ○ C mrs. Sloan
6. On ____ , I showed Grandma the trees.
   - ○ A september
   - ○ B saturday
   - ⊗ C Saturday

School + Home **Home Activity** Your child prepared for taking tests on using capital letters. Look through a newspaper article together. Ask your child to circle days of the week, months, holidays, or titles of people.

© Pearson Education, Inc., 2

492 **Conventions** Capital Letters

Reader's and Writer's Notebook, p. 492

Bridge to Common Core

CONVENTIONS OF STANDARD ENGLISH

As children identify, form, and use capital letters, they are gaining control of the conventions of standard English. Your guidance will help them correctly capitalize proper nouns, adjectives, and abbreviations as well as titles when they write.

Daily Fix-It

7. We shou'ldve wun the game.
We should've won the game.

8. We wouldv'e, if w'ed scored!
We would've, if we'd scored!

Discuss the Daily Fix-It corrections with children. Review contractions and the correct spelling of the word *won.*

Common Core State Standards

Writing 3. Write narratives in which they recount a well-elaborated event or short sequence of events, include details to describe actions, thoughts, and feelings, use temporal words to signal event order, and provide a sense of closure. **Writing 5.** With guidance and support from adults and peers, focus on a topic and strengthen writing as needed by revising and editing.

Writing

Zoom in on

Realistic Fiction

Mini-Lesson Revise: Adding Words and Phrases

- Yesterday we wrote realistic fiction about characters who wanted to be like sports heroes. Today we will revise to help people who read the stories. We can use words that tell what happens first, next, and last.

- Display the Revising Tips. Explain that revising is a time for making the story clear. Tomorrow they will proofread to correct any errors such as misspellings or missing capital letters.

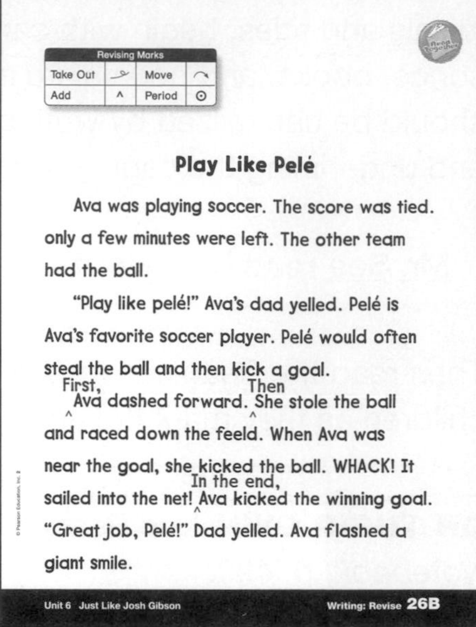

Revising Marks			
Take Out		Move	
Add	^	Period	⊙

Play Like Pelé

Ava was playing soccer. The score was tied. only a few minutes were left. The other team had the ball.

"Play like pelé!" Ava's dad yelled. Pelé is Ava's favorite soccer player. Pelé would often steal the ball and then kick a goal.

First, Ava dashed forward. Then She stole the ball and raced down the feeld. When Ava was near the goal, she kicked the ball. WHACK! It sailed into the net! In the end, Ava kicked the winning goal. "Great job, Pelé!" Dad yelled. Ava flashed a giant smile.

Unit 6 Just Like Josh Gibson Writing: Revise 26B

Writing Transparency 26B TR DVD

Revising Tips

✔ Add words to tell what happens first, next, and last.

✔ Add a clear, interesting ending to your story.

- Use Writing Transparency 26B to model adding time-order words. At the end of "Play Like Pelé," Ava kicked the winning goal. I want to make the ending clear, so I will add the words *first, then,* and *in the end.* Then readers can easily understand what is happening in the end of my story. Make the revisions on the transparency.

  Tell children that they can add time-order words to clarify what is happening in their stories.

PEER CONFERENCING • PEER REVISION Pair children and have them read their partner's story. Allow one to two minutes. Then have the readers use one or two minutes to tell what happens at the beginning, middle, and end. Have readers comment if the ending of the story is clear. Have each writer listen for any part of the story that the reader has not understood. Then have partners exchange roles. Circulate to assist children planning to revise their stories. As appropriate, suggest adding **time-order transition words.**

GUIDE PRACTICE Have children revise their stories. For those not sure how to revise, have children refer to the Revising Tips or the Key Features of Realistic Fiction.

Corrective feedback Circulate to monitor and confer with children as they write. Remind them that they will have time to proofread and edit tomorrow. Today they can make changes in story events or make sentences clearer. Help them understand the benefits of adding or changing words, especially time-order transition words. Encourage them to write endings that are clear.

Routine Quick Write for Fluency

Team Talk

1. **Talk** Read these sentences aloud, and have children discuss time-order words that can be added to tie the ending ideas together.
   It was time for Jaime's party to end. Jaime said good-by to the last guest. He went to thank his mom for the wonderful birthday party.
2. **Write** Have children rewrite the ending to include time-order words.
3. **Share** Partners can read the sentences to one another and tell how the time-order words tie the ideas in the ending together.

Routines Flip Chart

Access for All

A Advanced

Fairy-Tale Ending Remind children that many fairy tales end with "And they lived happily ever after." Have children choose a fairy tale and add one or two sentences to the ending that include time-order words.

Academic Vocabulary 

time-order transition words words that show readers the order of events or steps: *first, next, then, later, now, tomorrow, last, finally* (and others)

Common Core State Standards

Speaking/Listening 4. Tell a story or recount an experience with appropriate facts and relevant, descriptive details, speaking audibly in coherent sentences. **Speaking/Listening 6.** Produce complete sentences when appropriate to task and situation in order to provide requested detail or clarification. **Also Speaking/Listening 1., Language 3.a.**

Bridge to Common Core

PRESENTATION OF KNOWLEDGE/ IDEAS

As children present their brief oral reports, they are learning to adapt their speech in a style that is appropriate to their communicative task and audience.

Listening and Speaking

Use Vocabulary to Express Ideas and Tone

TEACH Explain to children that good speakers use clear and specific vocabulary to convey their ideas.

- When good speakers give oral reports, they use clear and specific words. This helps the listener understand the facts and details in the report.
- Good speakers choose their words carefully so that what they say is clear to their audience.
- Good speakers use words that help set a tone and make clear how they feel about what they are saying.
- Good listeners pay close attention to facts and details being presented in an oral report. They ask questions if they do not understand how details relate to the facts.

MODEL Use the passage below to model using clear and specific vocabulary.

I am going to tell you about my family's tradition for celebrating birthdays. I am going to use clear and specific words. First, the entire family gets together at the birthday person's house. We bring something special to share. We might bring a favorite food, a special song, or a story we like. After we share what we brought, we tell about special moments we have had with the birthday person and celebrate how extraordinary he or she is.

GUIDE PRACTICE Ask children to share a tradition that their families follow on a special occasion. Encourage children to use specific, clear words in their descriptions.

ON THEIR OWN Divide the class into small groups. Tell children that they will present an oral report about a family tradition at the end of the unit. To begin preparing for the report, children should tell their group about one of their family traditions. Encourage children to share facts and details about the tradition, using specific, clear vocabulary to express their ideas and set a tone for their report. Remind them to use words that show how they feel about the tradition. Discuss with children whether they should use formal or informal language for their presentation. Instruct listeners to ask questions if they do not understand something the speaker says. After group members tell about their family traditions, have them prepare written descriptions of the traditions for their oral reports.

Research and Inquiry

Step 4 Synthesize

TEACH Tell children that the next step in their inquiry project is to review the topic to see if they have the information they set out to find or if the answers lead to a different topic.

MODEL We planned to find out more about how sports traditions help athletes. Display the list of inquiry questions and the answers recorded during research. The question I asked was *How do athletes learn the sport?* I answered the question using a book about a famous athlete. The answer was *They play the sport with other people.* So I have answered the topic, and it does not need to change.

GUIDE PRACTICE Read the remaining inquiry questions and answers. After each answer is read, have partners discuss whether or not the answer provides information about how sports traditions help athletes. Note any new questions the children have and revise the original topic if necessary. Finally, tell children that tomorrow they will organize all the information in order to share it with others.

Access for All

 Strategic Intervention

More Research If a question has not been answered, provide children with athletes' biographies and guide them through each step to locate information that will answer the question.

A Advanced

Answer Extension Have partners review their question and answer and discuss specific ways the tradition helps athletes. For example, with the model answer, children could include that children learn the rules of the sport, they learn to play as a team, an adult coaches them, and they are challenged to improve.

Wrap Up Your Day!

✔ **Phonics** Write *hopped, flies,* and *raking.* Have children read the words and identify the base word and ending in each. Repeat with *smarter* and *happiest.*

✔ **Fluency** Display *Greg was happiest when he batted balls that sailed past the tallest part of the fence.* Have children read the sentence three or four times until they can do so fluently.

Preview DAY 5

Remind children that they heard about struggling baseball players. Tomorrow they will hear about the players again.

DAY 5 at a Glance

Content Knowledge
Oral Vocabulary

Phonics/Spelling
Review Inflected Endings

Text-Based Comprehension
Review Compare and Contrast

Selection Vocabulary
Review

Assessment
Phonics
Selection Vocabulary
Fluency
Comprehension

Conventions
Review Using Capital Letters

Writing
Realistic Fiction: Proofread

Research and Inquiry
Communicate

Materials
- Student Edition
- Read Aloud Anthology
- Weekly Test

Bridge to Common Core

INTEGRATION OF KNOWLEDGE/IDEAS
This week children have integrated content presented in diverse formats and analyzed how different texts address similar topics. They have developed knowledge about sports traditions to expand the unit concept of traditions.

Social Studies Knowledge Goals
Children have learned that sports are
- an important tradition in our culture
- enjoyed by players and spectators
- played by both boys and girls

Content Knowledge

Sports Traditions

REVIEW CONCEPT This week we have read and listened to selections about how sports traditions are important to our country. Today you will listen to a story about a coach and a player. Read the story.

- How does the coach feel about Meg's playing ability? (He believes she has good skills, is a natural talent, and is a hard worker.)

"Yankee Doodle Shortstop"

Build Oral Language

REVIEW AMAZING WORDS Orally review the meaning of this week's Amazing Words. Then display this week's concept map. Have children use Amazing Words such as *challenge* and *effort,* as well as the concept map, to answer the question, *Why are sports traditions important in our country?*

Why are sports traditions important in our country?

- Families can share sports traditions.
  - Families play games together.
  - Parents teach children to play sports.
  - Families share sports memories.
- Everyone can enjoy watching or playing sports.
  - Girls and boys can play sports.
  - Girls and boys can play sports equally well.
  - Players love to hear people cheer for them.
- We can look up to and learn from athletes.
  - People can admire baseball players and try to be like them.
  - Coaches and others can help players play better.
- Sports challenge us to do our best.
  - Athletes give their best effort.

Build Oral Vocabulary

Team Talk **CONNECT TO AMAZING IDEAS** Pair children and have them discuss how the Question of the Week, *Why are sports traditions important in our country?,* connects to the question of this unit of study: *Are traditions and celebrations important in our lives?* Tell children to use the concept map and what they've learned from this week's discussions and reading selections to form an Amazing Idea—a realization or "big idea" about **traditions.** Use the following ideas as prompts:

- What sports interest you? Do you enjoy playing sports or watching them?
- How can sports traditions bring a family closer together?

Then ask pairs to share their Amazing Idea with the class. Encourage children to recall in which selection they learned their ideas.

Amazing Ideas might include these key concepts:

- All people can enjoy watching and playing sports.
- Sports traditions are important in many families.

Amazing Words

athlete	disguise
challenge	champion
effort	professional
dainty	shortstop

MONITOR PROGRESS Check Oral Vocabulary

FORMATIVE ASSESSMENT Call on individuals to use this week's Amazing Words to talk about sports traditions. Prompt discussion with the questions below. Monitor children's ability to use the Amazing Words and note which words children are unable to use.

- **What sport would you make the *effort* to be a *champion* at playing?**
- **What sports might require *dainty* moves?**
- **Why might a *professional athlete* have to wear a *disguise?***
- **What is the job of a *shortstop?***
- **When can playing sports be a *challenge?***

If... children have difficulty using the Amazing Words,

then... reteach the unknown words using the Robust Vocabulary Routines, pp. 361a, 366b, 382b, 386b.

Check Concepts and Language Use the Day 5 instruction on ELL Poster 26 to monitor children's understanding of the lesson concept.

Amazing Words Use pantomime and gestures to give children clues as you review the Amazing Words.

Common Core State Standards

Foundational Skills 3. Know and apply grade-level phonics and word analysis skills in decoding words. **Language 2.** Demonstrate command of the conventions of standard English capitalization, punctuation, and spelling when writing.

Phonics

Review Inflected Endings

TARGET PHONICS SKILL Write the following sentences on the board. Have children read each one, first quietly to themselves and then aloud as you track the print.

1. **We are hoping that Mom will let us help with baking and trimming the cake.**
2. **Grace danced into the room and hugged Grandma for the longest time.**
3. **The airplane roars loudly as it flies higher into the sky and vanishes in the clouds.**
4. **I grabbed the biggest, juiciest apple and hurried out the door.**

Team Talk Have children discuss with a partner which words have inflected endings. Have them identify the base word and any spelling change. Then call on individuals to share with the class.

Spelling Test

Inflected Endings

DICTATE SPELLING WORDS Say each word, read the sentence, repeat the word, and allow time for children to write the word.

1. liked	I **liked** the chicken we had for dinner.
2. lighter	Sal will carry the **lighter** box of books.
3. planned	Dad **planned** a summer trip for us.
4. tried	I **tried** to do the math problem.
5. liking	The baby seems to be **liking** the peas.
6. skipped	We **skipped** all the way to school.
7. heaviest	Two men must unload the **heaviest** sofa.
8. planning	We had fun **planning** the party.
9. lightest	My baby sister puts away the **lightest** toys.
10. skipping	Eve and I were **skipping** rope in the park.
11. heavier	Mother put a **heavier** blanket on the bed.
12. trying	Josh was **trying** to give the dog a bath.

High-Frequency Words

13. promise	I **promise** to clean my room tomorrow.
14. because	The picnic was cancelled **because** of rain.

Assess

- Spell words with inflected endings.
- Spell high-frequency words.

Access for All

Check Spelling Write the six base words. Have children refer to them as they spell the words.

A Advanced

Extend Spelling Have children who have demonstrated proficiency in spelling individual words spell each word in a self-made sentence that includes other words with inflected endings. Have them circle the words.

Day 5 SMALL GROUP TIME • Differentiate Reteaching, p. SG•1

OL On-Level

- **Develop** Capital Letters
- **Reread** *Reading Street Sleuth,* pp. 68–69

- **Review/Discuss** Capital Letters
- **Reread** *Reading Street Sleuth,* pp. 68–69

A Advanced

- **Extend** Capital Letters
- **Reread** *Reading Street Sleuth,* pp. 68–69
- **Communicate** Inquiry Project

If... children need more scaffolding and practice with **Conventions and Writing,**
then... use the Grammar Transition Lessons on pp. 310–385 in the *ELL Handbook.*

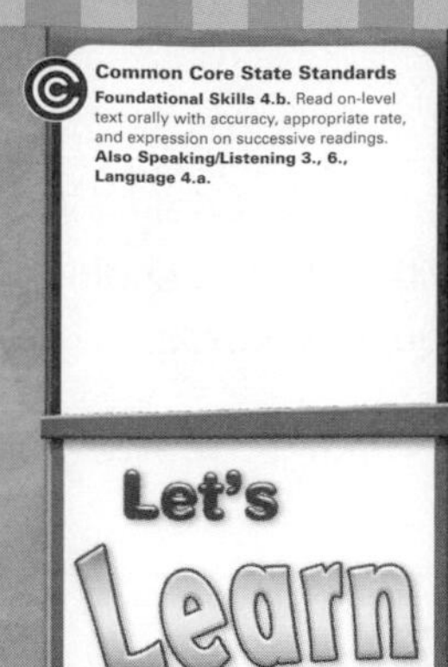

Vocabulary

Homophones

Context Clues Homophones are words that sound alike but have different spellings and meanings. Use the context to understand the meaning of a homophone.

The boat has a large **sail**.
The store had jackets on **sale**.

Practice It! Use the context to tell the meaning of each homophone.

1. A hare looks very much like a rabbit. She is wearing her hair in a ponytail.
2. I heard a loud noise when the plane took off. A herd of elephants is at the water hole.

Fluency

Accuracy and Appropriate Rate

Read with accuracy. Read the words you see. Do not omit or add words. Read at a comfortable pace. Read at the same pace as you speak.

Practice It! Read the text below to a partner.

1. Kim wants to be an airline pilot.
2. Jamal wants to be a racecar driver.

Listening and Speaking

Use clear and specific vocabulary words when you give an oral report.

Use Vocabulary to Express Ideas and Establish Tone

When giving an oral report, use clear and specific vocabulary to express ideas and establish tone. Choose your words carefully for reports. Specific words can make your meaning clear. For example, if you want to tell about a cherry tree, use the word *cherry*. Do not say fruit tree. When you use specific words, your listeners will know exactly what you mean. The words you choose can also let listeners know how you feel.

Sometimes when you are listening, you may not understand a word. You may not understand what a speaker means. Ask questions. The answers will help you understand the speaker's message.

Practice It! What activity do you like to do when you are not in school? Prepare a report. Tell the class about something you enjoy doing outside of school. Be sure to use common nouns correctly in your report. Remember to use formal language when giving your report. When others give their reports listen carefully. Ask questions if you do not understand.

390 391

Student Edition, pp. 390–391

Common Core State Standards

Foundational Skills 4.b. Read on-level text orally with accuracy, appropriate rate, and expression on successive readings. **Language 4.a.** Use sentence-level context as a clue to the meaning of a word or phrase.

Access for All

Strategic Intervention

Choose Meaning If children have difficulty distinguishing between homophones, provide them with a choice of meanings. For example: *A hare looks very much like a rabbit.* Is a hare an animal or something that grows on your head? Which words in the sentence tell you that?

Vocabulary

Homophones

TEACH Read and discuss the Vocabulary lesson on page 390 of the Student Edition. Use the model to explain that homophones are words that sound alike but are spelled differently and have different meanings.

GUIDE PRACTICE Read the instructions for the Vocabulary Practice It! activity. Then read the sentences in item 1 aloud with children.

Which two words sound alike but are spelled differently? *(hare* and *hair)* The context helps me understand that a *hare, h-a-r-e,* is an animal and *hair, h-a-i-r,* grows on your head.

ON THEIR OWN Have pairs complete item 2.

Corrective feedback	Circulate around the room and listen as children identify the homophones *heard* and *herd* and infer their meanings. Provide assistance as needed.

Fluency

Accuracy and Appropriate Rate

TEACH Read and discuss the Fluency instructions.

READ WORDS IN CONTEXT Give children a moment to look at the sentences. Then have them read each sentence three or four times until they can read each sentence with accuracy and at an appropriate rate.

Listening and Speaking

Use Vocabulary to Express Ideas and Establish Tone

TEACH Have children turn to page 391 of the Student Edition. Read and discuss the explanation of using vocabulary in an oral report together. Tell children that good speakers use specific words that express exactly what they mean, and they use words that help show how they feel. Remind children that good listeners who do not understand a word ask the speaker questions to clarify their understanding.

ANALYZE Have children discuss how using the word *cherry* instead of the word *fruit* to talk about a cherry tree helps the listener know exactly what kind of tree the speaker is referring to. What different kinds of fruit trees can you name? (Possible response: There are apple, peach, pear, orange, and lemon trees.)

INTRODUCE PROMPT Read the Practice It! prompt with the class. Remind children that they should use complete sentences in their oral reports and that their oral reports should use specific words that help express their ideas and show how they feel about their topic.

Team Talk Have children give their oral reports before the class. Encourage listeners to ask questions they may have. After each report, provide time for partners to discuss which specific words were used that helped make clear what the speaker enjoys doing outside school and how she or he feels about the activity.

Use Vocabulary to Express Ideas and Establish Tone

In addition to using clear, specific vocabulary in an oral report, children at Grade 3 should also be able to choose content that matches the topic and relate to the background and interest of the audience.

Homophones Point out that in English, words with different spellings can sometimes sound the same. Have children choose a pair of homophones, write them, and say them aloud to a partner. Monitor children's pronunciation.

Informational Text 7. Explain how specific images (e.g., a diagram showing how a machine works) contribute to and clarify a text.

Text-Based Comprehension

Review Compare and Contrast

Remember that we can look for ways in which characters, events, and other story elements are alike and different. What do we do when we identify likenesses and differences? (compare and contrast)

CHECK UNDERSTANDING Read aloud the following story and have children answer the questions that follow.

Sam and Teddy heard their school was planning a bake sale, and they both wanted to help. Sam made cookies to sell. Unlike Sam, Teddy decided to make muffins. Sam made cookies with oatmeal and raisins in them. Teddy's muffins also had raisins, but they did not have oatmeal. The day of the sale, Sam and Teddy sat at the same table. People bought all of both boys' homemade treats. Both boys felt great about helping their school.

1. How are Sam and Teddy alike? (Both boys bake items for the school bake sale.)
2. How are the boys' baked goods alike and different? (Sam and Teddy both use raisins in their recipes, but Sam uses oatmeal and Teddy does not use oatmeal. Sam makes cookies, and Teddy makes muffins.)
3. How do Teddy's feelings about the bake sale compare with Sam's feelings? (Their feelings are the same. They both feel great.)

Vocabulary

Review Selection Vocabulary

SELECTION WORDS Write this week's selection words: *threw, sailed, field, plate, bases,* and *cheers.* Read them aloud together. Then have children tell what each word means and pantomime the action or an appropriate baseball action that would be done with the word. For example, children can pantomime standing next to the *plate,* running the *bases,* or catching a ball in the *field.*

Corrective feedback	**If...** children cannot tell what the selection words mean, **then...** review the definitions on page 365a.

Genre

Review Expository Text

EXPOSITORY TEXT Review with children that **expository text,** or informational text, gives facts about real people, places, and events. Sometimes those facts are presented in **graphic sources,** such as charts, graphs, and maps.

TEACH The expository text "How Baseball Began" contains two graphs and three maps. Have children turn to pages 388–389 in their Student Edition. The graphs are drawn to look like scoreboards, but they show the number of teams in each league. The maps are of different parts of the world, and the numbers show the locations of countries where baseball is played today.

Think Aloud **MODEL** On the first graph, I can look at the year in the first column and count the number of baseballs in that row to see that the National League had eight teams in 1876 and the American League had eight teams in 1900.

GUIDE PRACTICE Ask the following questions to guide children in reading the graphs.

- For what year does the second graph compare the number of teams in the leagues? (2009)
- How many more teams were in the National League than the American League that year? (two)

MODEL When I read page 389, I see the number 1 in parentheses after the name of the United States. I know if I find the number 1 on one of the maps, it will show me where the United States is located.

GUIDE PRACTICE Ask the following questions to guide children in reading the maps.

- Which map shows where Japan is located—the left map, the middle map, or the right map? (middle map)
- Which map shows where South Africa is located—the left map, the middle map, or the right map? (right map)

ON THEIR OWN How many more teams did the National League have in 2009 than it had in 1876? (eight) Which two countries that play baseball are featured on the map on the left? (the United States and Canada)

Access for All

 Strategic Intervention

Reading Graphic Sources If children have difficulty answering the questions about the graphs and maps, suggest they use their fingers to guide their reading across the rows of the graphs and to match the numbers in the text with the numbers on the maps.

 Advanced

Summarizing Graphic Sources Have children write a sentence that sums up the information on the second graph and another sentence that sums up the information on the maps.

Academic Vocabulary 

expository text writing that contains facts and information; also called informational text

graphic sources visual representations of information, such as charts and graphs; also called graphics

Common Core State Standards

Foundational Skills 3. Know and apply grade-level phonics and word analysis skills in decoding words. **Foundational Skills 4.b.** Read on-level text orally with accuracy, appropriate rate, and expression on successive readings.

Assess

- Words with Inflected Endings
- Fluency: Rate
- Compare and Contrast

Fluency Goals

Set individual fluency goals for children to enable them to reach the end-of-the-year goal.

- **Current Goal:** 80–90 WCPM
- **End-of-Year Goal:** 90 WCPM

Assessment

Monitor Progress

For a written assessment of inflected endings and compare and contrast, use Weekly Test 26, pp. 151–156.

SENTENCE READING Use the following reproducible page to assess children's ability to read words in context. Call on children to read two sentences aloud. Start over with sentence one if necessary.

MONITOR PROGRESS Sentence Reading

If... children have trouble reading words with inflected endings,
then... use the Reteach Lesson in *First Stop.*

FLUENCY Take a one-minute sample of children's oral reading. Have children read the fluency passage on p. 391f.

COMPREHENSION Have the child read the entire passage. (If the child has difficulty with the passage, you may read it aloud.) Then have the child make a comparison and contrast based on the passage.

MONITOR ACCURACY Have children monitor their accuracy by recording their scores using the Sentence Reading Chart and by recording the number of words read correctly per minute on their Fluency Progress Chart in *First Stop.*

MONITOR PROGRESS Fluency and Comprehension

If... a child does not achieve the fluency goal on the timed reading,
then... copy the passage and send it home with the child for additional fluency practice, or have the child practice with a fluent reader.

If... a child cannot compare and contrast,
then... use the Reteach Lesson in *First Stop.*

Name ______________________________

Read the Sentences

1. The girl cried when the baby birds sailed into the sky without dropping.

2. The biggest player liked hearing our cheers as he walked toward the football.

3. The ball went bouncing off the field as the team tried to score.

4. Joking around, she threw her little sister's prettiest doll into the air.

5. Jake planned to throw his best pitch over the plate, but it dropped too soon.

6. "That was the luckiest hit ever!" I said as I was running around the bases.

MONITOR PROGRESS

- **Inflected Endings**
- **Selection Vocabulary**

Name ______________________________

Read the Story

Luke and Carlos

Luke and Carlos are best friends. They're the 8
same in many ways but different in other ways. 17
They have always lived on the same street. They 26
are both in the second grade. They each have an 36
older sister and a younger brother. They often ride 45
their bikes together. 48
While Luke and Carlos are the same in many 57
ways, they are different. Luke belongs to a soccer 66
team. He would rather play soccer than any other 75
sport. Carlos is on a baseball team. He is the best 86
player on the team. Carlos says that he does not like 97
soccer. Luke says he does not want to play baseball. 107
The boys would like to play a sport together. 116
But they don't know if they would like the same sport. 127
Luke says, "We would like to try playing basketball 136
on the same team. We're both ready to try it this year. 148
I hope it works out." 153

MONITOR PROGRESS

- Check Fluency
- Compare and Contrast

Conventions

Review Using Capital Letters

REVIEW Remind children that names of days, months, holidays, songs, poems, and books, as well as initials and titles in names, begin with capital letters. Have them give several examples of words that begin with capital letters.

GUIDE PRACTICE Write the following sentences. Have children state if they are correct or if there are errors in using capital letters or punctuation. Have children identify any errors and explain how to correct them.

1. **Mr low gave Sam a gift.**
2. **I will name my dog Bingo after the song "bingo."**
3. **Jack saw a movie every Saturday in july.**

APPLY Have children state a proper noun for each of the following nouns. Then have them say a sentence using the proper noun and tell what letter in the word should be capitalized.

day
month
teacher
holiday

ON THEIR OWN Use Let's Practice It!, p. 298 on the *Teacher Resources DVD-ROM.*

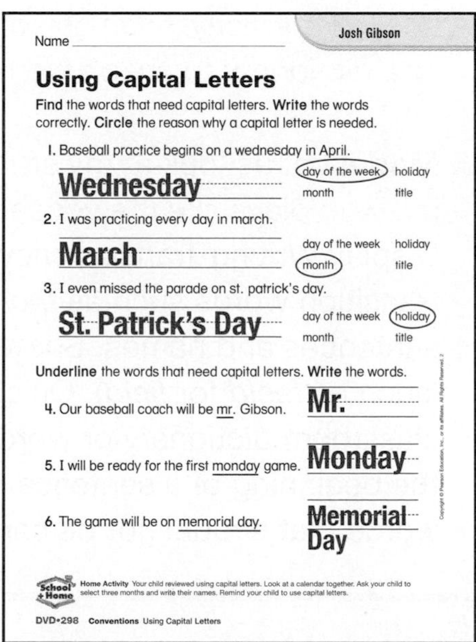
Name ______ Josh Gibson

Using Capital Letters

Find the words that need capital letters. **Write** the words correctly. **Circle** the reason why a capital letter is needed.

1. Baseball practice begins on a wednesday in April.
Wednesday — (day of the week) holiday month title
2. I was practicing every day in march.
March — day of the week holiday (month) title
3. I even missed the parade on st. patrick's day.
St. Patrick's Day — day of the week (holiday) month title

Underline the words that need capital letters. **Write** the words.

4. Our baseball coach will be mr. Gibson. Mr.
5. I will be ready for the first monday game. Monday
6. The game will be on memorial day. Memorial Day

Home Activity Your child reviewed using capital letters. Look at a calendar together. Ask your child to select three months and write their names. Remind your child to use capital letters.

DVD•298 Conventions Using Capital Letters

Let's Practice It! TR DVD•298

Common Core State Standards

Foundational Skills 4.b. Read on-level text orally with accuracy, appropriate rate, and expression on successive readings. **Language 2.** Demonstrate command of the conventions of standard English capitalization, punctuation, and spelling when writing.

Daily Fix-It

9. We chear as Joe runs the baises.
We cheer as Joe runs the bases.
10. Center feald is not home playte.
Center field is not home plate.

Discuss the Daily Fix-It corrections with children. Review CVCe words, vowel pattern *ie,* and the spelling of *cheer.*

Common Core State Standards

Writing 3. Write narratives in which they recount a well-elaborated event or short sequence of events, include details to describe actions, thoughts, and feelings, use temporal words to signal event order, and provide a sense of closure. **Writing 5.** With guidance and support from adults and peers, focus on a topic and strengthen writing as needed by revising and editing. **Writing 6.** With guidance and support from adults, use a variety of digital tools to produce and publish writing, including in collaboration with peers.

Bridge to Common Core

PRODUCTION AND DISTRIBUTION OF WRITING

Children have developed and strengthened their drafts throughout the week. Their final well-structured drafts will reflect the changes they made to improve their realistic fiction stories. Children will present their stories by reading them aloud to a partner or by presenting them on screen to an audience of classmates.

Writing

Realistic Fiction

REVIEW REVISING Remind children that yesterday they revised their stories. They may have added time-order words to the end of their realistic stories to tie the ideas together. Today they will proofread their stories.

Mini-Lesson Proofread

Proofread for Transition Words and Capital Letters

■ **Teach** In our stories, if we spell the words correctly, readers will know what words we mean. When we proofread, we check to make sure the words are correct. We can check to make sure all sentences and names begin with a capital letter. We also can look at words such as *first, then,* and *end* to make sure they are used and spelled correctly. I can use our word lists or a dictionary to check them.

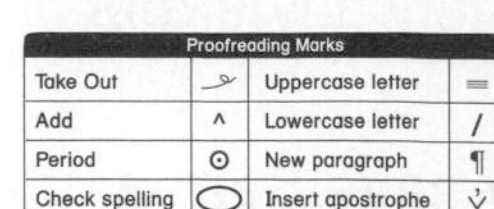

Proofreading Marks

Take Out		Uppercase letter	≡
Add	^	Lowercase letter	/
Period	⊙	New paragraph	¶
Check spelling	⬭	Insert apostrophe	∨

Play Like Pelé

Ava was playing soccer. The score was tied. only a few minutes were left. The other team had the ball.

"Play like pelé!" Ava's dad yelled. Pelé is Ava's favorite soccer player. Pelé would often steal the ball and then kick a goal.

First, Ava dashed forward. Then She stole the ball and raced down the feeld field. When Ava was near the goal, she kicked the ball. WHACK! It sailed into the net! In the end, Ava kicked the winning goal. "Great job, Pelé!" Dad yelled. Ava flashed a giant smile.

Unit 6 Just Like Josh Gibson Writing: Proofread 26C

Writing Transparency 26C TR DVD

■ **Model** Let us look at my story about the girl who plays like the soccer player Pelé. Display Writing Transparency 26C. Explain that you will look at time-order transition words such as *then* as well as the first letter in words that begin sentences and names. Show how you would change any misspellings (such as *feeld* for *field*). Quickly show how to check a word's spelling in a classroom dictionary or word list. Model how you would change a letter at the beginning of a sentence or a name if it were not capitalized and change words that should not be capitalized.

PROOFREAD Display the Proofreading Tips. Have children proofread their stories to correct any misspellings, missing capital letters, or errors with periods. Circulate to assist children with transition words or other words.

Proofreading Tips

- ✔ Are my words spelled correctly? Check a dictionary.
- ✔ Are words such as *first* and *then* spelled correctly?
- ✔ Do my sentences begin with a capital letter?
- ✔ Do names, months, and days of the week begin with a capital letter?

PRESENT Have children make a final draft of their stories, with their revisions and proofreading corrections. Help as appropriate. If possible, have children use a word processing program to produce their final copy.

Then choose an option for children to present their stories.

They might take turns reading them aloud to a partner.	Children might type their stories using computers and present them on screen for others to read.

When children have finished writing their realistic fiction, give them a copy of About My Writing, p. RR39 of the *Reader's and Writer's Notebook.* Then have children evaluate their writing by answering the questions on the page.

Routine Quick Write for Fluency

1. **Talk** Have partners take two minutes to think about actions of their sports hero.
2. **Write** Each child writes three sentences that tell a sequence of events the athlete might do.
3. **Share** Partners trade sentences and edit the sentences to include time-order transition words.

Routines Flip Chart

Support Editing For children to whom English conventions still are not very familiar, look for gradual improvement over the course of the year. Help children recognize the beginning of a sentence and the capital letters of the alphabet.

Common Core State Standards

Speaking/Listening 1. Participate in collaborative conversations with diverse partners about grade 2 topics and texts with peers and adults in small and larger groups. **Speaking/Listening 2.** Recount or describe key ideas or details from a text read aloud or information presented orally or through other media. **Also Speaking/Listening 1.c.**

Research and Inquiry

Step 5 Communicate

TEACH Tell children that today they will organize information they found in sources, create a poster that displays the information, and share the information with the class.

Think Aloud

MODEL Display the list of inquiry questions and the answers recorded during research. We have been asking and answering questions that tell how sports traditions help athletes. I was interested in the question *How do athletes learn the sport?* The answer I found was *They play the sport with other people.* We are going to show our information using a poster. So on my poster, one of the things I will show is children playing and learning a sport together.

GUIDE PRACTICE Review the answers on the chart with children, and lead a discussion identifying which ones identify ways sports traditions help athletes.

ON THEIR OWN Use *Reader's and Writer's Notebook,* p. 489.

Have children choose answers they want to share and create a poster that illustrates them. Have children share their posters in small groups. Remind them how to be good speakers and listeners:

- Good speakers choose words that clearly tell about ideas. They also speak at a pace that everyone can understand.
- Good listeners wait until the speaker has finished speaking before raising their hands to ask a question for clarification.

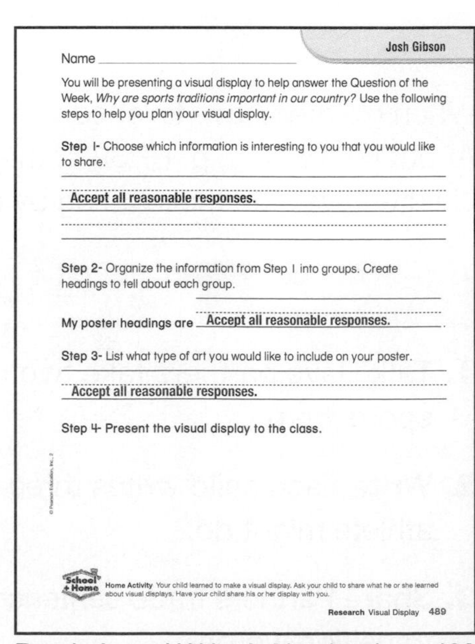

Josh Gibson

Name ____________

You will be presenting a visual display to help answer the Question of the Week, *Why are sports traditions important in our country?* Use the following steps to help you plan your visual display.

Step 1- Choose which information is interesting to you that you would like to share.

Accept all reasonable responses.

Step 2- Organize the information from Step 1 into groups. Create headings to tell about each group.

My poster headings are Accept all reasonable responses.

Step 3- List what type of art you would like to include on your poster.

Accept all reasonable responses.

Step 4- Present the visual display to the class.

© Pearson Education, Inc., 2

School + Home **Home Activity** Your child learned to make a visual display. Ask your child to share what he or she learned about visual displays. Have your child share his or her display with you.

Research Visual Display 489

Reader's and Writer's Notebook, p. 489

Wrap Up Your Week!

Sports Traditions

Why are sports traditions important in our country?

Think Aloud This week we found out why sports traditions are important in many people's lives. In the story "The Princesses Have a Ball," we read about how the princesses felt they had to hide their love of basketball. In the stories *Just Like Josh Gibson* and "Yankee Doodle Shortstop," we found out about girls who loved baseball and played with boys on a team.

Team Talk Have children recall their Amazing Ideas about sports traditions. Then have children use these ideas to help them demonstrate their understanding of the Question of the Week, *Why are sports traditions important in our country?*

Amazing Words

You've learned 008 words this week!

You've learned 209 words this year!

Next Week's Concept

The American Flag

What traditions and celebrations involve our country's flag?

Poster Preview Prepare children for next week by using Week 2, ELL Poster 27. Read the Poster Talk-Through to introduce the concept and vocabulary. Ask children to identify and describe objects and actions in the art.

Selection Summary Send home the summary of *Red, White, and Blue: The Story of the American Flag* in English and the child's home language if available. Children can read the summary with family members.

Tell children that next week they will read about the American flag.

Preview Next Week

Assessment Checkpoints for the Week

Weekly Assessment

Use pp. 151–156 of *Weekly Tests* to check:

✔ **Phonics** Inflected Endings

✔ **Comprehension** Compare and Contrast

✔ **Selection Vocabulary**

bases	plate
cheers	sailed
field	threw

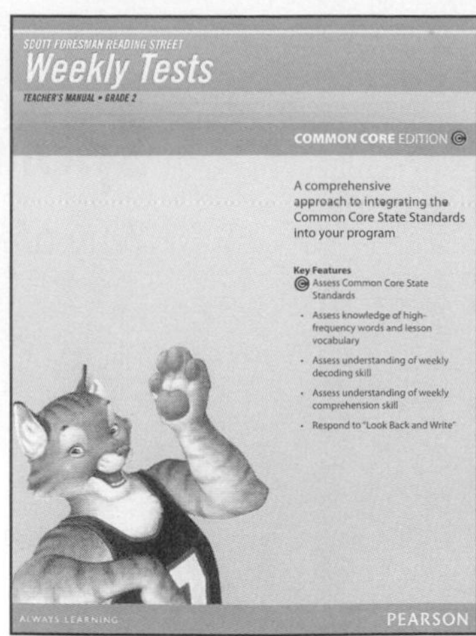

Weekly Tests

Differentiated Assessment

Advanced

On-Level

Strategic Intervention

Use pp. 151–156 of *Fresh Reads for Fluency and Comprehension* to check:

✔ **Comprehension** Compare and Contrast

 **Comprehension** Draw Conclusions

✔ **Fluency** Words Correct Per Minute

Fresh Reads for Fluency and Comprehension

Managing Assessment

Use *Assessment Handbook* for:

✔ **Weekly Assessment Blackline Masters for Monitoring Progress**

✔ **Observation Checklists**

✔ **Record-Keeping Forms**

✔ **Portfolio Assessment**

Assessment Handbook

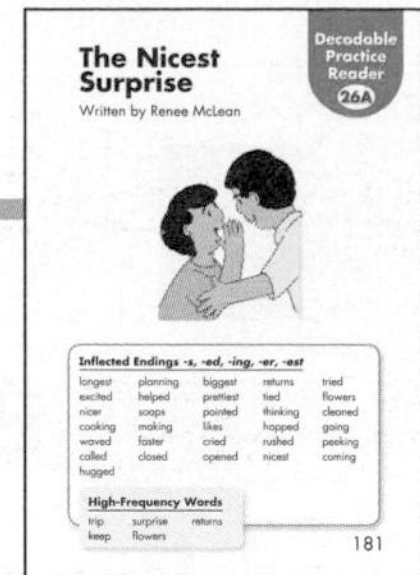

DAY 1 Differentiate Phonics

- Inflected Endings
- Decodable Practice Reader
- Advanced Selection "Babe Didrikson"
- **Inquiry** Identify Questions

DAY 2 Differentiate Comprehension

- Selection Vocabulary
- **Access Text** Read *Just Like Josh Gibson*
- **Inquiry** Investigate

DAY 3 Differentiate Close Reading

- Develop Vocabulary
- **Close Reading** Reread *Just Like Josh Gibson*
- **Inquiry** Investigate

"Josh Gibson, Home Run King," pp. 68–69

DAY 4 Differentiate Vocabulary

- Amazing Words
- **Read** "Josh Gibson, Home Run King" or Leveled Readers
- **Inquiry** Organize

DAY 5 Differentiate Reteaching

- **Conventions** Pronouns
- **Read** "Josh Gibson, Home Run King" or Leveled Readers
- **Inquiry** Communicate

Teacher Guides and student pages can be found in the Leveled Reader Database.

Place English Language Learners in the groups that correspond to their reading abilities.
If... children need scaffolding and practice,
then... use the ELL notes on the instructional pages.

Independent Practice

Independent Practice Stations

See pp. 360h and 360i for Independent Stations.

Pearson Trade Book Library

See the Leveled Reader Database for Lesson Plans and student pages.

Reading Street Digital Path

Independent Practice Activities available in the Digital Path.

Independent Reading

See p. 360i for independent reading suggestions.

On-Level

Common Core State Standards

Foundational Skills 3. Know and apply grade-level phonics and word analysis skills in decoding words. **Literature 1.** Ask and answer such questions as *who, what, where, when, why,* and *how* to demonstrate understanding of key details in a text. **Literature 10.** By the end of the year, read and comprehend literature, including stories and poetry, in the grades 2–3 text complexity band proficiently, with scaffolding as needed at the high end of the range. **Language 4.a.** Use sentence-level context as a clue to the meaning of a word or phrase.

1 Build Word Knowledge

Practice Phonics

INFLECTED ENDINGS Write the following words and have children practice reading the words.

tried	planned	liking	heavier	lightest

Then have them name the base word and identify any spelling change.

Spelling

INFLECTED ENDINGS Remind children that each spelling word has an inflected ending. Clarify the pronunciation and meaning of each word. For example, say: She tried to hit a home run, but she struck out. Have children identify the same letters and endings in words such as *planning, skipping, liking,* and *heaviest, lightest.*

2 Read

Decodable Reader 26A *The Nicest Surprise*

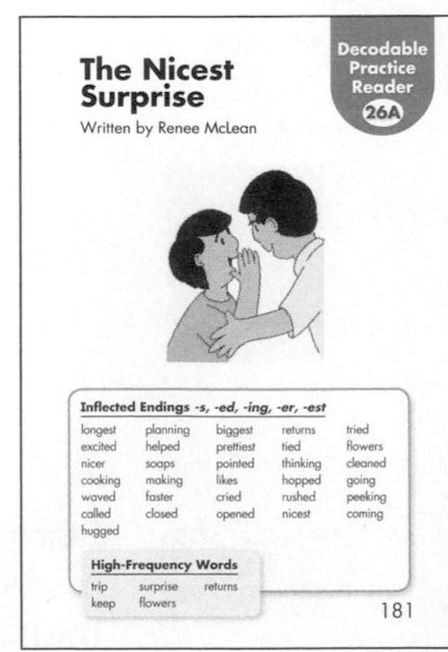

HIGH-FREQUENCY WORDS Have children read the decodable reader. Then have them reread the text to develop automaticity. Have children return to the text and find the previously taught high-frequency words. Help children demonstrate their understanding of the words. Provide sentence frames such as: I gave my mom _______ for her birthday. (flowers)

If... children need more scaffolding and practice with phonics, **then...** use the Phonics Transition Lessons on pages 213–309 in the *ELL Handbook.*

On-Level

1 Build Word Knowledge

Practice Selection Vocabulary

bases	cheers	field
plate	sailed	threw

DEFINE IT Discuss the definition for the word *cheers* with children. Ask: How would you describe *cheers* to a friend? (Possible response: *Cheers* are shouts or yells of encouragement.) Continue with the remaining words.

Team Talk **TALK ABOUT IT** Have pairs use the selection words in sentences to internalize meaning. Ask: How can you pair the selection words together in a sentence? (Possible response: After the ball sailed over the fence, the batter rounded the bases to the cheers of the crowd.) Allow time for children to play with the words and then share their sentences.

2 Read

Just Like Josh Gibson

If you read *Just Like Josh Gibson* during whole group time, then use the following instruction.

ACCESS TEXT Have children look at the pictures on pp. 372–373. Reread both pages.

- Look at the picture on p. 373. How can you tell Grandmama isn't allowed to play with the boys? (They are wearing uniforms and she is in a pink outfit. She is on the other side of the fence.)
- What is a *Louisville slugger?* (a bat)
- What clues help tell you what a *Louisville slugger* is? (After giving it to his daughter, the story says she would "make baseballs fly." She is holding a bat in the picture.)
- What other baseball equipment do you see on these pages? (ball, plate, gloves, uniforms)

If you are reading *Just Like Josh Gibson* during small group time, then return to pp. 367a–381a to guide the reading.

SMALL GROUP TIME

Independent Reading Options

Trade Book Library

eStreet Interactive
www.ReadingStreet.com
Teacher's Guides available on the Leveled Reader Database.

On-Level

Common Core State Standards

Literature 1. Ask and answer such questions as *who, what, where, when, why,* and *how* to demonstrate understanding of key details in a text. **Literature 3.** Describe how characters in a story respond to major events and challenges.

1 Build Word Knowledge

Develop Vocabulary

REREAD FOR VOCABULARY Have children reread p. 375 of *Just Like Josh Gibson.*

Read the following sentence and discuss words and phrases related to playing baseball. *(play, hit, throw, fly round the bases)*

Grandmama says she would play all day, with everybody saying she could do it all, hit, throw, and fly round the bases.

- What does *fly round the bases* mean? (run fast around the bases)
- What are some other words for running fast? (sprinting, darting, dashing)

2 Read

Just Like Josh Gibson

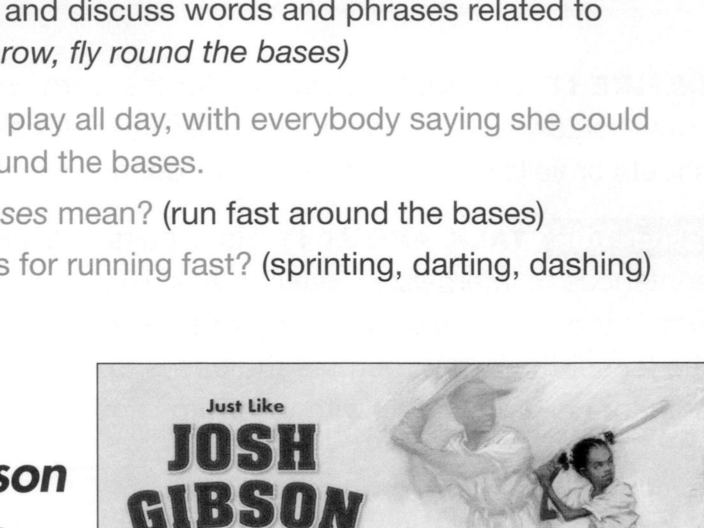

If you read *Just Like Josh Gibson* during whole group time, then use the following instruction.

CLOSE READING Reread pp. 376–377. Have children summarize the ideas presented on these pages. Ask questions to guide deeper understanding.

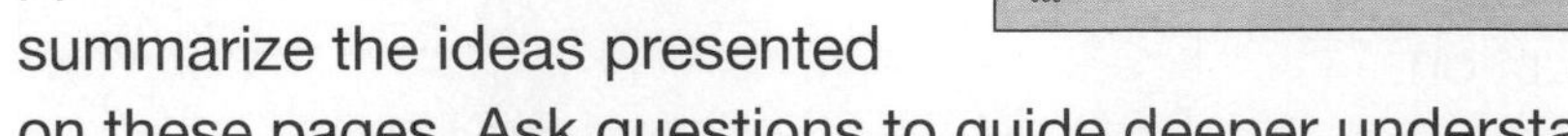

- How many baseball players does a team need to have to play a game? (nine) What clues in the text tell you this? (After Danny got hurt, there were only eight All-Stars. They needed another player to play.)
- Why do you think Grandmama reminded herself about all the simple and pleasant things about baseball as she went to bat? (She was a little nervous, but she knew she could do this.)

Have children read the following sentence from the story: *Until … two days, hot days after the Fourth of July, Danny hurt his arm sliding into second, and there were only eight All-Stars.* Explain that strong adjectives help the reader feel the atmosphere of a story. Ask children to rewrite the sentence, replacing *hot* with another adjective. (Until ... two days, scorching days after the Fourth of July …)

If you are reading *Just Like Josh Gibson* during small group time, then return to pp. 367a–381a to guide the reading.

If... children need more scaffolding and practice with the main selection, **then...** use the activities on p. DI•18 in the Teacher Resources section on SuccessNet.

On-Level

1 Build Word Knowledge

Practice Amazing Words

athlete	challenge	effort	dainty
disguise	champion	professional	shortstop

Team Talk **LANGUAGE DEVELOPMENT** Have children practice building sentences. Display a sentence starter and have children add an oral phrase or clause using the Amazing Words. For example: It is quite a challenge to _______. (Possible response: It is quite a challenge to play shortstop on a professional team.)

2 Text-Based Comprehension

READ ALOUD "Josh Gibson, Home Run King" Lead children in a choral reading of "Josh Gibson, Home Run King" from *Reading Street Sleuth* on pp. 68–69. Then have partners take turns reading the paragraphs of the selection.

ACCESS TEXT Guide children as they work on the Be a Sleuth section.

Look for Clues Have children reread the text. After reading, ask them to talk about Josh Gibson's feelings about baseball. Find sentences that show that baseball meant a lot to Gibson.

Ask Questions Talk to children about baseball. Then discuss things that might have changed over the years. I wonder if the uniforms have changed. I wonder what they might have looked like one hundred years ago. What do you wonder about baseball long ago?

Make Your Case Discuss the sports that children play or like to watch. Then have children state their opinion about which sport they think is most popular. Have children with the same opinion work together to identify reasons for the sport's popularity.

SMALL GROUP TIME

More Reading for Group Time

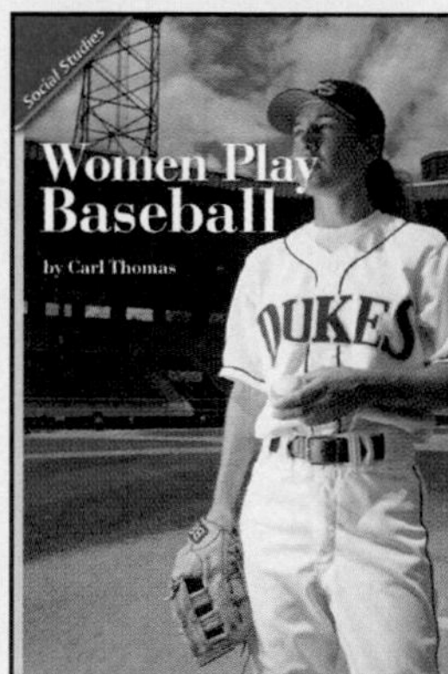

ON-LEVEL

Reviews
- Concept Vocabulary
- Compare and Contrast
- Monitor and Clarify

Use this suggested Leveled Reader or other text at children's instructional level.

eStreet Interactive
www.ReadingStreet.com

Use the Leveled Reader Database for lesson plans and student pages for *Women Play Baseball.*

Common Core State Standards

Language 2. Demonstrate command of the conventions of standard English capitalization, punctuation, and spelling when writing. **Foundational Skills 3.** Know and apply grade-level phonics and word analysis skills in decoding words. **Foundational Skills 4.** Read with sufficient accuracy and fluency to support comprehension.

1 Build Word Knowledge

Practice Using Capital Letters

REVIEW If needed, revisit the conventions lesson on p. 381c.

IDENTIFY CAPITAL LETTERS Have children identify capital letters in the selection "Josh Gibson, Home Run King." Point out some examples and ask children to identify why capital letters were used.

2 Text-Based Comprehension

REREAD "Josh Gibson, Home Run King" Have partners reread "Josh Gibson, Home Run King."

EXTEND UNDERSTANDING Briefly discuss segregation, pointing out that African Americans were not allowed to play in the same league as whites, so they formed their own baseball league.

PERFORMANCE TASK • Prove It! Collect resources on Josh Gibson, Satchel Paige, Jackie Robinson, or another Negro League baseball player or team. Help children learn more about one of the players and write a brief biography about that player.

COMMUNICATE Encourage children to include pictures with their reports. Provide time for children to share their reports with partners.

More Reading for Group Time

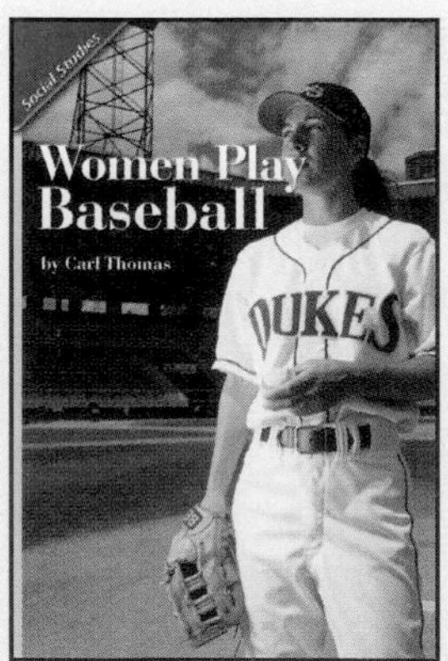

ON-LEVEL

Reviews
- Concept Vocabulary
- Compare and Contrast
- Monitor and Clarify

Use this suggested Leveled Reader or other text at children's instructional level.

eSTREET INTERACTIVE
www.ReadingStreet.com

Use the Leveled Reader Database for lesson plans and student pages for *Women Play Baseball.*

1 Build Word Knowledge

Reteach Phonics

INFLECTED ENDINGS Reteach the lesson on p. 362a, Inflected Endings. Use these additional practice words.

finished **runs** **working** **stronger**

Then have children blend and read these additional words and circle the inflected ending.

hugs **flies** **stopped** **driving** **bigger** **largest**

2 Read

Decodable Reader 26A *The Nicest Surprise*

DECODE WORDS Have children practice reading the words listed on p. 181.

Corrective feedback	**If...** children have difficulty reading the words independently, **then...** reteach the words prior to reading Decodable Reader 26A.

READ IN CONTEXT Have children take turns reading a page in *The Nicest Surprise.* Have them reread the text several times to ensure accuracy.

Corrective feedback	**If...** children have difficulty reading the selection independently, **then...** model reading a page and have children echo you.

3 Reread for Fluency

Have children reread the text to develop automaticity in their reading.

SMALL GROUP TIME

If... children need more scaffolding and practice with phonics, **then...** use the Phonics Transition Lessons on pages 213–309 in the *ELL Handbook.*

Common Core State Standards

Literature 1. Ask and answer such questions as *who, what, where, when, why,* and *how* to demonstrate understanding of key details in a text. **Literature 10.** By the end of the year, read and comprehend literature, including stories and poetry, in the grades 2–3 text complexity band proficiently, with scaffolding as needed at the high end of the range.

1 Build Word Knowledge

Reteach Selection Vocabulary

bases	cheers	field
plate	sailed	threw

DEFINE IT Describe a *field* to a friend. Restate the word in child-friendly terms. A *field* is a piece of land used for some special purpose. Page 373 discusses Grandmama's dream of playing a game on a baseball field.

Team Talk **TALK ABOUT IT** Have you played a sport on a field? Turn and talk to your partner about this. Allow time for children to discuss. Ask for examples. Rephrase their examples for usage when necessary or to correct misunderstandings. Continue with the remaining words.

Corrective feedback	**If...** children need more practice with selection vocabulary, **then...** use the *Envision It! Pictured Vocabulary Cards.*

2 Read

Just Like Josh Gibson

If you read *Just Like Josh Gibson* during whole group time, then use the instruction below.

ACCESS TEXT Have children look at the picture on pp. 374–375. Point to the plate in the picture. What else do you see in the picture? (houses, a baseball, baseball gloves, children, trees, a bat) Reread the text on these pages.

- Is someone who flies around the bases moving fast or slow? (fast)
- What clues in the sentence let you know that flying around the bases is a good skill in baseball? (The sentence says *she could do it all* in reference to baseball and then lists what she could do including flying around the bases.)

If you are reading *Just Like Josh Gibson* during small group time, then return to pp. 367a–381a to guide the reading.

Corrective feedback	**If...** children have difficulty understanding the section, **then...** read the section aloud using the Access Text Notes.

Independent Reading Options

Trade Book Library

eSTREET INTERACTIVE
www.ReadingStreet.com

Teacher's Guides available on the Leveled Reader Database.

Strategic Intervention

1 Build Word Knowledge

Develop Vocabulary

REREAD FOR VOCABULARY Have children reread the second paragraph on p. 374 of *Just Like Josh Gibson.* Let's read this paragraph to find out what the word *imagine* means. To help children understand the word *imagine,* ask questions related to the context, such as: Does Danny really play for the Dodgers? Do the children wish they could one day play professional baseball?

Corrective feedback	**If...** children have difficulty understanding the word *imagine,* **then...** guide children to use a dictionary to find definitions.

2 Read

Just Like Josh Gibson

If you read *Just Like Josh Gibson* during whole group time, then use the instruction below.

CLOSE READING Reread pp. 370–371. Ask questions related to the context.

- Look at the picture on pp. 370–371. Which person is Josh Gibson? (the one batting) How do you know? (The story is about a time he hit a baseball hard.)
- In the story Josh Gibson hits a ball in Pittsburgh. Where does the ball land? (Philadelphia) Could this have really happened? (no) What is the point of the story? (Josh Gibson could hit the ball really hard and far.)

Corrective feedback	**If...** children have trouble answering the questions, **then...** reread the page and have them fill in sentence frames to summarize the ideas. **Josh Gibson was a great ______. There was even a story told that he hit a baseball from ______ to ______.**

If you are reading *Just Like Josh Gibson* during small group time, then return to pp. 367a–381a to guide the reading.

SMALL GROUP TIME

ELL

If... children need scaffolding and practice with the main selection, **then...** use the activities on p. DI•18 in the Teacher Resources section on SuccessNet.

Strategic Intervention

Common Core State Standards

Language 2. Demonstrate command of the conventions of standard English capitalization, punctuation, and spelling when writing.

1 Build Word Knowledge

Review Amazing Words

athlete	challenge	effort	dainty
disguise	champion	professional	shortstop

Team Talk LANGUAGE DEVELOPMENT Help children practice building sentences. Display a sentence starter and have children add oral phrases using the Amazing Words. For example: The shortstop on the team is _______. (Possible response: The shortstop on the team is a good athlete.)

Corrective feedback | **If...** children have difficulty using Amazing Words orally, **then...** review the meaning of each of the words.

2 Text-Based Comprehension

READ ALOUD "Josh Gibson, Home Run King" Read aloud "Josh Gibson, Home Run King" from *Reading Street Sleuth* on pp. 68–69 as children follow along. Then lead a choral reading of the selection.

ACCESS TEXT Guide children as they work on the Be a Sleuth section.

Look for Clues Reread the sentences from the first paragraph. After reading a sentence, ask children how it helps them understand that baseball was important to Gibson. Discuss each sentence and the clues it provides.

Ask Questions If possible, show pictures of baseball players and ball fields from the past and those of today. Help children compare and contrast the pictures. Have them ask questions about what they see in the pictures.

Make Your Case Help children make a list of sports people play and watch. Then write the following sentence frame on the board. *I think America's favorite sport is _______ because _______, _______, and _______.* Have children work with partners to complete the sentence frame.

More Reading for Group Time

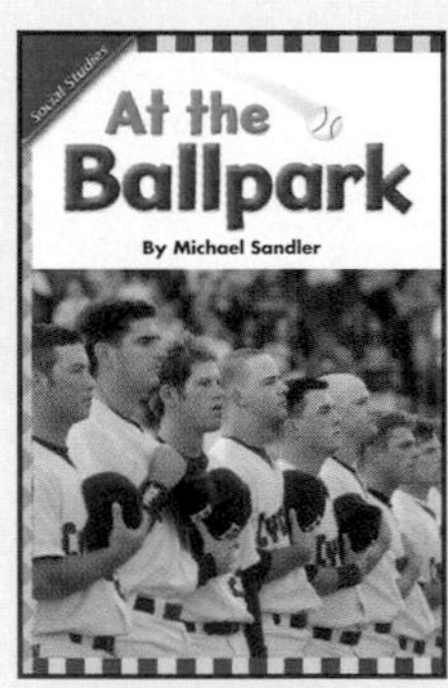

CONCEPT LITERACY

Practice
- Concept Words
- Selection Vocabulary

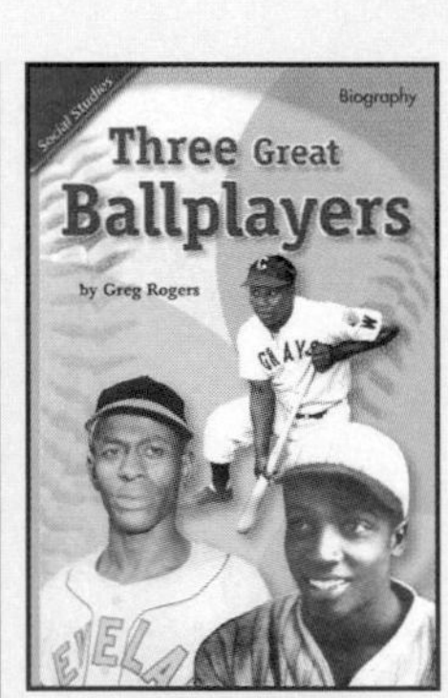

BELOW LEVEL

Review
- Compare and Contrast
- Monitor and Clarify
- Selection Vocabulary

Use these suggested Leveled Readers or other text at children's instructional level.

eStreet Interactive
www.ReadingStreet.com

Use the Leveled Reader Database for lesson plans and student pages for *At the Ballpark* and *Three Great Ballplayers.*

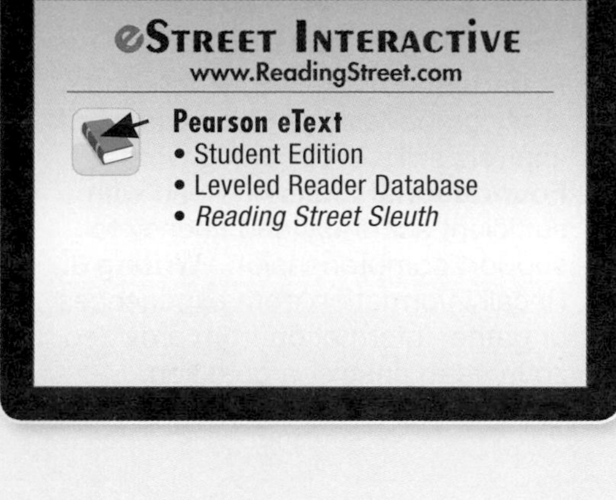

1 Build Word Knowledge

Review Using Capital Letters

IDENTIFY Choral read the Conventions note at the bottom of page 385 with children to review using capital letters. Have children reread the model story on p. 385 to find examples of how the author used capital letters. Allow time for children to discuss their examples and correct any misunderstandings.

2 Text-Based Comprehension

REREAD "Josh Gibson, Home Run King" Have partners reread "Josh Gibson, Home Run King."

EXTEND UNDERSTANDING Discuss why African Americans started their own baseball league. For a long time African Americans were not allowed to play in the same leagues as whites, so African Americans started their own league.

PERFORMANCE TASK • Prove It! Provide resources on Josh Gibson, Satchel Paige, Jackie Robinson, or other Negro League baseball players. Help each child identify a player and write at least two sentences that tell what position the player played and the teams he played on.

COMMUNICATE Have children share what they have learned about their player with the group.

SMALL GROUP TIME

More Reading for Group Time

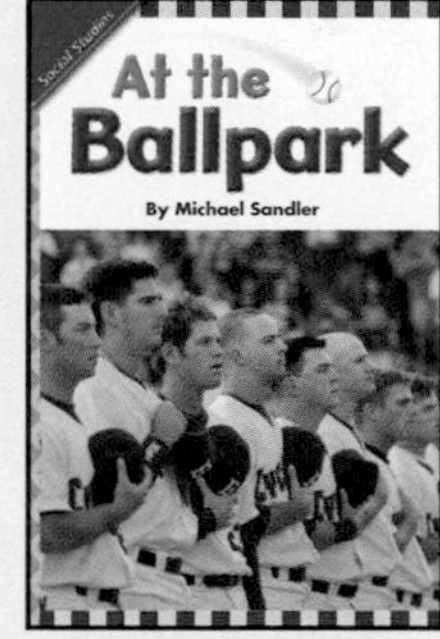

CONCEPT LITERACY

Practice
- Concept Words
- Selection Vocabulary

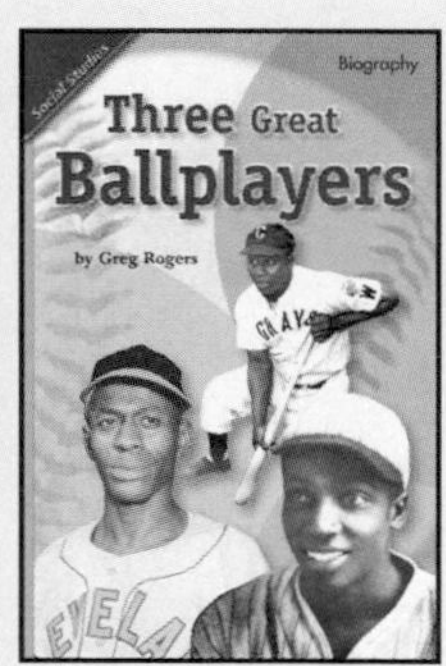

BELOW LEVEL

Review
- Compare and Contrast
- Monitor and Clarify
- Selection Vocabulary

Use these suggested Leveled Readers or other text at children's instructional level.

eStreet Interactive
www.ReadingStreet.com

Use the Leveled Reader Database for lesson plans and student pages for *At the Ballpark* and *Three Great Ballplayers*.

Common Core State Standards

Foundational Skills 3. Know and apply grade-level phonics and word analysis skills in decoding words. **Foundational Skills 4.** Read with sufficient accuracy and fluency to support comprehension. **Writing 8.** Recall information from experiences or gather information from provided sources to answer a question.

1 Build Word Knowledge

Extend Phonics

INFLECTED ENDINGS Have children practice with more complex words. Have children write the words on cards and sort by the inflected endings. Then have them use the words in sentences.

happier	potatoes	foxes	tried	lying
hitting	preferred	easiest	parties	does
buses	fattest	beginning	wetter	cried

2 Read

"Babe Didrikson"

TEACH VOCABULARY Before reading, introduce the selection words: *athlete, effort.* Help children determine the meaning of each word using these sentences:

1. Great **athletes** compete every four years in the Olympics.
2. Even though they lost, the players were proud of their **effort.**

Babe Didrikson

Today if a woman wishes to play a sport, she trains and plays and sometimes even wins. Back in the 1920s and 1930s, however, it was much rarer to find a woman athlete.

One of the first women in sports was Babe Didrikson. Babe was also one of the greatest athletes ever. Her real first name was Mildred. She grew up in Texas. She loved to play sports as a child. She especially liked to play baseball with the boys.

Young Mildred was a good baseball player. That might be the reason she got the name "Babe." Babe Ruth was a famous baseball player. He hit a lot of home runs, and Mildred hit a lot of home runs too.

Didrikson played many other sports and excelled at all of them. She played basketball. She also played golf and became a women's golf champion. They say that someone once asked Didrikson if there was anything she didn't play. She replied, "Dolls."

When she was twenty-one, Didrikson went to the 1932 Olympic Games. She entered three track and field events and won three medals—two gold and one silver. Not everyone was cheering and clapping for her because some people thought that sports should only be for men. But that didn't stop Didrikson. With her bravery and effort, she changed the way people thought about women in sports.

Advanced Selection 21 **Vocabulary:** athlete, effort

SMALL GROUP TIME

Just Like Josh Gibson SG•13

READ Have children read "Babe Didrikson" silently. Then have children take turns reading aloud. After reading, have children recall the two most important ideas of the selection using details from the text.

3 Inquiry: Extend Concepts

IDENTIFY QUESTIONS Have children choose two famous women athletes to compare and contrast. During the week, they should learn more about their choices from reading, studying pictures, and talking with adults or older children. On Day 5 they will share what they learned. Guide children in brainstorming possible choices.

- Think about your choices. Are they alike in some ways? Are they different in some ways?

If... children need practice with phonics,
then... use the Phonics Transition Lessons on pages 213–309 in the *ELL Handbook.*

Babe Didrikson

Today if a woman wishes to play a sport, she trains and plays and sometimes even wins. Back in the 1920s and 1930s, however, it was much rarer to find a woman athlete.

One of the first women in sports was Babe Didrikson. Babe was also one of the greatest athletes ever. Her real first name was Mildred. She grew up in Texas. She loved to play sports as a child. She especially liked to play baseball with the boys.

Young Mildred was a good baseball player. That might be the reason she got the name "Babe." Babe Ruth was a famous baseball player. He hit a lot of home runs, and Mildred hit a lot of home runs too.

Didrikson played many other sports and excelled at all of them. She played basketball. She also played golf and became a women's golf champion. They say that someone once asked Didrikson if there was anything she didn't play. She replied, "Dolls."

When she was twenty-one, Didrikson went to the 1932 Olympic Games. She entered three track and field events and won three medals—two gold and one silver. Not everyone was cheering and clapping for her because some people thought that sports should only be for men. But that didn't stop Didrikson. With her bravery and effort, she changed the way people thought about women in sports.

Advanced Selection 21 **Vocabulary:** athlete, effort

Advanced

Common Core State Standards

Literature 1. Ask and answer such questions as *who, what, where, when, why,* and *how* to demonstrate understanding of key details in a text. **Literature 3.** Describe how characters in a selection respond to major events and challenges. **Literature 7.** Use information gained from the illustrations and words in a print or digital text to demonstrate understanding of its characters, setting, or plot. **Language 1.** Demonstrate command of the conventions of standard English grammar and usage when writing or speaking.

1 Build Word Knowledge

Extend Selection Vocabulary

bases	cheers	field
plate	sailed	threw

Team Talk Have partners use the selection words in sentences to internalize their meanings. Have children use as many of the words as they can while making sure the sentence is grammatically correct. (Possible response: As the batter rounded the bases, the outfielder threw the ball toward the plate.)

2 Read

Just Like Josh Gibson

If you read *Just Like Josh Gibson* during whole group time, then use the instruction below.

ACCESS TEXT Have children silently reread *Just Like Josh Gibson,* retell the selection and complete a plot map. (Beginning: Grandmama tells the story of how she loved baseball as a little girl. Middle: Even though she is very talented, Grandmama can only practice with the boys, because girls aren't allowed to play baseball. End: Grandmama gets her chance to play in a game, and she is the star.)

DISCUSS GENRE Discuss what makes *Just Like Josh Gibson* realistic fiction. Point out that the selection tells about made-up events that seem like they could happen in real life.

If you are reading *Just Like Josh Gibson* during small group time, then return to pp. 367a–381a to guide the reading.

3 Inquiry: Extend Concepts

INVESTIGATE Guide children in choosing materials at their independent reading levels.

LOOK AHEAD Help children choose formats to present their information, such as dramatic presentations, illustrated posters, or three-dimensional displays.

Independent Reading Options

Trade Book Library

eStreet Interactive
www.ReadingStreet.com

Teacher's Guides available on the Leveled Reader Database.

Advanced

1 Build Word Knowledge

Develop Vocabulary

REREAD FOR VOCABULARY Have children reread *Just Like Josh Gibson* and make a two-column chart listing nouns from the selection associated with baseball and verbs used to describe playing baseball.

Nouns	Verbs
baseball	throw
glove	hit
Louisville slugger	practice
field	fly
plate	caught
bases	

2 Read

Just Like Josh Gibson

If you read *Just Like Josh Gibson* during whole group time, then use the instruction below.

CLOSE READING Reread pp. 372–375. Explain that at times in the past, people weren't allowed to do certain things because of their gender or race. Do you think Grandmama's Papa agreed with the idea that girls shouldn't be allowed to play with the boys? Explain. (He did not believe that. He showed up at her birth with baseball equipment and played often with her. He said she would make balls fly like Josh Gibson.) Why does everyone say, "too bad she's a girl …"? (She is good enough to play on a team and could probably help the team win games.)

If you are reading *Just Like Josh Gibson* during small group time, then return to pp. 367a–381a to guide the reading.

3 Inquiry: Extend Concepts

INVESTIGATE Give children time to investigate their compare and contrast project on two famous female athletes by reading and studying pictures. If necessary, help children make connections between players of the past and players of the present.

SMALL GROUP TIME

If... children need more scaffolding and practice with the main selection, **then...** use the activities on p. DI•18 in the Teacher Resources section on SuccessNet.

Advanced

Common Core State Standards

Writing 8. Recall information from experiences or gather information from provided sources to answer a question. **Language 1.** Demonstrate command of the conventions of standard English grammar and usage when writing or speaking. **Speaking/Listening 1.** Participate in collaborative conversations with diverse partners about grade 2 topics and texts with peers and adults in small and larger groups.

More Reading for Group Time

ADVANCED

- Extend Concept Vocabulary
- Review Target Skills

Use this suggested Leveled Reader or other text at children's instructional level.

eStreet Interactive
www.ReadingStreet.com

Use the Leveled Reader Database for lesson plans and student pages for *Baseball Heroes Make History.*

1 Build Word Knowledge

Extend Amazing Words and Selection Vocabulary

athlete	disguise
challenge	champion
effort	professional
dainty	shortstop

bases	cheers
field	plate
sailed	threw

Team Talk Have children ask each other questions using the Amazing Words and the selection vocabulary, such as: What kind of effort does it take to become a champion athlete?

2 Text-Based Comprehension

READ ALOUD "Josh Gibson, Home Run King" Have partners take turns reading paragraphs of "Josh Gibson, Home Run King" from *Reading Street Sleuth* on pp. 68–69. Then have children read the selection independently.

ACCESS TEXT Guide children as they work on the Be a Sleuth section.

Look for Clues Have children find clues that show baseball was important to Gibson and clues that show Gibson was important to baseball.

Ask Questions Talk to children about what they know about baseball. Then discuss things that might have changed over the years. Direct children to ask their questions. Have children choose one question to research and find the answer.

Make Your Case Have children identify the sport they think is most popular and cite reasons for its popularity. They might take a poll of classmates and adults they know to determine whether others agree with their opinion.

3 Inquiry: Extend Concepts

ORGANIZE INFORMATION Give children time to continue reading and preparing information. Provide any necessary materials, such as poster board and art supplies.

Advanced

1 Build Word Knowledge

Capital Letters

IDENTIFY CAPITAL LETTERS Have children return to the text of "Josh Gibson, Home Run King," identify words with capital letters, and tell why they begin with capital letters. Then have children write two sentences that have proper nouns in them.

2 Text-Based Comprehension

REREAD "Josh Gibson, Home Run King" Have partners reread "Josh Gibson, Home Run King." Then ask children to write a paragraph summarizing the article. Make sure they use capital letters correctly.

EXTEND UNDERSTANDING Briefly discuss segregation and its impact on sports. Ask, What does *segregation* mean?

PERFORMANCE TASK • Prove It! Collect resources on Josh Gibson, Satchel Paige, Jackie Robinson, or another Negro League baseball player. Direct children to choose a player, do research about the player's career in baseball, and then write a brief biography.

COMMUNICATE Have children present their reports and then display the reports with pictures of the players they researched.

3 Inquiry: Extend Concepts

COMMUNICATE Have children share their inquiry projects comparing and contrasting two woman athletes they have learned about.

More Reading for Group Time

ADVANCED

- Extend Concept Vocabulary
- Review Target Skills

Use this suggested Leveled Reader or other text at children's instructional level.

eStreet Interactive
www.ReadingStreet.com

Use the Leveled Reader Database for lesson plans and student pages for *Baseball Heroes Make History.*

TEACHER NOTES

Tennessee Common Core Edition 

This Week's Target Skills and Strategies

Target Skills and Strategies	Common Core State Standards for English Language Arts	Tennessee CUs and GLEs
Phonics and Spelling **Skill:** Abbreviations	**CCSS Foundational Skills 3.** Know and apply grade-level phonics and word analysis skills in decoding words. **(Also CCSS Language 2.)**	**TN CU 0201.1.11** Apply phonics generalizations in order to decode words.
Text-Based Comprehension **Skill:** Author's Purpose	**CCSS Informational Text 6.** Identify the main purpose of a text, including what the author wants to answer, explain, or describe. **(Also CCSS Informational Text 2.)**	**TN GLE 0201.6.2** Comprehend the main ideas and supporting details of informational texts.
Strategy: Summarize	**CCSS Informational Text 2.** Identify the main topic of a multiparagraph text as well as the focus of specific paragraphs within the text.	**TN GLE 0201.6.2** Comprehend the main ideas and supporting details of informational texts.
Vocabulary **Skill:** Multiple-Meaning Words **Strategy:** Context Clues	**CCSS Language 4.** Determine or clarify the meaning of unknown and multiple-meaning words and phrases based on grade 2 reading and content, choosing flexibly from an array of strategies. **(Also CCSS Language 4.a., CCSS Foundational Skills 4.c.)**	**TN CU 0201.1.9** Show evidence of expanding language through vocabulary growth. **(Also TN GLE 0201.1.2)**
Fluency **Skill:** Accuracy	**CCSS Foundational Skills 4.b.** Read on-level text orally with accuracy, appropriate rate, and expression on successive readings.	**TN CU 0201.8.9** Read orally with fluency and accuracy, using appropriate pacing and expression.
Listening and Speaking Evaluate Advertisements	**CCSS Speaking/Listening 1.** Participate in collaborative conversations with diverse partners about *grade 2 topics and texts* with peers and adults in small and larger groups. **(Also CCSS Speaking/Listening 3.)**	**TN CU 0201.2.8** Participate in group discussion. **(Also TN GLE 0201.2.1, TN GLE 0201.2.2)**
Six-Trait Writing **Trait of the Week:** Voice	**CCSS Writing 3.** Write narratives in which they recount a well-elaborated event or short sequence of events, include details to describe actions, thoughts, and feelings, use temporal words to signal event order, and provide a sense of closure.	**TN CU 0201.3.7** Arrange events in a logical and sequential order when writing. **(Also TN CU 0201.3.2, TN CU 0201.3.8)**
Writing Descriptive Poem or Song	**CCSS Writing 3.** Write narratives in which they recount a well-elaborated event or short sequence of events, include details to describe actions, thoughts, and feelings, use temporal words to signal event order, and provide a sense of closure. **(Also CCSS Literature 4.)**	**TN CU 0201.3.7** Arrange events in a logical and sequential order when writing. **(Also TN CU 0201.3.2, TN CU 0201.3.8)**
Conventions **Skill:** Quotation Marks	**CCSS Language 2.** Demonstrate command of the conventions of standard English capitalization, punctuation, and spelling when writing.	**TN GLE 0201.1.1** Demonstrate control of basic English usage, mechanics, spelling, and sentence structure.

Access for All to Differentiate Instruction

Reading Street Sleuth

Respecting the Star-Spangled Banner
pp. 70–71

Follow the path to close reading using the Super Sleuth tips:

- Look for Clues
- Ask Questions
- Make Your Case
- Prove it!

This Week's Optional Tennessee Readers Provide Informational Text

Concept Literacy

CCSS Informational Text 1.; TN CU 0201.8.6

Below Level

CCSS Informational Text 2., CCSS Informational Text 6.; TN GLE 0201.6.2

On Level

CCSS Informational Text 2., CCSS Informational Text 6.; TN GLE 0201.6.2

Advanced

CCSS Informational Text 2., CCSS Informational Text 6.; TN GLE 0201.6.2

ELL

CCSS Informational Text 2., CCSS Informational Text 6.; TN GLE 0201.6.2

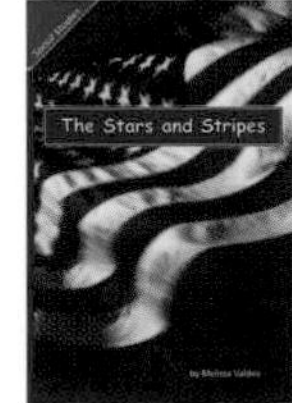

ELD

CCSS Informational Text 2., CCSS Informational Text 6.; TN GLE 0201.6.2

ISBN-13: 978-0-328-73472-6 ISBN-10: 0-328-73472-1

Assessment

Tennessee Assessment Resources for Common Core Test Success

Tennessee Daily Formative Assessment in Your Teacher's Edition

Baseline Group Tests

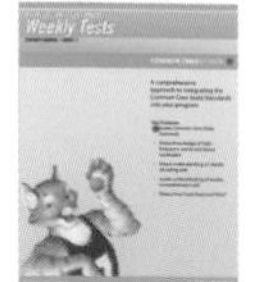

CCSS Weekly Tests, pp. 157–162

CCSS Fresh Reads, pp. 157–162

Unit 6 CCSS Benchmark Test

CCSS Success Tracker, ExamView, and Online Lesson Planner

RTI

Response to Intervention Kits Increase Instruction and Progress Monitoring

Intensive Intervention *My Sidewalks* Level B, Unit 6, pp. 178–193

Writing, Grammar, and Spelling

Six-Trait Writing

- Focus/Ideas
- Organization/Paragraphs
- Voice
  Trait of the Week
  CCSS Writing 3.
  TN CU 0201.3.7
- Word Choice
- Sentences
- Conventions

Resources for Six-Trait Writing, Grammar, and Spelling

Reader's and Writer's Notebook
- Practice Reading
- Practice Grammar
- Practice Spelling
- Practice Writing

Writing Rubrics and Anchor Papers

Digital Resources
- Online Journal
- Online Writing Transparencies
- Grammar Jammer

Teacher Resources DVD-ROM
- Reader's and Writer's Notebook
- Let's Practice It!
- Graphic Organizers
- Writing Transparencies

Grade 2 Skills Trace

Skills and Strategies	Looking Back	This Week's Selection	Looking Ahead
Phonics and Spelling **Skill:** Abbreviations	**Unit 6** 356b, 381c, 384a, 384–385, 389b	394a, 394–395, 395a, 395c–395d, 398c, 418c, 418d, 422d, 422e–422f, 424c, 425e	**Unit 6** 452c, 524d
Text-Based Comprehension **Skill:** Author's Purpose	**Unit 2** 223a, 224h, 228–229, 232–233 **Unit 3** 353a–353b, 354h, 356–357	396a, 396–397, 400a, 402–403, 404–405, 408–409, 410–411, 412–413, 414–415, 423a, 425b, 425f	**Unit 6** 487a, 489a, 521a
Strategy: Summarize	**Unit 2** 192h, 194–195, 200–201 **Unit 3** 424h, 430–431, 434–435	396a, 396–397, 400a, 404–405, 410–411, 414–415, 416–417, 419a, 422–423	Grade 3 **Units 1, 4, 5**
Vocabulary **Skill:** Multiple-Meaning Words **Strategy:** Context Clues	**Unit 4** 26g, 26–27, 32–33, 42g, 52–53, 126g, 126–127, 138–139, 144g, 153a	398g, 418g	Grade 3 **Units 1, 4**
Fluency **Skill:** Accuracy	**Unit 4** 76f, 81b, 83a **Unit 5** 212f, 219a, 221a, 221d	418f, 423b, 425a, 425d	**Unit 6** 488f, 493b, 495a, 495d
Listening and Speaking Evaluate Advertisements	Skill not previously taught	423f	Skill not subsequently taught
Six-Trait Writing **Trait of the Week:** Voice	**Unit 4** 143c–143d, 146–147, 147a **Unit 5** 277d–277e, 280–281, 281a	417d–417e, 420–421, 421a, 423d–423e	Grade 3 **Units 1, 3**
Writing Descriptive Poem or Song	Grade 1 **Unit 4**	397c–397d, 417d–417e, 420–421, 421a, 423d–423e, 425h–425i	Grade 3 **Unit 5**
Conventions **Skill:** Quotation Marks	Skill not previously taught	397b, 417c, 420a, 420–421, 423c, 425g	Grade 3 **Unit 6**

Tennessee Science and Social Studies Standards Taught During the Reading Lesson

TN CU 0207.T/E.3 Use tools to measure materials and construct simple products.

TN 2.4.04.c Explain the meaning of selected patriotic symbols and landmarks of Tennessee.

TN 2.5.01 Identify major events, people, and patterns Tennessee, United States, and world history.

Teaching the Common Core State Standards This Week

The Common Core State Standards for English Language Arts are divided into strands for **Reading** (including **Foundational Skills**), **Writing**, **Speaking and Listening**, and **Language**. The chart below shows some of the content you will teach this week, strand by strand. Turn to this week's 5-Day Planner on pages 392d–392e to see how this content is taught each day.

Reading Strand

- **Phonics:** Abbreviations
- **Text-Based Comprehension:** Author's Purpose; Summarize
- **Fluency:** Accuracy
- **Literary Text:** Main Idea and Topic
- **Genre:** Main Selection: Informational Text; Paired Selection: Poetry (Song)

Writing Strand

- **Writing Mini-Lesson:** Descriptive Poem or Story
- **Trait:** Voice
- **Look Back and Write:** Text Evidence

Common Core State Standards for English Language Arts

Speaking and Listening Strand

- **Content Knowledge:** Build Oral Language
- **Listening and Speaking:** Evaluate Advertisements
- **Research and Inquiry**

Language Strand

- **Oral Vocabulary: Amazing Words** *history*, *independence*, *symbol*, *patriotic*, *unfurl*, *frayed*, *allegiance*, *indivisible*
- **Vocabulary:** Multiple-Meaning Words; Context Clues
- **Selection Vocabulary:** *America*, *birthday*, *flag*, *freedom*, *nicknames*, *stars*, *stripes*
- **Academic Vocabulary:** *abbreviation, topic, author's purpose, dialogue, quotation marks, poem, summarize, chart, poetry, alliteration, topic, main idea*
- **Conventions:** Quotation Marks
- **Spelling:** Abbreviations

Text-Based Comprehension

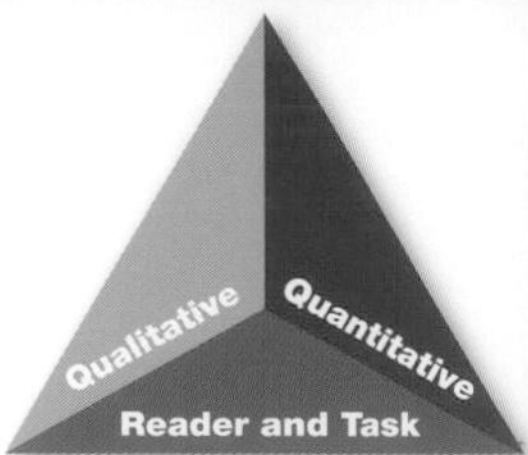

Text Complexity Measures

Use the rubric to familiarize yourself with the text complexity of ***Red, White, and Blue: The Story of the American Flag***.

Bridge to Complex Knowledge

Quantitative Measures	**Lexile**	480L
	Average Sentence Length	9.49
	Word Frequency	3.55

Qualitative Measures	**Levels of Meaning**	information is factual with a clearly stated purpose; understand that factual information can be gathered using text, maps, and images
	Structure	conventional structure; events happen chronologically; captions; maps
	Language Conventionality and Clarity	clear, literal language; academic language; use of signal words for sequence
	Theme and Knowledge Demands	text assumes no prior knowledge; singular perspective

Reader and Task Suggestions

FORMATIVE ASSESSMENT Based on assessment results, use the **Reader and Task Suggestions** in Access Main Selection to scaffold the selection or support independence for children as they read ***Red, White, and Blue: The Story of the American Flag***.

READER AND TASK SUGGESTIONS	
Preparing to Read the Text	**Leveled Tasks**
• Review strategies for understanding multiple-meaning words. Refer to the vocabulary skill lesson on p. 398g. • Point out the maps and illustrations used to enhance understanding of the text. • Remind children that this selection is informational. They may need to read more slowly to better understand the text.	• **Structure** If the chronological events are confusing for children, have them keep a list of dates and events from the text in the correct time order. • **Language Conventionality and Clarity** If children struggle with the academic language, have them list any words that they do not understand.

Recommended Placement Both the qualitative and quantitative measures suggest this text should be placed in the Grade 2–3 text complexity band, which is where both the Common Core State Standards and *Scott Foresman Reading Street* have placed it.

Focus on Common Core State Standards

Main Selection, pp. 400–417

Paired Selection, pp. 422–423

Text-Based Comprehension

Author's Purpose
CCSS Informational Text 2., CCSS Informational Text 6.

Summarize
CCSS Informational Text 2.

Fluency

Accuracy
CCSS Foundational Skills 4.b.

Writing and Conventions

Trait: Voice
CCSS Writing 3.

Writing Mini-Lesson: Descriptive Poem or Song
CCSS Literature 4., CCSS Writing 3.

Conventions: Quotation Marks
CCSS Language 2.

Oral Vocabulary

Amazing Words

history	independence
symbol	patriotic
unfurl	frayed
allegiance	indivisible

CCSS Language 6.

Vocabulary

Vocabulary
Skill: Multiple-Meaning Words
CCSS Language 4., CCSS Language 4.a.

Strategy: Context Clues
CCSS Foundational Skills 4.c., CCSS Language 4.a.

America	birthday	flag
freedom	nicknames	stars
stripes		

Phonics and Spelling

Abbreviations
CCSS Foundational Skills 3., CCSS Language 2.

Mr.	Mrs.	St.
Jan.	Feb.	Aug.
Dr.	Ms.	Rd.
Oct.	Nov.	Dec.

Listening and Speaking

Evaluate Advertisements
CCSS Speaking/Listening 1., CCSS Speaking/Listening 3.

Preview Your Week

What traditions and celebrations involve our country's flag?

Red, White, and Blue
The Story of THE AMERICAN FLAG
BY John Herman
ILLUSTRATED BY Shannan Stirnweiss
Genre **Informational Text** often gives facts about real people, places, and events that reflect history or the traditions of communities. Look for facts as you read.
Question of the Week
What traditions and celebrations involve our country's flag?
400 401

Main Selection, pp. 400–417

Common Core State Standards Literature 4. Describe how words and phrases (e.g., regular beats, alliteration, rhymes, repeated lines) supply rhythm and meaning in a story, poem, or song.
Social Studies in Reading
Genre
Poetry (Song)
- A song is a lyric poem set to music. Poetry shows lines of words that have rhythm.
- Poetry often rhymes.
- Poetry may tell about what the poet senses and feels.
- Read "You're a Grand Old Flag." As you read, think about how the songwriter feels about the American flag.
- Songs often use words that have different meanings from their ordinary meanings. Find the phrase "Ev'ry heart beats true." Is this the literal, or real, meaning of the words? Or do the words mean something else?

You're a Grand Old Flag
by George M. Cohan

You're a grand old flag,
You're a high flying flag
And forever in peace may
you wave.
You're the emblem of the
land I love.
The home of the free and
the brave.

Ev'ry heart beats true
'Neath the red, white, and blue,
Where there's never a boast
or brag.
Should auld acquaintance
be forgot,
Keep your eye on the grand
old flag.

Let's Think About
How do the words create a **rhythm**? Find the words that **rhyme**.

Let's Think About
Reading Across Texts "You're a Grand Old Flag" is one song about the flag of the United States. What other song about the flag did you read about in *Red, White, and Blue?*
Writing Across Texts Make a list of other traditional songs that you know.
422 423

Paired Selection, pp. 422–423

Genre: Informational Text
Phonics: Abbreviations
Text-Based Comprehension: Author's Purpose
Vocabulary: Multiple-Meaning Words

Social Studies in Reading
Genre: Poetry (Song)

Build Content Knowledge

KNOWLEDGE GOALS
Children will understand some of the traditions that honor the flag:
- the Pledge of Allegiance
- the National Anthem
- the Fourth of July

THIS WEEK'S CONCEPT MAP
Develop a concept-related graphic organizer like the one below over the course of this week.

BUILD ORAL VOCABULARY
This week, children will acquire the following academic vocabulary/domain-specific words.

Amazing Words

history	independence
symbol	patriotic
unfurl	frayed
allegiance	indivisible

OPTIONAL CONCEPT-BASED READING Use the Digital Path to access readers offering different levels of text complexity.

Concept Literacy

Below Level

On Level

Advanced

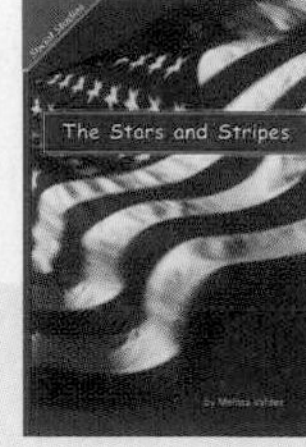

ELL

The Stars and Stripes
ELD

This Week's Digital Resources

eStreet Interactive

www.ReadingStreet.com

Get Ready to Read

Background Building Audio CD This audio CD provides valuable background information about the ways the American flag has changed over time and how the flag is used today to help children read and comprehend the weekly texts.

Concept Talk Video Use this video on the Digital Path to build momentum and introduce the weekly concept of the American flag.

Interactive Sing with Me Big Book "Our Flag, Our Symbol," sung to the tune of "Row, Row, Row Your Boat," introduces the Amazing Words with a catchy, concept-related song.

Interactive Sound-Spelling Cards With these interactive cards on the Digital Path, children see an image, hear the image name, and see the spelling for abbreviations.

Pearson eText Use the eText for the Decodable Readers on the Leveled Reader Database for phonics and fluency support.

Letter Tile Drag and Drop Using this interactive tool on Pearson SuccessNet, children click and spell words to enhance their phonics skills.

Read and Comprehend

Envision It! Animations Use this colorful animation on the Digital Path to explain the target comprehension skill, Author's Purpose.

Pearson eText Read the eText of the main selection, *Red, White, and Blue: The Story of the American Flag,* and the paired selection, "You're a Grand Old Flag," with audio support on Pearson SuccessNet.

Story Sort Use the Story Sort Activity on the Digital Path after reading *Red, White, and Blue: The Story of the American Flag* to involve children in summarizing.

Journal: Word Bank Use the Word Bank on the Digital Path to have children write sentences using this week's selection words.

Vocabulary Activities A variety of interactive vocabulary activities on the Digital Path help children practice concept-related words.

Language Arts

Grammar Jammer Choose a whimsical animation on the Digital Path to provide an engaging grammar lesson that will capture children's attention.

Pearson eText Find the Student Edition eText of the Let's Write It! and Let's Learn It! pages with audio support on Pearson SuccessNet.

Additional Resources

Teacher Resources DVD-ROM Use the following resources on the TR DVD or on Pearson SuccessNet throughout the week:

- Amazing Word Cards
- Reader's and Writer's Notebook
- Writing Transparencies
- Daily Fix-It Transparencies
- Scoring Rubrics
- Grammar Transparencies
- Research Transparencies
- Let's Practice It!
- Graphic Organizers
- Vocabulary Cards
- Vocabulary Transparencies

This Week's Skills

Phonics/Spelling
Abbreviations

Comprehension
Author's Purpose
Summarize

Language
Vocabulary: Multiple-Meaning Words
Conventions: Quotation Marks

Fluency
Accuracy

Writing
Descriptive Poem or Song

5-Day Planner

DAY 1

Get Ready to Read

Content Knowledge 392j
Oral Vocabulary: *history, independence, symbol*

Phonics/Spelling 394a
Abbreviations
Spelling Pretest
READ Decodable Reader 27A
Reread for Fluency

Monitor Progress
Check Word Reading

Read and Comprehend

Text-Based Comprehension 396a
Author's Purpose
Summarize

Selection Vocabulary 397a
Selection Words: *America, birthday, flag, freedom, nicknames, stars, stripes*

Language Arts

Conventions 397b
Quotation Marks

Writing 397c
Descriptive Poem or Song

Research and Inquiry 397e
Identify and Focus Topic

DAY 2

Get Ready to Read

Content Knowledge 398a
Oral Vocabulary: *patriotic, unfurl*

Phonics/Spelling 398c
Abbreviations
Review Contractions
Spelling: Abbreviations

Read and Comprehend

Selection Vocabulary 398e
Review Selection Words: *America, birthday, flag, freedom, nicknames, stars, stripes*
Skill: Multiple-Meaning Words
Reread for Fluency

Monitor Progress
Check Selection Words/ High-Frequency Words

Text-Based Comprehension 399a
READ *Red, White, and Blue: The Story of the American Flag*—1st Read

Informational Text 417b
Main Idea and Topic

Language Arts

Conventions 417c
Quotation Marks

Writing 417d
Descriptive Poem or Song

Handwriting 417f
Cursive *B, P, R, T, F*/Letter Smoothness

Research and Inquiry 417g
Research Skill: Chart

DAY 3

Get Ready to Read

Content Knowledge 418a
Oral Vocabulary: *frayed*

Phonics/Spelling 418c
Sort Words
Fluent Word Reading
Decode and Read
Spelling: Dictation

Read and Comprehend

Fluency 418f
Accuracy

Selection Vocabulary 418g
Selection Words: *America, birthday, flag, freedom, nicknames, stars, stripes*
Multiple-Meaning Words

Text-Based Comprehension 418h
READ *Red, White, and Blue: The Story of the American Flag*—2nd Read
Monitor Progress Check Retelling

Language Arts

Conventions 420a
Quotation Marks

Writing 420–421
Descriptive Poem or Song

Research and Inquiry 421b
Gather and Record Information

DAY 4

Get Ready to Read

Content Knowledge 422a
Oral Vocabulary: *allegiance, indivisible*

Phonics/Spelling 422c
Review Inflected Endings
Spiral Review Fluent Word Reading
READ Decodable Reader 27C
Spelling: Abbreviations

Read and Comprehend

Poetry in Reading 422h
READ "You're a Grand Old Flag" Paired Reading

Fluency 423b
Accuracy
Monitor Progress Fluency Check

Language Arts

Conventions 423c
Quotation Marks

Writing 423d
Descriptive Poem or Song

Listening and Speaking 423f
Evaluate Advertisements

Research and Inquiry 423g
Synthesize

DAY 5

Get Ready to Read

Content Knowledge 424a
Review Oral Vocabulary
Monitor Progress
Check Oral Vocabulary

Phonics/Spelling 424c
Review Abbreviations
Spelling Test

Read and Comprehend

Vocabulary 424–425
Fluency 425a
Listening and Speaking 425a

Text-Based Comprehension 425b
Review Author's Purpose

Vocabulary 425b
Review Selection Words: *America, birthday, flag, freedom, nicknames, stars, stripes*

Genre 425c
Review Informational Text

Assessment 425d
Monitor Progress
Sentence Reading; Fluency and Comprehension

Language Arts

Conventions 425g
Review Quotation Marks

Writing 425h
Descriptive Poem or Song

Research and Inquiry 425j
Communicate

Wrap Up Your Week! 425k

Access for All

What do I do in group time?

It's as easy as 1-2-3!

1 TEACHER-LED SMALL GROUPS → 2 INDEPENDENT PRACTICE STATIONS → 3 INDEPENDENT READING

Small Group Time

Bridge to Common Core

SKILL DEVELOPMENT

- Abbreviations
- Multiple-Meaning Words
- Author's Purpose
- Summarize

DEEP UNDERSTANDING

This Week's Knowledge Goals

Children will understand some of the traditions that honor the flag:

- the Pledge of Allegiance
- the National Anthem
- the Fourth of July

1 Small Group Lesson Plan

	DAY 1 Differentiate Phonics	DAY 2 Differentiate Comprehension
OL On-Level pp. SG•19–SG•23	**Practice Phonics** More Abbreviations **Decodable Reader** Read *Mrs. Jenkins*	**Build Word Knowledge** Practice Selection Vocabulary **Access Text** Read *Red, White, and Blue: The Story of the American Flag*
SI Strategic Intervention pp. SG•24–SG•28	**Reteach Phonics** Blend Abbreviations **Decodable Reader** Read *Mrs. Jenkins*	**Build Word Knowledge** Reteach Selection Vocabulary **Access Text** Read *Red, White, and Blue: The Story of the American Flag*
A Advanced pp. SG•29–SG•34	**Extend Phonics** More Abbreviations **Advanced Selection** Read "Raising the Stars and Stripes"	**Build Word Knowledge** Extend Selection Vocabulary **Access Text** Read *Red, White, and Blue: The Story of the American Flag*
Independent Inquiry Project	Introduce	Investigate
ELL **If...** children need more scaffolding and practice with...	**Phonics** **then...** use the ELL activities on p. DI•37 in the Teacher Resources section on SuccessNet.	**Comprehension Skill** **then...** use the ELL activities on p. DI•38 in the Teacher Resources section on SuccessNet.

Reading Street Sleuth

- Provides access to grade-level text for all children
- Focuses on finding clues in text through close reading
- Builds capacity for complex text

Build Text-Based Comprehension

Red, White, and Blue: The Story of the American Flag

Optional Leveled Readers

Concept Literacy

Below Level

On Level

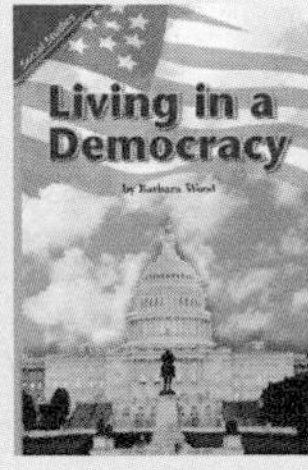

Advanced

ELL

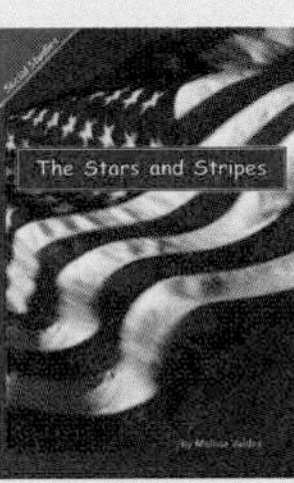

ELD

DAY 3 Differentiate Close Reading	DAY 4 Differentiate Vocabulary	DAY 5 Differentiate Reteaching
Reread to Develop Vocabulary **Close Reading** Reread *Red, White, and Blue: The Story of the American Flag*	**Build Word Knowledge** Develop Language Using Amazing Words **Text-Based Comprehension** Read *Reading Street Sleuth,* pp. 70–71, or Leveled Readers	**Practice** Quotation Marks **Text-Based Comprehension** Reread *Reading Street Sleuth,* pp. 70–71, or Leveled Readers
Reread to Develop Vocabulary **Close Reading** Reread *Red, White, and Blue: The Story of the American Flag*	**Build Word Knowledge** Review/Discuss Amazing Words **Text-Based Comprehension** Read *Reading Street Sleuth,* pp. 70–71, or Leveled Readers	**Review** Quotation Marks **Text-Based Comprehension** Reread *Reading Street Sleuth,* pp. 70–71, or Leveled Readers
Reread to Develop Vocabulary **Close Reading** Reread *Red, White, and Blue: The Story of the American Flag* Investigate	**Build Word Knowledge** Extend Amazing Words and Selection Vocabulary **Text-Based Comprehension** Read *Reading Street Sleuth,* pp. 70–71, or Leveled Readers Organize	**Extend** Quotation Marks **Text-Based Comprehension** Reread *Reading Street Sleuth,* pp. 70–71, or Leveled Readers Communicate
Main Selection **then...** use the activities on p. DI•39 in the Teacher Resources section on SuccessNet.	**Amazing Words** **then...** use the routine on pp. xxxvi–xxxvii in the *ELL Handbook.*	**Conventions and Writing** **then...** use the activities on pp. DI•41–DI•42 in the Teacher Resources section on SuccessNet.

2 Independent Stations

Practice Last Week's Skills

 Focus on these activities when time is limited.

ACCESS FOR ALL
- ● Below-Level Activities
- ▲ On-Level Activities
- ■ Advanced Activities

WORD WISE

Use inflected endings.

OBJECTIVES
- Spell words with inflected endings *-ed, -s, -es, -ing, -er,* and *-est.*

MATERIALS
- *Word Wise* Flip Chart, Letter Tiles, paper, pencils

 **Interactive Sound-Spelling Cards**  **Letter Tile Drag and Drop**

● Children spell *plays, liked, heavier, lightest, ranches,* and *skipping* with the Letter Tiles. They write the words and circle the endings. They illustrate and label three words.

▲ Children spell *tried, lighter, prettiest, liking, planning,* and *ranches.* They write the words and circle the endings. They pick endings for *heavy* and write the words.

■ Children add endings to the words *earn, knit, circle, distinguish, crumble, excite, happy,* and *thin.* They then write a sentence for each word.

WORD WORK

Identify inflected endings.

OBJECTIVES
- Identify and add to words *-ed, -s, -es, -ing, -er,* or *-est.*

MATERIALS
- *Word Work* Flip Chart; Sound-Spelling Cards: 118, 119, 121, 123–129; Teacher-made word cards: *running, stopped, sillier, wettest, tap, ride, ranch, happy, fast, nice, pretty, long, look, find, hop, hope;* paper; pencils; crayons

 **Interactive Sound-Spelling Cards**

● Children say each Sound-Spelling Card word. They find two word cards that show words with inflected endings and illustrate them.

▲ Children say each Sound-Spelling Card word. They select eight base word cards and write the words with inflected endings.

■ Children say each Sound-Spelling Card word. They add an ending to each of the base word cards.

LET'S WRITE!

Write fiction.

OBJECTIVES
- Write a piece of realistic fiction with organization to get a sharp beginning, a middle, and a strong ending.

MATERIALS
- *Let's Write!* Flip Chart, paper, pencils

 **Grammar Jammer**

● Children choose a favorite character or celebrity. They write two sentences about someone who wants to be like that person and illustrate the sentences.

▲ Children select a favorite character or celebrity. They write a realistic story about someone who wants to be just like that person. They write three sentences.

■ Children select a favorite character or celebrity. They write a realistic story about someone who wants to be like that person.

WORDS TO KNOW

Identify homophones.

OBJECTIVES
- Identify and choose the correct homophone in context.

MATERIALS
- *Words to Know* Flip Chart; Teacher-made word cards: *wear/ware, blew/blue, steel/steal, read/red, pause/paws, ad/add, past/passed, too/two, write/right, would/wood;* paper; pencils; crayons

 **Vocabulary Activities**

● Children choose one homophone card and say the words. They illustrate the difference between the words' meanings and use each word in a sentence.

▲ Children choose three homophone cards and say the words. They create a poster that shows the different meanings of the word pairs.

■ Children use the homophone cards to write a funny story. They use as many homophone pairs as possible.

READ FOR MEANING

Use text-based comprehension tools.

OBJECTIVES

- Compare and contrast elements in a story.

MATERIALS

- *Read for Meaning* Flip Chart, 2.6.1 Leveled Readers, compare-and-contrast graphic organizer, paper, pencils, crayons

 **Pearson eText**
- Leveled eReaders

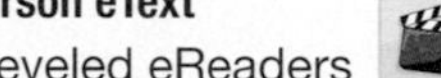

 **Envision It! Animations**

● Children read *Three Great Ballplayers.* They choose two characters and draw a picture showing how they are alike or different, listing their traits below.

▲ Children read *Women Play Baseball.* They use the organizer to compare and contrast two characters. They write two comparable traits and two contrasting traits.

■ Children read *Baseball Heroes Make History* and list comparable and contrasting traits in the organizer. They write two paragraphs comparing and contrasting the characters.

GET FLUENT

Practice fluent reading.

OBJECTIVES

- Read aloud with accuracy and at an appropriate rate.

MATERIALS

- *Get Fluent* Flip Chart, 2.6.1 Leveled Readers

 **Pearson eText**
- Leveled Readers

● Children work with a partner to take turns reading from *Three Great Ballplayers.* They use punctuation clues and monitor reading rate.

▲ Children work with a partner to take turns reading from *Women Play Baseball.* They use punctuation clues and monitor reading rate.

■ Children work with a partner to take turns reading from *Baseball Heroes Make History.* They use punctuation clues and monitor reading rate.

Manage the Stations

Use these management tools to set up and organize your Practice Stations:

Practice Station Flip Charts

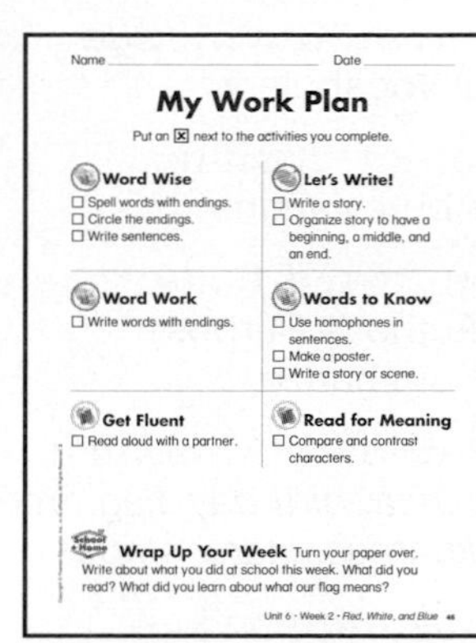
Name ______ Date ______

My Work Plan

Put an ☒ next to the activities you complete.

Word Wise
- ☐ Spell words with endings.
- ☐ Circle the endings.
- ☐ Write sentences.

Let's Write!
- ☐ Write a story.
- ☐ Organize story to have a beginning, a middle, and an end.

Word Work
- ☐ Write words with endings.

Words to Know
- ☐ Use homophones in sentences.
- ☐ Make a poster.
- ☐ Write a story or scene.

Get Fluent
- ☐ Read aloud with a partner.

Read for Meaning
- ☐ Compare and contrast characters.

Wrap Up Your Week Turn your paper over. Write about what you did at school this week. What did you read? What did you learn about what our flag means?

Unit 6 • Week 2 • *Red, White, and Blue* 45

Classroom Management Handbook for Differentiated Instruction Practice Stations, p. 45

3 Independent Reading

Children should select appropriately complex texts to read and write about independently every day before, during, and after school.

Suggestions for this week's independent reading:
- Fictional texts on last week's social studies topic: Why are sports traditions important in our country?
- Fiction selections about why sports traditions are important in our country
- Fiction book by a favorite author

BOOK TALK Have partners discuss their independent reading for the week. Tell them to refer to their Reading Log and paraphrase what the selection was about. To focus the discussion, prompt them to talk about one or more of the following:

Key Ideas and Details
- Who was the author? Why did he or she write the selection?
- What did I learn from this text?
- How do the characters interact with each other?

Craft and Structure
- Did I understand the main idea and why events happened?
- Did the events flow smoothly, or were they confusing?

Integration of Ideas
- Did the story seem believable? Why or why not?
- Was this book like others I have read?

 **Pearson eText**
- Student Edition
- Decodable Readers
- Leveled Readers

 **Trade Book Library**

 **Materials from School or Classroom Library**

DAY 1 at a Glance

Content Knowledge
Oral Vocabulary

Phonics/Spelling
Abbreviations

Text-Based Comprehension
Author's Purpose
Summarize

Selection Vocabulary
America, birthday, flag, freedom, nicknames, stars, stripes

Conventions
Quotation Marks

Writing
Descriptive Poem or Song

Research and Inquiry
Identify and Focus Topic

Materials

- Student Edition
- Sing with Me Big Book
- Sound-Spelling Cards
- Decodable Reader 27A
- Reader's and Writer's Notebook

Bridge to Common Core

INTEGRATION OF KNOWLEDGE/IDEAS
This week children read, write, and talk about the American flag.

Texts This Week

- "Our Flag, Our Symbol"
- "Flags"
- "Great-Grandmother's Secret"
- "America's Flag"
- *Red, White, and Blue: The Story of the American Flag*
- "Uncle Sam and Old Glory"
- "You're a Grand Old Flag"

Social Studies Knowledge Goals
Children will understand some of the traditions that honor the flag, including

- the Pledge of Allegiance
- the National Anthem
- the Fourth of July

Street Rhymes!

Let's all stand up for the red, white, and blue!
We honor its stripes and its many stars too.
It stands for America, land of the free.
Put your hand on your heart and sing with me
The song that praises the stars and stripes,
"Oh, say, can you see, by the dawn's early light."

- To introduce this week's concept, read aloud the poem several times and ask children to join you.

Content Knowledge

The American Flag

CONCEPT TALK To help children gain knowledge and understanding, tell them that this week they will talk, sing, read, and write about the flag of the United States. Write the Question of the Week, *What traditions and celebrations involve our country's flag?,* and track the print as you read it.

Build Oral Language

TALK ABOUT THE AMERICAN FLAG Have children turn to pages 392–393 in their Student Edition. Read the title and look at the photos. Use these questions to guide discussion and create a "What traditions and celebrations involve our country's flag?" concept map.

- Look at the picture of the fireworks display. What day do you think these people are celebrating? (Fourth of July) *We see our flag on the Fourth of July,* so we'll write this idea on our map.
- What celebration are the girl and her mother at? (Fourth of July parade) Let's add *We wave flags at parades* to our map.
- Now look at the picture with the large flag. Where are these people celebrating our flag? (a baseball game) People celebrate the flag at sports events and sing the National Anthem. Let's add these ideas to our map.

Common Core State Standards
Language 6. Use words and phrases acquired through conversations, reading and being read to, and responding to texts, including using adjectives and adverbs to describe (e.g., *When other kids are happy that makes me happy*).
Also Speaking/Listening 1.

Oral Vocabulary

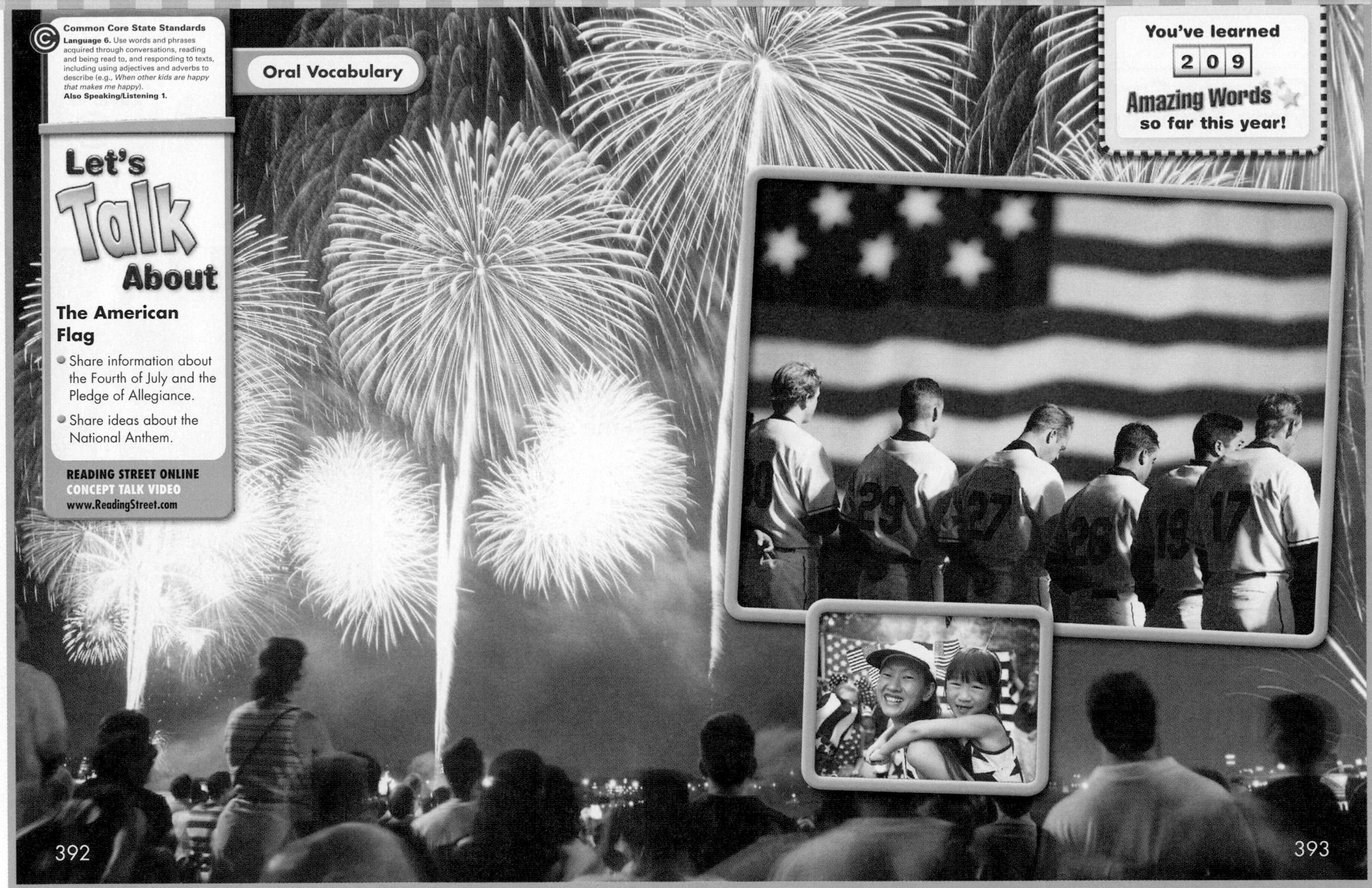

Let's Talk About
The American Flag
Share information about the Fourth of July and the Pledge of Allegiance.
Share ideas about the National Anthem.
READING STREET ONLINE
CONCEPT TALK VIDEO
www.ReadingStreet.com
You've learned 209 Amazing Words so far this year!
392
393
Student Edition, pp. 392–393

CONNECT TO READING Explain that this week, children will read about our flag in the past and about some of the traditions and celebrations that involve our flag.

What traditions and celebrations involve our country's flag?

- We see our flag on the Fourth of July.
  - We wave flags at parades.
- We celebrate our flag at sports events.
  - We sing the National Anthem.

eSTREET INTERACTIVE
www.ReadingStreet.com

- **Pearson eText**
  - Student Edition
- **Concept Talk Video**

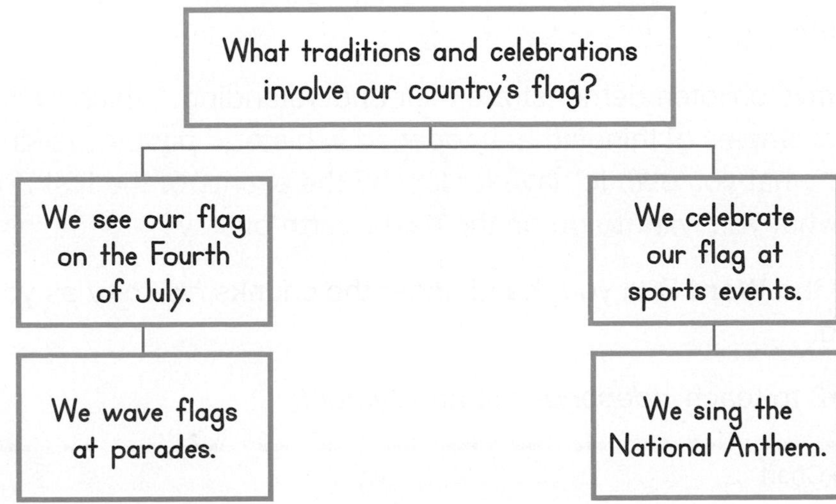

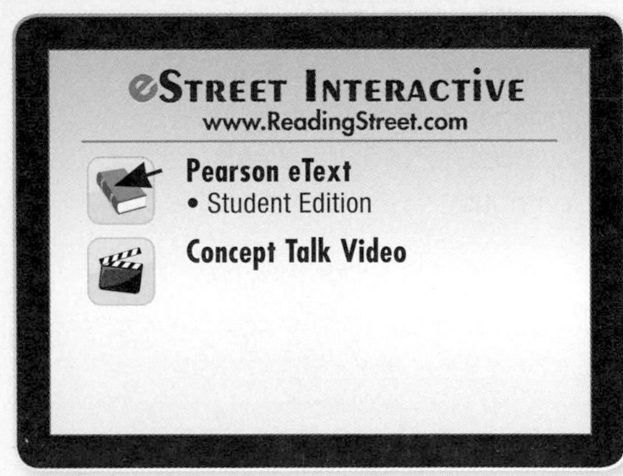

ELL

Preteach Concepts Use the Day 1 instruction on ELL Poster 27 to assess and build background knowledge, develop concepts, and build oral vocabulary.

ELL Support Additional support is provided in the *ELL Handbook* and in the ELL Support Lessons on the *Teacher Resources DVD-ROM.*

Common Core State Standards

Language 6. Use words and phrases acquired through conversations, reading and being read to, and responding to texts, including using adjectives and adverbs to describe (e.g., *When other kids are happy that makes me happy*).

Content Knowledge

Build Oral Vocabulary

INTRODUCE AMAZING WORDS Display page 27 of the *Sing with Me* Big Book. Tell children they are going to sing about the flag of our country. Ask children to listen for the Amazing Words *history, independence,* and *symbol* as you sing. Sing the song again and have children join you.

Sing with Me Big Book, p. 27

Amazing Words

You've learned 209 words so far.

You'll learn 008 words this week!

history	unfurl
independence	frayed
symbol	allegiance
patriotic	indivisible

Amazing Words — Robust Vocabulary Routine

1. **Introduce the Word** Relate the word *history* to the song. The song says we all share the history of our flag. Supply a child-friendly definition. History is everything that has happened in the past to a group of people or a country. Have children say the word.

2. **Demonstrate** Provide examples to show meaning. In school we study the *history* of the United States. George Washington was an important man in our *history.*

3. **Apply** Have children demonstrate their understanding. Which of the following are examples of things that happened in history: people walking on the moon or what you plan to have for lunch? the events of the first Fourth of July or what you want to do on the next Fourth of July?

4. **Display the Word** Run your hand under the chunks *his-tor-y* as you read the word.

See p. OV•2 to teach *independence* and *symbol.*

Routines Flip Chart

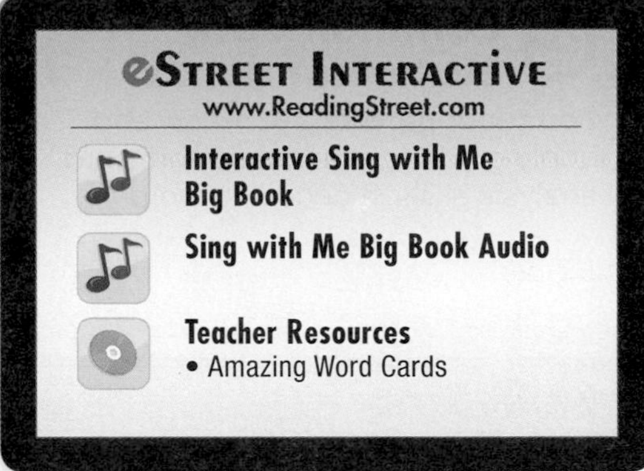

AMAZING WORDS AT WORK Have children look at the picture on page 27.

- I see children saying the Pledge of Allegiance to the flag. Why do we pledge allegiance to the flag? Use the word *symbol* in your answer. (The flag is the symbol of our country.)
- What are some things our country has that the flag stands for? Use *independence* in your answer. (Possible response: The flag stands for the independence of our country. Some children might know the stars on the flag stand for the states that make up the country.)
- We share independence. What else does the song say that we all share? Use *history* in your answer. (Possible response: We are Americans, so we share the history of the flag and the history of the United States of America.)

APPLY AMAZING WORDS Have children demonstrate their understanding of the Amazing Words by completing these sentences orally.

One thing that happened in our country's **history** is ______.

My **independence** makes me feel ______.

______ is a **symbol** of ______.

Corrective feedback | **If...** children have difficulty using the Amazing Words, **then...** remind them of the definitions and provide opportunities for children to use the words in sentences.

Access for All

Advanced

Expand Vocabulary Have children research other symbols of the United States (the bald eagle, Uncle Sam). Children may illustrate and label the symbols and then explain to the class why they are symbols.

Cognates All three Amazing Words have cognates that Spanish speakers may recognize: *historia, independencia,* and *símbolo.* Point out how this prior knowledge can help children with learning new words.

Common Core State Standards

Foundational Skills 3. Know and apply grade-level phonics and word analysis skills in decoding words.

Skills Trace

Abbreviations

Introduce U6W2D1

Practice U6W2D2; U6W2D3; U6W2D4

Reteach/Review U6W2D5; U6W3D4

Assess/Test Weekly Test U6W2
Benchmark Test U6

KEY: U=Unit W=Week D=Day

Academic Vocabulary 

abbreviation a shortened form of one word. It begins with a capital letter and ends with a period.

Phonics

Teach/Model

Abbreviations

CONNECT Write *it's* and *haven't.* Point out to children that they have already studied shortened words like these. Ask them to read the words. Explain that today they will learn how to read shortened forms of words called abbreviations.

Sound-Spelling Card 107

USE SOUND-SPELLING CARD An **abbreviation** is a shortened form of a word. Display Card 107. Point to *Ave.* This is an abbreviation for the word *avenue.* It begins with a capital letter (point to *A*) and ends with a period (point to the period).

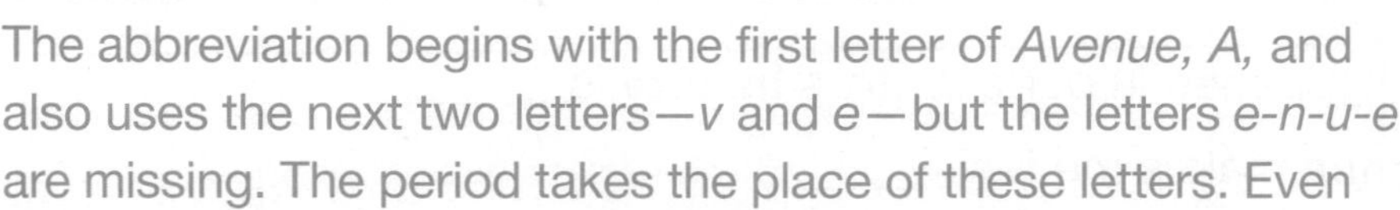

MODEL Write *Greenleaf Avenue* and below it *Greenleaf Ave.* The abbreviation begins with the first letter of *Avenue, A,* and also uses the next two letters—*v* and *e*—but the letters *e-n-u-e* are missing. The period takes the place of these letters. Even though some letters are missing, I read the abbreviation as if all the letters are there—*Greenleaf Avenue.* Have children say *Avenue* several times as you point to *Ave.* Follow this procedure to teach and model *Mr. (Mister Carlos, Mr. Carlos), Apr. (April),* and *Mon. (Monday).* Write and explain the abbreviations and pronunciations of *Mrs.* and *Ms.* as exceptions.

GROUP PRACTICE Have children read the abbreviations above with you. Then write the words and abbreviations below. Have the group read each word in the top row separately. Then point to the appropriate abbreviation. Read the abbreviation and have children echo it. Identify the capital letter, missing letters, and period. Have children tell if the abbreviation names part of an address, a person, a month, or a day.

Street	Doctor	Road	Friday	August	October	Sunday
St.	Dr.	Rd.	Fri.	Aug.	Oct.	Sun.

REVIEW What do you know about reading abbreviations? (You read the abbreviation as if all the letters of the word are there.)

Phonics

Abbreviations

Words I Can Blend

Mr.

Ave.

Dr.

Feb.

Mon.

Sentences I Can Read

1. Mr. Jones lives at 235 Elm Ave.
2. I will see Dr. Lopez on Feb. 21.
3. Our last day of school is Mon., June 8.

394

From: Ms. Sophie Martin

Subject: Oct. 14 party at 320 S. Main Ave.

Date: Thur., Sept. 29

To: Mrs. Grace Timmons; Dr. Abby Gomez; Mr. Albert Soto Jr.; Ms. Susan Nelson

Dear Friends,

Mrs. Wilson and her class at Big Hollow School are grateful to you. Without your help, our new playground would not have been built. Please come to a party to celebrate its grand opening. The party will be held at 320 S. Main Ave., on Fri., Oct. 14, from 1:00 P.M. until 3:00 P.M. We would love to see you there.

Abbreviations

395

Student Edition, pp. 394–395

Guide Practice

BLEND WORDS Have children turn to page 394 in their Student Edition. Look at the picture on this page. It shows street signs with capital *A,* lowercase *v,* lowercase *e, period* on it. That is the abbreviation for the complete word *avenue. Avenue* is another word that names a street. Even though letters are missing, we say the word as if all the letters are showing.

GUIDE PRACTICE For each word in "Words I Can Blend," ask children to say each abbreviation. You may wish to write the corresponding word for each abbreviation. Then have children blend the whole word and say the abbreviation.

Corrective feedback	**If...** children have difficulty reading an abbreviation, **then...** write the complete word for the abbreviation. Model sound-by-sound blending or the word parts strategy for decodable words. Then have children read the word and its abbreviation.

Access for All

SI Strategic Intervention

Context Explain that *Dr.* can stand for the title *doctor* or the address *drive.* Children will need to use context clues to determine which word the abbreviation represents.

Common Core State Standards

Foundational Skills 4. Read with sufficient accuracy and fluency to support comprehension. **Language 2.** Demonstrate command of the conventions of standard English capitalization, punctuation, and spelling when writing. **Language 2.e.** Consult reference materials, including beginning dictionaries, as needed to check and correct spellings.

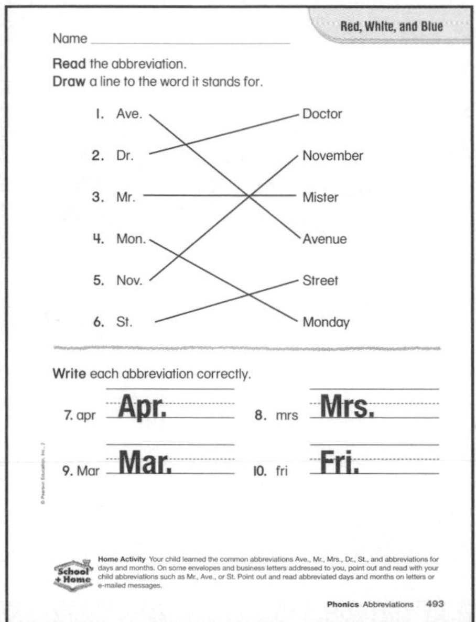

Name ____________ Red, White, and Blue

Read the abbreviation.
Draw a line to the word it stands for.

1. Ave.	Doctor
2. Dr.	November
3. Mr.	Mister
4. Mon.	Avenue
5. Nov.	Street
6. St.	Monday

Write each abbreviation correctly.

7. apr **Apr.** 8. mrs **Mrs.**
9. Mar **Mar.** 10. fri **Fri.**

School + Home **Home Activity** Your child learned the common abbreviations Ave., Mr., Mrs., Dr., St., and abbreviations for days and months. On some envelopes and business letters addressed to you, point out and read with your child abbreviations such as Mr., Ave., or St. Point out and read abbreviated days and months on letters or e-mailed messages.

Phonics Abbreviations 493

Reader's and Writer's Notebook, p. 493

Phonics

DECODE WORDS IN ISOLATION After children can successfully identify abbreviations and read the words they stand for on page 394 in their Student Edition, point to them in random order and ask children to read them naturally.

DECODE WORDS IN CONTEXT Have children read each of the sentences on page 394. Have them identify the abbreviations.

Team Talk Pair children and have them take turns reading each of the sentences aloud. Have them tell how they identify abbreviations by the capital letter and the period.

Chorally read the "I Can Read!" passage on page 395 along with the children. Then have them read the passage aloud to themselves.

ON THEIR OWN Use *Reader's and Writer's Notebook,* p. 493.

Abbreviations

FORMATIVE ASSESSMENT Write the following abbreviations and have the class read them. Notice which abbreviations children miss during the group reading. Call on individuals to read some of the words.

					Spiral Review
Mr.	**Rd.**	**Mon.**	**Oct.**	**Ave.**	
hawk	**squall**	**stalk**	**August**	**daughter** ←	Row 2 reviews *aw, au, au(gh), al.*
praised	**player**	**sailing**	**explain**	**holiday** ←	Row 3 reviews *ai, ay.*

If... children cannot read abbreviations at this point,
then... use the Small Group Time Strategic Intervention lesson, p. SG•24, to reteach abbreviations. Continue to monitor children's progress using other instructional opportunities during the week. See the Skills Trace on p. 394a.

Spelling Pretest

Abbreviations

DICTATE SPELLING WORDS Dictate the abbreviations. Have children write them. Have children check their pretests and correct misspellings. Have them use resources, such as a dictionary, to find correct spellings.

1. **Mr.** **Mr.** Chavez is my neighbor.
2. **Mrs.** **Mrs.** Knox walks her dog in the park.
3. **St.** The bus will stop on Eagle **St.** to pick us up.
4. **Jan.** We leave for vacation on **Jan.** 9.
5. **Feb.** Valentine's Day is **Feb.** 14.
6. **Aug.** School will start on **Aug.** 30 this year.
7. **Dr.** Lee went to see **Dr.** Jones when he was sick.
8. **Ms.** **Ms.** Thomas is a new teacher in our school.
9. **Rd.** The house on Beach **Rd.** is for sale.
10. **Oct.** My grandfather is coming to visit us on **Oct.** 5.
11. **Nov.** John is having a birthday party on **Nov.** 3.
12. **Dec.** **Dec.** 31 is the last day of the year.

ON THEIR OWN Use Let's Practice It!, p. 305 on the *Teacher Resources DVD-ROM.*

Access for All

 Advanced

Extend Spelling Allow children who spell words correctly to spell more challenging abbreviations, such as *Gov., Ave., Sr., Jr., Tues.,* and *Thurs.*

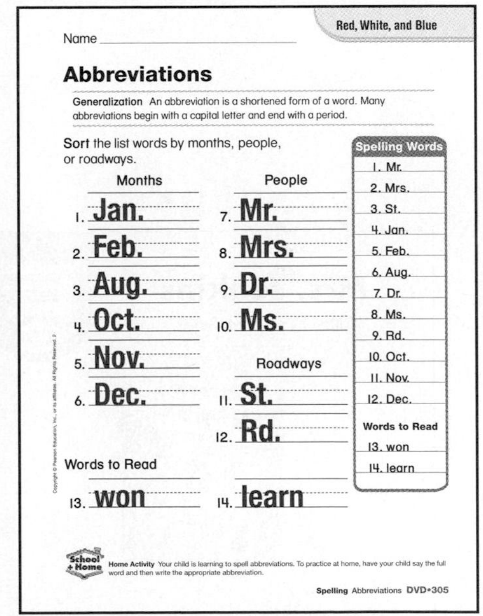

Name ______ Red, White, and Blue

Abbreviations

Generalization An abbreviation is a shortened form of a word. Many abbreviations begin with a capital letter and end with a period.

Sort the list words by months, people, or roadways.

Months
1. Jan.
2. Feb.
3. Aug.
4. Oct.
5. Nov.
6. Dec.

People
7. Mr.
8. Mrs.
9. Dr.
10. Ms.

Roadways
11. St.
12. Rd.

Words to Read
13. won
14. learn

Spelling Words: 1. Mr. 2. Mrs. 3. St. 4. Jan. 5. Feb. 6. Aug. 7. Dr. 8. Ms. 9. Rd. 10. Oct. 11. Nov. 12. Dec.
Words to Read: 13. won 14. learn

School + Home Home Activity Your child is learning to spell abbreviations. To practice at home, have your child say the full word and then write the appropriate abbreviation.

Spelling Abbreviations DVD•305

Let's Practice It! TR DVD•305

Day 1 SMALL GROUP TIME • Differentiate Phonics, p. SG•18

OL On-Level
- **Practice Phonics** Additional Abbreviations
- **Read** Decodable Reader *Mrs. Jenkins*

SI Strategic Intervention
- **Reteach Phonics** Blend Abbreviations
- **Read** Decodable Reader *Mrs. Jenkins*

A Advanced
- **Extend Phonics** More Abbreviations
- **Read** Advanced Selection for Abbreviations of Words
- **Introduce** Inquiry Project

If... children need more scaffolding and practice with **Phonics, then...** use the ELL activities on p. DI•37 in the Teacher Resources section on SuccessNet.

Common Core State Standards

Foundational Skills 3. Know and apply grade-level phonics and word analysis skills in decoding words.

Decodable Reader 27A

If children need help, then...

Read *Mrs. Jenkins*

DECODE WORDS IN ISOLATION Have children turn to page 199 in *Decodable Practice Readers* 2.2 and decode each word.

READ HIGH-FREQUENCY WORDS Have children identify and read the high-frequency words *important, mountain, bike,* and *south* on the first page.

PREVIEW DECODABLE READER Have children read the title and preview the story. Tell them they will read a story that has abbreviations.

DECODE WORDS IN CONTEXT Pair children for reading and listen as they decode. One child begins. Children read the entire story, switching readers after each page. Partners reread the story. This time the other child begins.

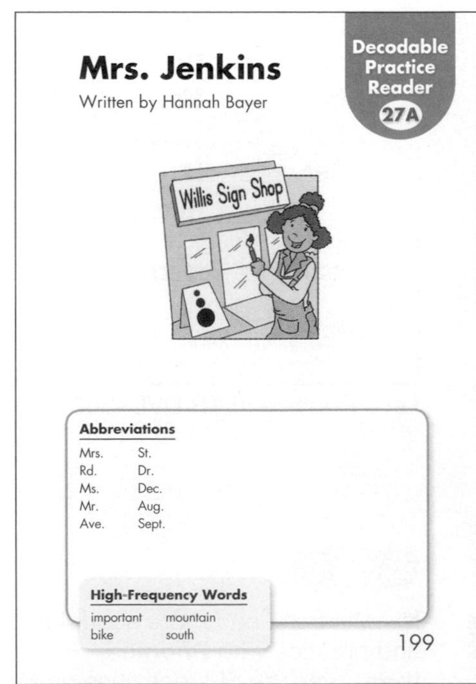

Decodable Practice Reader 27A

Mrs. Jenkins
Written by Hannah Bayer

Abbreviations

Mrs.	St.
Rd.	Dr.
Ms.	Dec.
Mr.	Aug.
Ave.	Sept.

High-Frequency Words

important	mountain
bike	south

199

Decodable Practice Reader 27A

Mrs. Rose Jenkins works at Willis Sign Shop.
Mrs. Jenkins has an important job there.
She is the dot lady.
She paints dots on signs.

200

What kind of dots?
Have you seen street signs that say "Main St." or "Mountain Rd." or other names?
Mrs. Jenkins painted those dots!

201

Have you seen mailboxes that say "Dr. Silva" or "Ms. Smith?"
The dot lady painted those dots, too.
Did she paint your mailbox?

202

Mrs. Jenkins paints dots on posters, too.
For example, have you seen a poster about a "Dec. 12" music concert?
She may have painted that dot!

203

Once Mr. Ellis replaced Mrs. Jenkins with a dot-painting machine.
That was a mistake!
It painted dots in the wrong places!

204

The machine did not know that "St." meant street or that "Aug." meant August.
Mr. Ellis sold the machine and hired Mrs. Jenkins back.
She was happy.

205

So if you see a sign that reads "Bike Race! South Maple Ave. closed to traffic on Sept. 15," remember Mrs. Jenkins.
The dot lady may have painted it!

206

Corrective feedback	**If...** children have difficulty decoding a word or an abbreviation, **then...** refer them to the Sound-Spelling Cards to identify the sounds in a decodable word; prompt them to blend the word. If the word is an abbreviation, review the abbreviation and its corresponding word. • What is the new word? • Is the new word a word you know? • Does it make sense in the story?

CHECK DECODING AND COMPREHENSION Have children retell the story to include characters, setting, and events. Then have children find abbreviations in the story. Children should supply *Mrs., St., Rd., Dr., Ms., Dec., Mr., Aug., Ave.,* and *Sept.*

Reread for Fluency

REREAD DECODABLE READER Have children reread Decodable Practice Reader 27A to develop automaticity decoding abbreviations.

Routine Oral Rereading

1. **Read** Have children read the entire book orally.
2. **Reread** To achieve optimal fluency, children should reread the text three or four times.
3. **Corrective Feedback** Listen as children read. Provide corrective feedback regarding their fluency and decoding.

Routines Flip Chart

Abbreviations

Beginning Before reading, write your name on the board. Say it, underlining the title, as you point to yourself. Guide children to find the same abbreviation in the story (*Mrs.*, p. 200; *Ms.*, p. 202; *Mr.*, p. 204). Then read that page aloud and tell children to raise their hands each time they hear the abbreviation. Preview the story to point out and say the other abbreviations.

Intermediate Write the corresponding word for each abbreviation in the story (except *Mrs.* and *Ms.*). Read each page of the story aloud as children follow along in their books. Pause after each sentence that has an abbreviation of one of the words on the board. Ask children to point to the corresponding word on the board.

Advanced After reading, have children summarize the text on each page. Every time the child says a word written as an abbreviation, tell the others to raise their hands.

Common Core State Standards

Informational Text 6. Identify the main purpose of a text, including what the author wants to answer, explain, or describe.

Skills Trace

Author's Purpose

Introduce U2W2D1; U3W1D1; U6W2D1

Practice U2W2D2; U2W2D3; U2W2D4; U3W1D2; U3W1D3; U3W1D4; U6W2D2; U6W2D3; U6W2D4

Reteach/Review U1W2D3; U2W2D5; U2W5D3; U3W1D5; U5W1D3; U6W2D5

Assess/Test Weekly Tests U2W2; U3W1; U6W2
Benchmark Tests U2; U3; U6

KEY: U=Unit W=Week D=Day

Academic Vocabulary 

topic the subject of an article

author's purpose the reason an author wrote about a topic

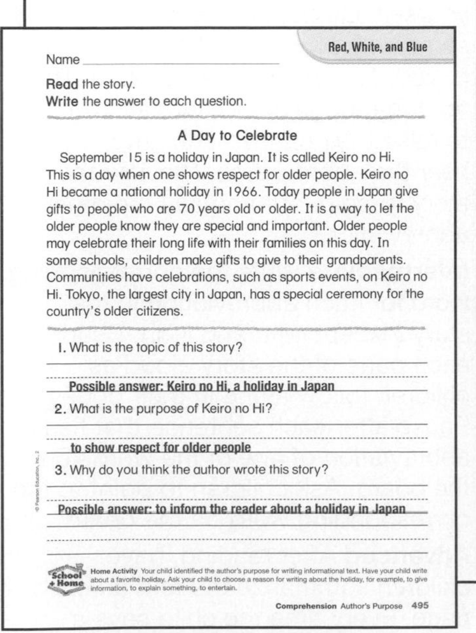

Red, White, and Blue

Name ____________

Read the story.
Write the answer to each question.

A Day to Celebrate

September 15 is a holiday in Japan. It is called Keiro no Hi. This is a day when one shows respect for older people. Keiro no Hi became a national holiday in 1966. Today people in Japan give gifts to people who are 70 years old or older. It is a way to let the older people know they are special and important. Older people may celebrate their long life with their families on this day. In some schools, children make gifts to give to their grandparents. Communities have celebrations, such as sports events, on Keiro no Hi. Tokyo, the largest city in Japan, has a special ceremony for the country's older citizens.

1. What is the topic of this story?
Possible answer: Keiro no Hi, a holiday in Japan

2. What is the purpose of Keiro no Hi?
to show respect for older people

3. Why do you think the author wrote this story?
Possible answer: to inform the reader about a holiday in Japan

School + Home **Home Activity** Your child identified the author's purpose for writing informational text. Have your child write about a favorite holiday. Ask your child to choose a reason for writing about the holiday, for example, to give information, to explain something, to entertain.

Comprehension Author's Purpose 495

Reader's and Writer's Notebook, pp. 495 and 503

Zoom in on

Text-Based Comprehension

Author's Purpose

Summarize

READ Remind children of the weekly concept—the American Flag. Have children follow along as you read "Flags" on page 397 of the Student Edition.

MODEL A CLOSE READ Demonstrate close reading for children. Before I begin reading, I read the title and look at the pictures. Have children follow along as you read the first paragraph of "Flags." In the first paragraph, the author tells me that a flag is a symbol. This information along with the title and the pictures gives me clues about what the **topic** of the article might be. I will continue reading to see what the author tells me next. I'll also look for parts of the article that help me decide if the **author's purpose** is to entertain, to describe, or to explain.

INTRODUCE Have children read p. 396. Explain that the skill of author's purpose and the strategy of summarizing are tools they can use to deepen their understanding. Review the bulleted items and explanations on p. 396. Then have children use a graphic organizer like the one shown to identify the author's purpose for writing the article.

IDENTIFY TEXT EVIDENCE Have children reread "Flags" using the callouts as guides. Then ask volunteers to respond to the callouts, citing specific examples from the text to support their answers.

APPLY Use *Reader's and Writer's Notebook,* pp. 495 and 503 for additional practice with identifying author's purpose. Children may also turn to pp. EI•2 and EI•25 to review the skill and strategy if necessary.

Comprehension Skill

Author's Purpose

- An author has a purpose, or reason, for writing.
- An author might write to entertain, to describe, or to explain.
- As you read "Flags," use a chart like this to identify the topic and explain the author's purpose.

Topic	Author's Purpose

Comprehension Strategy

Summarize

A summary is a brief retelling of a paragraph or a story. You summarize by telling only the most important ideas in your own words. Summarizing as you read can help you remember main events. It is a strategy that good readers use to check their understanding.

396

Flags

A flag is a piece of cloth. But it is much more. A flag is a symbol. It can stand for a country.

A flag sends a message. Each color and picture on a flag tells something. The color red stands for courage. The color white stands for peace. The color blue stands for freedom. The flags of the United States, France, and Laos are red, white, and blue.

Many flags have pictures. A picture of an eagle might stand for freedom. The flags of Egypt and Ecuador each have an eagle on them. Other flags, like the U.S. flag, have stars. The flag of China has five stars. The flag of Ghana has one big star. The Turkish flag has a star and the shape of the moon.

The flags of Canada, the United States, and Mexico use different colors and symbols.

Strategy Summarize this paragraph in your own words.

Skill Explain why the author wrote this text.

Your Turn!

Need a Review? See the *Envision It! Handbook* for additional help with author's purpose and summarize.

Ready to Try It? As you read *Red, White, and Blue,* use what you learned to help you understand the text.

397

Student Edition, pp. 396–397

Model Fluent Reading

ACCURACY Have children listen as you model how to read paragraphs 1 and 2 of "Flags" without mistakes. Then have children reread paragraphs 1 and 2.

Routine Paired Reading

1. **Reread** To achieve optimal fluency, have partners reread the text three or four times.
2. **Corrective Feedback** Listen as children read. Provide corrective feedback regarding their fluency and decoding.

Routines Flip Chart

eSTREET INTERACTIVE
www.ReadingStreet.com

Pearson eText
- Student Edition

Teacher Resources
- Reader's and Writer's Notebook

Envision It! Animations

Skills/Strategies

Strategy A flag's colors and pictures send a message. Different countries use red, white, and blue on their flags to stand for courage, peace, and freedom.

Skill The author wrote this text to explain about flags as symbols.

Common Core State Standards

Informational Text 4. Determine the meaning of words and phrases in a text relevant to a grade 2 topic or subject area. **Language 2.** Demonstrate command of the conventions of standard English capitalization, punctuation, and spelling when writing.

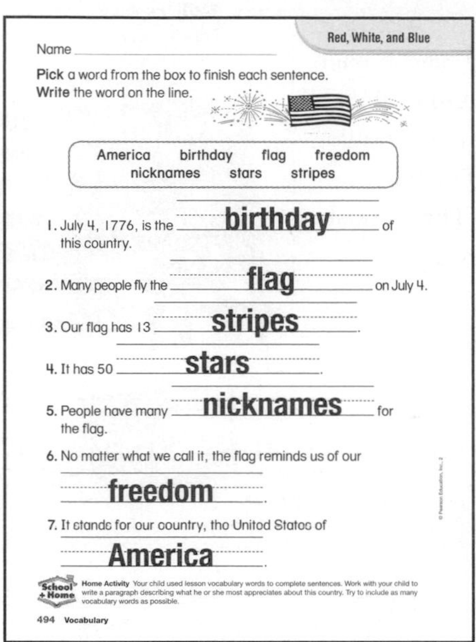

Name ____________ Red, White, and Blue

Pick a word from the box to finish each sentence. **Write** the word on the line.

America birthday flag freedom nicknames stars stripes

1. July 4, 1776, is the **birthday** of this country.
2. Many people fly the **flag** on July 4.
3. Our flag has 13 **stripes**.
4. It has 50 **stars**.
5. People have many **nicknames** for the flag.
6. No matter what we call it, the flag reminds us of our **freedom**.
7. It stands for our country, the United States of **America**.

Home Activity Your child used lesson vocabulary words to complete sentences. Work with your child to write a paragraph describing what he or she most appreciates about this country. Try to include as many vocabulary words as possible.

494 Vocabulary

Reader's and Writer's Notebook, p. 494

Selection Vocabulary

Use the following routine to introduce this week's tested selection vocabulary.

America the United States of America

birthday the day that somebody was born or something began, usually celebrated yearly

flag a piece of cloth, usually with square corners, with a picture or pattern that stands for a place or country

freedom the condition of not being under someone else's control

nicknames names used instead of real names

stars shapes that have five or more points

stripes long, narrow bands of color

SEE IT/SAY IT Write *America.* Scan across the word with your finger as you say it: A-mer-i-ca.

HEAR IT Use the word in a sentence. Fifty states make up America.

DEFINE IT Elicit definitions from children. How would you tell another child what *America* is? Clarify or give a definition when necessary. Yes, *America* is "the United States of America." Restate the word in child-friendly terms. America is the country we live in.

Team Talk What makes America a great country to live in? Turn to your partner and talk about this. Be prepared to explain your answers. Allow children time to discuss. Ask for examples. Rephrase their examples for usage when necessary or to correct misunderstandings.

MAKE CONNECTIONS Have children discuss the word. Where are some places in America you would like to visit? Turn and talk to your partner about this. Then be prepared to share. Have children share. Rephrase their ideas for usage when necessary or to correct misunderstandings.

RECORD Have children write the word and its meaning.

Continue this routine to introduce the remaining words in this manner.

ON THEIR OWN Use *Reader's and Writer's Notebook,* p. 494.

Corrective feedback	**If...** children are having difficulty understanding, **then...** review the definitions in small groups.

Conventions

Quotation Marks

MAKE CONNECTIONS Write the following sentence from *Just Like Josh Gibson* on the board. *The umpire pointed at Josh and said, "You're out yesterday in Pittsburgh!"* Look at the sentence. What did the umpire say? Point to the quotation marks. We know what the umpire said because the words are surrounded by quotation marks.

TEACH Explain that words the characters say to each other in a story are called **dialogue. Quotation marks** show the exact words a character says, or the words a person says in real life, such as *Trent said, "I like dogs."*

MODEL Display Grammar Transparency 27. Read the definition aloud. Model identifying where to put the quotation marks in each example. Then read the directions and model number 1.

GUIDE PRACTICE Continue with items 2–6, having children identify where quotation marks should be placed in each sentence.

APPLY Write the following sentences on the board. Have the class read the sentences orally. Then ask children where the quotation marks should go.

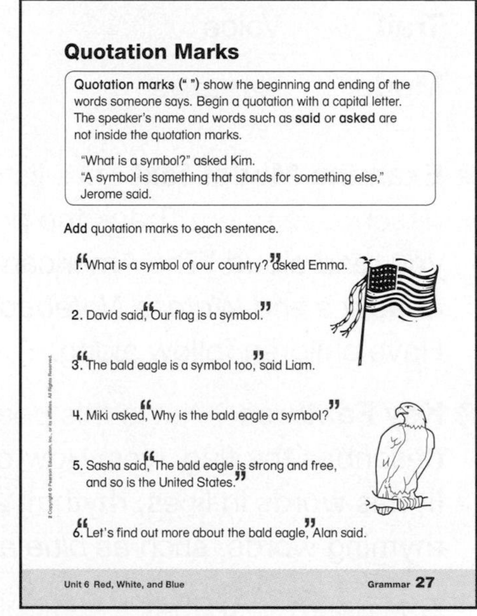

Quotation Marks

Quotation marks (" ") show the beginning and ending of the words someone says. Begin a quotation with a capital letter. The speaker's name and words such as **said** or **asked** are not inside the quotation marks.

"What is a symbol?" asked Kim.
"A symbol is something that stands for something else," Jerome said.

Add quotation marks to each sentence.

1. "What is a symbol of our country?" asked Emma.
2. David said, "Our flag is a symbol."
3. "The bald eagle is a symbol too," said Liam.
4. Miki asked, "Why is the bald eagle a symbol?"
5. Sasha said, "The bald eagle is strong and free, and so is the United States."
6. "Let's find out more about the bald eagle," Alan said.

Unit 6 Red, White, and Blue — Grammar 27

Grammar Transparency 27 TR DVD

1. **Dr. Martin Luther King Jr. said, I have a dream.**
2. **There's no place like home, said Dorothy.**

Team Talk Pair children and have them take turns making a brief statement about their favorite sport or activity. Have partners work together to write these statements as dialogue, adding clue words, such as *Ella said,* and quotation marks. Have children share examples with the class.

eSTREET INTERACTIVE
www.ReadingStreet.com

Teacher Resources
- Daily Fix-It Transparency
- Grammar Transparency

Access for All

A Advanced

Sentence Production Allow children who demonstrate an understanding of quotation marks to share examples of dialogue with the class by writing them on the board.

Academic Vocabulary 

dialogue written conversation

quotation marks the punctuation marks (" ") used to indicate the beginning and end of a speaker's exact words

Daily Fix-It

1. Hour flag has stars and strips.
   Our flag has stars and stripes.
2. We will cook diner for thanksgiving.
   We will cook dinner for Thanksgiving.

Discuss the Daily Fix-It corrections with children. Review homophones, CVCe words, the capitalization of proper nouns, and the spelling of *dinner.*

Dialogue To help children locate a speaker's words in a sentence, point out that words such as *said, asked,* and *shouted* usually are found just before or after the speaker's words.

Options for Conventions Support To provide children with practice with quotation marks, use the lesson on p. 350 in the *ELL Handbook.*

DAY 1

Common Core State Standards

Literature 4. Describe how words and phrases (e.g., regular beats, alliteration, rhymes, repeated lines) supply rhythm and meaning in a story, poem, or song. **Writing 3.** Write narratives in which they recount a well-elaborated event or short sequence of events, include details to describe actions, thoughts, and feelings, use temporal words to signal event order, and provide a sense of closure.

Bridge to Common Core

TEXT TYPES AND PURPOSES

This week children write a descriptive poem or song about an American symbol.

Narrative Writing

Through reading and discussion, children will gain a deeper understanding of the American flag. They will use the knowledge from the texts to write and support a descriptive poem or song.

Throughout the week, children will improve the range and content of their writing through daily mini-lessons.

5-Day Plan

DAY 1	Read Like a Writer
DAY 2	Description
DAY 3	Writer's Craft: Express Feelings
DAY 4	Revise: Rearranging Words in Sentences
DAY 5	Proofread

Writing Zoom in on

Descriptive Poem or Song

Mini-Lesson Read Like a Writer

- **Introduce** This week you will write a descriptive poem or song. A descriptive poem or song tells about a topic using clear description and expresses a feeling.

  Prompt Think about American symbols and traditions. Now write a poem or song about one of those symbols or traditions.

  Trait Voice

  Mode Narrative

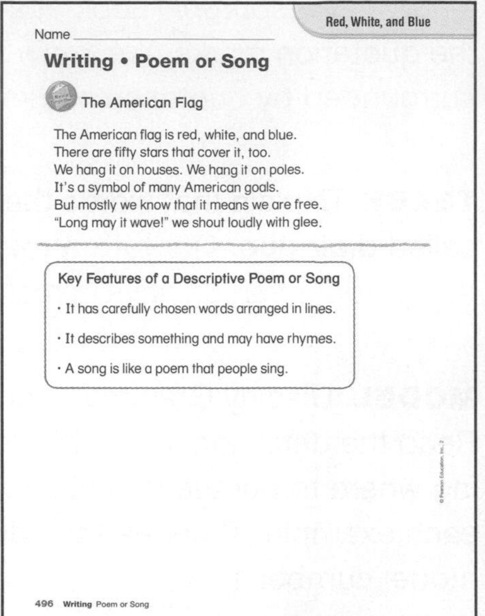
Red, White, and Blue

Name

Writing • Poem or Song

The American Flag

The American flag is red, white, and blue.
There are fifty stars that cover it, too.
We hang it on houses. We hang it on poles.
It's a symbol of many American goals.
But mostly we know that it means we are free.
"Long may it wave!" we shout loudly with glee.

Key Features of a Descriptive Poem or Song

- It has carefully chosen words arranged in lines.
- It describes something and may have rhymes.
- A song is like a poem that people sing.

496 Writing Poem or Song

Reader's and Writer's Notebook, p. 496

- **Examine Model Text** Let's listen to a descriptive poem. Track the print as you read aloud "The American Flag" on *Reader's and Writer's Notebook,* p. 496. Have children follow along.

- **Key Features** What is this poem about? (the American flag) Ask if the poem describes the flag. (yes) How do you know "The American Flag" is a poem? (It has words in lines, rhythm, and rhyming words.) Help children circle rhyming words, such as *blue* and *too,* and clap the rhythm.

  This poem describes a symbol of the United States—the American flag. It uses words that help you see what the flag looks like.

  In the poem, the author shares his or her feelings for the flag. The author uses the words *shout* and *glee.* There is a quote, too. What feeling is the author sharing? (pride)

- **Model Free Verse** Write this free verse poem on the board and read it aloud.

  The Pledge
  We stand,
  Hands over our hearts,
  And pledge allegiance.
  We're proud to be Americans.

  What does this poem describe? (saying the Pledge of Allegiance) How does this poem differ from the one on the transparency? (It is shorter and does not have rhyme or a regular rhythm.)

Review Key Features

Review key features of a descriptive **poem** or song with children. You may want to post these key features in the classroom to allow children to refer to them as they work on their poem.

Key Features of a Descriptive Poem or Song

- has carefully chosen words arranged in lines
- describes something and may have rhymes
- A song is like a poem that people sing.
- A free verse poem may not have rhyme or a regular rhythm.

Connect to Familiar Texts

Use examples from "Our Flag, Our Symbol" (*Sing with Me* Big Book) or another song or poem familiar to children. Point out that "Our Flag, Our Symbol," is a song. Explain that it is a poem, too. The words form a rhythm, and they are organized in lines. The song describes the American flag and expresses a love of the flag. Point out the rhyming words *country, free, history,* and *me.*

Remind children that they have read a descriptive poem written in free verse. Have them turn to pages 252–253 in their Student Edition and reread "Fishermen." Point out that this descriptive poem is organized in lines but does not have rhyme or a regular rhythm.

Routine Quick Write for Fluency

Team Talk

1. **Talk** Read these questions aloud, and have children respond.
   What is one of your favorite American symbols or traditions?
   What makes this symbol or tradition special?
2. **Write** Have children write sentences to answer the questions. Tell children to use words that clearly describe their topic.
3. **Share** Partners can read their sentences, or couplets, to one another and identity rhyming words.

Routines Flip Chart

Write Guy *by Jeff Anderson*

Let Me Check My List

Encourage children to keep lists of words they come across that are exciting or interesting to them. They can use their lists to increase their vocabulary and incorporate the words in their own writing. This is a great way to improve vocabulary and word choice.

Academic Vocabulary 

poem an expressive, imaginative piece of writing often arranged in lines having rhythm and rhyme. In a poem, the patterns made by the sounds of the words have special importance.

Common Core State Standards

Speaking/Listening 1. Participate in collaborative conversations with diverse partners about grade 2 topics and texts with peers and adults in small and larger groups.

21st Century Skills

Internet Guy *Don Leu*

Weekly Inquiry Project

STEP 1	Identify and Focus Topic
STEP 2	Research Skill
STEP 3	Gather and Record Information
STEP 4	Synthesize
STEP 5	Communicate

Research and Inquiry

Step 1 Identify and Focus Topic

TEACH Display and review the concept web that explores this week's question: *What traditions and celebrations involve our country's flag?* What ideas about our country's traditions and celebrations would you like to learn more about? Ask children to share their interests. Help them identify celebrations in the United States that use the flag.

Think Aloud **MODEL** Our country has many celebrations. We use the flag at many of them. One way to learn about them is to ask questions and then look for the answers. For example, we might begin by asking on which holidays we use the flag. I'll record that question.

GUIDE PRACTICE Give children time to think about questions that, when answered, would help them learn more about celebrations that use the American flag. Record questions in a chart.

Topic: Celebrations That Use the American Flag

Question	Answer
On which holidays do we use the American flag?	

Wrap Up Your Day!

✔ **Phonics: Abbreviations** Write *Mr.* and *Rd.* Ask children to read the abbreviations and use them in example sentences.

✔ **Spelling: Abbreviations** Have children write abbreviations for *Doctor, Street,* and *January.*

✔ **Content Knowledge** Have children recall the *Sing with Me* song "Our Flag, Our Symbol." Why is the our flag part of important traditions in our country? (Possible response: The flag stands for freedom and independence.)

✔ **Homework** Send home this week's Family Times Newsletter from Let's Practice It!, pp. 301–302 on the *Teacher Resources DVD-ROM.*

Name

Family Times

You are your child's first and best teacher!

This week we're

Reading Red, White, and Blue: The Story of the American Flag

Talking About What our flag means

Learning About Abbreviations, Author's Purpose

1

Let's Practice It!
TR DVD•301–302

Tell children that tomorrow they will read about how the flag became part of our tradition.

DAY 2 at a Glance

Content Knowledge
Oral Vocabulary

Phonics/Spelling
Abbreviations

Selection Vocabulary
America, birthday, flag, freedom, nicknames, stars, stripes
Multiple-Meaning Words

Text-Based Comprehension
Author's Purpose
Summarize

Conventions
Quotation Marks

Writing
Descriptive Poem or Song
Writing Trait: Voice

Handwriting
Cursive *B, P, R, T, F*/Letter Smoothness

Research and Inquiry
Research Skill: Chart

Materials

- Student Edition
- Sing with Me Big Book
- Read Aloud Anthology
- Sound-Spelling Cards
- Reader's and Writer's Notebook

Common Core State Standards

Speaking/Listening 2. Recount or describe key ideas or details from a text read aloud or information presented orally or through other media. **Language 6.** Use words and phrases acquired through conversations, reading and being read to, and responding to texts, including using adjectives and adverbs to describe (e.g., *When other kids are happy that makes me happy*).

Content Knowledge

The American Flag

EXPAND THE CONCEPT To reinforce concepts and to focus children's attention, have them sing "Our Flag, Our Symbol" from the *Sing with Me* Big Book. In the song we sing that our flag is a symbol. What is our flag a symbol of? (The flag is a symbol of our country and our independence.)

Build Oral Language

INTRODUCE AMAZING WORDS Display the *Read Aloud Anthology* story "Great-Grandmother's Secret." Read the title and identify the author. Explain that in the story, the author uses some Amazing Words. Read the story and have children listen for the word *patriotic.*

"Great-Grandmother's Secret"

TALK ABOUT SENTENCES AND WORDS Reread this sentence from the story.

"I want to hang our flag and be patriotic like everyone else," replied William.

- Have children repeat the sentence with you. What does *I want to hang our flag* and *be patriotic* mean? (The speaker wants to hang the flag to show support of his country.)
- **Team Talk** What other words could we use in place of *patriotic?* Have children share their suggestions.
- After children have tried other words, ask: Why do you think the author chose the word *patriotic?* (The author wanted a word that strongly expresses pride in country.)
- **Team Talk** Turn to your partner and talk about ways people can show they are patriotic.

Build Oral Vocabulary

Amazing Words Robust Vocabulary Routine

1. **Introduce the Word** Relate the word *patriotic* to the story. William wants to hang the flag and be *patriotic.* Supply a child-friendly definition. People who love and are loyal to their country are *patriotic.* Have children say the word.
2. **Demonstrate** Provide examples to show meaning. It is *patriotic* to defend your country. People who work to improve their country are *patriotic.*
3. **Apply** Have children demonstrate their understanding. How might people show they are *patriotic?*
4. **Display the Word** Run your hand under the four syllables *pa-tri-ot-ic* as you read the word.

See p. OV•2 to teach *unfurl.*

Routines Flip Chart

ADD TO THE CONCEPT MAP Discuss flag traditions and celebrations children have read about.

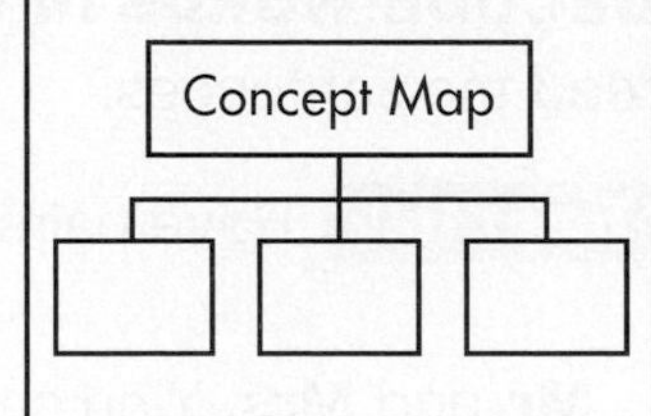

- In "Great-Grandmother's Secret," what did William want to do? (He wanted to fly the flag on the Fourth of July.) He wanted to fly it because everyone else was flying it from their homes and cars. We can add *People fly flags from homes and cars* under our Fourth of July box.
- What flag did his great-grandmother give to William to fly? (the flag that had been draped over her husband's casket) Let's add this as another important tradition: *We drape the flag over the caskets of soldiers.*
- What had William's mother done with their old flag? (His mother had given it to the American Legion to be disposed of properly.) Also, his great-grandmother's flag had been carefully folded in a triangle. We'll add *The flag is handled in special ways* to our map.

Amazing Words

history	unfurl
independence	frayed
symbol	allegiance
patriotic	indivisible

Access for All

SI Strategic Intervention

Word Part Strategy Break the word *unfurl* into its word parts: *un* and *furl.* Remind children that the prefix *un-* can mean "to do the opposite of; to undo." *Furl* means "to roll up." Ask children to put the meanings of the parts together to define *unfurl.*

ELL

Reinforce Vocabulary Use the Day 2 instruction on ELL Poster 27 to teach selection vocabulary and discuss the lesson concept.

Common Core State Standards

Language 2. Demonstrate command of the conventions of standard English capitalization, punctuation, and spelling when writing. **Language 2.e.** Consult reference materials, including beginning dictionaries, as needed to check and correct spellings.

Phonics

Review Contractions

Abbreviations

REVIEW SOUND-SPELLINGS Review reading contractions using Sound-Spelling Cards 110, 111, 112, and 114 and reading abbreviations using Sound-Spelling Card 107.

DECODE WORDS IN ISOLATION Display these contractions and abbreviations. Have the class identify them as contractions or abbreviations and read them aloud. Then point to the words in random order and ask children to read them quickly.

Dr.	**he's**	**St.**
I'm	**wasn't**	**Apr.**
she'll	**Mon.**	**Dec.**

Corrective feedback | Model identifying and reading contractions and abbreviations and then ask children to read them with you.

DECODE WORDS IN CONTEXT Display these sentences. Have the class read the sentences.

Team Talk Have pairs take turns reading the sentences naturally.

Mr. and **Mrs.** Ying can't go to the beach until **Fri., Aug. 5.**

I'll walk to the park on Post **Ave.** this **Sun.** if **it's** sunny.

Ms. Jones **doesn't** want to go to the game **Nov.** 9 if her daughter **isn't** playing.

Spelling

Abbreviations

GUIDE PRACTICE Remind children that the words on the spelling list are abbreviations. Review that many abbreviations begin with a capital letter and end with a period. Tell children that you will either say the complete word for an abbreviation or, for titles, you will segment the sounds. They should repeat the sounds in each word, think about its abbreviation, and write the abbreviation. Check the spelling of each abbreviation before saying the next one. Have children use resources such as a dictionary to find correct spellings.

1. February **Feb.**
2. August **Aug.**
3. /m/ /i/ /s/ /t/ /ər/ **Mr.**
4. Street **St.**
5. January **Jan.**
6. /m/ /i/ /z/ **Ms.**
7. December **Dec.**
8. /d/ /o/ /k/ /t/ /ər/ **Dr.**
9. October **Oct.**
10. Road **Rd.**
11. November **Nov.**
12. /m/ /i/ /s/ /i/ /z/ **Mrs.**

ON THEIR OWN Use *Reader's and Writer's Notebook,* p. 497.

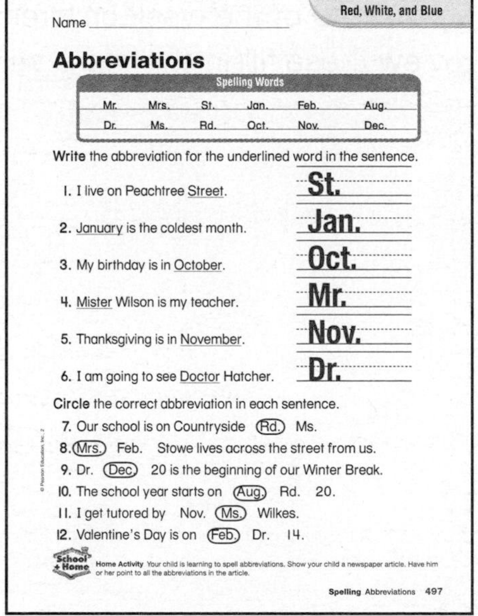

Red, White, and Blue

Name

Abbreviations

Spelling Words					
Mr.	Mrs.	St.	Jan.	Feb.	Aug.
Dr.	Ms.	Rd.	Oct.	Nov.	Dec.

Write the abbreviation for the underlined word in the sentence.

1. I live on Peachtree Street. **St.**
2. January is the coldest month. **Jan.**
3. My birthday is in October. **Oct.**
4. Mister Wilson is my teacher. **Mr.**
5. Thanksgiving is in November. **Nov.**
6. I am going to see Doctor Hatcher. **Dr.**

Circle the correct abbreviation in each sentence.

7. Our school is on Countryside (Rd.) Ms.
8. (Mrs.) Feb. Stowe lives across the street from us.
9. Dr. (Dec) 20 is the beginning of our Winter Break.
10. The school year starts on (Aug.) Rd. 20.
11. I get tutored by Nov. (Ms.) Wilkes.
12. Valentine's Day is on (Feb.) Dr. 14.

School + Home **Home Activity** Your child is learning to spell abbreviations. Show your child a newspaper article. Have him or her point to all the abbreviations in the article.

Spelling Abbreviations 497

Reader's and Writer's Notebook, p. 497

Professional Development

Labeling classroom items such as calendars and photographs with abbreviations for the names of titles, days of the week, and months of the year can help children become accustomed to their use. Have children go on a hunt to find the abbreviations. Have them record the abbreviations and read them.

Spelling Capitalization In languages such as Spanish, French, and Portuguese, the days and months are not usually capitalized. Provide practice with this English spelling convention.

Common Core State Standards

Informational Text 4. Determine the meaning of words and phrases in a text relevant to a grade 2 topic or subject area. **Language 4.d.** Use knowledge of the meaning of individual words to predict the meaning of compound words (e.g., *birdhouse, lighthouse, housefly; bookshelf, notebook, bookmark*).

Selection Vocabulary

ACTIVATE PRIOR KNOWLEDGE Display the selection words and discuss what children already know about them.

Write incomplete sentences, such as those below. Have children identify the word that completes each sentence. Children may need to use the glossary.

- A _______ flies on a flagpole in front of the school. (flag)
- We celebrate our country's _______ on July 4. (birthday)
- People living in the thirteen colonies wanted _______ from English rule. (freedom)
- The American flag has red and white _______. (stripes)
- The American flag has fifty white ________. (stars)
- People come from many different countries to live in _______. (America)
- We can look at a list of state _______ to see that Delaware is also called *The First State.* (nicknames)

REVIEW Explain that *birthday* is a compound word. Have children identify the two words in the compound word *(birth* and *day).* Ask if the two smaller words help them understand the compound word.

By the end of the week children should know the selection words. Have them review these fill-in-the-blank sentences and create their own with a partner.

MONITOR PROGRESS Check Selection Vocabulary/ High-Frequency Words

FORMATIVE ASSESSMENT Write the following words and have the class read them. Listen for children who miss words during the reading. Call on those children to read some of the words individually.

				Spiral Review
freedom	stars	flag	nicknames	Rows 3 and 4 review previously taught high-frequency words.
America	birthday	stripes		
picture	school	answer	faraway ←	
parents	wash	company	←	

If... children cannot read these words,

then... use the Small Group Time Strategic Intervention lesson, p. SG•25, to reteach the words. Monitor children's fluency with these words during reading and provide additional practice.

Access for All

SI Strategic Intervention

Illustrate It Write the selection vocabulary on separate sheets of drawing paper. Distribute a word to each child. Have children draw a picture on the back of the paper to illustrate the word. Then have children take turns showing their pictures to the class. The first child to identify the word goes next.

Visual Support Write these selection words: *America, flag, stars,* and *stripes.* Point to each word and say it. Then point to a United States map, flag, or design on the flag to support understanding. Repeat the process and have children echo the word.

Multilingual Vocabulary Lists Children can apply knowledge of their home languages to acquire new English vocabulary by using the Multilingual Vocabulary Lists (*ELL Handbook,* pages 429–440).

Common Core State Standards

Language 4. Determine or clarify the meaning of unknown and multiple-meaning words and phrases based on grade 2 reading and content, choosing flexibly from an array of strategies. **Language 4.a.** Use sentence-level context as a clue to the meaning of a word or phrase.

Selection Vocabulary

America the United States of America

birthday the day someone was born or something began, usually celebrated every year

flag a piece of cloth, usually with square corners, with a picture or pattern that stands for a place or a country

freedom the condition of not being under someone else's control

nicknames names used instead of real names

stars shapes that have five or more points

stripes long, narrow bands of color

Bridge to Common Core

VOCABULARY ACQUISITION AND USE

As children interact with this week's selection words, they are learning academic vocabulary and domain-specific words they will encounter as they read and write in school and beyond. Teaching how to use context clues to help determine or clarify the meanings of multiple-meaning words will help children gain independence as they encounter multiple-meaning words in other contexts.

Vocabulary Skill

Multiple-Meaning Words

TEACH Explain that some words have more than one meaning. Discuss how readers can use context clues—the words and sentences around a word—to decide which meaning is relevant in a particular sentence. Refer children to Words! on p. W•7 in the Student Edition for additional practice. Then read "America's Flag" on p. 399 with children.

Think Aloud

MODEL Write on the board: *The flag has stars and stripes on it.* The word *stars* can mean "small, bright objects in the night sky." It can mean "five-pointed shapes." It can also mean "famous people, like movie actors." I can tell that in this sentence the relevant meaning is "five-pointed shapes" because the flag has those shapes on it.

GUIDE PRACTICE Write these sentences on the board: *We saw three stars walk into the movie. We saw three stars shining brightly.* Have children identify the context clues that show which meaning of *stars* is relevant in each sentence.

ON THEIR OWN Read "America's Flag" on page 399. Have children identify other multiple-meaning words and use the context clues to determine their relevant meanings. Then have them use context clues to determine the meanings of the other Words to Know. For additional practice, use *Reader's and Writer's Notebook,* p. 498.

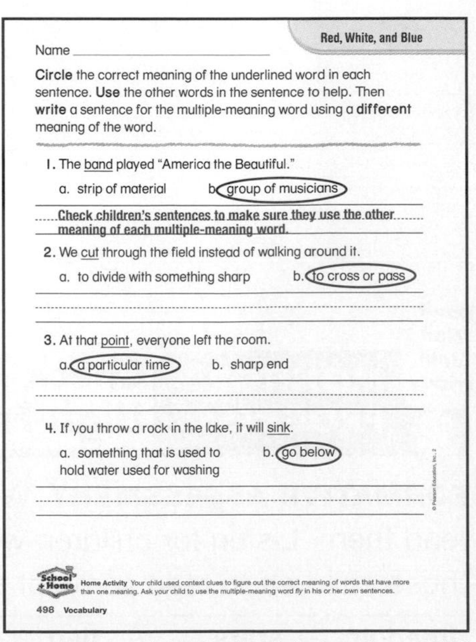

Red, White, and Blue

Name ____________

Circle the correct meaning of the underlined word in each sentence. **Use** the other words in the sentence to help. Then **write** a sentence for the multiple-meaning word using a **different** meaning of the word.

1. The band played "America the Beautiful."
   a. strip of material b. group of musicians

   Check children's sentences to make sure they use the other meaning of each multiple-meaning word.
2. We cut through the field instead of walking around it.
   a. to divide with something sharp b. to cross or pass
3. At that point, everyone left the room.
   a. a particular time b. sharp end
4. If you throw a rock in the lake, it will sink.
   a. something that is used to hold water used for washing b. go below

School + Home **Home Activity** Your child used context clues to figure out the correct meaning of words that have more than one meaning. Ask your child to use the multiple-meaning word *fly* in his or her own sentences.

© Pearson Education, Inc., 2

498 Vocabulary

Reader's and Writer's Notebook, p. 498

Vocabulary Strategy for

Multiple-Meaning Words

Context Clues While reading, you may come across a word that has more than one meaning. For example, *bat* means "a stick used to hit a ball." *Bat* also means "a flying animal." You can use context clues to determine the relevant meaning.

1. Try the meaning you know. Does it make sense? If not, the word may have more than one meaning.
2. Read on and look at the nearby words. Can you figure out the meaning from the context?
3. Try the new meaning in a sentence. Does it make sense?

Read "America's Flag." Use context clues to find the relevant meaning of the multiple-meaning words.

Words to Write Reread "America's Flag." Write about what the flag means to you. Use words from the *Words to Know* list.

398

AMERICA'S FLAG

We call it the Red, White, and Blue. We call it the Stars and Stripes too. These are nicknames for the American flag. You can probably guess why people call the flag by those names. Look at the picture of the flag. What colors do you see? You see red, white, and blue. What patterns do you see? You see stars and stripes.

People hang the flag outside their homes on special holidays such as the Fourth of July. That is our country's birthday.

On that day long ago, the American colonies declared their freedom from England. But you don't have to wait for a holiday. You can fly your flag anytime you want. When you look at it, think of what it stands for—America and freedom.

Your Turn!

Need a Review? For more help with context clues and multiple-meaning words, see *Words!* on pp. W•7 and W•10.

Ready to Try It? Read *Red, White, and Blue* on pp. 400–417.

399

Student Edition, pp. 398–399

Reread for Fluency

Have children reread paragraph 3 of "America's Flag."

Routine Paired Reading

1. **Reread** To achieve optimal fluency, have partners reread the text three or four times.
2. **Corrective Feedback** Listen as children read. Provide corrective feedback regarding their fluency and decoding.

Routines Flip Chart

eStreet Interactive
www.ReadingStreet.com

Pearson eText
- Student Edition

Teacher Resources
- Envision It! Pictured Vocabulary Cards
- Tested Vocabulary Cards
- Reader's and Writer's Notebook

Zoom in on

Text-Based Comprehension

Introduce Main Selection

Student Edition, pp. 400–401

GENRE Informational text often gives facts about real people, places, and events. In some informational texts the facts given reflect history or the traditions of communities. As they read *Red, White, and Blue,* ask children to look for facts that describe the history of the American flag.

PREVIEW AND PREDICT Have children identify the title of the selection, the author, and the illustrator. Help children activate prior knowledge and use what they know and the title of the selection to predict some of the traditions or ways people use the American flag.

PURPOSE By analyzing *Red, White, and Blue,* children learn about the American flag.

SUMMARIZE Good readers stop to **summarize** to check their understanding of what they are reading. Summarizing helps them identify the most important information in a selection. Have children turn to page EI•25 in their Student Edition.

What are these pictures mostly about? When I summarize, I retell the most important events in a few sentences. I leave out details. As I read *Red, White, and Blue,* I will summarize to check my understanding.

Student Edition, p. EI•25

Common Core State Standards

Informational Text 2. Identify the main topic of a multiparagraph text as well as the focus of specific paragraphs within the text. **Also Informational Text 10.**

Strategy Response Log

Predict Have children use p. RR33 in their *Reader's and Writer's Notebook* and use their background knowledge to write their predictions about the selection and the American flag.

Bridge to Common Core

CRAFT AND STRUCTURE

As children preview the selection and predict what it is about, they are determining how the purpose is connected to the content and style of informational text. This sets the stage for children to see how different parts of informational text, including graphics and text, are connected to each other and the whole.

Academic Vocabulary 

summarize to retell the most important ideas of what was read

Access Main Selection

READER AND TASK SUGGESTIONS	
Preparing to Read the Text	**Leveled Tasks**
• Review strategies for understanding multiple-meaning words. Refer to the vocabulary skill lesson on p. 398g. • Point out the maps and illustrations used to enhance understanding of the text. • Remind children that this selection is informational. They may need to read more slowly to better understand the text.	• **Structure** If the chronological events are confusing for children, have them keep a list of dates and events from the text in the correct time order. • **Language Conventionality and Clarity** If children struggle with the academic language, have them list any words that they do not understand.

See Text Complexity Measures for *Red, White, and Blue* on the tab at the beginning of the week.

READ Tell children that today they will read *Red, White, and Blue* for the first time. Use the Read for Understanding routine.

Routine Read for Understanding

Deepen understanding by reading the selection multiple times.

1. **First Read**—If children need support, use the **Access Text** notes to help them clarify understanding.
2. **Second Read**—Use the **Close Reading** notes to help children draw knowledge from the text.

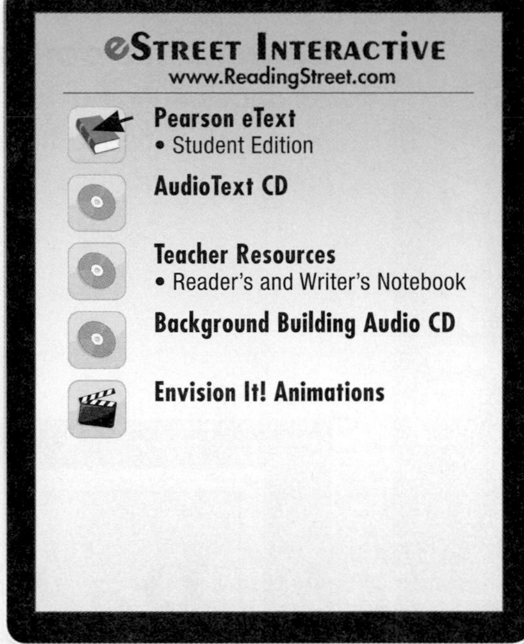

Preview Main Selection Ask children what they already know about the American flag. Then do a picture walk of the selection so children can talk about and see the activities in which people use the American flag.

1ST READ

Access Text If children need help, then...

CONNECT TO CONCEPT Look at the picture on pages 400 and 401. What are the children carrying? (a flag, a flute, a drum) Do the children look happy or upset? (happy) What American tradition might these children be celebrating? (They might be marching in a parade for the Fourth of July.)

Student Edition, pp. 400–401

2ND READ

Close Reading

ANALYSIS • TEXT EVIDENCE Look carefully at the flag and the children in this picture. Do you think this is a scene from America's past or its present? Why do you think so? What clues from the picture tell you this? (It's from the past; the flag looks different and so do the children's clothes.)

AUTHOR'S PURPOSE What is the topic of this selection? What does the author want to inform you about with this selection? (The topic of the selection is the American flag. The author wants to inform me about the flag's history.)

REVIEW SELECTION VOCABULARY Have children locate the selection word *nicknames* on page 402. What does it mean that our flag has many nicknames? (People call the flag many names other than its real name.)

Common Core State Standards

Informational Text 4. Determine the meaning of words and phrases in a text relevant to a grade 2 topic or subject area. **Informational Text 6.** Identify the main purpose of a text, including what the author wants to answer, explain, or describe. **Also Informational Text 1.**

We all know the American flag. Its bright colors fly at baseball games. It flies at Fourth of July parades. We even see it on clothes!

Our flag has lots of nicknames—like Old Glory and the Red, White, and Blue. Sometimes it's called the Stars and Stripes. But where did our flag come from? Who decided what it would look like? The truth is that no one knows for sure.

Back in the 1700s, America didn't have a flag. It didn't need one. It wasn't even a country yet.

It was just thirteen colonies. The colonies belonged to England. The English flag flew in towns from New Hampshire to Georgia.

But as time went on, the thirteen colonies didn't want to belong to England anymore. Americans decided to fight for their freedom.

A war began. It was the American Revolution. Now a new flag was needed—an American flag.

402 403

Student Edition, pp. 402–403

INFERENCE • TEXT EVIDENCE What event is pictured on page 403? Which country is each group of soldiers fighting for? (A war is pictured. The soldiers flying the British flag are fighting for England, and the soldiers with the Stars and Stripes flag are fighting for the thirteen colonies.)

1ST READ

Access Text If children need help, then...

SUMMARIZE Briefly summarize how the first flag may have been made. (George Washington wanted a flag for his army. He drew a picture of what he wanted and showed it to Betsy Ross. Ross made some changes, which Washington liked. Then, she sewed the first flag.)

AUTHOR'S PURPOSE • REREAD CHALLENGING TEXT Why does the author include details about Betsy Ross's grandson on page 405? Reread the page to help you find the answer to the question. (The author includes details about what Ross's grandson said to support the idea that the story about the first American flag is in fact true.)

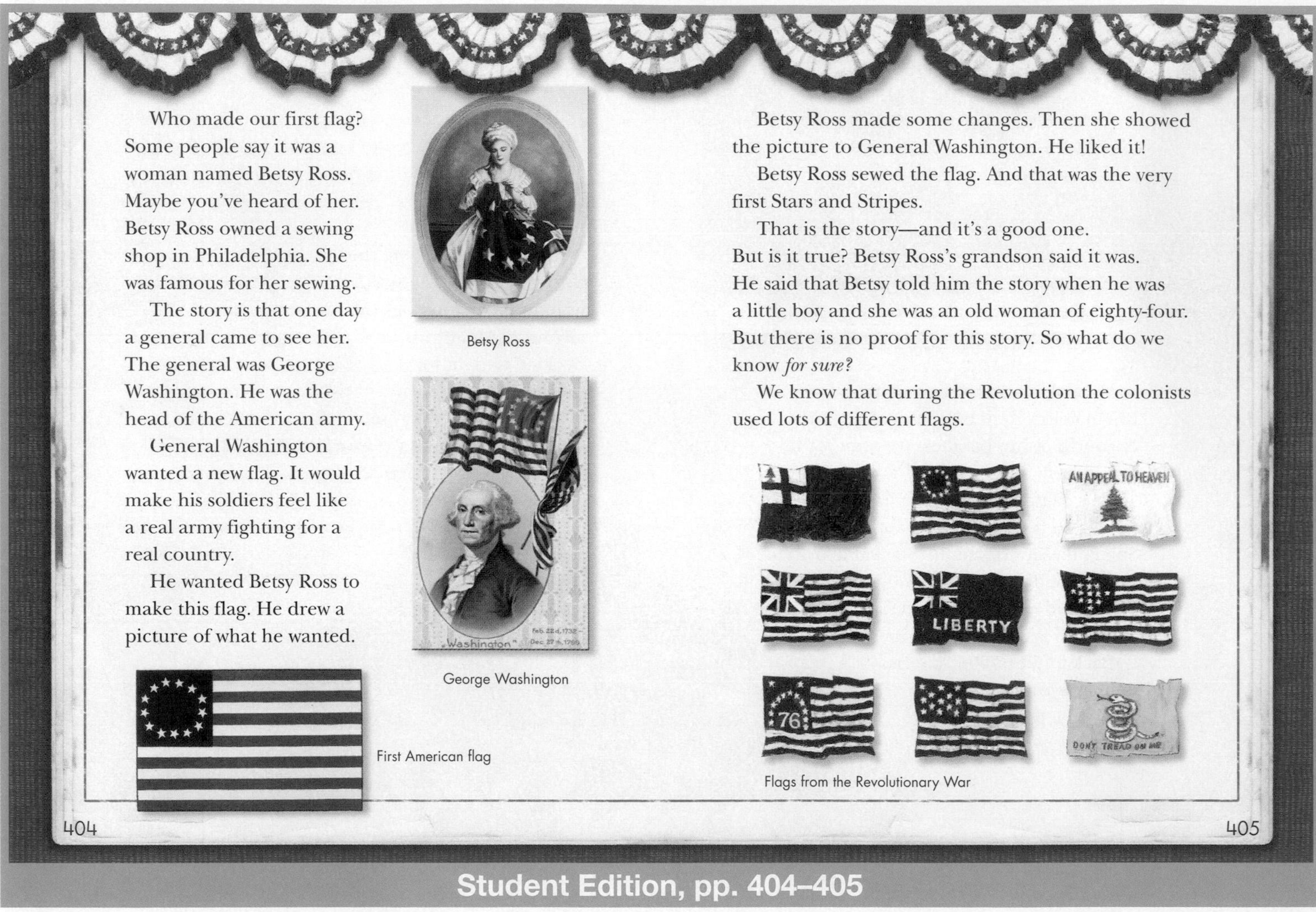

Who made our first flag? Some people say it was a woman named Betsy Ross. Maybe you've heard of her. Betsy Ross owned a sewing shop in Philadelphia. She was famous for her sewing.

The story is that one day a general came to see her. The general was George Washington. He was the head of the American army.

General Washington wanted a new flag. It would make his soldiers feel like a real army fighting for a real country.

He wanted Betsy Ross to make this flag. He drew a picture of what he wanted.

Betsy Ross

George Washington

First American flag

404

Betsy Ross made some changes. Then she showed the picture to General Washington. He liked it!

Betsy Ross sewed the flag. And that was the very first Stars and Stripes.

That is the story—and it's a good one. But is it true? Betsy Ross's grandson said it was. He said that Betsy told him the story when he was a little boy and she was an old woman of eighty-four. But there is no proof for this story. So what do we know *for sure?*

We know that during the Revolution the colonists used lots of different flags.

Flags from the Revolutionary War

405

Student Edition, pp. 404–405

2ND READ

Close Reading

Review FACT AND OPINION • EVALUATION The author writes that the story of the first American flag is a good one. Is this a statement of fact or of opinion? (opinion) How do you know? (It cannot be proved true.) Have children find a fact on p. 405. (Colonists used lots of different flags.)

SYNTHESIS Describe some of the flags shown on page 405. How are they different from the current American flag?

REVIEW MULTIPLE-MEANING WORDS I can use context clues to help determine the relevant meaning of a multiple-meaning word. I see the word *look* in the third paragraph on page 406. This word can mean "to see" or "to appear." Which meaning is correct here? (to appear) Which context clues helped you? ("where stars and stripes had to go," "the same")

Common Core State Standards

Informational Text 6. Identify the main purpose of a text, including what the author wants to answer, explain, or describe. **Foundational Skills 3.** Know and apply grade-level phonics and word analysis skills in decoding words. **Also Language 4.a., Informational Text 8.**

But once the colonies became the United States of America, the country needed *one* flag—the same flag for everybody.

So on June 14, 1777, a decision was made. The flag was going to have thirteen red and white stripes. The flag was also going to have thirteen white stars on a blue background, one for each of the thirteen colonies. Now the United States had a flag.

Congress had picked the colors and the stars and stripes. But Congress did not say where the stars and stripes had to go. So the flag still did not always look the same!

People could put them any way they liked. Sometimes the stripes were up and down, like this.

Sometimes the stars were in a circle, like this.

But nobody minded. Up and down or side to side, the stars and stripes still stood for the United States.

Over the years, the flag became more and more important to people.

In 1812, the United States was at war with England again. British soldiers came to America. They sailed up our rivers. They marched down our streets. They even burned down the White House—the home of the President.

406

407

Student Edition, pp. 406–407

ANALYSIS What did Congress decide the first national flag should look like? (It should have 13 red and white stripes, 13 white stars, and a blue background.) Why did people continue making more than one kind of flag? (Congress did not say how the stars and stripes should appear on the flag.)

ANALYSIS • TEXT EVIDENCE What clues in the text and picture on p. 407 tell you that the War of 1812 was a very dangerous time for our young country? (British soldiers are burning the White House. They sailed up our rivers and marched down our streets.)

1ST READ

Access Text If children need help, then...

AUTHOR'S PURPOSE What is the main topic on pages 408–409? What does the author want us to know about how the flag was involved? (The topic is the bombing of a fort by the British. When Francis Scott Key saw the flag still flying, he wrote a poem, which is now a song that stands for our country.)

Student Edition, pp. 408–409

2ND READ

Close Reading

ANALYSIS • TEXT EVIDENCE Look at the picture of the flag on page 408. What does the flag look like? Where and when was this flag flown? Why is this flag an important treasure? (The flag looks ripped and dirty. It flew over Fort McHenry during the war with Britain. It is the flag that inspired Francis Scott Key to write the poem "The Star-Spangled Banner.")

AUTHOR'S PURPOSE Why does the author give details about people moving out west? (to explain that the country was getting bigger and that more states would be added to the country) What does the author want us to know about how these details connect to the history of the flag? (There was not going to be enough room to add stripes on the flag for all of the new states.)

Common Core State Standards

Informational Text 2. Identify the main topic of a multiparagraph text as well as the focus of specific paragraphs within the text. **Also Informational Text 3. and 6.**

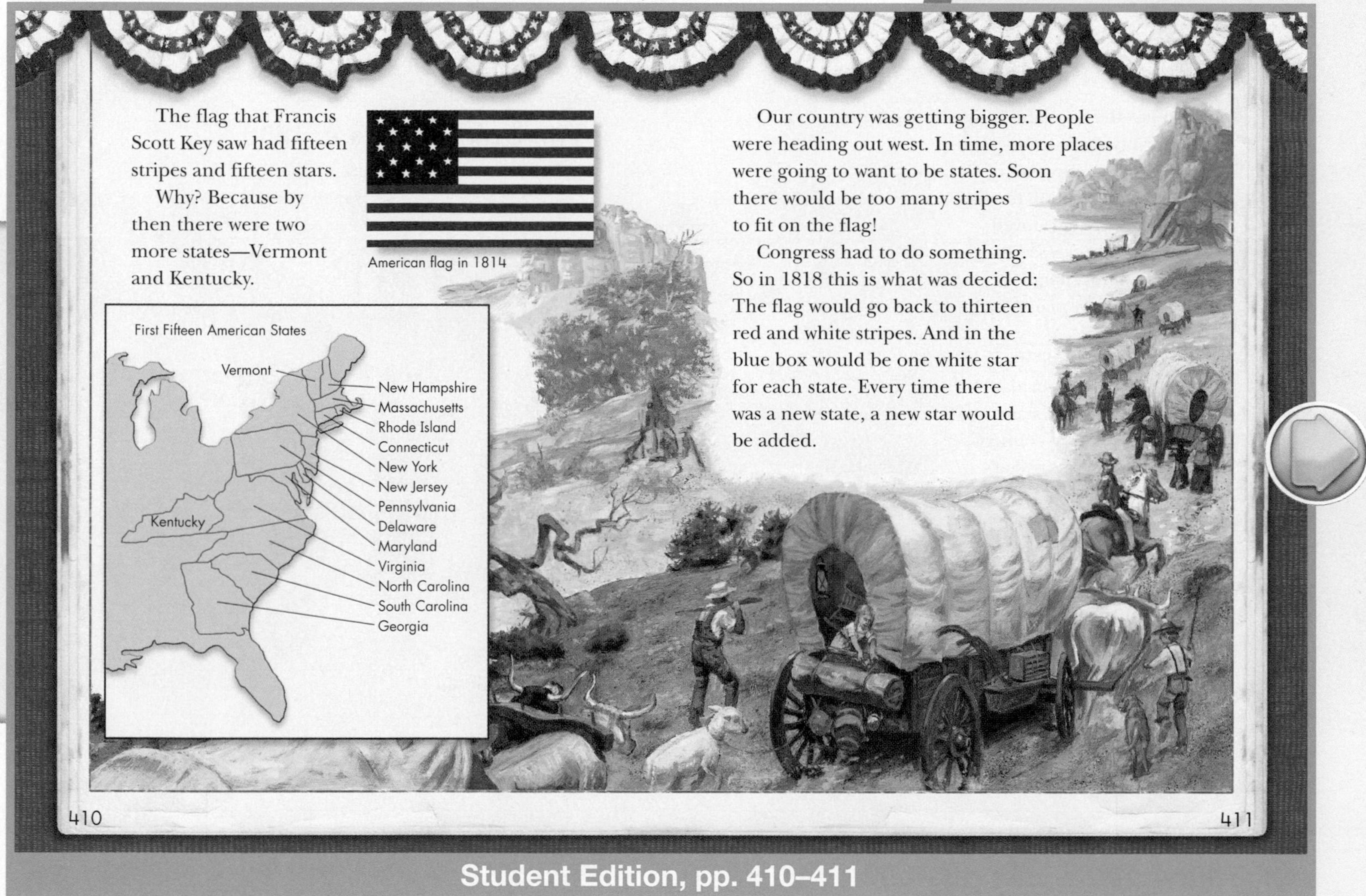

Student Edition, pp. 410–411

EVALUATION • TEXT EVIDENCE Why do you think Congress decided the flag should always have only 13 red and white stripes? Use clues in the text to help you answer the question. (The flag would get too big if we added a stripe every time we added a state. It also honored the original thirteen colonies.)

1ST READ

Access Text If children need help, then...

AUTHOR'S PURPOSE What is shown on pages 412–413? (a map and a flag) What is the author's purpose for including pictures of maps and flags throughout the selection? (The pictures show how the flag and the United States have changed over time.)

USE DECODING Have children check their reading of new words using these questions:

- Did I blend the sounds to read the word?
- Did I put the new word in the sentence to make sure it made sense?
- Did I look for word parts to help me understand the word?

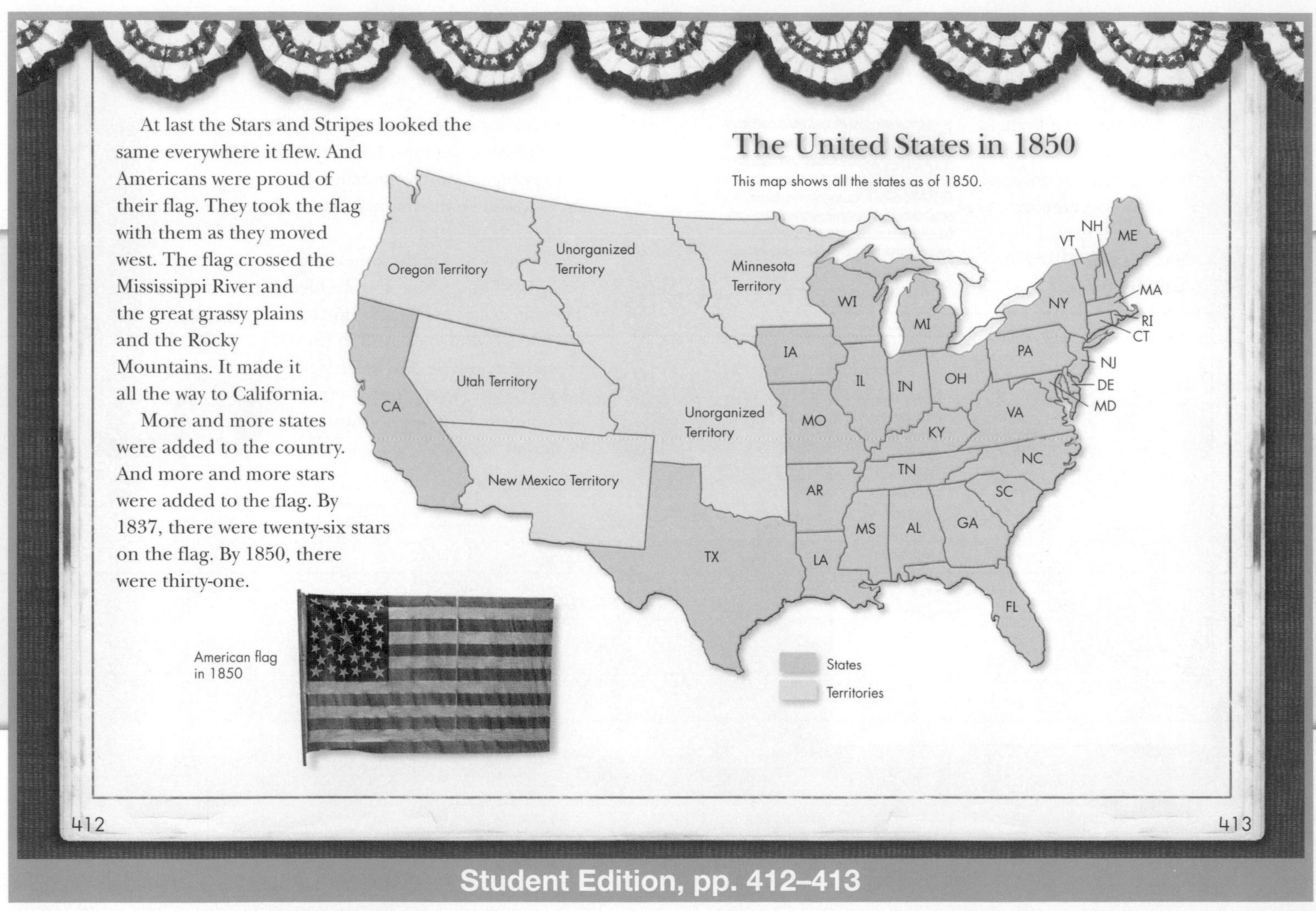

Student Edition, pp. 412–413

2ND READ

Close Reading

ANALYSIS I see that the map on pages 412–413 has two shades of blue. What do these colors show? (states and territories in the United States) What do you think territories are? (Territories are places where people live and have laws but have not organized to become states yet.)

SUMMARIZE Summarize the main events of the Civil War and how the American flag was involved. (Part of the South broke away from the United Sates to start its own country. The North fought the South to keep the country together. The South made its own flag. The North won the war, and the Southern states rejoined the country.)

Common Core State Standards

Informational Text 2. Identify the main topic of a multiparagraph text as well as the focus of specific paragraphs within the text. **Informational Text 6.** Identify the main purpose of a text, including what the author wants to answer, explain, or describe. **Also Foundational Skills 4.c.**

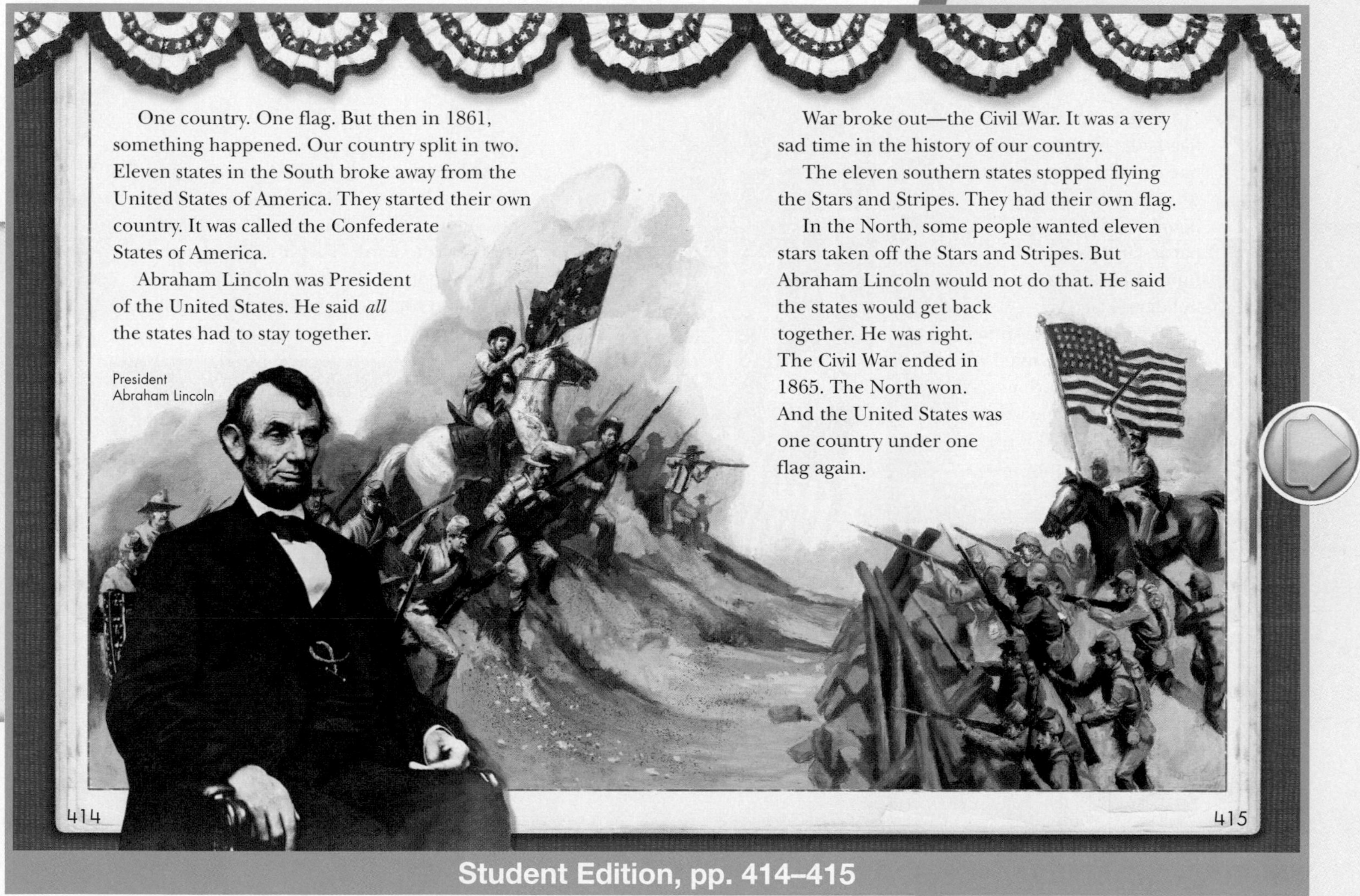

One country. One flag. But then in 1861, something happened. Our country split in two. Eleven states in the South broke away from the United States of America. They started their own country. It was called the Confederate States of America.

Abraham Lincoln was President of the United States. He said *all* the states had to stay together.

President Abraham Lincoln

War broke out—the Civil War. It was a very sad time in the history of our country.

The eleven southern states stopped flying the Stars and Stripes. They had their own flag.

In the North, some people wanted eleven stars taken off the Stars and Stripes. But Abraham Lincoln would not do that. He said the states would get back together. He was right. The Civil War ended in 1865. The North won. And the United States was one country under one flag again.

414 415

Student Edition, pp. 414–415

ANALYSIS • TEXT EVIDENCE Why did some people in the North want to take eleven stars off the flag? Look for clues in the text to support your answer. (They believed the eleven states fighting the war in the South would never be part of the United States again.)

CONNECT TO SOCIAL STUDIES In a speech given at the end of the Civil War, Lincoln said, "Let us ... strive to bind up the nation's wounds ... and achieve ... a lasting peace." His actions and words helped reunite the North and the South.

1ST READ

Access Text Ⓒ If children need help, then...

CROSS-TEXT EVALUATION

Use a Strategy to Self-Check How did the story "Great-Grandmother's Secret" from the *Read Aloud Anthology* help you understand this selection?

Continue to DAY 2
Text-Based Comprehension
p. 417a

Student Edition, pp. 416–417

2ND READ

Close Reading Ⓒ

SYNTHESIS • TEXT EVIDENCE Using what you learned in this selection, tell why the American flag is an important American symbol. Have children cite examples from the text.

Continue to DAY 3
Think Critically
p. 418–419

Text-Based Comprehension

Check Understanding

Have children discuss each question with a partner. Ask several pairs to share their responses.

- ☑ **Informational text** How do you know this selection is informational text? (The text includes facts that happened in real life. The facts describe something about history—the history of the American flag.)
- ☑ **Confirm predictions** How did you use the title of the selection to predict what the selection would be about? Were your predictions correct? (Possible response: The phrase "the Story of the American Flag" helped me predict that I would read about the history of the American flag.)
- ☑ **Draw conclusions** How would the American flag change if Puerto Rico became a state? (The flag would have one more star.)
- ☑ **Cause and effect** Why was June 14 chosen for Flag Day? (The flag turned 100 years old on June 14, 1877.)
- ☑ **Compare and contrast** *Red, White, and Blue* and the short selection "America's Flag" on page 399 are both about the American flag. How are the two selections alike and how are they different? (Both discuss nicknames for the flag, the United States independence from Britain, and the flag's appearance. *Red, White, and Blue* has far more facts and details and traces the history of the flag.)
- ☑ **Facts and details** The text points out that some Northerners wanted stars taken off the flag during the Civil War, but Lincoln refused to do that. What reasons does the text give for wanting the stars off and for keeping them on? (Some Northerners wanted stars taken off because the Southern states had left the Union and were flying their own flag. Lincoln would not agree to take them off because he said the states would get back together.)

Day 2 SMALL GROUP TIME • Differentiate Comprehension, p. SG•18

OL On-Level	SI Strategic Intervention	A Advanced
• **Practice** Selection Vocabulary • **Read** *Red, White, and Blue*	• **Reteach** Selection Vocabulary • **Read** *Red, White, and Blue*	• **Extend** Selection Vocabulary • **Read** *Red, White, and Blue* • **Investigate** Inquiry Project

Common Core State Standards

Informational Text 1. Ask and answer such questions as *who, what, where, when, why,* and *how* to demonstrate understanding of key details in a text. **Informational Text 3.** Describe the connection between a series of historical events, scientific ideas or concepts, or steps in technical procedures in a text. **Informational Text 8.** Describe how reasons support specific points the author makes in a text. **Informational Text 9.** Compare and contrast the most important points presented by two texts on the same topic.

Support Discussion Help English learners answer the third question by rephrasing it if necessary. Why would a star be added to the American flag if Puerto Rico became a state?

If... children need more scaffolding and practice with the **Comprehension Skill,**
then... use the ELL activities on p. DI•38 in the Teacher Resources section on SuccessNet.

Common Core State Standards

Informational Text 2. Identify the main topic of a multiparagraph text as well as the focus of specific paragraphs within the text. **Language 2.** Demonstrate command of the conventions of standard English capitalization, punctuation, and spelling when writing.

Informational Text

Main Idea and Topic

IDENTIFY THE MAIN IDEA AND TOPIC Explain that the topic of an informational article is the subject that it is about. The main idea is the most important thing that the author is saying about the topic. Use "America's Flag" on page 399 in the Student Edition to distinguish the main idea from the topic of an informational article.

- What is the topic of "America's Flag"? (the flag of the United States)
- What does the first paragraph say about the flag? (It has nicknames because of its colors and patterns.)
- What does the second paragraph say about the flag? (People hang the flag to celebrate holidays such as the Fourth of July.)
- What does the third paragraph say about the flag? (You can fly the flag anytime to celebrate freedom.)
- If you sum up those details from the paragraphs, what is the main idea of the whole article? (America's flag, with its colors and patterns, is flown to celebrate freedom.)

GUIDE PRACTICE Explain that a long selection such as *Red, White, and Blue* often has several main ideas. Then use Graphic Organizer 16 to help the class identify the main idea on pages 404–405 of the selection. Write *Topic: The Beginning of the United States Flag* on the organizer. Work with children to list supporting details and determine the main idea.

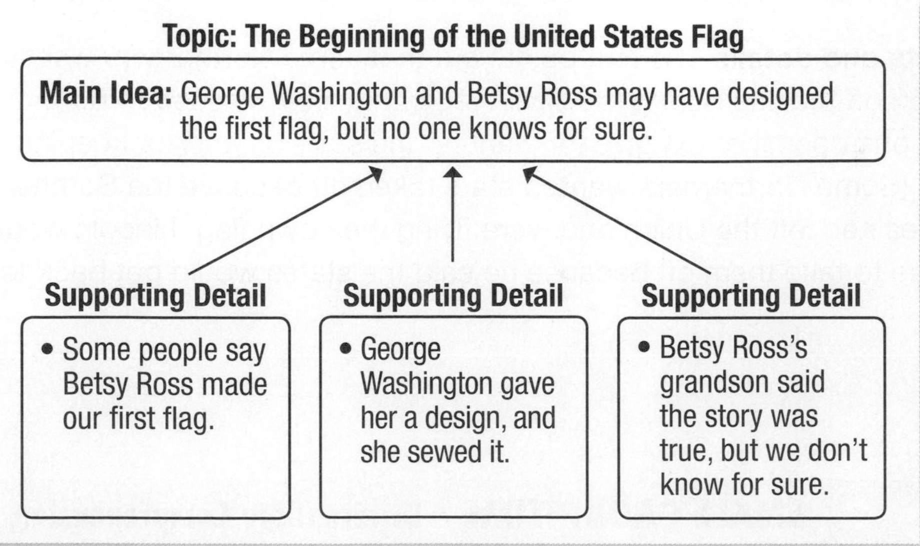

Graphic Organizer 16

ON THEIR OWN Assign small groups a section of *Red, White, and Blue.* Have them identify the main idea of the section and share their information with the class.

Conventions

Quotation Marks

TEACH Write *"I'm coming," said Maria.* Point to each word as you read it. Ask children to identify who is speaking in this sentence. (Maria) What did Maria say? ("I'm coming.") I know what words Maria said because there are special marks that tell me the words people say. What do we call these marks? (quotation marks)

GUIDE PRACTICE Write the following sentence frames on the board. Have children complete each sentence with a speaker's name and something the speaker might say. Write children's responses on the board.

1. **_______ shouted, "_______!"**
2. **"_______?" asked _______.**
3. **_______ said, "_______."**

APPLY Have volunteers orally answer each of the following questions. Then have the class restate the responses as quotations. Write the quotations children suggest and have them add the quotation marks.

1. **What do you know about the flag?**
2. **What colors are on the flag?**
3. **What shapes are on the flag?**

ON THEIR OWN Use *Reader's and Writer's Notebook,* p. 499.

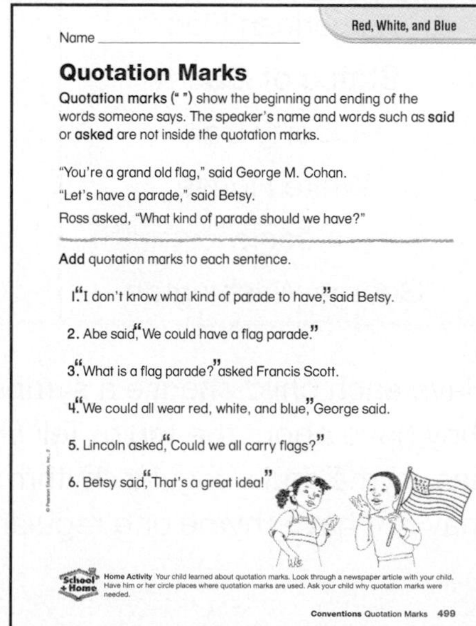

Name ________________

Red, White, and Blue

Quotation Marks

Quotation marks (" ") show the beginning and ending of the words someone says. The speaker's name and words such as **said** or **asked** are not inside the quotation marks.

"You're a grand old flag," said George M. Cohan.

"Let's have a parade," said Betsy.

Ross asked, "What kind of parade should we have?"

Add quotation marks to each sentence.

1. "I don't know what kind of parade to have," said Betsy.
2. Abe said, "We could have a flag parade."
3. "What is a flag parade?" asked Francis Scott.
4. "We could all wear red, white, and blue," George said.
5. Lincoln asked, "Could we all carry flags?"
6. Betsy said, "That's a great idea!"

School + Home **Home Activity** Your child learned about quotation marks. Look through a newspaper article with your child. Have him or her circle places where quotation marks are used. Ask your child why quotation marks were needed.

Conventions Quotation Marks 499

Reader's and Writer's Notebook, p. 499

Access for All

Strategic Intervention

Practice Quotation Marks If children have difficulty understanding when to use quotation marks, play a written game of Simon Says. Write the words Simon says in quotation marks and have children follow the written directions.

Daily Fix-It

3. the flag stands for freedum
   The flag stands for freedom.
4. Our fleg has stars and sripes.
   Our flag has stars and stripes.

Discuss the Daily Fix-It corrections with children. Review sentence capitalization, short *a,* consonant blend *str,* and the spelling of *freedom.*

Punctuation Point out that the punctuation that comes before the second quotation mark tells how the words should be read. Have children recall that a question mark shows that the speaker is asking a question, an exclamation point shows excitement, and within quotation marks, a comma may take the place of a period.

Common Core State Standards

Writing 3. Write narratives in which they recount a well-elaborated event or short sequence of events, include details to describe actions, thoughts, and feelings, use temporal words to signal event order, and provide a sense of closure.

Writing

Descriptive Poem or Song

Writing Trait: Voice

INTRODUCE THE PROMPT Review with children the key features of a descriptive poem. Point out that "The American Flag" is a descriptive poem. Assure children that they can write a poem that gives vivid descriptions. Explain that today children will plan their own poem about an American symbol or tradition. It will express a feeling. Read aloud the writing prompt.

Writing Prompt

Think about American symbols and traditions. Now write a poem about one of those symbols or traditions.

GENERATE POEM IDEAS

To plan a new poem, think about different American symbols and traditions. A symbol stands for something. Our flag is a symbol of our country. A tradition is something people have done for a long time. Let's make a list of them. Display a two-column chart. Label the columns *Symbols* and *Traditions.* I'll start with the American flag. It was the symbol we read about in *Red, White, and Blue.*

Guide children in completing the chart. Possible ideas are shown. Record the responses. Keep the chart available while children plan their poems.

Symbols	Traditions
American Flag	Thanksgiving
Statue of Liberty	Fourth of July
Liberty Bell	baseball games
White House	
eagle	
George Washington	

Have each child choose a symbol or tradition. Tell children to identify a feeling they have about the topic. Tell children they can write a poem or a song that has rhyme and a regular rhythm or they can write a poem in free verse, which may not have rhyme or a regular rhythm. Circulate to guide them.

Mini-Lesson Description

Introduce Use *Reader's and Writer's Notebook,* p. 500 to model poem planning. Thanksgiving is my topic. The feeling I will express is that I think it is the best holiday. Now I will use a web to plan my poem. I'll write the topic in the center circle. I'll write words and phrases that describe Thanksgiving in the outer circles.

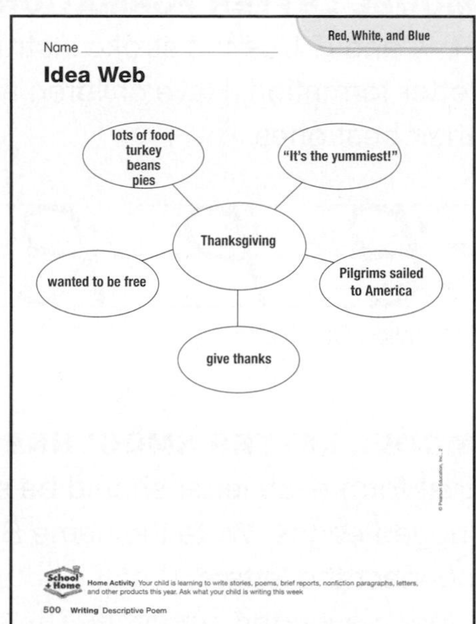
Name
Red, White, and Blue
Idea Web

Home Activity Your child is learning to write stories, poems, brief reports, nonfiction paragraphs, letters, and other products this year. Ask what your child is writing this week.
500 Writing Descriptive Poem

Reader's and Writer's Notebook, p. 500

Model When I think about Thanksgiving, I think about lots of food, such as turkey, beans, and pies. I'll write these descriptions in a circle. I want to include a quote. I say, "It's the yummiest!" Because it is a quote, I will include quotation marks around the exact words. Thanksgiving is a time we give thanks. I am thankful for the Pilgrims. They came to America to be free. I will include all these descriptions in my web. Now it's your turn. Plan the ideas you will describe in your poem. Circulate to guide and assist children.

Routine Quick Write for Fluency

Team Talk

1. **Talk** Have partners take two minutes to name the symbol or tradition they chose and a description about it.
2. **Write** Each child briefly writes two sentences using the description.
3. **Share** Each child reads the sentences to the partner.

Routines Flip Chart

Access for All

Advanced

Research a Symbol or Tradition
Encourage children to find three facts about their topic. Have them include the facts in their poems.

Support Prewriting

Beginning Show children pictures of American symbols and traditions. Point out the details of each using vivid description. Review each and have children say them.

Intermediate Have children draw pictures and write phrases to describe the symbol or tradition. Have them describe the items to other children.

Advanced Have children draw pictures and write short sentences in their webs. As they share the ideas with partners, children can clarify and add details.

Common Core State Standards

Writing 7. Participate in shared research and writing projects (e.g., read a number of books on a single topic to produce a report; record science observations). **Speaking/ Listening 2.** Recount or describe key ideas or details from a text read aloud or information presented orally or through other media.

Handwriting

Cursive *B, P, R, T, F*/Letter Smoothness

MODEL LETTER FORMATION Display uppercase cursive letters: *B, P, R, T,* and *F.* Use the stroke instructions pictured below to model proper letter formation. Have children write each letter several times and circle their best ones.

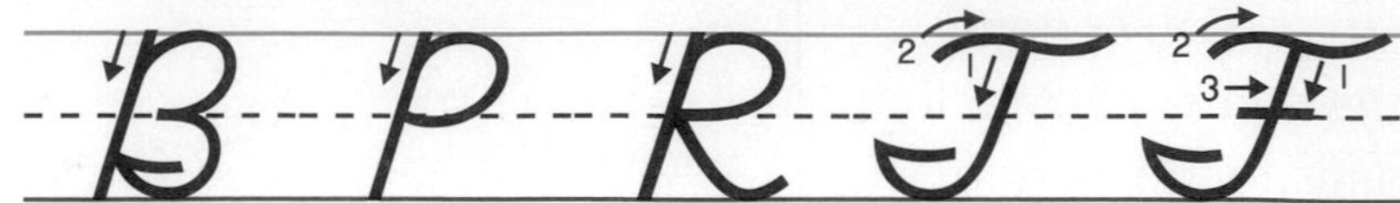

D'Nealian Cursive™

MODEL LETTER SMOOTHNESS Explain that when we write, the strokes that form each letter should be smooth. Lines should not have any shaky or jagged edges. Write the name *Ben Rush* using smooth strokes to form and connect the letters. When I write this name, I make sure the lines of each letter are written smoothly. The end stroke of one letter flows neatly into the beginning stroke of the next letter. Write *Ben Rush* again, with strokes that are jagged and shaky, and include some broken lines. The lines of my letters should not look jagged or broken. It should not seem as if I wrote them with a shaky hand. By writing letters smoothly, I make it easier for others to understand what I write. Ask children which of the two writing examples is easiest to read and have them explain why.

GUIDE PRACTICE Write the following sentence, using strokes that look jagged and shaky.

Mrs. Tate is in town.

Team Talk Have children work in pairs to discuss what is wrong with the sentence and how to fix it. Have children write the sentence correctly.

Research and Inquiry

Step 2 Research Skill: Chart

TEACH Remind children that a **chart** is a good way to organize information. They might read charts when they do research to get information. They might make a chart to organize the information as they learn it. They can also make a chart to share the information they learn.

Think Aloud **MODEL** Display Research Transparency 27. Let's see how a chart is organized. Point out the title, columns, headings, and recorded information. Looking at the title, I can see this chart lists traditions in the United States that use the American flag. The chart has two columns: Tradition and The Flag's Use. I can see that one tradition that uses the flag is a parade, and that the flag is used to lead the parade.

GUIDE PRACTICE Ask questions about the chart for children to answer.

ON THEIR OWN Use *Reader's and Writer's Notebook,* p. 501.

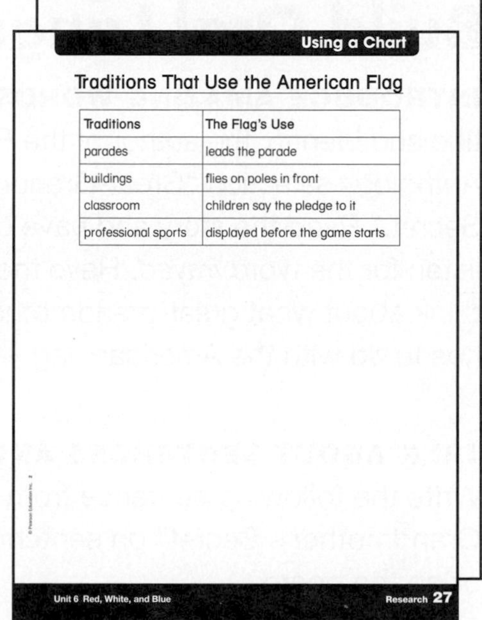
Using a Chart

Traditions That Use the American Flag

Traditions	The Flag's Use
parades	leads the parade
buildings	flies on poles in front
classroom	children say the pledge to it
professional sports	displayed before the game starts

Unit 6 Red, White, and Blue Research 27

Research Transparency 27 TR DVD; Reader's and Writer's Notebook, p. 501

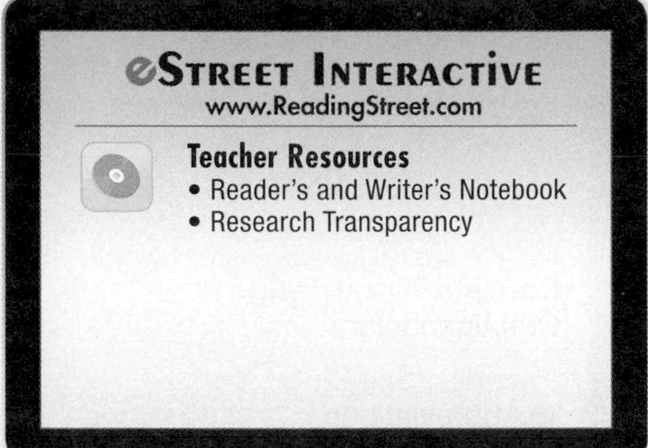

Bridge to Common Core

RESEARCH TO BUILD AND PRESENT KNOWLEDGE

Children will gather evidence from texts and other sources to use in answering questions for their research projects. They will also

- learn to locate information in a chart
- learn to organize information in a chart

Academic Vocabulary

chart a visible display of information organized in columns

Wrap Up Your Day!

✔ **Content Knowledge** Monitor children's use of oral vocabulary as they respond. What is the flag a symbol for? (America, freedom, independence) Why is "The Star-Spangled Banner" a patriotic song? (It is about loving and being loyal to our country.)

Preview DAY 3

Tell children that tomorrow they will reread *Red, White, and Blue: The Story of the American Flag.*

DAY 3 at a Glance

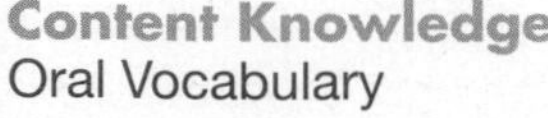

Content Knowledge
Oral Vocabulary

Phonics/Spelling
Abbreviations

Fluency
Accuracy

Selection Vocabulary
America, birthday, flag, freedom, nicknames, stars, stripes
Multiple-Meaning Words

Text-Based Comprehension
Review Fact and Opinion

Conventions
Quotation Marks

Writing
Descriptive Poem or Song

Research and Inquiry
Gather and Record Information

Materials

- Student Edition
- Sing with Me Big Book
- Read Aloud Anthology
- Reader's and Writer's Notebook
- Decodable Reader 27B
- Retelling Cards

Common Core State Standards

Speaking/Listening 2. Recount or describe key ideas or details from a text read aloud or information presented orally or through other media. **Language 6.** Use words and phrases acquired through conversations, reading and being read to, and responding to texts, including using adjectives and adverbs to describe (e.g., *When other kids are happy that makes me happy*).

Content Knowledge

The American Flag

EXPAND THE CONCEPT To reinforce concepts and to focus children's attention, have children sing "Our Flag, Our Symbol" from the *Sing with Me* Big Book. What does the flag say about our country? (The flag says that we are free.)

Build Oral Language

INTRODUCE AMAZING WORDS Read the title and identify the author of the *Read Aloud Anthology* selection "Great-Grandmother's Secret." Read the story and have children listen for the word *frayed.* Have them also think about what great-grandmother's secret has to do with the American flag.

"Great-Grandmother's Secret"

TALK ABOUT SENTENCES AND WORDS Write the following sentence from "Great-Grandmother's Secret" on sentence strips or on the board.

The flag we used last summer was frayed and worn, so I took it to the American Legion.

- Ask children to read it with you as you track the print.
- Point to and read *The flag we used last summer was frayed and worn.* What does this mean? (The flag had edges coming apart and was old.) Why does the author use the word *frayed?* (It describes the way the flag was falling apart.) What other words could the author have used?
- Now point to and read *frayed and worn* again. Point out that *worn* is a word with multiple meanings. What does *worn* mean here? ("damaged by use") Why do you think the author chose the word *worn?* (It shows the flag had been used a lot.)

- **Team Talk** Now have children work with a partner to replace key words in the sentence with simpler words or synonyms. Use the following sentence frame.

The flag we used last summer was ______ and ______, so I took it to the American Legion.

Build Oral Vocabulary

Amazing Words Robust Vocabulary Routine

1. **Introduce the Word** Relate the word *frayed* to the story. William's mother gets rid of their old flag because it is *frayed.* Supply a child-friendly definition. When something is *frayed,* it is worn away at the edges, and threads are hanging loose. Have children say the word.
2. **Demonstrate** Provide examples to show meaning. A pair of jeans might be *frayed* at the bottom. An old rug may be *frayed* around the edges.
3. **Apply** Have children demonstrate their understanding. Name some things that might be *frayed.*
4. **Display the Word** Have children decode the word by identifying the initial blend *fr* /f//r/; the long *a* sound, /ā/, spelled *ay;* and the final /d/ sound, spelled *ed.*

Routines Flip Chart

ADD TO THE CONCEPT MAP Discuss the history of the flag and how traditions and celebrations involving it developed over the years.

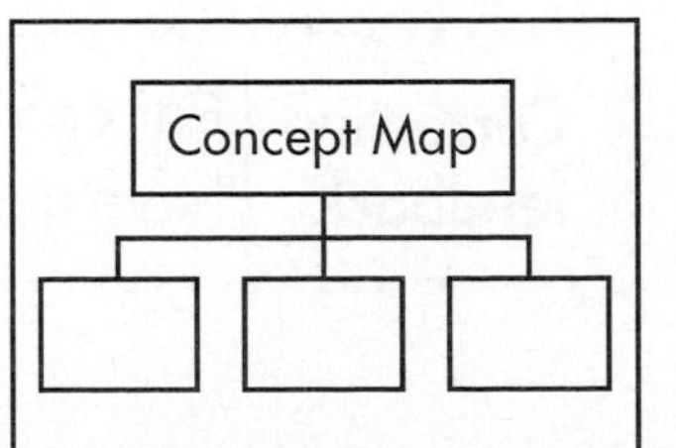

- In *Red, White, and Blue: The Story of the American Flag,* what did Francis Scott Key do? (He saw the flag was still flying after a battle, and he wrote a poem about it.) What happened to the poem? (It was set to music and became the National Anthem.) Let's add this information to the map.
- When do we celebrate the birthday of the flag? (June 14 is Flag Day.) We'll include *We celebrate Flag Day on June 14* as an important celebration. Why is June 14 considered to be the flag's birthday? (The flag was first designed on June 14, 1777.) Let's add this supporting detail to the map too.

Amazing Words

history	unfurl
independence	frayed
symbol	allegiance
patriotic	indivisible

ELL **Expand Vocabulary** Use the Day 3 instruction on ELL Poster 27 to help children expand vocabulary.

Common Core State Standards

Foundational Skills 3. Know and apply grade-level phonics and word analysis skills in decoding words. **Foundational Skills 4.** Read with sufficient accuracy and fluency to support comprehension.

Phonics

Sort Words

MODEL WORD BUILDING Write *Word* and *Abbreviation* as headings on a two-column chart. Write the individual words and abbreviations from the chart below on self-stick notes. Now we are going to sort words and their abbreviations. Display *Ln.* I know that these letters form an abbreviation. This abbreviation begins with a capital letter and ends with a period. Attach *Ln.* in the Abbreviation column.

GUIDE PRACTICE Display each self-stick note one at a time. Have children take turns reading the word or abbreviation and attaching it in the appropriate column.

When all words and abbreviations have been sorted, remove only the notes containing abbreviations from the chart. Then as you point to each word remaining on the chart, have children read it and attach the self-stick note containing the word's abbreviation next to it. When the chart is complete, have children read each column as you point to it.

Word	Abbreviation
Lane	Ln.
Mister	Mr.
Circle	Cir.
April	Apr.
December	Dec.
Thursday	Thurs.

Corrective feedback For corrective feedback, model reading the abbreviation and have children repeat it.

Fluent Word Reading

MODEL Write *Avenue* and *Ave.* Point to *Avenue.* This word is *Avenue.* Point to *Ave.* This is the abbreviation for *Avenue.* I read it as if all the letters are written.

GUIDE PRACTICE Write the abbreviations below. You may wish to review the complete words. Think about what the whole word might look like. Say the whole word in your head. When I point to the abbreviation, we'll read it together. Allow one second per sound previewing time for the first reading.

Sept.	Rd.	Sat.	Mon.	Wed.	Jan.

ON THEIR OWN Have children read the list above three or four times, until they can read one word per second.

Decode and Read

DECODE WORDS IN ISOLATION Have children turn to page 207 in *Decodable Practice Readers* 2.2 and find the first list of words. Each word in this list is an abbreviation. Let's read these abbreviations. Be sure that children correctly read each abbreviation.

Next, have children read the high-frequency words.

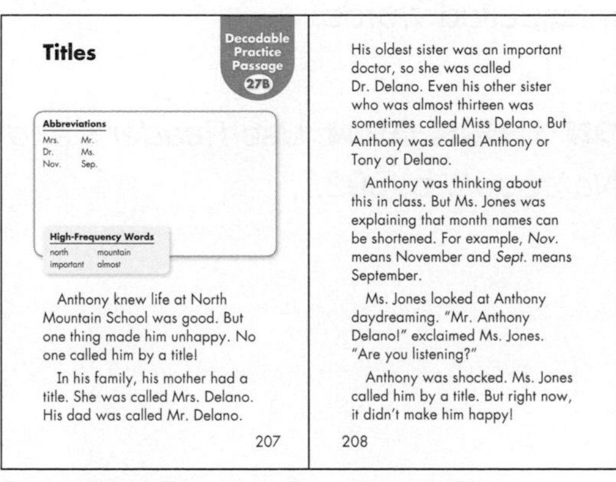

Titles

Decodable Practice Passage 27B

Abbreviations

Mrs. Mr.
Dr. Ms.
Nov. Sep.

High-Frequency Words

north mountain
important almost

Anthony knew life at North Mountain School was good. But one thing made him unhappy. No one called him by a title!

In his family, his mother had a title. She was called Mrs. Delano. His dad was called Mr. Delano.

207

His oldest sister was an important doctor, so she was called Dr. Delano. Even his other sister who was almost thirteen was sometimes called Miss Delano. But Anthony was called Anthony or Tony or Delano.

Anthony was thinking about this in class. But Ms. Jones was explaining that month names can be shortened. For example, *Nov.* means November and *Sept.* means September.

Ms. Jones looked at Anthony daydreaming. "Mr. Anthony Delano!" exclaimed Ms. Jones. "Are you listening?"

Anthony was shocked. Ms. Jones called him by a title. But right now, it didn't make him happy!

208

Decodable Practice Passage 27B

DECODE WORDS IN CONTEXT Chorally read the story along with children. Have children identify abbreviations in the story.

Team Talk Pair children and have them take turns reading the story aloud to each other. Monitor children as they read to check for proper pronunciation and appropriate pacing.

Access for All

SI Strategic Intervention

Read Abbreviations If children have trouble reading the abbreviations in the Fluent Word Reading activity, write the complete words. Guide children to decode each word using letter-sound correspondences and syllable patterns. Then write the abbreviation and have children read it.

Common Core State Standards

Language 2. Demonstrate command of the conventions of standard English capitalization, punctuation, and spelling when writing. **Foundational Skills 4.b.** Read on-level text orally with accuracy, appropriate rate, and expression on successive readings.

Spelling Words

Abbreviations

1. Mr.	**7. Dr.**
2. Mrs.	**8. Ms.**
3. St.	**9. Rd.**
4. Jan.	**10. Oct.**
5. Feb.	**11. Nov.**
6. Aug.	**12. Dec.**

High-Frequency Words

13. won	**14. learn**

Spelling

Abbreviations

SPELL HIGH-FREQUENCY WORDS Write *won* and *learn* and point them out on the Word Wall. Have children say and spell the words with you and then without you.

DICTATION Have children write these sentences. Explain that they should write abbreviations for addresses, months, and titles of people. Then say each sentence. Repeat it slowly, one word at a time.

1. **Mr. Hawk won the race on Oct. 9.**
2. **The green house on Dash Rd. belongs to Ms. Rich.**
3. **The children learn that Mrs. Fly will move Nov. 20.**

PROOFREAD AND CORRECT Write each sentence, spelling words one at a time. Have children circle and rewrite any misspelled words.

ON THEIR OWN Use *Reader's and Writer's Notebook,* p. 502.

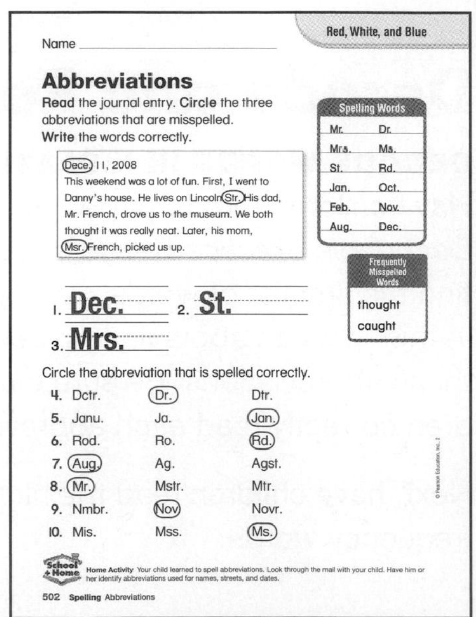
Red, White, and Blue

Name ______

Abbreviations

Read the journal entry. **Circle** the three abbreviations that are misspelled.
Write the words correctly.

Dece. 11, 2008
This weekend was a lot of fun. First, I went to Danny's house. He lives on Lincoln Str. His dad, Mr. French, drove us to the museum. We both thought it was really neat. Later, his mom, Msr. French, picked us up.

Spelling Words

Mr.	Dr.
Mrs.	Ms.
St.	Rd.
Jan.	Oct.
Feb.	Nov.
Aug.	Dec.

Frequently Misspelled Words
thought
caught

1. Dec. 2. St.
3. Mrs.

Circle the abbreviation that is spelled correctly.

4.	Dctr.	Dr.	Dtr.
5.	Janu.	Ja.	Jan.
6.	Rod.	Ro.	Rd.
7.	Aug.	Ag.	Agst.
8.	Mr.	Mstr.	Mtr.
9.	Nmbr.	Nov	Novr.
10.	Mis.	Mss.	Ms.

School + Home **Home Activity** Your child learned to spell abbreviations. Look through the mail with your child. Have him or her identify abbreviations used for names, streets, and dates.

502 **Spelling** Abbreviations

© Pearson Education, Inc., 2

Reader's and Writer's Notebook, p. 502

ELL

If... children need more scaffolding and practice with reading the **Main Selection,**
then... use the ELL activities on p. DI•39 in the Teacher Resources section on SuccessNet.

Day 3 SMALL GROUP TIME • Differentiate Close Reading, p. SG•18

OL On-Level	SI Strategic Intervention	A Advanced
• **Reread** to Develop Vocabulary • **Reread** *Red, White, and Blue*	• **Reread** to Develop Vocabulary • **Reread** *Red, White, and Blue*	• **Reread** to Develop Vocabulary • **Reread** *Red, White, and Blue* • **Investigate** Inquiry Project

Fluency

Accuracy

MODEL FLUENT READING Have children turn to Student Edition, pp. 402–403. Point to the second line on p. 402. When I see a word I don't know, I try to sound it out. When I come to the word *bright,* I break it down into sounds I already know, *br-igh-t.* I know that *igh* sounds like the long *i* from other words I know.

GUIDE PRACTICE Have children read the pages with you. Then have them reread the pages as a group without you until they read with no hesitation and no mistakes. Continue in the same way with pp. 404–405.

Corrective feedback	**If...** children have difficulty reading with accuracy, **then...** prompt: • Do you read groups of words, not word-by-word? • Where did you get stuck? • Should you try sounding out a word by syllables?

Reread for Fluency

Routine Choral Reading

1. **Select a Passage** For *Red, White, and Blue,* use pp. 406–409.
2. **Model** First, have children track the print as you read.
3. **Guide Practice** Then have children read along with you.
4. **Corrective Feedback** Have the class read aloud without you. Monitor progress and provide feedback. For optimal fluency, children should reread three to four times.

Routines Flip Chart

CHECK COMPREHENSION Have children use the illustration of the flags on page 406 to explain why the American flags do not look alike.

Access for All

Strategic Intervention

Breaking Words into Smaller Parts Remind children that long words sometimes contain prefixes and suffixes. When they come across a long word, children should look for word parts, and then use their knowledge of them in chunking and decoding the word.

Options for Oral Rereading

Use *Red, White, and Blue* or the Day 1 Decodable Practice Reader.

Common Core State Standards

Language 4. Determine or clarify the meaning of unknown and multiple-meaning words and phrases based on grade 2 reading and content, choosing flexibly from an array of strategies. **Informational Text 1.** Ask and answer such questions as *who, what, where, when, why,* and *how* to demonstrate understanding of key details in a text. **Informational Text 3.** Describe the connection between a series of historical events, scientific ideas or concepts, or steps in technical procedures in a text.

Selection Vocabulary

America the United States of America

birthday the day that somebody was born or something began, usually celebrated yearly

flag a piece of cloth, usually with square corners, with a picture or pattern that stands for a place or country

freedom the condition of not being under someone else's control

nicknames names used instead of real names

stars shapes that have five or more points

stripes long, narrow bands of color

Vocabulary

Selection Vocabulary

REVIEW SELECTION WORDS Display and review the selection words *freedom, flag, stripes, stars, nicknames, birthday,* and *America.* Have children read the words aloud.

Team Talk Provide graph paper. Have partners use the selection words to make a crossword puzzle. Clues can be fill-in-the-blank sentences or glossary definitions. Have pairs of children exchange papers to solve the puzzles.

Multiple-Meaning Words

REVIEW MULTIPLE-MEANING WORDS Remind children that some words can have more than one meaning. Point out that the selection word *stars* can mean "shapes that have five or more points": *There are fifty stars on the American flag.* It can also mean "plays an important part in a play, television show, or movie": *My favorite actor stars in a new television show.* Tell children that they can usually determine the relevant meaning of a multiple-meaning word by using context clues.

Write *flies. Flies* is a multiple-meaning word. It can mean "black insects that have wings": *The flies buzzed around the food.* It can also mean "moves in the air": *A flag flies at the top of a flagpole.*

GUIDE PRACTICE Write the following words.

light **bark** **ring** **fall**

Have children give multiple meanings for each word and use the word in sentences to show the relevant meaning.

light—a device that makes it possible to see; not heavy
bark—the covering of a tree; the sound a dog makes
ring—a circle; a kind of jewelry worn on a finger
fall—a tumble to the ground; a season

Team Talk Have children work in pairs to think of more multiple-meaning words. Have them choose one word and draw pictures to show each meaning.

Text-Based Comprehension

Read Main Selection

REVIEW FACT AND OPINION Remind children that authors use facts and opinions when writing about real people, places, events, or things. Facts are true statements that can be proved, while opinions are what someone believes or thinks. Identifying facts and opinions can help us better understand what the author is saying. Have children turn to page 406 in their Student Edition. Which sentence in the last paragraph on the page is an opinion? How do you know it is an opinion? (*But nobody minded.* It cannot be proved.) For additional practice with fact and opinion, see Let's Practice It!, p. 304 on the *Teacher Resources DVD-ROM.*

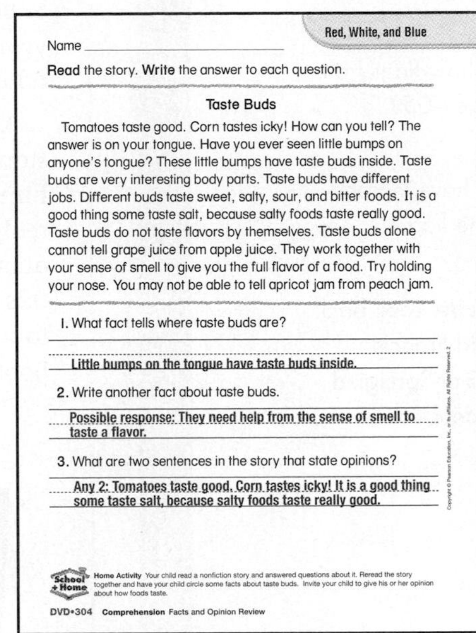

Red, White, and Blue

Name ______________________

Read the story. **Write** the answer to each question.

Taste Buds

Tomatoes taste good. Corn tastes icky! How can you tell? The answer is on your tongue. Have you ever seen little bumps on anyone's tongue? These little bumps have taste buds inside. Taste buds are very interesting body parts. Taste buds have different jobs. Different buds taste sweet, salty, sour, and bitter foods. It is a good thing some taste salt, because salty foods taste really good. Taste buds do not taste flavors by themselves. Taste buds alone cannot tell grape juice from apple juice. They work together with your sense of smell to give you the full flavor of a food. Try holding your nose. You may not be able to tell apricot jam from peach jam.

1. What fact tells where taste buds are?

Little bumps on the tongue have taste buds inside.

2. Write another fact about taste buds.

Possible response: They need help from the sense of smell to taste a flavor.

3. What are two sentences in the story that state opinions?

Any 2: Tomatoes taste good. Corn tastes icky! It is a good thing some taste salt, because salty foods taste really good.

School + Home **Home Activity** Your child read a nonfiction story and answered questions about it. Reread the story together and have your child circle some facts about taste buds. Invite your child to give his or her opinion about how foods taste.

DVD•304 **Comprehension** Facts and Opinion Review

Let's Practice It! TR DVD•304

GENRE: INFORMATIONAL TEXT Remind children that informational text gives facts about real people, places, or events that reflect history or the traditions of communities. Have children recall facts from *Red, White, and Blue: The Story of the American Flag* that reflect history and traditions. (The American flag was made when the original 13 colonies fought for independence, and it has changed as the country has grown and changed.)

READ Return to pages 400–417 and use the **2nd Read/Close Reading Notes** to reread *Red, White, and Blue.*

Routine — Read for Understanding

Deepen understanding by reading the selection multiple times.

1. **First Read**—If children need support, use the **Access Text** notes to help them clarify understanding.
2. **Second Read**—Use the **Close Reading** notes to help children draw knowledge from the text.

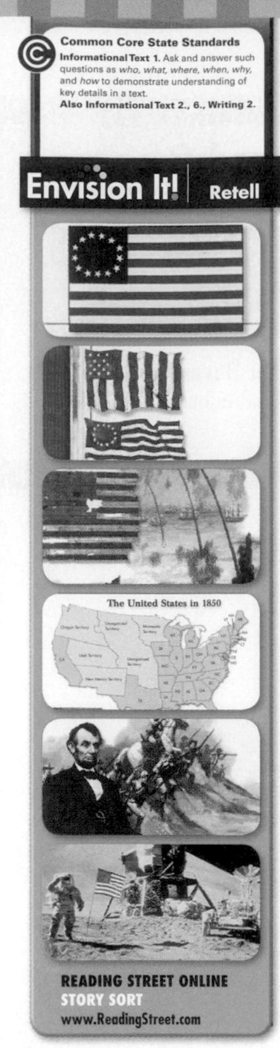

Think Critically

1. Where in your community might you see the flag flying, based on what you learned in the text? Text to World
2. Why do you think the author wrote about the American flag? Think Like an Author
3. Why did the author show flags from the Revolution on page 405? Author's Purpose
4. Summarize what you have learned about the design of the flag. Summarize
5. **Look Back and Write** Look back at page 409. Why did Francis Scott Key write "The Star-Spangled Banner"? Provide evidence to support your answer. Key Ideas and Details • Text Evidence

418

Meet the Author

John Herman

John Herman grew up near New York City. He knew he wanted to be a writer when he was twelve years old. Now he writes books for adults, teenagers, and children.

Mr. Herman likes to make up stories. *Red, White, and Blue* gave him a chance to write about real events. He loves reading about American history, so this was a new thing for him to try. He hopes to write more books like this in the future!

Read more books about the American flag.

The Flag We Love by Pam Muñoz Ryan

Betsy Ross by Alexandra Wallner

Use the *Reader's and Writer's Notebook* to record your independent reading.

419

Student Edition, pp. 418–419

Common Core State Standards

Informational Text 1. Ask and answer such questions as *who, what, where, when, why,* and *how* to demonstrate understanding of key details in a text. **Also Informational Text 2., 3., 6. and Writing 2.**

Bridge to Common Core

KEY IDEAS AND DETAILS

By reading the text multiple times, children will make logical inferences from the text and cite textual evidence when writing or discussing the knowledge they have gained.

Use the Think Critically page to ensure a thorough understanding of *Red, White, and Blue: The Story of the American Flag.*

Think Critically

1. **TEXT TO WORLD** I might see the flag flying outside our school, the library, and the post office.
2. **THINK LIKE AN AUTHOR** The author wanted to inform readers about the history of the flag.
3. **AUTHOR'S PURPOSE** The author wanted to show how the flag did not always look the same.
4. **SUMMARIZE** I learned that the flag may have first been designed by George Washington and Betsy Ross, but it has changed over the years. The stars stand for the numbers of states, and the stripes stand for the thirteen original colonies.
5. **LOOK BACK AND WRITE • TEXT EVIDENCE** For writing fluency, assign a five-minute time limit. As children finish, encourage them to reread their response and proofread for errors.

Scoring Rubric Look Back and Write

TOP-SCORE RESPONSE A top-score response uses details from the text and the picture to explain why Francis Scott Key wrote "The Star-Spangled Banner."

A top-score response might include:
Francis Scott Key wrote "The Star-Spangled Banner" to show his pride. He was watching a battle. British soldiers were attacking an American Fort all night long. When the morning came and the flag was still flying, he knew the Americans had won. He was so proud that he wrote "The Star-Spangled Banner."

Retell

Have children work in pairs, retelling the selection to one another. Remind children that their partners should include the topic, main ideas, and what they learned from the reading. Have children use the retelling strip in the Student Edition or the Story Sort to retell the selection. Monitor children's retellings.

Scoring Rubric Expository Retelling

	4	3	2	1
Connections	Makes connections and generalizes beyond the text	Makes connections to other events, texts, or experiences	Makes a limited connection to another event, text, or experience	Makes no connection to another event, text, or experience
Author's Purpose	Elaborates on author's purpose	Tells author's purpose with some clarity	Makes some connection to author's purpose	Makes no connection to author's purpose
Topic	Describes the main topic	Identifies the main topic with some details early in retelling	Identifies the main topic	Retelling has no sense of topic
Important Ideas	Gives accurate information about ideas using key vocabulary	Gives accurate information about ideas with some key vocabulary	Gives limited or inaccurate information about ideas	Gives no information about ideas
Conclusions	Draws conclusions and makes inferences to generalize beyond the text	Draws conclusions about the text	Is able to tell some learnings about the text	Is unable to draw conclusions or make inferences about the text

Don't Wait Until Friday

MONITOR PROGRESS Check Retelling

If... children have difficulty retelling the selection,
then... use the Retelling Cards/Story Sort to scaffold their retelling.

Strategy Response Log

Summarize Have children revisit p. RR33 in their *Reader's and Writer's Notebook* to review their predictions about the selection and the flag. Did they accurately predict what they would read about? Then have them write a sentence or draw a picture that tells about an important fact they learned from the selection.

Plan to Assess Retelling

- ☐ **Week 1** Strategic Intervention
- ☑ **This Week** Assess Advanced children.
- ☐ **Week 3** Strategic Intervention
- ☐ **Week 4** On-Level
- ☐ **Week 5** Strategic Intervention
- ☐ **Week 6** Assess any children you have not yet checked during this unit.

Meet the Author

Read aloud page 419 as children follow along. Discuss why John Herman might love reading about American history.

Read Independently

Have children enter their independent reading into their Reading Logs.

Common Core State Standards

Language 2. Demonstrate command of the conventions of standard English capitalization, punctuation, and spelling when writing. **Writing 3.** Write narratives in which they recount a well-elaborated event or short sequence of events, include details to describe actions, thoughts, and feelings, use temporal words to signal event order, and provide a sense of closure.

Daily Fix-It

5. some of the strippes are white.
Some of the stripes are white.

6. People move to america
People move to America.

Discuss the Daily Fix-It corrections with children. Review sentence and proper noun capitalization, punctuation, and the correct spelling of *stripes.*

Conventions

Quotation Marks

REVIEW Remind children that quotation marks show the beginning and end of the words someone says. Add that writing with quotation marks lets readers know that someone is talking. *"Please, can I have a snack?" begged Sue.*

GUIDE PRACTICE Write this quotation on the board and have children read it aloud.

Abraham Lincoln said, "If there is anything that a man can do well, I say let him do it. Give him a chance."

What is the first word that Abraham Lincoln said? What is the last word Abraham Lincoln said?

Team Talk Have partners work together to think of a sentence they could say about giving people a chance to do something. Have them write their sentence as dialogue, putting quotation marks around the words they would say.

APPLY Have children orally complete the following dialogue.

1. **"_______?" asked Stan.**
2. **"_______," answered Mike.**
3. **"_______," said Stan.**
4. **"_______!" shouted Mike.**

ON THEIR OWN Use Let's Practice It!, p. 307 on the *Teacher Resources DVD-ROM.*

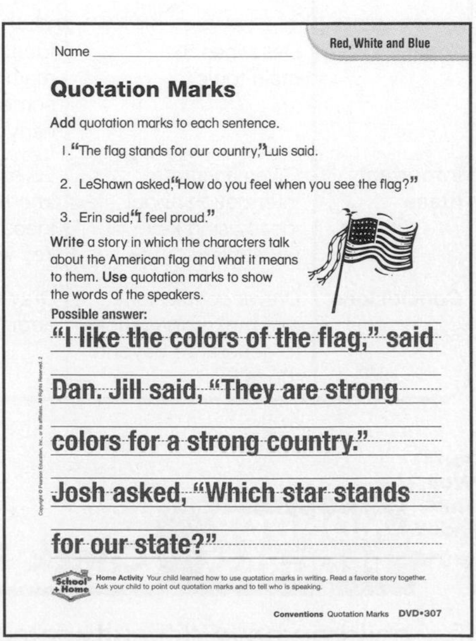
Name ______________ Red, White and Blue

Quotation Marks

Add quotation marks to each sentence.

1. "The flag stands for our country," Luis said.
2. LeShawn asked, "How do you feel when you see the flag?"
3. Erin said, "I feel proud."

Write a story in which the characters talk about the American flag and what it means to them. **Use** quotation marks to show the words of the speakers.

Possible answer:

"I like the colors of the flag," said Dan. Jill said, "They are strong colors for a strong country." Josh asked, "Which star stands for our state?"

Home Activity Your child learned how to use quotation marks in writing. Read a favorite story together. Ask your child to point out quotation marks and to tell who is speaking.

Conventions Quotation Marks DVD•307

Let's Practice It! TR DVD•307

Common Core State Standards
Writing 3. Write narratives in which they recount a well-elaborated event or short sequence of events, include details to describe actions, thoughts, and feelings, use temporal words to signal event order, and provide a sense of closure.
Also Language 2.

Let's Write It!

Key Features of a Descriptive Poem or Song

- has carefully chosen words arranged in lines
- describes something and may have rhymes
- A song is like a poem that people sing.

READING STREET ONLINE
GRAMMAR JAMMER
www.ReadingStreet.com

Descriptive

Descriptive Poem or Song

A descriptive poem or song describes something. It may tell how someone feels too. Many poems and songs have words that rhyme. The student model on the next page is an example of a descriptive poem.

Writing Prompt Think about American symbols and traditions. Now write a poem about one of those symbols or traditions.

Writer's Checklist

Remember, you should ...

- ✓ include words that describe.
- ✓ express your interest in the topic.
- ✓ use sentence punctuation and quotation marks correctly.

420

Student Model

The Statue of Liberty

The Statue of Liberty is so grand.
She welcomes people to our land.
She holds her torch of light so high.
It looks like it could touch the blue sky.
She seems to say, "Come in and be free."
She is a great symbol of our country.

Genre This **descriptive poem** has words that rhyme and words that describe.

Writing Trait Voice The writer expresses feelings about the topic.

The writer uses **quotation marks** to show spoken words.

Conventions

Using Quotation Marks

- **Quotation marks (" ")** show the beginning and end of the words someone says. A word such as *said* and the speaker's name are not inside the quotation marks.
- Place a period in a quotation inside the marks.

421

Student Edition, pp. 420–421

Let's Write It!

WRITE A DESCRIPTIVE POEM OR SONG Use pp. 420–421 in the Student Edition. Read aloud the Key Features of a Descriptive Poem or Song and the definition. Read aloud the Writing Prompt and discuss the Writer's Checklist.

REVIEW THE STUDENT MODEL Read aloud "The Statue of Liberty." Ask children to identify some of the descriptions. Then read aloud and briefly discuss the side notes about genre, the writing trait, and using quotation marks.

Scoring Rubric

TOP-SCORE RESPONSE Help children understand that a top-score response includes description, shares a feeling, and uses a quote. For a complete rubric see Writing Rubric 27 from the *Teacher Resources DVD-ROM.*

CONNECT TO CONVENTIONS Read to children the Conventions note about using quotation marks.

eStreet Interactive
www.ReadingStreet.com

Pearson eText
- Student Edition

Teacher Resources
- Let's Practice It!
- Daily Fix-It Transparency
- Scoring Rubric

ELL

Guide Writing Explain that poems do not have to rhyme. Then present this frame for children to complete:

The ________ is an American symbol.
It is ________ and ________.
It stands for ________.
It makes me feel ________.

Writing 3. Write narratives in which they recount a well-elaborated event or short sequence of events, include details to describe actions, thoughts, and feelings, use temporal words to signal event order, and provide a sense of closure. **Writing 8.** Recall information from experiences or gather information from provided sources to answer a question.

Writing

Descriptive Poem or Song

Mini-Lesson Writer's Craft: Express Feelings

- **Introduce** Use the web from yesterday and Writing Transparency 27A to model a descriptive poem. Yesterday I chose Thanksgiving as the topic of my poem. I wrote in the web that Thanksgiving made me think about food, such as turkey, beans, and pie. I added details that help the reader see and almost taste the food. My quote was "It's the yummiest!" I also included details about the Pilgrims and giving thanks at a feast. Here is the poem I wrote. I used the web to help me write descriptions. I also directly stated my feelings for Thanksgiving in the first sentence and I used words that rhyme. Read aloud the draft on the Transparency.

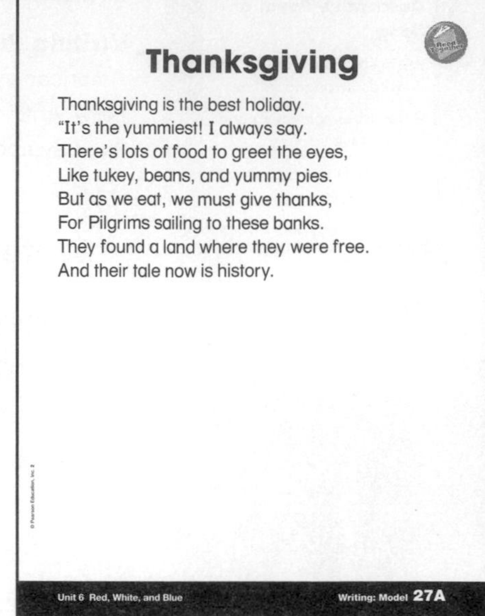

Thanksgiving

Thanksgiving is the best holiday.
"It's the yummiest! I always say.
There's lots of food to greet the eyes,
Like tukey, beans, and yummy pies.
But as we eat, we must give thanks,
For Pilgrims sailing to these banks.
They found a land where they were free.
And their tale now is history.

Unit 6 Red, White, and Blue — Writing: Model 27A

Writing Transparency 27A TR DVD

- Explain how children can use their webs to draft the poem to describe and add sensory details to their topic. Explain they can write a song or a poem in free verse, if they prefer. Remind children that the goal is to write the ideas on paper. They can edit later to correct the words.

GUIDE WRITING Now it is time to draft your poem or song. Tell about an American symbol or tradition and how you feel about it. Have children use their webs. Help them finish the ideas. Then guide children as they draft the poems or songs.

Routine Quick Write for Fluency

Team Talk

1. **Talk** Have partners take one minute to talk about how they feel about the symbol or tradition they chose.
2. **Write** Each child writes the partner's ideas as a quote.
3. **Share** Partners point out the quotation marks in the other's sentences.

Routines Flip Chart

Research and Inquiry

Step 3 Gather and Record Information

TEACH Tell children that today they will gather information about U.S. celebrations. Their goal is to find out more about celebrations that use the American flag.

Think Aloud **MODEL** Display the list of questions from Day 1. We asked the question *On which holidays do we use the American flag?* In *Red, White, and Blue,* we learned June 14 is Flag Day. Ask children what other information you might include about Flag Day. Record the information in the inquiry chart.

GUIDE PRACTICE Provide books and others sources for children to use in their research. Have partners use the sources to answer the first question and research other questions. Compile their information. Tell children that tomorrow they will review the topic to make sure their questions were answered.

Topic: Celebrations That Use the American Flag

Question	Answer
On which holidays do we use the American flag?	Flag Day—June 14. We fly the flag.

Access for All

SI Strategic Intervention

Charts Review with children that there are many different kinds of charts: T-charts, three-column charts, four-column charts, K-W-L charts, and so on. Help them make a three-column chart to organize the information about holidays with the heads *Holiday, Date,* and *How We Use the Flag.*

Wrap Up Your Day!

✔ **Author's Purpose** Why did the author write *Red, White, and Blue: The Story of the American Flag?* How can you tell?

✔ **Summarize** Have children tell why it is important to recall important selection ideas while reading.

Tell children that tomorrow they will read about the American flag and what it stands for.

DAY 4 at a Glance

Content Knowledge
Oral Vocabulary

Phonics
Review Inflected Endings

High-Frequency Words
Review

Spelling
Abbreviations

Poetry in Reading
Poetry (Song)

Fluency
Accuracy

Conventions
Quotation Marks

Writing
Descriptive Poem or Song: Revise

Listening and Speaking
Evaluate Advertisements

Research and Inquiry
Synthesize

Materials

- Student Edition
- Sing with Me Big Book
- Read Aloud Anthology
- Decodable Reader 27C
- Reader's and Writer's Notebook

Common Core State Standards

Speaking/Listening 2. Recount or describe key ideas or details from a text read aloud or information presented orally or through other media. **Language 6.** Use words and phrases acquired through conversations, reading and being read to, and responding to texts, including using adjectives and adverbs to describe (e.g., *When other kids are happy that makes me happy*).

Content Knowledge

The American Flag

EXPAND THE CONCEPT To reinforce concepts and to focus children's attention, have children sing "Our Flag, Our Symbol" from the *Sing with Me* Big Book. What do we love about our flag? (We love its stars and stripes.)

Build Oral Language

REVIEW GENRE: INFORMATIONAL TEXT Have children tell the key features of informational text: it often gives facts about real people, places, and events that reflect history or the traditions of communities. Explain that today you will read more facts about the history of our flag in "Uncle Sam and Old Glory: Symbols of America" by Delno C. West and Jean M. West.

"Uncle Sam and Old Glory"

MONITOR LISTENING COMPREHENSION Recall the story of how George Washington and Betsy Ross created the first flag with stars and stripes. Have children listen to "Uncle Sam and Old Glory."

Team Talk **TALK ABOUT THE AMERICAN FLAG** Read aloud the first paragraph of page 151 of "Uncle Sam and Old Glory." Display it on a whiteboard if possible, and track the print as you read.

- Have pairs of children generate questions for each other about what they visualize about the morning routine at school when they hear this paragraph.
- Add words generated in the discussion to the concept map.

Build Oral Vocabulary

Amazing Words **Robust Vocabulary Routine**

1. **Introduce the Word** Relate the word *allegiance* to the story. Children say the Pledge of *Allegiance* in classrooms every morning. Supply a child-friendly definition. *Allegiance* is the loyalty a person feels to his or her country, school, family, friends, or a leader. Have children say the word.
2. **Demonstrate** Provide examples to show meaning. A young man or woman might join the army because of *allegiance* to his or her country. Children say the pledge to show their *allegiance* to the United States.
3. **Apply** Have children demonstrate their understanding. How would you show your *allegiance* to something or someone important to you?
4. **Display the Word** Run your hand under the three chunks *al-le-giance* as you read the word.

See p. OV•2 to teach *indivisible.*

Routines Flip Chart

ADD TO THE CONCEPT MAP Discuss the flag and its traditions.

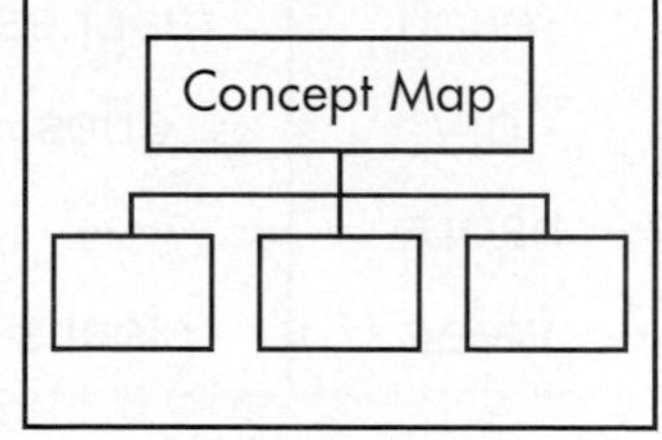

- What happens every morning in classrooms across the country? (Children say the Pledge of Allegiance.) We'll add *We say the Pledge of Allegiance* as our last important tradition.
- Why does the flag we pledge allegiance to look the way it does? (The red, white, and blue colors stand for courage, liberty, and loyalty. The stripes are symbols of the first thirteen colonies, and the stars are symbols of the states.) Let's add this idea to our chart: *Our flag's colors, stars, and stripes are symbols.*

Amazing Words

history	unfurl
independence	frayed
symbol	allegiance
patriotic	indivisible

Produce Oral Language Use the Day 4 instruction on ELL Poster 27 to extend and enrich language.

Preview Comprehension Refer children to the map of the thirteen colonies on p. 403 and the first flag pictured on p. 404 in their Student Edition. Have them compare the number of stars and stripes with the number of colonies. Then have them compare a current map of the United States with today's flag.

Common Core State Standards

Foundational Skills 3. Know and apply grade-level phonics and word analysis skills in decoding words.

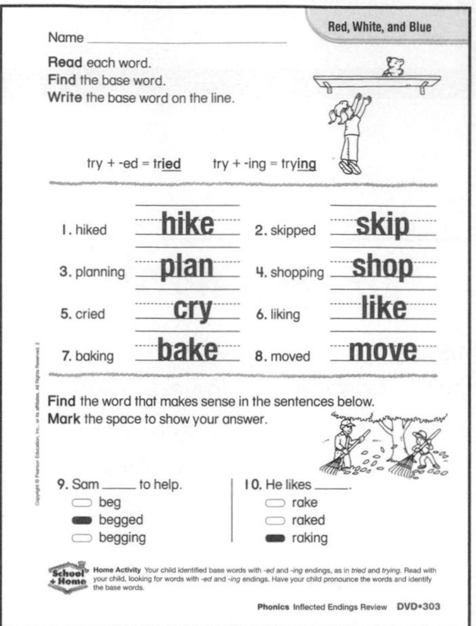
Red, White, and Blue

Name ____________

Read each word.
Find the base word.
Write the base word on the line.

try + -ed = tr**ied** try + -ing = try**ing**

1. hiked hike
2. skipped skip
3. planning plan
4. shopping shop
5. cried cry
6. liking like
7. baking bake
8. moved move

Find the word that makes sense in the sentences below.
Mark the space to show your answer.

9. Sam ____ to help.
- beg
- begged
- begging

10. He likes ____.
- rake
- raked
- raking

Home Activity Your child identified base words with *-ed* and *-ing* endings, as in *tried* and *trying*. Read with your child, looking for words with *-ed* and *-ing* endings. Have your child pronounce the words and identify the base words.

Phonics Inflected Endings Review DVD•303

Let's Practice It! TR DVD•303

Phonics

Review Inflected Endings

REVIEW INFLECTED ENDINGS To review last week's phonics skill, write *fixes, driving, chatted,* and *spicier.* You studied words like these last week. What do you know about reading them? (These words have endings. If a word has an ending, look closely at the base word because it may have a spelling change. Read the base word and then read the ending.)

Corrective feedback	If children are unable to answer the question about inflected endings, refer them to Sound-Spelling Cards 121, 122, 123, 124, 125, 126, 127, 128, 129, and 130.

GUIDE PRACTICE Draw a six-column chart. Write the headings and base words in the first column as shown. Have children read each base word, determine which endings can be added to the word, and identify any spelling changes. As children respond, write the words in the chart. Then have them read the rows of words.

Base Word	*-s* or *-es*	*-ed*	*-ing*	*-er*	*-est*
step	steps	stepped	stepping	—	—
funny	—	—	—	funnier	funniest
bounce	bounces	bounced	bouncing	—	—
reach	reaches	reached	reaching	—	—
dry	dries	dried	drying	drier	driest
happy	—	—	—	happier	happiest
clean	cleans	cleaned	cleaning	cleaner	cleanest

ON THEIR OWN Use Let's Practice It!, p. 303 on the *Teacher Resources DVD-ROM.*

Fluent Word Reading

Spiral Review

READ WORDS IN ISOLATION Display these words and abbreviations. Tell children that they can blend some words on this list and others are abbreviations or Word Wall words.

Have children read the list three or four times until they can read at the rate of two to three seconds per word.

drawing	**because**	**wash**	**Mr.**	**picture**
raise	**Mrs.**	**chalk**	**taught**	**answer**
school	**Ave.**	**company**	**always**	**Aug.**
Mon.	**walkway**	**parents**	**faraway**	**laundry**

Corrective feedback

Word Reading

If... children have difficulty reading whole words or abbreviations,
then... have them blend decodable words, work on identifying abbreviations, or say and spell high-frequency words.

If... children cannot read fluently at a rate of two to three seconds per word,
then... have pairs practice the list until they can read it fluently.

READ WORDS IN CONTEXT Display these sentences. Call on individuals to read a sentence. Then randomly point to review words for children to read. To help you monitor word reading, high-frequency words are underlined and decodable words are italicized.

We are *drawing* a *chalk* <u>picture</u> on the *walkway* by First *Ave*.

My <u>parents</u> <u>wash</u> our *laundry* every *Mon*. *because* it's dirty!

***Mr. Brainerd* started his <u>company</u> last *Aug*. in a <u>faraway</u> city.**

In <u>school</u> *Mrs. Crawford taught* us *always* to *raise* our hands before *saying* the <u>answer</u>.

Corrective feedback

Sentence Reading

If... children cannot read an underlined high-frequency word,
then... read the word for them and spell it, having them echo you.

If... children have difficulty reading an italicized decodable word,
then... guide them in blending or identifying abbreviations.

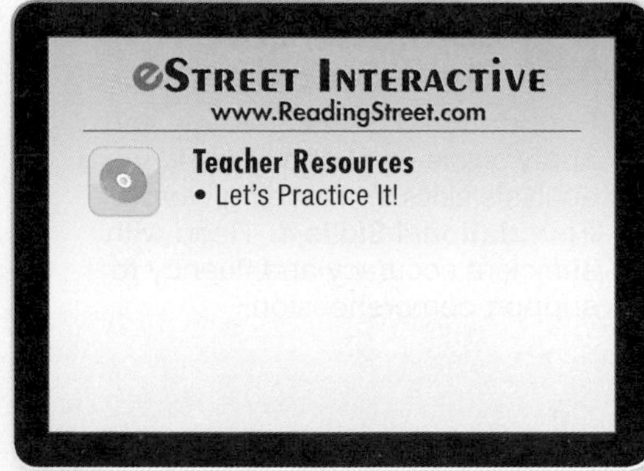

Spiral Review

These activities review

- your previously taught high-frequency words *answer, company, faraway, parents, picture, school, wash.*
- abbreviations.
- vowel patterns *aw, au, au(gh), al.*
- vowel digraphs *ai, ay.*

Fluent Word Reading Have children listen to a more fluent reader model the words or have pairs read the words together.

Common Core State Standards

Foundational Skills 3. Know and apply grade-level phonics and word analysis skills in decoding words. **Foundational Skills 4.** Read with sufficient accuracy and fluency to support comprehension.

Decodable Reader 27C

If children need help, then...

Read *North Hall Street*

DECODE WORDS IN ISOLATION Have children turn to page 209 in *Decodable Practice Readers* 2.2 and decode each word.

READ HIGH-FREQUENCY WORDS Have children identify and read the high-frequency words *almost, dog,* and *north* on the first page.

PREVIEW Have children read the title and preview the story. Tell them they will read a story that has abbreviations.

DECODE WORDS IN CONTEXT Pair children for reading and listen as they decode. One child begins. Children read the entire story, switching readers after each page. Partners reread the story. This time the other child begins.

North Hall Street

Written by Jake Swanson

Decodable Practice Reader 27C

Abbreviations

Sat., Aug., St.
Mr., Mrs., Dr.
Ms., Ave.

High-Frequency Words

north dog almost

209

Decodable Practice Reader 27C

A sign said, "Yard Sale on Sat., Aug. 17 at 123 North Hall St." Mr. Walter Hanks saw the sign. He wrote down the day and address.

210

At home, Mr. Hanks told Mrs. Hanks about the yard sale. Mr. and Mrs. Hanks planned to go. Yard sales were important to them.

211

Mrs. Hanks took her dog to a vet. Mrs. Hanks told Dr. Sara Woo about the sale. Dr. Woo planned to go.

212

Dr. Woo told Ms. Nevins. Hall St. was close to Ms. Nevins' house on Elm Ave. She planned on going with her family.

213

Mr. and Mrs. Hanks, Dr. Woo, and Ms. Nevins told more pals. Almost all of them planned to go to the sale. They told other people, too.

214

On Saturday, Mr. and Mrs. Hanks went to the yard sale at 132 South Hall St. So did all a lot of other people. But there was no yard sale!

215

Mr. Hanks looked at his note. "Whoops, it's not 132, but 123 North Hall St.," he said. And that is where all the shoppers went!

216

Corrective feedback	**If...** children have difficulty decoding a word or abbreviation, **then...** refer them to the Sound-Spelling Cards to identify the sounds in a decodable word; prompt them to blend the word. If the word is an abbreviation, review the abbreviation and its corresponding word. • What is the new word? • Is the new word a word you know? • Does it make sense in the story?

CHECK DECODING AND COMPREHENSION Have children retell the story to include characters, setting, and events. Then have children find abbreviations in the story. They should supply *Sat., Aug., St., Mr., Mrs., Dr., Ms.,* and *Ave.*

Reread for Fluency

REREAD DECODABLE READER Have children reread Decodable Practice Reader 27C to develop automaticity decoding abbreviations.

Routine Oral Rereading

1. **Read** Have children read the entire book orally.
2. **Reread** To achieve optimal fluency, children should reread the text three or four times.
3. **Corrective Feedback** Listen as children read. Provide corrective feedback regarding their fluency and decoding.

Routines Flip Chart

Leveled Support

Beginning After reading, write an abbreviation from the story on the board. Next to it write a pair of similar words, one of which is the corresponding word. Examples: ***Mister****/Mark; Gas/****August;*** *Stop/****Street; Mistress****/Missing;* ***Doctor****/Drip; Moss/****Miss; Avenue****/Van.* Read the sentence from the story and ask children to identify which word you read.

Intermediate Have partners write the abbreviations from the first page as a list. Have children review the story and record with a tally the number of times each word appears. Partners chorally read the sentences.

Advanced Pair children. Have them use the list on the first page to write abbreviations on small pieces of paper. Have them sort the words into three groups: people, places, and days and months.

Common Core State Standards

Language 2. Demonstrate command of the conventions of standard English capitalization, punctuation, and spelling when writing. **Literature 4.** Describe how words and phrases (e.g., regular beats, alliteration, rhymes, repeated lines) supply rhythm and meaning in a story, poem, or song.

Spelling

Abbreviations

PARTNER REVIEW Supply pairs of children with index cards on which the spelling words have been written. Have one child read a word while the other writes it. Then have children switch roles. Have them use the cards to check their spelling and correct any misspelled words.

ON THEIR OWN Use Let's Practice It!, p. 306 on the *Teacher Resources DVD-ROM.*

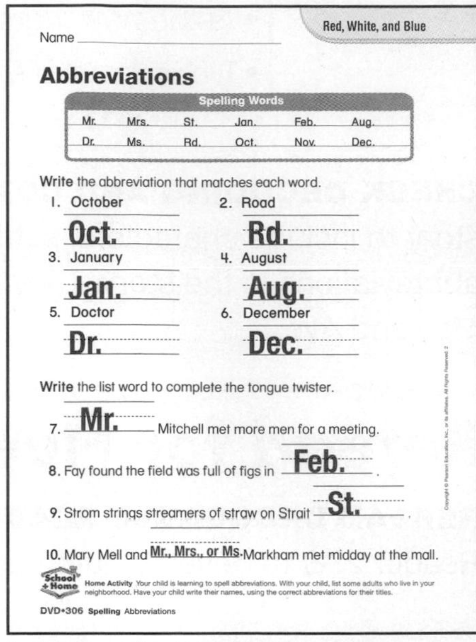

Name ____________ Red, White, and Blue

Abbreviations

Spelling Words					
Mr.	Mrs.	St.	Jan.	Feb.	Aug.
Dr.	Ms.	Rd.	Oct.	Nov.	Dec.

Write the abbreviation that matches each word.

1. October — Oct.
2. Road — Rd.
3. January — Jan.
4. August — Aug.
5. Doctor — Dr.
6. December — Dec.

Write the list word to complete the tongue twister.

7. Mr. Mitchell met more men for a meeting.
8. Fay found the field was full of figs in Feb.
9. Strom strings streamers of straw on Strait St.
10. Mary Mell and Mr., Mrs., or Ms. Markham met midday at the mall.

DVD•306 Spelling Abbreviations

Let's Practice It! TR DVD•306

If... children need more scaffolding and practice with **Amazing Words, then...** use the routine on pp. xxxvi–xxxvii in the *ELL Handbook.*

Day 4 SMALL GROUP TIME • Differentiate Vocabulary, p. SG•18

OL On-Level	SI Strategic Intervention	A Advanced
• **Develop** Language Using Amazing Words • **Read** *Reading Street Sleuth,* pp. 70–71	• **Review/Discuss** Amazing Words • **Read** *Reading Street Sleuth,* pp. 70–71	• **Extend** Amazing Words and Selection Vocabulary • **Read** *Reading Street Sleuth,* pp. 70–71 • **Organize** Inquiry Project

Poetry in Reading

Poetry (Song)

ACTIVATE PRIOR KNOWLEDGE Remind children that poems often show feelings. Ask them to recall from *Red, White, and Blue* how Francis Scott Key felt when he wrote the poem "The Star-Spangled Banner." (He was proud that the flag was still flying after a battle.)

PREVIEW AND PREDICT Have children turn to pages 422–423 in their Student Edition. Read the title and the author's name. Have children look through the selection and predict what it might be about. (a poem about the United States flag)

READ POETRY (SONG) Tell children that they will read the words to a song, which is a form of **poetry.** Review the key features of poetry: it creates an image and expresses feelings. It is written in lines, and the lines are often arranged in groups called verses. The lines have a rhythm, or beat, and words sometimes rhyme or are repeated. Explain that in some poems consonant sounds at the beginning of words or within words are repeated, such as "broad stripes and bright stars." This kind of sound repetition is called **alliteration.**

Genre

LET'S THINK ABOUT... As children read "You're a Grand Old Flag," use Let's Think About in the Student Edition to help them focus on the features and structure of poetry.

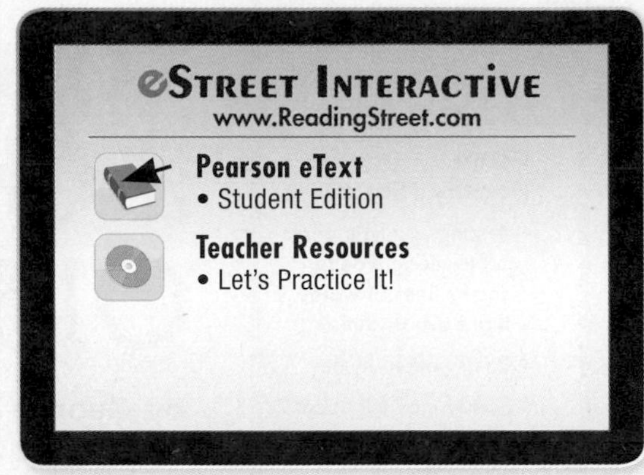

Academic Vocabulary

poetry carefully chosen words, arranged in lines that create an image and express thoughts and feelings. A poem usually has a rhythm and sometimes has rhyme or repetition.

alliteration the repetition of consonants sounds at the beginning of words or within words

Social Studies in Reading

Genre
Poetry (Song)

- A song is a lyric poem set to music. Poetry shows lines of words that have rhythm.
- Poetry often rhymes.
- Poetry may tell about what the poet senses and feels.
- Read "You're a Grand Old Flag." As you read, think about how the songwriter feels about the American flag.
- Songs often use words that have different meanings from their ordinary meanings. Find the phrase "Ev'ry heart beats true." Is this the literal, or real, meaning of the words? Or do the words mean something else?

You're a Grand Old Flag

by George M. Cohan

You're a grand old flag,
You're a high flying flag
And forever in peace may
  you wave.
You're the emblem of the
  land I love.
The home of the free and
  the brave.

Ev'ry heart beats true
'Neath the red, white, and blue,
Where there's never a boast
  or brag.
Should auld acquaintance
  be forgot,
Keep your eye on the grand
  old flag.

Let's Think About...

How do the words create a **rhythm**? Find the words that **rhyme**. 1

Let's Think About...

Reading Across Texts "You're a Grand Old Flag" is one song about the flag of the United States. What other song about the flag did you read about in *Red, White, and Blue*?

Writing Across Texts Make a list of other traditional songs that you know.

422 423

Student Edition, pp. 422–423

Common Core State Standards

Literature 4. Describe how words and phrases (e.g., regular beats, alliteration, rhymes, repeated lines) supply rhythm and meaning in a story, poem, or song. **Literature 10.** By the end of the year, read and comprehend literature, including stories and poetry, in the grades 2–3 text complexity band proficiently, with scaffolding as needed at the high end of the range.

Access Text

Think Aloud **SUMMARIZE** To summarize, I think about the most important ideas I've read. In the poem the most important ideas are these: The flag is grand because it stands for the country that the speaker loves. That country is the home of free, brave people, where the writer hopes there will always be peace.

Think Aloud **DRAW CONCLUSIONS** I can use clues in the text to draw a conclusion about how the author feels about the flag. He calls it a "grand" flag and a "high flying" flag, and he calls it an emblem of the land he loves. I can conclude that he loves the flag.

ALLITERATION What is alliteration? (the repetition of consonant sounds in two or more words) What are some examples of alliteration in the song? *(flying flag, land I love, boast or brag)*

AUTHOR'S PURPOSE Why do you think George M. Cohan wrote this song? (to express his love of the flag and his country)

LET'S THINK ABOUT... features of poetry

1. Possible response: When you read the words aloud, you hear a beat. The words that rhyme are *wave/brave, true/blue,* and *brag/flag.*

Reading Across Texts

Children should name "The Star-Spangled Banner" as the song they read about in *Red, White, and Blue.* Suggest children reread pages 408–409 to review when and why the poem was written.

Writing Across Texts

If children have difficulty thinking of songs, have them work in groups. Possible responses: "America the Beautiful," "Yankee Doodle," "My Country, 'Tis of Thee," "God Bless America." Children might also name folk tunes such as "On Top of Old Smoky."

Vocabulary Support

auld acquaintance Explain to children that the line "Should auld acquaintance be forgot" comes from a popular old Scottish song and means "Should old friends be forgotten?"

Common Core State Standards

Foundational Skills 4.b. Read on-level text orally with accuracy, appropriate rate, and expression on successive readings. **Language 2.** Demonstrate command of the conventions of standard English capitalization, punctuation, and spelling when writing.

Access for All

Advanced

Rate If children already read at 90 words correct per minute, have them read more challenging text.

Fluency Assessment Plan

Do a formal fluency assessment with eight to ten children every week. Assess four or five children on Day 4 and four or five children on Day 5. Use the reproducible fluency passage, Teacher's Edition, p. 425f.

Options for Oral Rereading

Use *Red, White, and Blue* or one of the week's Decodable Practice Readers.

Fluency

Accuracy

- Have children turn to pp. 404–405 in *Red, White, and Blue.*
- Have children follow along as you read the pages accurately without making a mistake.
- Have the class read the pages with you and then reread the pages as a group until they read without making mistakes. To provide additional fluency practice, pair nonfluent readers with fluent readers.

Routine Paired Reading

1. **Select a Passage** For *Red, White, and Blue,* use pp. 406–409.
2. **Model** First, have children track the print as you read.
3. **Guide Practice** Then have children read along with you.
4. **On Their Own** For optimal fluency, have partners reread three or four times.

Routines Flip Chart

Fluency Check

As children reread, monitor their progress toward their individual fluency goals. Current Goal: 80–90 words correct per minute. End-of-Year-Goal: 90 words correct per minute.

If... children cannot read fluently at a rate of 80–90 words correct per minute,
then... have children practice with text at their independent level.

Conventions

Quotation Marks

TEST PRACTICE Use *Reader's and Writer's Notebook,* p. 504 to help children understand identifying dialogue with quotation marks in test items. Recall that quotation marks show the beginning and ending words that someone says: *Jon ordered, "Get that book."* Model identifying words that should appear in quotation marks by writing this sentence on the board, reading it aloud, and underlining words within the quotation marks.

> **"Can I see the movie?" asked Bretta.**

Then read the *Reader's and Writer's Notebook,* p. 504 directions. Guide children as they mark the answer for number 1.

ON THEIR OWN Use *Reader's and Writer's Notebook,* p. 504.

APPLY After children mark the answers to numbers 1–6, review the correct choices aloud, and have children read each sentence aloud and point out words that appear in quotation marks.

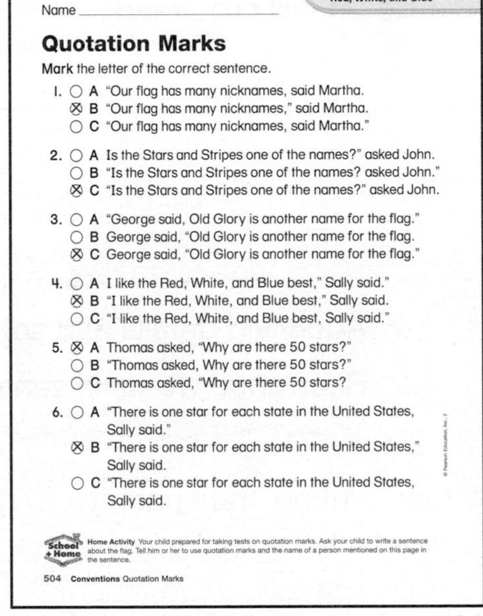

Red, White, and Blue

Name ____________

Quotation Marks

Mark the letter of the correct sentence.

1. ○ A "Our flag has many nicknames, said Martha.
   ⊗ B "Our flag has many nicknames," said Martha.
   ○ C "Our flag has many nicknames, said Martha."
2. ○ A Is the Stars and Stripes one of the names?" asked John.
   ○ B "Is the Stars and Stripes one of the names? asked John."
   ⊗ C "Is the Stars and Stripes one of the names?" asked John.
3. ○ A "George said, Old Glory is another name for the flag."
   ○ B George said, "Old Glory is another name for the flag.
   ⊗ C George said, "Old Glory is another name for the flag."
4. ○ A I like the Red, White, and Blue best," Sally said."
   ⊗ B "I like the Red, White, and Blue best," Sally said.
   ○ C "I like the Red, White, and Blue best, Sally said."
5. ⊗ A Thomas asked, "Why are there 50 stars?"
   ○ B "Thomas asked, Why are there 50 stars?"
   ○ C Thomas asked, "Why are there 50 stars?
6. ○ A "There is one star for each state in the United States, Sally said."
   ⊗ B "There is one star for each state in the United States," Sally said.
   ○ C "There is one star for each state in the United States, Sally said.

School + Home **Home Activity** Your child prepared for taking tests on quotation marks. Ask your child to write a sentence about the flag. Tell him or her to use quotation marks and the name of a person mentioned on this page in the sentence.

504 **Conventions** Quotation Marks

Reader's and Writer's Notebook, p. 504

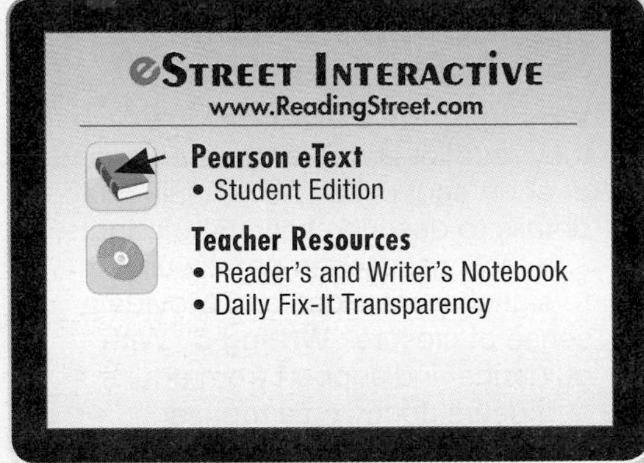

Bridge to Common Core

CONVENTIONS OF STANDARD ENGLISH

As children identify and use quotation marks, they are gaining control of the conventions of standard English. Your guidance will help them use quotation marks effectively as they write.

Daily Fix-It

7. america's birthdaiy is July 4th.
   America's birthday is July 4th.
8. i painted sturs and stripes.
   I painted stars and stripes.

Discuss the Daily Fix-It corrections with children. Review spelling and capitalization.

Common Core State Standards

Writing 3. Write narratives in which they recount a well-elaborated event or short sequence of events, include details to describe actions, thoughts, and feelings, use temporal words to signal event order, and provide a sense of closure. **Writing 5.** With guidance and support from adults and peers, focus on a topic and strengthen writing as needed by revising and editing.

Writing

Descriptive Poem or Song

Mini-Lesson Revise: Rearranging Words in Sentences

- Yesterday we wrote descriptive poems and songs. Today we will revise and look for ways to add details. We will also look to see whether we can rearrange words to improve the rhythm of the poem.

- Display the Revising Tips. Explain that revising is a time for making the description vivid and looking at the rhythm and rhyme of the poem or song. Tomorrow children will proofread.

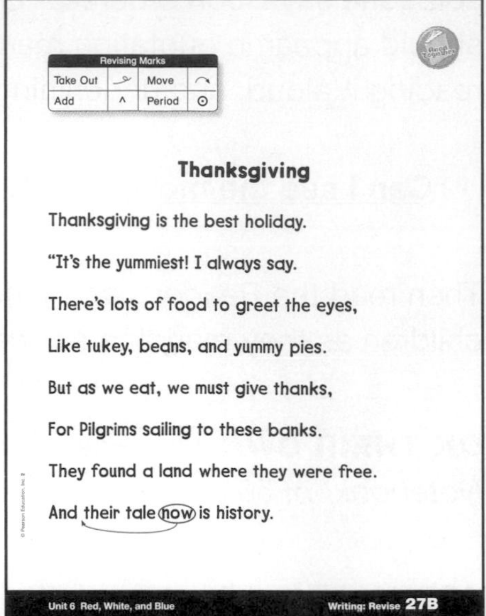

Revising Marks			
Take Out	⟋	Move	⌒
Add	^	Period	⊙

Thanksgiving

Thanksgiving is the best holiday.

"It's the yummiest! I always say.

There's lots of food to greet the eyes,

Like tukey, beans, and yummy pies.

But as we eat, we must give thanks,

For Pilgrims sailing to these banks.

They found a land where they were free.

And their tale now is history.

Unit 6 Red, White, and Blue — Writing: Revise 27B

Writing Transparency 27B TR DVD

Revising Tips

✔ Add vivid details and sensory details.

✔ Rearrange words in sentences to make ideas clear.

- Use Writing Transparency 27B to model adding vivid details and rearranging words. Look at the last sentence: *And their tale now is history.* The rhythm does not follow the rest of the poem. I'll rearrange the words so the line reads: And now their tale is history. Tell children to add words to give vivid details and rearrange or delete words to improve rhythm.

PEER CONFERENCING • PEER REVISION Have children take turns reading their poems in a small group. Children should listen for any part of each poem that may not have a smooth rhythm. Ask listeners to identify whether each poem is a poem or song with rhyme and a regular rhythm or a free verse poem without rhyme or a regular rhythm. Then have listeners take turns sharing descriptions they like in the poems. Circulate to assist children planning to revise their poem. As appropriate, suggest adding vivid and sensory details and rearranging words to smooth the rhythm.

GUIDE PRACTICE Have children revise their poems. For those not sure how to revise, have children refer to the Revising Tips or the Key Features of a Descriptive Poem or Song.

Corrective feedback Circulate to monitor and confer with children as they write. Remind them that they will have time to proofread and edit tomorrow. Today they can make changes in details and word order. Help them understand the benefits of adding or changing words, especially to improve rhythm.

Routine Quick Write for Fluency

Team Talk

1. **Talk** Read this couplet aloud, and have children tell how to rearrange words to improve the rhythm.
   On the Fourth of July, the fireworks fly.
   In the air they burst and color the sky.
   (They burst in the air and color the sky.)
2. **Write** Have children write another couplet about the Fourth of July.
3. **Share** Partners read their couplets and discuss if the lines rhyme and have rhythm. They can work together to improve couplets when needed.

Routines Flip Chart

Access for All

Strategic Intervention

Computer Rhyming Words Show children how to find a child-friendly rhyming word Web site. Let them search for words to complete rhymes.

Listening and Speaking

Evaluate Advertisements

TEACH Explain to children that one purpose for speaking is to persuade—to get listeners to agree with an idea or argument. Advertisements are a powerful example of persuasive speaking. The speaker's goal is to get listeners to buy a product or service. Explain that advertisements seek to persuade by

- identifying the target audience, or people most likely to be persuaded to buy a product or service.
- using "loaded" words: words that make listeners feel they need the product or service.
- including facts that prove why the product or service is better than competing products or services.

Explain that good listeners evaluate advertising by

- asking if the product or service is one they really need.
- identifying opinions and loaded words in the advertisement.
- identifying facts that prove the product or service is the best choice.

MODEL Use the passage below to model evaluating advertisements.

Yesterday, I heard an advertisement for laundry detergent. I buy laundry detergent, so I listened carefully. The speaker used the word *concentrated,* saying I could wash 16 more loads of laundry than with the same amount of regular detergent. He also said the product was *tough on stains.* That made me think it was a good product. The speaker then said the product costs 20 percent less than other detergents. This fact made me decide to buy this product, because I want to save money.

GUIDE PRACTICE Read these ad pitches aloud and evaluate their effectiveness as a class. Encourage children to identify target audience, loaded words, and facts.

number-one selling vacuum cleaner
uses half the energy to wash dishes
take years off your face with this cream
tastes as good as Grandma's
gets 20 more miles to the gallon
your friends will want these shoes

ON THEIR OWN Divide the class into small groups. Tell children they will work together to write a script for the purpose of selling a product. Remind them to identify their target audience, to choose words that get listeners excited about the product, and to support their product with facts. Allow groups to perform their scripts for the class or to record them and present them. Have classmates evaluate the effectiveness of each group's advertisement.

Common Core State Standards

Writing 1. Write opinion pieces in which they introduce the topic or book they are writing about, state an opinion, supply reasons that support the opinion, use linking words (e.g., *because, and, also*) to connect opinion and reasons, and provide a concluding statement or section. **Speaking/Listening 3.** Ask and answer questions about what a speaker says in order to clarify comprehension, gather additional information, or deepen understanding of a topic or issue. **Also Speaking/Listening 1.**

Bridge to Common Core

COMPREHENSION AND COLLABORATION

As children collaborate to produce, perform, and evaluate scripts, they are learning to present information in a way that enables listeners to follow the line of reasoning and to evaluate information presented.

Research and Inquiry

Step 4 Synthesize

TEACH Tell children that the next step in their inquiry project is to review the topic to see if they have the information they set out to find or if their answers lead to a different topic.

MODEL We planned to find out more about celebrations that use the American flag. Display the list of inquiry questions and the answers recorded during research. The first question was *On which holidays do we use the American flag?* One answer was *Flag Day.* This is a good example of a celebration with the flag. So we have answered the topic, and it does not need to change.

GUIDE PRACTICE Read the remaining inquiry questions and answers. After each answer is read, have partners discuss whether or not the answer provides information about celebrations that use the American flag. Note any new questions the children have and revise the original topic if necessary. Finally, tell children that tomorrow they will organize all the information in order to share it with others.

Access for All

SI Strategic Intervention

Answer Questions If a question has not been answered, provide sources and guide children through each step to locate information that will answer the question.

A Advanced

Answer Extension Have children choose a celebration or tradition to research in more detail. Have them present the information to the class with their chart on Day 5.

Wrap Up Your Day!

✔ **Phonics** Write sentences that have abbreviations. Have children read the sentences and identify the abbreviations.

✔ **Fluency** Display the sentence *On Jan. 6, Mr. and Mrs. Jeffers will host a party at 753 North St.* Have children read the sentence three or four times until they can do so fluently.

Preview DAY 5

Remind children that they heard about the flag's history today. Tomorrow they will hear about the flag's history again.

DAY 5 at a Glance

Content Knowledge
Oral Vocabulary

Phonics/Spelling
Review Abbreviations

Text-Based Comprehension
Review Author's Purpose

Selection Vocabulary
Review

Assessment
Phonics
Selection Vocabulary
Fluency
Comprehension

Conventions
Review Quotation Marks

Writing
Descriptive Poem or Song: Proofread

Research and Inquiry
Communicate

Materials

- Student Edition
- Read Aloud Anthology
- Weekly Test

Bridge to Common Core

INTEGRATION OF KNOWLEDGE/IDEAS
This week children have integrated content presented in diverse formats and analyzed how different texts address similar topics. They have developed knowledge about the American flag to expand the unit concept of traditions.

Social Studies Knowledge Goals
Children have learned some of the traditions that honor the flag, including

- the Pledge of Allegiance
- the National Anthem
- the Fourth of July

Content Knowledge

The American Flag

REVIEW CONCEPT We have read and listened to selections about our country's flag. Today you will listen to find out how different people view the flag. Read the selection.

- What does the flag remind many people of? (It reminds many people of the great things about the country.)

"Uncle Sam and Old Glory"

Build Oral Language

REVIEW AMAZING WORDS Orally review the meaning of this week's Amazing Words. Then display this week's concept map. Have children use Amazing Words such as *symbol* and *independence,* as well as the concept map, to answer the question, *What traditions and celebrations involve our country's flag?*

What traditions and celebrations involve our country's flag?

- We see our flag on the Fourth of July.
  - We wave flags at parades.
  - People fly flags from homes and cars.
- We celebrate our flag at sports events.
  - We sing the National Anthem.
  - Francis Scott Key's poem about the flag flying after a battle became the National Anthem.
- We drape the flag over the caskets of soldiers.
  - The flag is handled in special ways.
- We celebrate Flag Day on June 14.
  - The flag was first designed on June 14, 1777.
- We say the Pledge of Allegiance.
  - Our flag's colors, stars, and stripes are symbols.

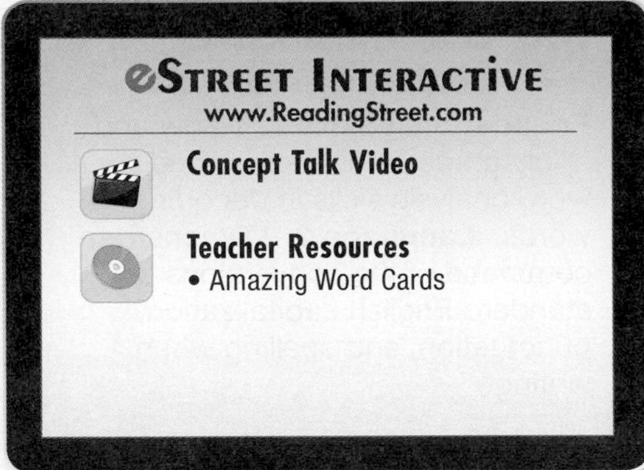

Build Oral Vocabulary

Team Talk **CONNECT TO AMAZING IDEAS** Pair children and have them discuss how the Question of the Week, *What traditions and celebrations involve our country's flag?,* connects to the question of this unit of study: *Are traditions and celebrations important in our lives?* Tell children to use the concept map and what they've learned from this week's discussions and reading selections to form an Amazing Idea—a realization or "big idea" about **traditions.** Use the following ideas as prompts:

- Why do we pay respect to the American flag?
- On what special occasions do we display the flag?

Then ask pairs to share their Amazing Idea with the class. Encourage children to recall in which selection they learned their ideas.

Amazing Ideas might include these key concepts:

- We pledge allegiance to the flag because it is a symbol of our country.
- We fly the flag on special days, such as the Fourth of July and Flag Day.

Check Oral Vocabulary

FORMATIVE ASSESSMENT Call on individuals to use this week's Amazing Words to talk about traditions and our flag. Prompt discussion with the questions below. Monitor children's ability to use the Amazing Words and note which words children are unable to use.

- **How does the *history* of our country's flag show that the United States is *indivisible?***
- **How is the flag a *symbol* of our *independence?***
- **How might a *patriotic* person show *allegiance* to his or her country?**
- **If you saw someone *unfurl* a *frayed* flag, what would you do?**

If... children have difficulty using the Amazing Words,
then... reteach the unknown words using the Robust Vocabulary Routines, pp. 393a, 398b, 418b, 422b.

Amazing Words

history	unfurl
independence	frayed
symbol	allegiance
patriotic	indivisible

ELL

Check Concepts and Language Use the Day 5 instruction on ELL Poster 27 to monitor children's understanding of the lesson concept.

Amazing Words To aid children's responses, supply sentence starters, such as *The history of our country's flag shows that the United States is indivisible because . . .*

Common Core State Standards

Foundational Skills 3. Know and apply grade-level phonics and word analysis skills in decoding words. **Language 2.** Demonstrate command of the conventions of standard English capitalization, punctuation, and spelling when writing.

Phonics

Review Abbreviations

TARGET PHONICS SKILL Write the following sentences on the board. Have children read each one, first quietly to themselves and then aloud as you track the print.

1. **Mr. and Mrs. Bono visited us this weekend.**
2. **The first Fri. in Dec. is my birthday.**
3. **Go to the corner of Bean St. and Knot Ave. to catch the bus.**
4. **The games we planned for Aug. and Sept. will not take place.**

Team Talk Have children discuss with a partner what the abbreviations stand for and if they are part of an address, a person's name, a month, or a day. Then call on individuals to share with the class.

Spelling Test

DICTATE SPELLING WORDS Say each abbreviation, read the sentence, repeat the abbreviation, and allow time for children to write the abbreviation.

1. Dec.	The school's winter break begins **Dec.** 15.
2. St.	The restaurant on Third **St.** has tasty pizza.
3. Mr.	**Mr.** Reese walks his dog each morning.
4. Nov.	Jill has a math test **Nov.** 3.
5. Dr.	We see **Dr.** Mason when we are sick.
6. Jan.	**Jan.** 1 is the first day of the year.
7. Ms.	**Ms.** Picket is the school media assistant.
8. Rd.	The shoe store on Deck **Rd.** is having a sale.
9. Feb.	We send Valentines on **Feb.** 14.
10. Mrs.	**Mrs.** Atkins teaches piano lessons.
11. Aug.	Lee's favorite band will give a concert **Aug.** 8.
12. Oct.	My birthday is **Oct.** 27.

High-Frequency Words

13. won	Jung Hee **won** the tennis game.
14. learn	I would like to **learn** how to read music.

Assess

- Spell abbreviations.
- Spell high-frequency words.

Access for All

SI Strategic Intervention

Check Spelling Have children choose the correct spelling of each abbreviation from three random spellings.

A Advanced

Extend Spelling Have children who have demonstrated proficiency in spelling individual words spell each word in a self-made sentence.

Day 5 SMALL GROUP TIME • Differentiate Reteaching, p. SG•18

OL On-Level

- **Develop** Quotation Marks
- **Reread** *Reading Street Sleuth,* pp. 70–71

SI Strategic Intervention

- **Review/Discuss** Quotation Marks
- **Reread** *Reading Street Sleuth,* pp. 70–71

A Advanced

- **Extend** Quotation Marks
- **Reread** *Reading Street Sleuth,* pp. 70–71
- **Communicate** Inquiry Project

If... children need more scaffolding and practice with **Conventions and Writing,**
then... use the activities on pp. DI•41–DI•42 in the Teacher Resources section on SuccessNet.

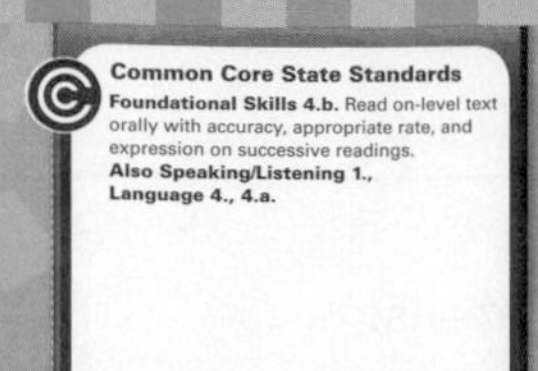

READING STREET ONLINE
ONLINE STUDENT EDITION
www.ReadingStreet.com

Vocabulary

Multiple-Meaning Words

Context Clues A multiple-meaning word is a word that has more than one meaning. You can use context clues to determine what the relevant meaning is.

Practice It! Read each sentence. Choose the meaning of the bold word.

1. The boat started to **sink**.
   go under water
   a small tub with a drain
2. **Fall** is my favorite season.
   drop or come down autumn

Fluency

Read with Accuracy

Be sure you read every word. Blend the sounds to read new words. Ask yourself if it is a word you know. Check the new word in the sentence to see if it makes sense.

Practice It! Choose a page from *Red, White, and Blue*. Read the page aloud to a partner. Check each other's understanding of the text.

424

Listening and Speaking

Share how ads use facts and opinions to sell goods.

Evaluate Advertisements

Companies use advertisements to sell their goods. You can see the ads on the Internet and television. You can see them in magazines and newspapers. Look at some ads. What do ads tell you about a product? Do they tell you what the product does? Do they say that everyone wants the product? Decide whether the ad gives mostly facts or mostly opinions.

Practice It! Work in groups. Look on the Internet or in a magazine for an ad. Write what the ad is for. Write what facts and opinions you find. Then share the information and your ideas with the class. Remember to speak clearly and use specific words. Remember to pay attention to others when they speak.

Tips

- Show the class a copy of your ad and point out its graphics and words.
- Speak at an appropriate pace.
- Use proper conventions of language.

425

Student Edition, pp. 424–425

Common Core State Standards

Foundational Skills 4.b. Read on-level text orally with accuracy, appropriate rate, and expression on successive readings. **Speaking/ Listening 3.** Ask and answer questions about what a speaker says in order to clarify comprehension, gather additional information, or deepen understanding of a topic or issue. **Also Speaking/Listening 1., 2. and Language 4., 4.a.**

Access for All

 Strategic Intervention

Choose Meaning Some children may find it helpful to insert both meanings of the multiple-meaning word into the sentence and see which makes sense. Give additional practice if necessary.

Vocabulary

Multiple-Meaning Words

TEACH Read and discuss the Vocabulary lesson on page 424 of the Student Edition. Explain that some words have more than one meaning. The words around a multiple-meaning word can tell a reader which meaning is being used.

GUIDE PRACTICE Read the instructions for the Vocabulary Practice It! activity. Then read the sentence in item 1 aloud with children.

Which meaning makes sense in the sentence? (go under water)

ON THEIR OWN Have pairs complete item 2.

Corrective feedback	Circulate around the room and listen as children identify which meaning of *fall* is used in the sentence. Provide assistance as needed.

Fluency

Accuracy

TEACH Read and discuss the Fluency instructions.

READ WORDS IN CONTEXT Give children a few minutes to look through *Red, White, and Blue,* choose a page, and practice reading it silently three or four times. Then have partners take turns reading the page to each other with accuracy.

Listening and Speaking

Evaluate Advertisements

TEACH Read the explanation of evaluating advertisements on page 425 of the Student Edition together. Remind children that advertisements are persuasive writing. They are meant to persuade people to buy something or do something. Review with children the difference between a fact and an opinion.

ANALYZE Have children discuss some of the ads they see on television. What product is being advertised? What is memorable about the ad? What does the ad do to make you want the product? Have children talk about how advertising influences them to buy products.

INTRODUCE PROMPT Read the Practice It! prompt with the class. Remind children to speak clearly and listen closely to each other as they work in their groups.

Team Talk Have small groups choose an ad from a magazine or the Internet, note what the ad is for, and identify facts and opinions in it. As groups make their oral presentations to the class, ask each member to report at least one finding his or her group made.

Evaluate Advertisements

In addition to working in small groups to accomplish tasks such as identifying facts and opinions, children at Grade 3 should also be able to take turns speaking, respond appropriately when asked a question, and acknowledge the contributions of others.

Multiple-Meaning Words Provide visual clues and use gestures to help children understand the two meanings of *sink* and *fall.*

Common Core State Standards

Informational Text 2. Identify the main topic of a multiparagraph text as well as the focus of specific paragraphs within the text. **Informational Text 4.** Determine the meaning of words and phrases in a text relevant to a grade 2 topic or subject area. **Informational Text 6.** Identify the main purpose of a text, including what the author wants to answer, explain, or describe.

Text-Based Comprehension

Review Author's Purpose

Remember that authors have certain reasons for writing, such as to entertain or inform. What do we call an author's reason for writing? (author's purpose)

CHECK UNDERSTANDING Read aloud the following selection and have children answer the questions that follow.

If you want to buy a pet, a guinea pig is the best choice. Guinea pigs make good pets for several reasons. First, a guinea pig does not cost a lot of money. Its cage and its food are not expensive, either. Second, guinea pigs are very gentle. They rarely bite and will sit quietly in your lap. Third, guinea pigs are very little bother to have around. They are not noisy, messy, or smelly. Best of all, guinea pigs are fun to hold, and you can feed them treats and teach them their name. So, pick a guinea pig for your next pet!

1. What is the topic of the selection I just read? (Guinea pigs are the best pets.)
2. What is the author's purpose? (The author's purpose is to persuade the reader that guinea pigs make the best pets.)
3. How do you know the author's purpose is to persuade? (The author uses several arguments to support the opinion that guinea pigs make the best pets, so that readers will agree that it is true.)

Vocabulary

Review Selection Vocabulary

SELECTION WORDS Review this week's selection words: *flag, nicknames, stars, stripes, America, freedom,* and *birthday.* Say a cloze sentence that uses context clues for each of the words, such as: Our _______ is red, white, and blue. (flag) Have children name the selection word that completes the sentence.

Corrective feedback	**If...** children cannot tell what the words mean, **then...** review the definitions on page 397a.

Genre

Review Informational Text

INFORMATIONAL TEXT Review with children that informational text gives facts about real people, places, and events that reflect history or the traditions of communities. An informational article has a topic and a main idea about that topic.

TEACH Remember that the **topic** is the subject that the author is writing about. The **main idea** is the most important thing that the author is saying about the topic. You consider the most important details about the topic and sum them up to state the main idea. Let's look again at *Red, White, and Blue* for main ideas. Have children turn to pages 402–403 in their Student Edition. Read the first two paragraphs aloud.

Think Aloud **MODEL** The topic of these two paragraphs is the American flag. The first paragraph talks about how we know and see the flag in lots of places. The second paragraph asks where the flag came from and answers that no one knows. I'll sum up those details to state this main idea: Today we see the American flag in lots of places, but no one knows where the flag first came from.

GUIDE PRACTICE Ask the following questions to guide children in determining the main idea of the rest of pages 402–403.

- What is the topic of this section? (the flag)
- What does the last paragraph on page 402 say about the flag? (In the 1700s America didn't have a flag.)
- What does the first paragraph on page 403 say about the flag? (The thirteen colonies flew the English flag because they belonged to England.)
- What does the second paragraph say? (The colonies decided to fight for their freedom.)
- What does the third paragraph say about the flag? (An American flag was needed once war began.)
- What is the main idea of this section? (Americans didn't need their own flag until they decided to be free of England.)

ON THEIR OWN How do you identify the topic? (You decide what the subject is.) How do you identify the main idea? (You sum up the most important details about the topic.)

Access for All

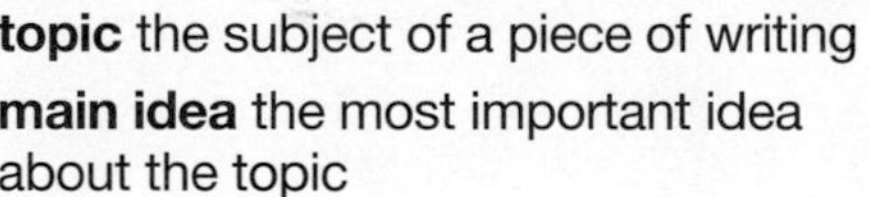

Distinguishing Topic from Main Idea
If children have difficulty distinguishing between the topic and the main idea, explain that the topic can usually be expressed in a word or phrase, while the main idea is a statement about the topic and is expressed in a complete sentence.

Academic Vocabulary

topic the subject of a piece of writing

main idea the most important idea about the topic

Common Core State Standards

Foundational Skills 4.a. Read on-level text with purpose and understanding. **Foundational Skills 4.b.** Read on-level text orally with accuracy, appropriate rate, and expression on successive readings.

Assess

- Abbreviations
- Fluency: Rate
- Author's Purpose

Fluency Goals

Set individual fluency goals for children to enable them to reach the end-of-the-year goal.

- **Current Goal:** 80–90 WCPM
- **End-of-Year Goal:** 90 WCPM

Assessment

Monitor Progress

For a written assessment of abbreviations and author's purpose, use Weekly Test 27, pp. 157–162.

SENTENCE READING Use the following reproducible page to assess children's ability to read words in context. Call on children to read two sentences aloud. Start over with sentence one if necessary.

MONITOR PROGRESS Sentence Reading

If... children have trouble reading abbreviations,
then... use the Reteach Lesson in *First Stop.*

FLUENCY Take a one-minute sample of children's oral reading. Have children read the fluency passage on p. 425f.

COMPREHENSION Have the child read the entire passage. (If the child has difficulty with the passage, you may read it aloud.) Then have the child tell the topic of the passage and the author's purpose in writing it.

MONITOR ACCURACY Have children monitor their accuracy by recording their scores using the Sentence Reading Chart and by recording the number of words read correctly per minute on their Fluency Progress Chart in *First Stop.*

MONITOR PROGRESS Fluency and Comprehension

If... a child does not achieve the fluency goal on the timed reading,
then... copy the passage and send it home with the child for additional fluency practice, or have the child practice with a fluent reader.

If... a child cannot identify the topic and the author's purpose,
then... use the Reteach Lesson in *First Stop.*

Name ____

Read the Sentences

1. Mr. and Mrs. Hines shopped for Seth's birthday.

2. Dr. Lott had the flag flying on Harkins St. outside her office.

3. If you stood outside on Becker Blvd. last Tues., you could see the stars shining.

4. On the house at the corner of Shaw St. and Marine Ave., they are painting stripes.

5. On the fourth Thurs. in Nov. of each year, America celebrates Thanksgiving.

6. I call my cats, Mr. Prince and Ms. Hawkeye, by the nicknames of Princer and Hawks.

7. School usually starts in Aug. or Sept., so that's when children end their summer freedom.

MONITOR PROGRESS

- **Abbreviations**
- **Selection Vocabulary**

Name ____________________

Read the Story

The Grand Canyon

The Grand Canyon is in Arizona. It is 277 miles long 11
and one mile deep. A river flows through the bottom 21
of the canyon. Many, many years ago this river cut 31
through the rock and made the canyon. 38

There are many amazing colors of rocks on the 47
steep walls of the canyon. You can see pink, red, and 58
orange rocks. 60

The Grand Canyon contains different kinds of 67
plants and animals. Willow trees grow near the river. 76
Cactus plants grow in the sand. Foxes, deer, bobcats, 85
and rabbits can be found in many places. 93

Today, people who visit the canyon like to go 102
down to the river. They can hike along the sloping trail. 113
Some people think it is easier to ride a mule though. 124
By riding a mule, they won't have any worries about 134
tripping. When people get to the bottom of the canyon, 144
they can take a raft trip. 150

MONITOR PROGRESS

- Check Fluency
- Author's Purpose

Conventions

Review Quotation Marks

REVIEW Remind children that quotation marks show the beginning and end of the words someone says. The speaker's name is written outside the quotation marks. Have children give several examples of quotes, including their own names in each example.

GUIDE PRACTICE Write the following sentences. Have individuals supply quotation marks for each sentence.

1. **Please stand for The Star-Spangled Banner, said the principal.**
2. **The mayor said, Fly your flag on the Fourth of July.**
3. **Sarita asked, What time is it?**

APPLY Call on a pair of children. Ask them to have a brief dialogue about the following topics. Choose a quotation, and ask children how to punctuate it.

favorite foods
after-school activities
summer plans
a school subject

Have others explain where quotation marks would be placed if the dialogue were written. For example, *Maria said, "My favorite food is spaghetti."*

ON THEIR OWN Use Let's Practice It!, p. 308 on the *Teacher Resources DVD-ROM.*

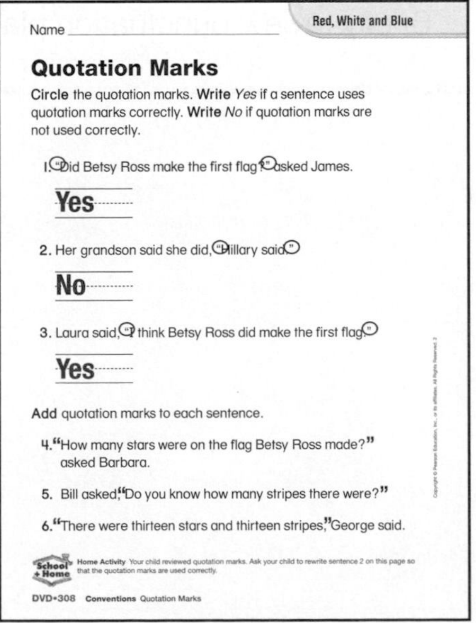
Name ______ Red, White and Blue

Quotation Marks

Circle the quotation marks. **Write** *Yes* if a sentence uses quotation marks correctly. **Write** *No* if quotation marks are not used correctly.

1. "Did Betsy Ross make the first flag?" asked James.
Yes

2. Her grandson said she did, "Hillary said."
No

3. Laura said, "I think Betsy Ross did make the first flag."
Yes

Add quotation marks to each sentence.

4. "How many stars were on the flag Betsy Ross made?" asked Barbara.
5. Bill asked, "Do you know how many stripes there were?"
6. "There were thirteen stars and thirteen stripes," George said.

Home Activity Your child reviewed quotation marks. Ask your child to rewrite sentence 2 on this page so that the quotation marks are used correctly.

DVD•308 **Conventions** Quotation Marks

Let's Practice It! TR DVD•308

Common Core State Standards

Foundational Skills 4.b. Read on-level text orally with accuracy, appropriate rate, and expression on successive readings. **Language 2.** Demonstrate command of the conventions of standard English capitalization, punctuation, and spelling when writing.

Daily Fix-It

9. Our flagg has fifty stars?
Our flag has fifty stars.
10. this is my eighth Birthday.
This is my eighth birthday.

Discuss the Daily Fix-It corrections with children. Review capitalization, punctuation, and the spelling of *flag*.

Common Core State Standards

Writing 3. Write narratives in which they recount a well-elaborated event or short sequence of events, include details to describe actions, thoughts, and feelings, use temporal words to signal event order, and provide a sense of closure. **Writing 5.** With guidance and support from adults and peers, focus on a topic and strengthen writing as needed by revising and editing. **Speaking/Listening 5.** Create audio recordings of stories or poems; add drawings or other visual displays to stories or recounts of experiences when appropriate to clarify ideas, thoughts, and feelings. **Also Language 2.e.**

Bridge to Common Core

PRODUCTION AND DISTRIBUTION OF WRITING

Children have developed and strengthened their drafts throughout the week. Their final well-structured drafts will reflect the changes they made to improve their descriptive poems or songs. Children will present their poems by making and playing audio recordings of them or binding illustrated copies into a class book.

Writing

Descriptive Poem or Song

REVIEW REVISING Remind children that yesterday they revised their poems and songs. They may have rearranged words to make the rhythm smoother. They added vivid details and sensory details too. Today they will proofread their descriptive poems or songs.

Mini-Lesson Proofread

Proofread for Quotation Marks

- **Teach** If we spell the words correctly in poems and songs, readers will know what words we mean. When we proofread, we check to make sure the words are correct. I can use our word lists or a dictionary to check them. We can check to make sure the punctuation is correct, especially in sentences that have quotes.

- **Model** Let us look at my poem about Thanksgiving. Display Writing Transparency 27C. Explain that you will look at all words to make sure they are spelled correctly. Show how you would change any misspellings (such as *tukey* for *turkey*). Quickly show how to check a word's spelling in a classroom dictionary or word list. Model how you would add a missing quotation mark by inserting a caret and writing the quotation marks. Briefly review punctuation placement in or out of the quotation marks.

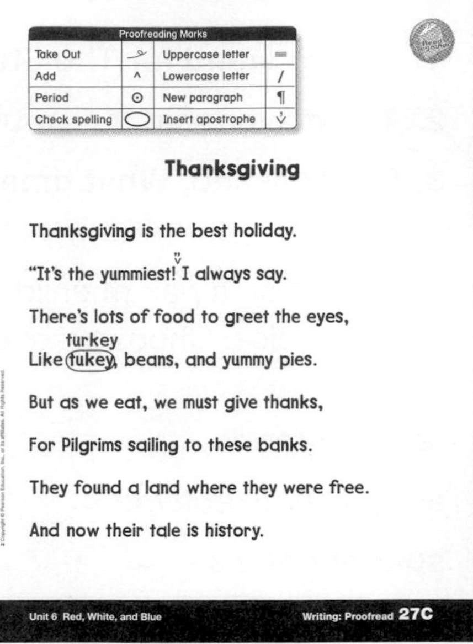

Proofreading Marks

Take Out		Uppercase letter	
Add	^	Lowercase letter	/
Period	⊙	New paragraph	¶
Check spelling	◯	Insert apostrophe	

Thanksgiving

Thanksgiving is the best holiday.
"It's the yummiest! I always say.
There's lots of food to greet the eyes,
Like ~~tukey~~ turkey, beans, and yummy pies.
But as we eat, we must give thanks,
For Pilgrims sailing to these banks.
They found a land where they were free.
And now their tale is history.

Unit 6 Red, White, and Blue — Writing: Proofread 27C

Writing Transparency 27C TR DVD

PROOFREAD Display the Proofreading Tips. Have children proofread their poems and songs to correct any misspellings, missing capital letters, or punctuation errors. Circulate to assist children with quotation marks.

Proofreading Tips

- ✔ Are my words spelled correctly? Check a dictionary.
- ✔ Do my sentences begin with a capital letters?
- ✔ Do my sentences have ending punctuation?
- ✔ Do I have quotations marks around words someone says?

PRESENT Have children make a final draft of their poems or songs, with their revisions and proofreading corrections. Help as appropriate.

Choose an option for children to present their descriptive poems or songs. Provide a tape recorder so that children can make an audio presentation of their poems or songs.

Help children make an audio of their poems and songs.	They might copy the poem and illustrate it. Then bind the pages to make a class book about American symbols and traditions.

When children have finished writing their realistic fiction, give them a copy of About My Writing, p. RR39 of the *Reader's and Writer's Notebook.* Then have children evaluate their writing by answering the questions on the page.

Routine Quick Write for Fluency — Team Talk

1. **Talk** Have partners take one minute to find a vivid description in each of their poems or songs.
2. **Write** Each child writes a sentence explaining why the description is good.
3. **Share** Partners trade sentences and read them aloud.

Routines Flip Chart

Support Editing For children to whom English conventions still are not very familiar, look for gradual improvement over the course of the year. Help children recognize the different ending marks and their uses.

Common Core State Standards

Speaking/Listening 1.a. Follow agreed-upon rules for discussions (e.g., gaining the floor in respectful ways, listening to others with care, speaking one at a time about the topics and texts under discussion). **Speaking/Listening 2.** Recount or describe key ideas or details from a text read aloud or information presented orally or through other media.

Research and Inquiry

Step 5 Communicate

TEACH Tell children that today they will review their information, create their own charts, and share the information with the class.

Think Aloud **MODEL** Display the list of inquiry questions and the answers recorded during research. We have been asking and answering questions about the celebrations that use the flag. I was interested in the question *On which holidays do we use the American flag?* The answer I found was *Flag Day.* We are going to show our information on a chart. So on my chart one of the celebrations I will include is Flag Day, and I will include some details about it.

GUIDE PRACTICE Review the answers on the chart with children. Have them prompt you to circle the celebrations that may be included on their charts.

ON THEIR OWN Have children make their charts to show celebrations involving the American flag. Discuss how many columns they want on their charts. A sample three-column chart is shown below. Have children share their charts with a small group. Remind them how to be good speakers and listeners:

- Good speakers think about the audience. They use words and a tone that the audience will understand.
- Good listeners think about the information shared and decide if it makes sense. If they have a question, they raise their hand to ask a question.

Topic: Celebrations That Involve the Flag

Holiday	Date	Use
Flag Day	June 14	fly the flag

Wrap Up Your Week!

The American Flag

What traditions and celebrations involve our country's flag?

Think Aloud This week we discovered traditions and celebrations that involve our country's flag. In the selection *Red, White, and Blue,* we read about the history of our flag. In the poem "You're a Grand Old Flag," we read a song that expresses patriotic feelings about the flag.

Team Talk Have children discuss their Amazing Ideas about traditions and the flag with a partner. Then have children use these ideas to help them demonstrate their understanding of the Question of the Week, *What traditions and celebrations involve our country's flag?*

Amazing Words

You've learned 008 words this week!

You've learned 217 words this year!

Next Week's Concept

Family Celebrations

Why are family celebrations special?

Poster Preview Prepare children for next week by using Week 3, ELL Poster 28. Read the Poster Talk-Through to introduce the concept and vocabulary. Ask children to identify and describe objects and actions in the art.

Selection Summary Send home the summary of *A Birthday Basket for Tía,* in English and the children's home languages, if available. Children can read the summary with family members.

Tell children that next week they will read about more traditions and family celebrations.

Preview Next Week

Assessment Checkpoints for the Week

Weekly Assessment

Use pp. 157–162 of *Weekly Tests* to check:

✔ **Phonics** Abbreviations

✔ **Comprehension** Author's Purpose

✔ **Selection Vocabulary**

America	nicknames
birthday	stars
flag	stripes
freedom	

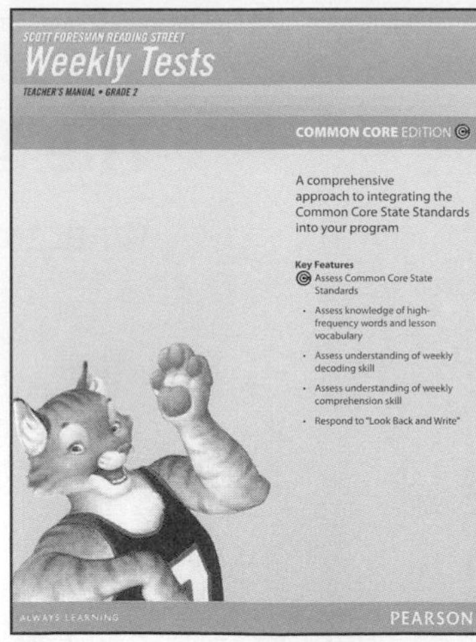

Weekly Tests

Differentiated Assessment

Advanced

On-Level

Strategic Intervention

Use pp. 157–162 of *Fresh Reads for Fluency and Comprehension* to check:

✔ **Comprehension** Author's Purpose

✔ Review **Comprehension** Fact and Opinion

✔ **Fluency** Words Correct Per Minute

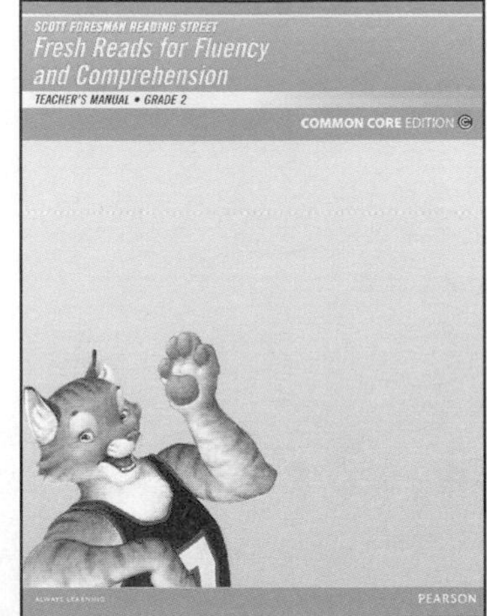

Fresh Reads for Fluency and Comprehension

Managing Assessment

Use *Assessment Handbook* for:

✔ **Weekly Assessment Blackline Masters for Monitoring Progress**

✔ **Observation Checklists**

✔ **Record-Keeping Forms**

✔ **Portfolio Assessment**

Assessment Handbook

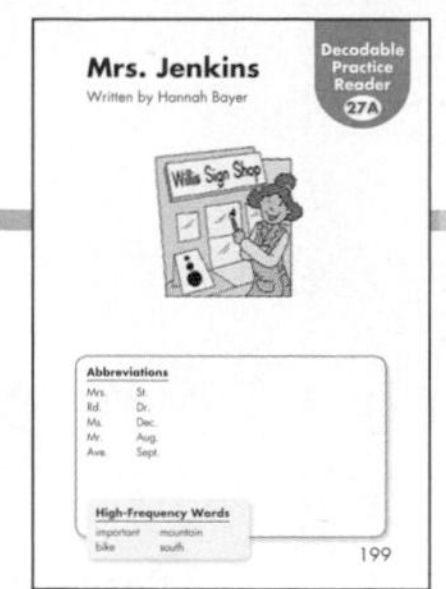

DAY 1 Differentiate Phonics

- Abbreviations
- Decodable Practice Reader
- Advanced Selection "Raising the Stars and Stripes"
- **Inquiry** Identify Questions

DAY 2 Differentiate Comprehension

- Selection Vocabulary
- **Access Text** Read *Red, White, and Blue*
- **Inquiry** Investigate

DAY 3 Differentiate Close Reading

- Develop Vocabulary
- **Close Reading** Reread *Red, White, and Blue*
- **Inquiry** Investigate

DAY 4 Differentiate Vocabulary

- Amazing Words
- **Read** "Respecting the Star-Spangled Banner" or Leveled Readers
- **Inquiry** Organize

"Respecting the Star-Spangled Banner," pp. 70–71

DAY 5 Differentiate Reteaching

- **Conventions** Quotation Marks
- **Read** "Respecting the Star-Spangled Banner" or Leveled Readers
- **Inquiry** Communicate

Teacher Guides and student pages can be found in the Leveled Reader Database.

Place English Language Learners in the groups that correspond to their reading abilities.
If... children need scaffolding and practice,
then... use the ELL notes on the instructional pages.

Independent Practice

Independent Practice Stations

See pp. 392h and 392i for Independent Stations.

Pearson Trade Book Library

See the Leveled Reader Database for Lesson Plans and student pages.

Reading Street Digital Path

Independent Practice Activities available in the Digital Path.

Independent Reading

See p. 392i for independent reading suggestions.

On-Level

Common Core State Standards

Foundational Skills 3. Know and apply grade-level phonics and word analysis skills in decoding words. **Informational Text 1.** Ask and answer such questions as *who, what, where, when, why,* and *how* to demonstrate understanding of key details in a text. **Informational Text 4.** Determine the meaning of words and phrases in a text relevant to a grade 2 topic or subject area. **Also Foundational Skills 4.c.**

1 Build Word Knowledge

Practice Phonics

ABBREVIATIONS Write the following abbreviations and have children practice reading them.

Mrs.	Aug.	St.	Dec.	Dr.

Spelling

ABBREVIATIONS Remind children that each spelling word is an abbreviation, or shortened form of a longer word. Clarify the meaning of each word. For example, write an abbreviation such as *Rd.* or *Oct.,* and ask children to give the word it stands for.

2 Read

Decodable Reader 27A *Mrs. Jenkins*

HIGH-FREQUENCY WORDS Have children read the decodable reader. Then have them reread the text to develop automaticity. Have children return to the text and find the previously taught high-frequency words. Help children demonstrate their understanding of the words. Provide sentence frames such as: It takes special skills to climb a ______. (mountain)

If... children need more scaffolding and practice with phonics, **then...** use the ELL activities on p. DI•37 in the Teacher Resources section on SuccessNet.

On-Level

1 Build Word Knowledge

Practice Selection Vocabulary

America	birthday	flag	freedom
nicknames	stars	stripes	

DEFINE IT Discuss the definition for the word *freedom* with children. Ask: How would you describe *freedom* to a friend? (It's being able to do anything you want.) Continue with the remaining words.

Team Talk **TALK ABOUT IT** Have pairs use the selection words in sentences to internalize meaning. Ask: How can you pair the selection words together in a sentence? (Possible response: I think the American flag stands for freedom.) Allow time for children to play with the words and then share their sentences.

2 Read

Red, White, and Blue

If you read *Red, White, and Blue: The Story of the American Flag* during whole group time, then use the following instruction.

ACCESS TEXT Have children look at the pictures on pp. 408–409. Reread both pages.

- Are the Americans on land or at sea? (The Americans are on land.) How can you tell? (An American flag is flying over the fort.) What clues in the pictures tell you this was a difficult and dangerous battle for the Americans? (There are many explosions taking place on the beach and at the fort. The fort is surrounded by a number of ships.)
- What are *soldiers?* (people who serve in the military)
- What other words on p. 408 give you a clue that soldiers are people who serve in the military? *(fighting, fort)*

If you are reading *Red, White, and Blue: The Story of the American Flag* during small group time, then return to pp. 399a–417a to guide the reading.

SMALL GROUP TIME

Independent Reading Options

Trade Book Library

eStreet Interactive
www.ReadingStreet.com
Teacher's Guides available on the Leveled Reader Database.

Common Core State Standards

Informational Text 1. Ask and answer such questions as *who, what, where, when, why,* and *how* to demonstrate understanding of key details in a text. **Informational Text 4.** Determine the meaning of words and phrases in a text relevant to a grade 2 topic or subject area.

1 Build Word Knowledge

Develop Vocabulary

REREAD FOR VOCABULARY Have children reread *Red, White, and Blue: The Story of the American Flag,* p. 406.

Read the following sentence and discuss words and phrases related to the American flag. *(colors, stars, stripes)*

Congress had picked the colors and the stars and stripes.

- What did the thirteen stars and thirteen stripes initially stand for? (the thirteen American colonies)
- What are some other phrases on this page that further describe the American flag? *(thirteen red and white stripes; thirteen white stars; blue background)*

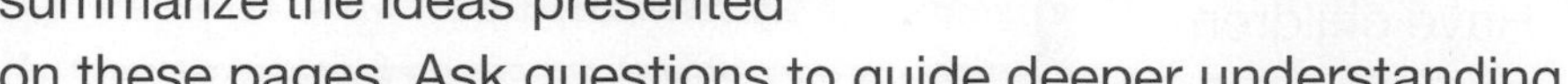

2 Read

Red, White, and Blue

If you read *Red, White, and Blue: The Story of the American Flag* during whole group time, then use the following instruction.

CLOSE READING Reread pp. 404–407. Have children summarize the ideas presented on these pages. Ask questions to guide deeper understanding.

- Did Betsy Ross make the first American flag? (We aren't sure. There is no proof.) What evidence supports the claim that she did make the first flag? (She was famous for her sewing. Her grandson claims she told him it happened.)
- Why were early American flags different from one another? (Congress did not say exactly where the stars and stripes should go.)
- How can you tell that the war with Great Britain in 1812 was a serious threat to our new country? (They were able to burn down the home of the President. They marched down American streets and sailed up American rivers.)

Have children read these sentences from page 407 and use a connecting word to combine them into one sentence: *They sailed up our rivers. They marched down our streets.* (They sailed up our rivers and marched down our streets.)

If you are reading *Red, White, and Blue: The Story of the American Flag* during small group time, then return to pp. 399a–417a to guide the reading.

If... children need more scaffolding and practice with the main selection, **then...** use the activities on p. DI•39 in the Teacher Resources section on SuccessNet.

On-Level

1 Build Word Knowledge

Practice Amazing Words

history	independence	symbol	patriotic
unfurl	frayed	allegiance	indivisible

Team Talk **LANGUAGE DEVELOPMENT** Have children practice building more sentences. Display a sentence starter and have children add oral phrases or clauses using the Amazing Words. For example: It is patriotic to ______. (Possible response: It is patriotic to say the Pledge of Allegiance.)

2 Text-Based Comprehension

READ ALOUD "Respecting the Star-Spangled Banner" Lead children in a choral reading of "Respecting the Star-Spangled Banner" from *Reading Street Sleuth* on pp. 70–71. Then have partners take turns reading the paragraphs of the selection.

ACCESS TEXT Guide children as they work on the Be a Sleuth section.

Look for Clues Have children look for clue words in the text that help tell the order of steps for folding a flag. What would happen if the steps were not in order?

Ask Questions Ask, Where do you see the American flag displayed? After discussing this question, have children ask questions about putting a flag on display, taking it down, and putting it away.

Make Your Case Have children discuss why the flag is important. What does the flag represent? Why should we show respect for our country and its flag? Have children write a list of reasons for showing respect to the flag and use their list as they discuss the issue with a partner.

eStreet Interactive
www.ReadingStreet.com

Pearson eText
- Student Edition
- Leveled Reader Database
- *Reading Street Sleuth*

SMALL GROUP TIME

More Reading for Group Time

ON-LEVEL

Reviews
- Concept Vocabulary
- Author's Purpose
- Summarize

Use this suggested Leveled Reader or other text at children's instructional level.

eStreet Interactive
www.ReadingStreet.com

Use the Leveled Reader Database for lesson plans and student pages for *American Revolution Heroes.*

On-Level

Common Core State Standards

Language 2. Demonstrate command of the conventions of standard English capitalization, punctuation, and spelling when writing. **Foundational Skills 3.** Know and apply grade-level phonics and word analysis skills in decoding words. **Foundational Skills 4.** Read with sufficient accuracy and fluency to support comprehension.

More Reading for Group Time

ON-LEVEL

Reviews
- Concept Vocabulary
- Author's Purpose
- Summarize

Use this suggested Leveled Reader or other text at children's instructional level.

eSTREET INTERACTIVE
www.ReadingStreet.com

Use the Leveled Reader Database for lesson plans and student pages for *American Revolution Heroes.*

1 Build Word Knowledge

Practice Quotation Marks

REVIEW If needed, revisit the conventions lesson on p. 417c.

IDENTIFY QUOTATION MARKS Have children turn to "Respecting the Star-Spangled Banner" to identify quotation marks in the selection and state the reason for their use.

2 Text-Based Comprehension

REREAD "Respecting the Star-Spangled Banner" Have partners reread "Respecting the Star-Spangled Banner."

EXTEND UNDERSTANDING Identify other symbols that represent the United States, such as the American bald eagle, the Statue of Liberty, and the Liberty Bell. Display pictures of the symbols and discuss their meaning.

PERFORMANCE TASK • Prove It! Organize children in small groups. Assign each group a question related to the Flag Code, such as: *How do you display the American flag together with the flag of another country? How do you display the American flag together with our state flag? How and when is the American flag flown at half-mast? What is the proper way to salute the flag?* Have groups create posters and/or written reports to answer their assigned questions.

COMMUNICATE Invite children to present their posters or reports. Provide time for a question-and-answer period after each presentation.

1 Build Word Knowledge

Reteach Phonics

ABBREVIATIONS Reteach the lesson on p. 394a, Abbreviations. Then write the following abbreviations and ask children to name the word.

Mr. **Feb.** **Ave.** **Dec.** **Sat.**

2 Read

Decodable Reader 27A *Mrs. Jenkins*

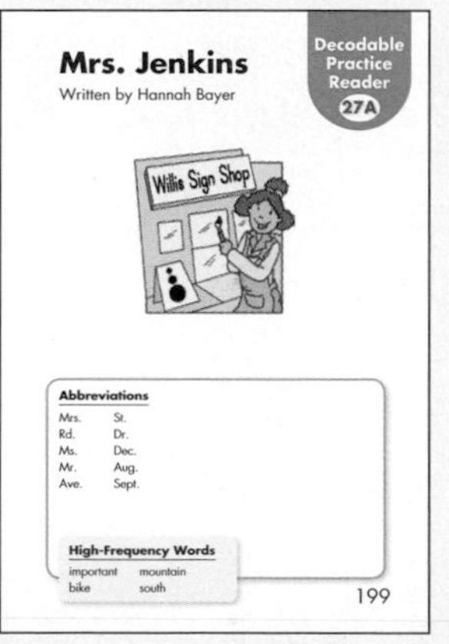

DECODE WORDS Have children practice reading the words listed on p. 199.

Corrective feedback	**If...** children have difficulty reading the words independently, **then...** reteach the words prior to reading Decodable Reader 27A.

READ IN CONTEXT Have children take turns reading a page in *Mrs. Jenkins.* Have them reread the text several times to ensure accuracy.

Corrective feedback	**If...** children have difficulty reading the selection independently, **then...** model reading a page and have children echo you.

3 Reread for Fluency

Have children reread the text to develop automaticity in their reading.

SMALL GROUP TIME

If... children need more scaffolding and practice with phonics, **then...** use the ELL activities on p. DI•37 in the Teacher Resources section on SuccessNet.

Common Core State Standards

Informational Text 1. Ask and answer such questions as *who, what, where, when, why,* and *how* to demonstrate understanding of key details in a text. **Informational Text 4.** Determine the meaning of words and phrases in a text relevant to a grade 2 topic or subject area. **Also Language 4.**

1 Build Word Knowledge

Reteach Selection Vocabulary

America	birthday	flag	freedom
nickname	stars	stripes	

DEFINE IT Describe the word *nickname* to a friend. Restate the word in child-friendly terms. A *nickname* is a name used instead of a real name. Jeff is a nickname for Jeffrey. Old Glory is one of the nicknames for the American flag listed on page 402.

Team Talk **TALK ABOUT IT** What are some ways that people get nicknames? Turn and talk to your partner about this. Allow time for children to discuss. Ask for examples. Rephrase their examples for usage when necessary or to correct misunderstandings. Continue with the remaining words.

Corrective feedback | **If...** children need more practice with selection vocabulary, **then...** use the *Envision It! Pictured Vocabulary Cards.*

2 Read

Red, White, and Blue

If you read *Red, White, and Blue: The Story of the American Flag* during whole group time, then use the instruction below.

ACCESS TEXT Have children look at the picture on pp. 410–411. What is happening in this picture? (A wagon train of people are headed west.) Reread the text on these pages.

- How was the American flag different in 1814 from what it was right after the American Revolution? (There are fifteen stars and fifteen stripes in 1814. After the Revolution there were thirteen of each.)
- What does the author mean when he says our country was "getting bigger"? (The United States was adding more states.)

If you are reading *Red, White, and Blue: The Story of the American Flag* during small group time, then return to pp. 399a–417a to guide the reading.

Corrective feedback | **If...** children have difficulty understanding the section, **then...** read the section aloud using the Access Text Notes.

Independent Reading Options

Trade Book Library

eStreet Interactive
www.ReadingStreet.com

Teacher's Guides available on the Leveled Reader Database.

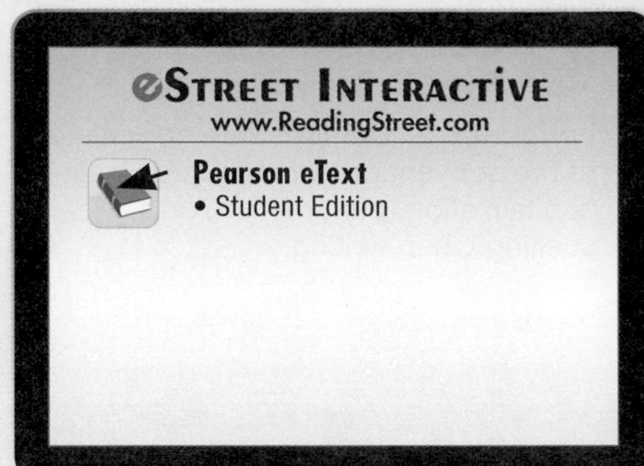

1 Build Word Knowledge

Develop Vocabulary

REREAD FOR VOCABULARY Have children reread p. 417 of *Red, White, and Blue.* Let's read this text to find out what the word *astronaut* means. To help children understand the word *astronaut,* ask questions, such as: Can anyone just go into space? (no) What special equipment would it take to get someone to the moon? (a spaceship, a lunar module, a space suit)

Corrective feedback	**If...** children have difficulty understanding the word *astronaut,* **then...** guide children to use online sources to find more information.

2 Read

Red, White, and Blue

If you read *Red, White, and Blue: The Story of the American Flag* during whole group time, then use the instruction below.

CLOSE READING Reread pp. 402–403. Ask questions related to the context.

- Why did America need a new flag in the 1700s? (Americans didn't want to be a part of England anymore. They wanted to have their own country.)
- Look at the picture of the battle. Which are the British soldiers? How can you tell? (The British soldiers are on the left. They have a flag I don't recognize and are fighting against people carrying an American flag.)

Corrective feedback	**If...** children have trouble answering the questions, **then...** reread the page and have them fill in sentence frames to summarize the ideas. **Americans decided they wanted their freedom from ______. A new ______ was needed for the colonies.**

If you are reading *Red, White, and Blue: The Story of the American Flag* during small group time, then return to pp. 399a–417a to guide the reading.

If... children need scaffolding and practice with the main selection, **then...** use the activities on p. DI•39 in the Teacher Resources section on SuccessNet.

SMALL GROUP TIME

SI Strategic Intervention

Language 2. Demonstrate command of the conventions of standard English capitalization, punctuation, and spelling when writing.

1 Build Word Knowledge

Review Amazing Words

history	independence	symbol	patriotic
unfurl	frayed	allegiance	indivisible

Team Talk **LANGUAGE DEVELOPMENT** Help children practice building sentences. Display a sentence starter and have children add oral phrases or clauses using the Amazing Words. For example: This history book tells about _______. (Possible response: This history book tells about the Americans' fight for independence.)

Corrective feedback	**If...** children have difficulty using Amazing Words orally, **then...** review the meaning of each of the words.

2 Text-Based Comprehension

READ ALOUD "Respecting the Star-Spangled Banner" Read aloud "Respecting the Star-Spangled Banner" from *Reading Street Sleuth* on pp. 70–71 as children follow along. Then lead a choral reading of the selection.

ACCESS TEXT Guide children as they work on the Be a Sleuth section.

Look for Clues Reread the text aloud. Tell children to listen for clue words, such as *first, next,* and *then,* that help show the sequence of the steps for folding a flag. Then read the steps out of order. What would happen if you tried to fold a flag this way?

Ask Questions Where are there flags at school? Who do you think put the flags there? Who takes care of the flags? Have children think of questions they could ask the person who cares for the school's flags.

Make Your Case Have children discuss why the flag is important. What does it represent? Help children understand that the flag represents the United States of America and its values such as freedom and justice. Then have children say why they believe it is important to respect the flag.

More Reading for Group Time

CONCEPT LITERACY

Practice
- Concept Words
- Selection Vocabulary

BELOW LEVEL

Review
- Author's Purpose
- Summarize
- Selection Vocabulary

Use these suggested Leveled Readers or other text at children's instructional level.

eSTREET INTERACTIVE
www.ReadingStreet.com

Use the Leveled Reader Database for lesson plans and student pages for *Flag Day* and *America's Birthday.*

Strategic Intervention

1 Build Word Knowledge

Review Quotation Marks

IDENTIFY Choral read the Conventions note at the bottom of page 421 with children to review quotation marks. Have children reread the model poem on p. 421 to find examples of how the author used quotation marks. Allow time for children to discuss the examples and correct any misunderstandings.

2 Text-Based Comprehension

REREAD "Respecting the Star-Spangled Banner" Have partners reread "Respecting the Star-Spangled Banner."

EXTEND UNDERSTANDING Identify other symbols representing the United States, such as the American bald eagle, Uncle Sam, the Liberty Bell, and the Statue of Liberty. Display pictures of the symbols.

PERFORMANCE TASK • Prove It! Organize children into small groups. Assign each group a question related to the Flag Code, such as: *How do you display the American flag together with the flag of another country? How do you display the American flag together with our state flag? What is the proper way to salute the flag?* Provide resources that the groups can use to find answers to the questions. Have groups illustrate their answers.

COMMUNICATE Have children share their illustrations with other groups and, if possible, demonstrate the answer to the questions as well.

SMALL GROUP TIME

More Reading for Group Time

CONCEPT LITERACY

Practice
- Concept Words
- Selection Vocabulary

BELOW LEVEL

Review
- Author's Purpose
- Summarize
- Selection Vocabulary

Use these suggested Leveled Readers or other text at children's instructional level.

eStreet Interactive
www.ReadingStreet.com

Use the Leveled Reader Database for lesson plans and student pages for *Flag Day* and *America's Birthday.*

Advanced

Common Core State Standards

Foundational Skills 3. Know and apply grade-level phonics and word analysis skills in decoding words. **Writing 8.** Recall information from experiences or gather information from provided sources to answer a question.

1 Build Word Knowledge

Extend Phonics

ABBREVIATIONS Have children practice with state abbreviations. Explain that state abbreviations on mail have two capital letters and no period. Have them find each state on a United States map.

TX	IL	NY	VA	CA
ND	FL	AK	OR	CO

2 Read

"Raising the Stars and Stripes"

TEACH VOCABULARY Before reading, introduce the selection words: *allegiance, indivisible.* Help children determine the meaning of each word using these sentences:

1. Every morning, children in Mr. Hull's class said the Pledge of **Allegiance.**
2. The founders wanted to make our country **indivisible.**

Raising the Stars and Stripes

It was a sunny Mon. morning, but Jawon and his friends were not studying in school. Instead, they were marching in a parade!

Their teacher, Ms. Chang, was leading her class down Washington St. In front of them, all in straight rows, the high school band played "The Stars and Stripes Forever." Behind them, all in straight rows, soldiers and sailors marched proudly.

When the parade turned left onto Jefferson Rd., Jawon spotted his mother and her friend, Mrs. Ortiz, watching the parade from the curb. He waved happily to them, and they smiled and waved back.

Soon the parade entered the park at Lincoln Ave. and stopped. The spectators had followed along, and all quietly assembled around a small hill. Dr. Stein delivered a short speech on service to our country. Then two soldiers slowly raised the American flag. Once it reached the top of the flagpole, everyone solemnly said the Pledge of Allegiance.

Was it the 4th of July? No, the date was Nov. 11. It was Veterans Day, and the town was honoring men and women who had fought for our country. As Jawon finished the pledge with "indivisible, with liberty and justice for all," he never felt more thankful.

Advanced Selection 27 **Vocabulary:** allegiance, indivisible

Red, White, and Blue SG•30

READ Have children read "Raising the Stars and Stripes" silently. Then have children take turns reading aloud. After reading, have children recall the two most important ideas of the selection using details from the text.

3 Inquiry: Extend Concepts

IDENTIFY QUESTIONS Have partners choose a national monument to research. During the week, they should learn more about the monument from reading, studying pictures, and talking with adults or older children. On Day 5 they will share what they learned. Guide children in brainstorming possible choices.

- Think about important monuments in our country. Where are they located? Why are they important?

If... children need practice with phonics,
then... use the ELL activities on p. DI•37 in the Teacher Resources section on SuccessNet.

Raising the Stars and Stripes

It was a sunny Mon. morning, but Jawon and his friends were not studying in school. Instead, they were marching in a parade!

Their teacher, Ms. Chang, was leading her class down Washington St. In front of them, all in straight rows, the high school band played "The Stars and Stripes Forever." Behind them, all in straight rows, soldiers and sailors marched proudly.

When the parade turned left onto Jefferson Rd., Jawon spotted his mother and her friend, Mrs. Ortiz, watching the parade from the curb. He waved happily to them, and they smiled and waved back.

Soon the parade entered the park at Lincoln Ave. and stopped. The spectators had followed along, and all quietly assembled around a small hill. Dr. Stein delivered a short speech on service to our country. Then two soldiers slowly raised the American flag. Once it reached the top of the flagpole, everyone solemnly said the Pledge of Allegiance.

Was it the 4th of July? No, the date was Nov. 11. It was Veterans Day, and the town was honoring men and women who had fought for our country. As Jawon finished the pledge with "indivisible, with liberty and justice for all," he never felt more thankful.

Advanced Selection 27 **Vocabulary:** allegiance, indivisible

SMALL GROUP TIME

Advanced

Common Core State Standards

Informational Text 1. Ask and answer such questions as *who, what, where, when, why,* and *how* to demonstrate understanding of key details in a text. **Informational Text 2.** Identify the main topic of a multiparagraph text as well as the focus of specific paragraphs within the text. **Informational Text 4.** Determine the meaning of words and phrases in a text relevant to a grade 2 topic or subject area.

1 Build Word Knowledge

Extend Selection Vocabulary

Team Talk Have partners use the selection words in sentences to internalize their meanings. Have children use as many of the words as they can while making sure the sentence is grammatically correct. (Possible response: Many people celebrate America's birthday by flying the flag.)

America	birthday	flag	freedom
nicknames	stars	stripes	

2 Read

Red, White, and Blue

If you read *Red, White, and Blue: The Story of the American Flag* during whole group time, then use the instruction below.

ACCESS TEXT Have children silently reread *Red, White, and Blue: The Story of the American Flag,* summarize the selection, and identify the main idea and details. (Main Idea: The American flag has changed to represent the growth of our country. Details: The first flag had thirteen stars and thirteen stripes. Congress decided to keep the original thirteen stripes but to add one star for each new state. Today the flag has fifty stars.)

DISCUSS GENRE Discuss what makes *Red, White, and Blue: The Story of the American Flag* an informational text. Point out that the selection tells about real people, places, and events that reflect the history of the country.

If you are reading *Red, White, and Blue: The Story of the American Flag* during small group time, then return to pp. 399a–417a to guide the reading.

3 Inquiry: Extend Concepts

INVESTIGATE Guide children in choosing materials at their independent reading levels.

LOOK AHEAD Help children choose formats to present their information, such as illustrated posters or three-dimensional displays.

Independent Reading Options

Trade Book Library

eSTREET INTERACTIVE
www.ReadingStreet.com

Teacher's Guides available on the Leveled Reader Database.

Advanced

1 Build Word Knowledge

Develop Vocabulary

REREAD FOR VOCABULARY Have children reread *Red, White, and Blue: The Story of the American Flag* and make a two-column chart listing different nicknames for the American flag in the first column and nicknames for the United States and their state or city in the second column.

Nicknames for the American flag	Nicknames for Our Country, State, or City
Old Glory	(Possible Response: Land of Opportunity)
Red, White, and Blue	
Stars and Stripes	
Star-Spangled Banner	

2 Read

Red, White, and Blue

If you read *Red, White, and Blue* during whole group time, then use the instruction below.

CLOSE READING Reread pp. 408–411. Explain that war and change have been a part of our nation's history. What did the flag still flying in the morning at Fort McHenry symbolize to Francis Scott Key? (It meant that the Americans had won the battle.) There is a famous saying that "the pen is mightier than the sword." Explain how the poem that Key wrote became more important than the battle itself. (Key wrote a poem that inspired Americans.) How did the growth of the country force Congress to change the design of the flag? (The country was gaining too many new states to keep adding stripes. Congress had to come up with a new way of changing the flag that made sense.)

If you are reading *Red, White, and Blue: The Story of the American Flag* during small group time, then return to pp. 399a–417a to guide the reading.

3 Inquiry: Extend Concepts

INVESTIGATE Give children time to investigate their projects on national monuments by reading and studying pictures.

SMALL GROUP TIME

ELL

If... children need more scaffolding and practice with the main selection, **then...** use the activities on p. DI•39 in the Teacher Resources section on SuccessNet.

Writing 7. Participate in shared research and writing projects (e.g., read a number of books on a single topic to produce a report; record science observations). **Language 2.** Demonstrate command of the conventions of standard English capitalization, punctuation, and spelling when writing.

More Reading for Group Time

ADVANCED

- Extend Concept Vocabulary
- Review Target Skills

Use this suggested Leveled Reader or other text at children's instructional level.

eSTREET INTERACTIVE
www.ReadingStreet.com

Use the Leveled Reader Database for lesson plans and student pages for *Living in a Democracy.*

1 Build Word Knowledge

Extend Amazing Words and Selection Vocabulary

history	unfurl
independence	frayed
symbol	allegiance
patriotic	indivisible

America	birthday
flag	freedom
nicknames	stars
stripes	

Team Talk Have children ask each other questions using the Amazing Words and the Selection Vocabulary, such as: What is another patriotic symbol for America?

2 Text-Based Comprehension

READ ALOUD "Respecting the Star-Spangled Banner" Have partners take turns reading paragraphs of "Respecting the Star-Spangled Banner" from *Reading Street Sleuth* on pp. 70–71. Then have children read the selection independently.

ACCESS TEXT Guide children as they work on the Be a Sleuth section.

Look for Clues Have children reread the text and identify clue words that help show the order of the steps for folding a flag. Then provide a flag for them to fold.

Ask Questions Encourage children to generate questions as you discuss the selection.

Make Your Case Have children write a letter to the editor of the school newspaper or a local newspaper explaining why it is important to show respect for the flag.

3 Inquiry: Extend Concepts

ORGANIZE INFORMATION Give children time to continue reading and preparing information. Provide any necessary materials, such as poster board, materials to create three-dimensional displays or models, and art supplies.

Advanced

1 Build Word Knowledge

Quotation Marks

IDENTIFY QUOTATION MARKS Have children find the quotation marks in the selection "Respecting the Star-Spangled Banner" and explain why they are used. Encourage children to find quotation marks in another *Sleuth* selection and explain their use.

2 Text-Based Comprehension

REREAD "Respecting the Star-Spangled Banner" Have partners reread "Respecting the Star-Spangled Banner."

EXTEND UNDERSTANDING Ask children to name other symbols for the United States of America. Encourage them to find facts about one of the symbols and to share their findings with the group.

PERFORMANCE TASK • Prove It! Organize children into small groups. Assign each group a question related to the Flag Code, such as: *How do you display the American flag together with the flag of another country? How do you display the American flag together with our state flag? How and when is the American flag flown at half-mast? What is the proper way to salute the flag?* Ask groups to research their questions and create posters that provide the answers.

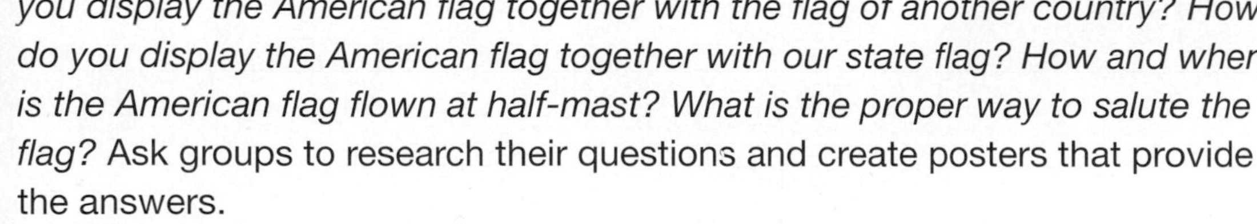

COMMUNICATE Invite children to present their posters and field questions after their presentations.

3 Inquiry: Extend Concepts

COMMUNICATE Have children share their inquiry projects about a national monument.

SMALL GROUP TIME

More Reading for Group Time

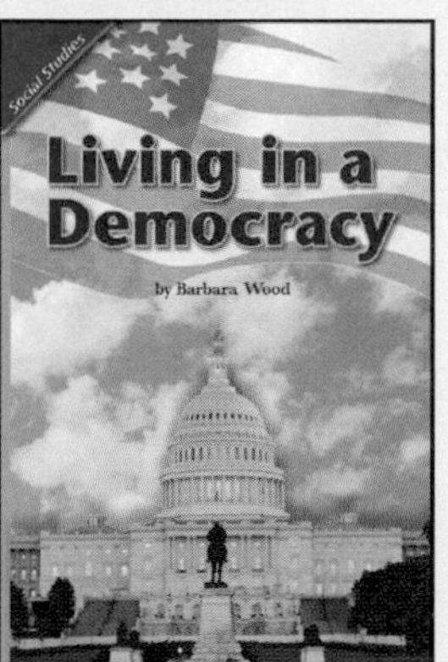

ADVANCED

- Extend Concept Vocabulary
- Review Target Skills

Use this suggested Leveled Reader or other text at children's instructional level.

eStreet Interactive
www.ReadingStreet.com

Use the Leveled Reader Database for lesson plans and student pages for *Living in a Democracy.*

TEACHER NOTES

Tennessee Common Core Edition 

This Week's Target Skills and Strategies

Target Skills and Strategies	Common Core State Standards for English Language Arts	Tennessee CUs and GLEs
Phonics and Spelling **Skill:** Final Syllables *-tion, -ture, -ion*	**CCSS Foundational Skills 3.** Know and apply grade-level phonics and word analysis skills in decoding words. **(Also CCSS Language 2.)**	**TN CU 0201.1.11** Apply phonics generalizations in order to decode words.
Text-Based Comprehension **Skill:** Draw Conclusions	**CCSS Literature 5.** Describe the overall structure of a story, including describing how the beginning introduces the story and the ending concludes the action.	**TN CU 0201.8.10** Identify the characters, plot, and setting of a story.
Strategy: Questioning	**CCSS Literature 1.** Ask and answer such questions as who, what, where, when, why, and how to demonstrate understanding of key details in a text.	**TN CU 0201.8.6** Derive meaning while reading by employing strategies.
Vocabulary **Skill:** Words from Other Languages **Strategy:** Context Clues	**CCSS Language 4.a.** Use sentence-level context as a clue to the meaning of a word or phrase. **(Also CCSS Language 5.a.)**	Reviews Grade K **TN CU 0001.1.8** Use context clues to identify vocabulary in text.
Fluency **Skill:** Appropriate Phrasing	**CCSS Foundational Skills 4.a.** Read on-level text with purpose and understanding.	**TN CU 0201.8.6** Derive meaning while reading by employing strategies. **(Also TN CU 0201.8.1, TN CU 0201.8.8)**
Listening and Speaking Listen to a Description	**CCSS Speaking/Listening 1.a.** Follow agreed-upon rules for discussions (e.g., gaining the floor in respectful ways, listening to others with care, speaking one at a time about the topics and texts under discussion). **(Also CCSS Listening and Speaking 3.)**	**TN CU 0201.2.5** Use rules for conversation. **(Also TN CU 0201.2.1)**
Six-Trait Writing **Trait of the Week:** Sentences	**CCSS Language 1.f.** Produce, expand, and rearrange complete simple and compound sentences (e.g., The boy watched the movie; The little boy watched the movie; The action movie was watched by the little boy).	**TN CU 0201.1.6** Identify and correctly write complete sentences.
Writing Invitation Letter	**CCSS Writing 1.** Write opinion pieces in which they introduce the topic or book they are writing about, state an opinion, supply reasons that support the opinion, use linking words (e.g., *because, and, also*) to connect opinion and reasons, and provide a concluding statement or section.	**TN CU 0201.3.7** Arrange events in a logical and sequential order when writing. **(Also TN GLE 0201.3.1, TN GLE 0201.3.3)**
Conventions **Skill:** Prepositions and Prepositional Phrases	**CCSS Language 1.** Demonstrate command of the conventions of standard English grammar and usage when writing or speaking.	**TN GLE 0201.1.1** Demonstrate control of basic English usage, mechanics, spelling, and sentence structure.

Access for All to Differentiate Instruction

Reading Street Sleuth

Another Movie Night to Remember
pp. 72–73

Follow the path to close reading using the Super Sleuth tips:

- Look for Clues
- Ask Questions
- Make Your Case
- Prove it!

This Week's Optional Tennessee Readers Provide Informational Text

Concept Literacy

CCSS Informational Text 1.; TN CU 0201.8.6

Below Level

CCSS Informational Text 1.; TN CU 0201.8.6

On Level

CCSS Informational Text 1.; TN CU 0201.8.6

Advanced

CCSS Informational Text 1.; TN CU 0201.8.6

ELL

CCSS Literature 1. CCSS Literature 5.; TN CU 0201.8.6, TN CU 0201.8.10

ELD

CCSS Literature 1. CCSS Literature 5.; TN CU 0201.8.6, TN CU 0201.8.10

ISBN-13: 978-0-328-73472-6 ISBN-10: 0-328-73472-1

Assessment

Tennessee Assessment Resources for Common Core Test Success

Tennessee Daily Formative Assessment in Your Teacher's Edition

Baseline Group Tests

CCSS Weekly Tests, pp. 163–168

CCSS Fresh Reads, pp. 163–168

Unit 6 CCSS Benchmark Test

CCSS Success Tracker, ExamView, and Online Lesson Planner

RTI

Response to Intervention Kits Increase Instruction and Progress Monitoring

Intensive Intervention *My Sidewalks* Level B, Unit 6, pp. 194–209

Writing, Grammar, and Spelling

Six-Trait Writing

- Focus/Ideas
- Organization/Paragraphs
- Voice
- Word Choice
- Sentences
  Trait of the Week
  CCSS Language 1.f.
  TN CU 0201.1.6
- Conventions

Resources for Six-Trait Writing, Grammar, and Spelling

Reader's and Writer's Notebook
- Practice Reading
- Practice Grammar
- Practice Spelling
- Practice Writing

Writing Rubrics and Anchor Papers

Digital Resources
- Online Journal
- Online Writing Transparencies
- Grammar Jammer

Teacher Resources DVD-ROM
- Reader's and Writer's Notebook
- Let's Practice It!
- Graphic Organizers
- Writing Transparencies

Grade 2 Skills Trace

Skills and Strategies	Looking Back	This Week's Selection	Looking Ahead
Phonics and Spelling **Skill:** Final Syllables *-tion, -ture, -ion*	Skill not previously taught	428a, 428–429, 429a, 429c–429d, 432c, 448c, 448d, 452d, 452e–452f, 456c, 457e	**Unit 6** 464c, 492c, 524d
Text-Based Comprehension **Skill:** Draw Conclusions	**Unit 3** 387a, 388h, 390–391, 394–395 **Unit 4** 24a, 24–25, 28a, 30–31	430a, 430–431, 434a, 436–437, 447a, 449a, 454–455, 457b, 457f	Grade 3 **Units 2, 3, 4, 5**
Strategy: Questioning	**Unit 3** 354h, 358–359, 362–363 **Unit 4** 88a, 88–89, 92a, 94–95	430a, 430–431, 433a, 438–439, 442–443, 444–445, 446–447, 449a, 452–453, 454–455	Grade 3 **Units 2, 4, 6**
Vocabulary **Skill:** Words from Other Languages **Strategy:** Context Clues	**Unit 4** 26g, 26–27, 32–33, 42g, 52–53	432g, 432–433, 442–443, 448g, 456–457	Grade 3 **Units 2, 3, 4, 5**
Fluency **Skill:** Appropriate Phrasing	**Unit 4** 110f, 117a, 119a **Unit 5** 348f, 355a, 357a	448f, 455a, 457a	**Unit 6** 520f, 527a, 527f, 529a
Listening and Speaking Listen to a Description	Skill not previously taught	455e	Skill not subsequently taught
Six-Trait Writing **Trait of the Week:** Sentences	**Unit 4** 109d–109e, 112–113, 113a **Unit 5** 329c–329d, 347c–347d	431c–431d, 447d–447e, 450–451, 451a, 455c–455d	Grade 3 **Units 1, 3, 4**
Writing Invitation Letter	Grade 1 **Unit 4**	431c–431d, 447d–447e, 450–451, 451a, 455c–455d, 457h–457i	Grade 3 **Unit 5**
Conventions **Skill:** Prepositions and Prepositional Phrases	Grade 1 **Unit 5**	431b, 447c, 450a, 450–451, 455b, 457g	Grade 3 **Unit 4**

Tennessee Social Studies Standards Taught During the Reading Lesson

TN 2.1.01.c Recognize patterns of cultural traits such as language, religion, and family structure.

TN 2.5.02.c Describe and measure calendar time by days, weeks, months, and years.

TN 2.6.02.a Identify and describe ways family, groups, and community influence an individual's daily life and personal choices.

Teaching the Common Core State Standards This Week

The Common Core State Standards for English Language Arts are divided into strands for **Reading** (including **Foundational Skills**), **Writing**, **Speaking and Listening**, and **Language**. The chart below shows some of the content you will teach this week, strand by strand. Turn to this week's 5-Day Planner on pages 426d–426e to see how this content is taught each day.

Reading Strand

- **Phonics:** Final Syllables *-tion*, *-ture*, *-ion*
- **Text-Based Comprehension:** Draw Conclusions; Questioning
- **Fluency:** Appropriate Phrasing
- **Literary Text:** Setting and Plot
- **Genre:** Main Selection: Realistic Fiction; Paired Selection: Online Directories

Common Core State Standards for English Language Arts

Writing Strand

- **Writing Mini-Lesson:** Invitation Letter
- **Trait:** Sentences
- **Look Back and Write:** Text Evidence

Speaking and Listening Strand

- **Content Knowledge:** Build Oral Language
- **Listening and Speaking:** Listen to a Description
- **Research and Inquiry**

Language Strand

- **Oral Vocabulary: Amazing Words** *celebration*, *custom*, *tradition*, *create*, *inspect*, *angle*, *brilliant*, *snapshot*
- **Vocabulary:** Words from Other Languages; Context Clues
- **Selection Vocabulary:** *aunt*, *bank*, *basket*, *collects*, *favorite*, *present*
- **Academic Vocabulary:** *draw conclusions, preposition, prepositional phrase, invitation, interview, questioning, source, plot, setting, myth*
- **Conventions:** Prepositions and Prepositional Phrases
- **Spelling:** Final Syllables *-tion*, *-ture*, *-ion*

Text-Based Comprehension

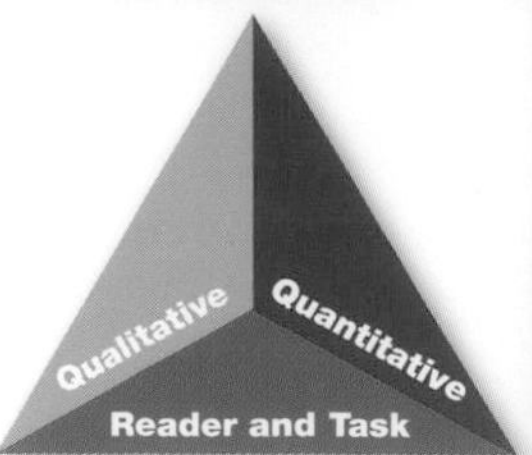

Text Complexity Measures

Use the rubric to familiarize yourself with the text complexity of ***A Birthday Basket for Tía***.

Bridge to Complex Knowledge

Quantitative Measures	**Lexile**	580L
	Average Sentence Length	7.91
	Word Frequency	3.54

Qualitative Measures	**Levels of Meaning**	understand realistic fiction; character motivation
	Structure	conventional structure; events happen chronologically
	Language Conventionality and Clarity	simple sentence structure; non-English words
	Theme and Knowledge Demands	simple theme; common experiences; references to another culture

Reader and Task Suggestions

FORMATIVE ASSESSMENT Based on assessment results, use the **Reader and Task Suggestions** in Access Main Selection to scaffold the selection or support independence for children as they read ***A Birthday Basket for Tía***.

READER AND TASK SUGGESTIONS

Preparing to Read the Text	Leveled Tasks
• Review strategies for understanding words from other languages. See the vocabulary skill lesson on p. 432g. • Review the importance of realistic fiction that is written in chronological order. • Remind children that as they encounter unfamiliar words, they may need to read more slowly to better understand the text.	• **Language Conventionality and Clarity** If children struggle with non-English words, have them identify the words and use context clues to determine the meanings. • **Theme and Knowledge Demands** If children do not have difficulty with references to another culture, have them identify events in the text that are familiar to them.

Recommended Placement Both the qualitative and quantitative measures suggest this text should be placed in the Grade 2–3 text complexity band, which is where both the Common Core State Standards and *Scott Foresman Reading Street* have placed it. Encourage children to access any unfamiliar vocabulary using the context clues and images.

Focus on Common Core State Standards

Main Selection, pp. 434–447

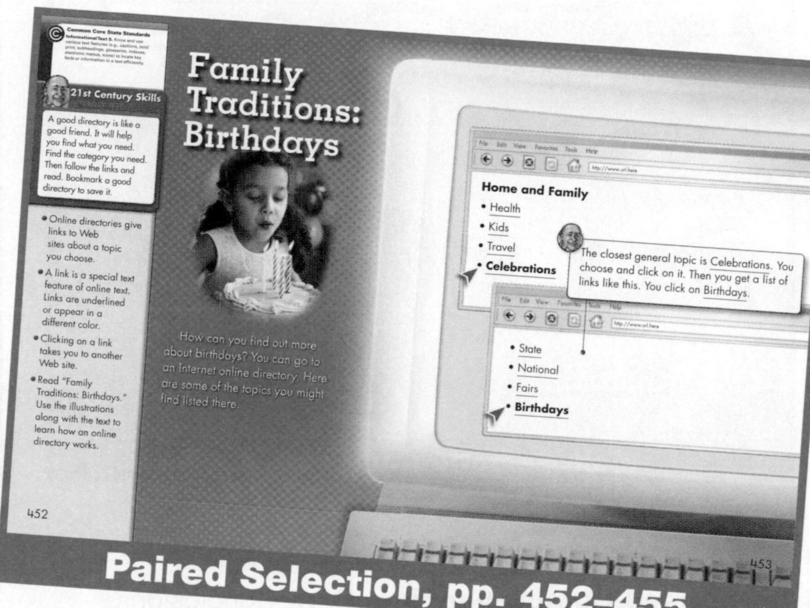

Paired Selection, pp. 452–455

Text-Based Comprehension

Draw Conclusions
CCSS Literature 5.

Questioning
CCSS Literature 1.

Fluency

Appropriate Phrasing
CCSS Foundational Skills 4.a.

Writing and Conventions

Trait: Sentences
CCSS Language 1.f.

Writing Mini-Lesson: Invitation Letter
CCSS Writing 1.

Conventions: Prepositions and Prepositional Phrases
CCSS Language 1.

Oral Vocabulary

Amazing Words

celebration	custom
tradition	create
inspect	angle
brilliant	snapshot

CCSS Language 6.

Vocabulary

Vocabulary Skill: Words from Other Languages
CCSS Language 4.a.

Strategy: Context Clues
CCSS Language 4.a.,
CCSS Language 5.a.

aunt	bank	basket
collects	favorite	present

Phonics and Spelling

Final Syllables *-tion, -ture, -ion*
CCSS Foundational Skills 3.,
CCSS Language 2.

mixture	nation	section
future	picture	action
caution	station	fixture
motion	nature	feature

Listening and Speaking

Listen to a Description
CCSS Speaking/Listening 1.a.,
CCSS Speaking/Listening 3.

Preview Your Week

Why are family celebrations special?

Main Selection, pp. 434–447

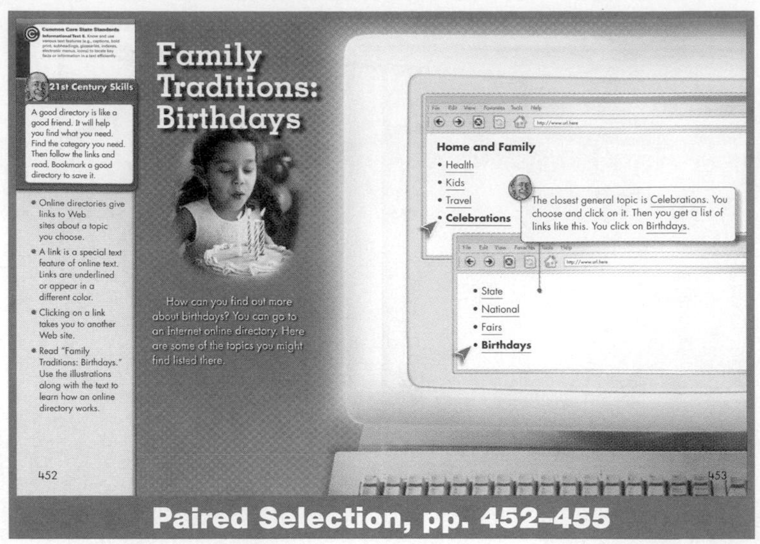

Paired Selection, pp. 452–455

Genre: Realistic Fiction

Phonics: Final Syllables *-tion, -ture, -ion*

Text-Based Comprehension: Draw Conclusions

Vocabulary: Words from Other Languages

21st Century Skills

Genre: Online Directories

Build Content Knowledge

KNOWLEDGE GOALS

Children will understand that family celebrations:

- involve cultural traditions
- include certain activities
- include special foods

THIS WEEK'S CONCEPT CHART

Develop a concept-related graphic organizer like the one below over the course of this week.

Why are family celebrations special?

We Celebrate Special Events	Family Members Get Together	We Do Special Activities
We celebrate the birth of a baby. We celebrate birthdays.	We dress up in special clothes.	

BUILD ORAL VOCABULARY

This week, children will acquire the following academic vocabulary/domain-specific words.

Amazing Words

celebration	custom
tradition	create
inspect	angle
brilliant	snapshot

OPTIONAL CONCEPT-BASED READING Use the Digital Path to access readers offering different levels of text complexity.

Concept Literacy

Below Level

On Level

Advanced

ELL

ELD

This Week's Digital Resources

eSTREET INTERACTIVE
www.ReadingStreet.com

Get Ready to Read

Background Building Audio CD This audio CD provides valuable background information about ways children celebrate their birthdays to help children read and comprehend the weekly texts.

Concept Talk Video Use this video on the Digital Path to build momentum and introduce the weekly concept of family celebrations.

Interactive Sing with Me Big Book "Family Traditions," sung to the tune of "The More We Get Together," introduces the Amazing Words with a catchy, concept-related song.

Interactive Sound-Spelling Cards With these interactive cards on the Digital Path, children see an image, hear the image name, and see the spelling for final syllables *-tion, -ture,* and *-ion.*

Pearson eText Use the eText for the Decodable Readers on the Leveled Reader Database for phonics and fluency support.

Letter Tile Drag and Drop Using this interactive tool on Pearson SuccessNet, children click and spell words to enhance their phonics skills.

Read and Comprehend

Envision It! Animations Use this colorful animation on the Digital Path to explain the target comprehension skill, Draw Conclusions.

Pearson eText Read the eText of the main selection, *A Birthday Basket for Tía*, and the paired selection, "Family Traditions: Birthdays," with audio support on Pearson SuccessNet.

Story Sort Use the Story Sort Activity on the Digital Path after reading *A Birthday Basket for Tía* to involve children in summarizing.

Journal: Word Bank Use the Word Bank on the Digital Path to have children write sentences using this week's selection words.

Vocabulary Activities A variety of interactive vocabulary activities on the Digital Path help children practice concept-related words.

Language Arts

Grammar Jammer Choose a whimsical animation on the Digital Path to provide an engaging grammar lesson that will capture children's attention.

Pearson eText Find the Student Edition eText of the Let's Write It! and Let's Learn It! pages with audio support on Pearson SuccessNet.

Additional Resources

Teacher Resources DVD-ROM Use the following resources on the TR DVD or on Pearson SuccessNet throughout the week:

- Amazing Word Cards
- Reader's and Writer's Notebook
- Writing Transparencies
- Daily Fix-It Transparencies
- Scoring Rubrics
- Grammar Transparencies
- Research Transparencies
- Let's Practice It!
- Graphic Organizers
- Vocabulary Cards
- Vocabulary Transparencies

This Week's Skills

Phonics/Spelling
Final Syllables *-tion, -ture, -ion*

Comprehension
Draw Conclusions
Questioning

Language
Vocabulary: Words from Other Languages
Conventions: Prepositions and Prepositional Phrases

Fluency
Appropriate Phrasing

Writing
Invitation Letter

5-Day Planner

DAY 1

Get Ready to Read

Content Knowledge 426j
Oral Vocabulary: *celebration, custom, tradition*

Phonics/Spelling 428a
Final Syllables *-tion, -ture, -ion*
Spelling Pretest
READ Decodable Reader 28A
Reread for Fluency

Monitor Progress
Check Word Reading

Read and Comprehend

Text-Based Comprehension 430a
Draw Conclusions
Questioning

Vocabulary 431a
Selection Words: *aunt, bank, basket, collects, favorite, present*

Language Arts

Conventions 431b
Prepositions and Prepositional Phrases

Writing 431c
Invitation Letter

Research and Inquiry 431e
Identify and Focus Topic

DAY 2

Get Ready to Read

Content Knowledge 432a
Oral Vocabulary: *create*

Phonics/Spelling 432c
Final Syllables *-tion, -ture, -ion*
Review Final Syllables *-le*
Spelling: Final Syllables *-ture, -tion*

Read and Comprehend

Vocabulary 432e
Review Selection Words: *aunt, bank, basket, collects, favorite, present*
Skill: Words from Other Languages
Strategy: Context Clues
Reread for Fluency

Monitor Progress
Check Selection Words

Text-Based Comprehension 433a
READ *A Birthday Basket for Tía*—1st Read

Literary Text 447b
Setting and Plot

Language Arts

Conventions 447c
Prepositions and Prepositional Phrases

Writing 447d
Invitation Letter

Handwriting 447f
Cursive *G, S, I*/Letter Size

Research and Inquiry 447g
Research Skill: Interview and Natural Sources

DAY 3

Get Ready to Read

Content Knowledge 448a
Oral Vocabulary: *inspect*

Phonics/Spelling 448c
Sort Words
Fluent Word Reading
Decode and Read
Spelling: Dictation

Read and Comprehend

Fluency 448f
Appropriate Phrasing

Selection Vocabulary 448g
Selection Words: *aunt, bank, basket, collects, favorite, present*
Words from Other Languages

Text-Based Comprehension 448h
READ *A Birthday Basket for Tía*—2nd Read
Monitor Progress Check Retelling

Language Arts

Conventions 450a
Prepositions and Prepositional Phrases

Writing 450–451
Invitation Letter

Research and Inquiry 451b
Gather and Record Information

DAY 4

Get Ready to Read

Content Knowledge 452a
Oral Vocabulary: *angle, brilliant, snapshot*

Phonics/Spelling 452c
Review Abbreviations
Spiral Review Fluent Word Reading
READ Decodable Reader 28C
Spelling: Final Syllables *-tion, -ture*

Read and Comprehend

21st Century Skills 452h
Online Directories
READ "Family Traditions: Birthdays" Paired Reading

Fluency 455a
Appropriate Phrasing
Monitor Progress Fluency Check

Language Arts

Conventions 455b
Prepositions and Prepositional Phrases

Writing 455c
Invitation Letter

Listening and Speaking 455e
Listen to a Description

Research and Inquiry 455f
Synthesize

DAY 5

Get Ready to Read

Content Knowledge 456a
Review Oral Vocabulary
Monitor Progress
Check Oral Vocabulary

Phonics/Spelling 456c
Review Final Syllables *-tion, -ture, -ion*
Spelling Test

Read and Comprehend

Vocabulary 456–457
Fluency 457a
Listening and Speaking 457a

Text-Based Comprehension 457b
Review Draw Conclusions

Vocabulary 457b
Review Selection Words: *aunt, bank, basket, collects, favorite, present*

Genre 457c
Review Realistic Fiction

Assessment 457d
Monitor Progress
Sentence Reading; Fluency and Comprehension

Language Arts

Conventions 457g
Review Prepositions and Prepositional Phrases

Writing 457h
Invitation Letter

Research and Inquiry 457j
Communicate

Wrap Up Your Week! 457k

Access for All

What do I do in group time?

It's as easy as 1-2-3!

1. TEACHER-LED SMALL GROUPS
2. INDEPENDENT PRACTICE STATIONS
3. INDEPENDENT READING

Small Group Time

Bridge to Common Core

SKILL DEVELOPMENT

- Final Syllables *-tion, -ture, -ion*
- Words from Other Languages
- Draw Conclusions
- Questioning

DEEP UNDERSTANDING

This Week's Knowledge Goals

Children will understand that family celebrations:
- involve cultural traditions
- include certain activities
- include special foods

1 Small Group Lesson Plan

	DAY 1 Differentiate Phonics	DAY 2 Differentiate Comprehension
OL On-Level pp. SG•36–SG•40	**Practice Phonics** Additional Words with Final Syllables *-tion, -ture, -ion* **Decodable Reader** Read *My Future*	**Build Word Knowledge** Practice Selection Vocabulary **Access Text** Read *A Birthday Basket for Tía*
SI Strategic Intervention pp. SG•41–SG•45	**Reteach Phonics** Blend Words with Final Syllables *-tion, -ture, -ion* **Decodable Reader** Read *My Future*	**Build Word Knowledge** Reteach Selection Vocabulary **Access Text** Read *A Birthday Basket for Tía*
A Advanced pp. SG•46–SG•51	**Extend Phonics** More Words with Final Syllables *-tion, -ture, -ion* **Advanced Selection** Read "A Naming Celebration"	**Build Word Knowledge** Extend Selection Vocabulary **Access Text** Read *A Birthday Basket for Tía*
Independent Inquiry Project	Introduce	Investigate
ELL **If...** children need more scaffolding and practice with...	**Phonics** **then...** use the Phonics Transition Lessons on pp. 213–309 in the *ELL Handbook.*	**Comprehension Skill** **then...** use the ELL activities on p. DI•59 in the Teacher Resources section on SuccessNet.

Reading Street Sleuth

- Provides access to grade-level text for all children
- Focuses on finding clues in text through close reading
- Builds capacity for complex text

Build Text-Based Comprehension

A Birthday Basket for Tía

Optional Leveled Readers

Concept Literacy

Below Level

On Level

Advanced

ELL

ELD

DAY 3 Differentiate Close Reading	DAY 4 Differentiate Vocabulary	DAY 5 Differentiate Reteaching
Reread to Develop Vocabulary **Close Reading** Reread *A Birthday Basket for Tía*	**Build Word Knowledge** Develop Language Using Amazing Words **Text-Based Comprehension** Read *Reading Street Sleuth,* pp. 72–73, or Leveled Readers	**Practice** Prepositions and Prepositional Phrases **Text-Based Comprehension** Reread *Reading Street Sleuth,* pp. 72–73, or Leveled Readers
Reread to Develop Vocabulary **Close Reading** Reread *A Birthday Basket for Tía*	**Build Word Knowledge** Review/Discuss Amazing Words **Text-Based Comprehension** Read *Reading Street Sleuth,* pp. 72–73, or Leveled Readers	**Review** Prepositions and Prepositional Phrases **Text-Based Comprehension** Reread *Reading Street Sleuth,* pp. 72–73, or Leveled Readers
Reread to Develop Vocabulary **Close Reading** Reread *A Birthday Basket for Tía* Investigate	**Build Word Knowledge** Extend Amazing Words and Selection Vocabulary **Text-Based Comprehension** Read *Reading Street Sleuth,* pp. 72–73, or Leveled Readers Organize	**Extend** Prepositions and Prepositional Phrases **Text-Based Comprehension** Reread *Reading Street Sleuth,* pp. 72–73, or Leveled Readers Communicate
Main Selection **then...** use the activities on p. DI•60 in the Teacher Resources section on SuccessNet.	**Amazing Words** **then...** use the routine on pp. xxxvi–xxxvii in the *ELL Handbook.*	**Conventions and Writing** **then...** use the Grammar Transition Lessons on pp. 310–385 in the *ELL Handbook.*

2 Independent Stations

Practice Last Week's Skills

★ Focus on these activities when time is limited.

ACCESS FOR ALL
- ● Below-Level Activities
- ▲ On-Level Activities
- ■ Advanced Activities

★ WORD WISE

Spell abbreviations.

OBJECTIVES
- Spell words with abbreviations.

MATERIALS
- *Word Wise* Flip Chart, Letter Tiles, paper, pencils

 **Interactive Sound-Spelling Cards**  **Letter Tile Drag and Drop**

● Children spell *Mister* with Letter Tiles. They say and write the word. They then write the abbreviation. They repeat with *February, Doctor,* and *Road.*

▲ Children spell *November, Street, January, October,* and *Monday* with Letter Tiles. They write the abbreviated forms and use each in a sentence.

■ Children spell *Governor, Avenue, Senior, Junior, Tuesday, Thursday, December,* and *August.* They write the abbreviated forms and use five in a story.

WORD WORK

Identify abbreviations.

OBJECTIVES
- Identify and use abbreviations

MATERIALS
- *Word Work* Flip Chart; Teacher-made abbreviation cards: *Mr., S., Ave., Dr., Jan., Mon.;* Teacher-made word cards: *Road, Junior, February, Street, North, Friday;* paper; pencils

 **Interactive Sound-Spelling Cards**

● Children take an abbreviation card and say the word that goes with it. They use the abbreviation to write a sentence.

▲ Children take three abbreviation cards and use each one in a sentence. They take three word cards, say the words, and write the abbreviations in sentences.

■ Children take five abbreviation cards and say the words. They take five word cards and write the abbreviation for each and use them in sentences.

LET'S WRITE!

Write a song or poem.

OBJECTIVES
- Write a descriptive song or poem.
- Express feelings through the use of voice.

MATERIALS
- *Let's Write!* Flip Chart, paper, pencils

 **Grammar Jammer**

● Children choose their favorite tradition and write a short song or poem about it. They use rhyming words. They should make up a tune to go with their song.

▲ Children write a song or poem about their favorite tradition. They express feelings and use sensory details to describe sights and sounds.

■ Children write a song or poem about their favorite tradition. They express feelings and use sensory details to describe sights and sounds. They should craft a melody for a song.

WORDS TO KNOW

Use context clues.

OBJECTIVES
- Use context clues to determine the relative meaning of multiple-meaning words.

MATERIALS
- *Words to Know* Flip Chart; Teacher-made word cards: *run, cold, call, bat, stand;* paper, pencils

 **Vocabulary Activities**

● Children read two sentences: *The owner may fire the coach. A fire blazed in the old house.* They determine the meaning of *fire* in each and write down the meanings.

▲ Children pick a word card and write two meanings for it. They read two sentences: *The soldiers faced grave danger. We laid flowers at his grave.* They write the two meanings of the word *grave.*

■ Children choose five word cards and write two meanings for each. They write five sentences that include context clues.

Manage the Stations

Use these management tools to set up and organize your Practice Stations:

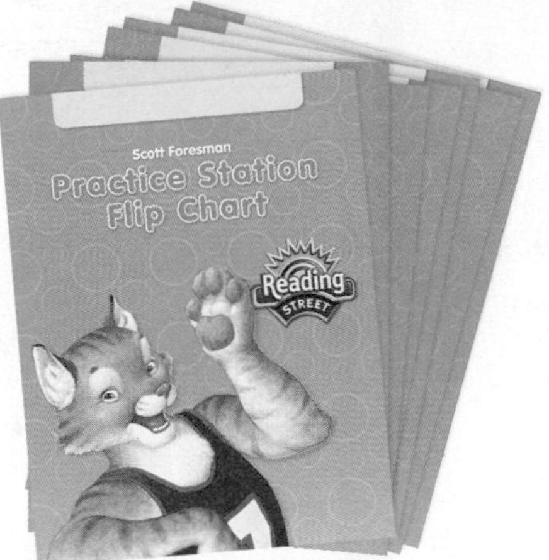

Practice Station Flip Charts

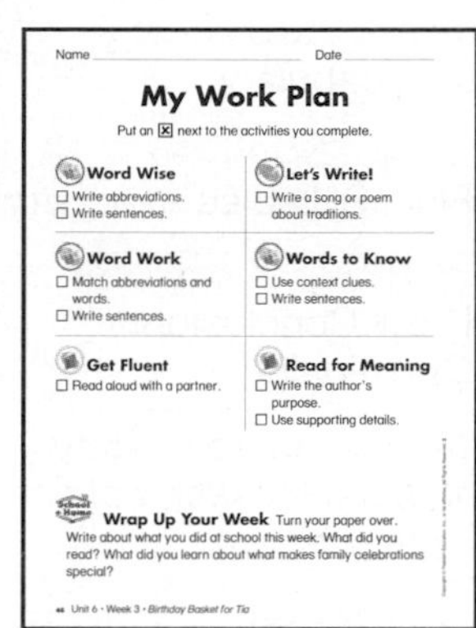

Name ______ Date ______

My Work Plan

Put an ☒ next to the activities you complete.

Word Wise
- ☐ Write abbreviations.
- ☐ Write sentences.

Let's Write!
- ☐ Write a song or poem about traditions.

Word Work
- ☐ Match abbreviations and words.
- ☐ Write sentences.

Words to Know
- ☐ Use context clues.
- ☐ Write sentences.

Get Fluent
- ☐ Read aloud with a partner.

Read for Meaning
- ☐ Write the author's purpose.
- ☐ Use supporting details.

Wrap Up Your Week Turn your paper over. Write about what you did at school this week. What did you read? What did you learn about what makes family celebrations special?

46 Unit 6 • Week 3 • *Birthday Basket for Tía*

Classroom Management Handbook for Differentiated Instruction Practice Stations, p. 46

READ FOR MEANING

Use text-based comprehension tools.

OBJECTIVES

- Identify the author's purpose in a story.

MATERIALS

- *Read for Meaning* Flip Chart, 2.6.2 Leveled Readers, paper, pencils, crayons

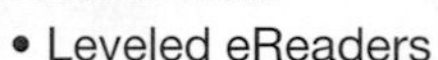

Pearson eText
- Leveled eReaders

Envision It! Animations

● Children read *America's Birthday.* They determine the author's purpose and draw a picture illustrating the author's feelings on the topic.

▲ Children read *American Revolution Heroes* and determine the author's purpose. They write a paragraph, using details from the text to tell the author's purpose.

■ Children read *Living in a Democracy* and determine the author's purpose. They write a paragraph, using details from the text to explain the author's purpose.

GET FLUENT

Practice fluent reading.

OBJECTIVES

- Read aloud with accuracy.

MATERIALS

- *Get Fluent* Flip Chart, 2.6.2 Leveled Readers

Pearson eText
- Leveled Readers

● Children work with a partner to take turns reading from *America's Birthday.* They use punctuation to aid accuracy.

▲ Children work with a partner to take turns reading from *American Revolution Heroes.* They use punctuation to aid accuracy.

■ Children work with a partner to take turns reading from *Living in a Democracy.* They use punctuation to aid accuracy.

3 Independent Reading

Children should select appropriately complex texts to read and write about, independently every day before, during, and after school.

Suggestions for this week's independent reading:
- Informational texts on last week's social studies topic: What traditions and celebrations involve our country's flag?
- Nonfiction selections about what traditions and celebrations involve our country's flag
- Nonfiction book by a favorite author

BOOK TALK Have partners discuss their independent reading for the week. Tell them to refer to their Reading Log and paraphrase what the selection was about. To focus the discussion, prompt them to talk about one or more of the following:

Key Ideas and Details
- Who is the author? Why did he or she write this piece?
- What did I learn from this text?

Craft and Structure
- Did the author use words that were interesting and clear?
- How well did the author explain the topic?

Integration of Ideas
- How could I use the information in this work?
- Was this book like others I have read?

Pearson eText
- Student Edition
- Decodable Readers
- Leveled Readers

Trade Book Library

Materials from School or Classroom Library

DAY 1 at a Glance

Content Knowledge
Oral Vocabulary

Phonics/Spelling
Final Syllables *-tion, -ture, -ion*

Text-Based Comprehension
Draw Conclusions
Questioning

Selection Vocabulary
aunt, bank, basket, collects, favorite, present

Conventions
Prepositions and Prepositional Phrases

Writing
Invitation Letter

Research and Inquiry
Identify and Focus Topic

Materials

- Student Edition
- Sing with Me Big Book
- Sound-Spelling Cards
- Decodable Reader 28A
- Reader's and Writer's Notebook

Bridge to Common Core

INTEGRATION OF KNOWLEDGE/IDEAS
This week children read, write, and talk about family celebrations.

Texts This Week

- "Family Tradition"
- "Empty Eggshells"
- *Magda's Tortillas*
- "A Party and a Present"
- *A Birthday Basket for Tía*
- Poetry Selections
- "Family Traditions: Birthdays"

Social Studies Knowledge Goals
Children will understand that family celebrations

- involve cultural traditions
- include certain activities
- include special foods

Street Rhymes!

On birthdays, how do you celebrate?
With a big cake you can decorate?
With a piñata and flowers
Or wrapped gifts stacked in towers?
Will you have a party with all your friends,
Who will laugh and play til the party ends?

- To introduce this week's concept, read aloud the poem several times and ask children to join you.

Content Knowledge

Family Celebrations

CONCEPT TALK To help children gain knowledge and understanding, tell them that this week they will talk, sing, read, and write about family celebrations. Write the Question of the Week, *Why are family celebrations special?*, and track the print as you read it.

Build Oral Language

TALK ABOUT FAMILY CELEBRATIONS Have children turn to pages 426–427 in their Student Edition. Read the title and look at the photos. Use these questions to guide discussion and create a "Why are family celebrations special?" chart.

- Look at the picture of the two boys and the baby. What do you think this family is celebrating? (the birth of the baby) Let's make one column head *We Celebrate Special Events* and write *We celebrate the birth of a baby* under it.
- Who is pictured in the big photo? (Possible response: a boy and his grandfather) Family members get together for celebrations. Let's make that our second column head. What is special about the boy? (He's dressed in traditional clothes.) We dress up in special clothes when we get together for celebrations. We'll add that to the chart.
- What is the woman celebrating? (her 100th birthday) Let's add *We celebrate birthdays* to the events we celebrate.

Common Core State Standards
Language 6. Use words and phrases acquired through conversations, reading and being read to, and responding to texts, including using adjectives and adverbs to describe (e.g., *When other kids are happy that makes me happy*).
Also Speaking/Listening 1.

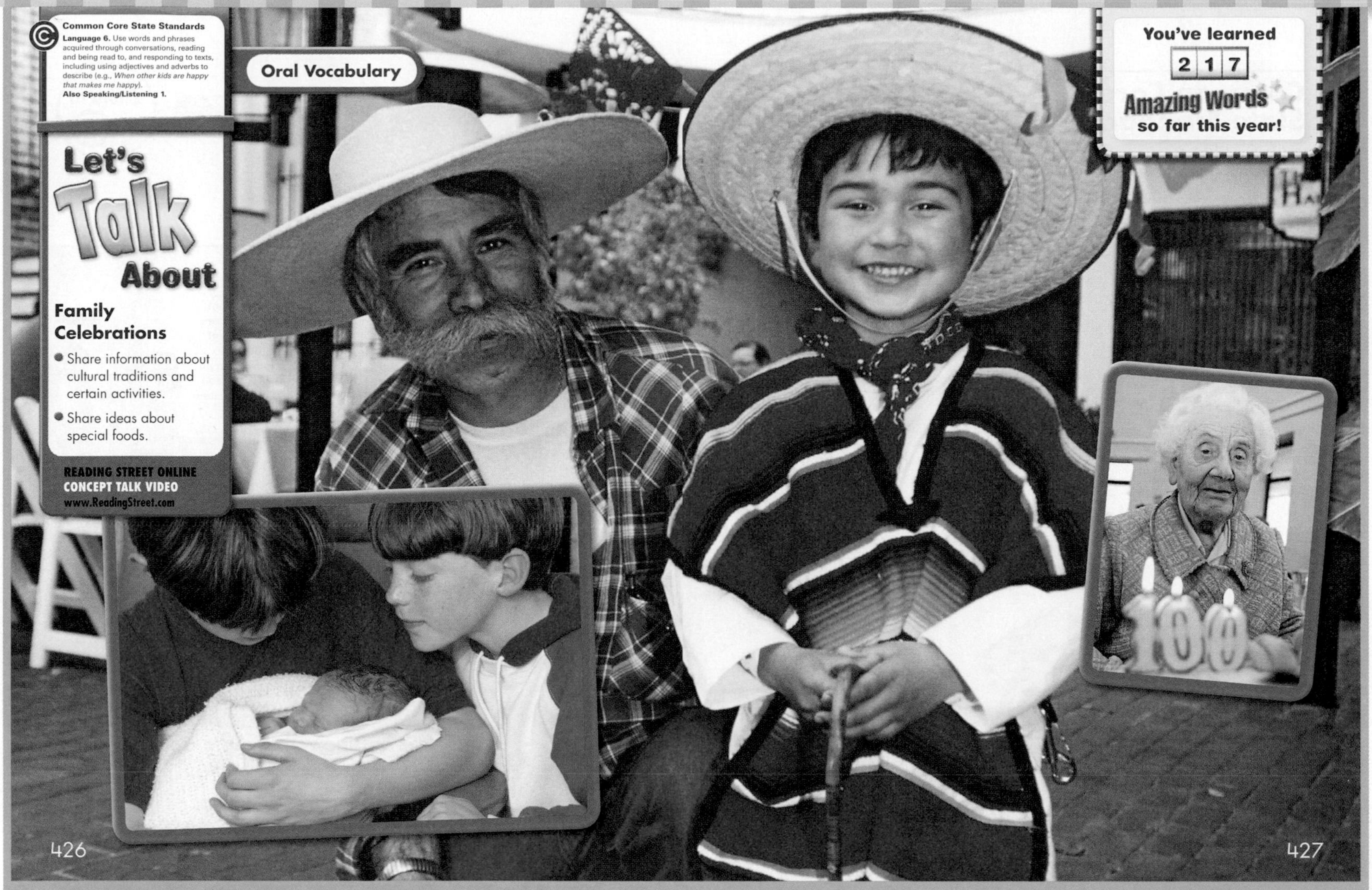

Oral Vocabulary
Let's Talk About
Family Celebrations
• Share information about cultural traditions and certain activities.
• Share ideas about special foods.
READING STREET ONLINE
CONCEPT TALK VIDEO
www.ReadingStreet.com
You've learned
2 1 7
Amazing Words
so far this year!
100
426
427

Student Edition, pp. 426–427

CONNECT TO READING Explain that this week, children will read about a special birthday. The family does many special activities to celebrate. Let's add *We Do Special Activities* to our chart.

Why are family celebrations special?

We Celebrate Special Events	Family Members Get Together	We Do Special Activities
We celebrate the birth of a baby. We celebrate birthdays.	We dress up in special clothes.	

eStreet Interactive
www.ReadingStreet.com
- **Pearson eText**
  - Student Edition
- **Concept Talk Video**

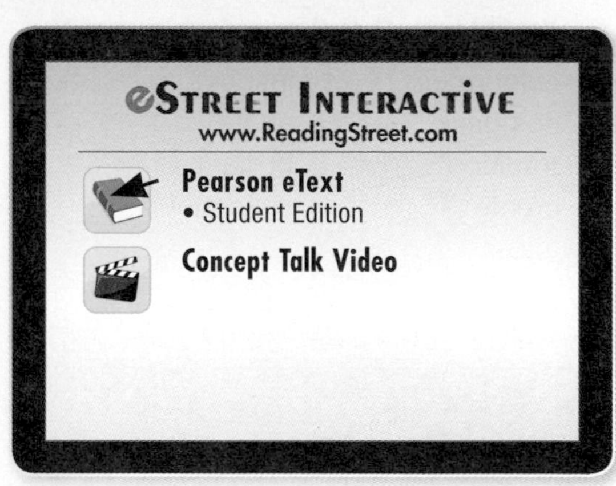

ELL

Preteach Concepts Use the Day 1 instruction on ELL Poster 28 to assess and build background knowledge, develop concepts, and build oral vocabulary.

ELL Support Additional support is provided in the *ELL Handbook* and in the ELL Support Lessons on the *Teacher Resources DVD-ROM.*

Common Core State Standards

Language 6. Use words and phrases acquired through conversations, reading and being read to, and responding to texts, including using adjectives and adverbs to describe (e.g., *When other kids are happy that makes me happy*).

Amazing Words

You've learned 217 words so far.

You'll learn 008 words this week!

celebration	inspect
custom	angle
tradition	brilliant
create	snapshot

Content Knowledge

Build Oral Vocabulary

INTRODUCE AMAZING WORDS Display page 28 of the *Sing with Me* Big Book. Tell children they are going to sing about families. Ask children to listen for the Amazing Words *celebration, custom,* and *tradition* as you sing. Sing the song again and have children join you.

Sing with Me Big Book, p. 28

Amazing Words **Robust Vocabulary Routine**

1. **Introduce the Word** Relate the word *celebration* to the song. A *celebration* is a time when families come together. Supply a child-friendly definition. A *celebration* is a party for a special day. Have children say the word.
2. **Demonstrate** Provide examples to show meaning. We usually have a *celebration* for our birthday. My family had a *celebration* when my brother graduated from college.
3. **Apply** Have children demonstrate their understanding. Describe your favorite *celebration.*
4. **Display the Word** Run your hand under the four syllables *cel-e-bra-tion* as you read the word. Point out the syllable *-tion* at the end of the word.

See p. OV•3 to teach *custom* and *tradition.*

Routines Flip Chart

AMAZING WORDS AT WORK Have children look at the picture on page 28.

- It looks like a family is visiting their grandparents for a party. What are some reasons a family might get together? Use the word *celebration* in your answer. (Possible response: A family might get together for a celebration of a birthday or holiday.)
- What are some things that this family might do when they get together? Use *custom* in your answer. (Possible response: Their family customs might include eating certain foods or playing certain games.)
- Why is *tradition* important to families? (Possible response: Tradition is important because it unites families.)

APPLY AMAZING WORDS Have children demonstrate their understanding of the Amazing Words by completing these sentences orally.

He has planned a **celebration** for ______.

On Thanksgiving we have a **custom** of ______.

In my family it is a **tradition** to ______.

Corrective feedback	**If...** children have difficulty using the Amazing Words, **then...** remind them of the definitions and provide opportunities for children to use the words in sentences.

Access for All

 Advanced

Synonyms Have children explain why the Amazing Words *custom* and *tradition* are synonyms.

Cognates The Amazing Words *celebration* and *tradition* have cognates that Spanish speakers may recognize: *celebración* and *tradición.* Point out how this prior knowledge can help children with learning new words.

Common Core State Standards

Foundational Skills 3. Know and apply grade-level phonics and word analysis skills in decoding words.

Skills Trace

Final Syllables: *-tion, -ture, -ion*

Introduce U6W3D1

Practice U6W3D2; U6W3D3; U6W3D4

Reteach/Review U6W3D5; U6W4D4

Assess/Test Weekly Test U6W3 Benchmark Test U6

KEY: U=Unit W=Week D=Day

Vocabulary Support

You may wish to explain the meaning of these words.

fracture break

stallion a male horse

Phonics

Teach/Model

Final Syllables *-tion, -ture, -ion*

CONNECT Write *candle.* Point out that children have already studied words like this. Ask what they know about the last syllable in *candle.* (It is the consonant *d* and *-le.*) Explain that today they will learn that *-tion, -ture,* and *-ion* can also make up a word's last syllable.

Sound-Spelling Card 135

USE SOUND-SPELLING CARDS Display Card 135. Point to *-tion.* The letters *-tion* form the last syllable in the word *lotion.* They stand for the sounds /sh/ /ə/ /n/. Have children say /sh/ /ə/ /n/ several times as you point to *-tion.* Repeat for *-ture* (/ch/ /ər/) using Card 136 and for *-ion* (/y/ /ə/ /n/) using Card 131.

MODEL Write *lotion.* I see a word ending in *-tion.* Point to *-tion.* I know that these four letters form their own syllable. I divide the word before the consonant *t* and read each syllable. Frame the first syllable. The first syllable ends in a vowel, so the vowel will be long: /l/ /ō/. Frame the second syllable. The sounds in the second syllable are /sh/ /ə/ /n/. I read the syllables together—*lotion.* Repeat with *mixture,* pointing out that the vowel sound in the first syllable will be short because the syllable ends with a consonant.

Sound-Spelling Card 136

Write *companion.* This word has several syllable patterns. First, I notice the ending pattern *-ion.* Point to *-ion.* These letters form their own syllable and stand for the sounds /y/ /ə/ /n/ or /ə/ /n/. I will divide the word before the vowel *i.* I also see two consonants together—*mp*—so I will divide the word between them. Then I read each syllable (frame each syllable): /k/ /ə/ /m/, /p/ /a/ /n/, /y/ /ə/ /n/—*companion.*

GROUP PRACTICE Write the following words. Have the group read the words with you. Then identify the final syllable in each word.

future	**stallion**	**action**	**fracture**	**station**	**signature**
section	**pasture**	**opinion**	**addition**	**creature**	**contraction**

REVIEW What do you know about reading words with the endings *-tion, -ture,* and *-ion?* (The letters make up the word's last syllable.)

Sound-Spelling Card 131

Phonics

Final Syllables *-tion, -ture, -ion*

Words I Can Blend

picture
station
question
fashion
future

Sentences I Can Read

1. A picture of that train is hanging in the station.
2. Can you answer my question about the latest fashion?
3. In the future James will ask for things he needs.

Julie likes books! What kind of books? Julie likes all kinds. She would read a million books if she could. She reads fiction and nonfiction. She reads action stories and adventure stories. She reads math books about fractions and art books about sculpture. She even reads picture books. If you ask Julie a question about the book she liked most, she will tell you. The most exciting book she ever read was about creatures on a space station in the future.

You've learned

Final Syllables *-tion, -ture, -ion*

428 429

Student Edition, pp. 428–429

Guide Practice

BLEND WORDS Have children turn to page 428 in their Student Edition. Look at the pictures on this page. I see a picture of *lotion,* a picture of an *onion,* and a picture of *furniture.* The word *lotion* ends with the syllable /sh/ /ə/ /n/. It is spelled *-tion.* The word *onion* ends with the syllable /y/ /ə/ /n/. It is spelled *-ion.* The word *furniture* ends with the syllable /ch/ /ə/ /r/. It is spelled *-ture.*

GROUP PRACTICE For each word in "Words I Can Blend," ask children to say each word part. Make sure children identify the word parts and say the correct vowel sound in the first syllable. Then have children blend the whole word. Point out that *-tion* in *question* spells /ch/ /ə/ /n/ and *-ion* in *fashion* spells /ə/ /n/.

Corrective feedback	**If...** children have difficulty decoding a word, **then...** model sound-by-sound blending or the word parts strategy for decodable words.

Language Transfer For children whose home language is Spanish, point out the cognates for the following words: *future/futuro, section/sección, fracture/fractura, addition/adición, action/acción; precaution/precaución, adventure/aventura.*

Common Core State Standards

Foundational Skills 3. Know and apply grade-level phonics and word analysis skills in decoding words. **Language 2.** Demonstrate command of the conventions of standard English capitalization, punctuation, and spelling when writing.

Name ______ A Birthday Basket for Tía

Circle a word with -tion, -ture, or -ion to finish each sentence.

nation mixture 1,000,000 million

1. I saw a horse in the ______. portion (pasture)
2. I watched from one ______ of the yard. (section) suction
3. I moved with ______. culture (caution)
4. I walked in slow ______. (motion) station
5. I'd like to see a ______ horses. (million) cushion

Home Activity Your child wrote words that include the syllables -tion as in nation, -ture as in mixture, and -ion as in onion. Write some other words with -tion, -ion, or -ture, such as future, nature, texture, action, station, and opinion. Have your child read each word and identify the final syllable pattern.

Phonics Final Syllables -tion, -ture, -ion 505

Reader's and Writer's Notebook, p. 505

Phonics

DECODE WORDS IN ISOLATION After children can successfully combine the word parts to read the words on page 428 in their Student Edition, point to words in random order and ask children to read them naturally.

DECODE WORDS IN CONTEXT Have children read each of the sentences on page 428. Have them identify words in the sentences that have final syllables *-tion, -ture,* and *-ion.*

Team Talk Pair children and have them take turns reading each of the sentences aloud.

Chorally read the "I Can Read!" passage on page 429 along with the children. Then have them read the passage aloud to themselves.

ON THEIR OWN Use *Reader's and Writer's Notebook,* p. 505.

Syllables *-tion, -ture, -ion*

FORMATIVE ASSESSMENT Write the following words and have the class read them. Notice which words children miss during the group reading. Call on individuals to read some of the words.

potion	**moisture**	**adventure**	**location**	**million**	**Spiral Review**
pictured	**captured**	**cautions**	**lecturing**	**motions** ←	Row 2 reviews endings.
fraction	**creature**	**sculpture**	**fracture**	**station** ←	Row 3 reviews consonant blends.

If... children cannot read words with *-tion, -ture,* and *-ion* at this point,

then... use the Small Group Time Strategic Intervention lesson, p. SG•41 to reteach final syllables *-tion, -ture,* and *-ion.* Continue to monitor children's progress using other instructional opportunities during the week. See the Skills Trace on p. 428a.

Spelling Pretest

Final Syllables *-tion, -ture*

DICTATE SPELLING WORDS Dictate the spelling words and read the sentences. Have children write the words. If needed, chunk the words, clarify pronunciations, and give meanings. Have children correct misspelled words.

1. mixture	This salad has a **mixture** of different fruits.
2. nation	Who is the President of our **nation?**
3. section	This **section** of the fence is broken.
4. future	We plan to move in the **future.**
5. picture*	Camille painted a **picture** of a zebra.
6. action	I'll say a word, and you act out the **action.**
7. caution	Drive with **caution** on an icy road.
8. station	We will pick up my aunt at the bus **station.**
9. fixture	The plumber fixed the bathroom **fixture.**
10. motion	The rocking **motion** helps the baby sleep.
11. nature	We hiked the **nature** trail by the lake.
12. feature	A nose is one **feature** on your face.

* Word marked with asterisk comes from the selection *A Birthday Basket for Tía.*

ON THEIR OWN Use Let's Practice It!, p. 315 on the *Teacher Resources DVD-ROM.*

Access for All

Advanced

Extend Spelling Allow children who spell words correctly to spell more challenging words such as *furniture, region, fracture, adventure, religion,* and *contraction.*

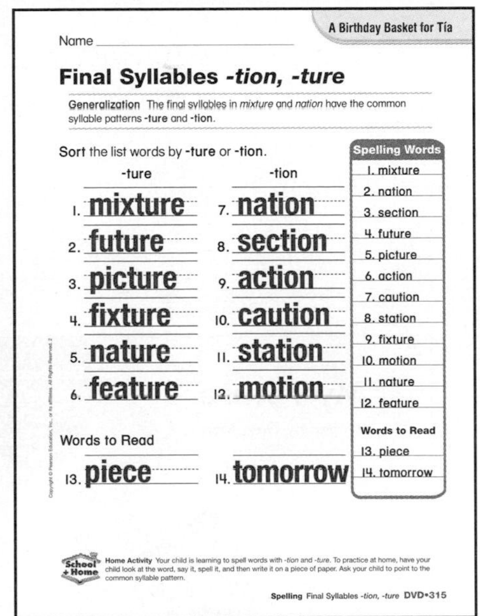

A Birthday Basket for Tía

Name

Final Syllables *-tion, -ture*

Generalization The final syllables in *mixture* and *nation* have the common syllable patterns **-ture** and **-tion**.

Sort the list words by **-ture** or **-tion**.

-ture	-tion
1. mixture	7. nation
2. future	8. section
3. picture	9. action
4. fixture	10. caution
5. nature	11. station
6. feature	12. motion

Words to Read

13. piece 14. tomorrow

Spelling Words
1. mixture
2. nation
3. section
4. future
5. picture
6. action
7. caution
8. station
9. fixture
10. motion
11. nature
12. feature

Words to Read
13. piece
14. tomorrow

Home Activity Your child is learning to spell words with -tion and -ture. To practice at home, have your child look at the word, say it, spell it, and then write it on a piece of paper. Ask your child to point to the common syllable pattern.

Spelling Final Syllables -tion, -ture DVD•315

Let's Practice It! TR DVD•315

Day 1 SMALL GROUP TIME • Differentiate Phonics, p. SG•35

OL On-Level
- **Practice Phonics** Additional Words with Final syllables *-tion, -ture, -ion*
- **Read** Decodable Reader *My Future*

SI Strategic Intervention
- **Reteach Phonics** Blend Words with Final syllables *-tion, -ture, -ion*
- **Read** Decodable Reader *My Future*

A Advanced
- **Extend Phonics** More Words with Final syllables *-tion, -ture, -ion*
- **Read** Advanced Selection for Words with Final syllables *-tion, -ture, -ion*
- **Introduce** Inquiry Project

If... children need more scaffolding and practice with **Phonics,** **then...** use the Phonics Transition Lessons on pp. 213–309 in the *ELL Handbook.*

Common Core State Standards

Foundational Skills 3. Know and apply grade-level phonics and word analysis skills in decoding words.

Decodable Reader 28A

If children need help, then...

Read *My Future*

DECODE WORDS IN ISOLATION Have children turn to page 217 in *Decodable Practice Readers* 2.2 and decode each word.

READ HIGH-FREQUENCY WORDS Have children identify and read the high-frequency words *might, paint, smile, move,* and *take* on the first page.

PREVIEW DECODABLE READER Have children read the title and preview the story. Tell them they will read words with syllables *-tion* and *-ture.*

DECODE WORDS IN CONTEXT Pair children for reading and listen as they decode. One child begins. Children read the entire story, switching readers after each page. Partners reread the story. This time the other child begins.

My Future

Written by Greg Morton

Decodable Practice Reader 28A

Final Syllables *-tion, -ture*

future picture(s) mixture
action stations nation
locations nature motion

High-Frequency Words

might paint smile
move take

217

Decodable Practice Reader 28A

There are many jobs
that people have.
When I think about my future,
I try to picture what I might be.
I have many choices!
218

Maybe I will be an artist.
I can paint fine pictures,
using a mixture of colors.
My pictures will make people smile.
219

Maybe I will be a firefighter.
I can take action to protect my city.
Maybe I will work at stations
all over the nation!
220

Maybe I will be a builder.
I can make skyscrapers
and houses in many locations.
I could even make a house for myself!
221

Maybe I will be a park ranger.
I can see wild animals and enjoy
nature.
I will show people how to be safe
and keep things clean in my park.
222

Maybe I will be a dancer.
I will be in motion every day.
I will dance in shows
and teach kids
how to move nicely.
223

My future might hold anything!
I know that I will be happy
if I do something that I like
and that makes other people glad.
224

Corrective feedback

If... children have difficulty decoding a word,
then... refer them to the Sound-Spelling Cards to identify sounds in a decodable word; prompt them to blend the word. If the word has a syllable with *-tion* or *-ture,* have them identify the word parts and read them together to say the word.

- What is the new word?
- Is the new word a word you know?
- Does it make sense in the story?

CHECK DECODING AND COMPREHENSION Have children retell the story to include characters, setting, and events. Then have children find words that include syllables *-tion* and *-ture.* Children should supply the following words:

-tion: *action, stations, nation, locations, motion*

-ture: *future, picture(s), mixture, nature*

Reread for Fluency

REREAD DECODABLE READER Have children reread Decodable Practice Reader 28A to develop automaticity decoding words with final syllables *-tion* and *-ture.*

Routine Oral Rereading

1. **Read** Have children read the entire book orally.
2. **Reread** To achieve optimal fluency, children should reread the text three or four times.
3. **Corrective Feedback** Listen as children read. Provide corrective feedback regarding their fluency and decoding.

Routines Flip Chart

Final Syllables *-tion, -ture*

Beginning Before reading, preview the selection, using illustrations to scaffold meaning. Say words from the story ending in *-tion* and *-ture* and have children repeat them. Have children give thumbs up if they hear *-tion* and thumbs down if they hear *-ture.*

Intermediate After reading, have children supply words ending in *-tion* or *-ture,* to complete sentences such as the following:
A dancer will be in ________ (motion); A firefighter will work at a ________ (station).
Have children read each complete sentence aloud.

Advanced Have children name a job they would like to have in the future. Have them describe the job using words with syllables *-tion* and *-ture.*

Text-Based Comprehension

Draw Conclusions

Questioning

READ Remind children of the weekly concept—family celebrations. Have children follow along as you read "Empty Eggshells" on page 431.

MODEL A CLOSE READ Demonstrate close reading for children. Before I begin reading, I read the title and look at the pictures. Have children follow along as you read the first two paragraphs of "Empty Eggshells." The story tells me that Danny came early to Jorge's party. I know people invite friends to parties, so I can draw the conclusion that Jorge and Danny are friends, and Jorge invited Danny to his party. Then the text tells me that Danny sees empty eggshells and asks what they will do with them. I can draw the conclusion that Jorge might have asked Danny to come early to help him do something, and that something involves empty eggshells.

INTRODUCE Have children read p. 430. Explain that the skill of **draw conclusions** and the strategy of questioning are tools they can use to deepen their understanding. Review the bulleted items and explanations on p. 430. Then have children use a graphic organizer like the one shown to draw a conclusion from the story.

IDENTIFY TEXT EVIDENCE Have children reread "Empty Eggshells" using the callouts as guides. Then ask volunteers to respond to the callouts, citing specific examples from the text to support their answers.

APPLY Use Reader's and Writer's Notebook, pp. 507 and 515 for additional practice with drawing conclusions. Children may also turn to pp. EI•7 and EI•23 to review the skill and strategy if necessary.

Common Core State Standards

Literature 1. Ask and answer such questions as *who, what, where, when, why,* and *how* to demonstrate understanding of key details in a text.

Skills Trace

Draw Conclusions

Introduce U3W2D1; U4W1D1; U6W3D1

Practice U3W2D2; U3W2D3; U3W2D4; U4W1D2; U4W1D3; U4W1D4; U6W3D2; U6W3D3; U6W3D4

Reteach/Review U3W2D5; U3W3D3; U4W1D5; U4W4D3; U6W1D3; U6W3D5

Assess/Test Weekly Tests U3W2; U4W1; U6W3
Benchmark Tests U4; U6

KEY: U=Unit W=Week D=Day

Academic Vocabulary

draw conclusions use details from text and background knowledge to decide something about characters and events in a story

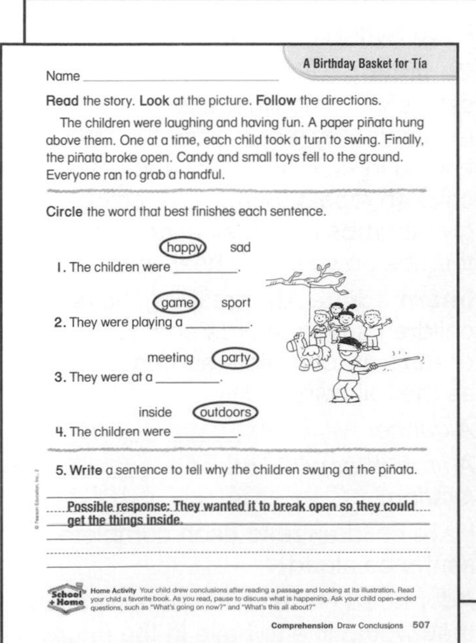

Name ____________ A Birthday Basket for Tía

Read the story. **Look** at the picture. **Follow** the directions.

The children were laughing and having fun. A paper piñata hung above them. One at a time, each child took a turn to swing. Finally, the piñata broke open. Candy and small toys fell to the ground. Everyone ran to grab a handful.

Circle the word that best finishes each sentence.

1. The children were ________. (happy) sad
2. They were playing a ________. (game) sport
3. They were at a ________. meeting (party)
4. The children were ________. inside (outdoors)

5. **Write** a sentence to tell why the children swung at the piñata.

Possible response: They wanted it to break open so they could get the things inside.

Home Activity Your child drew conclusions after reading a passage and looking at its illustration. Read your child a favorite book. As you read, pause to discuss what is happening. Ask your child open-ended questions, such as "What's going on now?" and "What's this all about?"

Comprehension Draw Conclusions 507

Reader's and Writer's Notebook, pp. 507 and 515

Comprehension Skill

Draw Conclusions

- When you read, you can draw conclusions or figure out more about the characters and events in a story.
- Use evidence from the text to make conclusions.
- Use what you learned about draw conclusions and a diagram like the one below as you read "Empty Eggshells."

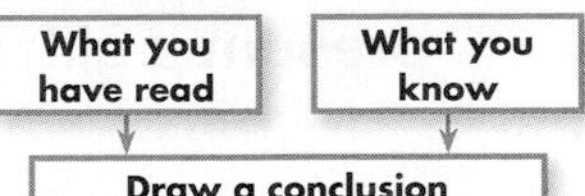

Comprehension Strategy

Questioning

Good readers ask themselves literal and relevant questions before, during, and after they read. As you read "Empty Eggshells," write your questions about the text on a sheet of paper. Look for evidence from the text to answer your questions. Share your questions with a partner.

430

Empty Eggshells

When Danny arrived early for Jorge's party, he saw a carton of eggs. But they were just empty eggshells, with a hole at the top. No egg inside.

"What do we do with these?" Danny asked.

"First, we will paint the eggshells. Next, we will fill each egg with tiny bits of paper," Jorge told him. "Then, my mother will glue paper over each hole."

Strategy Ask a question here, such as "What does the family do with the empty eggshells first? What do they do next?"

Before the party, Jorge's father hid the painted eggs in the apartment. All the children went on an egg hunt, and all the eggs were found. Then—surprise! Jorge cracked one open over the top of Danny's head! The colored paper rained down! Danny laughed and laughed. Soon everyone at the party was cracking *cascarones* over one another's heads!

Skill Here you can make a conclusion about Jorge and Danny. Do you think they are friends? How do you know?

Your Turn!

Need a Review? See the *Envision It! Handbook* for additional help with draw conclusions and questioning.

Ready to Try It? As you read the story, use what you've learned to understand the text.

431

Student Edition, pp. 430–431

Model Fluent Reading

APPROPRIATE PHRASING Have children listen as you read the first three paragraphs of "Empty Eggshells" and model how to use punctuation cues to achieve appropriate phrasing. Explain that you are coming to a full stop at end punctuation and pausing after commas.

Have children reread paragraph 1 of "Empty Eggshells" orally.

Routine Oral Rereading

1. **Reread** To achieve optimal fluency, children should reread the text three or four times with appropriate phrasing.
2. **Corrective Feedback** Listen as children read. Provide corrective feedback regarding their phrasing, fluency, and decoding.

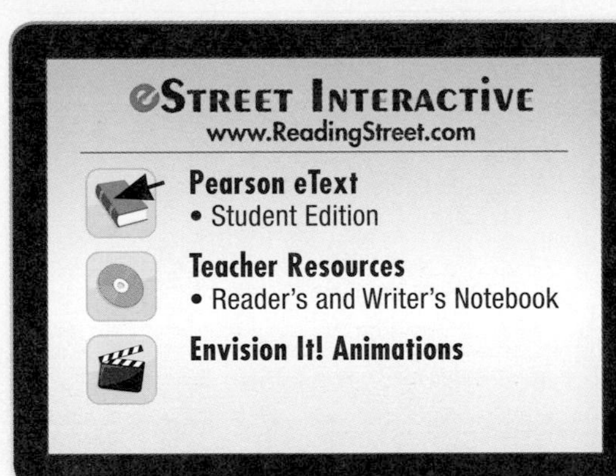

Skills/Strategies

Strategy First, the family paints the eggshells. Then they fill them with bits of paper.

Skill Yes, they are friends because Jorge invited Danny to his party, Danny helped Jorge make the eggs, and Danny laughed when Jorge cracked the egg on his head.

Common Core State Standards

Language 1. Demonstrate command of the conventions of standard English grammar and usage when writing or speaking. **Language 4.** Determine or clarify the meaning of unknown and multiple-meaning words and phrases based on grade 2 reading and content, choosing flexibly from an array of strategies.

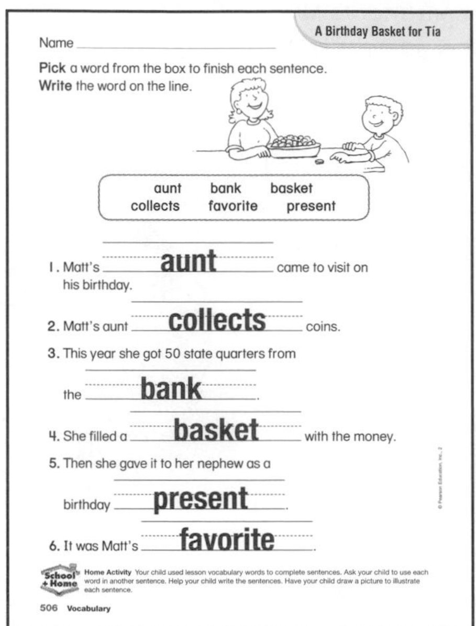

A Birthday Basket for Tía

Name ______________

Pick a word from the box to finish each sentence.
Write the word on the line.

aunt bank basket
collects favorite present

1. Matt's **aunt** came to visit on his birthday.
2. Matt's aunt **collects** coins.
3. This year she got 50 state quarters from the **bank**.
4. She filled a **basket** with the money.
5. Then she gave it to her nephew as a birthday **present**.
6. It was Matt's **favorite**.

School + Home **Home Activity** Your child used lesson vocabulary words to complete sentences. Ask your child to use each word in another sentence. Help your child write the sentences. Have your child draw a picture to illustrate each sentence.

506 Vocabulary

Reader's and Writer's Notebook, p. 506

Selection Vocabulary

Use the following routine to introduce this week's tested selection vocabulary.

aunt your father's sister, your mother's sister, or your uncle's wife

bank a place where people keep their money

basket a container made of twigs, grasses, or strips of wood woven together

collects brings things together or gathers them together

favorite the thing liked better than others

present a gift; something given

SEE IT/SAY IT Write *aunt.* Scan across the word with your finger as you say it: aunt.

HEAR IT Use the word in a sentence. My mother and my aunt are very close.

DEFINE IT Elicit definitions from children. How would you tell another child who an *aunt* is? Clarify or give a definition when necessary. Yes, an *aunt* is your father's sister, your mother's sister, or your uncle's wife. Restate the word in child-friendly terms. An *aunt* is one of your parent's sisters.

Team Talk If your father does not have a sister, can you still have an aunt? Turn to your partner and talk about this. Be prepared to explain your answers. Allow children time to discuss. Ask for examples. Rephrase their examples for usage when necessary or to correct misunderstandings.

MAKE CONNECTIONS Have children discuss the word. Do you have any aunts? Are you close? Do you and your aunt(s) get together for family celebrations? Have children share. Rephrase their ideas for usage when necessary or to correct misunderstandings.

RECORD Have children write the word and its meaning.

Continue this routine to introduce the remaining words in this manner.

ON THEIR OWN Use *Reader's and Writer's Notebook,* p. 506.

Corrective feedback	**If...** children are having difficulty understanding, **then...** review the definitions in small groups.

Conventions

Prepositions and Prepositional Phrases

MAKE CONNECTIONS Write the following sentence from "Empty Eggshells" on the board: *"Then, my mother will glue paper over each hole."* Where will his mother glue the paper? (over each hole) Explain that *over each hole* is a prepositional phrase.

TEACH Explain that a **preposition** is a word that is used with a noun or pronoun to make up a **prepositional phrase.** A preposition can help tell where someone or something is or when something happens. He sat *on* the chair. The movie begins *at* eight o'clock.

MODEL Display Grammar Transparency 28. Read the definition aloud. Model identifying the preposition and the prepositional phrase in each example. Then read the directions and model number 1.

Prepositions

A **preposition** is the first word in a **prepositional phrase.**

What is **in** the birthday basket?

The preposition shows more about the rest of the sentence.

Cecilia filled the basket **with care.**
Tía will come **in the morning.**
The cat sits **on the book.**

Common Prepositions

about	across	after	around	at
before	below	between	by	during
except	for	from	in	into
near	of	on	onto	out
over	through	to	under	until
upon	with			

Write the preposition in ( ) that completes each sentence.

1. Cecilia made a basket (out, for) Tía. **for**
2. She put a book (in, except) the basket. **in**
3. Tía brings tea (across, at) night. **at**
4. Tía sits outside (from, during) warm days. **during**
5. Tía looked (under, onto) my bed. **under**
6. The cat jumped (until, into) the basket. **into**

Unit 6 A Birthday Basket for Tía — Grammar 28

Grammar Transparency 28 TR DVD

GUIDE PRACTICE Continue with items 2–6, having children identify the preposition in each sentence and then identifying and reading the prepositional phrase.

APPLY Have the class complete these sentence frames orally. Have children identify the preposition and the prepositional phrase in each sentence.

1. **We ran to ______.**
2. **Sasha stopped at ______.**
3. **Grandpa walked from ______.**
4. **Mary put her cloths in ______.**

Team Talk Pair children and have them use the preposition *to* as they write an answer to the question *Where will you go after school?* Have children share examples with the class.

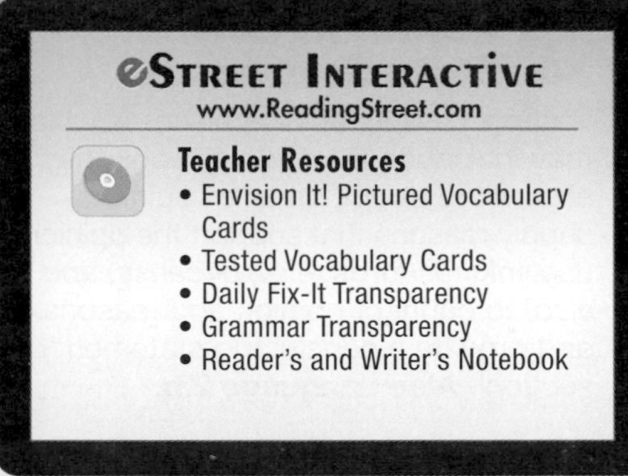

Access for All

 Strategic Intervention

Support Conventions Write the prepositions *at, in, on, after, around,* and *under* on index cards. Have children choose an index card and use the word in a sentence.

Academic Vocabulary 

preposition a word that shows the relationship of a noun or pronoun to another word or words.

prepositional phrase a group of words that begins with a preposition and ends with a noun or pronoun

Daily Fix-It

1. My favorit aunt collects baskets? My favorit<u>e</u> aunt collects baskets<u>.</u>
2. Where are we meeting? she asked. <u>"</u>Where are we meeting?<u>"</u> she asked.

Discuss the Daily Fix-It corrections with children. Review quotation marks, end punctuation, and the spelling of *favorite.*

Visual Support Point to various items at your desk. Describe the relationship of each item to the desk. *(The dictionary is on the desk.)* Then ask a question: *Where is the dictionary?*

Common Core State Standards

Writing 1. Write opinion pieces in which they introduce the topic or book they are writing about, state an opinion, supply reasons that support the opinion, use linking words (e.g., *because, and, also*) to connect opinion and reasons, and provide a concluding statement or section. **Also Language 2.b.**

Academic Vocabulary 

invitation a polite request asking someone to come to some place or to do something

Bridge to Common Core

TEXT TYPES AND PURPOSES

This week children write an invitation letter for a family event.

Opinion Writing

Through reading and discussion, children will gain a deeper understanding of family celebrations. They will use the knowledge from the texts to write and support an invitation letter.

Throughout the week, children will improve the range and content of their writing through daily mini-lessons.

5-Day Plan

DAY 1	Read Like a Writer
DAY 2	Sentences
DAY 3	Writer's Craft: Choosing Details
DAY 4	Revise: Deleting Sentences
DAY 5	Proofread

Writing

Invitation Letter

Mini-Lesson Read Like a Writer

- **Introduce** This week you will write an invitation letter. An **invitation** letter asks someone to come to a planned event. It tells details about where and when the event will take place.

Prompt Think about family parties and how to plan a family party. Write an invitation letter to invite a relative to an event.

Trait Sentences

Mode Opinion

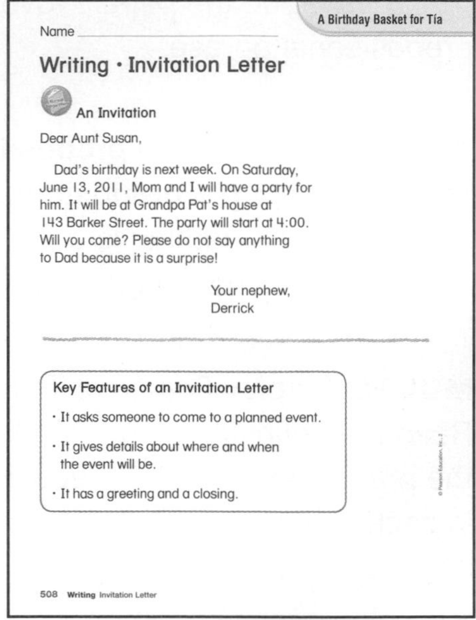

A Birthday Basket for Tía

Name

Writing • Invitation Letter

An Invitation

Dear Aunt Susan,

Dad's birthday is next week. On Saturday, June 13, 2011, Mom and I will have a party for him. It will be at Grandpa Pat's house at 143 Barker Street. The party will start at 4:00. Will you come? Please do not say anything to Dad because it is a surprise!

Your nephew,
Derrick

Key Features of an Invitation Letter

- It asks someone to come to a planned event.
- It gives details about where and when the event will be.
- It has a greeting and a closing.

508 Writing Invitation Letter

Reader's and Writer's Notebook, p. 508

- **Examine Model Text** Let's listen to an invitation letter. Track the print as you read aloud the invitation letter to a birthday party on *Reader's and Writer's Notebook,* p. 508. Have children follow along.

- **Key Features** Who is being invited? (Aunt Susan) What is the event? (Dad's birthday) Discuss the features that make it an invitation letter, such as the greeting and closing, and the details telling about the event. Have children circle the details of the event's date, time, and place. Point out the commas at the end of the greeting and closing.

This invitation letter is a letter because it has a greeting that names a person who will read the letter. It has a closing and a signature that tells who wrote the letter.

In the invitation letter, the event is named. The details of the day, time, and place are also included so the person reading the letter will know all the important information about the event.

Review Key Features

Review key features of an invitation letter with children. You may want to post these key features in the classroom to allow children to refer to them as they work on their invitation letters.

Key Features of an Invitation Letter

- asks someone to come to a planned event
- gives details about where and when the event will be
- has a greeting and a closing

Connect to Familiar Texts

Use the example from *Dear Juno* (Unit 3) or another letter familiar to children. Point out the letter format with the greeting and closing. Explain that the letter from Grandma is a friendly letter, which gives details that are interesting to the reader. However, the purpose of an invitation letter is to ask someone to come to an event.

Routine Quick Write for Fluency — Team Talk

1. **Talk** Read these questions aloud, and have children respond.
   What community events have you gone to?
   Why should people in a community go to these events?
2. **Write** Have children write a sentence that persuades a community member to come to an event.
3. **Share** Partners can read their sentences to each other.

Routines Flip Chart

Write Guy *by Jeff Anderson*

Show Off—In a Good Way

Post children's successful sentences or short paragraphs. Celebrate children as writers. Select a sentence of the week, and write it large! Display it as a poster inside or outside the classroom door. Children learn from each other's successes.

Common Core State Standards

Writing 8. Recall information from experiences or gather information from provided sources to answer a question. **Speaking/Listening 1.b.** Build on others' talk in conversations by linking their comments to the remarks of others.

Academic Vocabulary 

interview a conversation in which one person asks questions about a topic and the other person provides answers

21st Century Skills

Internet Guy *Don Leu*

Weekly Inquiry Project

STEP 1	Identify and Focus Topic
STEP 2	Research Skill
STEP 3	Gather and Record Information
STEP 4	Synthesize
STEP 5	Communicate

Research and Inquiry

Step 1 Identify and Focus Topic

TEACH Display and review the chart that explores this week's question: *Why are family celebrations special?* What ideas about family celebrations would you like to learn more about? Ask children to share their interests. Help them identify ways their family celebrations are special.

Think Aloud **MODEL** One way to learn about people is to conduct an **interview.** During an interview, one person asks questions about a topic, and the other person provides the answers. For example, if I wanted to learn more about celebrations in your family, I might ask questions about how you celebrate certain events. Then you would give me your answers.

GUIDE PRACTICE Give children time to think about interview questions that, when answered, would help them learn more about ways their family celebrations are special. Tell children that the questions asked by others may help them think of questions of their own. Encourage them to listen carefully and to use each other's questions as springboards for additional questions. Record children's questions in a chart.

Topic: Family Celebrations Are Special

Question	Answer
What does your family do at a birthday party?	

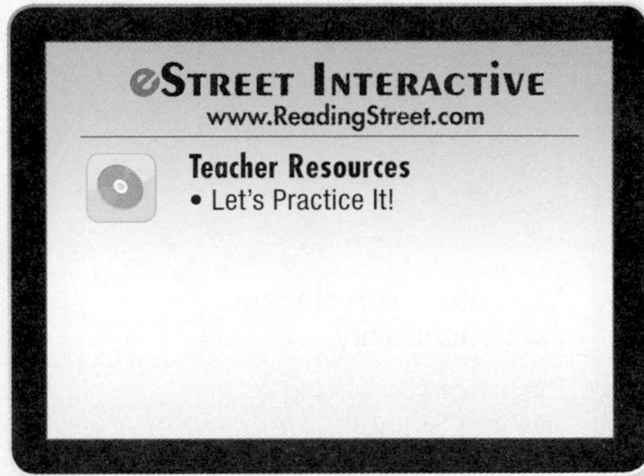

Wrap Up Your Day!

- ✔ **Phonics: Final Syllables *-tion, -ture, -ion*** Write *lotion, nature,* and *fashion.* Ask children to decode the words.
- ✔ **Spelling Final Syllables *-tion, -ture*** Have children name the letters for each sound in *nation* and *mixture.* Write the letters as children write them in the air.
- ✔ **Content Knowledge** Have children recall what happened in the *Sing with Me* song "Family Tradition." Why are family traditions and celebrations important? (Possible response: They unite people.)
- ✔ **Homework** Send home this week's Family Times Newsletter from Let's Practice It!, pp. 311–312 on the *Teacher Resources DVD-ROM.*

Let's Practice It!
TR DVD•311–312

Tell children that tomorrow they will read about a family celebration—a birthday party.

DAY 2 at a Glance

Content Knowledge
Oral Vocabulary

Phonics/Spelling
Final Syllables *-tion, -ture, -ion*

Selection Vocabulary
aunt, bank, basket, collects, favorite, present
Words from Other Languages

Text-Based Comprehension
Draw Conclusions
Questioning

Conventions
Prepositions and Prepositional Phrases

Writing
Invitation Letter
Writing Trait: Sentences

Handwriting
Cursive *G, S, I*/Letter Size

Research and Inquiry
Research Skill: Interview and Sources

Materials

- Student Edition
- Sing with Me Big Book
- Big Book
- Reader's and Writer's Notebook
- Sound-Spelling Cards

Common Core State Standards

Speaking/Listening 2. Recount or describe key ideas or details from a text read aloud or information presented orally or through other media. **Language 6.** Use words and phrases acquired through conversations, reading and being read to, and responding to texts, including using adjectives and adverbs to describe (e.g., *When other kids are happy that makes me happy*).

Content Knowledge

Family Celebrations

EXPAND THE CONCEPT To reinforce concepts and to focus children's attention, have children sing "Family Tradition" from the *Sing with Me* Big Book. In the song we sing that tradition is important. To whom is tradition important? (Tradition is important to all cultures and to family groups too.)

Build Oral Language

INTRODUCE AMAZING WORDS Display the Big Book *Magda's Tortillas.* Read the title and identify the author. Explain that in the story, the author uses some Amazing Words. Read the story and have children listen for the word *create.*

Big Book

TALK ABOUT SENTENCES AND WORDS Reread this sentence from the story.

"I don't care how many tortillas I make, or how many shapes I create," she said.

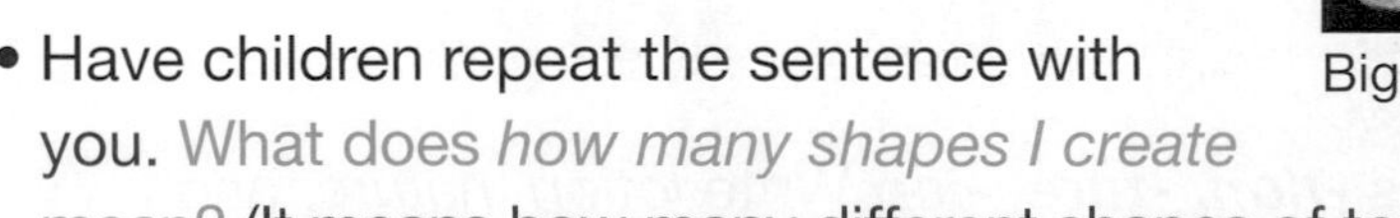

- Have children repeat the sentence with you. What does *how many shapes I create* mean? (It means how many different shapes of tortillas she makes.)
- 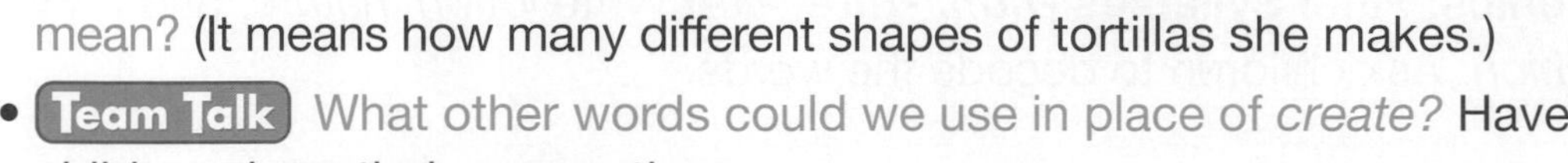 Team Talk What other words could we use in place of *create?* Have children share their suggestions.
- After children have tried other words, ask: Why do you think the author chose the word *create?* (It is an interesting synonym for *make*.)
- Team Talk Turn to your partner and talk about something you have created or built.

Build Oral Vocabulary

Amazing Words Robust Vocabulary Routine

1. **Introduce the Word** Relate the word *create* to the story. Magda is able to *create* tortillas in different shapes. Supply a child-friendly definition. If you *create* something, you make something that hasn't been made before. Have children say the word.
2. **Demonstrate** Provide examples to show meaning. An artist *creates* a beautiful statue out of clay. My father *creates* delicious new recipes for dinner.
3. **Apply** Have children demonstrate their understanding. What is something you would like to *create?*
4. **Display the Word** Run your hand under the two syllables *cre-ate* as you read the word. Emphasize that create is a two-syllable word, and both syllables have a long vowel sound.

Routines Flip Chart

ADD TO THE CONCEPT CHART Discuss family celebrations and why they are special.

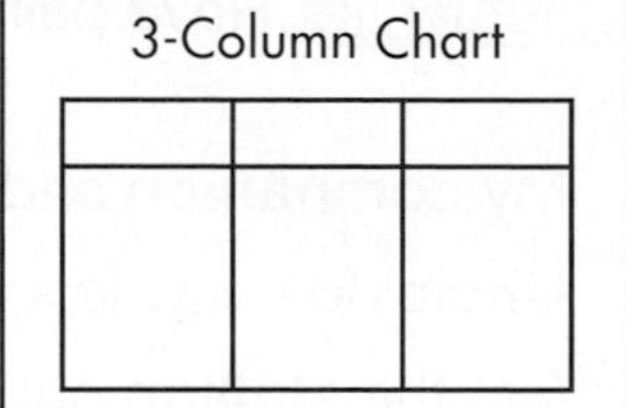

- Look at the picture that goes with our song "Family Tradition." What does it show? (A family getting together with their grandparents. They're bringing food.) We often share special dishes when we have a celebration. We'll add *People share special foods* under *Family Members Get Together.*
- In the Big Book story *Magda's Tortillas,* what does Magda do on her seventh birthday? (Her grandmother teaches her to make tortillas, and she makes them in special shapes.) Magda learns how to create a special food for her birthday. Let's add this as a special activity: *We sometimes learn special things.*
- What does Tío Manuel do when he sees Magda's tortillas? (He takes a picture before they are all eaten.) We'll add *We take photos to save memories* under *We Do Special Activities.*

Amazing Words

celebration	inspect
custom	angle
tradition	brilliant
create	snapshot

Access for All

 Strategic Intervention

Realistic Fiction To help children gain a greater understanding of realistic fiction, have them look at the pictures accompanying *Magda's Tortillas.* Then have the children tell you what is real, or realistic, about the pictures.

Reinforce Vocabulary Use the Day 2 instruction on ELL Poster 28 to teach selection vocabulary and discuss the lesson concept.

Common Core State Standards

Foundational Skills 3. Know and apply grade-level phonics and word analysis skills in decoding words. **Language 2.** Demonstrate command of the conventions of standard English capitalization, punctuation, and spelling when writing. **Language 2.e.** Consult reference materials, including beginning dictionaries, as needed to check and correct spellings.

Phonics

Review Final Syllable *-le*

Final Syllables *-tion, -ture, -ion*

REVIEW SOUND-SPELLINGS Review final syllables *-le, -tion, -ture,* and *-ion* using Sound-Spelling Cards 134, 135, 136, and 131.

DECODE WORDS IN ISOLATION Display these words. Have the class read the words. Then point to the words in random order and ask children to read them quickly.

fiction	**station**	**table**
feature	**apple**	**billion**
wiggle	**furniture**	**contraction**

Corrective feedback | Model reading decodable words and then ask children to read them with you.

DECODE WORDS IN CONTEXT Display these sentences. Have the class read the sentences.

Team Talk Have pairs take turns reading the sentences naturally.

My **companion** and I **giggle** at the **mixture** of **riddles** in this book.
Uncle Joe saw lots of **creatures** on his **nature adventure.**
Get the **stallion** out of the **stable** and put him in the **pasture.**

Spelling

Final Syllables *-tion, -ture*

GUIDE PRACTICE Tell children you will chunk the spelling words. They should say the parts of each word aloud as they write them. Check the spelling of each word before saying the next word. Have children use resources such as a dictionary to find correct spellings.

1. mix ture **mixture**
2. na tion **nation**
3. sec tion **section**
4. fu ture **future**
5. pic ture **picture**
6. ac tion **action**
7. cau tion **caution**
8. sta tion **station**
9. fix ture **fixture**
10. mo tion **motion**
11. na ture **nature**
12. fea ture **feature**

ON THEIR OWN Use *Reader's and Writer's Notebook*, p. 509.

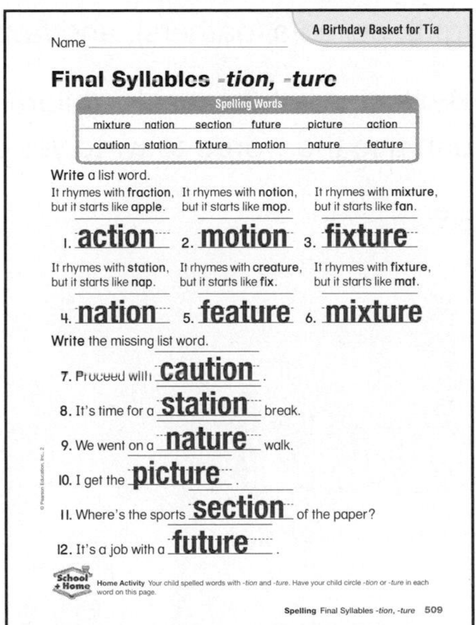
Name

A Birthday Basket for Tía

Final Syllables *-tion, -ture*

Spelling Words					
mixture	nation	section	future	picture	action
caution	station	fixture	motion	nature	feature

Write a list word.

It rhymes with **fraction**, but it starts like **apple**. 1. action
It rhymes with **notion**, but it starts like **mop**. 2. motion
It rhymes with **mixture**, but it starts like **fan**. 3. fixture
It rhymes with **station**, but it starts like **nap**. 4. nation
It rhymes with **creature**, but it starts like **fix**. 5. feature
It rhymes with **fixture**, but it starts like **mat**. 6. mixture

Write the missing list word.

7. Proceed with caution.
8. It's time for a station break.
9. We went on a nature walk.
10. I get the picture.
11. Where's the sports section of the paper?
12. It's a job with a future.

School + Home — Home Activity Your child spelled words with -tion and -ture. Have your child circle -tion or -ture in each word on this page.

Spelling Final Syllables -tion, -ture 509

Reader's and Writer's Notebook, p. 509

Pronounce *-ture* Children of various language backgrounds may have trouble articulating the *r*-controlled sound in *-ture*. Learners must bunch up the tongue and constrict the throat. Point to and say the spelling words ending in *-ture*. Have children echo.

Common Core State Standards

Language 4. Determine or clarify the meaning of unknown and multiple-meaning words and phrases based on grade 2 reading and content, choosing flexibly from an array of strategies.

Selection Vocabulary

ACTIVATE PRIOR KNOWLEDGE Display the words and ask oral questions like those below.

- Is an *aunt* a family member?
- Would you put a desk in a *basket?*
- If you have a *favorite* song, do you like to hear it on the radio?
- Would you go to a *bank* to buy clothes?
- If a girl *collects* seashells on a beach, would she bury them in the sand?
- Would you give a *present* to your mom on Mother's Day?

Children should respond yes or no and give reasons for their choice. To broaden children's understanding of words, have them change the questions where they responded no, so the response is yes.

USE SYNONYMS Ask children to name synonyms for these words: *present* (gift), *collects* (gathers), and *favorite* (most liked).

By the end of the week, children should know the selection words. Children can use the words to write yes and no questions for classmates to answer.

Don't Wait Until Friday

MONITOR PROGRESS

Check Selection Vocabulary/ High-Frequency Words

FORMATIVE ASSESSMENT Write the following words and have the class read them. Listen for children who miss words during the reading. Call on those children to read some of the words individually.

				Spiral Review
basket	**present**	**aunt**	**favorite**	Rows 3 and 4 review previously taught high-frequency words.
collects	**bank**			
finally	**whatever**	**caught**	**believe** ←	
been	**tomorrow**		←	

If... children cannot read these words,

then... use the Small Group Time Strategic Intervention lesson, p. 42, to reteach the words. Monitor children's fluency with these words during reading and provide additional practice.

Access for All

SI Strategic Intervention

Share Answers Pair children and ask the questions below. Have each child share answers to the questions to reinforce understanding of the selection vocabulary.

- *How many aunts do you have?*
- *Have you ever been in a bank? What did you see in the bank?*
- *What have you put in a basket?*
- *What is one thing you like to collect?*
- *What is your favorite activity?*
- *What is the best present you have ever received?*

Visual Support English learners will benefit from additional visual support to understand selection vocabulary. Gather pictures of a basket, present, and piggy bank. Then write *basket, present,* and *bank.* Point to and say each word. Then point to the picture and repeat the word. Have children echo. Continue the process while pantomiming the motion of picking up toys for *collects* and hugging a personal item for *favorite.*

Multilingual Vocabulary Lists Children can apply knowledge of their home languages to acquire new English vocabulary by using the Multilingual Vocabulary Lists (*ELL Handbook,* pages 429–440).

Common Core State Standards

Language 4.a. Use sentence-level context as a clue to the meaning of a word or phrase.

Selection Vocabulary

aunt your father's sister, your mother's sister, or your uncle's wife

bank a place where people keep their money

basket a container made of twigs, grass, or strips of wood woven together

collects brings things together or gathers them together

favorite the thing liked better than others

present a gift; something given

Bridge to Common Core

VOCABULARY ACQUISITION AND USE

When children interact with this week's selection words, they are learning grade-appropriate words that they will encounter in school and beyond. Teaching the strategy of using context clues to help determine the meanings of words from other languages will help children gain independence as they encounter words from other languages in other contexts.

Vocabulary Skill

Words from Other Languages

READ Have children read "A Party and a Present" on p. 433 with you. Use the vocabulary skill and strategy as tools to build comprehension.

TEACH Explain that sometimes a word from another language is used in a story. Discuss how readers can often use context clues—the words and sentences around a word—to help them figure out its meaning. Refer children to Words! on p. W•7 in the Student Edition for additional practice. Then reread "A Party and a Present" on page 433 with children.

Think Aloud **MODEL** Write on the board: *The town held a fiesta to celebrate the holiday.* The word *fiesta* is not an English word; it is Spanish. If I look at the words *celebrate the holiday,* that clue helps me figure out that the town held a festival, or big party. That's what *fiesta* means.

GUIDE PRACTICE Tell children to find the slanted, or italicized, word *fiesta* in the second sentence on page 433. Ask them to identify the context clue that shows them what the word means. (a party)

ON THEIR OWN Read "A Party and a Present" on page 433. Have children identify other Spanish words and use the context to determine their meanings. If there is not enough context to determine the meaning of a word, suggest that asking a classmate or teacher is another way to learn the meaning. Then have children use context to determine the meanings of the Words to Know.

For additional practice, use *Reader's and Writer's Notebook,* p. 510.

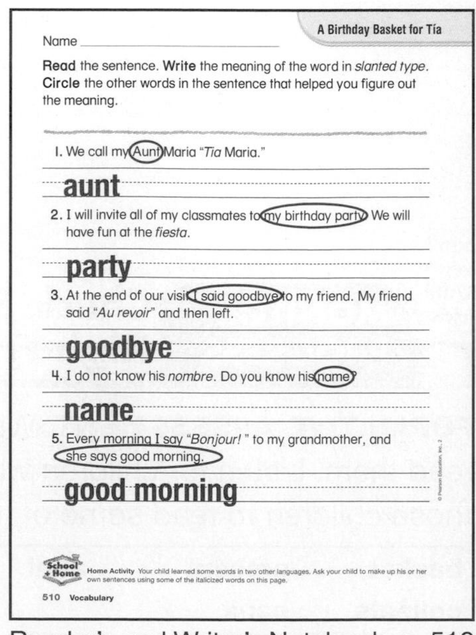

A Birthday Basket for Tía

Name

Read the sentence. **Write** the meaning of the word in *slanted type*. **Circle** the other words in the sentence that helped you figure out the meaning.

1. We call my Aunt Maria "*Tía* Maria."

aunt

2. I will invite all of my classmates to my birthday party. We will have fun at the *fiesta*.

party

3. At the end of our visit I said goodbye to my friend. My friend said "*Au revoir*" and then left.

goodbye

4. I do not know his *nombre*. Do you know his name?

name

5. Every morning I say "*Bonjour!*" to my grandmother, and she says good morning.

good morning

School + Home **Home Activity** Your child learned some words in two other languages. Ask your child to make up his or her own sentences using some of the italicized words on this page.

510 Vocabulary

Reader's and Writer's Notebook, p. 510

Vocabulary Strategy for

Words from Other Languages

Context Clues When you read, you may come to a word from another language. These words are sometimes in slanted type, or italics. If you do not know the word, you can sometimes learn its meaning from the context.

1. Look at the new word.
2. Use the context to determine the new word's relevant meaning.
3. Try the meaning of the word in the sentence. Does it make sense?

Read "A Party and a Present." Look for Spanish words. Use the context to figure out the relevant meaning of each word.

Words to Write Reread "A Party and a Present." Write sentences about a special gift you can give to someone. Use words from the *Words to Know* list.

A Party and a Present

Is someone you know having a birthday soon? Is he or she having a party, or a *fiesta*? What will you give that person? It is not hard to think of a present. Ask yourself what the person likes. What is his or her favorite game? Does he or she have a favorite hobby? favorite color? favorite food? See if the answers give you an idea.

You do not have to break your piggy bank to buy a present. Buy flowers at the grocery store. Find a basket or bowl at home. Arrange the flowers in it. This makes a nice present for your aunt, or *tía*.

Maybe this special person collects things such as baseball cards, photos, or rings. Decorate a box that has a lid. Find or draw pictures that match what the person collects.

Is your gift ready? Soon it will be *fiesta* time. Everyone will have fun. There will be games. There might even be a *piñata!*

Your Turn!

Need a Review? For more help with using context clues to determine the meaning of words from other languages, see *Words!* on p. W•7.

Ready to Try It? Read *A Birthday Basket for Tía* on pp. 434–447.

432 433

Student Edition, pp. 432–433

Reread for Fluency

Have children reread paragraph 1 of "A Party and a Present."

Routine Paired Reading

1. **Reread** To achieve optimal fluency, have partners reread the text three or four times.
2. **Corrective Feedback** Listen as children read. Provide corrective feedback regarding their fluency and decoding.

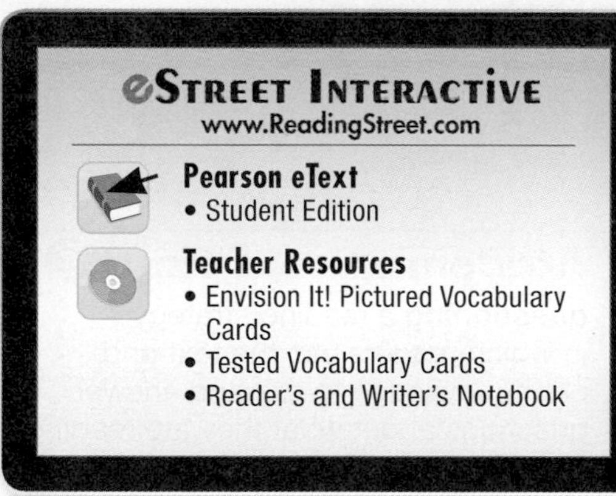

Zoom in on 

Text-Based Comprehension

Introduce Main Selection

Student Edition, pp. 434–435

GENRE Realistic fiction is a made-up story that could happen in real life. As they read *A Birthday Basket for Tía,* ask children to look for facts that indicate this story could happen in real life.

PREVIEW AND PREDICT Have children identify the title of the story, the author, and the illustrator. Help children look through the selection and use the illustrations to predict what the selection will be about.

PURPOSE By analyzing *A Birthday Basket for Tía,* children learn about family celebrations.

QUESTIONING Good readers ask questions as they read. Readers can use evidence in the text, prior knowledge, or a combination of both to answer questions and clarify meaning. Have children turn to page EI•23 in their Student Edition.

Look at this picture. What question is the child asking? How will this help him as he reads the text on the case? Asking questions before, during, and after reading helps me understand what I read. When I ask questions about a story, I may find the answers in the text or use what I know to figure out the answer. As I read today, I will ask questions to help me understand.

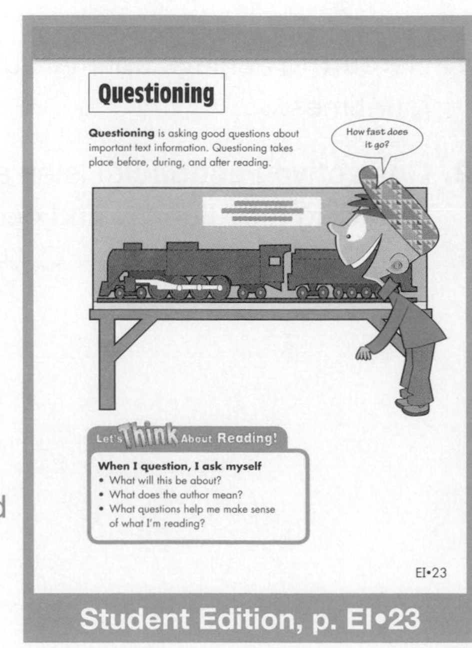

Student Edition, p. EI•23

Common Core State Standards

Literature 1. Ask and answer such questions as *who, what, where, when, why,* and *how* to demonstrate understanding of key details in a text.

Strategy Response Log

Questioning Before reading, have children use p. RR34 in their *Reader's and Writer's Notebook* to write questions they have about the story. Encourage them to look for the answers to their questions when they read.

Bridge to Common Core

CRAFT AND STRUCTURE

As children preview the selection and predict what it is about, they are determining how the purpose is connected to the content and style of realistic fiction. This sets the stage for children to see how different parts of realistic stories are connected to each other and the whole.

Academic Vocabulary 

questioning a reading strategy in which readers use the text and prior knowledge to ask and answer questions about what they are reading

Access Main Selection

READER AND TASK SUGGESTIONS	
Preparing to Read the Text	**Leveled Tasks**
• Review strategies for understanding words from other languages. See the vocabulary skill lesson on p. 432g. • Review the importance of realistic fiction that is written in chronological order. • Remind children that as they encounter unfamiliar words, they may need to read more slowly to better understand the text.	• **Language Conventionality and Clarity** If children struggle with non-English words, have them identify the words and use context clues to determine the meanings. • **Theme and Knowledge Demands** If children do not have difficulty with references to another culture, have them identify events in the text that are familiar to them.

See Text Complexity Measures for *A Birthday Basket for Tía* on the tab at the beginning of the week.

READ Tell children that today they will read *A Birthday Basket for Tía* for the first time. Use the Read for Understanding routine.

Routine Read for Understanding

Deepen understanding by reading the selection multiple times.

1. **First Read**—If children need support, use the **Access Text** notes to help them clarify understanding.
2. **Second Read**—Use the **Close Reading** notes to help children draw knowledge from the text.

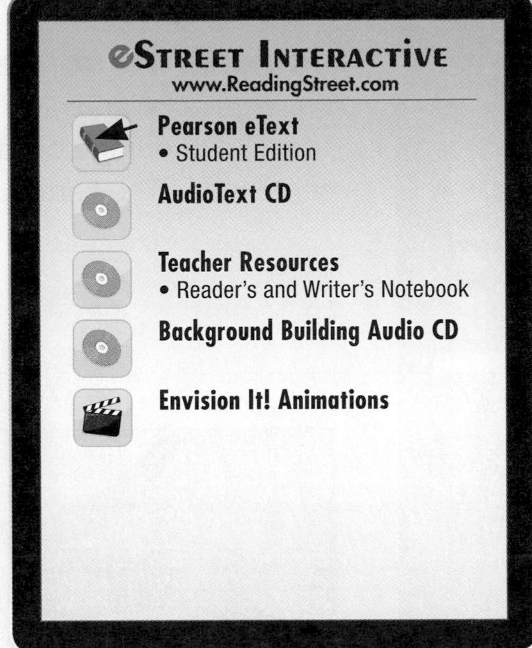

Preview Main Selection Ask children what they already know about birthday parties. Then do a picture walk of the selection so children can talk about how they prepare for a birthday party and what they do at the party.

1ST READ

Access Text If children need help, then...

CONNECT TO CONCEPT Look at the picture on pages 434 and 435. What are the people doing? Encourage children to answer in complete sentences. (They are hugging, playing music, and smiling.) What tradition has this family gathered to celebrate? (The family has gathered to celebrate a birthday.)

Student Edition, pp. 434–435

2ND READ

Close Reading

EVALUATION • TEXT EVIDENCE How do you think the family members in the picture are feeling? Why do you think so? Use clues from the picture to help answer. (They are happy. They are smiling. Two people are hugging. They are listening to music.)

DRAW CONCLUSIONS • REREAD CHALLENGING TEXT Remind children that good readers draw conclusions as they read. Have children reread pages 436 and 437. How do Cecilia and Mamá feel about Tía? How do you know? (Cecilia and Mamá love Tía and want to honor her on her birthday. Mamá cooks beans and prepares other food for Tía's surprise party. Cecilia draws a picture of Tía and thinks about what to give her for her birthday.)

Common Core State Standards

Literature 1. Ask and answer such questions as *who, what, where, when, why,* and *how* to demonstrate understanding of key details in a text. **Also Literature 7. and Speaking/Listening 6.**

Today is secret day. I curl my cat into my arms and say, "Ssshh, Chica. Can you keep our secret, silly cat?"

Today is special day. Today is my great-aunt's ninetieth birthday. Ten, twenty, thirty, forty, fifty, sixty, seventy, eighty, ninety. Ninety years old. *¡Noventa años!*

436

At breakfast Mamá asks, "What is today, Cecilia?" I say, "Special day. Birthday day."

Mamá is cooking for the surprise party. I smell beans bubbling on the stove. Mamá is cutting fruit—pineapple, watermelon, mangoes. I sit in the backyard and watch Chica chase butterflies. I hear bees bzzzzz.

I draw pictures in the sand with a stick. I draw a picture of my aunt, my *Tía*. I say, "Chica, what will we give Tía?"

437

Student Edition, pp. 436–437

ANALYSIS Why does Mamá ask Cecilia what day it is? (Mamá wants to make sure Cecilia remembers that today is Tía's birthday.) Who also has been told that it's Tía's birthday? (Chica the cat has been told it's Tía's birthday.)

Time for Science **CONNECT TO SCIENCE** A fruit is the part of a plant that grows around the seed and can be used for food. A vegetable is a part of the plant that can be used for food, such as lettuce (leaves), carrots (roots), broccoli (stems and flowers), and beans (seeds).

1ST READ

Access Text ◎ If children need help, then...

◎ QUESTIONING On page 438, Cecilia asks Mamá if she can use a basket. What does Cecilia want to use the basket for? (It's a birthday basket for Tía.) Where did you find your answer? (It's written in the last line on page 438.)

REVIEW SELECTION VOCABULARY Have children locate the selection word *favorite* on page 439. What does it mean that Cecilia calls the book her *favorite*? (Cecilia likes that book more than all her other books.)

Chica and I walk around the front yard and the backyard looking for a good present. We walk around the house. We look in Mamá's room. We look in my closet and drawers.

I say, "Chica, shall we give her my little pots, my piggy bank, my tin fish, my dancing puppet?"

I say, "Mamá, can Chica and I use this basket?"

Mamá asks, "Why, Cecilia?"

"It's a surprise for the surprise party," I answer. Chica jumps into the basket. "No," I say. "Not for you, silly cat. This is a birthday basket for Tía."

438

I put a book in the basket. When Tía comes to our house, she reads it to me. It's our favorite book. I sit close to her on the sofa. I smell her perfume. Sometimes Chica tries to read with us. She sits on the book. I say, "Silly cat. Books are not for sitting."

I put Tía's favorite mixing bowl on the book in the basket. Tía and I like to make *bizcochos*, sugary cookies for the family.

Tía says, "Cecilia, help me stir the cookie dough." She says, "Cecilia, help me roll the cookie dough." When we take the warm cookies from the oven, Tía says, "Cecilia, you are a very good cook."

439

Student Edition, pp. 438–439

2ND READ

Close Reading ◎

ANALYSIS Why does Cecilia consider giving Tía her little pots, piggy bank, tin fish, and puppet? (They are things Cecilia loves.) Why does Cecilia decide against these things as a present? (She wants to give things that Tía likes.)

INFERENCE • TEXT EVIDENCE How do you think Cecilia feels about her cat, Chica? Use clues from the text and the pictures to answer the question. (Cecilia loves her cat and finds her funny. She calls her "silly cat" whenever she tries to take Tia's presents. They are together a lot.)

CHECK DECODING Have children check their reading of new words using these questions:

- Did I blend the sounds to read the word?
- Did I put the new word in the sentence to make sure it made sense?
- Did I look for word parts to help me understand the word?

Common Core State Standards

Literature 4. Describe how words and phrases (e.g., regular beats, alliteration, rhymes, repeated lines) supply rhythm and meaning in a story, poem, or song. **Also Literature 1., 7. and Foundational Skills 3., 4.c.**

I put a flowerpot in the mixing bowl on the book in the basket. Tía and I like to grow flowers for the kitchen window. Chica likes to put her face in the flowers. "Silly cat," I say.

I put a teacup in the flowerpot that is in the mixing bowl on the book in the basket. When I'm sick, my aunt makes me hot mint tea, *hierbabuena*. She brings it to me in bed. She brings me a cookie too.

440

I put a red ball in the teacup that is in the flowerpot in the mixing bowl on the book in the basket. On warm days Tía sits outside and throws me the ball.

She says, "Cecilia, when I was a little girl in Mexico, my sisters and I played ball. We all wore long dresses and had long braids."

Chica and I go outside. I pick flowers to decorate Tía's basket.

On summer days when I am swinging high up to the sky, Tía collects flowers for my room.

441

Student Edition, pp. 440–441

ANALYSIS Why does Cecilia put the items she does in the basket? (Each item reminds her of a special time she has had with Tía.)

ANALYSIS How does the author use repetition, or repeated words and phrases, on these pages? What effect does this have? (The author repeats what is in the basket each time an item is added. The repetition gives the story a rhythm and also shows how the gifts are accumulating and filling the basket.)

1ST READ

Access Text If children need help, then…

QUESTIONING What might you ask about Chica as you read page 442? (Why does Chica rub the closet door?) What is the answer? (She shows where the present is hidden.) What text clues helped you? (Mamá asks, "Chica, where is the birthday basket?")

REREAD CHALLENGING TEXT Have children reread page 443 to find and determine the meaning of words from another language. Point out that the words appear in italic, or slanted, type. Which words are from another language? *(qué pasa)* Use context clues to help you tell what they mean. (What is this?)

Mamá calls, "Cecilia, where are you?"

Chica and I run and hide our surprise.

I say, "Mamá, can you find the birthday basket for Tía?"

Mamá looks under the table. She looks in the refrigerator. She looks under my bed. She asks, "Chica, where is the birthday basket?"

Chica rubs against my closet door. Mamá and I laugh. I show her my surprise.

After my nap, Mamá and I fill a piñata with candy. We fill the living room with balloons. I hum, mmmmm, a little work song like the one Tía hums when she sets the table or makes my bed. I help Mamá set the table with flowers and tiny cakes.

442

"Here come the musicians," says Mamá. I open the front door. Our family and friends begin to arrive too.

I curl Chica into my arms. Then Mamá says, "Sshh, here comes Tía."

I rush to open the front door. "Tía! Tía!" I shout. She hugs me and says,

"Cecilia, *¿qué pasa?* What is this?"

443

Student Edition, pp. 442–443

2ND READ

Close Reading

ANALYSIS Why can't Mamá find the birthday basket? (Mamá cannot find the birthday basket because Cecilia has hidden it in her closet.)

SYNTHESIS How do Cecilia and Mamá decorate for the party? How is this alike and different from parties you have been to?

DRAW CONCLUSIONS Why does Cecilia's family have a party with friends, family, and musicians to celebrate Tía's birthday? (The family wants to show Tía how much they love her and to celebrate that she is 90 years old.)

Common Core State Standards

Literature 1. Ask and answer such questions as *who, what, where, when, why,* and *how* to demonstrate understanding of key details in a text. **Language 4.a.** Use sentence-level context as a clue to the meaning of a word or phrase.

Student Edition, pp. 444–445

INFERENCE • TEXT EVIDENCE If you were at this surprise party, what would you hear? (the sounds of music, laughter, and talking) How do you know? (I can use the text, the picture that shows men with instruments in their hands, and what I know about parties.)

1ST READ

Access Text If children need help, then...

QUESTIONING Have children talk about questions they had as they read and how they used evidence from the text to help answer these questions.

CROSS-TEXT EVALUATION

Use a Strategy to Self-Check How did the short selection "A Party and a Present" help you understand this selection?

Continue to DAY 2
Text-Based Comprehension
p. 447a

I give her the birthday basket. Everyone gets close to see what's inside. Slowly Tía smells the flowers. She looks at me and smiles. Then she takes the red ball out of the teacup and the teacup out of the flowerpot.

She pretends to take a sip of tea and we all laugh.

Carefully, Tía takes the flowerpot out of the bowl and the bowl off of the book. She doesn't say a word. She just stops and looks at me. Then she takes our favorite book out of the basket.

And guess who jumps into the basket?

446

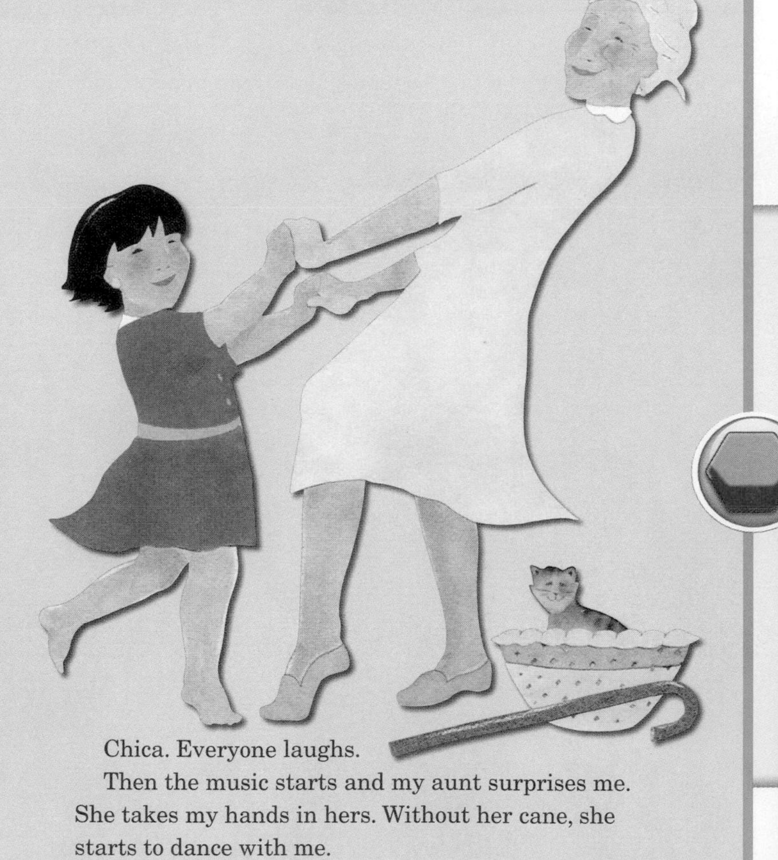

Chica. Everyone laughs.

Then the music starts and my aunt surprises me. She takes my hands in hers. Without her cane, she starts to dance with me.

447

Student Edition, pp. 446–447

2ND READ

Close Reading

SYNTHESIS • TEXT EVIDENCE Using what you learned in this selection, tell how family celebrations are important to family members. Have children cite examples from the text.

Continue to DAY 3
Think Critically
p. 448–449

Text-Based Comprehension

Check Understanding

Have children discuss each question with a partner. Ask several pairs to share their responses.

☑ **Realistic fiction** How are the events in this story like events in real life? (The characters in the story plan a surprise birthday party for a relative, just like people sometimes do in real life. They invite friends and family to their home to join the celebration. Their daily activities are similar to things that people do in real life.)

☑ **Confirm predictions** How did you use the illustrations to predict what would happen in the story? Were your predictions correct? (I used the picture on page 434 to predict that the person celebrating a birthday would be a girl's older relative.)

☑ **Inference** Does Tía like her surprise party and her gift from Cecilia? What clues from the text help support your answer? (Tía seems delighted with the party and with her gift from Cecilia. The text says Tía smiles, laughs, and stops to look at Cecilia. Then she gets up to dance with Cecilia.)

☑ **Draw conclusions** How would you describe the relationship between Cecilia and Tía? (They have a close and loving relationship. They also enjoy spending time together and sharing many different activities.)

☑ **Connect text to self** What are some special traditions you and your family have to celebrate birthdays? How are they similar to and different from how Cecilia's family celebrates Tía's birthday? (Children might say that their family gathers for parties, like Cecilia's family does. Also at the parties, they might eat special foods, give gifts, and sing "Happy Birthday.")

Day 2 SMALL GROUP TIME • Differentiate Comprehension, p. SG•35

OL On-Level	SI Strategic Intervention	A Advanced
• **Practice** Selection Vocabulary • **Read** *A Birthday Basket for Tía*	• **Reteach** Selection Vocabulary • **Read** *A Birthday Basket for Tía*	• **Extend** Selection Vocabulary • **Read** *A Birthday Basket for Tía* • **Investigate** Inquiry Project

Common Core State Standards

Literature 1. Ask and answer such questions as *who, what, where, when, why,* and *how* to demonstrate understanding of key details in a text.

Support Discussion To help children answer the last question, have them use some words from their primary language to describe the customs, activities, and foods that are part of their birthday celebrations. Have children draw or act out the words to show their meanings.

If... children need more scaffolding and practice with the **Comprehension Skill,**
then... use the ELL activities on p. DI•59 in the Teacher Resources section on SuccessNet.

Common Core State Standards

Literature 5. Describe the overall structure of a story, including describing how the beginning introduces the story and the ending concludes the action. **Language 1.** Demonstrate command of the conventions of standard English grammar and usage when writing or speaking.

Literary Text

Setting and Plot

IDENTIFY SETTINGS AND PLOTS Review with children that each story has a setting, where and when the story takes place, and a plot, the story's action. Explain that comparing and contrasting settings and plots of stories can be interesting, especially if they are written by the same author. Use *A Birthday Basket for Tía* and *The Night the Moon Fell* (pp. 128–143) to describe similarities and differences in the settings and plots of these two stories by Pat Mora.

- What is the setting of *A Birthday Basket for Tía?* (The story takes place in the home of Cecilia on her great-aunt's birthday.)
- What is the setting of *The Night the Moon Fell?* (The story takes place in the sky and the ocean during one night.)
- What is the plot in *A Birthday Basket for Tía?* (Cecilia doesn't know what to give her great-aunt for her birthday. She decides to put all the things her great-aunt loves in a basket. Tía comes and is surprised. She loves Cecilia's present, and the family celebrates with music and dancing.)
- What is the plot in *The Night the Moon Fell?* (The moon falls into the ocean and breaks into pieces on the bottom. Fish help roll the pieces of Luna together and lift her back into the sky. They stay in the sky with her.)

GUIDE PRACTICE Work with children to describe how the settings of the stories are similar and different. Use Graphic Organizer 18.

ON THEIR OWN Give small groups copies of Graphic Organizer 18 to describe how the plots are similar and different. Then create a consensus answer and enter it on the chart. Keep this organizer for discussion on Day 5.

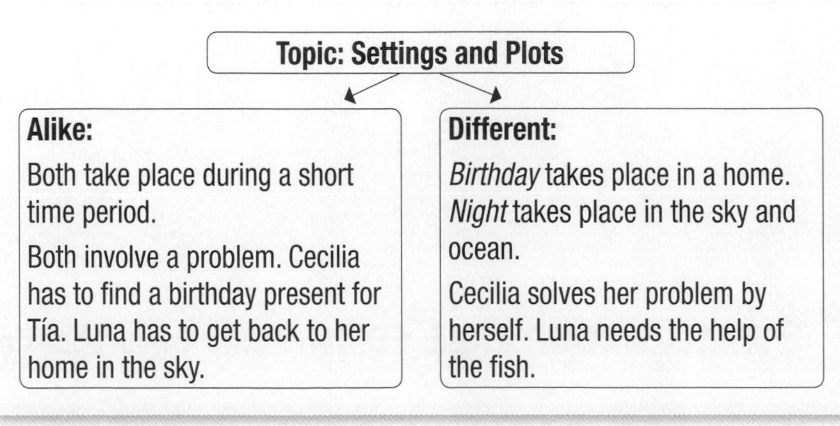

Graphic Organizer 18

Conventions

Prepositions and Prepositional Phrases

TEACH Write *The dog jumped on the bed.* Point to each word as you read it. Ask children where the dog jumped. (on the bed) What is the preposition in the phrase *on the bed? (on)* This preposition tells me that the dog is *on* the bed, not *under* the bed or *near* the bed. The prepositions *for, from, of,* and *with* help me understand other ideas in sentences.

GUIDE PRACTICE Write the following sentence frames on the board. Have children complete each sentence using any of the following prepositions: *in, for, from, of, with,* or *at.* Then have them read each prepositional phrase.

1. **The gift is ______.**
2. **Len found his book ______.**
3. **Mom will wait ______.**

APPLY Have children orally answer the following questions in complete sentences, using prepositional phrases.

1. **Where might a mouse hide?**
2. **Where do you go to buy bread?**
3. **Where can you find a nest?**

ON THEIR OWN Use *Reader's and Writer's Notebook,* p. 511.

Access for All

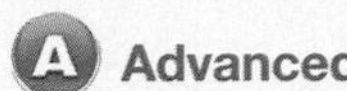

Using Prepositions Allow children who demonstrate proficiency in identifying prepositions to create a written "tour" of the school. Have them describe what is found where in the area. Have children underline the prepositions in their writing.

Daily Fix-It

3. Jordan colects baseball cards
   Jordan collects baseball cards.
4. My favrite aunt salls flowers.
   My favorite aunt sells flowers.

Discuss the Daily Fix-It corrections with children. Review sentence punctuation and the spelling of *collects, favorite,* and *sells.*

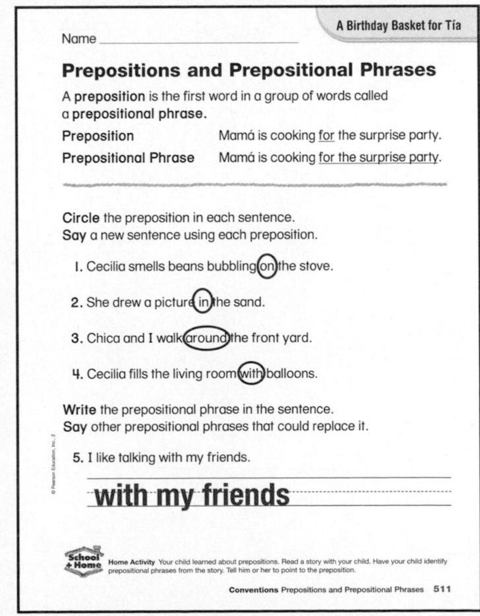

Name ______________ A Birthday Basket for Tía

Prepositions and Prepositional Phrases

A **preposition** is the first word in a group of words called a **prepositional phrase.**

Preposition	Mamá is cooking for the surprise party.
Prepositional Phrase	Mamá is cooking for the surprise party.

Circle the preposition in each sentence.
Say a new sentence using each preposition.

1. Cecilia smells beans bubbling on the stove.
2. She drew a picture in the sand.
3. Chica and I walk around the front yard.
4. Cecilia fills the living room with balloons.

Write the prepositional phrase in the sentence.
Say other prepositional phrases that could replace it.

5. I like talking with my friends.

with my friends

Home Activity Your child learned about prepositions. Read a story with your child. Have your child identify prepositional phrases from the story. Tell him or her to point to the preposition.

Conventions Prepositions and Prepositional Phrases 511

Reader's and Writer's Notebook, p. 511

Common Core State Standards

Language 1.f. Produce, expand, and rearrange complete simple and compound sentences (e.g., The boy watched the movie; The little boy watched the movie; The action movie was watched by the little boy). **Language 2.b.** Use commas in greetings and closings of letters.

Writing

Invitation Letter

Writing Trait: Sentences

INTRODUCE THE PROMPT Review with children the key features of an invitation letter. Point out that they read an invitation letter to a surprise birthday party yesterday. Assure children that they can write an invitation letter. Explain that today children will plan their own invitation letter to a family event. It will provide all the details about the event. The letter will also have a greeting and a closing. Read aloud the writing prompt.

Writing Prompt

Think about family parties and how to plan a family party. Write an invitation letter to invite a relative to an event.

GENERATE INVITATION LETTER IDEAS

Let's make a list of family events to help plan the invitation letter. I'll start with birthday party. It was the family event we read about in *A Birthday Basket for Tía.*

Guide children in completing the chart. Possible ideas are shown. Record the responses. Keep the chart available while children plan their invitations.

Family Events
birthday
reunion
wedding
anniversary
holiday

Have each child choose a family event. Circulate to guide children. Tell them to think about the details related to the event.

Mini-Lesson Sentences

■ **Introduce** Use *Reader's and Writer's Notebook,* p. 512 to model planning an invitation letter. I will plan an invitation letter for a family reunion using a T-chart. In the left column I will write the five *Ws*—*Who, What, Where, When,* and *Why.* If I answer these five questions, I will have all the details I need to write sentences.

Name ______________ A Birthday Basket for Tía

T-Chart

Details	Sentences and Phrases
Who: Grandpa Jim	Dear Grandpa Jim,
What: Carter family reunion	I am planning the Carter family reunion.
Where: Hamilton Park	It will be at Hamilton Park.
When: Saturday, June 16, 2012 12:00 until dark	The relatives in the Carter family will meet for a picnic on Saturday, June 16, 2012. It will begin at 12:00 and end when it gets dark.
Why: eat play games look at photos	We will eat lots of good food, play games, and look at family photos.

School + Home Home Activity Your child is learning to write stories, poems, brief reports, nonfiction paragraphs, letters, and other products this year. Ask what your child is writing this week.

512 Writing Invitation Letter

Reader's and Writer's Notebook, p. 512

■ **Model** The *Who* is the person who will read the letter. I am inviting Grandpa Jim, so I will write *Grandpa Jim* in the Details column. This is the greeting, so in the Sentences and Phrases column I will write *Dear Grandpa Jim* and end it with a comma. The *What* in my letter is the event. I am planning the Carter family reunion. I write that under Details. My sentence is *I am planning the Carter family reunion.* The words are in an order that makes sense. Continue to model details and sentences. Focus on word order so that sentences are clear. Point out the comma in the date and colon in the time. Circulate to guide children as they complete their charts.

Routine Quick Write for Fluency

Team Talk

1. **Talk** Have partners take two minutes to share the details of their family event.
2. **Write** Each child chooses one detail on his or her chart. Both children write the detail in a sentence in which the word order is clear.
3. **Share** Each child reads the sentence aloud.

Routines Flip Chart

Access for All

Advanced

Party Planning Encourage children to plan a party, including elements such as a guest list, the supplies needed, and a time schedule for the events.

Support Prewriting

Beginning Children can draw a picture of the event and the people who will attend. Have them write the names of the family members. Encourage them to share the illustration with a partner, possibly one who speaks the same home language.

Intermediate Have children draw pictures or write phrases to describe the family event. Have them describe the details in the illustration to other children.

Advanced Have children write short sentences in their charts and share them with a partner. As they share the ideas, children can clarify and add details.

Common Core State Standards

Writing 8. Recall information from experiences or gather information from provided sources to answer a question.

Handwriting

Cursive *G, S,* and *I*/Letter Size

MODEL LETTER FORMATION Display uppercase cursive letters *G, S,* and *I.* Use the stroke instructions pictured below to model proper letter formation. Have children write each letter several times and circle their best ones.

D'Nealian Cursive™

MODEL LETTER SIZE Explain that when we write, similarly shaped letters should be the same height. Draw a pair of writing lines on the chalkboard, adding a dotted midline. Write the sentence *I like Gus and Sam* using proper letter proportion. When I write this sentence, I make sure my tall letters touch the top line. I make sure my small letters are half the size of my tall letters. Write *I like Gus and Sam* again and make uppercase letters too short. My uppercase letters should not be too short to touch the top line. Write *I like Gus and Sam* again and make lowercase letters too tall. My lowercase letters should not be so tall they touch the top line. By writing letters that are the correct size, I make it easier for others to read what I write. Ask children which of the three writing examples is easiest to read and have them explain why.

GUIDE PRACTICE Write the following sentence, using incorrect letter size.

I asked Sal a question.

Team Talk Have children work in pairs to discuss what is wrong with the sentence and how to fix it. Have them discuss why proper letter size is important and share with the class. Have them write the sentence correctly.

Research and Inquiry

Step 2 Research Skill: Interview and Sources

TEACH Review with children that an interview is a way to gather information by asking people questions and recording their answers. Remind children that such people are **sources** and that sources may be found inside school.

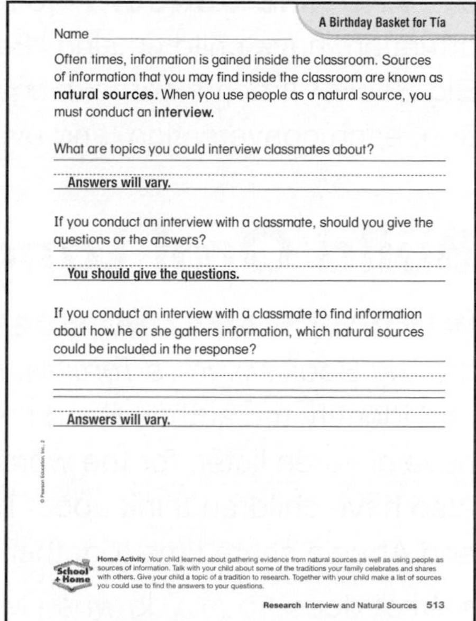

A Birthday Basket for Tía

Name ____________

Often times, information is gained inside the classroom. Sources of information that you may find inside the classroom are known as **natural sources.** When you use people as a natural source, you must conduct an **interview.**

What are topics you could interview classmates about?

Answers will vary.

If you conduct an interview with a classmate, should you give the questions or the answers?

You should give the questions.

If you conduct an interview with a classmate to find information about how he or she gathers information, which natural sources could be included in the response?

Answers will vary.

© Pearson Education, Inc., 2

School + Home **Home Activity** Your child learned about gathering evidence from natural sources as well as using people as sources of information. Talk with your child about some of the traditions your family celebrates and shares with others. Give your child a topic of a tradition to research. Together with your child make a list of sources you could use to find the answers to your questions.

Research Interview and Natural Sources 513

Reader's and Writer's Notebook, p. 513

Think Aloud **MODEL** When I interview, I plan ahead. I think of questions beforehand to ask my source and write them down. Then I listen carefully and take notes on the answers. If I were interviewing another teacher at school about birthdays, I would ask questions such as *How did you celebrate your last birthday? Who came to visit? What did you have to eat?*

GUIDE PRACTICE Have children use classmates as sources. Provide them with this topic: *How did you celebrate your last birthday?* Have partners generate a list of interview questions. Then have children take turns interviewing each other.

ON THEIR OWN Use *Reader's and Writer's Notebook,* p. 513.

Academic Vocabulary 

source a person or thing that can give information

Bridge to Common Core

RESEARCH TO BUILD AND PRESENT KNOWLEDGE

Children will gather evidence from personal sources to use in answering questions for their research projects. They will also

- learn to write interview questions
- learn to conduct an interview
- learn to record responses to interview questions

Wrap Up Your Day!

✔ **Content Knowledge** Monitor children's use of oral vocabulary as they respond. Ask: What did Cecilia use to create her birthday basket? (book, mixing bowl, flowerpot, teacup, ball, flowers) Why do you think it was a fun celebration? (It was a party with food, music, dancing, a piñata, friends, and family.)

Tell children that tomorrow they will reread *A Birthday Basket for Tía.*

DAY 3 at a Glance

Content Knowledge
Oral Vocabulary

Phonics/Spelling

Final Syllables *-tion, -ture, -ion*

Fluency
Appropriate Phrasing

Selection Vocabulary
aunt, bank, basket, collects, favorite, present
Words from Other Languages

Text-Based Comprehension
Review Cause and Effect

Conventions
Prepositions and Prepositional Phrases

Writing
Invitation Letter

Research and Inquiry
Gather and Record Information

Materials

- Student Edition
- Sing with Me Big Book
- Big Book
- Reader's and Writer's Notebook
- Decodable Reader 28B
- Retelling Cards

Common Core State Standards

Speaking/Listening 2. Recount or describe key ideas or details from a text read aloud or information presented orally or through other media. **Language 6.** Use words and phrases acquired through conversations, reading and being read to, and responding to texts, including using adjectives and adverbs to describe (e.g., *When other kids are happy that makes me happy*).

Content Knowledge

Family Celebrations

EXPAND THE CONCEPT To reinforce concepts and to focus children's attention, have children sing "Family Tradition" from the *Sing with Me* Big Book. What are some things that unite family members? (Each celebration, each conversation, and every family custom unites family members.)

Build Oral Language

INTRODUCE AMAZING WORDS Display the Big Book *Magda's Tortillas.* Read the title and identify the author. Read the story and have children listen for the word *inspect.* Also have children think about how Magda and Abuela share time together.

Big Book

- What does Abuela do when Magda gets upset because she cannot make round tortillas? (She points out that Magda makes her tortillas in shapes such as a heart and a star. Later she compliments Magda and calls her an artist.)
- What does Magda do when Abuela compliments her? (She tells Abuela that Abuela's round tortillas will always be her favorite, and she hugs Abuela.)

TALK ABOUT SENTENCES AND WORDS Write the following sentence from *Magda's Tortillas* on sentence strips or on the board.

Magda Madrigal had just washed her little hands, and now she presented them for inspection.

- Ask children to read it with you as you track the print.
- Point to and read *she presented them for inspection.* What does this mean? (She showed her hands so her grandmother could see they were clean.) Why does the author use the word *presented* instead of *showed?* (It sounds more formal and helps creates a string of words with the long and short *e* sounds.) What other words could the author have used?

- Now point to and reread *she presented them for inspection.* What does the word *inspection* mean? ("checking," or "examination") Why do you think the author chose the word *inspection?* (It is a precise word, and it fits with the other words with long and short *e* sounds.)
- **Team Talk** Now have children work with a partner to replace key words in the sentence with simpler words or synonyms. Use the following sentence frame.

Magda Madrigal had just washed her little hands, and now she _______ them for _______.

Build Oral Vocabulary

Amazing Words — Robust Vocabulary Routine

1. **Introduce the Word** Relate the word *inspect* to the story. Magda presents her hands for her grandmother to *inspect.* Supply a child-friendly definition. When you *inspect* something, you look at it very carefully. Have children say the word.
2. **Demonstrate** Provide examples to show meaning. Mom will *inspect* my room after I clean it to make sure I did a good job. The police will *inspect* the house for clues.
3. **Apply** Have children demonstrate their understanding. Why is it a good idea to *inspect* a used toy you want to buy?
4. **Display the Word** Run your hand under the two syllables *in-spect* as you read the word.

Routines Flip Chart

ADD TO THE CONCEPT CHART Use these questions to discuss family celebrations and what makes them special as you add to the concept chart.

3-Column Chart

- What does Cecilia do to celebrate Tía's ninetieth birthday? (She makes Tía a special gift basket that reminds her of good times they spent together.) We can add *We share memories* under *We Do Special Activities* in our chart.
- What are some things the family does to celebrate Tía's ninetieth birthday? (They have music.) Where shall we add this idea?

Amazing Words

celebration	inspect
custom	angle
tradition	brilliant
create	snapshot

ELL

Expand Vocabulary Use the Day 3 instruction on ELL Poster 28 to help children expand vocabulary.

Physical Response Help children understand the word *inspect* by demonstrating how to inspect an object, such as a book or photograph. Then have children do the same. Ask what they notice when they inspect it. Ask what other items they sometimes inspect.

Common Core State Standards

Foundational Skills 3. Know and apply grade-level phonics and word analysis skills in decoding words.

Phonics

Sort Words

MODEL WORD SORTING Write *-tion, -ture,* and *-ion* as headings on a three-column chart. Write the words from the chart below on self-stick notes in random order. Now we are going to read and sort words with the final syllables *-tion, -ture,* and *-ion.* Display *motion.* I see the spelling pattern *-tion* forms the final syllable of this word. I know the first syllable *mo-* has a long vowel sound because it ends in a vowel. I can read the word *motion.* Attach the note in the appropriate column.

GUIDE PRACTICE Distribute the self-stick notes to children. Have them take turns reading the words and attaching them under the appropriate heading. Monitor children's work. When the chart is complete, have children read each column of words as you point to it.

-tion	*-ture*	*-ion*
motion	mixture	million
caution	culture	onion
fraction	lecture	rebellion
direction	departure	scallion

Corrective feedback For corrective feedback, explain where to divide the words. Then have children echo read the syllables with you.

Fluent Word Reading

MODEL Write *adventure.* I can look for word parts I know in this word. I see that the spelling pattern *-ture* forms the final syllable. At the beginning of the word, I see the pattern of two consonants between two vowels. I divide the word between the two consonants to make two syllables. I read each word part and then read the parts together: *ad-ven-ture—adventure.*

GUIDE PRACTICE Write the words below. Look for word parts you know. When I point to the word, we'll read it together. Allow one second per word part previewing time for the first reading.

question **million** **fracture** **capture** **direction** **vacation**

ON THEIR OWN Have children read the list above three or four times, until they can read one word per second.

Decode and Read

DECODE WORDS IN ISOLATION Have children turn to page 225 in *Decodable Practice Readers* 2.2 and find the first list of words. Each word in this list ends in *-tion, -ture,* or *-ion.* Let's blend and read these words. Be sure that children correctly read each word part.

Next, have children read the high-frequency words.

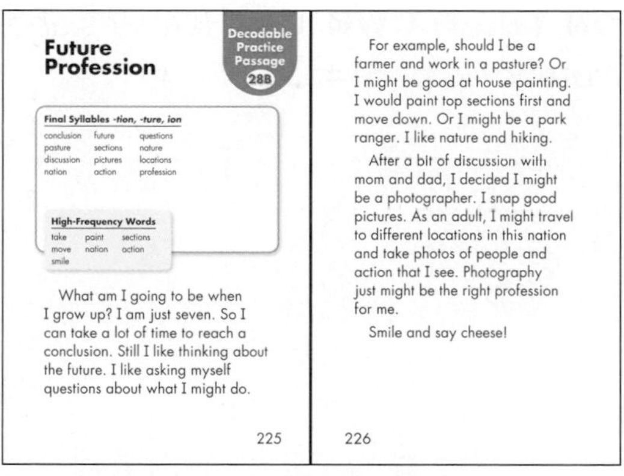
Future Profession

Decodable Practice Passage 28B

Final Syllables -tion, -ture, -ion
conclusion future questions
posture sections nature
discussion pictures locations
nation action profession

High-Frequency Words
take paint sections
move nation action
smile

What am I going to be when I grow up? I am just seven. So I can take a lot of time to reach a conclusion. Still I like thinking about the future. I like asking myself questions about what I might do.

225

For example, should I be a farmer and work in a pasture? Or I might be good at house painting. I would paint top sections first and move down. Or I might be a park ranger. I like nature and hiking.

After a bit of discussion with mom and dad, I decided I might be a photographer. I snap good pictures. As an adult, I might travel to different locations in this nation and take photos of people and action that I see. Photography just might be the right profession for me.

Smile and say cheese!

226

Decodable Practice Passage 28B

DECODE WORDS IN CONTEXT Chorally read the story along with children. Have children identify words in the story that end in *-tion, -ture,* and *-ion.*

Team Talk Pair children and have them take turns reading the story aloud to each other. Monitor children as they read to check for proper pronunciation and appropriate pacing.

Access for All

SI Strategic Intervention

Practice Final Syllables Write on cards additional words with final syllables *-tion, -ture,* and *-ion* and underline the final syllable. Mix the cards and have children sort them by final syllable. Then guide children in dividing each word into syllables. Model blending the words and have children repeat.

A Advanced

Extend Fluent Word Reading Have children write a story using the words from Fluent Word Reading. Allow them to read their stories to the class.

Cognates Children literate in Spanish may recognize many of the words as cognates, including: *cuestíon/question, vacaciones/vacation, dirección/direction, cultura/culture.*

Common Core State Standards

Language 2. Demonstrate command of the conventions of standard English capitalization, punctuation, and spelling when writing. **Foundational Skills 4.a.** Read on-level text with purpose and understanding.

Access for All

 Advanced

Spelling Have children assist classmates who are having difficulty making corrections to their sentences.

Spelling Words

Final Syllables *-tion, -ture*

1. mixture	**7. caution**
2. nation	**8. station**
3. section	**9. fixture**
4. future	**10. motion**
5. picture	**11. nature**
6. action	**12. feature**

High-Frequency Words

13. piece	**14. tomorrow**

Spelling

Final Syllables *-tion, -ture*

SPELL HIGH-FREQUENCY WORDS Write *pieces* and *tomorrow* and point them out on the Word Wall. Then write *piece* underneath *pieces.* Review that *-s* was added to *piece* to show more than one. Have children say and spell *piece* and *tomorrow* with you and then without you.

DICTATION Have children write these sentences. Say each sentence. Then repeat it slowly, one word at a time.

1. **Tomorrow I will see a motion picture.**
2. **A piece fell off that section of the light fixture.**
3. **The park will build a nature station in the future.**

PROOFREAD AND CORRECT Write each sentence, spelling words one at a time. Have children circle and rewrite any misspelled words.

ON THEIR OWN Use *Reader's and Writer's Notebook,* p. 514.

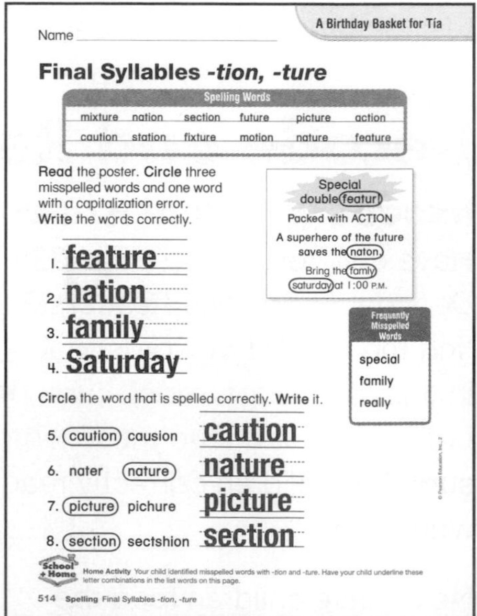

Name ____________ A Birthday Basket for Tía

Final Syllables *-tion, -ture*

Spelling Words					
mixture	nation	section	future	picture	action
caution	station	fixture	motion	nature	feature

Read the poster. **Circle** three misspelled words and one word with a capitalization error. **Write** the words correctly.

Special double featur
Packed with ACTION
A superhero of the future saves the naton.
Bring the famly saturday at 1:00 P.M.

1. feature
2. nation
3. family
4. Saturday

Frequently Misspelled Words: special, family, really

Circle the word that is spelled correctly. **Write** it.

5. caution causion — caution
6. nater nature — nature
7. picture pichure — picture
8. section sectshion — section

School + Home **Home Activity** Your child identified misspelled words with *-tion* and *-ture*. Have your child underline these letter combinations in the list words on this page.

514 **Spelling** Final Syllables *-tion, -ture*

Reader's and Writer's Notebook, p. 514

ELL

If... children need more scaffolding and practice with reading the **Main Selection,**
then... use the ELL activities on p. DI•60 in the Teacher Resources section on SuccessNet.

Day 3 SMALL GROUP TIME • Differentiate Close Reading, p. SG•35

OL On-Level
- **Reread** to Develop Vocabulary
- **Reread** *A Birthday Basket for Tía*

SI Strategic Intervention
- **Reread** to Develop Vocabulary
- **Reread** *A Birthday Basket for Tía*

A Advanced
- **Reread** to Develop Vocabulary
- **Reread** *A Birthday Basket for Tía*
- **Investigate** Inquiry Project

Fluency

Appropriate Phrasing

MODEL FLUENT READING Have children turn to Student Edition, pp. 436–437. Point to the quotation marks. Quotation marks show that someone is talking. I will read the part in quotation marks the way someone would say it. I pause when I see commas.

GUIDE PRACTICE Have children read the pages with you. Then have them reread the pages as a group without you until they read with appropriate phrasing. Continue in the same way with pp. 438–439.

Corrective feedback

If... children have difficulty reading with appropriate phrasing,
then... prompt:

- Are there commas to tell you that a group of words belongs together?
- Are there groups of words that that you would say together if you were speaking?
- Try to read groups of words, not word by word.

Reread for Fluency

Routine Choral Reading

1. **Select a Passage** For *A Birthday Basket for Tía,* use pp. 440–441.
2. **Model** First, have children track the print as you read.
3. **Guide Practice** Then have children read along with you.
4. **Corrective Feedback** Have the class read aloud without you. Monitor progress and provide feedback. For optimal fluency, children should reread three to four times.

Routines Flip Chart

CHECK COMPREHENSION Have children explain why Cecilia adds flowers to Tía's birthday basket.

Options for Oral Rereading

Use *A Birthday Basket for Tía* or the Day 1 Decodable Reader.

Reading with Quotation Marks If children have trouble knowing that quotation marks enclose a speaker's words, continue to model other sentences and guide practice until the children feel more comfortable reading with quotation marks.

Common Core State Standards

Language 4. Determine or clarify the meaning of unknown and multiple-meaning words and phrases based on grade 2 reading and content, choosing flexibly from an array of strategies. **Language 5.** Demonstrate understanding of word relationships and nuances in word meanings.

Selection Vocabulary

aunt your father's sister, your mother's sister, or your uncle's wife

basket a container made of twigs, grasses, or strips of wood woven together

collects brings things together or gathers them together

bank a place where people keep their money

favorite the thing liked better than others

present a gift; something given

Vocabulary

Selection Vocabulary

REVIEW SELECTION WORDS Display and review the selection words *present, aunt, basket, collects, bank,* and *favorite.* Have children read the words aloud.

Team Talk Have partners compile a list of related words for each selection word without writing the word. For example, they could write *uncle, cousin, grandmother,* and *grandfather* to relate to *aunt.* (All words name family members.) Have pairs exchange papers to identify the selection words and the relationships.

Words from Other Languages

REVIEW WORDS FROM OTHER LANGUAGES Remind children that sometimes when they are reading, they may come to a word or words from another language. These words are often in italics, or slanted type. Remind children of the Spanish words they read in the story *A Birthday Basket for Tía.* Have children look through the selection again and identify words from Spanish on pages 436, 437, 439, 440, 443, and 444.

GUIDE PRACTICE Write *tortilla*. This word is pronounced /t/ /ôr/ • /t/ /ē/ • /y/ /ə/. A tortilla is a round, flat bread made from corn or flour. It is a Spanish word, so the pronunciation is different from English. In Spanish, the letter *i* is pronounced /ē/, and the letter pair *ll* is pronounced /y/.

Write the following words.

tea (Chinese)	**cookie (Dutch)**	**spaghetti (Italian)**
tomato (Spanish)	**yogurt (Turkish)**	**karate (Japanese)**

Say the words and have children repeat them. Discuss the meanings of the words, and have children use the words in sentences. Tell the origin of the word and discuss if it follows English spelling or pronunciation patterns.

Team Talk Write and say these words adapted from Spanish: *potato, fiesta, mosquito.* Have children work in pairs to define the words and use them in sentences. Then have partners discuss if the words follow familiar spelling and pronunciation patterns.

Text-Based Comprehension

Read Main Selection

REVIEW CAUSE AND EFFECT Remind children that what happens and why it happens is known as cause and effect. Thinking about the effect, or what happens, and the cause, or why it happens, helps us better understand the characters and events we read about. Have children turn to pages 446–447 in their Student Edition. Why does everyone laugh after Tía empties the birthday basket? (Chica jumps into the basket.) For additional practice with cause and effect, use Let's Practice It!, p. 314 on the *Teacher Resources DVD-ROM.*

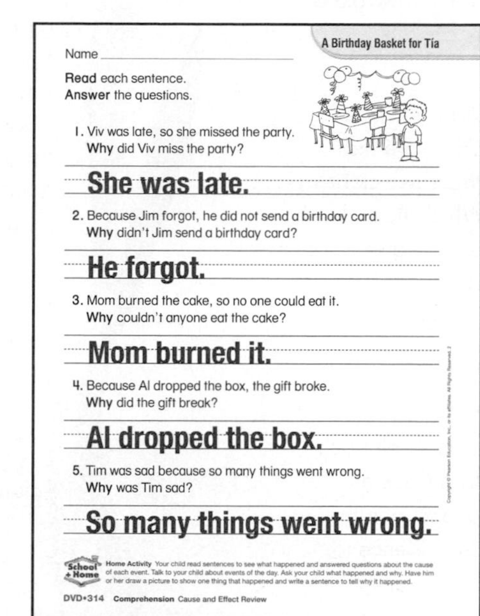
Name ______ A Birthday Basket for Tía

Read each sentence.
Answer the questions.

1. Viv was late, so she missed the party.
Why did Viv miss the party?
She was late.

2. Because Jim forgot, he did not send a birthday card.
Why didn't Jim send a birthday card?
He forgot.

3. Mom burned the cake, so no one could eat it.
Why couldn't anyone eat the cake?
Mom burned it.

4. Because Al dropped the box, the gift broke.
Why did the gift break?
Al dropped the box.

5. Tim was sad because so many things went wrong.
Why was Tim sad?
So many things went wrong.

DVD•314 Comprehension Cause and Effect Review

Let's Practice It! TR DVD•314

GENRE: REALISTIC FICTION Remind children that realistic fiction is a made-up story that could happen in real life. Have children recall details from *A Birthday Basket for Tía* that indicate this story could happen in real life. (It has characters, a plot, and a setting that come from real life.)

READ Return to pages 434–447 and use the **2nd Read/Close Reading Notes** to reread *A Birthday Basket for Tía.*

Routine Read for Understanding

Deepen understanding by reading the selection multiple times.

1. **First Read**—If children need support, use the **Access Text** notes to help them clarify understanding.
2. **Second Read**—Use the **Close Reading** notes to help children draw knowledge from the text.

Think Critically

1. Cecilia puts six things in the birthday basket. Would you put the same six things in a gift basket? Explain.
   Text to Self
2. Why do you think the author wrote a story about a birthday basket?
   Think Like an Author
3. Pat Mora wrote this story and *The Night the Moon Fell.* How are the plots and settings of these two stories alike and different? Which story do you think she enjoyed writing more? Why? Draw Conclusions
4. Did anything in the story confuse you? What questions did you ask as you read? Questioning
5. **Look Back and Write** Look back at page 440. Why does Cecilia put a flowerpot and a teacup in the basket for Tía? Provide evidence to support your answer.
   Key Ideas and Details • Text Evidence

448

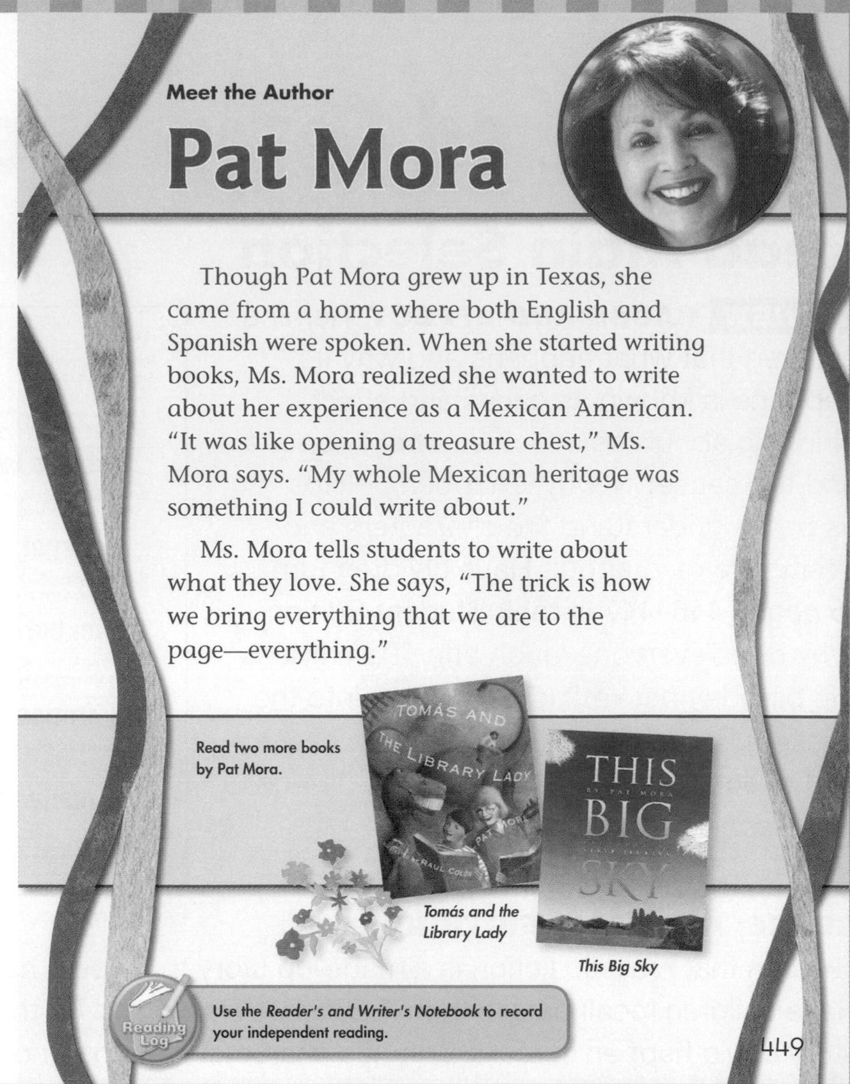
Meet the Author

Pat Mora

Though Pat Mora grew up in Texas, she came from a home where both English and Spanish were spoken. When she started writing books, Ms. Mora realized she wanted to write about her experience as a Mexican American. "It was like opening a treasure chest," Ms. Mora says. "My whole Mexican heritage was something I could write about."

Ms. Mora tells students to write about what they love. She says, "The trick is how we bring everything that we are to the page—everything."

Read two more books by Pat Mora.

Tomás and the Library Lady

This Big Sky

Reading Log

Use the *Reader's and Writer's Notebook* to record your independent reading.

449

Student Edition, pp. 448–449

Common Core State Standards

Literature 1. Ask and answer such questions as *who, what, where, when, why,* and *how* to demonstrate understanding of key details in a text. **Also Literature 2., 7. and Writing 3.**

Bridge to Common Core

KEY IDEAS AND DETAILS

By reading the text multiple times, children will make logical inferences from the text and cite textual evidence when writing or discussing the knowledge they have gained.

Use the Think Critically page to ensure a thorough understanding of *A Birthday Basket for Tía.*

Think Critically

1. **TEXT TO SELF** I would put in things special to the person getting the basket.
2. **THINK LIKE AN AUTHOR** The author wanted to entertain us with a story about a girl who shows her love for her great-aunt.
3. **DRAW CONCLUSIONS** *A Birthday Basket for Tía* takes place in a girl's home during one day. *The Night the Moon Fell* takes place in the night sky and the ocean. In each story, the main character has a problem to solve. Pat Mora might have liked writing *A Birthday Basket for Tía* more because the family may be like her own family.
4. **QUESTIONING** I wondered why Chica rubbed against the closet door, so I asked myself about that. Then I realized that the basket was in the closet.
5. **LOOK BACK AND WRITE • TEXT EVIDENCE** For writing fluency, assign a five-minute time limit. As children finish, encourage them to reread their response and proofread for errors.

Scoring Rubric Look Back and Write

TOP-SCORE RESPONSE A top-score response uses details from the text and the picture to tell why Cecilia put a flowerpot and a teacup in the basket.

A top-score response might include:
Cecilia put a flowerpot in the basket because she and Tía grow flowers for the kitchen window. She put a teacup in the basket because Tía makes tea for her when she is sick.

Retell

Have children work in pairs, retelling the story to one another. Remind children that their partners should include the characters, setting, and events from the beginning, middle, and end of the story. Have children use the retelling strip in the Student Edition or the Story Sort to retell the selection. Monitor children's retellings.

Scoring Rubric Narrative Retelling

	4	3	2	1
Connections	Makes connections and generalizes beyond the text	Makes connections to other events, stories, or experiences	Makes a limited connection to another event, story, or experience	Makes no connection to another event, story, or experience
Author's Purpose	Elaborates on author's purpose	Tells author's purpose with some clarity	Makes some connection to author's purpose	Makes no connection to author's purpose
Characters	Describes the main character(s) and any character development	Identifies the main character(s) and gives some information about them	Inaccurately identifies some characters or gives little information about them	Inaccurately identifies the characters or gives no information about them
Setting	Describes the time and location	Identifies the time and location	Omits details of time or location	Is unable to identify time or location
Plot	Describes the events in sequence using rich detail	Tells the plot with some errors in sequence that do not affect meaning	Tells parts of plot with gaps that affect meaning	Retelling has no sense of story

Don't Wait Until Friday **MONITOR PROGRESS** Check Retelling

If... children have difficulty retelling the selection,
then... use Story Sequence Graphic Organizer 23 and the Retelling Cards/ Story Sort to scaffold their retelling.

Strategy Response Log

Questioning Have children revisit p. RR34 in their *Reader's and Writer's Notebook* to answer the questions they had about the story before they read it.

Plan to Assess Retelling

- ☐ **Week 1** Strategic Intervention
- ☐ **Week 2** Advanced
- ☑ **This Week** Assess Strategic Intervention children.
- ☐ **Week 4** On-Level
- ☐ **Week 5** Strategic Intervention
- ☐ **Week 6** Assess any children you have not yet checked during this unit.

Meet the Author

Read aloud page 449 as children follow along. Ask what it means when Pat Mora says, "We bring everything that we are to the page."

Read Independently

Have children enter their independent reading into their Reading Logs.

Common Core State Standards

Language 1. Demonstrate command of the conventions of standard English grammar and usage when writing or speaking. **Writing 1.** Write opinion pieces in which they introduce the topic or book they are writing about, state an opinion, supply reasons that support the opinion, use linking words (e.g., *because, and, also*) to connect opinion and reasons, and provide a concluding statement or section.

Daily Fix-It

5. Aunt sue cullects dolls.
Aunt Sue collects dolls.

6. Is that your faverite basket.
Is that your favorite basket?

Discuss the Daily Fix-It corrections with children. Review proper name capitalization, sentence punctuation, and referring to a dictionary to check spelling.

Conventions

Prepositions and Prepositional Phrases

REVIEW Remind children that prepositions are words that are used with a noun or a pronoun to connect them to another word. Prepositions usually give information about things such as place, direction, or time: The school bus stops *at* this corner. In this sentence the preposition is *at* and the prepositional phrase is *at this corner.* A prepositional phrase begins with a preposition and end with a noun or pronouns.

GUIDE PRACTICE Write this sentence on the board and have children read it aloud.

I put the book on the box.

What does the preposition tell you about the book and the box? What is the prepositional phrase?

Team Talk Have partners work together to restate the sentence above using a new preposition. Have them write the new sentence and share with the class.

APPLY Have children orally complete each sentence by supplying an appropriate preposition.

1. **Tess will dance _______ Greg.**
2. **We walked home _______ the theater.**
3. **The race starts _______ noon.**
4. **I want a computer _______ my birthday.**

Have them complete these sentences by supplying a prepositional phrase.

1. **School starts _______.**
2. **I found my book _______.**
3. **The party will be _______.**

ON THEIR OWN Use Let's Practice It!, p. 317 on the *Teacher Resources DVD-ROM.*

Name ____________ A Birthday Basket for Tía

Prepositions and Prepositional Phrases

Imagine you are helping to plan a surprise party.

Write about what you will have at your surprise party.
Use prepositional phrases.

Possible response: I will have a party at my house. We will hide behind the couch. We will yell, "Surprise!" after Kurt walks inside.

Choose other prepositions. **Say** a sentence for each preposition.

Home Activity Your child learned how to use prepositions in writing. Take turns with your child writing sentences using prepositional phrases.

Conventions Prepositions and Prepositional Phrases DVD•317

Let's Practice It! TR DVD•317

Common Core State Standards
Writing 1. Write opinion pieces in which they introduce the topic or book they are writing about, state an opinion, supply reasons that support the opinion, use linking words (e.g., *because, and, also*) to connect opinion and reasons, and provide a concluding statement or section.
Also Language 1.

Let's Write It!

Key Features of an Invitation Letter
- asks someone to come to a planned event
- gives details about where and when the event will be
- has a greeting and a closing

READING STREET ONLINE
GRAMMAR JAMMER
www.ReadingStreet.com

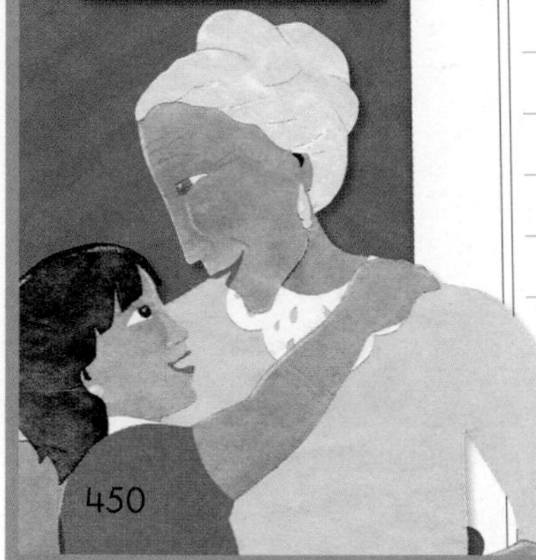

Persuasive

Invitation Letter

An invitation letter asks someone to come to an event. The student model on the next page is an example of an invitation letter.

Writing Prompt Think about family parties and how to plan a family party. Write an invitation letter to invite a relative to an event.

Writer's Checklist

Remember, you should . . .
- ✓ write clear sentences to invite the person.
- ✓ begin the greeting and closing with a capital letter.
- ✓ use prepositional phrases correctly.

Student Model

Dear Uncle Ed,
We are having a party to celebrate Luz coming home. It will be fun.
The day will be Sunday, June 24, 2011. The party will start at 1:00 in the afternoon. It will be at Grandma's house in La Porte.
Please come. We enjoy seeing you when you visit.
Your niece,
Briana

Genre An **invitation letter** has a greeting and a closing.

Writing Trait Sentences The writer uses words in an order that makes sense.

Writer uses **prepositions** correctly.

Conventions

Prepositions and Prepositional Phrases

A **preposition** is the first word in a prepositional phrase. Prepositions may tell where something is or when something happens. The words **on, at,** and **in** are prepositions.

450 451

Student Edition, pp. 450–451

Let's Write It!

WRITE AN INVITATION LETTER Use pp. 450–451 in the Student Edition. Read aloud the Key Features of an Invitation Letter and the definition of invitation letter. Read aloud the Writing Prompt and discuss the Writer's Checklist.

REVIEW THE STUDENT MODEL Then read the Student Model on p. 451 aloud. Point out the greeting and closing and the comma that ends each. Read aloud and briefly discuss the side notes about genre, the writing trait, and prepositions.

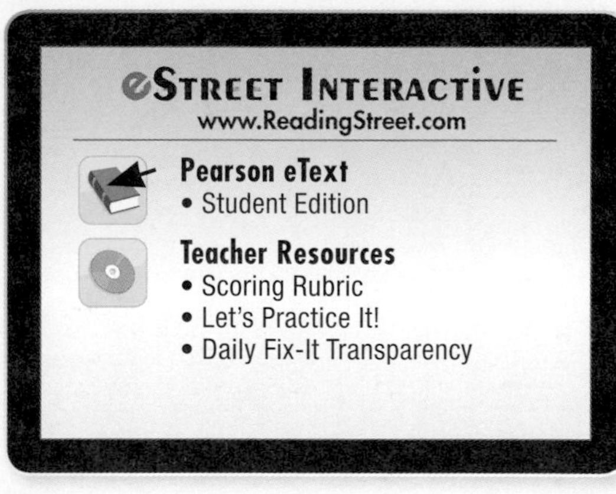

Scoring Rubric

TOP-SCORE RESPONSE Help children understand that a top-score response has a greeting and closing, gives details about the event, and uses prepositions correctly. For a complete rubric see Writing Rubric 28 from the *Teacher Resources DVD-ROM.*

CONNECT TO CONVENTIONS Read to children the Conventions note about prepositions and prepositional phrases.

eStreet Interactive
www.ReadingStreet.com

Pearson eText
- Student Edition

Teacher Resources
- Scoring Rubric
- Let's Practice It!
- Daily Fix-It Transparency

Common Core State Standards

Writing 1. Write opinion pieces in which they introduce the topic or book they are writing about, state an opinion, supply reasons that support the opinion, use linking words (e.g., *because, and, also*) to connect opinion and reasons, and provide a concluding statement or section.

Writing

Invitation Letter

Mini-Lesson Writer's Craft: Choosing Details

- **Introduce** Use the T-chart from yesterday and Writing Transparency 28A to model writing details in an invitation letter. Yesterday I made a chart using the 5 *W*s to plan the details for a family event. The Who is Grandpa Jim. The What is the Carter family reunion. The Where is Hamilton Park. The When is Saturday, June 16, 2012 from 12:00 until dark. The Why is to eat, play games, and look at photos. The ideas are in an order that make sense. Also by including these details, I am persuading Grandpa Jim to attend. Here is my draft. I used the chart to help write. I used the prepositions *at, in,* and *on* so the sentences are clear. I also added the last two sentences to get Grandpa Jim to want to come. Read aloud the draft on the Transparency.

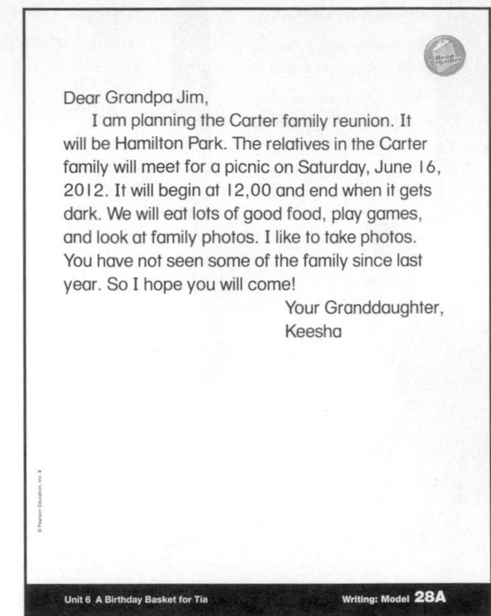
Dear Grandpa Jim,
I am planning the Carter family reunion. It will be Hamilton Park. The relatives in the Carter family will meet for a picnic on Saturday, June 16, 2012. It will begin at 12,00 and end when it gets dark. We will eat lots of good food, play games, and look at family photos. I like to take photos. You have not seen some of the family since last year. So I hope you will come!
Your Granddaughter,
Keesha

Unit 6 A Birthday Basket for Tia Writing: Model 28A

Writing Transparency 28A TR DVD

- Explain how children can use their T-chart to draft the invitation letter. Remind them that the goal is to write their ideas. They can edit later.

GUIDE WRITING Now it is time to write your invitation letter. Include all the details about the family event so that you can persuade your relative to attend. Put the details in an order so they are easy to understand. Have children use their T-charts. Help them finish the ideas. Then guide children as they draft the invitation letters.

Routine Quick Write for Fluency

Team Talk

1. **Talk** Have partners take two minutes to talk about a recent family event.
2. **Write** Each child writes sentences that include two or three details.
3. **Share** Partners circle the prepositions in the others' sentences.

Routines Flip Chart

Research and Inquiry

Step 3 Gather and Record Information

TEACH Tell children that today they will conduct an interview in class. Their goal is to find out more about ways that family celebrations are special. Review and model the steps of how to conduct an interview.

Think Aloud **MODEL** Display the list of questions that the class created on Day 1. Before the interview, we know we have to prepare a list of questions. We already have our list. I'm interested in learning more about the activities families do at a birthday party. So I'll ask *What does your family do at a birthday party?* Ask a child to answer the question. Record the answer next to the question.

GUIDE PRACTICE Have children use each other as school sources by pairing up to ask each other one of the inquiry questions. Compile their information. Explain that tomorrow they will review their topic and make sure all of their questions have been answered.

Topic: Family Celebrations Are Special

Question	Answer
What does your family do at a birthday party?	We break a piñata.

Access for All

SI Strategic Intervention

Taking Notes Give children practice in taking interview notes by responding to a few questions and allowing them time to record your answers. Explain that they do not have to record every word, just key words that tell the most important meaning.

Wrap Up Your Day!

✔ **Draw Conclusions** Why do you think Magda will continue to make her special tortillas?

✔ **Questioning** Have children tell why it is important to ask questions about the selection details as they read.

Preview DAY 4

Tell children that tomorrow they will hear poems about family celebrations.

DAY 4 at a Glance

- **Content Knowledge** Oral Vocabulary
- **Phonics** **Review** Abbreviations
- **High-Frequency Words** **Review**
- **Spelling** Final Syllables *-tion, -ture*
- **21st Century Skills** Online Directories
- **Fluency** Appropriate Phrasing
- **Conventions** Prepositions and Prepositional Phrases
- **Writing** Invitation Letter: Revise
- **Listening and Speaking** Listen to a Description
- **Research and Inquiry** Synthesize

Materials

- Student Edition
- Sing with Me Big Book
- Read Aloud Anthology
- Decodable Reader 28C
- Reader's and Writer's Notebook

Common Core State Standards

Speaking/Listening 2. Recount or describe key ideas or details from a text read aloud or information presented orally or through other media. **Language 6.** Use words and phrases acquired through conversations, reading and being read to, and responding to texts, including using adjectives and adverbs to describe (e.g., *When other kids are happy that makes me happy*).

Content Knowledge

Family Celebrations

EXPAND THE CONCEPT To reinforce concepts and to focus children's attention, have children sing "Family Tradition" from the *Sing with Me* Big Book. What do you think it means to be united like glue? (Family members stick together as one.)

Build Oral Language

REVIEW GENRE: POETRY Have children tell the key features of a poem: it is an imaginative piece of writing that expresses feelings. It is often arranged in lines that have rhythm and rhyme, and the patterns of the sounds have special importance. Explain that today you will read three poems about family celebrations: "Happy Birthday, Mother Dearest" by Jack Prelutsky, "Ode to Family Photographs" by Gary Soto, and "Seeing All My Family" by Claire Salama.

Poetry Selections

MONITOR LISTENING COMPREHENSION Recall the birthday celebration for Tía. Have children listen to the three poems.

Team Talk **TALK ABOUT FAMILY CELEBRATIONS** Read aloud the poem "Seeing All My Family" on page 155 of the *Read Aloud Anthology.* Display it on a whiteboard if possible, and track the print as you read.

- Have pairs of children describe the sights and sounds of one of their own family celebrations.
- Add words generated in the discussion to the concept chart.

Build Oral Vocabulary

Amazing Words Robust Vocabulary Routine

1. **Introduce the Word** Relate the word *brilliant* to the poem "Seeing All My Family." On special occasions the speaker's family is like a *brilliant* fireworks show. Supply a child-friendly definition. If something is *brilliant,* it is very bright and sparkling. Have children say the word.
2. **Demonstrate** Provide examples to show meaning. A diamond ring is *brilliant.* The colored lights at night are especially *brilliant.*
3. **Apply** Have children demonstrate their understanding. Name some things that are *brilliant.*
4. **Display the Word** Run your hand under the two chunks *bril-liant* as you read the word.

See p. OV•3 to teach *angle* and *snapshot.*

Routines Flip Chart

ADD TO THE CONCEPT CHART Discuss family celebrations and what makes them special.

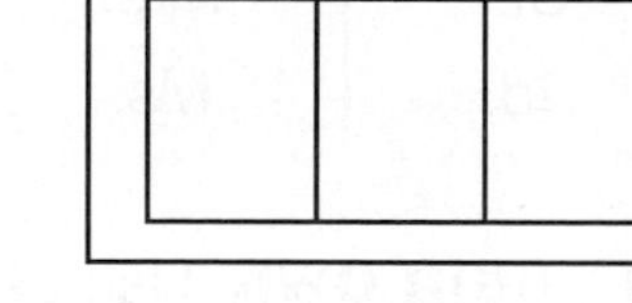

- What do the children do in "Happy Birthday, Mother Dearest"? (They make their mother a special birthday breakfast of strange foods.)
- What does the mother do in "Ode to Family Photographs"? (She takes bad funny pictures of the family.)
- How does the speaker in "Seeing All My Family" picture her family? (She compares each one to a special kind of firework.)
- What do all these poems have in common? (The family members are special in some way.) Let's add *We enjoy the special qualities of our family* under *Family Members Get Together* in our chart.

Amazing Words

celebration	inspect
custom	angle
tradition	brilliant
create	snapshot

Produce Oral Language Use the Day 4 instruction on ELL Poster 28 to extend and enrich language.

Preview Listening Read aloud a few short simple poems, clapping out the rhythm as you read and then having children clap along with you. Remind children that many poems have rhythm. Hearing the rhythm of the lines is part of the pleasure of listening to a poem and can help you understand the meaning.

Common Core State Standards

Foundational Skills 3. Know and apply grade-level phonics and word analysis skills in decoding words. **Foundational Skills 4.** Read with sufficient accuracy and fluency to support comprehension.

Name ____________ A Birthday Basket for Tía

Pick an abbreviation word from the box to replace the word in ( ). Write the word on the line.

1. We live on Maple (Avenue). Ave.
2. (Doctor) Moreno lives next to us. Dr.
3. (Mister) Chang lives in the house on our south side. Mr.
4. We will have a block party on (Wednesday). Wed.
5. The last party was on (September) 9, 2009. Sept.
6. We will also invite the people from Elm (Street). St.

Write each abbreviation correctly.

7. octob Oct. 8. Mrs Mrs.
9. Decem Dec. 10. Sat Sat.

School + Home **Home Activity** Your child learned the common abbreviations *Ave., Mr., Mrs., Dr., St.*, and abbreviations for days and months. Have your child use abbreviations to address some envelopes, using mail sent to you as models. Point out and read abbreviated days and months on letters or e-mailed messages.

Phonics Abbreviations Review DVD•313

Let's Practice It! TR DVD•313

Phonics

Review Abbreviations

REVIEW ABBREVIATIONS To review last week's phonics skill, write *Mr.* and *St.* You studied words like these last week. What kind of words are they? (They are abbreviations.) How do you know they are abbreviations? (They are shortened forms of words. They begin with a capital letter and end with a period.) How do you read abbreviations? (You read them as if all the letters are there.)

Corrective feedback | If children are unable to answer the questions about abbreviations, refer them to Sound-Spelling Card 107.

GUIDE PRACTICE Write *Address, Title, Month,* and *Day* as heads in a four-column chart. I will write some abbreviations. Read each abbreviation in your head. Then say *address* if the abbreviation might be part of an address. Say *title* if the abbreviation is a title. Say *month* if the abbreviation names a month. Say *day* if the abbreviation names a day. Write: *Mr., Sun., Ave., Mrs., Jan., Oct., St., Mon., Aug., Rd., Wed., Ms.* As children respond, write each abbreviation in the appropriate column. Then have children read the columns of abbreviations.

Address	Title	Month	Day
Ave.	Mr.	Jan.	Sun.
St.	Mrs.	Oct.	Mon.
Rd.	Ms.	Aug.	Wed.

ON THEIR OWN Use Let's Practice It!, p. 313 on the *Teacher Resources DVD-ROM.*

Fluent Word Reading

Spiral Review

READ WORDS IN ISOLATION Display these words. Tell children that they combine word parts for some words on this list and others are Word Wall words.

Have children read the list three or four times until they can read at the rate of two to three seconds per word.

can't	**been**	**picture**	**it's**	**believe**
mention	**action**	**future**	**caught**	**I'd**
haven't	**we'll**	**motion**	**finally**	**millions**
didn't	**whatever**	**station**	**vacation**	**tomorrow**

Corrective feedback
Word Reading

If... children have difficulty reading whole words,
then... have them combine word parts for decodable words or have them say and spell high-frequency words.

If... children cannot read fluently at a rate of two to three seconds per word,
then... have pairs practice the list until they can read it fluently.

READ WORDS IN CONTEXT Display these sentences. Call on individuals to read a sentence. Then randomly point to review words and have children read them. To help you monitor word reading, high-frequency words are underlined and decodable words are italicized.

I *can't* <u>believe</u> we *haven't* <u>caught</u> a fish on this *vacation*.

Didn't* I *mention* that *it's* <u>finally</u> time to go to the *station?

<u>Whatever</u> will happen in the *future? I'd* pay *millions* to know!

<u>Tomorrow</u> *we'll* see the *action motion picture* I have <u>been</u> waiting to see.

Corrective feedback
Sentence Reading

If... children are unable to read an underlined high-frequency word,
then... read the word for them and spell it, having them echo you.

If... children have difficulty reading an italicized decodable word,
then... guide them in combining word parts.

Access for All

A Advanced

Related Ending Write these words: *mission, vision, mansion, television, tension, confusion.* Point out that the spelling pattern *-sion* forms a syllable at the end of the word. Read and explain the words. Have children use the words in sentences. Then have them list other words ending in *-sion.*

Spiral Review

These activities review

- your previously taught high-frequency words *been, believe, caught, finally, tomorrow, whatever.*
- final syllables *-tion, -ture, -ion.*
- contractions.

Fluent Word Reading Have children listen to a more fluent reader model the words or have pairs read the words together.

Common Core State Standards

Foundational Skills 3. Know and apply grade-level phonics and word analysis skills in decoding words.

Decodable Reader 28C

If children need help, then...

Read *Action at the Game*

DECODE WORDS IN ISOLATION Have children turn to page 227 in *Decodable Practice Readers* 2.2 and decode each word.

READ HIGH-FREQUENCY WORDS Have children identify and read the high-frequency words *left, found, section, nation, action, team,* and *ball* on the first page.

PREVIEW Have children read the title and preview the story. Tell them they will read words with syllables *-tion* and *-ture.*

DECODE WORDS IN CONTEXT Pair children for reading and listen carefully as they decode. One child begins. Children read the entire story, switching readers after each page. Partners reread the story. This time the other child begins.

Decodable Practice Reader 28C

Action at the Game

Written by Kelley Fulsom

Final Syllables *-tion, -ture*

station section caution nation mentioned
action motion captured picture future

High-Frequency Words

left found section
nation action team
ball

227

Decodable Practice Reader 28C

My sister is taking me
to my first football game.
I can hardly wait!

228

We left the station
and walked to the school.
We found our seats
in the lower section.

229

"Why do those players have on
such big shirts?" I asked.
"There are pads under them," my
sister replied. "The players must use
caution so that they don't get hurt."

230

"This team is one of the best
in the nation," my sister mentioned.
I can tell that she is proud
of her school's team.

231

We saw lots of action
in this game.
It was hard to see it all
because the motion was so fast.

232

We saw action in the stands too.
Fans clapped and yelled for each
team. When our team captured the
ball and won, my sister jumped up
and hugged me.

233

We took a picture
with the winning players.
When I see that picture in the
future, it will remind me of the fun
we had.

234

Corrective feedback

If... children have difficulty decoding a word,
then... refer them to the Sound-Spelling Cards to identify sounds in a decodable word; prompt them to blend the word. If the word has a syllable with *-tion* or *-ture,* have them identify the word parts and read them together to say the word.

- What is the new word?
- Is the new word a word you know?
- Does it make sense in the story?

CHECK DECODING AND COMPREHENSION Have children retell the story to include characters, setting, and events. Then have children find words that include final syllables *-tion* and *-ture.* Children should supply the following words:

-tion: *station, section, caution, nation, mentioned, action, motion*

-ture: *captured picture, future*

Reread for Fluency

REREAD DECODABLE READER Have children reread Decodable Practice Reader 28C to develop automaticity decoding words with final syllables *-tion* and *-ture.*

Routine Oral Rereading

1. **Read** Have children read the entire book orally.
2. **Reread** To achieve optimal fluency, children should reread the text three or four times.
3. **Corrective Feedback** Listen as children read. Provide corrective feedback regarding their fluency and decoding.

Routines Flip Chart

Leveled Support

Beginning Before children read, preview the illustrations of *Action at the Game.* Write words with syllables *-tion* and *-ture* from the story, and say each word aloud, underlining *-tion* or *-ture.* Have children repeat the words with you.

Intermediate After reading, have children find words with final syllables *-tion* and *-ture.* Have them say the words and use each word in a sentence, for example: *I took a picture of a dog.*

Advanced After reading, have partners ask each other a question about the story, using words with final syllables *-tion* and *-ture,* such as *Where did the boy and his sister sit?* (in the lower section); *Whom did the boy take a picture with?* (the winning players)

Common Core State Standards

Language 2. Demonstrate command of the conventions of standard English capitalization, punctuation, and spelling when writing. **Informational Text 5.** Know and use various text features (e.g., captions, bold print, subheadings, glossaries, indexes, electronic menus, icons) to locate key facts or information in a text efficiently.

Spelling

Final Syllables *-tion, -ture*

PARTNER REVIEW Supply pairs of children with index cards on which the spelling words have been written. Have one child read a word while the other writes it. Then have children switch roles. Have them use the cards to check their spelling and correct any misspelled words.

ON THEIR OWN Use Let's Practice It!, p. 316 on the *Teacher Resources DVD-ROM.*

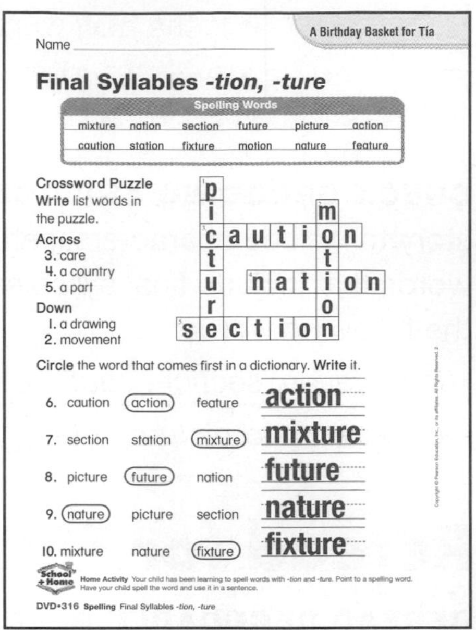

Name ____________ A Birthday Basket for Tia

Final Syllables *-tion, -ture*

Spelling Words					
mixture	nation	section	future	picture	action
caution	station	fixture	motion	nature	feature

Crossword Puzzle
Write list words in the puzzle.

Across
3. care
4. a country
5. a part

Down
1. a drawing
2. movement

Answers: 1. picture, 2. motion, 3. caution, 4. nation, 5. section

Circle the word that comes first in a dictionary. **Write** it.

6. caution (action) feature — action
7. section station (mixture) — mixture
8. picture (future) nation — future
9. (nature) picture section — nature
10. mixture nature (fixture) — fixture

School + Home: **Home Activity** Your child has been learning to spell words with -tion and -ture. Point to a spelling word. Have your child spell the word and use it in a sentence.

DVD•316 Spelling Final Syllables -tion, -ture

Let's Practice It! TR DVD•316

If... children need more scaffolding and practice with **Amazing Words, then...** use the routine on pp. xxxvi–xxxvii in the *ELL Handbook.*

Day 4 SMALL GROUP TIME • Differentiate Vocabulary, p. SG•35

OL On-Level
- **Develop** Language Using Amazing Words
- **Read** *Reading Street Sleuth,* pp. 72–73

SI Strategic Intervention
- **Review/Discuss** Amazing Words
- **Read** *Reading Street Sleuth,* pp. 72–73

A Advanced
- **Extend** Amazing Words and Selection Vocabulary
- **Read** *Reading Street Sleuth,* pp. 72–73
- **Organize** Inquiry Project

21st Century Skills

Online Directories

ACTIVATE PRIOR KNOWLEDGE Ask children to think about the selection *A Birthday Basket for Tía.* Ask what the family did to celebrate Tía's birthday. (Cecilia gave her a present. They had a piñata and balloons. They listened to music and danced.)

PREVIEW AND PREDICT Have children turn to page 452 in their Student Edition. Read the sidebar information on online directories and the title "Family Traditions: Birthdays." Have children look through the selection and predict what they might learn. (Children might say they will learn how people celebrate birthdays or how to find out about birthdays on the Internet.) Ask children what clues helped them make their predictions. (the selection title or the headings on the Web sites)

USE AN ONLINE DIRECTORY Tell children that they will read about how to use an online directory. An **online directory** is a **Web site** that people use to get information about a topic quickly and easily on the **Internet.** The directory lists links to other Web sites with information on the topic. The **links** are underlined words and phrases that a person can click on to make another Web site appear on the screen.

Academic Vocabulary 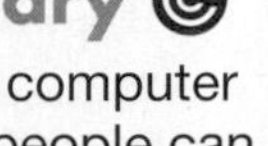

Internet an extremely large computer network. With the Internet, people can exchange information and messages around the world.

links areas on a Web page that you can click on to take you to another page or to a different area on the same page. Also called *hyperlinks.*

online directory Internet site that lists links to many other Web sites and is used to get information about a topic

Web site a place on the Internet where information can be found

Student Edition, pp. 452–453

Common Core State Standards

Informational Text 5. Know and use various text features (e.g., captions, bold print, subheadings, glossaries, indexes, electronic menus, icons) to locate key facts or information in a text efficiently. **Speaking/Listening 1.c.** Ask for clarification and further explanation as needed about the topics and texts under discussion.

Access Text

Think Aloud **QUESTIONING** Remind children that good readers ask themselves questions before, during, and after reading. Then they look for answers in the text. Suppose I look at page 453 and see *Celebrations* on one screen and *Birthdays* on the next. I ask myself, "If I was using this online directory, how would I get from Celebrations to Birthdays?" I keep that question in mind as I read. When I read the text in the yellow box, I find the answer: I would choose the word *Celebrations* and click on it.

Think Aloud **21ST CENTURY SKILLS** I know that "click on" means to move the mouse until the cursor on the screen is over the link and then press the left button on the mouse. The link on this page is underlined; sometimes links are in a different color so that you can recognize them. Look at the bar at the top of the screen. What commands do you see? (File, Edit, View, Favorites, Tools, Help) What command would show you a list of Web sites that you visit often? (Favorites)

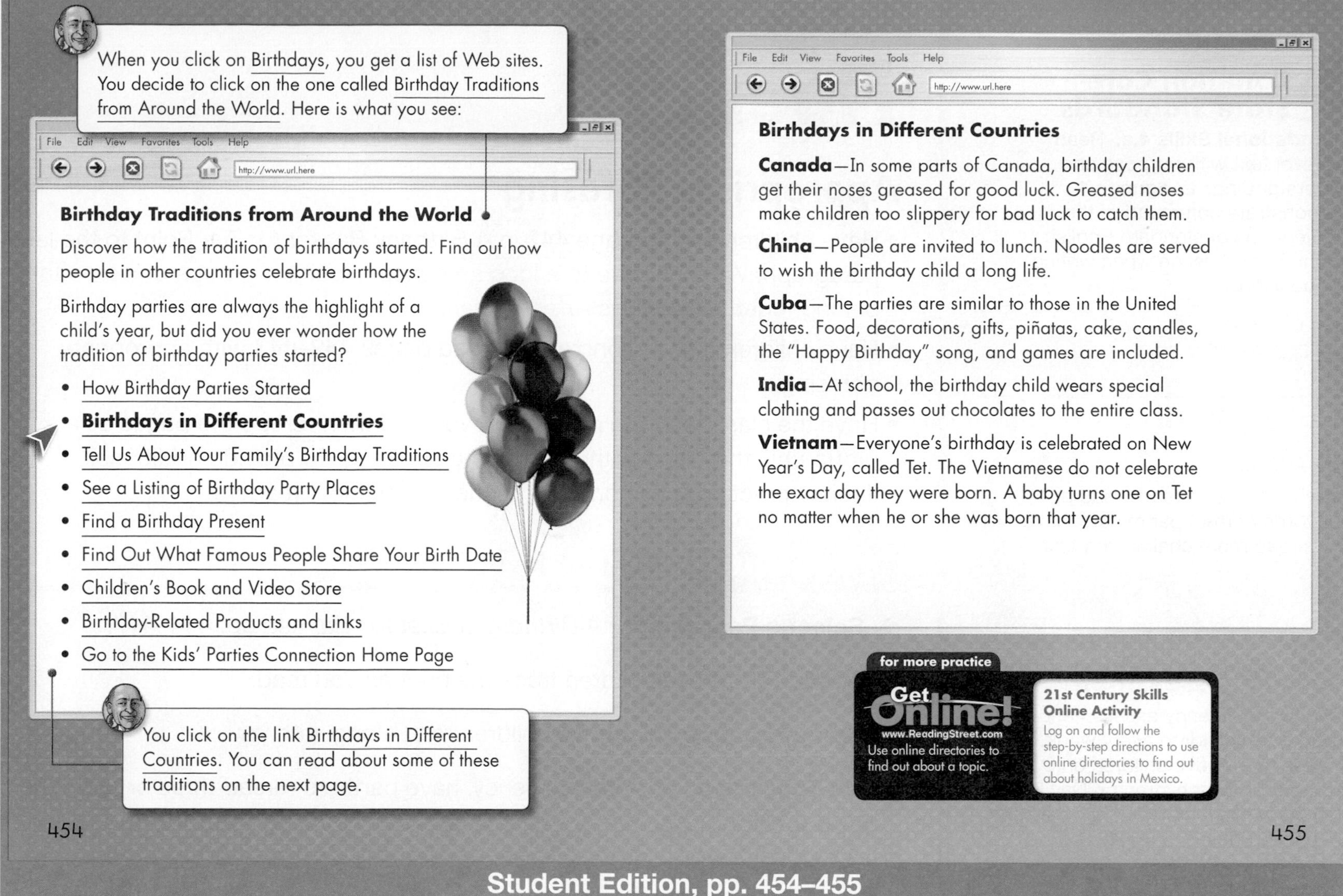

Student Edition, pp. 454–455

DRAW CONCLUSIONS What would you probably have to do if you clicked on the link *Find Out What Famous People Share Your Birth Date?* (You would probably have to enter your birth date and then click to find out which famous people were born on the same day.)

QUESTIONING What question might you ask yourself as you see the link *Birthdays in Different Countries* on page 454? (Children might ask this question: What countries are discussed on that Web site?) What would you do to answer that question? (Read on to find the list of countries on the next page.)

GET ONLINE! Begin the activity by logging on to the site listed in the Student Edition. Have children follow the directions to search for Internet sites in a protected environment.

Common Core State Standards

Foundational Skills 4.a. Read on-level text with purpose and understanding. **Language 1.** Demonstrate command of the conventions of standard English grammar and usage when writing or speaking.

Access for All

 Advanced

Rate If children already read at 90 words correct per minute, have them read more challenging text.

Fluency Assessment Plan

Do a formal fluency assessment with eight to ten children every week. Assess four or five children on Day 4 and four or five children on Day 5. Use the reproducible fluency passage, Teacher's Edition, p. 457f.

Options for Oral Rereading

Use *A Birthday Basket for Tía* or one of this week's Decodable Practice Readers.

Fluency

Appropriate Phrasing

- Have children turn to page 442 in *A Birthday Basket for Tía.* Point to the last paragraph. When I come to a long sentence, I look for groups of words that belong together, such as *After my nap.*
- Have children follow along as you read pages 442–443 with appropriate phrasing.
- Have the class read the pages with you and then reread the pages as a group until they read with appropriate phrasing. To provide additional fluency practice, pair nonfluent readers with fluent readers.

Routine Paired Reading

1. **Select a Passage** For *A Birthday Basket for Tía,* use pp. 444–447.
2. **Model** First, have children track the print as you read.
3. **Guide Practice** Then have children read along with you.
4. **On Their Own** For optimal fluency, have partners reread three or four times.

Routines Flip Chart

Fluency Check

As children reread with a partner, monitor their progress toward their individual fluency goals. Current Goal: 80–90 words correct per minute. End-of-Year-Goal: 90 words correct per minute.

If... children cannot read fluently at a rate of 80–90 words correct per minute,
then... have children practice with text at their independent level.

Conventions

Prepositions and Prepositional Phrases

TEST PRACTICE Use *Reader's and Writer's Notebook,* p. 516 to help children understand identifying prepositions in test items. Recall that prepositions are used with a noun or a pronoun to connect them to another word and usually give information about place, direction, or time: I crawled *under* the covers. Model identifying prepositions by writing this sentence on the board, reading it aloud, and underlining the preposition twice and the prepositional phrase once.

Juan's father is from Mexico.

Then read the *Reader's and Writer's Notebook,* p. 516 directions. Guide children as they mark the answer for number 1.

ON THEIR OWN Use *Reader's and Writer's Notebook,* p. 516.

APPLY After children mark the answers to numbers 1–6, review the correct choices aloud, and have children point out the prepositions and the prepositional phrases in each sentence.

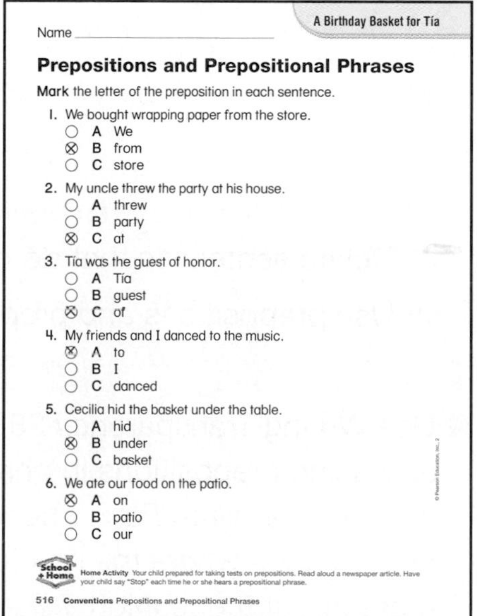

Name ____________ A Birthday Basket for Tía

Prepositions and Prepositional Phrases

Mark the letter of the preposition in each sentence.

1. We bought wrapping paper from the store.
   - ○ A We
   - ⊗ B from
   - ○ C store
2. My uncle threw the party at his house.
   - ○ A threw
   - ○ B party
   - ⊗ C at
3. Tía was the guest of honor.
   - ○ A Tía
   - ○ B guest
   - ⊗ C of
4. My friends and I danced to the music.
   - ⊗ A to
   - ○ B I
   - ○ C danced
5. Cecilia hid the basket under the table.
   - ○ A hid
   - ⊗ B under
   - ○ C basket
6. We ate our food on the patio.
   - ⊗ A on
   - ○ B patio
   - ○ C our

School + Home **Home Activity** Your child prepared for taking tests on prepositions. Read aloud a newspaper article. Have your child say "Stop" each time he or she hears a prepositional phrase.

© Pearson Education, Inc., 2

516 **Conventions** Prepositions and Prepositional Phrases

Reader's and Writer's Notebook, p. 516

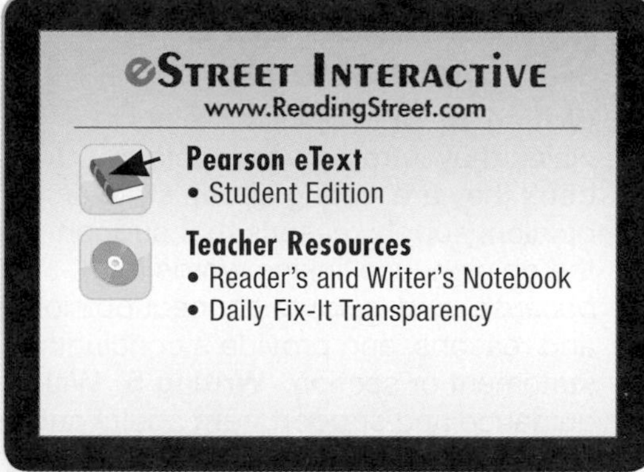

Bridge to Common Core

CONVENTIONS OF STANDARD ENGLISH

As children identify, form, and use prepositional phrases, they are gaining control of the conventions of standard English. Your guidance will help them use prepositions in prepositional phrases effectively as they speak and write.

Daily Fix-It

7. my aunt gave me a presint.
   My aunt gave me a present.
8. i gave hir my piggy bank.
   I gave her my piggy bank.

Discuss the Daily Fix-It corrections with children. Review capitalization and the correct spelling for *present* and *her.*

Common Core State Standards

Writing 1. Write opinion pieces in which they introduce the topic or book they are writing about, state an opinion, supply reasons that support the opinion, use linking words (e.g., *because, and, also*) to connect opinion and reasons, and provide a concluding statement or section. **Writing 5.** With guidance and support from adults and peers, focus on a topic and strengthen writing as needed by revising and editing.

Writing

Zoom in on ©

Invitation Letter

Mini-Lesson Revise: Deleting Sentences

- Yesterday we wrote invitation letters. Today we will revise and look for ways to make the letters clearer. We will also look to see if all the details in the invitation letter tell about the event.

- Display the Revising Tips. Explain that revising is a time to make sure all the details tell about the event. Tomorrow children will proofread.

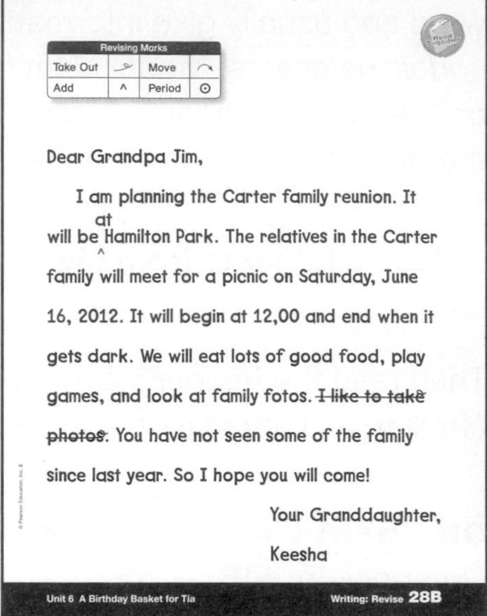

Revising Marks

Take Out	~~	Move	⌒
Add	^	Period	⊙

Dear Grandpa Jim,

I am planning the Carter family reunion. It will be ^at Hamilton Park. The relatives in the Carter family will meet for a picnic on Saturday, June 16, 2012. It will begin at 12,00 and end when it gets dark. We will eat lots of good food, play games, and look at family fotos. ~~I like to take photos~~. You have not seen some of the family since last year. So I hope you will come!

Your Granddaughter,
Keesha

Unit 6 A Birthday Basket for Tia — Writing: Revise 28B

Writing Transparency 28B TR DVD

Revising Tips

✔ Delete sentences that do not tell about the event.

✔ Use prepositions and prepositional phrases correctly.

- Use Writing Transparency 28B to model deleting unnecessary sentences and using prepositions in phrases correctly. Look at the second sentence: *It will be Hamilton Park.* I need the preposition *at* to make sure Grandpa Jim understands where the reunion will be. Here is a sentence that does not tell more about the reunion: *I like to take photos.* I will remove it. Tell children to delete sentences that do not tell details about the event and to check that prepositions are used to make the details easy to understand.

PEER CONFERENCING • PEER REVISION Tell partners to trade their invitation letters. Allow a few minutes for children to read the letters. Then have the readers use one or two minutes to comment if there is a sentence that will persuade the reader to attend the event. Circulate to assist children planning to revise their invitation letters. As appropriate, suggest adding persuasive sentences and deleting unnecessary sentences.

GUIDE PRACTICE Have children revise their invitation letters. For those not sure how to revise, have children refer to the Revising Tips or the Key Features of an Invitation Letter.

Corrective feedback Circulate to monitor and confer with children as they write. Remind them that they will have time to proofread and edit tomorrow. Today they can make changes in event details or make sentences clearer. Help them understand the benefits of adding or changing words, especially prepositions. Encourage them to write a sentence that will persuade the reader to attend the event.

Routine Quick Write for Fluency

1. **Talk** Discuss issues that are important to the community such as park playgrounds or community gardens.
2. **Write** Have children write persuasive statements to encourage a community leader to speak to the class about an important issue.
3. **Share** Partners exchange and evaluate statements.

Routines Flip Chart

Access for All

SI Strategic Intervention

Deleting Sentences Remind children that at least one sentence should persuade the reader to come to the event. It is not a detail about the event, but it should stay in the letter because it is of interest to the reader.

Listening and Speaking

Listen to a Description

INTRODUCE Explain to children that *caring* is about being kind and helpful to others. When we care about others, we show that we are good citizens.

- A caring person helps others who are in need.
- A caring person is kind to others.
- A caring person thinks about the feelings of others.

TEACH Explain to children that when good speakers prepare descriptive presentations, they consider the age, gender, and interests of their audience. Knowing the audience helps a speaker choose words that enable listeners to better understand and appreciate what is said. For their part, good listeners should demonstrate the traits of an attentive, active listener.

When listening to a description, attentive, active listeners

- can retell the details or summarize the information.
- think about what is being said and ask questions or make comments.
- try to form a mental image of the object being described.

MODEL Use the passage below to model attentive, active listening.

When I listen to someone giving a description, I give him or her my undivided attention. I listen very carefully to what the speaker says and try to imagine in my mind what he or she is describing. If I am unclear about anything, I ask the speaker a question.

GUIDE PRACTICE Describe to the class a classroom item. Remind children to demonstrate caring by using the traits of attentive, active listeners. Allow children to ask questions for clarification. Then have children identify the object you described. Discuss which part of your description helped children figure out what the object was.

ON THEIR OWN Remind children that as they prepare to give an oral report, they will want to think about their audience—their classmates. Have children take out their report about a family tradition that they worked on last week. Divide the class into pairs. Have partners first discuss audience, in terms of age, gender, and interests. Then, have partners take turns reading their reports to each other. Listeners should ask questions and suggest descriptions that demonstrate caring.

Common Core State Standards

Speaking/Listening 1.a. Follow agreed-upon rules for discussions (e.g., gaining the floor in respectful ways, listening to others with care, speaking one at a time about the topics and texts under discussion). **Speaking/Listening 3.** Ask and answer questions about what a speaker says in order to clarify comprehension, gather additional information, or deepen understanding of a topic or issue.

Bridge to Common Core

PRESENTATION OF KNOWLEDGE/ IDEAS

As children prepare for and deliver an oral report to a classmate, they are learning to present their information in an appropriate style, adapt their speech to the communicative task, and demonstrate their command of formal English.

Research and Inquiry

Step 4 Synthesize

TEACH Tell children that the next step in their inquiry project is to review the topic to see if they have the information they set out to find or if their answers led to a different topic.

MODEL We planned to find out more about ways that family celebrations are special. Display the list of inquiry questions and the answers recorded during research. The question I asked was *What does your family do at a birthday party?* The answer was *We break a piñata.* That is a special activity, so we have answered the topic, and it does not need to change.

GUIDE PRACTICE Read the remaining inquiry questions and answers. After each answer is read, have partners discuss whether or not the answer provides information about why family celebrations are special. Note any new questions the children have and revise the original topic if necessary. Finally, tell children that tomorrow they will organize all the information in order to share it with others.

Access for All

 Strategic Intervention

New Questions If new questions have been raised, restate the questions in simplified terms. Then pair children and have them interview each other to answer them.

 Advanced

More Questions During Guide Practice, have partners note any additional questions they would like to ask concerning specific information the partner shared. Have them write questions to find out more about it and then conduct an interview.

Wrap Up Your Day!

- ✔ **Phonics** List words with final syllables *-tion, -ture,* and *-ion.* Have children read the words.
- ✔ **Fluency** Display the sentence *Sandy took a million pictures of creatures in action while on her vacation.* Have children read the sentence three or four times until they can do so fluently.

Preview DAY 5

Tell children that tomorrow they will hear the poetry about family celebrations again.

DAY 5 at a Glance

Content Knowledge
Oral Vocabulary

Phonics/Spelling
Review Final Syllables *-tion, -ture, -ion*

Text-Based Comprehension
Review Draw Conclusions

Selection Vocabulary
Review

Assessment
Phonics
Selection Vocabulary
Fluency
Comprehension

Conventions
Review Prepositions and Prepositional Phrases

Writing
Invitation Letter: Proofread

Research and Inquiry
Communicate

Materials

- Student Edition
- Read Aloud Anthology
- Weekly Test

Bridge to Common Core

INTEGRATION OF KNOWLEDGE/IDEAS
This week children have integrated content presented in diverse formats and analyzed how different texts address similar topics. They have developed knowledge about family celebrations to expand the unit concept of traditions.

Social Studies Knowledge Goals
Children have learned that family celebrations

- involve cultural traditions
- include certain activities
- include special foods

Content Knowledge

Family Celebrations

REVIEW CONCEPT This week we have read and listened to selections about family celebrations. Today you will listen again to "Seeing All My Family" to find out how the speaker feels about her family. Read the poem on page 155 of the *Read Aloud Anthology.*

- How do you think the speaker feels about family get-togethers? Why? (She enjoys them and thinks they're fun and lively because she describes each family member as a certain kind of firework.)

Poetry Selections

Build Oral Language

REVIEW AMAZING WORDS Orally review the meanings of this week's Amazing Words. Then display this week's concept chart. Have children use Amazing Words such as *celebration* and *custom,* as well as the chart, to answer the question, *Why are family celebrations special?*

Why are family celebrations special?

We Celebrate Special Events	Family Members Get Together	We do Special Activities
We celebrate the birth of a baby.	We dress up in special clothes.	We sometimes learn special things.
We celebrate birthdays.	People share special foods.	We take photos to save memories.
	We enjoy the special qualities of our family.	We share memories.
		We listen to music.

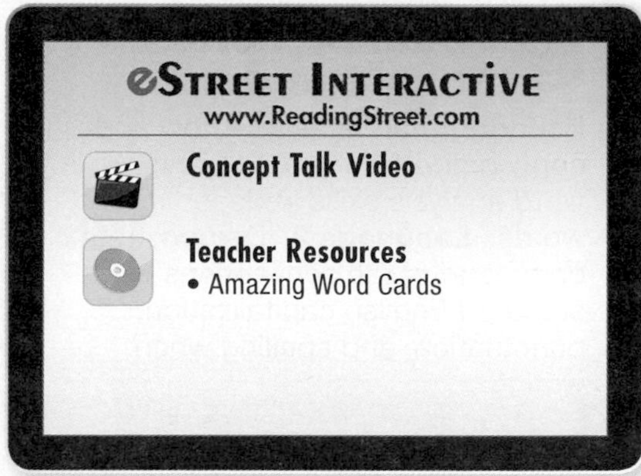

Build Oral Vocabulary

Team Talk **CONNECT TO AMAZING IDEAS** Pair children and have them discuss how the Question of the Week, *Why are family celebrations special?*, connects to the question of this unit of study: *Are traditions and celebrations important in our lives?* Tell children to use the chart and what they've learned from this week's discussions and reading selections to form an Amazing Idea—a realization or "big idea" about **traditions.** Use the following ideas as prompts:

- Why are celebrations important?
- What do family members celebrate together?
- What are some different ways people celebrate?

Then ask pairs to share their Amazing Idea with the class. Encourage children to recall in which selection they learned their ideas.

Amazing Ideas might include these key concepts:

- Celebrations bring families closer together.
- Families often celebrate events with food and music.

Amazing Words

celebration	inspect
custom	angle
tradition	brilliant
create	snapshot

Check Oral Vocabulary

FORMATIVE ASSESSMENT Call on individuals to use this week's Amazing Words to talk about family celebrations. Prompt discussion with the questions below. Monitor children's ability to use the Amazing Words and note which words children are unable to use.

- **What are some *traditions* at birthday *celebrations?***
- **Why are *customs* important?**
- **What things might you *create* for a family celebration?**
- **What might an adult *inspect* before a family celebration?**
- **What is something *brilliant* you might see at a family celebration?**
- **Why do we take *snapshots* at family gatherings?**

If... children have difficulty using the Amazing Words,

then... reteach the unknown words using the Robust Vocabulary Routines, pp. 427a, 432b, 448b, 452b.

Check Concepts and Language Use the Day 5 instruction on ELL Poster 28 to monitor children's understanding of the lesson concept.

Amazing Words As children answer each question, write their responses on the board and read them aloud to help English learners gain understanding from seeing and hearing the responses.

Common Core State Standards

Foundational Skills 3. Know and apply grade-level phonics and word analysis skills in decoding words. **Language 2.** Demonstrate command of the conventions of standard English capitalization, punctuation, and spelling when writing.

Phonics

Review Final Syllables *-tion, -ture, -ion*

Write the following sentences on the board. Have children read each one, first quietly to themselves and then aloud as you track the print.

1. **Use caution when you set the sculpture beside the furniture.**
2. **A vulture is a creature that no one likes to see or mention.**
3. **A million is just a fraction of a billion.**
4. **The hero in this fiction book rode off on his stallion to seek adventure.**

Team Talk Have children discuss with a partner which words have final syllables *-tion, -ture,* and *-ion.* Then call on individuals to share with the class.

Spelling Test

Final Syllables *-tion, -ture*

DICTATE SPELLING WORDS Say each word, read the sentence, repeat the word, and allow time for children to write the word.

1. nation	The **nation** watched the first moon landing.
2. section	You may read this **section** of the book.
3. future	I don't know what will happen in the **future.**
4. mixture	Let's make a bean **mixture** for the tacos.
5. caution	Use **caution** when you ride your bike.
6. motion	The rocking **motion** of a boat makes me ill.
7. feature	The **feature** movie begins in five minutes.
8. station	Aunt Susan works at the fire **station.**
9. picture	Look at the **picture** I took of you.
10. nature	It is fun to sit and look at **nature.**
11. action	Reid likes to play sports with lots of **action.**
12. fixture	Dad replaced the old light **fixture.**

High-Frequency Words

13. tomorrow	It is supposed to rain **tomorrow.**
14. piece	May I draw on this **piece** of paper?

Assess

- Spell words with final syllables *-tion, -ture.*
- Spell high-frequency words.

Access for All

SI Strategic Intervention

Check Spelling Have children choose the correct spelling of each word from three random spellings.

A Advanced

Extend Spelling Have children who have demonstrated proficiency in spelling individual words write a riddle for each word. For example, *I am the great outdoors. What am I?*

Day 5 SMALL GROUP TIME • Differentiate Reteaching, p. SG•35

OL On-Level

- **Develop** Prepositions and Prepositional Phrases
- **Reread** *Reading Street Sleuth,* pp. 72–73

SI Strategic Intervention

- **Review/Discuss** Prepositions and Prepositional Phrases
- **Reread** *Reading Street Sleuth,* pp. 72–73

A Advanced

- **Extend** Prepositions and Prepositional Phrases
- **Reread** *Reading Street Sleuth,* pp. 72–73
- **Communicate** Inquiry Project

If... children need more scaffolding and practice with **Conventions and Writing,**
then... use the Grammar Transition Lessons on pp. 310–385 in the *ELL Handbook.*

Vocabulary

Words from Other Languages

Context Clues Sometimes stories and articles have words that come from other languages. You can use the context around the word to determine its meaning.

Practice It! Find these words in *A Birthday Basket for Tía*. Use the context to determine their relevant meaning. Write a sentence with each word.

bizcochos **hierbabuena**
piñata **feliz cumpleaños**

Fluency

Appropriate Phrasing

When reading, look for groups of words that go together. Commas and periods often show how words are grouped. Be sure you understand what you're reading.

Practice It! Read the text aloud to a partner.

Yesterday, I took my dog for a walk to the dog park. When we came to the big pond, I let him play in the water. He jumped into the water and swam. Then he shook himself off, and we left.

Listening and Speaking

Get Ready For Grade 3: Think about your listeners' interests when preparing a descriptive report.

Listen to a Description

Listen carefully to descriptions. When preparing a description for an oral report, remember your listeners. Think about their interests. Ask yourself, "What will they like to hear?" Use sensory words in the description. Tell how something looks, feels, sounds, and smells. Then your listeners can visualize what you are describing. Listen carefully when others give a report. Try to visualize what the speakers are describing.

Practice It! Plan a report to describe an object or a story. As you prepare your description, think of sensory words you can use. Also think of prepositions and prepositional phrases you can use. Then give your report to the class. Listen to the reports other students give. Visualize what they are describing.

Tips

- Use sensory words so listeners can visualize what you are describing.
- Speak clearly and at an appropriate pace so listeners can hear and understand you.

456 457

Student Edition, pp. 456–457

Common Core State Standards

Foundational Skills 4.a. Read on-level text with purpose and understanding. **Speaking/Listening 1.a.** Follow agreed-upon rules for discussions (e.g., gaining the floor in respectful ways, listening to others with care, speaking one at a time about the topics and texts under discussion). **Also Speaking/Listening 3. and Language 4.a., 5.a.**

Vocabulary

Words from Other Languages

TEACH Read and discuss the Vocabulary lesson on page 456. Explain that some words we read are from other languages. We can use the context to help determine meaning.

GUIDE PRACTICE Read the instructions for the Vocabulary Practice It! activity. Read the first word and then have children repeat after you.

I can find this word on page 439. Clues in the sentence tell me that *bizcochos* are sugar cookies.

ON THEIR OWN Have pairs continue saying and finding the words in the story, determining their meanings, and writing a sentence with each word.

Corrective feedback | Circulate around the room and listen as children determine meanings for the words. Provide assistance as needed.

Access for All

Strategic Intervention

Words from Other Languages Have children of differing abilities work in pairs to look up words from other languages. Each partner should then write a sentence with the word. Tell partners to exchange papers and read each other's sentence.

Fluency

Appropriate Phrasing

TEACH Read and discuss the Fluency instructions.

READ WORDS IN CONTEXT Give children a moment to look at the paragraph. Then have partners take turns reading it to each other with appropriate phrasing.

Listening and Speaking

Listen to a Description

TEACH Read the explanation of listening to a description together. Discuss how good speakers keep their listeners' interests in mind and use sensory words and prepositional phrases. Prepositional phrases, such as *in a brown basket* and *of scratchy cloth,* can help describe objects. Good listeners listen attentively and try to visualize what the speaker is describing.

ANALYZE Remind children that sensory words tell how something looks, feels, sounds, and smells and help listeners make a picture in their minds. I'm thinking of an object that is white, black, and round and hangs on the wall. Its face is smooth. It ticks as its hands move in a circle. What object am I describing? (a clock) Have volunteers use sensory words to describe a classroom object as classmates identify it.

INTRODUCE PROMPT Read the Practice It! prompt with the class. Have each child select an object to describe. Remind children to speak clearly and keep their classmates' interests in mind and use sensory words and prepositional phrases as they plan their oral presentations.

Team Talk Have children give their descriptive reports before the class. Encourage listeners to ask questions if they need clarification or would like additional information. After each report, discuss which sensory words and prepositional phrases were used that helped listeners visualize the object being described.

Listen to a Description

In addition to trying to visualize when listening to a descriptive report, children at Grade 3 should also be able to maintain attention when listening, listen for a specific purpose, make pertinent comments, and summarize what is heard.

Develop Descriptive Vocabulary Help children make a chart with appropriate headings and pictures for the object they chose for their descriptive report—*looks (eyes), feels (hand), sounds (ears), smells (nose),* and/or *tastes (mouth)*—and help them develop a list of sensory terms they can use in their descriptive presentations. Encourage them to listen carefully and ask the meanings of sensory terms they hear in their classmates' presentations but do not understand.

Common Core State Standards

Literature 1. Ask and answer such questions as *who, what, where, when, why,* and *how* to demonstrate understanding of key details in a text. **Literature 5.** Describe the overall structure of a story, including describing how the beginning introduces the story and the ending concludes the action.

Text-Based Comprehension

Review Draw Conclusions

Remember that we can think about clues from the text to understand what the author is telling us. What do we call thinking about facts and details and interpreting what we read? (drawing conclusions)

CHECK UNDERSTANDING Read aloud the following story and have children answer the questions that follow.

Rosa's heart was pounding. Her knees were shaking. She felt like she could not get enough air to breathe. Rosa was next in line to jump off the diving board at the pool. Katie had just jumped, and she made it look so easy. Rosa climbed the ladder and took a few shaky steps onto the board. She was about to turn back when she heard someone call her name. It was Katie, and she was swimming just beyond the board. "You can do it!" yelled Katie. "Jump, and we'll swim together to the other side." Rosa smiled, took a deep breath, and gave a shout as her feet left the board.

1. What conclusion might you draw from reading the opening sentences? (Rosa feels very scared.)
2. What conclusion might you draw about Rosa and Katie? (Rosa and Katie are good friends.)
3. Why do you think Rosa decides to jump? (Katie gives Rosa help by telling her she can do it and saying they will swim together to the other side.)

Vocabulary

Review Selection Vocabulary

SELECTION WORDS Review this week's selection words: *aunt, present, bank, basket, favorite,* and *collects.* Say a list of related words for one of the words, such as *gift* and *package (present).* Have children say the selection word that belongs with the other words in the list.

Corrective feedback	**If...** children cannot tell what the words mean, **then...** review the definitions on page 431a.

Genre

Review Realistic Fiction

REALISTIC FICTION Review with children that realistic fiction is not a story that actually happened, but it seems real, and it could happen in real life. Realistic fiction has a **setting** and a **plot.**

TEACH Remember that we identified the setting and plot of *A Birthday Basket for Tía,* and we compared and contrasted them with those of *The Night the Moon Fell.* That story is a myth. In a **myth,** things that could not happen in real life usually occur. Let's think again about the settings and plots of these two different kinds of stories by the same author. Display the graphic organizer from Day 2.

Topic: Settings and Plots

Alike:	Different:
Both take place during a short time period. Both involve a problem. Cecilia has to find a birthday present for Tía. Luna has to get back to her home in the sky.	*Birthday* takes place in a home. *Night* takes place in the sky and ocean. Cecilia solves her problem by herself. Luna needs the help of the fish.

Graphic Organizer 18

Think Aloud **MODEL** *A Birthday Basket for Tía* takes place in a home. That's a realistic setting. *The Night the Moon Fell* takes place in the sky and the ocean. These are real settings, but they are not realistic in the story because the moon and fish talk.

GUIDE PRACTICE Guide children in comparing and contrasting the plots.

- What was realistic about the way Cecilia solved her problem? (She found things that Tía loved.) How does the story end? (happily, with the family celebrating)
- What was not realistic about the way Luna solved her problem? (She needed the fish to roll all her pieces together and lift her into the sky.) How does the story end? (happily, with the fish staying with her)

ON THEIR OWN Have children identify other ways in which the settings and plots of the two stories are similar and different.

Access for All

SI Strategic Intervention

Comparing and Contrasting Setting and Plot If children have difficulty describing the similarities and differences between plots and settings, they might find it helpful to use a T-chart with the titles of the selections as headings. Have them list the setting and plot events of the selections side by side.

A Advanced

Comparing and Contrasting Setting and Plot Encourage children to choose two other stories they have read by the same author and compare and contrast the settings and plots.

Academic Vocabulary

plot the events that take place in a story

setting where and when a story takes place

myth a story that attempts to explain something in nature

Assessment

Monitor Progress

For a written assessment of final syllables *-tion, -ture, -ion* and drawing conclusions, use Weekly Test 28, pp. 163–168.

SENTENCE READING Use the following reproducible page to assess children's ability to read words in context. Call on children to read two sentences aloud. Start over with sentence one if necessary.

MONITOR PROGRESS Sentence Reading

If... children have trouble reading words with final syllables *-tion, -ture,* and *-ion,*
then... use the Reteach Lesson in *First Stop.*

FLUENCY Take a one-minute sample of children's oral reading. Have children read the fluency passage on p. 457f.

COMPREHENSION Have the child read the entire passage. (If the child has difficulty with the passage, you may read it aloud.) Then have the child draw a conclusion based on information in the passage.

MONITOR ACCURACY Have children monitor their accuracy by recording their scores using the Sentence Reading Chart and by recording the number of words read correctly per minute on their Fluency Progress Chart in *First Stop.*

MONITOR PROGRESS Fluency and Comprehension

If... a child does not achieve the fluency goal on the timed reading,
then... copy the passage and send it home with the child for additional fluency practice, or have the child practice with a fluent reader.

If... a child cannot draw a conclusion,
then... use the Reteach Lesson in *First Stop.*

Common Core State Standards

Foundational Skills 3. Know and apply grade-level phonics and word analysis skills in decoding words. **Foundational Skills 4.a.** Read on-level text with purpose and understanding.

Assess

- Words with Final Syllables *-tion, -ture, -ion*
- Fluency: Rate
- Draw Conclusions

Fluency Goals

Set individual fluency goals for children to enable them to reach the end-of-the-year goal.

- **Current Goal:** 80–90 WCPM
- **End-of-Year Goal:** 90 WCPM

Name ______________________________

Read the Sentences

1. I took a picture of my aunt at the station.
2. The basket held a collection of dollhouse furniture.
3. One section of the bank features paintings.
4. Use caution when moving your favorite fixture.
5. Jordan collects plastic action creatures.
6. Ella gave me a mixture of lotions for a present.
7. The painting did not capture my vision of our favorite waterfall.
8. My aunt has a section of land that is a pasture.
9. Jill collects stamps from nations where she vacations.
10. The present was a picture of a calm nature scene.

MONITOR PROGRESS

- **Final Syllables *-tion, -ture, -ion***
- **Selection Vocabulary**

Name ______________________________

Read the Story

Tim's Pictures

Tim likes to take pictures. His mother lets him use 10
her new camera if he is very careful. The camera lets 21
him look at the pictures right after he takes them. 31
If Tim does not like a photo, he can remove it. 42

Tim likes taking pictures of all creatures, large or 51
small. Sometimes he can capture the moment of an 60
animal in motion. These action pictures are great. 68
Once he got a picture of a bird with its wings out. 80

Of course, he must use caution. He never gets too 90
close to an animal that may sting or bite him. Once he 102
thought he was taking a picture of some ladybugs. 111
When he saw the photo, there was a snake under a 122
plant. That's one reason he must be careful. 130

Taking photos is what Tim likes to do. He collects 140
his pictures in a book. Now and then he looks at them 152
and thinks about his future. 157

MONITOR PROGRESS
- Check Fluency
- Draw Conclusions

Conventions

Review Prepositions and Prepositional Phrases

REVIEW Remind children that prepositions are used with a noun or a pronoun and another word to form a prepositional phrase and can show place, direction, or time. Have children give several examples of prepositions and prepositional phrases.

GUIDE PRACTICE Write the following poem. Have children read and identify the six prepositions and prepositional phrases that appear in the poem.

I am looking for my red hat.
It is not on my bed.
It is not under the table.
It is not in the shed.
It is not with my other hats.
Oops, it is on my head!

APPLY Write the following prepositions on the board. Have children say a sentence using each preposition in a prepositional phrase.

at	**on**
for	**to**
with	**in**

ON THEIR OWN Have children write a sentence using one of the prepositions listed above. Then have them underline the prepositional phrase in the sentence they wrote. Use Let's Practice It!, p. 318 on the *Teacher Resources DVD-ROM.*

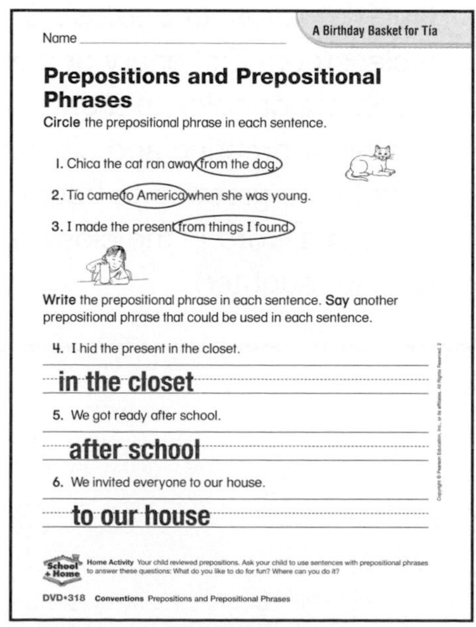

Name ______________ A Birthday Basket for Tía

Prepositions and Prepositional Phrases

Circle the prepositional phrase in each sentence.

1. Chica the cat ran away from the dog.
2. Tia came to America when she was young.
3. I made the present from things I found.

Write the prepositional phrase in each sentence. **Say** another prepositional phrase that could be used in each sentence.

4. I hid the present in the closet.
in the closet
5. We got ready after school.
after school
6. We invited everyone to our house.
to our house

Home Activity Your child reviewed prepositions. Ask your child to use sentences with prepositional phrases to answer these questions: What do you like to do for fun? Where can you do it?

DVD•318 **Conventions** Prepositions and Prepositional Phrases

Let's Practice It! TR DVD•318

Common Core State Standards

Foundational Skills 4.b. Read on-level text orally with accuracy, appropriate rate, and expression on successive readings. **Language 1.** Demonstrate command of the conventions of standard English grammar and usage when writing or speaking.

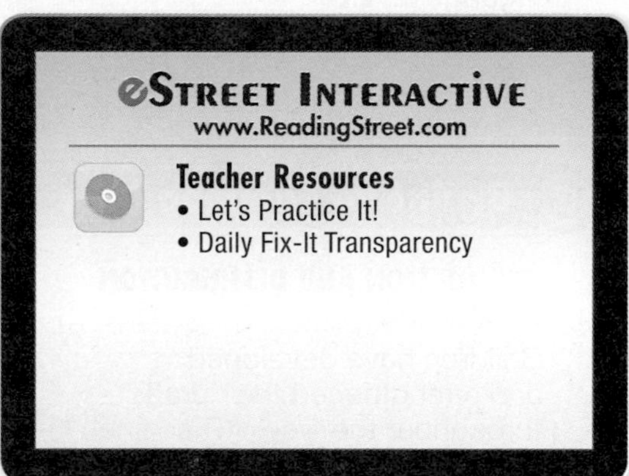

Daily Fix-It

9. that was my favurite present.
That was my favorite present.

10. i use a basket to collekt.
I use a basket to collect.

Discuss the Daily Fix-It corrections with children. Review sentence capitalization and the correct spelling of *favorite* and *collect.*

Common Core State Standards

Writing 5. With guidance and support from adults and peers, focus on a topic and strengthen writing as needed by revising and editing. **Writing 6.** With guidance and support from adults, use a variety of digital tools to produce and publish writing, including in collaboration with peers. **Language 2.e.** Consult reference materials, including beginning dictionaries, as needed to check and correct spellings. **Also Language 2., 2.b.**

Bridge to Common Core

PRODUCTION AND DISTRIBUTION OF WRITING

Children have developed and strengthened their drafts throughout the week. Their final well-structured drafts will reflect the changes they made to improve their invitation letters. Children type their letters on a computer and take them home to share with an audience of family members.

Writing

Zoom in on Ⓒ

Invitation Letter

REVIEW REVISING Remind children that yesterday they revised their invitation letters. They may have deleted sentences that did not tell more about the event. They checked prepositions, too. Today they will proofread their invitation letters.

Mini-Lesson Proofread

Proofread for Capital Letters

- **Teach** In our invitation letters, if we spell the words correctly, readers will know what words we mean. When we proofread, we check to make sure the words are correct. I can use our word lists or a dictionary to check them. Also, we are using a letter format, so I need to follow the rules of which words should and should not be capitalized in the greeting and closing and use commas after the greeting and closing. We have dates and times that use commas and colons, so I will pay attention to how I write them.

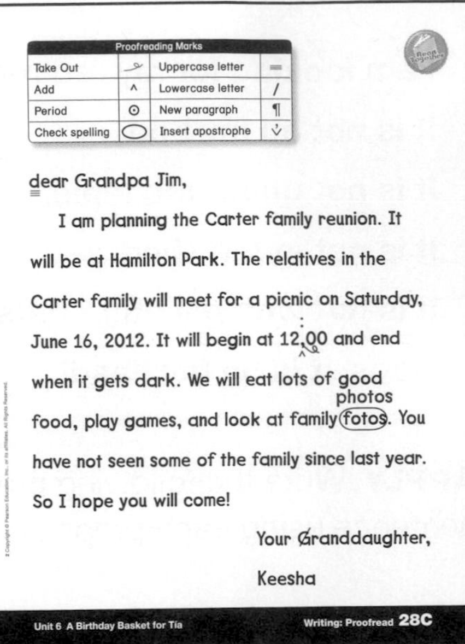

Proofreading Marks			
Take Out	⤼	Uppercase letter	≡
Add	^	Lowercase letter	/
Period	⊙	New paragraph	¶
Check spelling	◯	Insert apostrophe	✓

dear Grandpa Jim,

I am planning the Carter family reunion. It will be at Hamilton Park. The relatives in the Carter family will meet for a picnic on Saturday, June 16, 2012. It will begin at 12:00 and end when it gets dark. We will eat lots of good food, play games, and look at family photos fotos. You have not seen some of the family since last year. So I hope you will come!

Your Granddaughter,

Keesha

Unit 6 A Birthday Basket for Tia — Writing: Proofread 28C

Writing Transparency 28C TR DVD

- **Model** Let us look at my invitation letter about a family reunion. Display Writing Transparency 28C. Show how you would change any misspellings (such as *fotos* for *photos*). Quickly show how to check a word's spelling in a classroom dictionary or word list. Model how you would change or add a comma or colon in a date or time. Finally, review the format of words in a letter greeting and closing. Show how you would change the word *dear* in the greeting to begin with a capital letter. Show how you would change a word in the closing that should not begin with a capital letter. (Granddaughter)

PROOFREAD Display the Proofreading Tips. Have children proofread their invitation letters to correct any misspellings, missing capital letters, or errors with punctuation. Circulate to assist children with capitalization related to a letter format.

Proofreading Tips

- ✔ Are my words spelled correctly? Check a dictionary.
- ✔ Do I use a colon in times?
- ✔ Do I use a comma in dates?
- ✔ Do my greeting and closing follow the rules of a letter?

PRESENT Have children make a final draft of their letters, with their revisions and proofreading corrections. If possible, have children prepare the final draft using a computer word processing program. Help as appropriate. Choose an option for children to present their invitation letters.

They might prepare a neat copy of the letter and take it home to read aloud to the family.	They might type the letter on a computer. Once children print it out, they can add margin designs to make it look like stationary.

When children have finished writing their invitation letters, give them a copy of About My Writing, p. RR39 of the *Reader's and Writer's Notebook.* Then have children evaluate their writing by answering the questions on the page.

Routine Quick Write for Fluency

1. **Talk** Have partners take two minutes to think about an activity they will do with the family during the weekend.
2. **Write** Each child writes two sentences that give the details of the activity, including the day, date, and time.
3. **Share** Partners trade sentences and read them aloud.

Routines Flip Chart

Write Guy *by Jeff Anderson*

Focus Your Editing

In the editing process, children can get bogged down by everything that needs to be fixed. Editing one aspect at a time helps children focus their efforts and concentrate on one task, while making it easier for you as a teacher to fully explain and reteach the concept, moving children toward correctness. Sometimes less really is more.

Support Editing For children who are still unfamiliar with English conventions, look for gradual improvement over the course of the year. Help children recognize the differences in a period, colon, and comma.

Common Core State Standards

Speaking/Listening 2. Recount or describe key ideas or details from a text read aloud or information presented orally or through other media. **Speaking/Listening 3.** Ask and answer questions about what a speaker says in order to clarify comprehension, gather additional information, or deepen understanding of a topic or issue.

Research and Inquiry

Step 5 Communicate

TEACH Tell children that today they will organize information they found in the sources, create a Venn diagram that displays the information, and share the information with the class.

Think Aloud

MODEL Display the list of inquiry questions and the answers recorded during research. I was interested in the question *What does your family do at a birthday party?* The answer I found was *We break a piñata.* You are going to work with the partner you interviewed and think about how the celebrations in your families are alike and different. You will show the information on a Venn diagram. So on my Venn diagram, the celebrations are alike because the celebration is a birthday party. They are different because one family breaks a piñata, and another family plays Pin the Tail on the Donkey.

GUIDE PRACTICE Review the chart answers with children, and guide which ones should be circled because they identify ways family celebrations are special.

ON THEIR OWN Have partners choose a question and make a Venn diagram that shows how the celebrations are alike and different. Have children share their diagrams with the class. Remind them to be good speakers and listeners:

- Good speakers plan what they are going to say, especially if two people are speaking together.
- Good listeners remember the most important details so they can summarize the information for easier recall. They ask questions if something seems unclear.

Topic: Family Celebrations are Special

Question	Answer	Evidence to Change Topic
What does your family do at a birthday party?	We break a piñata.	No change. The answer gives us information about the topic.

Family Celebrations

Why are family celebrations special?

Think Aloud This week we explored family celebrations. In the selection *A Birthday Basket for Tía,* we read about a family birthday celebration for a ninety-year-old great-aunt. In "Family Traditions: Birthdays," we learned how to do Internet research on birthdays around the world.

Team Talk Have children discuss their Amazing Ideas about family celebrations with a partner. Then have children use these ideas to help them demonstrate their understanding of the Question of the Week, *Why are family celebrations special?*

Amazing Words

You've learned 008 words this week!

You've learned 225 words this year!

Next Week's Concept

Cowboys

What can we learn about cowboy traditions?

ELL

Poster Preview Prepare children for next week by using Week 4, ELL Poster 29. Read the Poster Talk-Through to introduce the concept and vocabulary. Ask children to identify and describe objects and actions in the art.

Selection Summary Send home the summary of *Cowboys* in English and the child's home language if available. Children can read the summary with family members.

Tell children that next week they will read about more traditions.

Preview Next Week

Assessment Checkpoints for the Week

Weekly Assessment

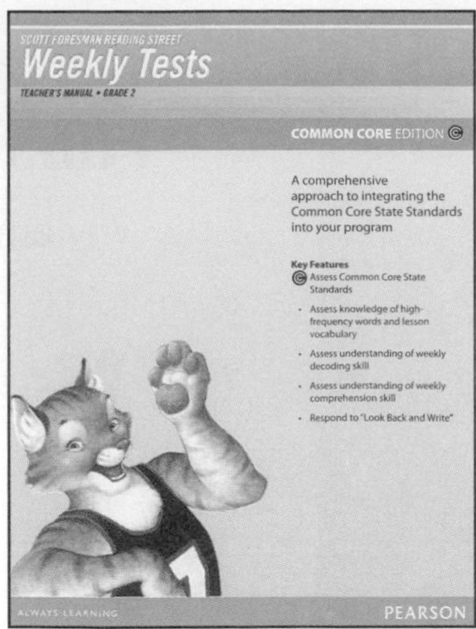

Weekly Tests

Use pp. 163–168 of *Weekly Tests* to check:

✔ **Phonics** Final Syllables *-tion, -ture, -ion*

✔ **Comprehension** Draw Conclusions

✔ **Selection Vocabulary**

aunt	**collects**
bank	**favorite**
basket	**present**

Differentiated Assessment

Fresh Reads for Fluency and Comprehension

Advanced

On-Level

Use pp. 163–168 of *Fresh Reads for Fluency and Comprehension* to check:

✔ **Comprehension** Draw Conclusions

✔ **Review Comprehension** Cause and Effect

✔ **Fluency** Words Correct Per Minute

Strategic Intervention

Fresh Reads for Fluency and Comprehension

Managing Assessment

Assessment Handbook

Use *Assessment Handbook* for:

✔ **Weekly Assessment Blackline Masters for Monitoring Progress**

✔ **Observation Checklists**

✔ **Record-Keeping Forms**

✔ **Portfolio Assessment**

DAY 1 Differentiate Phonics

- Final Syllables *-tion, -ture, -ion*
- Decodable Practice Reader
- Advanced Selection "A Naming Celebration"
- **Inquiry** Identify Questions

DAY 2 Differentiate Comprehension

- Selection Vocabulary
- **Access Text** Read *A Birthday Basket for Tía*
- **Inquiry** Investigate

DAY 3 Differentiate Close Reading

- Develop Vocabulary
- **Close Reading** Reread *A Birthday Basket for Tía*
- **Inquiry** Investigate

DAY 4 Differentiate Vocabulary

"Another Movie Night to Remember," pp. 72–73

- Amazing Words
- **Read** "Another Movie Night to Remember" or Leveled Readers
- **Inquiry** Organize

DAY 5 Differentiate Reteaching

- **Conventions** Pronouns
- **Read** "Another Movie Night to Remember" or Leveled Readers
- **Inquiry** Communicate

Teacher Guides and student pages can be found in the Leveled Reader Database.

Place English Language Learners in the groups that correspond to their reading abilities.
If... children need scaffolding and practice,
then... use the ELL notes on the instructional pages.

Independent Practice

Independent Practice Stations

See pp. 426h and 426i for Independent Stations.

Pearson Trade Book Library

See the Leveled Reader Database for Lesson Plans and student pages.

Reading Street Digital Path

Independent Practice Activities available in the Digital Path.

Independent Reading

See p. 426i for independent reading suggestions.

Common Core State Standards

Foundational Skills 3. Know and apply grade-level phonics and word analysis skills in decoding words. **Literature 1.** Ask and answer such questions as *who, what, where, when, why,* and *how* to demonstrate understanding of key details in a text. **Literature 10.** By the end of the year, read and comprehend literature, including stories and poetry, in the grades 2–3 text complexity band proficiently, with scaffolding as needed at the high end of the range.

1 Build Word Knowledge

Practice Phonics

FINAL SYLLABLES *-tion, -ture, -ion* Write the following words and have children practice reading them.

action	feature	cushion	moisture	nation

Spelling

FINAL SYLLABLES *-tion, -ture* Remind children that each spelling word ends in *-tion* or *-ture.* Clarify the pronunciation and meaning of each word. For example, say: Purple is a mixture of red and blue. Have children identify the final syllable endings in the words *nature, feature, picture* and *nation, section, caution.*

2 Read

Decodable Reader 28A *My Future*

HIGH-FREQUENCY WORDS Have children read the decodable reader. Then have them reread the text to develop automaticity. Have children return to the text and find the previously taught high-frequency words. Help children demonstrate their understanding of the words. Provide sentence frames such as: Her big _______ told me my aunt loved the present. (smile)

ELL

If... children need more scaffolding and practice with phonics, **then...** use the Phonics Transition Lessons on pp. 213–309 in the *ELL Handbook.*

On-Level

1 Build Word Knowledge

Practice Selection Vocabulary

aunt	bank	basket
collects	favorite	present

DEFINE IT Discuss the definition for the word *basket* with children. Ask: How would you describe a *basket* to a friend? (a container made of sticks or grasses) Continue with the remaining words.

Team Talk **TALK ABOUT IT** Have pairs use the selection words in sentences to internalize meaning. Ask: How can you pair the selection words together in a sentence? (Possible response: For my birthday present, my aunt gave me a bottle of my favorite perfume.) Allow time for children to play with the words and then share their sentences.

2 Read

A Birthday Basket for Tía

If you read *A Birthday Basket for Tía* during whole group time, then use the following instruction.

ACCESS TEXT Have children look at the pictures on pp. 436–437. Reread both pages.

- What fruit do you see in the picture that the author does not mention? (bananas)
- What does *secret* mean? (something not well-known; something you keep from others.)
- What other word gives you a clue that *secret* means something that you keep from others? *(surprise)*
- What secret are Cecilia and her mamá keeping? (They are having a surprise party for the great-aunt.)

If you are reading *A Birthday Basket for Tía* during small group time, then return to pp. 433a–447a to guide the reading.

SMALL GROUP TIME

Independent Reading Options

Trade Book Library

eStreet Interactive
www.ReadingStreet.com
Teacher's Guides available on the Leveled Reader Database.

On-Level

Common Core State Standards

Language 5.a. Identify real-life connections between words and their use (e.g., describe foods that are *spicy* or *juicy*). **Literature 1.** Ask and answer such questions as *who, what, where, when, why,* and *how* to demonstrate understanding of key details in a text. **Literature 10.** By the end of the year, read and comprehend literature, including stories and poetry, in the grades 2–3 text complexity band proficiently, with scaffolding as needed at the high end of the range.

1 Build Word Knowledge

Develop Vocabulary

REREAD FOR VOCABULARY Have children reread *A Birthday Basket for Tía,* pp. 444–445.

Read the following sentence and discuss words and phrases related to parties. *(birthday, surprise)*

It's your ninetieth birthday surprise party!

- What is a *surprise?* (something unexpected)
- What are some other words on these pages related to parties? *(shout, Happy Birthday, musicians, special)*

2 Read

A Birthday Basket for Tía

If you read *A Birthday Basket for Tía* during whole group time, then use the following instruction.

CLOSE READING Reread pp. 440–441. Have children summarize the ideas presented on these pages. Ask questions to guide deeper understanding.

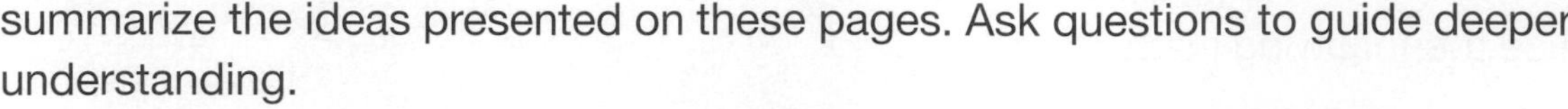

- What does Tía bring Cecilia when she is sick? (mint tea and cookies)
- What clues on this page show how much Tía loves Cecilia? (Tía brings Cecilia special things to eat and drink when she is sick, plays ball with Cecilia, tells Cecilia stories, and collects flowers for Cecilia's room.)
- What is special about all of the items that Cecilia is putting in the birthday basket for Tía? (They are all items that mean something special to the two of them. They are all things Cecilia and Tía share together.)

Have children read the following sentence from page 441: *I pick flowers to decorate Tía's basket.* Ask children to rewrite the sentence using an adjective to describe the flowers or the basket. (Possible response: I pick colorful flowers to decorate Tía's basket.)

If you are reading *A Birthday Basket for Tía* during small group time, then return to pp. 433a–447a to guide the reading.

If... children need more scaffolding and practice with the main selection, **then...** use the activities on p. DI•60 in the Teacher Resources section on SuccessNet.

On-Level

1 Build Word Knowledge

Practice Amazing Words

celebration	custom	tradition	create
inspect	angle	brilliant	snapshot

Team Talk **LANGUAGE DEVELOPMENT** Have children practice sentences. Display a sentence starter and have children add an oral phrase or clause using the Amazing Words. For example: It is a tradition in my family _______. (Possible response: It is a tradition in my family to have a big celebration when someone turns fifty.)

2 Text-Based Comprehension

READ ALOUD "Another Movie Night to Remember" Lead children in a choral reading of "Another Movie Night to Remember" from *Reading Street Sleuth* on pp. 72–73. Then have partners take turns reading the paragraphs of the selection.

ACCESS TEXT Guide children as they work on the Be a Sleuth section.

Look for Clues Reread the text with children. Explain that descriptions and actions can show a character's feelings. Have children write the clues that show the parents were not upset by the problems.

Ask Questions Tell children to think of a celebration that they have participated in. What was the occasion? What did you do? Then have children think about questions someone might ask them about the celebration.

Make Your Case Tell children to make a list of traditions and celebrations that are important to them. Have them write details that explain why each event is important. Allow children to use the list as they answer the Make Your Case question.

SMALL GROUP TIME

More Reading for Group Time

ON-LEVEL

Reviews
- Concept Vocabulary
- Draw Conclusions
- Questioning

Use this suggested Leveled Reader or other text at children's instructional level.

eSTREET INTERACTIVE
www.ReadingStreet.com

Use the Leveled Reader Database for lesson plans and student pages for *A World of Birthdays.*

On-Level

Common Core State Standards

Foundational Skills 3. Know and apply grade-level phonics and word analysis skills in decoding words. **Foundational Skills 4.** Read with sufficient accuracy and fluency to support comprehension. **Language 1.** Demonstrate command of the conventions of standard English grammar and usage when writing or speaking.

More Reading for Group Time

ON-LEVEL

Reviews
- Concept Vocabulary
- Draw Conclusions
- Questioning

Use this suggested Leveled Reader or other text at children's instructional level.

eSTREET INTERACTIVE
www.ReadingStreet.com

Use the Leveled Reader Database for lesson plans and student pages for *A World of Birthdays.*

1 Build Word Knowledge

Practice Prepositions and Prepositional Phrases

REVIEW If needed, revisit the conventions lesson on p. 447c.

IDENTIFY PREPOSITIONS AND PREPOSITIONAL PHRASES Have children turn to "Another Movie Night to Remember" to identify prepositions and prepositional phrases in the selection. Have them make a list of three prepositional phrases they find in the story, underlining the prepositions in each phrase. If necessary, distinguish infinitive phrases from prepositional phrases for children.

2 Text-Based Comprehension

REREAD "Another Movie Night to Remember" Have partners reread "Another Movie Night to Remember."

EXTEND UNDERSTANDING Discuss with children what makes holidays or celebrations important. Have children ask their parents or other family members to describe holiday activities they participated in when they were children. Then have a group discussion about family celebrations.

PERFORMANCE TASK • Prove It! Ask children to think of a short story about their family that they might one day want to share with their own children or other members of their family. You might suggest that they think of a special family celebration or some other fun memory. Have children write the story and draw a picture to accompany it.

COMMUNICATE Invite children to read their stories to the class. Have children mat the stories and pictures on construction paper and take the stories home to share with family members.

1 Build Word Knowledge

Reteach Phonics

FINAL SYLLABLES *-tion, -ture, -ion* Reteach the lesson on p. 428a, Final Syllables *-tion, -ture, -ion.* Use these additional practice words.

vacation **culture** **future** **affection** **scallion**

Then have children sort the following *-tion, -ture,* and *-ion* words and circle the letters that stand for those syllables.

section	**emission**	**mixture**	**caution**	**edition**
lotion	**feature**	**champion**	**sculpture**	**million**

2 Read

Decodable Reader 28A *My Future*

DECODE WORDS Have children practice reading the words listed on p. 217.

Corrective feedback **If...** children have difficulty reading the words independently, **then...** reteach the words prior to reading Decodable Reader 28A.

READ IN CONTEXT Have children take turns reading a page in *My Future.* Have them reread the text several times to ensure accuracy.

Corrective feedback **If...** children have difficulty reading the selection independently, **then...** model reading a page and have children echo you.

3 Reread for Fluency

Have children reread the text to develop automaticity in their reading.

SMALL GROUP TIME

If... children need more scaffolding and practice with phonics, **then...** use the Phonics Transition Lessons on pp. 213–309 in the *ELL Handbook.*

Common Core State Standards

Language 4.a. Use sentence-level context as a clue to the meaning of a word or phrase. **Literature 1.** Ask and answer such questions as *who, what, where, when, why,* and *how* to demonstrate understanding of key details in a text. **Literature 3.** Describe how characters in a story respond to major events and challenges.

1 Build Word Knowledge

Reteach Selection Vocabulary

aunt	bank	basket
collects	favorite	present

DEFINE IT Describe the word *aunt* to a friend. Restate the word in child-friendly terms. My *aunt* is the sister of my mom or dad. In the selection, they are celebrating the ninetieth birthday of Cecilia's great-aunt.

Team Talk **TALK ABOUT IT** Do you have an aunt? Turn and talk to your partner about this. Allow time for children to discuss. Rephrase their examples for usage when necessary or to correct misunderstandings. Continue with the remaining words.

Corrective feedback | **If...** children need more practice with selection vocabulary, **then...** use the *Envision It! Pictured Vocabulary Cards.*

2 Read

A Birthday Basket for Tía

If you read *A Birthday Basket for Tía* during whole group time, then use the instruction below.

ACCESS TEXT Have children look at the picture on pp. 444–445. Are the people having a good time? (yes) How can you tell? (They are smiling and dancing. There are people playing music.) Reread these pages.

- What do people say as Tía walks in? ("SURPRISE!") Why did the author put the word in all capital letters? (It shows that the word is being shouted.)
- What does *feliz cumpleaños* mean? (happy birthday) What clue does the author give to help you understand the Spanish words? (The author says the words in English right after the Spanish words.)

If you are reading *A Birthday Basket for Tía* during small group time, then return to pp. 433a–447a to guide the reading.

Corrective feedback | **If...** children have difficulty understanding the section, **then...** read the section aloud using the Access Text Notes.

Independent Reading Options

Trade Book Library

eSTREET INTERACTIVE
www.ReadingStreet.com

Teacher's Guides available on the Leveled Reader Database.

1 Build Word Knowledge

Develop Vocabulary

REREAD FOR VOCABULARY Have children reread p. 438 of *A Birthday Basket for Tía.* Let's read this text to find out what the word *present* means. To help children understand the word *present,* ask questions related to the context, such as: What does Cecilia decide to give Tía for her birthday? What are some customary things to give someone on his or her birthday?

Corrective feedback	**If...** children have difficulty understanding the word *present,* **then...** guide children to use online sources to find more information.

2 Read

A Birthday Basket for Tía

If you read *A Birthday Basket for Tía* during whole group time, then use the instruction below.

CLOSE READING Reread pp. 446–447. To help children understand what is going on in the selection, ask questions related to the context.

- What is in the basket at the end of the story? (Chica, the cat)
- How can you tell that Tía likes the basket? (She smiles. She dances with Cecilia.)
- How does Tía surprise Cecilia? (She dances without her cane.)

Corrective feedback	**If...** children have trouble answering questions about the text on pp. 446–447, **then...** reread the page and have them fill in sentence frames to summarize the ideas. **Tía is very _______ to get the present from Cecilia. She and Cecilia dance, and Tía doesn't even use her _______.**

If you are reading *A Birthday Basket for Tía* during small group time, then return to pp. 433a–447a to guide the reading.

If... children need scaffolding and practice with the main selection, **then...** use the activities on p. DI•60 in the Teacher Resources section on SuccessNet.

SMALL GROUP TIME

SI Strategic Intervention

Common Core State Standards

Language 1. Demonstrate command of the conventions of standard English grammar and usage when writing or speaking.

1 Build Word Knowledge

Review Amazing Words

celebration	custom	tradition	create
inspect	angle	brilliant	snapshot

Team Talk **LANGUAGE DEVELOPMENT** Help children practice building sentences. Display a sentence starter and have children add an oral phrase or clause using the Amazing Words. For example: Take a snapshot of _______. (Possible response: Take a snapshot of the big celebration.)

Corrective feedback | **If...** children have difficulty using Amazing Words orally, **then...** review the meaning of each of the words.

2 Text-Based Comprehension

READ ALOUD "Another Movie Night to Remember" Read aloud "Another Movie Night to Remember" from *Reading Street Sleuth* on pp. 72–73 as children follow along. Then lead a choral reading of the selection.

ACCESS TEXT Guide children as they work on the Be a Sleuth section.

Look for Clues Reread the last paragraph aloud. Ask, Is Dad angry that the girls burned the popcorn? How do you know? Tell children to look for other clues that show the parents were not upset about the problems.

Ask Questions Tell children to imagine a friend just went to a big family celebration. Ask, What questions would you ask your friend about the event? If children are having difficulty, prompt them with questions of your own.

Make Your Case Have children identify their favorite yearly tradition or celebration. Ask, Why are you most excited about this tradition or celebration? Have children share their responses with the class.

More Reading for Group Time

CONCEPT LITERACY

Practice
- Concept Words
- Selection Vocabulary

BELOW LEVEL

Review
- Draw Conclusions
- Questioning
- Selection Vocabulary

Use these suggested Leveled Readers or other text at children's instructional level.

eSTREET INTERACTIVE
www.ReadingStreet.com

Use the Leveled Reader Database for lesson plans and student pages for *Happy Birthday!* and *Special Chinese Birthdays.*

1 Build Word Knowledge

Review Prepositions and Prepositional Phrases

IDENTIFY Choral read the Conventions note at the bottom of page 451 with children to review using prepositions and prepositional phrases. Have children reread the model letter on p. 451 to find examples of how the author used prepositions and prepositional phrases. Allow time for children to discuss their examples and correct any misunderstandings.

2 Text-Based Comprehension

REREAD "Another Movie Night to Remember" Have partners reread "Another Movie Night to Remember."

EXTEND UNDERSTANDING With children, generate a list of special events or traditions that families celebrate. Provide an example of a special event your family celebrates, identifying the activities, people, and objects that help make the event important. Ask each child to describe an event his or her family celebrates.

PERFORMANCE TASK • Prove It! Ask children to think of a family story related to a special family celebration or some other fun memory. Help children write the story. Be sure they describe the event, identify the people who participated in it, and tell what made the event special.

COMMUNICATE Invite children to share their stories with group members. Then have children mat their stories on construction paper and take the stories home to share with their families.

SMALL GROUP TIME

More Reading for Group Time

CONCEPT LITERACY

Practice
- Concept Words
- Selection Vocabulary

BELOW LEVEL

Review
- Draw Conclusions
- Questioning
- Selection Vocabulary

Use these suggested Leveled Readers or other text at children's instructional level.

eSTREET INTERACTIVE
www.ReadingStreet.com

Use the Leveled Reader Database for lesson plans and student pages for *Happy Birthday!* and *Special Chinese Birthdays.*

Advanced

Common Core State Standards

Foundational Skills 3. Know and apply grade-level phonics and word analysis skills in decoding words. **Writing 8.** Recall information from experiences or gather information from provided sources to answer a question.

1 Build Word Knowledge

Extend Phonics

FINAL SYLLABLES *-tion, -ture, -ion* Have children practice with more complex words. Have them write the words in a list and sort by final syllables. Then have them use the words in sentences.

decision	mixture	traction	nature	furniture
ration	creature	motion	fission	adventure
station	delusion	tuition	billion	fracture

2 Read

"A Naming Celebration"

TEACH VOCABULARY Before reading, introduce the selection words: *celebration, tradition.* Help children determine the meaning of each word using these sentences:

1. They served delicious food at the holiday **celebration.**
2. Many weddings include the **tradition** of the bride and groom cutting a cake.

A Naming Celebration

What a lot of commotion there was at Della's house. Her newborn baby brother was wailing loudly for food. Her cousins Jacob and Ava were hurrying to make decorations and arrange the furniture. They were preparing for the big celebration when the baby would receive his name. The naming celebration was a tradition in Della's family.

"Della, your beautiful hair needs my attention. Come here so I can brush it," called Mama. As Mama wove long, shiny braids, she asked, "Della, what is your opinion about the baby's name?"

Della hoped to have adventures with her brother in the future. She had pictures in her imagination of how they would go on exciting explorations and discover sparkly rocks and other treasures!

"Christopher Columbus went on ocean explorations, and Michael Collins went on space explorations. My opinion is that the baby's name should be Christopher or Michael," Della declared.

After Della, Mama, and Papa had a conversation, they made the decision together. Della had permission to tell everyone the baby's real name. When it was time for the celebration, everyone circled around the baby's little bed. Della took a deep breath and said, "I want to make an important introduction. Meet my brother. His name is Christopher Michael."

Advanced Selection 28 Vocabulary: celebration, tradition

SMALL GROUP TIME

A Birthday Basket for Tía SG•47

READ Have children read "A Naming Celebration" silently. Then have children take turns reading aloud. After reading, have children recall the two most important ideas of the selection using details from the text.

3 Inquiry: Extend Concepts

IDENTIFY QUESTIONS Have children choose two traditions or customs to investigate. During the week, they should learn more about their choices from reading, studying pictures, and talking with adults or older children. On Day 5 they will share what they learned. Guide children in brainstorming possible choices.

- Think about your choices. In which countries are these traditions practiced? Do you practice them in your family?

If... children need practice with phonics,
then... use the Phonics Transition Lessons on pp. 213–309 in the *ELL Handbook.*

A Naming Celebration

What a lot of commotion there was at Della's house. Her newborn baby brother was wailing loudly for food. Her cousins Jacob and Ava were hurrying to make decorations and arrange the furniture. They were preparing for the big celebration when the baby would receive his name. The naming celebration was a tradition in Della's family.

"Della, your beautiful hair needs my attention. Come here so I can brush it," called Mama. As Mama wove long, shiny braids, she asked, "Della, what is your opinion about the baby's name?"

Della hoped to have adventures with her brother in the future. She had pictures in her imagination of how they would go on exciting explorations and discover sparkly rocks and other treasures!

"Christopher Columbus went on ocean explorations, and Michael Collins went on space explorations. My opinion is that the baby's name should be Christopher or Michael," Della declared.

After Della, Mama, and Papa had a conversation, they made the decision together. Della had permission to tell everyone the baby's real name. When it was time for the celebration, everyone circled around the baby's little bed. Della took a deep breath and said, "I want to make an important introduction. Meet my brother. His name is Christopher Michael."

Advanced Selection 28 **Vocabulary:** celebration, tradition

Common Core State Standards

Literature 1. Ask and answer such questions as *who, what, where, when, why,* and *how* to demonstrate understanding of key details in a text. **Literature 3.** Describe how characters in a selection respond to major events and challenges.

1 Build Word Knowledge

Extend Selection Vocabulary

Team Talk Have partners use the selection words in sentences to internalize their meanings. Have children use as many of the words as they can while making sure the sentence is grammatically correct. (Possible response: I deposited the check my aunt gave me for my birthday in the bank.)

aunt	bank	basket
collects	favorite	present

2 Read

A Birthday Basket for Tía

If you read *A Birthday Basket for Tía* during whole group time, then use the instruction below.

ACCESS TEXT Have children silently reread *A Birthday Basket for Tía,* retell the selection, and complete a plot map. (Beginning: Cecilia tries to think of a good gift for Tía on her ninetieth birthday. Middle: Cecilia collects things that are meaningful to her and Tía and puts them in a basket. End: Cecilia gives the basket to Tía. Tía is so pleased, she dances with Cecilia.)

DISCUSS GENRE Discuss what makes *A Birthday Basket for Tía* realistic fiction. Point out that the selection tells about made-up events that could happen in real life.

If you are reading *A Birthday Basket for Tía* during small group time, then return to pp. 433a–447a to guide the reading.

3 Inquiry: Extend Concepts

INVESTIGATE Guide children in choosing materials at their independent reading levels.

LOOK AHEAD Help children choose formats to present their information, such as illustrated posters, photographs, or three-dimensional displays.

Independent Reading Options

Trade Book Library

eSTREET INTERACTIVE
www.ReadingStreet.com

Teacher's Guides available on the Leveled Reader Database.

1 Build Word Knowledge

Develop Vocabulary

REREAD FOR VOCABULARY Have children reread *A Birthday Basket for Tía* and make a two-column chart. Have them list the Spanish words from the selection and their meaning in English.

Spanish Words	English Meaning
noventa años	ninety years
mamá	mom
tía	aunt
bizcochos	sugary cookies
hierbabuena	hot mint tea
¿que pasa?	What is this?
feliz cumpleaños	happy birthday

2 Read

A Birthday Basket for Tía

If you read *A Birthday Basket for Tía* during whole group time, then use the instruction below.

CLOSE READING Reread pp. 440–441. Explain that some relatives have special relationships. How do you know that Cecilia is special to Tía? (Tía does many things for her, such as cooking with her, bringing her treats, and playing ball with her.) What does Tía tell Cecilia about playing ball when she was young? (She says she played in Mexico as a girl. She says they wore long dresses and braided their hair.) Why do you think Tía tells Cecilia this story? (to share her youth)

If you are reading *A Birthday Basket for Tía* during small group time, then return to pp. 433a–447a to guide the reading.

3 Inquiry: Extend Concepts

INVESTIGATE Give children time to investigate their projects on traditions or customs by reading and studying pictures.

SMALL GROUP TIME

ELL

If... children need more scaffolding and practice with the main selection, **then...** use the activities on p. DI•60 in the Teacher Resources section on SuccessNet.

Common Core State Standards

Speaking/Listening 4. Tell a story or recount an experience with appropriate facts and relevant, descriptive details, speaking audibly in coherent sentences. **Language 1.** Demonstrate command of the conventions of standard English grammar and usage when writing or speaking.

1 Build Word Knowledge

Extend Amazing Words and Selection Vocabulary

celebration	inspect
custom	angle
tradition	brilliant
create	snapshot

aunt	bank
basket	collects
favorite	present

Team Talk Have children ask each other questions using the Amazing Words and the Selection Vocabulary, such as: What are some things people might collect in a basket?

2 Text-Based Comprehension

READ ALOUD "Another Movie Night to Remember" Have partners take turns reading paragraphs of "Another Movie Night to Remember" from *Reading Street Sleuth* on pp. 72–73. Then have children read the selection independently.

ACCESS TEXT Guide children as they work on the Be a Sleuth section.

Look for Clues Have children write the sentences that show how the parents reacted to the problems. Then have children look for clues showing that the children love their parents.

Ask Questions Have children think about what they would like to know about a particular celebration, such as a holiday or birthday celebration. Have them ask questions about that celebration.

Make Your Case Tell children to write a paragraph about a special celebration or tradition, explaining what makes the event special.

3 Inquiry: Extend Concepts

ORGANIZE INFORMATION Give children time to continue reading and preparing information. Provide any necessary materials, such as poster board, materials to create three-dimensional displays or models, and art supplies.

More Reading for Group Time

ADVANCED

- Extend Concept Vocabulary
- Review Target Skills

Use this suggested Leveled Reader or other text at children's instructional level.

eSTREET INTERACTIVE
www.ReadingStreet.com
Use the Leveled Reader Database for lesson plans and student pages for *Celebrations and Family Traditions.*

Advanced

1 Build Word Knowledge

Prepositions and Prepositional Phrases

PREPOSITIONS AND PREPOSITIONAL PHRASES Have children make a chart identifying prepositions and prepositional phrases in the selection "Another Movie Night to Remember." Then tell children to choose three of the prepositions and use them in sentences of their own.

2 Text-Based Comprehension

REREAD "Another Movie Night to Remember" Have partners reread "Another Movie Night to Remember."

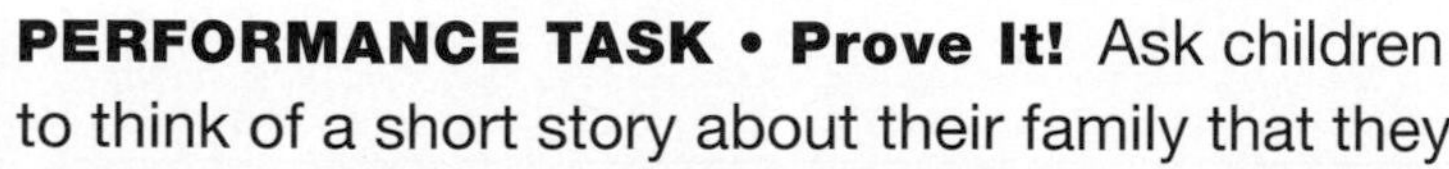

EXTEND UNDERSTANDING Encourage children to interview their parents about special events or traditions their families celebrated when they were children. Then hold a group discussion about ways past family celebrations are alike and different from those of today.

PERFORMANCE TASK • Prove It! Ask children to think of a short story about their family that they might one day want to share with their own children or other members of their family. Have children write the story and draw a picture to accompany it. Tell them to include dialogue and colorful descriptions in their stories.

COMMUNICATE Invite children to share their stories in small groups. Then have them mat the stories and pictures on construction paper and take the stories home to share with family members.

3 Inquiry: Extend Concepts

COMMUNICATE Have children share their inquiry projects about two different traditions or customs.

SMALL GROUP TIME

More Reading for Group Time

ADVANCED

- Extend Concept Vocabulary
- Review Target Skills

Use this suggested Leveled Reader or other text at children's instructional level.

eStreet Interactive
www.ReadingStreet.com

Use the Leveled Reader Database for lesson plans and student pages for *Celebrations and Family Traditions.*

TEACHER NOTES

Tennessee Common Core Edition 

This Week's Target Skills and Strategies

Target Skills and Strategies	Common Core State Standards for English Language Arts	Tennessee CUs and GLEs
Phonics and Spelling **Skill:** Suffixes *-ness, -less, -able, -ible*	**CCSS Foundational Skills 3.d.** Decode words with common prefixes and suffixes. **(Also CCSS Language 2.)**	**TN CU 0201.1.11** Apply phonics generalizations in order to decode words.
Text-Based Comprehension **Skill:** Sequence	**CCSS Informational Text 3.** Describe the connection between a series of historical events, scientific ideas or concepts, or steps in technical procedures in a text. **(Also CCSS Informational Text 1.)**	**TN CU 0201.5.4** Compare and contrast information and ideas.
Strategy: Text Structure	**CCSS Informational Text 3.** Describe the connection between a series of historical events, scientific ideas or concepts, or steps in technical procedures in a text. **(Also CCSS Informational Text 2.)**	**TN CU 0201.5.4** Compare and contrast information and ideas.
Vocabulary **Skill:** Unfamiliar Words **Strategy:** Context Clues	**CCSS Foundational Skills 4.c.** Use context to confirm or self-correct word recognition and understanding, rereading as necessary. **(Also CCSS Language 4., CCSS Language 4.a.)**	**TN GLE 0201.1.2** Employ a variety of strategies to decode words and expand vocabulary.
Fluency **Skill:** Accuracy and Appropriate Rate	**CCSS Foundational Skills 4.b.** Read on-level text orally with accuracy, appropriate rate, and expression on successive readings.	**TN CU 0201.8.9** Read orally with fluency and accuracy, using appropriate pacing and expression.
Listening and Speaking Identify Written Conventions	**CCSS Speaking/Listening 2.** Recount or describe key ideas or details from a text read aloud or information presented orally or through other media.	**TN CU 0201.2.4** Summarize what has been heard using the logical sequence of events. **(Also TN CU 0201.2.9, TN CU 0201.7.1)**
Six-Trait Writing **Trait of the Week:** Focus/Ideas	**CCSS Writing 2.** Write informative/explanatory texts in which they introduce a topic, use facts and definitions to develop points, and provide a concluding statement or section.	**TN CU 0201.3.1** Write to describe, entertain, and inform. **(Also TN GLE 0201.3.1, TN GLE 0201.3.3)**
Writing Compare-and-Contrast Text	**CCSS Writing 2.** Write informative/explanatory texts in which they introduce a topic, use facts and definitions to develop points, and provide a concluding statement or section. **(Also CCSS Writing 8.)**	**TN CU 0201.3.1** Write to describe, entertain, and inform. **(Also TN GLE 0201.3.1, TN GLE 0201.3.3)**
Conventions **Skill:** Commas	**CCSS Language 2.** Demonstrate command of the conventions of standard English capitalization, punctuation, and spelling when writing.	**TN GLE 0201.1.1** Demonstrate control of basic English usage, mechanics, spelling, and sentence structure.

Access for All to Differentiate Instruction

Reading Street Sleuth

Curtis the Cowboy Cook
pp. 74–75

Follow the path to close reading using the Super Sleuth tips:

- Look for Clues
- Ask Questions
- Make Your Case
- Prove it!

This Week's Optional Tennessee Readers Provide Informational Text

Concept Literacy

CCSS Informational Text 1.; TN CU 0201.8.6

Below Level

CCSS Literature 5.; TN CU 0201.8.10

On Level

CCSS Literature 5.; TN CU 0201.8.10

Advanced

CCSS Literature 5.; TN CU 0201.8.10

ELL

CCSS Informational Text 3.; TN CU 0201.5.4

ELD

CCSS Informational Text 3.; TN CU 0201.5.4

ISBN-13: 978-0-328-73472-6 ISBN-10: 0-328-73472-1

Assessment

Tennessee Assessment Resources for Common Core Test Success

Tennessee Daily Formative Assessment in Your Teacher's Edition

Baseline Group Tests

CCSS Weekly Tests, pp. 169–174

CCSS Fresh Reads, pp. 169–174

Unit 6 CCSS Benchmark Test

CCSS Success Tracker, ExamView, and Online Lesson Planner

RTI

Response to Intervention Kits
Increase Instruction and Progress Monitoring

Intensive Intervention
My Sidewalks
Level B, Unit 6, pp. 210–225

Writing, Grammar, and Spelling

Six-Trait Writing

- Focus/Ideas
  Trait of the Week
  CCSS Writing 2.
  TN CU 0201.3.1
- Organization/Paragraphs
- Voice
- Word Choice
- Sentences
- Conventions

Resources for Six-Trait Writing, Grammar, and Spelling

Reader's and Writer's Notebook
- Practice Reading
- Practice Grammar
- Practice Spelling
- Practice Writing

Writing Rubrics and Anchor Papers

Digital Resources
- Online Journal
- Online Writing Transparencies
- Grammar Jammer

Teacher Resources DVD-ROM
- Reader's and Writer's Notebook
- Let's Practice It!
- Graphic Organizers
- Writing Transparencies

Grade 2 Skills Trace

Skills and Strategies	Looking Back	This Week's Selection	Looking Ahead
Phonics and Spelling **Skill:** Suffixes *-ness, -less, -able, -ible*	**Unit 5** 192a, 192–193, 193a, 193c–193d, 195a	460a, 460–461, 461a, 461c–461d, 464c, 488c, 488d, 492d, 492e–492f, 494c, 495e	**Unit 6** 495e
Text-Based Comprehension **Skill:** Sequence	**Unit 3** 457a–457b, 458h, 464–465 **Unit 4** 58a, 58–59, 62a, 66–67	462a, 462–463, 466a, 468–469, 472–473, 476–477, 480–481, 484–485, 486–487, 489a, 495b, 495f	Grade 3 **Units 1, 5**
Strategy: Text Structure	**Unit 1** 58h, 62–63, 68–69 **Unit 2** 224h, 226–227, 230–231	466a, 470–471, 474–475, 478–479, 482–483, 484–485, 489a	Grade 3 **Units 2, 3**
Vocabulary **Skill:** Unfamiliar Words **Strategy:** Context Clues	**Unit 4** 126g, 126–127, 138–139, 144g, 153a	464g, 464–465, 476–477, 488g, 494–495	Grade 3 **Units 2, 3, 4, 5**
Fluency **Skill:** Accuracy and Appropriate Rate	**Unit 4** 42f, 51b, 53a **Unit 5** 248f, 253b, 255a, 255d	488f, 493b, 495a, 495d	Grade 3 **Units 1, 2, 3, 4, 5, 6**
Listening and Speaking Identify Written Conventions	Skill not previously taught	493f	Skill not subsequently taught
Six-Trait Writing **Trait of the Week:** Focus/Ideas	**Unit 3** 405d–405e, 408–409, 409a **Unit 4** 177c–177d, 180–181	487d–487e, 491a, 493d–493e	Grade 3 **Units 2, 4, 5**
Writing Compare-and-Contrast Text	Skill not previously taught	463c–463d, 487d–487e, 491a, 493d–493e, 495h–495i	Grade 3 **Unit 3**
Conventions **Skill:** Commas	Skill not previously taught	463b, 487c, 490a, 490–491, 493c, 495g	Grade 3 **Unit 6**

Tennessee Science and Social Studies Standards Taught During the Reading Lesson

TN CU 0207.5.2 Infer the characteristics needed by an organism to survive in a particular environment.
TN 2.3.02 Recognize the interaction between human and physical systems around the world.
TN 2.5.02.d Comprehend that physical and human characteristics of communities change over time.

Teaching the Common Core State Standards This Week

The Common Core State Standards for English Language Arts are divided into strands for **Reading** (including **Foundational Skills**), **Writing**, **Speaking and Listening**, and **Language**. The chart below shows some of the content you will teach this week, strand by strand. Turn to this week's 5-Day Planner on pages 458d–458e to see how this content is taught each day.

Reading Strand

- **Phonics:** Suffixes *-ness*, *-less*, *-able*, *-ible*
- **Text-Based Comprehension:** Sequence; Text Structure
- **Fluency:** Accuracy and Appropriate Rate
- **Literary Text:** Graphic Sources
- **Genre:** Main Selection: Informational Text; Paired Selection: Informational Text

Writing Strand

- **Writing Mini-Lesson:** Compare-and-Contrast Text
- **Trait:** Focus/Ideas
- **Look Back and Write:** Text Evidence

Common Core State Standards for English Language Arts

Speaking and Listening Strand

- **Content Knowledge:** Build Oral Language
- **Media Literacy:** Identify Written Conventions
- **Research and Inquiry**

Language Strand

- **Oral Vocabulary: Amazing Words** *climate*, *livestock*, *occupation*, *buckaroo*, *drover*, *lariat*, *legend*, *rawhide*
- **Vocabulary:** Unfamiliar Words; Context Clues
- **Selection Vocabulary:** *campfire*, *cattle*, *cowboy*, *galloped*, *herd*, *railroad*, *trails*
- **Academic Vocabulary:** *suffix, sequence, text structure, punctuation, comma, compare, contrast, text structure, schedule, source, main idea, details, informational text, author's message*
- **Conventions:** Commas
- **Spelling:** Suffixes *-ness*, *-less*, *-able*, *-ible*

Text-Based Comprehension

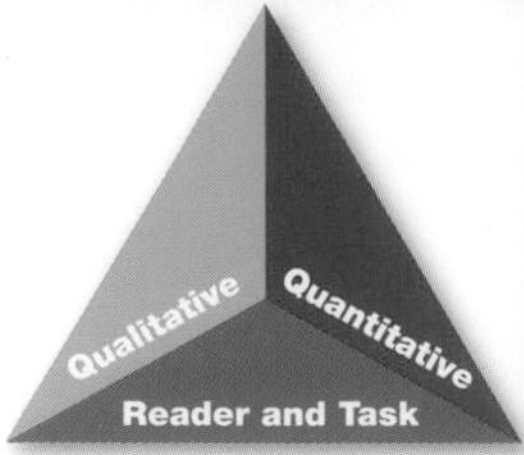

Text Complexity Measures

Use the rubric to familiarize yourself with the text complexity of ***Cowboys***.

Bridge to Complex Knowledge

Quantitative Measures	**Lexile**	630L
	Average Sentence Length	9.47
	Word Frequency	3.54

Qualitative Measures	**Levels of Meaning**	understand setting in informational text; information is factual with a clearly stated purpose
	Structure	simple, conventional structure; map
	Language Conventionality and Clarity	academic language; complex sentence structure
	Theme and Knowledge Demands	a basic knowledge of trail drives; experiences that are very different from one's own

Reader and Task Suggestions

FORMATIVE ASSESSMENT Based on assessment results, use the **Reader and Task Suggestions** in Access Main Selection to scaffold the selection or support independence for children as they read ***Cowboys***.

READER AND TASK SUGGESTIONS	
Preparing to Read the Text	**Leveled Tasks**
• Review strategies for understanding unfamiliar words. See the vocabulary skill lesson on p. 464g. • Point out the author's use of a map on pp. 486–487. • Remind children that this text is informational. They may need to read more slowly to better understand the text.	• **Language Conventionality and Clarity** If children have difficulty with complex sentence structure, have them identify confusing sentences and work with them to interpret meanings. • **Language Conventionality and Clarity** If children have no difficulty with complex sentence structure, have them identify and explain examples.

Recommended Placement Both the qualitative and quantitative measures suggest this text should be placed in the Grade 2–3 text complexity band, which is where both the Common Core State Standards and *Scott Foresman Reading Street* have placed it. Encourage children to stretch to access some of the unfamiliar words using context clues and the images on the page.

Focus on Common Core State Standards

COWBOYS

by Lucille Recht Penner
illustrated by Ben Carter

Genre
Informational Text often gives facts about real people, places, and events that reflect history or the traditions of communities. Look for facts about cowboys.

Question of the Week
What can we learn about cowboy traditions?

466

467

Main Selection, pp. 466–487

Common Core State Standards
Informational Text 6. Identify the main purpose of a text, including what the author wants to answer, explain, or describe.

Social Studies in Reading

Genre
Informational Text

- Informational text often gives facts about real people, places, and events that reflect history or the traditions of communities.
- Informational text may describe objects and their uses.
- Informational text may use pictures and headings.
- Read "Cowboy Gear." What is the topic, or the "big idea," of this text?

COWBOY GEAR

from *The Cowboy's Handbook*
★ by Tod Cody ★

A cowboy's clothes and equipment had to be hard-wearing. There was no room for luggage on the trail drive, and most cowboys wore the same thing for months. Mud-caked and smelly, these clothes were often burned at the end of the journey.

READY TO HIT THE TRAIL!
What to Wear When You're Riding the Range

HAT
You can use it to signal to other cowboys, beat trail dust off your clothes, and hold food for your horse. A true cowboy wears his hat when he's sleeping.

PANTS
Cowboys originally refused to wear jeans because they were worn by miners and farm laborers. Pants (trousers) made of thick woolen material are more comfortable to wear on horseback.

BOOTS
The pointed toes and high heels are designed for riding, not for walking. That's why cowboys in the movies walk the way they do!

BANDANNA
Soak it in water, roll it up into a wad, and place it under your hat to keep cool during a hot spell. You can also use it to filter muddy water and blindfold a "spooked" horse.

CHAPS
These thick leather leg-coverings will protect your legs from cow horns, rope burns, scrapes, and scratches. They also give a better grip to the saddle.

Think
Why does the author tell what cowboys did with their clothing at the end of a trail drive? **Informational Text**

1

Think
Reading Across Texts What information did each selection give about hats, bandannas, chaps, and boots?

Writing Across Texts Write a paragraph explaining which piece of gear you think cowboys needed most.

492

493

Paired Selection, pp. 492–493

Text-Based Comprehension

Sequence
CCSS Informational Text 1., CCSS Informational Text 3.

Text Structure
CCSS Informational Text 2., CCSS Informational Text 3.

Fluency

Accuracy and Appropriate Rate
CCSS Foundational Skills 4.b.

Writing and Conventions

Trait: Focus/Ideas
CCSS Writing 2.

Writing Mini-Lesson: Compare-and-Contrast Text
CCSS Writing 2., CCSS Writing 8.

Conventions: Commas
CCSS Language 2.

Oral Vocabulary

Amazing Words

climate	livestock
occupation	buckaroo
drover	lariat
legend	rawhide

CCSS Language 6.

Selection Vocabulary

Unfamiliar Words
CCSS Language 4., CCSS Language 4.a.

Context Clues
CCSS Foundational Skills 4.c. CCSS Language 4.

campfire	cattle	cowboy
galloped	herd	railroad
trails		

Phonics and Spelling

Suffixes *-ness, -less, -able, -ible*
CCSS Foundational Skills 3.d., CCSS Language 2.

kindness	careless	goodness
useless	fearless	darkness
sadness	sickness	helpless
thankless	fitness	weakness

Media Literacy

Identify Written Conventions
CCSS Speaking/Listening 2.

Preview Your Week

What can we learn about cowboy traditions?

COWBOYS

by Lucille Recht Penner
illustrated by Ben Carter

Genre **Informational Text** often gives facts about real people, places, and events that reflect history or the traditions of communities. Look for facts about cowboys.

Question of the Week
What can we learn about cowboy traditions?

466 467

Main Selection, pp. 466–487

Common Core State Standards
Informational Text 6. Identify the main purpose of a text, including what the author wants to answer, explain, or describe.

Social Studies in Reading

Genre Informational Text

- Informational text often gives facts about real people, places, and events that reflect history or the traditions of communities.
- Informational text may describe objects and their uses.
- Informational text may use pictures and headings.
- Read "Cowboy Gear." What is the topic, or the "big idea," of this text?

COWBOY GEAR

from *The Cowboy's Handbook*
★ by Tod Cody ★

A cowboy's clothes and equipment had to be hard-wearing. There was no room for luggage on the trail drive, and most cowboys wore the same thing for months. Mud-caked and smelly, these clothes were often burned at the end of the journey.

READY TO HIT THE TRAIL!
What to Wear When You're Riding the Range

HAT
You can use it to signal to other cowboys, beat trail dust off your clothes, and hold food for your horse. A true cowboy wears his hat when he's sleeping.

PANTS
Cowboys originally refused to wear jeans because they were worn by miners and farm laborers. Pants (trousers) made of thick woolen material are more comfortable to wear on horseback.

BOOTS
The pointed toes and high heels are designed for riding, not for walking. That's why cowboys in the movies walk the way they do!

BANDANNA
Soak it in water, roll it up into a wad, and place it under your hat to keep cool during a hot spell. You can also use it to filter muddy water and blindfold a "spooked" horse.

CHAPS
These thick leather leg-coverings will protect your legs from cow horns, rope burns, scrapes, and scratches. They also give a better grip to the saddle.

Think
Why does the author tell what cowboys did with their clothing at the end of a trail drive? **Informational Text**

1

Think
Reading Across Texts What information did each selection give about hats, bandannas, chaps, and boots?
Writing Across Texts Write a paragraph explaining which piece of gear you think cowboys needed most.

492 493

Paired Selection, pp. 492–493

Genre: Informational Text

Phonics: Suffixes *-ness, -less, -able, -ible*

Text-Based Comprehension: Sequence, Text Structure

Vocabulary: Unfamiliar Words

Social Studies in Reading

Genre: Informational Text

Build Content Knowledge

KNOWLEDGE GOALS
Children will understand that cowboys:

- worked hard
- had difficult working conditions
- wore protective clothing

THIS WEEK'S CONCEPT MAP
Develop a concept-related graphic organizer like the one below over the course of this week.

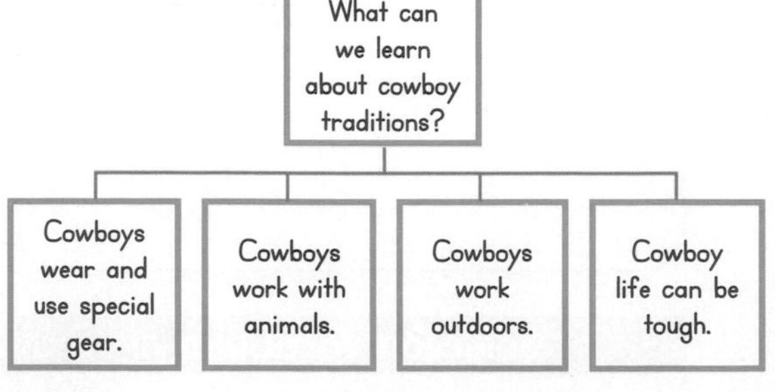

BUILD ORAL VOCABULARY
This week, children will acquire the following academic vocabulary/domain-specific words.

Amazing Words

climate	livestock
occupation	buckaroo
drover	lariat
legend	rawhide

OPTIONAL CONCEPT-BASED READING Use the Digital Path to access readers offering different levels of text complexity.

Concept Literacy

Below Level

On Level

Advanced

ELL

ELD

This Week's Digital Resources

eStreet Interactive
www.ReadingStreet.com

Get Ready to Read

Background Building Audio CD This audio CD provides valuable background information about cowboy traditions to help children read and comprehend the weekly texts.

Concept Talk Video Use this video on the Digital Path to build momentum and introduce the weekly concept of cowboy traditions.

Interactive Sing with Me Big Book "Occupation: Cowboy" sung to the tune of "If You're Happy and You Know It," introduces the Amazing Words with a catchy, concept-related song.

Interactive Sound-Spelling Cards With these interactive cards on the Digital Path children see an image, hear the image name, and see the spelling for the suffixes *-ness, -less, -able, -ible.*

Pearson eText Use the eText for the Decodable Readers on the Leveled Reader Database for phonics and fluency support.

Letter Tile Drag and Drop Using this interactive tool on Pearson SuccessNet, Children click and spell words to enhance their phonics skills.

Read and Comprehend

Envision It! Animations Use this colorful animation on the Digital Path to explain the target comprehension skill, Sequence.

Pearson eText Read the eText of the main selection, *Cowboys,* and the paired selection, "Cowboy Gear," with audio support on Pearson SuccessNet.

Story Sort Use the Story Sort Activity on the Digital Path after reading *Cowboys* to involve children in summarizing.

Journal: Word Bank Use the Word Bank on the Digital Path to have children write sentences using this week's selection words.

Vocabulary Activities A variety of interactive vocabulary activities on the Digital Path help children practice high-frequency and concept-related words.

Language Arts

Grammar Jammer Choose a whimsical animation on the Digital Path to provide an engaging grammar lesson that will capture children's attention.

Pearson eText Find the Student Edition eText of the Let's Write It! and Let's Learn It! pages with audio support on Pearson SuccessNet.

Additional Resources

Teacher Resources DVD-ROM Use the following resources on the TR DVD or on Pearson SuccessNet throughout the week:

- Amazing Word Cards
- Reader's and Writer's Notebook
- Writing Transparencies
- Daily Fix-It Transparencies
- Scoring Rubrics
- Grammar Transparencies
- Research Transparencies
- Let's Practice It!
- Graphic Organizers
- Vocabulary Cards
- Vocabulary Transparencies

This Week's Skills

Phonics
- Suffixes *-ness, -less, -able, -ible*

Comprehension
- Sequence
- Text Structure

Language
- **Vocabulary:** Unfamiliar Words

Conventions: Commas

Fluency
Accuracy and Appropriate Rate

Writing
Compare-and-Contrast Text

5-Day Planner

DAY 1

Get Ready to Read

Content Knowledge 458j
Oral Vocabulary: *climate, livestock, occupation*

Phonics/Spelling 460a
Suffixes *-ness, -less, -able, -ible*
Spelling Pretest
READ Decodable Reader 29A
Reread for Fluency 461d

Monitor Progress
Check Word Reading

Read and Comprehend

Text-Based Comprehension 462a
Sequence
Text Structure

Selection Vocabulary 463a
campfire, cattle, cowboy, galloped, herd, railroad, trails

Language Arts

Conventions 463b
Commas

Writing 463c
Compare-and-Contrast Text

Research and Inquiry 463e
Identify and Focus Topic

DAY 2

Get Ready to Read

Content Knowledge 464a
Oral Vocabulary: *buckaroo, drover*

Phonics/Spelling 464c
Suffixes *-ness, -less, -able, -ible*
Review Final Syllables *-tion, -ture, -ion*
Spelling: Suffixes *-ness, -less*

Read and Comprehend

Selection Vocabulary 464e
Review Selection Words: *campfire, cattle, cowboy, galloped, herd, railroad, trails*
Strategy: Unfamiliar Words
Reread for Fluency

Monitor Progress
Check Selection Words/
High-Frequency Words

Text-Based Comprehension 465a
READ *Cowboys*—1st Read

Informational Text 487b
Graphic Sources

Language Arts

Conventions 487c
Commas

Writing 487d
Compare-and-Contrast Text

Handwriting 487f
Cursive *Z, Q,* and *X*/Letter Slant

Research and Inquiry 487g
Research Skill: Schedule

DAY 3

Get Ready to Read

Content Knowledge 488a
Oral Vocabulary: *lariat*

Phonics/Spelling 488c
Build Words
Fluent Word Reading
Decode and Read
Spelling: Suffixes *-ness, -less*

Read and Comprehend

Fluency 488f
Accuracy and Appropriate Rate

Selection Vocabulary 488g
Selection Words: *campfire, cattle, cowboy, galloped, herd, railroad, trails*
Unfamiliar Words

Text-Based Comprehension 488h
READ *Cowboys*—2nd Read
Monitor Progress Check Retelling

Language Arts

Conventions 490a
Commas

Writing 490–491
Compare-and-Contrast Text

Research and Inquiry 491b
Gather and Record Information

DAY 4

Get Ready to Read

Content Knowledge 492a
Oral Vocabulary: *legend, rawhide*

Phonics/Spelling 492c
Review Final Syllables *-tion, -ture, -ion*
Spiral Review Fluent Word Reading
READ Decodable Reader 29C
Spelling: Suffixes *-ness, -less*

Read and Comprehend

Social Studies in Reading 492h
READ "Cowboy Gear" Paired Reading

Fluency 493b
Accuracy and Appropriate Rate
Monitor Progress Fluency Check

Language Arts

Conventions 493c
Commas

Writing 493d
Compare-and-Contrast Text

Media Literacy 493f
Identify Written Conventions

Research and Inquiry 493g
Review and Revise Topic

DAY 5

Get Ready to Read

Content Knowledge 494a
Review Oral Vocabulary
Monitor Progress
Check Oral Vocabulary

Phonics/Spelling 494c
Review Suffixes *-ness, -less, -able, -ible*
Spelling Test

Read and Comprehend

Vocabulary 494–495
Fluency 495a
Media Literacy 495a

Text-Based Comprehension 495b
Review Sequence

Vocabulary 495b
Review Selection Words: *campfire, cattle, cowboy, galloped, herd, railroad, trails*

Genre 495c
Review Informational Text

Assessment 495d
Monitor Progress
Sentence Reading; Fluency and Comprehension

Language Arts

Conventions 495g
Review Commas

Writing 495h
Compare-and-Contrast Text

Research and Inquiry 495j
Communicate

Wrap Up Your Week 495k
Cowboy Traditions

Access for All

What do I do in group time?

It's as easy as 1-2-3!

1 TEACHER-LED SMALL GROUPS → 2 INDEPENDENT PRACTICE STATIONS → 3 INDEPENDENT READING

Small Group Time

Bridge to Common Core

SKILL DEVELOPMENT
- Suffixes *-ness, -less, -able, -ible*
- Sequence
- Text Structure
- Unfamiliar Words

DEEP UNDERSTANDING

This Week's Knowledge Goals

Children will understand that cowboys:
- worked hard
- had difficult working conditions
- wore protective clothing

1 Small Group Lesson Plan

	DAY 1 Differentiate Phonics	DAY 2 Differentiate Comprehension
OL On-Level pp. SG•53–SG•57	**Practice Phonics** More Suffixes *-ness, -less, -able, -ible* **Decodable Reader** Read *Helpless Randy*	**Build Word Knowledge** Practice Selection Vocabulary **Access Text** Read *Cowboys*
SI Strategic Intervention pp. SG•58–SG•62	**Reteach Phonics** Blend Suffixes *-ness, -less, -able, -ible* **Decodable Reader** Read *Helpless Randy*	**Build Word Knowledge** Reteach Selection Vocabulary **Access Text** Read *Cowboys*
A Advanced pp. SG•63–SG•68	**Extend Phonics** More Suffixes *-ness, -less, -able, -ible* **Decodable Reader** **Advanced Selection** Read "Fearless Cowgirls"	**Build Word Knowledge** Extend Selection Vocabulary **Access Text** Read *Cowboys*
Independent Inquiry Project	Introduce	Investigate
ELL **If...** children need more scaffolding and practice with...	**Phonics** **then...** use the Grammar Transition Lessons on pp. 213–309 in the *ELL Handbook.*	**Comprehension Skill** **then...** use the ELL activities on p. DI•80 in the Teacher Resources section on SuccessNet.

Reading Street Sleuth

- Provides access to grade-level text for all children
- Focuses on finding clues in text through close reading
- Builds capacity for complex text

Build Text-Based Comprehension

Cowboys

Optional Leveled Readers

Concept Literacy

Below Level

On Level

Advanced

ELL

ELD

DAY 3 Differentiate Close Reading	DAY 4 Differentiate Vocabulary	DAY 5 Differentiate Reteaching
Reread to Develop Vocabulary **Close Reading** Reread *Cowboys*	**Build Word Knowledge** Develop Language Using Amazing Words **Text-Based Comprehension** Read *Reading Street Sleuth,* pp. 74–75, or Leveled Readers	**Practice** Commas **Text-Based Comprehension** Reread *Reading Street Sleuth,* pp. 74–75, or Leveled Readers
Reread to Develop Vocabulary **Close Reading** Reread *Cowboys*	**Build Word Knowledge** Review/Discuss Amazing Words **Text-Based Comprehension** Read *Reading Street Sleuth,* pp. 74–75, or Leveled Readers	**Review** Commas **Text-Based Comprehension** Reread *Reading Street Sleuth,* pp. 74–75, or Leveled Readers
Reread to Develop Vocabulary **Close Reading** Reread *Cowboys* **Investigate**	**Build Word Knowledge** Extend Amazing Words and Selection Vocabulary **Text-Based Comprehension** Read *Reading Street Sleuth,* pp. 74–75, or Leveled Readers **Organize**	**Extend** Commas **Text-Based Comprehension** Reread *Reading Street Sleuth,* pp. 74–75, or Leveled Readers **Communicate**
Main Selection **then...** use the activities on p. DI•81 on the Teacher Resources section on SuccessNet.	**Amazing Words** **then...** use the routine on pp. xxxvi–xxxvii in the *ELL Handbook.*	**Conventions and Writing** **then...** use the Grammar Transition Lessons on pp. 310–385 in the *ELL Handbook.*

Independent Stations

Practice Last Week's Skills

★ Focus on these activities when time is limited.

ACCESS FOR ALL
- ● Below-Level Activities
- ▲ On-Level Activities
- ■ Advanced Activities

WORD WISE

Spell words.

OBJECTIVES

- Spell words that end in *-tion, -ion,* and *-ture.*

MATERIALS

- *Word Wise* Flip Chart, Letter Tiles, note cards, paper, pencils, crayons

 **Interactive Sound-Spelling Cards**  **Letter Tile Drag and Drop**

● Children spell *nation, future, picture,* and *action.* They write each on a note card and circle the endings. They draw picture cards for *nation* and *future.*

▲ Children spell *mixture, section, caution, fixture, feature,* and *motion* and write them in a list. They make picture cards for *invention, adventure,* and *nature.*

■ Children spell *furniture, region, fracture,* and *contraction.* They think of two words each ending in *-tion* and *-ture* and use all four in a paragraph.

★ WORD WORK

Identify syllables.

OBJECTIVES

- Write and pronounce words with the final syllables *-tion, -ion,* and *-ture.*

MATERIALS

- *Word Wise* Flip Chart; Sound-Spelling Cards: 131, 135, 136; Teacher-made word cards for words ending in *-tion, -ion,* and *-ture;* paper; pencils

 **Interactive Sound-Spelling Cards**

● Children say the Sound-Spelling Card words. They choose two word cards for each ending. They say each word and write a sentence for each.

▲ Children say each Sound-Spelling Card word. They choose three cards for each ending. They write a sentence for each.

■ Children choose four cards for each ending. They list the words and use them to write a paragraph.

LET'S WRITE!

Write a letter.

OBJECTIVES

- Write an invitation letter.
- Make sure that the word order in each sentence makes sense.

MATERIALS

- *Let's Write!* Flip Chart, paper, pencils, crayons

 **Grammar Jammer**

● Children write an invitation to a surprise party. They write two sentences, using correct word order, and illustrate the invitation.

▲ Children use proper word order to write an invitation to a surprise party. They include information the guests need to know and illustrate the invitation.

■ Children use proper word order to plan and write an invitation to a surprise party. They include important information and illustrate the invitation.

WORDS TO KNOW

Identify words.

OBJECTIVES

- Identify and use words from other languages.

MATERIALS

- *Words to Know* Flip Chart, 2.6.3 Leveled Readers, paper, pencils, crayons

 **Vocabulary Activities**

● Children read *Special Chinese Birthdays.* They write one word from the story that comes from another language. They draw a picture that shows the word's meaning.

▲ Children read *A World of Birthdays.* They write two words from the story that come from another language. They write sentences illustrating each word's meaning.

■ Children read *Celebrations and Family Traditions* and record three words that come from another language. They write sentences illustrating each word's meaning.

READ FOR MEANING

Use text-based comprehension tools.

OBJECTIVES

- Draw conclusions.

MATERIALS

- *Read for Meaning* Flip Chart, 2.6.3 Leveled Readers

 **Pearson eText**
- Leveled eReaders

 **Envision It! Animations**

● Children read *Special Chinese Birthdays* and draw a conclusion. They illustrate the conclusion and label it with the conclusion and the details used to form it.

▲ Children read *A World of Birthdays* and draw a conclusion. They write a paragraph explaining the conclusion, including the details used to form it.

■ Children read *Celebrations and Family Traditions* and draw two conclusions. They use supporting facts and details to write a paragraph explaining their conclusions.

GET FLUENT

Practice fluent reading.

OBJECTIVES

- Read aloud with appropriate phrasing.

MATERIALS

- *Get Fluent* Flip Chart, 2.6.3 Leveled Readers

 **Pearson eText**
- Leveled Readers

● Children work with a partner to take turns reading from *Special Chinese Birthdays.* They note punctuation and phrasing.

▲ Children work with a partner to take turns reading from *A World of Birthdays.* They note punctuation and phrasing.

■ Children work with a partner to take turns reading from *Celebrations and Family Traditions.* They note punctuation and phrasing.

Manage the Stations

Use these management tools to set up and organize your Practice Stations:

Practice Station Flip Charts

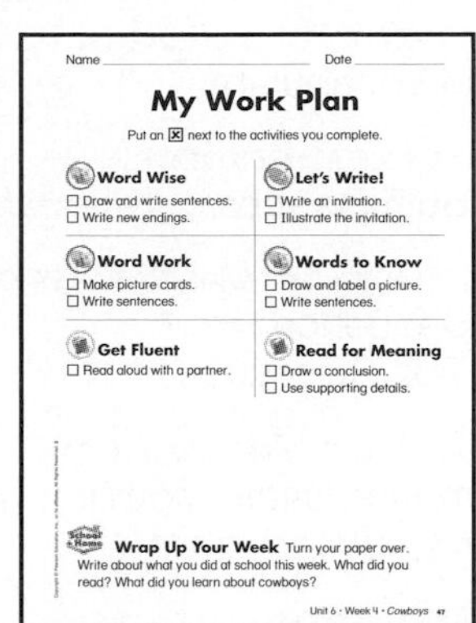

Name ____________ Date ________

My Work Plan

Put an ☒ next to the activities you complete.

Word Wise
- ☐ Draw and write sentences.
- ☐ Write new endings.

Let's Write!
- ☐ Write an invitation.
- ☐ Illustrate the invitation.

Word Work
- ☐ Make picture cards.
- ☐ Write sentences.

Words to Know
- ☐ Draw and label a picture.
- ☐ Write sentences.

Get Fluent
- ☐ Read aloud with a partner.

Read for Meaning
- ☐ Draw a conclusion.
- ☐ Use supporting details.

Wrap Up Your Week Turn your paper over. Write about what you did at school this week. What did you read? What did you learn about cowboys?

Unit 6 • Week 4 • *Cowboys* 47

Classroom Management Handbook for Differentiated Instruction Practice Stations, p. 47

3 Independent Reading

Children should select appropriately complex texts to read and write about independently every day before, during, and after school.

Suggestions for this week's independent reading:
- Fictional texts on last week's social studies topic: Why are family celebrations special?
- Fiction selections about why family celebrations are special
- Fiction book by a favorite author

BOOK TALK Have partners discuss their independent reading for the week. Tell them to refer to their Reading Log and paraphrase what the selection was about. To focus the discussion, prompt them to talk about one or more of the following:

Key Ideas and Details
- Who is the author? Why did he or she write the story?
- Who are the characters in the story? How do they interact with each other?
- What did I learn from this text?

Craft and Structure
- Did I understand the main idea and why events happened?
- Did the illustrations make the story more enjoyable?

Integration of Ideas
- Was this a realistic story? Why or why not?
- Was this book like others I have read?

 **Pearson eText**
- Student Edition
- Decodable Readers
- Leveled Readers

 **Trade Book Library**

 **Materials from School or Classroom Library**

DAY 1 at a Glance

Content Knowledge
Oral Vocabulary

Phonics/Spelling
Suffixes *-ness, -less, -able, -ible*

Text-Based Comprehension
Sequence
Text Structure

Selection Vocabulary
campfire, cattle, cowboy, galloped, herd, railroad, trails

Conventions
Commas

Writing
Compare-and-Contrast Text

Research and Inquiry
Identify and Focus Topic

Materials
- Student Edition
- Sing with Me Big Book
- Sound-Spelling Cards
- Decodable Reader 29A
- Reader's and Writer's Notebook

Bridge to Common Core

INTEGRATION OF KNOWLEDGE/IDEAS
This week children read, write, and talk about cowboys.

Texts This Week
- "Occupation: Cowboy"
- "The Stagecoach Driver"
- "B is for Buckaroo: A Cowboy Alphabet"
- "Like a Cowboy"
- *Cowboys*
- "Cowboy: An Album"
- "Cowboy Gear"

Social Studies Knowledge Goals
Children will understand that cowboys
- worked hard
- had difficult working conditions
- wore protective clothing

Street Rhymes!

In a cowboy hat, bandana at his neck,
Cowboy Rusty was on a long trek
Upon his horse to round up steers
Calming them from their wildest fears.
Then at day's end under the moon
He sat and sang a cowhand's tune.

- To introduce this week's concept, read aloud the poem several times and ask children to join you.

Content Knowledge

Cowboys

CONCEPT TALK To help children gain knowledge and understanding, tell them that this week they will talk, sing, read, and write about cowboy traditions. Write the Question of the Week, *What can we learn about cowboy traditions?,* and track the print as you read it.

Build Oral Language

TALK ABOUT COWBOYS Have children turn to pp. 458–459 in their Student Edition. Read the title and look at the photos. Use these questions to guide discussion and create the "What can we learn about cowboy traditions?" concept map.

- What kinds of clothing are the people wearing in these pictures? (They are wearing hats, jeans, and boots.) What is the group of young cowboys practicing with in the picture on page 458? (They are practicing with ropes.) Let's add *Cowboys wear and use special gear* to our concept map.
- Look at the picture of the cowgirl on page 459. What is the cowgirl doing in the picture? (She is working with a horse.) Let's add *Cowboys work with animals* to our map.
- Where do cowboys seem to do most of their work, indoors or outdoors? (outdoors) Let's add *Cowboys work outdoors* to our map.

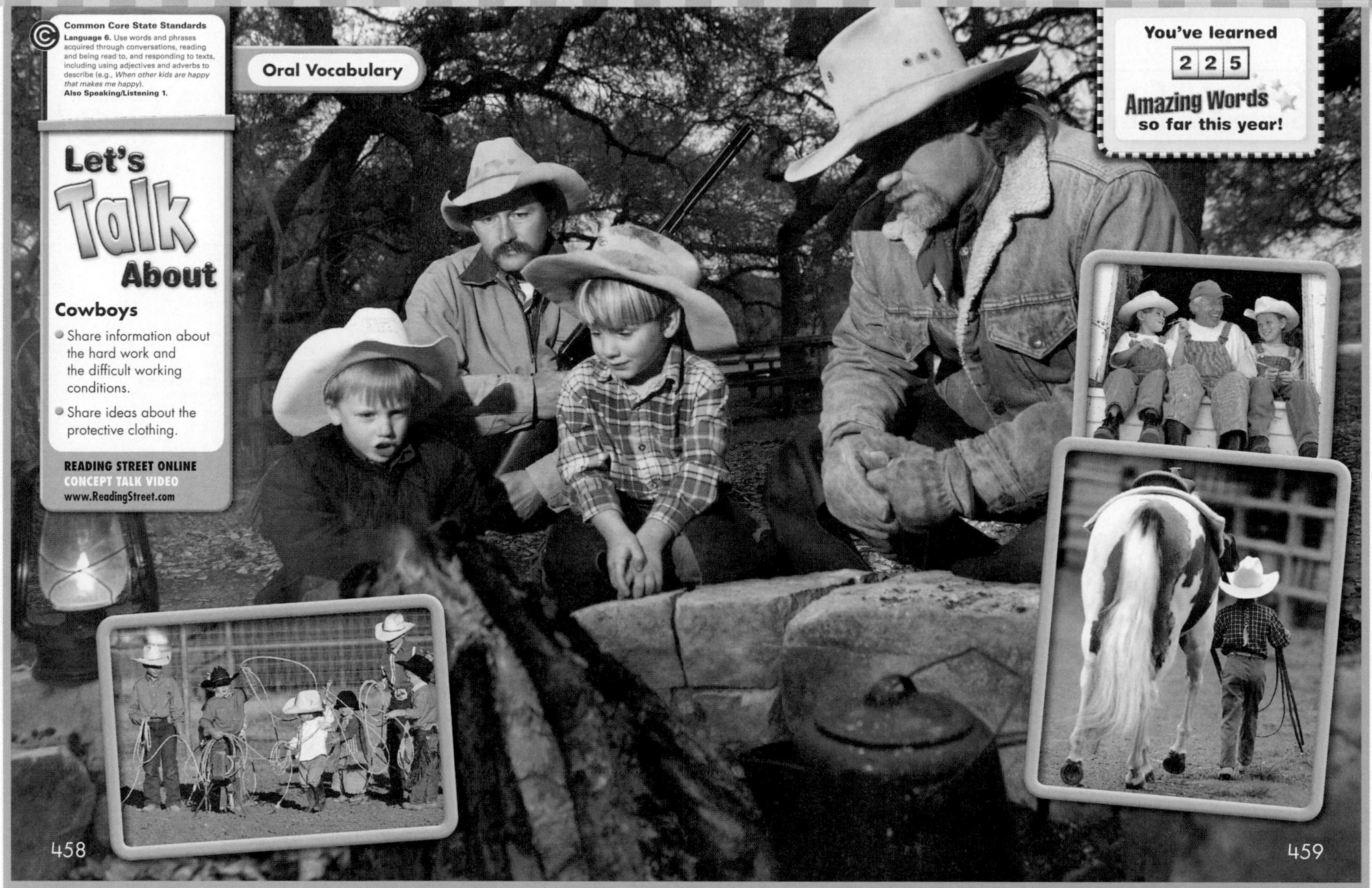

Common Core State Standards
Language 6. Use words and phrases acquired through conversations, reading and being read to, and responding to texts, including using adjectives and adverbs to describe (e.g., When other kids are happy that makes me happy).
Also Speaking/Listening 1.
Oral Vocabulary
Let's Talk About
Cowboys
Share information about the hard work and the difficult working conditions.
Share ideas about the protective clothing.
READING STREET ONLINE
CONCEPT TALK VIDEO
www.ReadingStreet.com
You've learned
2 2 5
Amazing Words
so far this year!
458
459

Student Edition, pp. 458–459

CONNECT TO READING Explain that this week, children will read about what it was like to be a cowboy one hundred years ago. Tell children that they will learn why a cowboy's occupation, or job, was so tough. Let's add *Cowboy life can be tough* to our map.

What can we learn about cowboy traditions?

- Cowboys wear and use special gear.
- Cowboys work with animals.
- Cowboys work outdoors.
- Cowboy life can be tough.

eSTREET INTERACTIVE
www.ReadingStreet.com

Pearson eText
- Student Edition

Concept Talk Video

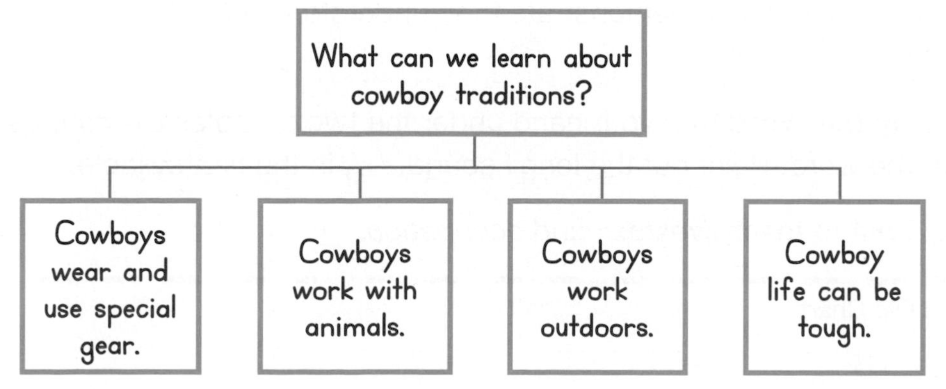

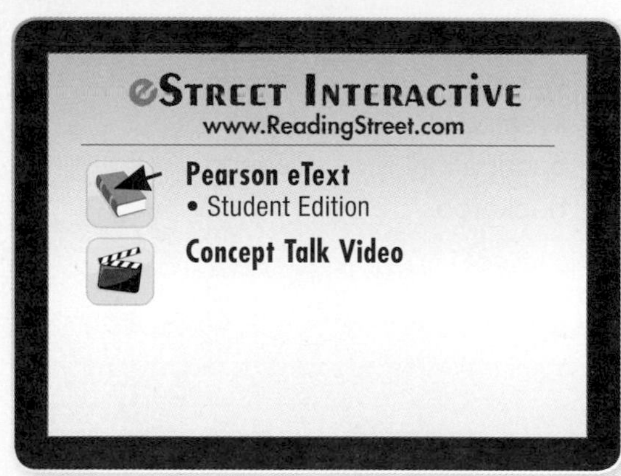

ELL

Preteach Concepts Use the Day 1 instruction on ELL Poster 29 to assess and build background knowledge, develop concepts, and build oral vocabulary.

ELL Support Additional support is provided in the *ELL Handbook* and in the ELL Support Lessons on the *Teacher Resources DVD-ROM.*

Common Core State Standards

Language 6. Use words and phrases acquired through conversations, reading and being read to, and responding to texts, including using adjectives and adverbs to describe (e.g., *When other kids are happy that makes me happy*).

Content Knowledge

Build Oral Vocabulary

INTRODUCE AMAZING WORDS Display page 29 of the *Sing with Me* Big Book. Tell children they are going to sing about being a cowboy. Ask children to listen for the Amazing Words *climate*, *livestock*, and *occupation* as you sing. Sing the song again and have children join you.

Sing with Me Big Book, p. 29

Amazing Words

You've learned **225** words so far.

You'll learn **008** words this week!

climate	drover
livestock	lariat
occupation	legend
buckaroo	rawhide

Amazing Words — Robust Vocabulary Routine

1. **Introduce the Word** Relate the word *climate* to the song. The *climate* makes things risky for a cowboy. Supply a child-friendly definition. *Climate* is the type of weather that happens in a particular place. Have children say the word.

2. **Demonstrate** Provide examples to show meaning. The desert has a dry *climate.* Florida has a much warmer *climate* than Alaska has.

3. **Apply** Have children demonstrate their understanding. What is the *climate* like where we live?

4. **Display the Word** Run your hand under the two syllables *cli-mate* as you read the word. Point out the long *i* sound, /ī/, in the first syllable.

See p. OV•4 to teach *livestock* and *occupation.*

Routines Flip Chart

AMAZING WORDS AT WORK Have children look at the picture on page 29.

- Where might this cowboy be taking his *livestock?* Use *livestock* in your answer. (Possible response: He might be taking the livestock to the barn; He might be taking his livestock to market.)
- Does the cowboy work in a wet or dry *climate?* Use *climate* in your answer. (Possible response: He works in a wet climate.)
- What kind of *occupation* would you like to have when you grow up? (Answers will vary.)

APPLY AMAZING WORDS Have children demonstrate their understanding of the Amazing Words by completing these sentences orally.

Our **climate** is ______ and ______.
My parents' **occupations** are ______ and ______.
The farmer's **livestock** are living in the ______ and ______.

Corrective feedback	**If...** children have difficulty using the Amazing Words, **then...** remind them of the definitions and provide opportunities for children to use the words in sentences.

Access for All

SI Strategic Intervention

Sentence Production If children have difficulty using *is* and *are,* then model the sentences several times and have children say them with you.

Pronunciation Speakers of mostly monosyllabic languages, such as Cantonese, Hmong, Khmer, Korean, and Vietnamese, may pronounce the syllables in a word with multiple syllables, such as *climate,* as separate words. Have children practice multisyllabic words with you.

Common Core State Standards

Foundational Skills 3.d. Decode words with common prefixes and suffixes.

Skills Trace

Suffixes: *-ness, -less, -able, -ible*

Introduce U6W4D1

Practice U6W4D2; U6W4D3; U6W4D4

Reteach/Review U6W4D5; U6W5D4

Assess/Test Weekly Test U6W4
Benchmark Test U6

KEY: U=Unit W=Week D=Day

Academic Vocabulary 

suffix letters added to the end of a word that change the meaning of the word.

Suffix Meanings

-ness the state of

-less without

-able, -ible able to

Phonics

Teach/Model

Suffixes *-ness, -less, -able, -ible*

CONNECT Write *sadly.* Point out to children that they have already studied words like this. Ask what they know about the ending of this word. (It is the suffix *-ly.*) Have them read the word. Explain that today they will learn about the suffixes *-ness, -less, -able,* and *-ible.*

USE SOUND-SPELLING CARDS Display Card 175. Point to the suffix *-ness. Kindness* has the base word *kind* and the suffix *-ness.* The suffix *-ness* means "the state or act of being," so *kindness* means "the act of being kind." Repeat this procedure with Card 172 for *-less* ("without"), Card 164 for *-able* ("able to"), and Card 169 for *-ible* ("has the quality of").

Sound-Spelling Card 175

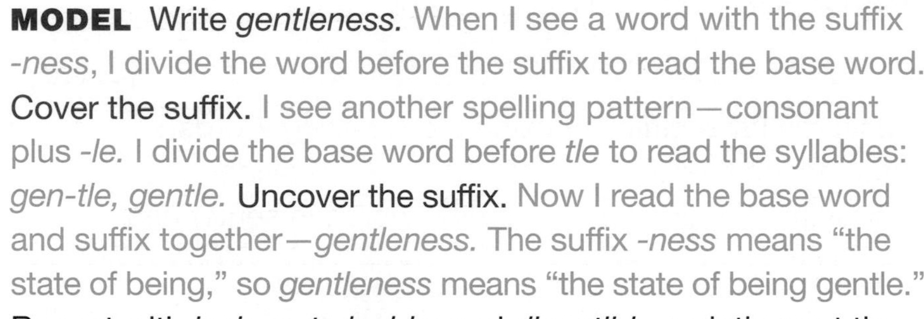

MODEL Write *gentleness.* When I see a word with the suffix *-ness*, I divide the word before the suffix to read the base word. Cover the suffix. I see another spelling pattern—consonant plus *-le.* I divide the base word before *tle* to read the syllables: *gen-tle, gentle.* Uncover the suffix. Now I read the base word and suffix together—*gentleness.* The suffix *-ness* means "the state of being," so *gentleness* means "the state of being gentle." Repeat with *joyless, trainable,* and *digestible*, pointing out the two syllables in the suffixes *-able* and *-ible.*

Sound-Spelling Card 172

Write *sensible.* Model breaking the word into the base word *sense* and the suffix *-ible,* pointing out that the final *e* was dropped from the base word before the suffix was added. Repeat with *laziness,* pointing out that *y* changed to *i.*

Write *usefulness.* Model breaking the word into a base word with two suffixes to read the word: *use-ful-ness, usefulness.*

GROUP PRACTICE Write the following words. Have the group read the words with you. Then identify the base word and suffix in each word.

sadness	**friendless**	**readable**	**collectible**	**goodness**
penniless	**reversible**	**heaviness**	**painlessly**	**hopelessness**

REVIEW What do you know about reading words with suffixes? (Read the base word, read the suffix or suffixes, and read the parts together.)

Sound-Spelling Card 164

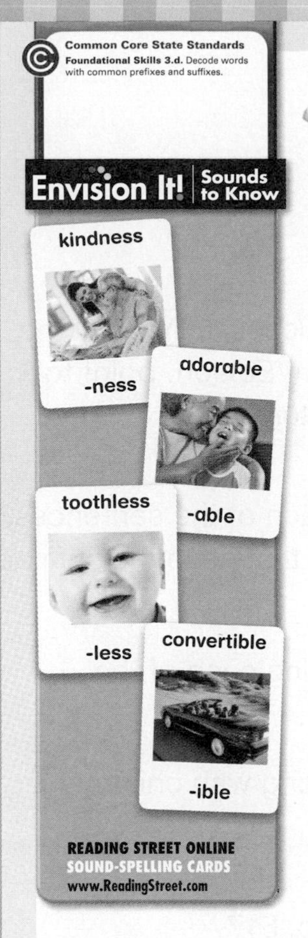

Phonics

Suffixes *-ness, -less, -able, -ible*

Words I Can Blend

comfortable
darkness
careless
reversible
seedless

Sentences I Can Read

1. Her sister felt comfortable walking in the darkness.
2. That was careless of him to leave his reversible jacket in the rain.
3. We enjoy eating seedless fruits.

460

My family has a fondness for fresh fruit. Every fall we pick fruit at Benson Farms near our home. Dad and Mom tell us to check the fruit for ripeness and redness before we pick it. They remind us not to be careless with the fruit. Needless to say, my sister and I are very capable of picking countless pieces of spotless fruit. We stay at that farm until darkness sets in. With some sadness we head home. It is the end of an incredible day.

You've learned

Suffixes *-ness, -less, -able, -ible*

461

Student Edition, pp. 460–461

Guide Practice

BLEND WORDS Have children turn to page 460 in their Student Edition. Look at the pictures on this page. I see a picture of a person showing *kindness,* a picture of an *adorable* child, a picture of a *toothless* baby, and a picture of a car that is a *convertible.* Each word has a base word and a suffix. In *kindness,* the base word is *kind* and the suffix is *-ness.* In *adorable,* the base word is *adore* and the suffix is *-able.* In *toothless,* the base word is *tooth* and the suffix is *-less.* In *convertible,* the base word is *convert,* which means "to change," and the suffix is *-ible.*

GROUP PRACTICE For each word in "Words I Can Blend," ask children to say each word part. Make sure they identify the base word or root and the suffix. Then have children say the parts to read the whole word.

Corrective feedback	**If...** children have difficulty decoding a word, **then...** model sound-by-sound blending or the word parts strategy for decodable words.

Access for All

 **Advanced**

Roots Tell children that a suffix can be added to another word part called a root. A ***root*** is a word part that tells the basic meaning of the word. It is not always a recognizable word itself. Point out that *visible* has the root *vis,* which means "see." *Portable* has the root word *port,* which means "carry."

Phonics

Apply

DECODE WORDS IN ISOLATION After children can successfully combine word parts to read the words on page 460 in their Student Edition, point to words in random order and ask children to read them naturally.

DECODE WORDS IN CONTEXT Have children read each of the sentences on page 460. Have them identify words in the sentences that have the suffixes *-ness, -less, -able,* and *-ible.*

Team Talk Pair children and have them take turns reading each of the sentences aloud.

Chorally read the "I Can Read!" passage on page 461 along with children. Then have them read the passage aloud to themselves.

ON THEIR OWN Use *Reader's and Writer's Notebook,* p. 517.

Common Core State Standards

Foundational Skills 3.d. Decode words with common prefixes and suffixes. **Language 2.** Demonstrate command of the conventions of standard English capitalization, punctuation, and spelling when writing.

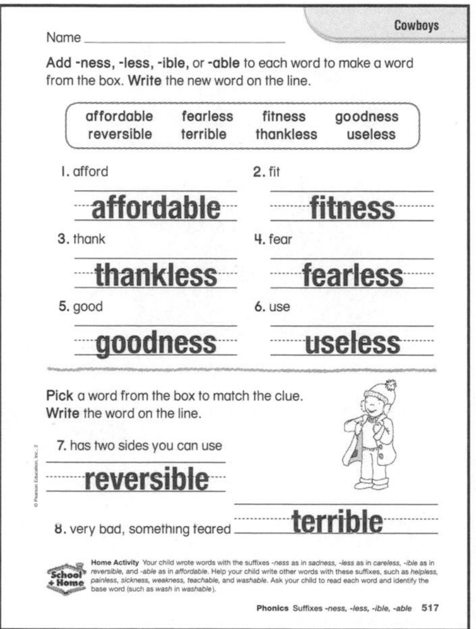

Cowboys

Name ______________

Add -ness, -less, -ible, or **-able** to each word to make a word from the box. **Write** the new word on the line.

affordable	fearless	fitness	goodness
reversible	terrible	thankless	useless

1. afford **affordable**
2. fit **fitness**
3. thank **thankless**
4. fear **fearless**
5. good **goodness**
6. use **useless**

Pick a word from the box to match the clue. **Write** the word on the line.

7. has two sides you can use **reversible**
8. very bad, something feared **terrible**

© Pearson Education, Inc., 2

School + Home **Home Activity** Your child wrote words with the suffixes *-ness* as in *sadness*, *-less* as in *careless*, *-ible* as in *reversible*, and *-able* as in *affordable*. Help your child write other words with these suffixes, such as *helpless, painless, sickness, weakness, teachable,* and *washable*. Ask your child to read each word and identify the base word (such as *wash* in *washable*).

Phonics Suffixes *-ness, -less, -ible, -able* 517

Reader's and Writer's Notebook, p. 517

Don't Wait Until Friday MONITOR PROGRESS *-ness, -less, -able, -ible*

FORMATIVE ASSESSMENT Write the following words and have the class read them. Notice which words children miss during the group reading. Call on individuals to read some of the words.

					Spiral Review
darkness	**fixable**	**tasteless**	**reversible**	**movable**	Row 3 reviews
penniless	**brightness**	**flexible**	**fearlessly**	**gracefulness**	long and short *ea.*
deafness	**weakness**	**dreamless**	**teachable**	**breathless** ←	

If... children cannot read words with these suffixes at this point,

then... use the Small Group Time Strategic Intervention lesson, p. SG•58, to reteach *-ness, -less, -able, -ible.* Continue to monitor children's progress using other instructional opportunities during the week. See the Skills Trace on p. 460a.

Spelling Pretest

Suffixes *-ness, -less*

DICTATE SPELLING WORDS Dictate the spelling words and read the sentences. Have children write the words. If needed, break the words into meaningful word parts, clarify the pronunciations, and give a definition for each word. Have children check their pretests and correct misspelled words. Have children use resources such as a dictionary to find correct spellings.

1. kindness	Jen showed **kindness** by helping the kitten.
2. careless	It was **careless** of you to lose the book.
3. goodness	I love the **goodness** of a fresh juicy peach.
4. useless	The car is **useless** without gas.
5. fearless*	Trey was **fearless** when he went skydiving.
6. darkness	We sat in the **darkness** at the movies.
7. sadness	Lia felt **sadness** when she moved.
8. sickness	I feel motion **sickness** on boats.
9. helpless	The h**elpless** baby needs to be fed.
10. thankless	Babysitting can be a **thankless** job.
11. fitness	Tran runs every day to improve his **fitness.**
12. weakness	I felt such **weakness** that I stayed in bed.

*Word marked with asterisk comes from the selection *Cowboys.*

ON THEIR OWN Use Let's Practice It!, p. 325 on the *Teacher Resources DVD-Rom.*

Access for All

Advanced

Extend Blending Ask children who spell words correctly to spell more difficult words, such as *awareness, wireless, cheerfulness, eagerness, paperless,* and *weightless.*

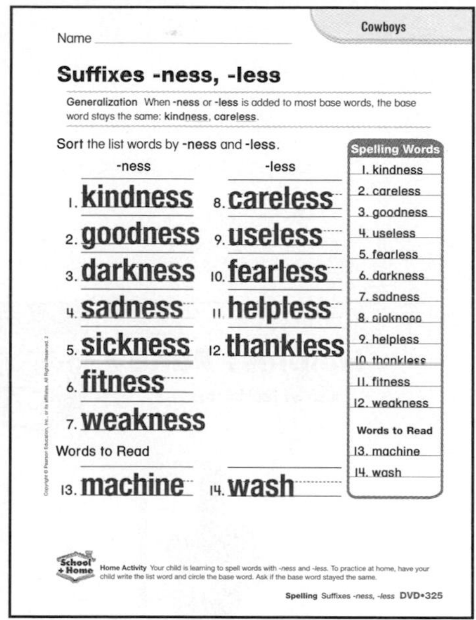
Cowboys

Name

Suffixes -ness, -less

Generalization When -ness or -less is added to most base words, the base word stays the same: kindness, careless.

Sort the list words by -ness and -less.

-ness	-less
1. kindness	8. careless
2. goodness	9. useless
3. darkness	10. fearless
4. sadness	11. helpless
5. sickness	12. thankless
6. fitness	
7. weakness	

Words to Read

13. machine 14. wash

Spelling Words: 1. kindness 2. careless 3. goodness 4. useless 5. fearless 6. darkness 7. sadness 8. sickness 9. helpless 10. thankless 11. fitness 12. weakness

Words to Read: 13. machine 14. wash

Home Activity Your child is learning to spell words with -ness and -less. To practice at home, have your child write the list word and circle the base word. Ask if the base word stayed the same.

Spelling Suffixes -ness, -less DVD•325

Let's Practice It! TR DVD•325

Day 1 SMALL GROUP TIME • Differentiate Phonics, p. SG•52

OL On-Level	SI Strategic Intervention	A Advanced
• **Practice Phonics** Additional Words with *Suffixes -ness, -less, -able, -ible* • **Read** Decodable Reader *Helpless Randy*	• **Reteach Phonics** Blend Words with *Suffixes -ness, -less, -able, -ible* • **Read** Decodable Reader *Helpless Randy*	• **Extend Phonics** More Words with *Suffixes -ness, -less, -able, -ible* • **Read** Advanced Selection for Words with *Suffixes -ness, -less, -able, -ible* • **Introduce** Inquiry Project

If... children need more scaffolding and practice with **Phonics,**
then... use the Phonics Transition Lessons on pages 213–309 in the *ELL Handbook.*

Decodable Reader 29A

If children need help, then...

Read *Helpless Randy*

DECODE WORDS IN ISOLATION Have children turn to page 235 in *Decodable Practice Readers* 2.2 and decode each word.

READ HIGH-FREQUENCY WORDS Have children identify and read the high-frequency words *without, life, please,* and *back* on the first page.

PREVIEW DECODABLE READER Have children read the title and preview the story. Tell them they will read words with suffixes *-ness, -less, -able,* and *-ible.*

DECODE WORDS IN CONTEXT Pair children for reading and listen as they decode. One child begins. Children read the entire story, switching readers after each page. Partners reread the story. This time the other child begins.

Common Core State Standards

Foundational Skills 3. Know and apply grade-level phonics and word analysis skills in decoding words. **Foundational Skills 3.d.** Decode words with common prefixes and suffixes.

Helpless Randy

Written by Liz Hornby

Decodable Practice Reader 29A

Suffixes *-ness, -less, -able, -ible*

lovable	useless	collectible	helpless
darkness	sadness	kindness	goodness
sweetness	weakness	fixable	brightness
colorless			

High-Frequency Words

without	life
please	back

235

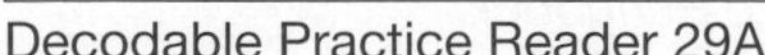

Decodable Practice Reader 29A

This is moving day.
Sandy did not grab Randy,
her old lovable bunny doll,
when she ran out the door.

236

"Did you pack that bunny?"
Mom asked Sandy.
"He's not old and useless.
He might be a collectible."

237

"Randy is helpless without me!"
Sandy cried.
"Without me his life will be filled
with darkness and sadness."

238

"Please show kindness," Sandy
begged. "Let me go back for my
bunny. "Mom's goodness shone
through. She smiled because of
Sandy's sweetness.

239

"You know my weakness,"
Mom laughed.
"This is fixable.
We will go get Randy."

240

Sandy picked up Randy and
hugged him.
Brightness had come back to her face.
"We'll make you new clothes,"
she said.
"Your old ones are colorless."

241

Sandy got in the car
and set Randy on her lap.
Mom smiled.
Mom knew that Sandy would have
missed her good friend.

242

Corrective feedback

If... children have difficulty decoding a word,
then... refer them to the Sound-Spelling Cards to identify sounds in a decodable word; prompt them to blend the word. If the word has a suffix with *-ness, -less, -able,* or *-ible,* have them identify the word parts and read them together to say the word.

- What is the new word?
- Is the new word a word you know?
- Does it make sense in the story?

CHECK DECODING AND COMPREHENSION Have children retell the story to include characters, setting, and events. Then have children find words that include suffixes *-ness, -less, -able,* and *-ible.* Children should supply the following words:

-ness: *darkness, sadness, kindness, goodness, sweetness, weakness, brightness*
-less: *useless, helpless, colorless*
-able: *lovable, fixable*
-ible: *collectible*

Reread for Fluency

REREAD DECODABLE READER Have children reread Decodable Practice Reader 29A to develop automaticity decoding words with suffixes *-ness, -less, -able,* and *-ible.*

Routine Oral Rereading

1. **Read** Have children read the entire book orally.
2. **Reread** To achieve optimal fluency, children should reread the text three or four times.
3. **Corrective Feedback** Listen as children read. Provide corrective feedback regarding their fluency and decoding.

Routines Flip Chart

Suffixes *-ness, -less, -able, -ible*
Beginning Before reading, preview the story, using illustrations to aid understanding. Write the story words on cards, with the base words and the suffixes in different colors. Say each word and have children repeat it. Have children sort the words by suffix.
Intermediate After reading, point out the words with suffixes and have children repeat them. Have children use story illustrations to make up a sentence about Sandy and Randy.
Advanced After reading, have children find words that end in suffixes and say them out loud. Then have each child tell a partner about Randy using two of the following words: *useless, helpless, colorless, lovable, fixable, collectible.*

Common Core State Standards

Informational Text 1. Ask and answer such questions as *who, what, where, when, why,* and *how* to demonstrate understanding of key details in a text.

Skills Trace

Sequence

Introduce U3W4D1; U4W2D1; U6W4D1

Practice U3W4D2; U3W4D3; U3W4D4; U4W2D2; U4W2D3; U4W2D4; U6W4D2; U6W4D3; U6W4D4

Reteach/Review U3W2D3; U3W4D5; U3W5D3; U4W2D5; U6W4D5

Assess/Test Weekly Tests U3W4; U4W2; U6W4
Benchmark Test U3

KEY: U=Unit W=Week D=Day

Academic Vocabulary

sequence the order of events in a text

text structure the way events or ideas in a text are organized

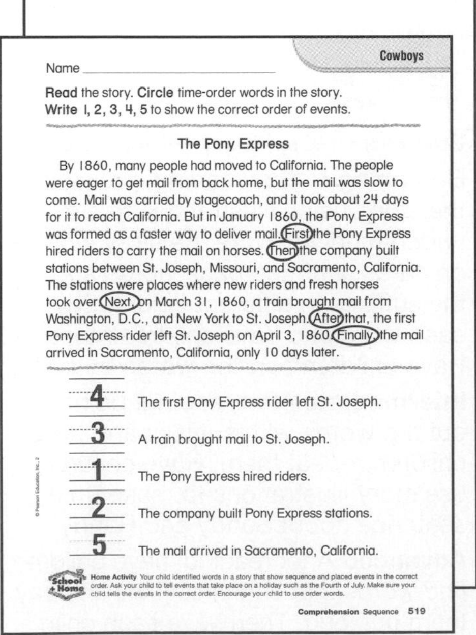

Name ____________ Cowboys

Read the story. **Circle** time-order words in the story.
Write 1, 2, 3, 4, 5 to show the correct order of events.

The Pony Express

By 1860, many people had moved to California. The people were eager to get mail from back home, but the mail was slow to come. Mail was carried by stagecoach, and it took about 24 days for it to reach California. But in January 1860, the Pony Express was formed as a faster way to deliver mail. First the Pony Express hired riders to carry the mail on horses. Then the company built stations between St. Joseph, Missouri, and Sacramento, California. The stations were places where new riders and fresh horses took over. Next, on March 31, 1860, a train brought mail from Washington, D.C., and New York to St. Joseph. After that, the first Pony Express rider left St. Joseph on April 3, 1860. Finally, the mail arrived in Sacramento, California, only 10 days later.

4 The first Pony Express rider left St. Joseph.
3 A train brought mail to St. Joseph.
1 The Pony Express hired riders.
2 The company built Pony Express stations.
5 The mail arrived in Sacramento, California.

Home Activity Your child identified words in a story that show sequence and placed events in the correct order. Ask your child to tell events that take place on a holiday such as the Fourth of July. Make sure your child tells the events in the correct order. Encourage your child to use order words.

Comprehension Sequence 519

Reader's and Writer's Notebook, pp. 519 and 527

Zoom in on

Text-Based Comprehension

Sequence

Text Structure

READ Remind children of the weekly concept—Cowboys. Have children follow along as you read "The Stagecoach Driver" on page 463.

Think Aloud **MODEL A CLOSE READ** Demonstrate close reading for children. Today we're going to read about the job of a stagecoach driver. Have children follow along as you read the title and the first three sentences of "The Stagecoach Driver." These opening sentences tell what the stagecoach driver did to start a trip. The word *first* is a clue to the first thing he did: he helped the riders get on the stagecoach. The next clue word, *then,* tells what happened next. I can tell that the events in this article are told in sequence. I can predict that the rest of the article will tell what happened during a trip and then what happened at the end.

INTRODUCE Have children read p. 462. Explain that the skill of **sequence** and the strategy of **text structure** are tools they can use to deepen their understanding. Review the bulleted items and explanations on p. 462. Then have children use a graphic organizer like the one shown to identify the sequence in the article.

IDENTIFY TEXT EVIDENCE Have children reread "The Stagecoach Driver" using the callouts as guides. Then ask volunteers to respond to the callouts, citing specific examples from the text to support their answers.

APPLY Use *Reader's and Writer's Notebook,* pp. 519 and 527 for additional practice with sequence. Students may also turn to pp. El•12 and El•26 to review the skill and strategy if necessary.

Comprehension Skill

Sequence

- Sequence is the order of events in a story.
- Clue words such as *first, next, then,* and *finally* will help you describe the order of events in a text.
- Use what you learned about sequence and complete an organizer like this as you read "The Stagecoach Driver."

What happens first	
What happens next	
What happens last	

Comprehension Strategy

Text Structure

Text structure is the way a selection is organized. Many stories are organized in time order. They are organized to tell what happened at the beginning, middle, and end. You can use text structure to help you remember what the selection says, and to retell it.

The Stagecoach Driver

To start a trip, a driver helped the riders and checked the horses. First, the driver helped riders get on the stagecoach. He helped them load their cases and bags. Then, he checked the horses. He made sure they were ready for the trip. He checked the wheels too. Then, he would get on the stagecoach, and the trip began!

Skill Describe what the stagecoach driver does before a trip. What are the clue words?

The stagecoach driver had to be careful. The trails and roads were muddy and rocky. He did not want the stagecoach to get stuck or tip over.

Finally, the stagecoach arrived after a long ride over the trail. The driver helped the riders off the stagecoach. He helped unload the cases and bags. Both the driver and the horses were tired after the trip. They needed to rest before the next trip.

Strategy What steps does the driver take when the ride is over?

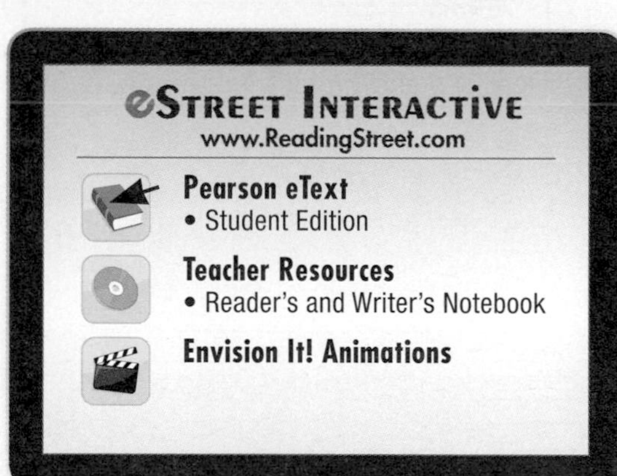

Your Turn!

Need a Review? See the *Envision It! Handbook* for additional help with sequence and text structure.

Ready to Try It? As you read *Cowboys,* use what you've learned to understand the text.

462 463

Student Edition, pp. 462–463

Model Fluent Reading

ACCURACY AND APPROPRIATE RATE Have children listen as you read the first three paragraphs of "The Stagecoach Driver" and model how to read with accuracy and at an appropriate rate.

Have children read paragraph 1 of "The Stagecoach Driver" orally.

Routine Oral Rereading

1. **Reread** To achieve optimal fluency, children should reread the text three or four times with appropriate phrasing.
2. **Corrective Feedback** Have children read aloud without you. Provide their corrective feedback regarding their accuracy, fluency, and decoding.

eStreet Interactive
www.ReadingStreet.com

Pearson eText
- Student Edition

Teacher Resources
- Reader's and Writer's Notebook

Envision It! Animations

Skills/Strategies

Skill The stagecoach driver helps the riders get on the stagecoach and load their cases and bags. Then he checks the horses and the wheels before getting on the coach himself. The clue words are *first* and *then.*

Strategy The driver helps the riders off the coach and helps unload their cases and bags.

Selection Vocabulary

Use the following routine to introduce this week's tested selection vocabulary.

campfire an outdoor fire used for cooking or warmth

cattle cows, bulls, and steers that are raised for their milk, meat, or skins

cowboy a man that works on a cattle ranch or in rodeos

galloped ran fast (referring to a horse)

herd a group of the same kind of animals that are kept or fed together

railroad a road or track of two steel rails on which trains run

trails overland paths

SEE IT/SAY IT Write *campfire.* Scan across the word with your finger as you say it: camp-fire.

HEAR IT Use the word in a sentence. We cooked our dinner over the campfire.

DEFINE IT Elicit definitions from children. How would you tell another child what a *campfire* is? Clarify or give a definition when necessary. Yes, a *campfire* is an outdoor fire used for cooking or warmth. Restate the word in child-friendly terms. A *campfire* is a fire built by campers.

Team Talk Is a campfire helpful or dangerous? Turn to your partner and talk about this. Be prepared to explain your answers. Allow children time to discuss. Ask for examples. Rephrase their examples for usage when necessary or to correct misunderstandings.

MAKE CONNECTIONS Have children discuss each word. Have you ever seen a campfire? Where were you? How do people use a campfire? Have children share. Rephrase their ideas for usage when necessary or to correct misunderstandings.

RECORD Have children write the word and its meaning.

Continue this routine to introduce the remaining words in this manner.

ON THEIR OWN Use *Reader's and Writer's Notebook,* p. 518.

Corrective feedback	**If...** children are having difficulty understanding, **then...** review the definitions in small groups.

Common Core State Standards

Informational Text 4. Determine the meaning of words and phrases in a text relevant to a grade 2 topic or subject area. **Language 2.** Demonstrate command of the conventions of standard English capitalization, punctuation, and spelling when writing. **Language 2.b.** Use commas in greetings and closings of letters.

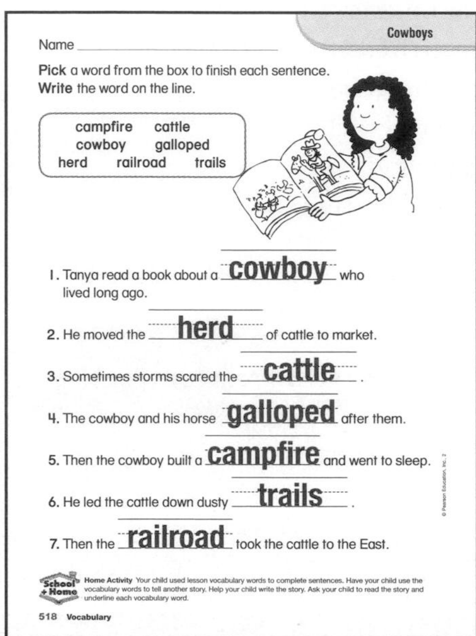
Cowboys

Name ______

Pick a word from the box to finish each sentence.
Write the word on the line.

campfire cattle cowboy galloped herd railroad trails

1. Tanya read a book about a **cowboy** who lived long ago.
2. He moved the **herd** of cattle to market.
3. Sometimes storms scared the **cattle**.
4. The cowboy and his horse **galloped** after them.
5. Then the cowboy built a **campfire** and went to sleep.
6. He led the cattle down dusty **trails**.
7. Then the **railroad** took the cattle to the East.

School + Home **Home Activity** Your child used lesson vocabulary words to complete sentences. Have your child use the vocabulary words to tell another story. Help your child write the story. Ask your child to read the story and underline each vocabulary word.

518 Vocabulary

Reader's and Writer's Notebook, p. 518

Multilingual Vocabulary Lists Children can apply knowledge of their home languages to acquire new English vocabulary by using the Multilingual Vocabulary Lists (*ELL Handbook,* pages 428–440).

Conventions

Commas

MAKE CONNECTIONS Write the following sentence from “The Stagecoach Driver” on the board. *Then, he would get on the stagecoach, and the trip began!* Read the sentence. Point to the commas. What are these punctuation marks? (commas)

TEACH Explain that **punctuation** marks are clues we use to help us understand what we read. **Commas** are used to separate words and phrases in writing.

MODEL Display Grammar Transparency 29. Read the definitions aloud. Model identifying the commas that appear in each example. Then read the directions and model the first part of the letter.

- The address at the top of this letter needs a comma.
- Commas should be placed between the names of cities and states. I will write a comma between *Syracuse* and *NY.*

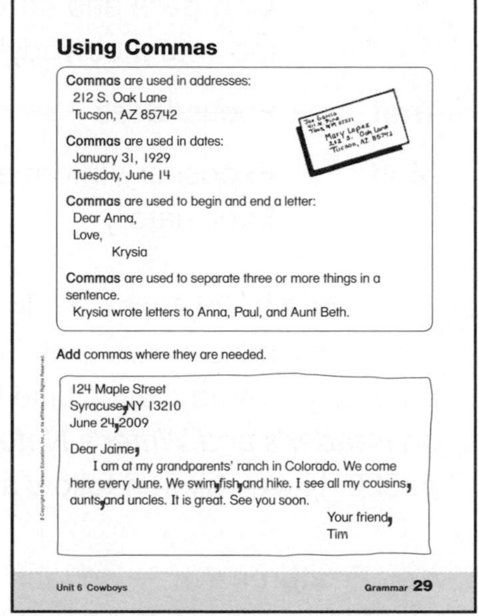

Using Commas

Commas are used in addresses:
212 S. Oak Lane
Tucson, AZ 85742

Commas are used in dates:
January 31, 1929
Tuesday, June 14

Commas are used to begin and end a letter:
Dear Anna,
Love,
Krysia

Commas are used to separate three or more things in a sentence.
Krysia wrote letters to Anna, Paul, and Aunt Beth.

Add commas where they are needed.

124 Maple Street
Syracuse, NY 13210
June 24, 2009

Dear Jaime,
I am at my grandparents' ranch in Colorado. We come here every June. We swim, fish, and hike. I see all my cousins, aunts, and uncles. It is great. See you soon.
Your friend,
Tim

Unit 6 Cowboys Grammar 29

Grammar Transparency 29 TR DVD

GUIDE PRACTICE Continue with the remainder of the letter, helping children identify where commas should be placed in the letter.

APPLY Have children complete these sentence frames orally with a city and state. Ask them where they should put a comma.

1. **I live in ______.**
2. **I was born in ______.**
3. **I would like to visit ______.**

Team Talk Pair children and have them work together to write their addresses and today’s date. Have them circle each comma.

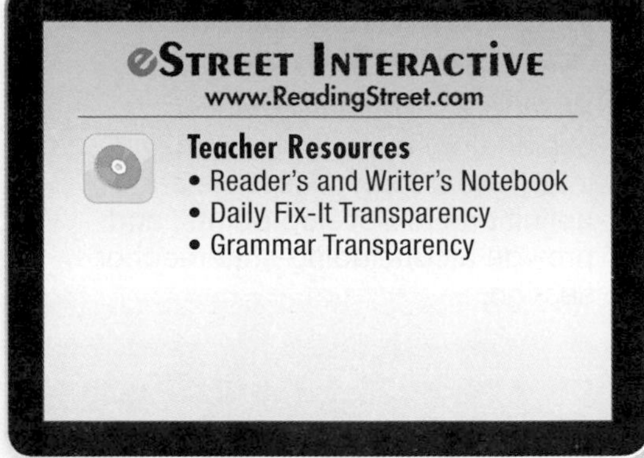

Access for All

 Strategic Intervention

Sentence Production If children fail to include a state name as they complete the sentences orally, model saying the answer correctly, emphasizing the state name, and have children repeat after you.

Academic Vocabulary 

punctuation marks used in writing to separate sentences and their elements and to make meaning clear

comma punctuation (,) that can be used, for example, to indicate a pause in a sentence and to separate items in a series

Daily Fix-It

1. A hurd wandered the trails?
   A herd wandered the trails.
2. “We will visit dr. Hino today, Mom said.
   “We will visit Dr. Hino today,” Mom said.

Discuss the Daily Fix-It corrections with children. Review end punctuation, quotation marks, capitalization of titles, and the spelling of *herd.*

Options for Conventions Support
To provide children with practice with commas, use the conventions lesson on p. DI•83 in the Teacher Resources section on SuccessNet.

DAY 1

Common Core State Standards

Writing 2. Write informative/explanatory texts in which they introduce a topic, use facts and definitions to develop points, and provide a concluding statement or section.

Academic Vocabulary 

compare tell how things are the same

contrast tell how things are different

Bridge to Common Core

TEXT TYPES AND PURPOSES

This week children write a text to compare and contrast their job at school or home with a cowboy's job.

Expository/Informative Writing

Through reading and discussion, children will gain a deeper understanding of cowboys. They will use the knowledge from the texts to write and support a compare-and-contrast text.

Throughout the week, children will improve the range and content of their writing through daily mini-lessons.

5-Day Plan

DAY 1	Read Like a Writer
DAY 2	Compare and Contrast
DAY 3	Writer's Craft: Compare/Contrast Words
DAY 4	Revise: Deleting Phrases
DAY 5	Proofread

Writing Zoom in on ©

Compare-and-Contrast Text

Mini-Lesson Read Like a Writer

Introduce This week you will write a compare-and-contrast text. A compare-and-contrast text tells how two things are alike and how they are different.

Prompt Think about a job you do at home or at school. Think about tasks that cowboys did. **Compare** and **contrast** your job with a cowboy's job.

Trait Focus/Ideas

Mode Expository/Informative/Explanatory

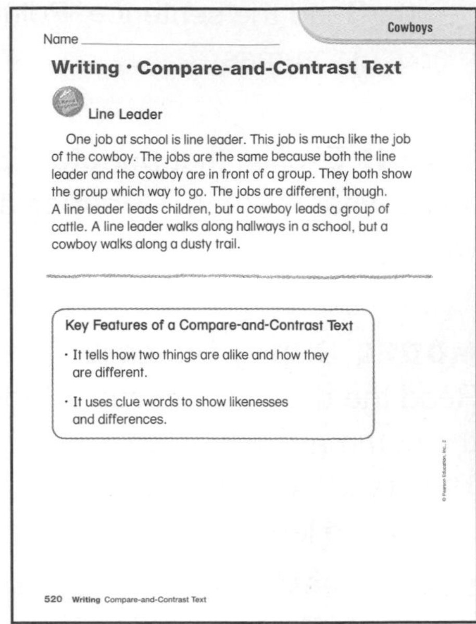

Name ________ Cowboys

Writing • Compare-and-Contrast Text

Line Leader

One job at school is line leader. This job is much like the job of the cowboy. The jobs are the same because both the line leader and the cowboy are in front of a group. They both show the group which way to go. The jobs are different, though. A line leader leads children, but a cowboy leads a group of cattle. A line leader walks along hallways in a school, but a cowboy walks along a dusty trail.

Key Features of a Compare-and-Contrast Text

- It tells how two things are alike and how they are different.
- It uses clue words to show likenesses and differences.

520 Writing Compare-and-Contrast Text

Reader's and Writer's Notebook, p. 520

Examine Model Text Let's listen to a compare-and-contrast text. Track the print as you read aloud "Line Leader" on *Reader's and Writer's Notebook,* p. 520. Have children follow along.

Key Features What two jobs are being compared and contrasted? (the job of a line monitor and cowboy's job of leading a cattle drive) How are the jobs the same? (Both show the group which way to go.) How are the jobs different? (The line leader leads children and walks along hallways. The cowboy leads cattle and walks along dusty trails.) Have children find clue words that show likenesses and differences, such as *like, same, both, different,* and *but.*

This paragraph is a compare-and-contrast text because it compares two things—the job of a line leader and the job of a cowboy leading the cattle drive.

Clue words help us understand how the jobs are alike. The words *like, same,* and *both* are clues that the author is comparing the jobs. The words *different* and *but* are clues that the author is contrasting the jobs.

Review Key Features

Review key features of a compare-and-contrast text with children. You may want to post these key features in the classroom to allow children to refer to them as they work on their compare-and-contrast text.

Key Features of a Compare-and-Contrast Text

- tells how two things are alike and how they are different
- uses clue words to show likenesses and differences

Connect to Familiar Texts

Use the example from *Just Like Josh Gibson* (Unit 6) or another selection familiar to children. During an important ball game Grandmama hit the ball, caught the ball, and did everything else just like the famous baseball player Josh Gibson.

Routine Quick Write for Fluency

Team Talk

1. **Talk** Read these questions aloud, and have children respond.
   How is the job of line leader like the job of a cowboy?
   How is the job of line leader different from the job of a cowboy?
2. **Write** Have children write short sentences to answer the questions.
3. **Share** Partners can read their sentences to each other and identify clue words that show likenesses and differences.

Routines Flip Chart

Write Guy *by Jeff Anderson*

What Do You Notice?

When children are examining the model text, ask, "What do you notice?" By having the responsibility of commenting on what they find effective in the text, children build self-confidence and often begin to notice features of the writing they might not have otherwise. Eventually they will start trying the features in their writing. Relish children's movement toward correctness and beauty.

Common Core State Standards

Speaking/Listening 1. Participate in collaborative conversations with diverse partners about grade 2 topics and texts with peers and adults in small and larger groups.

21st Century Skills

Internet Guy *Don Leu*

Weekly Inquiry Project

STEP 1	Identify and Focus Topic
STEP 2	Research Skill
STEP 3	Gather and Record Information
STEP 4	Synthesize
STEP 5	Communicate

Research and Inquiry

Step 1 Identify and Focus Topic

TEACH Display and review the concept chart that explores this week's question: *What can we learn about cowboy traditions?* What ideas about cowboy traditions would you like to learn more about? Ask children to share their interests. Help them identify that cowboys had routine tasks.

Think Aloud **MODEL** I want to learn about the different tasks a cowboy had and what a routine day for a cowboy was like. Let's record a question about that and other questions we have. Then we'll try to find the answers to our questions.

GUIDE PRACTICE Give children time to think about questions that, when answered, would help them learn about the routine tasks a cowboy had. Record children's questions in a chart.

Topic: Cowboy Routine

Question	Answer
What would a cowboy do at the beginning of the day?	

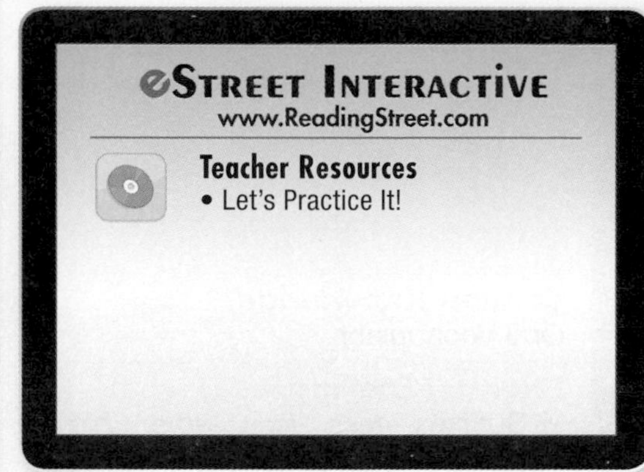

Wrap Up Your Day!

✔ **Phonics: Suffixes *-ness, -less, -able, -ible*** Write *cordless,* and ask children to decode the word and identify the base word and the suffix. Continue with *freshness, winnable,* and *sensible.*

✔ **Spelling: Suffixes *-ness, -less*** Have children add the suffix *-ness* to the words *kind* and *sick.* Have them add the suffix *-less* to *help* and *fear.*

✔ **Content Knowledge** Have children recall the *Sing with Me* song "Occupation: Cowboy." What did you learn about the cowboys' tradition of work? (Cowboys' jobs were very difficult, and they worked hard.)

✔ **Homework** Send home this week's Family Times Newsletter from Let's Practice It!, pp. 321–322 on the *Teacher Resources DVD–ROM.*

Let's Practice It!
TR DVD•321–322

Tell children that tomorrow they will read about cowboys and some of their traditions.

DAY 2 at a Glance

Content Knowledge
Oral Vocabulary

Phonics/Spelling
Suffixes *-ness, -less, -able, -ible*

Selection Vocabulary
campfire, cattle, cowboy, galloped, herd, railroad, trails
Unfamiliar Words

Text-Based Comprehension
Sequence
Text Structure

Conventions
Commas

Writing
Compare-and-Contrast Text
Writing Trait: Focus/Ideas

Handwriting
Cursive *Z, Q, X*/Letter Slant

Research and Inquiry
Research Skill: Schedule

Materials

- Student Edition
- Sing with Me Big Book
- Read Aloud Anthology
- Reader's and Writer's Notebook
- Sound-Spelling Cards

Common Core State Standards

Speaking/Listening 2. Recount or describe key ideas or details from a text read aloud or information presented orally or through other media. **Language 6.** Use words and phrases acquired through conversations, reading and being read to, and responding to texts, including using adjectives and adverbs to describe (e.g., *When other kids are happy that makes me happy*).

Content Knowledge

Cowboys

EXPAND THE CONCEPT To reinforce concepts and to focus children's attention, have children sing "Occupation: Cowboy" from the *Sing with Me* Big Book. What does the song say about a cowboy's occupation? (It was so tough.)

Build Oral Language

INTRODUCE AMAZING WORDS Read the title "B is for Buckaroo: A Cowboy Alphabet" of the *Read Aloud Anthology* selection. Identify the authors. Explain that in the selection the authors use some Amazing Words. Read the story and have children listen to the selection for the words *buckaroo* and *drover.*

"B is for Buckaroo: A Cowboy Alphabet"

TALK ABOUT SENTENCES AND WORDS Reread this sentence from the story.

B is for the Buckaroo, who's a cowboy through and through.

- Have children repeat the sentence with you. What does *B is for the Buckaroo* mean? (The letter *B* begins the word *buckaroo.*)
- **Team Talk** What other words could we use in place of *buckaroo?* Have children share their suggestions.
- After children have tried other words, ask: Why do you think the author chose the word *buckaroo?* (It begins with the letter *B* and it's another word for *cowboy.*)
- **Team Talk** Turn to your partner and talk about what a buckaroo might do.

Build Oral Vocabulary

Amazing Words Robust Vocabulary Routine

1. **Introduce the Word** Relate the word *buckaroo* to the selection. A *buckaroo* likes to ride on horseback. Supply a child-friendly definition. *Buckaroo* is another name for cowboy. Have children say the word.

2. **Demonstrate** Provide examples to show meaning. The *buckaroo* rode the wild horse. The *buckaroo* used his rope to catch a cow.

3. **Apply** Have children demonstrate their understanding. Where is a place a *buckaroo* might work? might not work?

4. **Display the Word** Run your hand under the three syllables *buck-a-roo* as you read the word.

See p. OV•4 to teach *drover.*

Routines Flip Chart

ADD TO THE CONCEPT MAP Discuss the work that cowboys do as you add to the concept map.

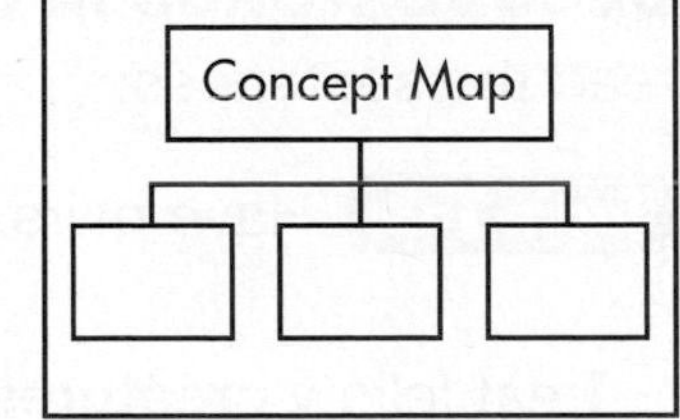

- In the song "Occupation: Cowboy," what kind of livestock do cowboys work with? (cattle) Where do the cowboys travel? (on the trail) How is climate important to a cowboy's occupation? (Climate can make things risky.) Let's add *Cowboys work with cattle, Cowboys travel on the trail,* and *Climate makes things risky* to the map. *Livestock, climate,* and *occupation* were our Amazing Words from yesterday.
- In "B is for Buckaroo," what kinds of gear do cowboys wear or use? (Cowboys wear boots, hats, jeans, chaps, and spurs and use lariats.) Let's add this information to our map. What do cowboys ride to do their work? (Cowboys ride horses.) Let's add *Cowboys ride horses* to the map.

Amazing Words

climate	drover
livestock	lariat
occupation	legend
buckaroo	rawhide

Access for All

SI Strategic Intervention

Access Content Help children recognize that many of the words in this selection rhyme. Share several examples of rhyming words, such as *make/brake* and *home/roam.* As you read the selection, stress the rhythm of the sentences as well as the words that rhyme.

Reinforce Vocabulary Use the Day 2 instruction on ELL Poster 29 to reinforce the meanings of lesson vocabulary.

Common Core State Standards

Foundational Skills 3.d. Decode words with common prefixes and suffixes. **Language 2.** Demonstrate command of the conventions of standard English capitalization, punctuation, and spelling when writing. **Language 2.e.** Consult reference materials, including beginning dictionaries, as needed to check and correct spellings.

Professional Development

Suffix Meaning Since the suffixes *-less* and *-ness* sound similar, children may get them confused. Tell children to think of the word *less* when they see the suffix *-less.* The word *less* can mean "without." Someone who is fearless is without fear.

Phonics

Review Final Syllables *-tion, -ture, -ion*

Suffixes *-ness, -less, -able, -ible*

REVIEW SOUND-SPELLINGS Review final syllables *-tion, -ture, -ion* using Sound-Spelling Cards 135, 136, and 131 and suffixes *-ness, -less, -able, -ible* using Sound-Spelling Cards 175, 172, 164, and 169.

DECODE WORDS IN ISOLATION Display these words. Have the class combine word parts to read the words. Then point to the words in random order and ask children to read them quickly.

fixture	**washable**	**slowness**
nation	**bunion**	**illness**
forcible	**painless**	**collectible**

Corrective feedback | Model combining word parts to read words and then ask children to combine and read with you.

DECODE WORDS IN CONTEXT Display these sentences. Have the class read the sentences.

Team Talk Have pairs take turns reading the sentences naturally.

Treat fellow **creatures** with **kindness** and **gentleness.**

The bone **fracture** in his leg caused him **countless sleepless** nights.

The **adventure** story in this book of **fiction** is **enjoyable,** in my **opinion.**

Spelling

Suffixes *-ness, -less*

GUIDE PRACTICE Tell children you will break the spelling words into meaningful word parts. They should repeat the parts of each word aloud as they write them. Check the spelling of each word before saying the next word. Have children use resources such as a dictionary to find correct spellings.

1.	kind ness	**kindness**
2.	care less	**careless**
3.	good ness	**goodness**
4.	use less	**useless**
5.	fear less	**fearless**
6.	dark ness	**darkness**
7.	sad ness	**sadness**
8.	sick ness	**sickness**
9.	help less	**helpless**
10.	thank less	**thankless**
11.	fit ness	**fitness**
12.	weak ness	**weakness**

ON THEIR OWN Use *Reader's and Writer's Notebook,* p. 521.

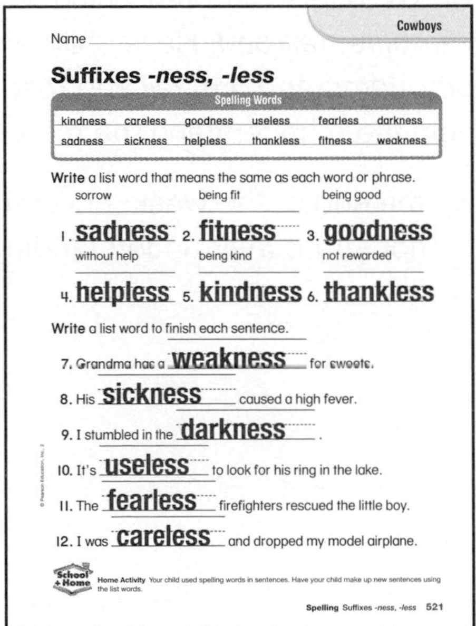
Name ____ Cowboys

Suffixes *-ness, -less*

Spelling Words					
kindness	careless	goodness	useless	fearless	darkness
sadness	sickness	helpless	thankless	fitness	weakness

Write a list word that means the same as each word or phrase.

1. sorrow — sadness
2. being fit — fitness
3. being good — goodness
4. without help — helpless
5. being kind — kindness
6. not rewarded — thankless

Write a list word to finish each sentence.

7. Grandma has a weakness for sweets.
8. His sickness caused a high fever.
9. I stumbled in the darkness.
10. It's useless to look for his ring in the lake.
11. The fearless firefighters rescued the little boy.
12. I was careless and dropped my model airplane.

School + Home **Home Activity** Your child used spelling words in sentences. Have your child make up new sentences using the list words.

Spelling Suffixes -ness, -less 521

Reader's and Writer's Notebook, p. 521

Extra Spelling Support Use facial expressions and body motions during dictation to help children understand the spelling words.

Common Core State Standards

Informational Text 4. Determine the meaning of words and phrases in a text relevant to a grade 2 topic or subject area. **Language 4.d.** Use knowledge of the meaning of individual words to predict the meaning of compound words (e.g., *birdhouse, lighthouse, housefly; bookshelf, notebook, bookmark*). **Language 5.** Demonstrate understanding of word relationships and nuances in word meanings.

Selection Vocabulary

ACTIVATE PRIOR KNOWLEDGE Display the selection words. Have children check their glossary for the meanings of unknown words.

Read aloud each list below. Ask children to name the vocabulary word that fits in the same category. Discuss reasons.

- cows, bulls, steers (*cattle*—all name specific kinds of cattle)
- paths, sidewalks, tracks (*trails*—all name places to walk)
- flock, pack, colony (*herd*—all name animal groups)
- stove, microwave, grill (*campfire*—all name places to cook food)
- highway, runway, bike lane (*railroad*—all name things that allow transportation to move)
- firefighter, police officer, doctor (*cowboy*—all name kinds of jobs)
- walked, trotted, cantered (*galloped*—all describe movements of horses)

REVIEW Ask children which words are made up of two smaller words. *(cowboy, campfire, railroad)* Have children identify the two words in each word. *(cow and boy, camp and fire, rail and road)* Have children tell how the two smaller words help them understand the meaning of the compound words.

By the end of the week, children should know the selection words. Have them demonstrate their understanding by creating new categories for the words.

MONITOR PROGRESS Check Selection Vocabulary/ High-Frequency Words

FORMATIVE ASSESSMENT Write the following words and have the class read them. Listen for children who miss words during the reading. Call on those children to read some of the words individually.

				Spiral Review
galloped	**cattle**	**railroad**	**trails**	Rows 3 and 4 review previously taught high-frequency words.
cowboy	**herd**	**campfire**		
buy	**alone**	**half**	**their** ←	
many	**youngest**		←	

If... children cannot read these words,

then... use the Small Group Time Strategic Intervention lesson, p. SG•59, to reteach the words. Monitor children's fluency with these words during reading and provide additional practice.

Access for All

SI Strategic Intervention

Illustrate It Write the selection words on index cards. Distribute cards to pairs of children. The first player picks a card and draws a picture to illustrate the word. The second player guesses the word. Each player, in turn, draws or guesses.

Visual Support English learners will benefit from additional visual support to understand selection vocabulary. Use the pictures in *Cowboys* to scaffold understanding. For example, use the words *galloped, cattle, cowboy,* and *herd* as you point to the picture on pages 472–473 and the word *campfire* as you display the picture on page 479.

Common Core State Standards

Foundational Skills 4.c. Use context to confirm or self-correct word recognition and understanding, rereading as necessary. **Language 4.a.** Use sentence-level context as a clue to the meaning of a word or phrase.

Selection Vocabulary

campfire an outdoor fire used for cooking or warmth

cattle cows, bulls, and steers that are raised for their milk, meat, or skins

cowboy a man who works on a cattle ranch or in rodeos

galloped ran fast (referring to a horse)

herd a group of the same kind of animals that are kept or fed together

railroad a road or track of two steel rails on which trains run

trails overland paths

Bridge to Common Core

VOCABULARY ACQUISITION AND USE

When children interact with this week's selection vocabulary, they are learning grade-appropriate domain-specific words that they will encounter in school and beyond. Teaching the strategy of using context to determine the meaning of unfamiliar words will help children gain independence as they encounter unfamiliar words in other contexts.

Vocabulary Skill

Unfamiliar Words

READ Have children read "Like a Cowboy" on p. 465 with you. Use the vocabulary skill and strategy to build comprehension.

TEACH Explain that readers sometimes come across words that they don't know. Discuss how readers can use context clues—the words and sentences around a word—to decide the meaning that is relevant in a particular sentence. Refer children to Words! on p. W•7 in the Student Edition for additional practice. Then read "Like a Cowboy" on p. 465 with children.

Think Aloud **MODEL** Write on the board, *The wild horse galloped away in a cloud of dust.* If I wasn't sure what *galloped* meant, I'd look at the other words in the sentence for clues. The fact that the horse was going away and a cloud of dust was stirred up makes me think that *galloped* means "ran fast." I'll try that meaning in the sentence: *The horse ran away fast in a cloud of dust.* That makes sense.

GUIDE PRACTICE Write this sentence on the board: *There were more than two hundred cattle in the herd.* Have children define the word *herd* and identify the context clues that helped them determine its relevant meaning.

ON THEIR OWN Have children reread "Like a Cowboy" on page 465. Have children use context clues to determine the relevant meanings of the other Words to Know. For additional practice, use *Reader's and Writer's Notebook,* p. 522.

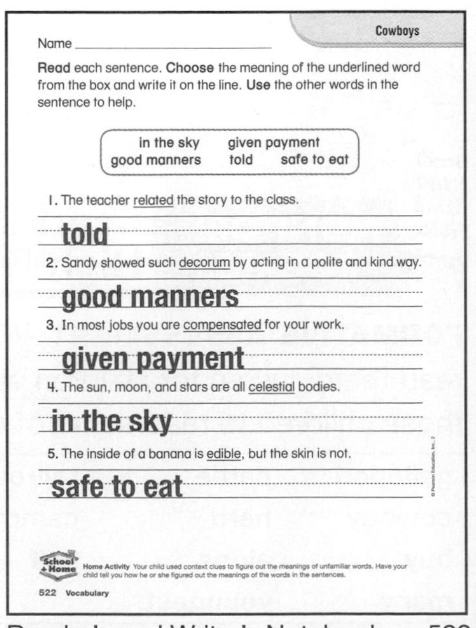

Name ______________ Cowboys

Read each sentence. **Choose** the meaning of the underlined word from the box and write it on the line. **Use** the other words in the sentence to help.

in the sky | given payment | good manners | told | safe to eat

1. The teacher related the story to the class.
told

2. Sandy showed such decorum by acting in a polite and kind way.
good manners

3. In most jobs you are compensated for your work.
given payment

4. The sun, moon, and stars are all celestial bodies.
in the sky

5. The inside of a banana is edible, but the skin is not.
safe to eat

School + Home **Home Activity** Your child used context clues to figure out the meanings of unfamiliar words. Have your child tell you how he or she figured out the meanings of the words in the sentences.

522 Vocabulary

© Pearson Education, Inc. 2

Reader's and Writer's Notebook, p. 522

Vocabulary Strategy for

Unfamiliar Words

Context Clues When you come to a word you don't know while reading, what can you do? You can look for context clues around the word. This strategy can help you figure out the relevant meaning of the word.

1. Read the words and sentences around the word you don't know. Sometimes the author explains the word.
2. Use context clues to develop a meaning for the word.
3. Try that meaning in the sentence. Does it make sense?

Read "Like a Cowboy." Look for context clues to help you understand the meanings of the *Words to Know.*

Words to Write Reread "Like a Cowboy." Would you like to be a cowboy or cowgirl? Why or why not? Write a paragraph. Use words from the *Words to Know* list.

464

LIKE A COWBOY

What was it like to be a cowboy long ago? To find out, some people stay on a ranch. They ride horses, and they chase and rope cattle, or cows. At night around a campfire, they tell stories and sing songs. They even take a herd of cattle on a cattle drive.

Long ago, cowboys took herds of cattle on long cattle drives. They traveled on trails that ran from Texas to Kansas. From there, the railroad took the cattle to cities in the East. The trail was a thousand miles long. The cattle drive lasted for months.

The cattle drive at the ranch today lasts only a day or two. Still, the cattle drive gives people an idea of what it was like to be a cowboy. They can imagine how hard the cowboys worked on the trail. They can imagine how happy the cowboys were as they galloped into town after a long cattle drive.

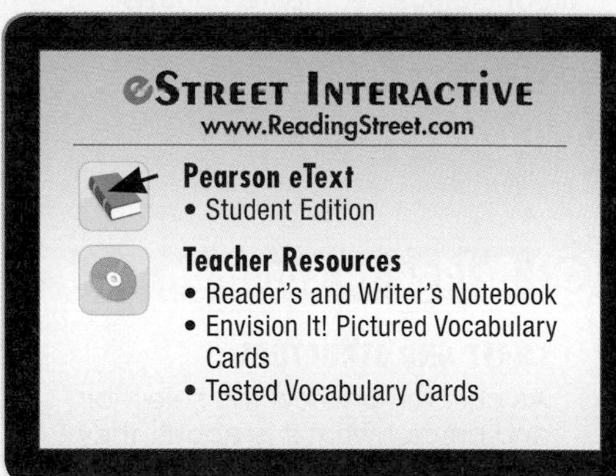

Your Turn!

Need a Review? For more help with using context clues to help you find the meanings of unfamiliar words, see *Words!* on p. W•7.

Ready to Try It? Read *Cowboys* on pp. 466–487.

465

Student Edition, pp. 464–465

Reread for Fluency

Have children reread paragraph 1 of "Like a Cowboy."

Routine Paired Reading

1. **Reread** To achieve optimal fluency, have partners reread the text three or four times.
2. **Corrective Feedback** Listen as children read. Provide corrective feedback regarding their fluency and decoding.

Routines Flip Chart

eSTREET INTERACTIVE
www.ReadingStreet.com

Pearson eText
- Student Edition

Teacher Resources
- Reader's and Writer's Notebook
- Envision It! Pictured Vocabulary Cards
- Tested Vocabulary Cards

Questions Ask children yes and no questions to reinforce word meaning, such as *Can people walk on trails?* Have them answer in complete sentences.

Common Core State Standards

Informational Text 1. Ask and answer such questions as *who, what, where, when, why,* and *how* to demonstrate understanding of key details in a text. **Informational Text 10.** By the end of year, read and comprehend informational texts, including history/social studies, science, and technical texts, in the grades 2–3 text complexity band proficiently, with scaffolding as needed at the high end of the range.

Strategy Response Log

Genre Before reading, have children use p. RR35 in their *Reader's and Writer's Notebook* to identify the characteristics of informational text. Have children look for these characteristics as they read the selection.

Academic Vocabulary 

text structure the organization of a piece of writing, such as cause/effect, chronological, compare/contrast, description, problem/solution, and proposition/support

Bridge to Common Core

CRAFT AND STRUCTURE

As children preview the selection and predict what it is about, they are determining how the purpose is connected to the content and style of an informational text. This sets the stage for children to see how different parts of informational text, including graphics, such as illustrations and a map, and text, are connected to each other and the whole.

Text-Based Comprehension

Introduce Main Selection

Student Edition, pp. 466–467

GENRE Informational text often gives facts about real people, places, and events that may reflect history or the traditions of communities. As they read *Cowboys,* ask children to look for facts that describe history or people's way of life.

PREVIEW AND PREDICT Have children identify the title, the author, and the illustrator. Remind them that the topic sentence is often the first sentence of a paragraph. Help children use topic sentences on pages 468–469 to predict what the main idea of the selection is.

PURPOSE By analyzing *Cowboys,* an informational text, children learn about cowboy traditions.

TEXT STRUCTURE Good readers think about how a piece of writing is organized, such as in sequence or with a problem and solution. Identifying **text structure** helps readers identify important ideas and see how ideas are related to the topic and each other. Have children turn to page EI•26 in their Student Edition.

How is the information on the poster organized? (in a sequence) When I read, I think about how the author has organized the text. As I read *Cowboys,* I will look for a pattern of ideas, such as the problems cowboys faced and how they solved them.

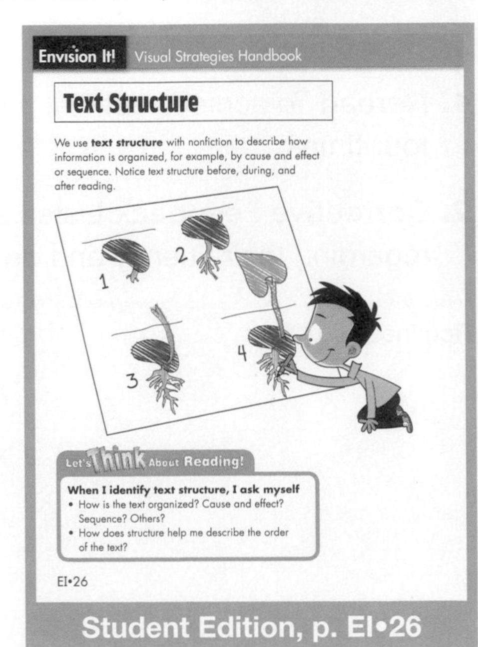

Student Edition, p. EI•26

Access Main Selection

READER AND TASK SUGGESTIONS	
Preparing to Read the Text	**Leveled Tasks**
• Review strategies for understanding unfamiliar words. See the vocabulary skill lesson on p. 464g. • Point out the author's use of a map on pp. 486–487. • Remind children that this text is informational. They may need to read more slowly to better understand the text.	• **Language Conventionality and Clarity** If children have difficulty with complex sentence structure, have them identify confusing sentences and work with them to interpret meanings. • **Language Conventionality and Clarity** If children have no difficulty with complex sentence structure, have them identify and explain examples.

See Text Complexity Measures for *Cowboys* on the tab at the beginning of the week.

READ Tell children that today they will read *Cowboys* for the first time. Use the Read for Understanding routine.

Routine Read for Understanding

Deepen understanding by reading the selection multiple times.

1. **First Read**—If children need support, use the **Access Text** notes to help them clarify understanding.
2. **Second Read**—Use the **Close Reading** notes to help children draw knowledge from the text.

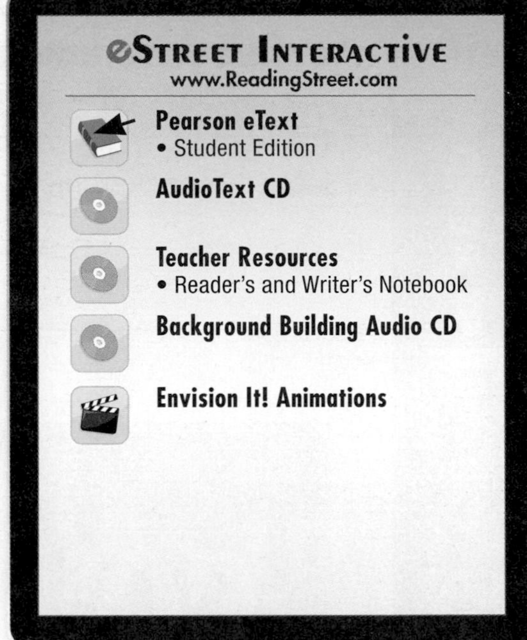

Preview Main Selection Ask children what they already know about cowboys. Then do a picture walk of the selection so children can talk about and see the activities that a cowboy did one hundred years ago.

1ST READ

Access Text If children need help, then...

CONNECT TO CONCEPT Look at the picture of the cowboys on page 467. What is the cowboy in the front wearing? (a cowboy hat, a long-sleeve jacket, a neckerchief) What tools is he using? (a rope, a saddle) Encourage children to answer the questions in complete sentences. What part of the traditional cowboy life does the picture show? (A cowboy working outdoors with animals.)

Student Edition, pp. 466–467

2ND READ

Close Reading

ANALYSIS What is the cowboy doing in the picture? (trying to lasso a wild horse) Why might the cowboy want to catch the horse that is running free? (He might want to catch the horse to tame it so he can ride it.)

SEQUENCE • REREAD CHALLENGING TEXT Remind children that good readers recognize sequence as they read. Have children reread pages 468 and 469. What happened first during a roundup? (Cowboys drove all the cattle together.) What did cowboys do after they drove all the cattle together? (They counted the baby calves that had been born since the last roundup and chose the biggest cattle to sell.)

Common Core State Standards

Informational Text 1. Ask and answer such questions as *who, what, where, when, why,* and *how* to demonstrate understanding of key details in a text. **Also Informational Text 3. and Speaking/Listening 6.**

If you were out west about a hundred years ago, you might have heard a cowboy yelling—*ti yi yippy yay!*—as he rode across the plains.

What was it like to be a cowboy way back then?

Cowboys lived on cattle ranches. A ranch had a house for the rancher and his family, barns for animals, and a bunkhouse where the cowboys slept.

468

The rancher owned thousands of cattle. They wandered for miles looking for grass and water.

Twice a year, the cowboys drove all the cattle together. This was called a roundup. The cowboys counted the baby calves that had been born since the last roundup. The biggest cattle were chosen to sell at market.

469

Student Edition, pp. 468–469

INFERENCE • TEXT EVIDENCE Who lived on a ranch? (The rancher and his family, as well as cowboys who worked for the rancher, lived on the ranch.) Were ranches large or small? What clues from the text and illustration tell you this? (They were large. I know because the rancher had thousands of cattle that wandered for miles.)

1ST READ

Access Text If children need help, then...

TEXT STRUCTURE Is the structure of the information on this page problem and solution or main idea and details? (problem and solution) What problem did cowboys face when rounding up Longhorns? (The Longhorns were wild, fast, and had sharp horns. They charged when they were mad.) How did cowboys solve the problem? (They used a long rope to catch the Longhorns.)

Student Edition, pp. 470–471

2ND READ

Close Reading

ANALYSIS Why did ranchers place brands on their cattle? (The brands proved the rancher owned the cattle.) Why would cattle with different brands be found mixed together? (The cattle roamed free for miles and might cross other ranchers' lands.)

SEQUENCE What happened after the roundup was over? (It was time to sell the Longhorns.) What did the cattle do after they had been walking a while? (The cattle tried to turn around and go home.) What happened next? (The cowboys rode up and down the sides of the herd and at the end to make sure cattle stayed in line and did not get left behind.)

Common Core State Standards

Informational Text 1. Ask and answer such questions as *who, what, where, when, why,* and *how* to demonstrate understanding of key details in a text. **Also Informational Text 3.**

After the roundup was over, it was time to sell the Longhorns. That meant taking them to big market towns. Back then, there were no roads across the wide plains—only dusty trails that cattle had made with their hooves as they tramped along. Some trails were a thousand miles long! Since cattle could walk only fifteen miles a day, the long, hard trip often lasted months. It was called a trail drive. There was a lot to do to get ready.

At the beginning of a trail day, one cowboy rode out in front of the herd. "Come on, boys," he called to the cattle. A few big Longhorns started after him. They bellowed and swung their heads from side to side. Other cattle followed, and soon they were all on their way.

Cattle didn't like so much walking. After a while, they wanted to turn around and go home. Cowboys rode up and down the sides of the herd to keep them in line. A few cowboys rode at the end of the herd to make sure no cattle were left behind.

472 473

Student Edition, pp. 472–473

SYNTHESIS How long could cattle drives last? (Cattle drives often lasted months.) What do you think were some important things that cowboys brought along on these drives?

EVALUATION • TEXT EVIDENCE What is shown in the illustration that is not talked about in the text? (extra horses and a wagon) Why do you think they are included in a cattle drive? (Horses could get hurt, and extra ones would be needed. The wagon carries supplies.)

1ST READ

Access Text If children need help, then...

TEXT STRUCTURE Does the author describe clothing as a problem or a solution for cowboys on the trail? (a solution) What problems did cowboys' clothing solve and how? (Clothes solved problems caused by the weather and the landscape. They kept cowboys comfortable and safe.)

CHECK DECODING Have children check their reading of new words using these questions:

- Did I blend the sounds to read the word?
- Did I put the new word in the sentence to make sure it made sense?
- Did I look for word parts to help me understand the word?

It was hot on the trail. Cowboys wore hats with wide brims to keep the sun out of their eyes. When it rained, the brims made good umbrellas. Around their necks, cowboys wore red bandannas. When it got dusty, they pulled the bandannas over their noses.

Leather leggings—called chaps—were tied over their pants to keep out thorns and cactus spines.

High leather boots kept out dirt and pebbles. Cowboy boots had handles called "mule ears." The cowboy grabbed the mule ears to pull his boots on.

474

475

Student Edition, pp. 474–475

2ND READ

Close Reading

ANALYSIS • TEXT EVIDENCE Explain how a bandana would help a cowboy when he pulled it over his nose. Use clues from the text to help you answer. (A bandanna worn over the nose let the cowboy breathe but blocked dust so the cowboy wouldn't choke.)

SEQUENCE What happened to a cow after it got stuck in the mud? (A cowboy would rope it and pull it out.)

REVIEW UNFAMILIAR WORDS The word *tramped* on page 477 is unfamiliar. Other words in the sentence might help. What tramped? (the herd) A bit further on, I read about the leaders walking. What might *tramped* mean? (walked along)

Common Core State Standards

Informational Text 1. Ask and answer such questions as *who, what, where, when, why,* and *how* to demonstrate understanding of key details in a text. **Also Foundational Skills 3., 4.c., Informational Text 2., and Language 4.a.**

What else did a cowboy need on his trail? A good horse. Cowboys spent the whole day on horseback. They rode little horses called cow ponies. A good cow pony was fearless. It could cross rough ground in the blackest night. It could swim a deep, wide river.

It could crash right through the bushes after a runaway cow. The cowboy had to hold on tight!

Every day the herd tramped the hot, dry plains. Two or three big steers were the leaders. They always walked in front. The cowboys got to know them well. They gave them pet names, like "Old Grumpy" and "Starface."

Cows could get in trouble. Sometimes one got stuck in the mud. The cowboy roped it and pulled it out. A cow might get hurt on the trail. A cowboy took care of that too.

476

477

Student Edition, pp. 476–477

Review MAIN IDEA AND DETAILS • ANALYSIS What is the main idea on page 476? (A cowboy needed a good horse.) What details support your answer? (Cowboys spent the day on horseback. Horses could get across rivers and chase runaway cows.)

CONNECT TO SCIENCE The plains described in the text are a type of grassland biome. Plains are mainly flat, and grasses are the dominant plants. Plains have few trees. Animals common to American plains are bison, prairie dogs, and pronghorn antelope.

1ST READ

Access Text — If children need help, then...

TEXT STRUCTURE What problem did the cowboys solve by using chuckwagons? (Cowboys faced the problem of not getting a hot, filling meal each night. The chuckwagon carried all the supplies the cook needed to make the meal, as well as water for cooking.)

REVIEW SELECTION VOCABULARY Have children locate the selection word *campfire* on page 479. How did the cowboys use their campfire? (The cowboys used their campfire to cook, for light to read or play cards, and to stay warm.)

At night the cowboys stopped to let the cattle eat, drink, and sleep. It was time for the cowboys to eat too. "Cookie" had a hot meal ready for them. That's what cowboys called the cook.

Cookie drove a special wagon called the chuckwagon. It had drawers for flour, salt, beans, and pots and pans. A water barrel was tied underneath.

Cookie gave every cowboy a big helping of biscuits, steak, gravy, and beans. He cooked the same meal almost every night, but the cowboys didn't mind. It tasted good!

There were no tables or chairs, so the cowboys sat right on the ground. After dinner they played cards or read by the flickering light of the campfire. The nights were chilly and bright with stars.

478 479

Student Edition, pp. 478–479

2ND READ

Close Reading

EVALUATION Why did the cook serve the same meal almost every night? Why didn't the cowboys mind? (The cook had limited kinds of food and little time to prepare meals. The cowboys were probably hungry and didn't care what they ate as long as they had food.)

INFERENCE • TEXT EVIDENCE Who set up camp each day? (The cook set up camp.) How do you know? Use clues from the text in your answer. (The cook had a wagon and had to ride ahead to have the meal ready for the cowboys.)

SEQUENCE What happens first, next, and last during a stampede? (First, something scares the cattle, such as a loud noise. Next, the cattle run wildly in all directions. Then cowboys must gallop to the front of the herd to make the leaders turn. They try to make the cattle run in a circle. At last, the cattle calm down and the stampede ends.)

Common Core State Standards

Informational Text 1. Ask and answer such questions as *who, what, where, when, why,* and *how* to demonstrate understanding of key details in a text. **Informational Text 4.** Determine the meaning of words and phrases in a text relevant to a grade 2 topic or subject area.

But the cowboys didn't stay up late. They were tired. At bedtime, they just pulled off their boots and crawled into their bedrolls. A cowboy never wore pajamas. What about a pillow? He used his saddle.

Trail drives were dangerous. Many things could go wrong. The herd might stampede if there was a loud noise—like a sudden crash of thunder. A stampede was scary. Cattle ran wildly in all directions, rolling their eyes and bellowing with fear. The ground shook under them. The bravest cowboys galloped to the front of the herd. They had to make

480

the leaders turn. They shouted at them and fired their six shooters in the air. They tried to make the cattle run in a circle until they calmed down.

Sometimes they'd run into rustlers. A rustler was a cow thief. Rustlers hid behind rocks and jumped out at the cattle to make them stampede. While the cowboys were trying to catch the terrified cattle and calm them down, the rustlers drove off as many as they could.

481

Student Edition, pp. 480–481

ANALYSIS Why didn't cowboys on a cattle drive ever wear pajamas? What other clothing requirements do you think cowboys had?

1ST READ

Access Text

If children need help, then...

TEXT STRUCTURE How did cowboys solve the problem of crossing big rivers? (Cowboys stayed on their horses as the horses swam across. If a cowboy fell off the horse, he held on to his horse's tail as the horse swam across.)

When the herd came to a big river, the cowboys in front galloped right into the water. The cattle plunged in after them. The cattle swam mostly under water. Sometimes the cowboys could see only the tips of their black noses and their long white horns.

Most cowboys didn't know how to swim. If a cowboy fell into the water, he grabbed the horse's tail and held on tight until they reached shore.

Trail drives often went through Indian Territory. The Indians charged ten cents a head to let the cattle cross their land. If the cowboys didn't pay, there might be a fight. But usually the money was handed over and the herd plodded on.

482 483

Student Edition, pp. 482–483

2ND READ

Close Reading

ANALYSIS On page 483, I read that Indians charged cowboys ten cents a head. Explain what this means. (Cowboys had to pay Indians ten cents for each Longhorn in the herd to cross their land.)

SEQUENCE What happened after cowboys got their pay? (They took a bath.)

TEXT STRUCTURE Have children recall some of the problems and solutions they identified in the selection. Then have children describe how this text structure helped connect ideas across the selection.

Common Core State Standards

Informational Text 1. Ask and answer such questions as *who, what, where, when, why,* and *how* to demonstrate understanding of key details in a text.

484

At last, the noisy, dusty cattle stamped into a market town. The cowboys drove them into pens near the railroad tracks. Then they got their pay. It was time for fun!

What do you think most cowboys wanted first? A bath! The barber had a big tub in the back of the shop. For a dollar, you could soak and soak. A boy kept throwing in pails of hot water. Ahh-h-h! Next it was time for a shave, a haircut, and some new clothes.

Tonight, the cowboys would sleep in real beds and eat dinner at a real table. They would sing, dance, and have fun with their friends.

But soon they would be heading back to Longhorn country. There would be many more hot days in the saddle. There would be many more cold nights under the stars.

485

Student Edition, pp. 484–485

EVALUATION • TEXT EVIDENCE What does the picture on page 484 show? What types of businesses and shops were important in a market town? Use clues from the illustration and text to help you answer. (a hotel, a barber, and a blacksmith shop, where cowboys could get their horses shoed)

CONNECT TO SOCIAL STUDIES Modern ranchers use machines to harvest hay for animals to eat. They transport animals using trains and trucks. Most ranches have telephones and Internet access so workers can communicate with others.

1ST READ

Access Text If children need help, then...

SEQUENCE Have children retell the selection in sequence.

CROSS-TEXT EVALUATION
Use a Strategy to Self-Check How did the article "Like a Cowboy" help you understand this selection?

Continue to DAY 2
Text-Based Comprehension
p. 487a

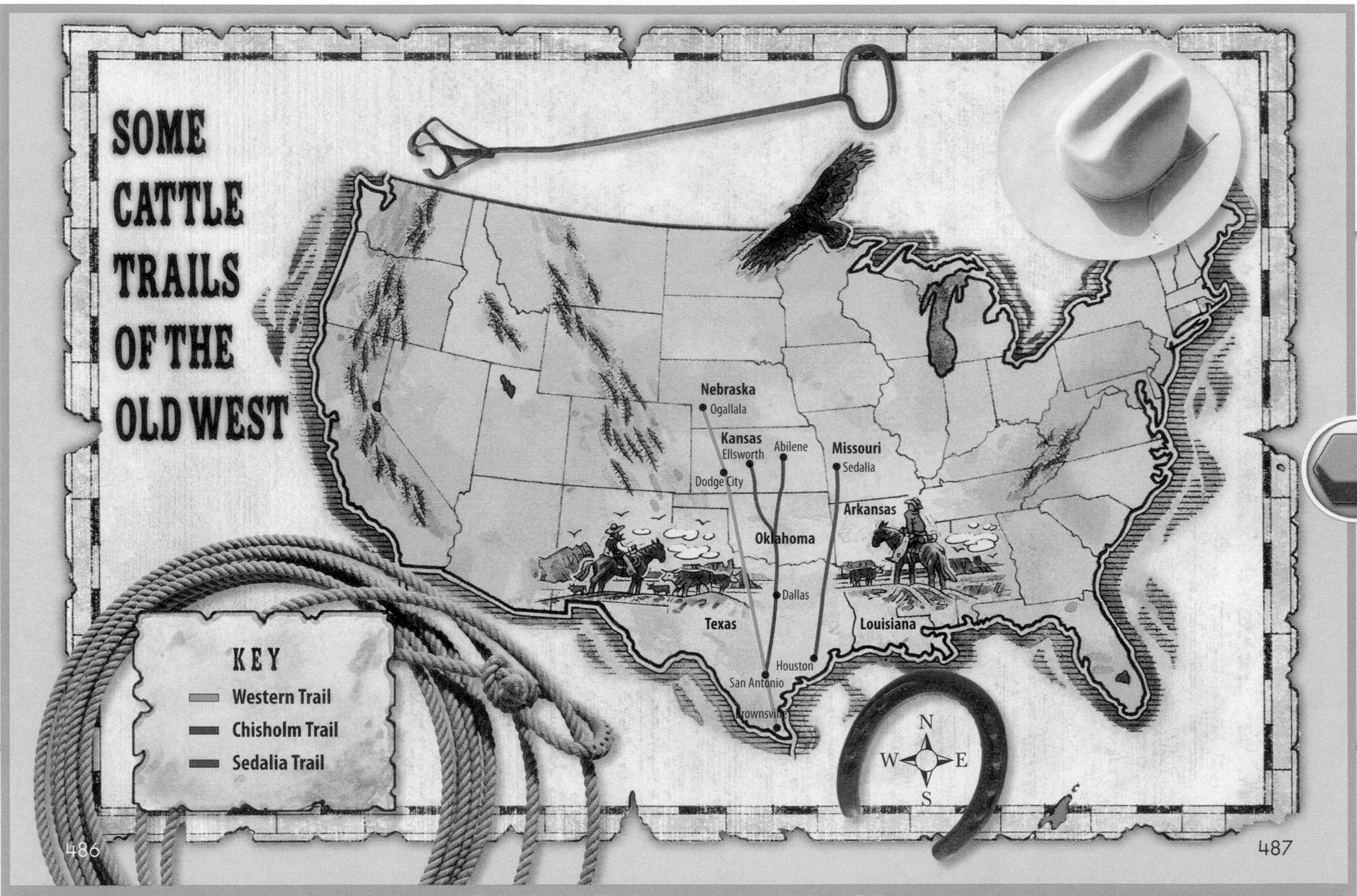

SOME CATTLE TRAILS OF THE OLD WEST
Nebraska
Ogallala
Kansas
Ellsworth
Abilene
Dodge City
Missouri
Sedalia
Arkansas
Oklahoma
Dallas
Texas
Louisiana
Houston
San Antonio
Brownsville
KEY
Western Trail
Chisholm Trail
Sedalia Trail
N
W
E
S
486
487

Student Edition, pp. 486–487

2ND READ

Close Reading

SYNTHESIS • TEXT EVIDENCE Using what you learned in this selection, tell about the traditional cowboy life. Have children cite examples from the text.

Continue to DAY 3
Think Critically
p. 488–489

Text-Based Comprehension

Check Understanding

Have children discuss each question with a partner. Ask several pairs to share their responses.

- **Informational text** What did you learn about the way cowboys lived while on a cattle drive in the Old West? (I learned that cowboys slept in their clothes and used a saddle for a pillow.)
- **Confirm predictions** How did you use the topic sentence on the top of page 470 to predict what would be described on the page? Were your predictions correct? (Children might say that they used the topic sentence to predict that the page would explain why a roundup was hard work.)
- **Compare and contrast** Both the article "Like a Cowboy" and the selection *Cowboys* discuss cowboys' lifestyles. How are the discussions alike? How are they different? (Both selections identify some of the duties of cowboys, including the trail drive. "Like a Cowboy" tells how people today can experience what it was like to be a cowboy long ago, whereas *Cowboys* tells how cowboys actually lived about 100 years ago.)
- **Author's purpose** Why do you think the author included a map in this selection? (The author wanted to share more information about cattle trails of the Old West. She wanted the reader to learn the names and locations of trails, and to see how long the trails were. She also wanted to show the towns where the trails began and ended.)
- **Identify reasons** What reasons does the author give to support the point that trail drives were dangerous? (The author supports the statement by explaining that cattle might stampede because of a loud noise or rustlers, the cowboys had to cross rivers and many of them could not swim, and a fight might break out if cowboys did not pay Indians for crossing Indian lands.)

Common Core State Standards

Informational Text 1. Ask and answer such questions as *who, what, where, when, why,* and *how* to demonstrate understanding of key details in a text. **Informational Text 6.** Identify the main purpose of a text, including what the author wants to answer, explain, or describe. **Informational Text 8.** Describe how reasons support specific points the author makes in a text. **Informational Text 9.** Compare and contrast the most important points presented by two texts on the same topic.

Access for All

Support Discussion If children struggle with the last question, show them a present-day map that includes the area featured on the Old West map in the selection. Guide children to recognize that this area probably has the same rivers and other land features but is much more populated.

Day 2 SMALL GROUP TIME • Differentiate Comprehension, p. SG•52

OL On-Level	SI Strategic Intervention	A Advanced
• **Practice** Selection Vocabulary • **Read** *Cowboys*	• **Reteach** Selection Vocabulary • **Read** *Cowboys*	• **Extend** Selection Vocabulary • **Read** *Cowboys* • **Investigate** Inquiry Project

If... children need more scaffolding and practice with the **Comprehension Skill,**
then... use the ELL activities on p. DI•80 in the Teacher Resources section on SuccessNet.

Common Core State Standards

Informational Text 7. Explain how specific images (e.g., a diagram showing how a machine works) contribute to and clarify a text. **Language 2.** Demonstrate command of the conventions of standard English capitalization, punctuation, and spelling when writing. **Language 2.b.** Use commas in greetings and closings of letters.

Informational Text

Graphic Sources

READ GRAPHIC SOURCES Use the cattle trails map on pages 486–487 in the Student Edition to demonstrate getting information from a graphic source.

- What kinds of information can we get from this map? (the names of the trails, where each trail began and ended, which trail was the longest, what states they passed through)
- How does the map help you understand the selection *Cowboys?* (It shows the cattle trails and helps me understand how long they were and why cowboys were so happy to get to the market towns.)

GUIDE PRACTICE Explain that the class will now outline the information that a reader can get from the map. Use Graphic Organizer 30. Write *Cattle Trails of the Old West* on the title line and *Western Trail* for point A. Work with children to complete the information for the Western Trail.

Title Cattle Trails of the Old West

A. Western Trail
1. Began in Brownsville, Texas, and ended in Ogallala, Nebraska
2. Passed through Texas, Oklahoma, Kansas, and Nebraska
3. Longest trail

B. Chisholm Trail
1. Began in San Antonio, Texas, and ended in Ellsworth, Kansas, and Abilene, Kansas
2. Passed through Texas, Oklahoma, and Kansas
3. Middle trail; split into two

C. Sedalia Trail
1. Began in Houston, Texas, and ended in Sedalia, Missouri
2. Passed through Texas, Oklahoma, Arkansas, and Missouri
3. Shortest trail

Graphic Organizer 30

ON THEIR OWN Distribute copies of Graphic Organizer 30 to small groups and have them complete the outline for the Chisholm and Sedalia Trails. Then have them share their work to compile a class outline.

Conventions

Commas

TEACH Write *Monday, June 2.* Point to each word as you read it. Ask children to identify how many commas appear in the date. (one) What kinds of words does the comma separate? (day and month) Repeat by writing and discussing *May 9, 2015.* I use a comma when I write a date. What other parts of a letter need a comma? (the address and the greeting and closing of the letter)

GUIDE PRACTICE Have children name dates and write them on the board. Ask children to add the commas in the correct places.

APPLY Have children orally answer each question in a complete sentence and clap to show where a comma should appear in the sentence.

1. **When were you born?**
2. **In what city and state were you born?**

ON THEIR OWN Use *Reader's and Writer's Notebook,* p. 523.

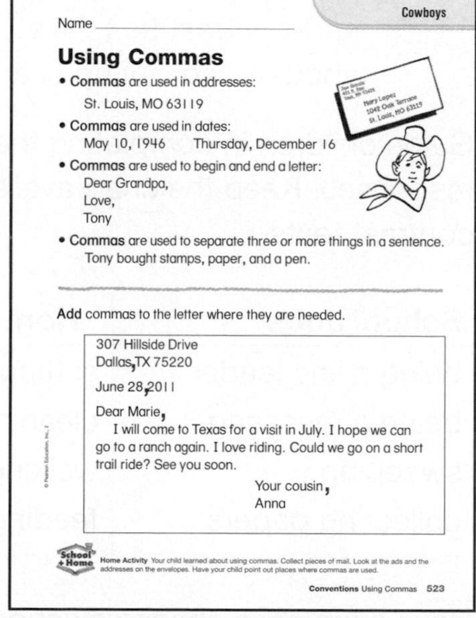

Name ____________ Cowboys

Using Commas

- **Commas** are used in addresses:
  St. Louis, MO 63119
- **Commas** are used in dates:
  May 10, 1946   Thursday, December 16
- **Commas** are used to begin and end a letter:
  Dear Grandpa,
  Love,
  Tony
- **Commas** are used to separate three or more things in a sentence.
  Tony bought stamps, paper, and a pen.

Add commas to the letter where they are needed.

307 Hillside Drive
Dallas, TX 75220

June 28, 2011

Dear Marie,
I will come to Texas for a visit in July. I hope we can go to a ranch again. I love riding. Could we go on a short trail ride? See you soon.

Your cousin,
Anna

Home Activity Your child learned about using commas. Collect pieces of mail. Look at the ads and the addresses on the envelopes. Have your child point out places where commas are used.

Conventions Using Commas 523

Reader's and Writer's Notebook, p. 523

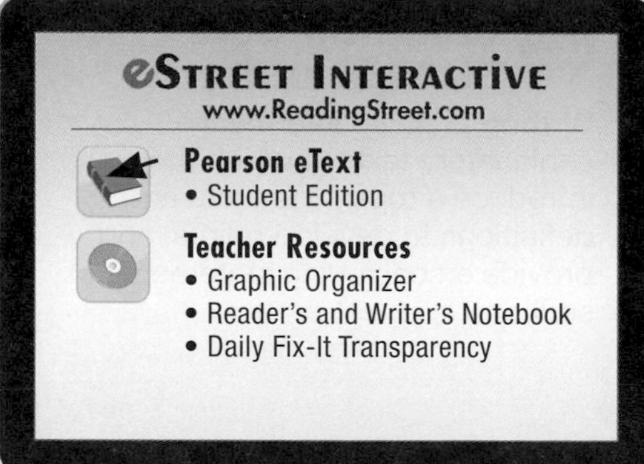

Access for All

Advanced

Practice Commas Challenge children who show a good understanding of comma usage to write a short letter that includes a return address, date, greeting, two body sentences, and closing. Have children circle each comma in their letter.

Daily Fix-It

3. Were sitting by the camfire.
   We're sitting by the campfire.
4. The Cowboy rode the tails.
   The cowboy rode the trails.

Discuss the Daily Fix-It corrections with children. Review contractions, capitalization, and the spelling of *campfire* and *trails.*

Subject/Verb Agreement Some children may need extra help given that the questions use the verb *were* and children will need to use the verb *was* in their answers. Model the sentences for children and have them repeat after you.

Common Core State Standards

Writing 2. Write informative/explanatory texts in which they introduce a topic, use facts and definitions to develop points, and provide a concluding statement or section.

Writing

Compare-and-Contrast Text

Writing Trait: Focus/Ideas

INTRODUCE THE PROMPT Review with children the key features of a compare-and-contrast text. Point out that "Line Leader" is a compare-and-contrast text. Assure children that they can write a text that tells how a job they do is the same as, and different from, the job a cowboy did. Explain that children will use clue words to make the ideas clear. Read aloud the writing prompt.

Writing Prompt

Think about a job you do at home or at school. Think about tasks that cowboys did. Compare and contrast your job with a cowboy's job.

GENERATE COMPARE-AND-CONTRAST TEXT IDEAS

Let's make a list of school and home jobs to help plan the compare-and-contrast text. I'll start with line leader since it was the job we read about in the writing example.

Guide children in completing the chart. Possible ideas are shown. Record the responses. Keep the chart available while children plan their compare-and-contrast texts.

School Jobs	Home Jobs
being a line leader	setting table
being a messenger	cleaning room
sweeping	walking dog
collecting papers	feeding pet

Have each child choose a school or home job. Circulate to guide children. Tell them to review *Cowboys* for ideas of how the job they chose compares and contrasts with the job of a cowboy.

Mini-Lesson Compare and Contrast

- **Introduce** Use *Reader's and Writer's Notebook,* p. 524 to model planning the compare-and-contrast text. To plan the text, I will use a Venn diagram. Raking leaves is my job choice. To begin, I will label the first section *Raking Leaves,* the middle section *Both,* and the last section *Rounding Up Cattle.* Now I will focus on details to show how the two jobs are alike and different.

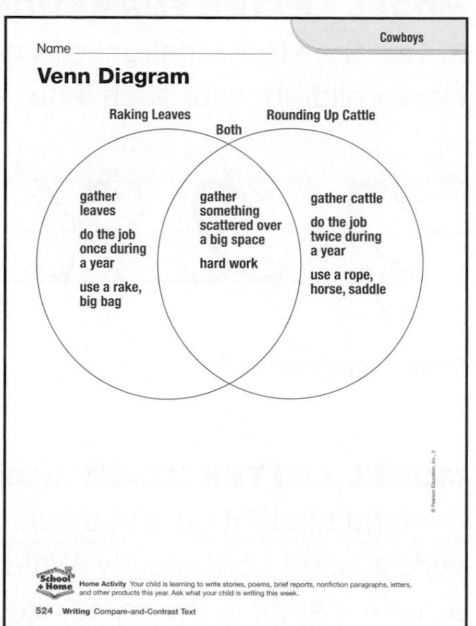
Name ______ Cowboys

Venn Diagram

Raking Leaves | Both | Rounding Up Cattle

Raking Leaves: gather leaves; do the job once during a year; use a rake, big bag

Both: gather something scattered over a big space; hard work

Rounding Up Cattle: gather cattle; do the job twice during a year; use a rope, horse, saddle

School + Home Home Activity Your child is learning to write stories, poems, brief reports, nonfiction paragraphs, letters, and other products this year. Ask what your child is writing this week.

524 Writing Compare-and-Contrast Text

Reader's and Writer's Notebook, p. 524

- **Model** First, I'll look at how the jobs are different. When I rake leaves, I gather leaves. I also do the job once during the year. I use a rake and bags. So I'll write these ideas in the left section. A cowboy gathered cattle. He did the job twice during the year. He used a horse, saddle, and rope. I'll write these details in the right section. The jobs are the same because both the cowboy and I gathered something that is scattered over a big space. Both jobs are hard work, too. Now it's your turn to plan your text. Circulate to guide children as they complete their diagrams.

Routine Quick Write for Fluency

1. **Talk** Have partners take two minutes to identify their jobs and tell how they compare and contrast with a cowboy's job.
2. **Write** Each child writes a sentence that either tells how the jobs are the same or different using a clue word such as *both, and,* and *but.*
3. **Share** Each child reads his or her sentence aloud. The partner tells if the sentence is a comparison or a contrast and explains the reasoning.

Routines Flip Chart

Access for All

SI Strategic Intervention

Completing the Diagram If children have difficulty completing the diagram, have them list details of the job they chose and the job of a cowboy. Have them review both lists to see what is different about the two jobs.

ELL

Support Prewriting

Beginning Children can pantomime the job they chose and say a word or phrase to identify the job.

Intermediate Have children pantomime the job they chose. Have them describe the details of the job to other children.

Advanced Have children write short sentences in their diagrams and share them with a partner. As they share the ideas, children can clarify and add details.

Common Core State Standards

Informational Text 5. Know and use various text features (e.g., captions, bold print, subheadings, glossaries, indexes, electronic menus, icons) to locate key facts or information in a text efficiently.

Handwriting

Cursive *Z*, *Q*, and *X*/Letter Slant

MODEL LETTER FORMATION Display uppercase cursive letters: *Z*, *Q*, and *X*. Use the stroke instructions pictured below to model proper letter formation. Have children write each letter several times and circle their best ones.

D'Nealian Cursive™

MODEL LETTER SLANT Explain that when we write, our letters may slant or stand straight up and down. Each of these styles is okay, as long as the style is used consistently. Write the sentence *Quinn is home,* making sure that all letters slant in the same direction. When I write this sentence, all my letters should lean, or slant, in the same direction. Write *Quinn is home* again, so that some letters slant one way and some slant the other way. My letters should not slant both left and right, so that they overlap, or bump into each other. By writing letters that always slant in the same direction, I make it easier for others to understand what I write. Ask children which of the two writing examples is easier to read and have them explain why.

GUIDE PRACTICE Write the following sentence, using inconsistent slant.

Zack always shows kindness.

Have children rewrite the sentence correctly.

Team Talk Have children work in pairs to discuss what was wrong with the sentence and how they corrected it. Have them write their first and last names at a slant and up and down and choose the style most comfortable for them.

Research and Inquiry

Step 2 Research Skill: Schedule

TEACH Tell children that a **source** is a person, place, or thing that provides information. Point out that a **schedule** can be a source of information. Explain that a schedule tells the activities or events that are planned and the order in which they will occur. Remind children that they follow a daily schedule in their class.

Think Aloud **MODEL** Display Research Transparency 29. This is an example of a schedule. Let's see how a schedule is organized. Point out the title, columns, headings, and rows of recorded information. The title is *Buckaroo Camp Schedule.* The title tells me that I will find out what campers do during the day at Buckaroo Camp. The schedule lists times and the activity that happens at each time. For example, I can see that the campers ride horses from 9:30 to 11:00.

Using a Schedule

Buckaroo Camp Schedule

Time	Activity
8:00 – 9:00	Clean stalls, water horses
9:00 – 9:30	Saddle horses
9:30 – 11:00	Ride horses
11:00 – 11:30	Unsaddle and wash horses
11:30 – 12:30	Lunch
12:30 – 1:30	Learn about horses
1:30 – 2:30	Saddle horses
2:30 – 3:30	Trail ride
3:30 – 4:00	Wash horses
4:00 – 4:30	Lariat practice
4:30 – 5:00	Feed and water horses
5:00	Camp Ends

Unit 6 Cowboys Research 29

Research Transparency 29

GUIDE PRACTICE Ask children other questions about the information on the schedule, such as: *When do campers learn about horses?* Remind children that a schedule is one kind of source that they may find helpful when gathering information.

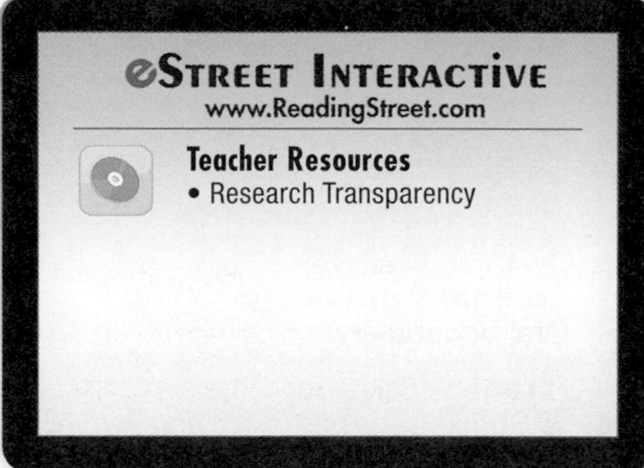

Academic Vocabulary

schedule a visible display of information organized on a table that tells activities or events and the time they will be done

source a person, place, or thing that provides information

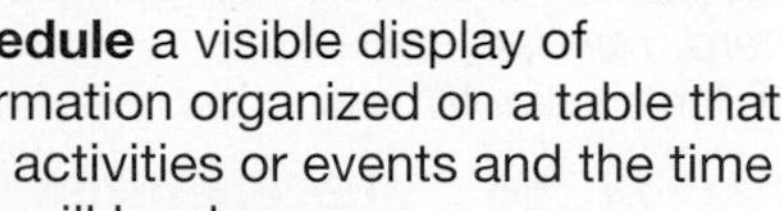

RESEARCH TO BUILD AND PRESENT KNOWLEDGE

Children will gather evidence from texts and other sources to use in answering questions for their research projects. They will also

- learn to use a schedule as a source
- learn to read a schedule

Wrap Up Your Day!

✔ **Content Knowledge** Monitor children's use of oral vocabulary as they respond. How was being a cowboy a tough occupation? (Cowboys worked in hot climates, and they worked along dangerous trails.) Describe the livestock cowboys handled. (Cowboys drove Longhorns and calves.)

Preview DAY 3

Tell children that tomorrow they will reread *Cowboys.*

DAY 3 at a Glance

Content Knowledge
Oral Vocabulary

Phonics/Spelling
Suffixes *-ness, -less, -able, -ible*

Fluency
Accuracy and Appropriate Rate

Selection Vocabulary
campfire, cattle, cowboy, galloped, herd, railroad, trails
Unfamiliar Words

Text-Based Comprehension
Review Main Idea and Details

Conventions
Commas

Writing
Compare-and-Contrast Text

Research and Inquiry
Gather and Record Information

Materials

- Student Edition
- Sing with Me Big Book
- Read Aloud Anthology
- Reader's and Writer's Notebook
- Decodable Reader 29B
- Retelling Cards

Common Core State Standards

Speaking/Listening 2. Recount or describe key ideas or details from a text read aloud or information presented orally or through other media. **Language 6.** Use words and phrases acquired through conversations, reading and being read to, and responding to texts, including using adjectives and adverbs to describe (e.g., *When other kids are happy that makes me happy*).

Content Knowledge

Cowboys

EXPAND THE CONCEPT To reinforce concepts and to focus children's attention, have children sing "Occupation: Cowboy" from the *Sing with Me* Big Book. What was the trail like? (The trail was rough.)

Build Oral Language

LISTEN FOR AMAZING WORDS Display the *Read Aloud Anthology* selection "B is for Buckaroo: A Cowboy Alphabet." Read the story and have children listen for the word *lariat.* Have them also think about cowboy traditions.

- Hats stand for the letter *H.* What is the traditional hat cowboys wore? ("Stetson," or "Ten Gallon")
- How did hats protect cowboys? (They kept sun, rain, and snow off the cowboys.)

"B is for Buckaroo: A Cowboy Alphabet"

TALK ABOUT SENTENCES AND WORDS Write the following sentence from "B is for Buckaroo: A Cowboy Alphabet" on sentence strips or on the board.

L is for Lariat or Lasso, a loop of rope coiled just so.

- Ask children to read it with you as you track the print.
- Point to and read *L is for Lariat or Lasso.* What does this mean? (The letter *L* is the first letter in the words *lariat* and *lasso.*) Why does the author use the word *lariat?* (It begins with the letter *L* and it's a tool cowboys use.) What other words could the author have used?
- Now point to and read ... *a loop of rope coiled just so.* What does *coiled* mean? ("twisted around") Why do you think the author chose the word *coiled?* (It has an *l* in it.)
- **Team Talk** Now have children work with a partner to replace key words in the sentence with simpler words or synonyms. Use the following sentence frame.

L is for ______ or lasso, a loop of rope ______ just so.

Build Oral Vocabulary

Amazing Words — Robust Vocabulary Routine

1. **Introduce the Word** Relate the word *lariat* to the book. The cowboys swing their *lariats* high and low. Supply a child-friendly definition. A *lariat* is a stiff length of rope with a sliding loop at one end, used for catching horses or cows. Have children say the word.
2. **Demonstrate** Provide examples to show meaning. A cowboy tosses a *lariat* over a cow's head to catch the cow. I am moving my arm to show how to swing and toss a *lariat.*
3. **Apply** Have children demonstrate their understanding. What would a cowboy catch with a *lariat*—a horse, a tree, or a shoe?
4. **Display the Word** Run your hand under the three syllables *lar-i-at* as you read the word.

Routines Flip Chart

ADD TO THE CONCEPT MAP Use these questions to discuss the importance of cowboy traditions as you add to the map.

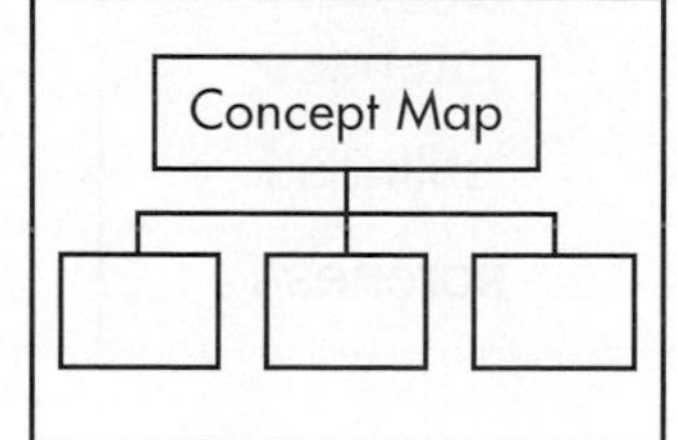

- In *Cowboys,* why was an Old West cattle roundup dangerous? (Cattle could hurt cowboys with their sharp horns.) Let's add *Cattle can be dangerous* to our map.
- Where did cowboys eat and sleep? (outdoors) Let's add *Old West cowboys ate and slept outdoors* to our map.
- How do cowboys' clothes protect them? (Clothes protect cowboys from sun, rain, dust, sharp plants, dirt, and rocks.) Let's add *Clothes protect against weather and injury* to the map.

Amazing Words

climate	drover
livestock	lariat
occupation	legend
buckaroo	rawhide

Expand Vocabulary Use the Day 3 instruction on ELL Poster 29 to expand children's use of English vocabulary to communicate about lesson concepts.

Access Content Many of the terms in "B is for Buckaroo" are adapted from Spanish terms, including *bronco (bronco), buckaroo (vaquero), chaps (chaperreras), lariat (la reata), lasso (lazo),* and *mustang (musteño)*. Point out these words to Spanish speakers to help them better understand the terms.

Common Core State Standards

Foundational Skills 3. Know and apply grade-level phonics and word analysis skills in decoding words. **Foundational Skills 3.d.** Decode words with common prefixes and suffixes.

Phonics

Build Words

MODEL WORD BUILDING Write *-ness, -less, -able,* and *-ible* as headings on a four-column chart. Now we are going to build words with the suffixes *-ness, -less, -able,* and *-ible.* Write *quick.* This word is *quick.* I will see which suffix I can add to *quick* to make a new word. Write *-ness* at the end of *quick.* When I write the suffix *-ness* at the end *quick,* I recognize the word *quickness.* Model reading *quickness.* Write *quickness* on the chart under *-ness* in the chart.

GUIDE PRACTICE Write the remaining base words from each column one at a time in random order. Have children add the appropriate suffix and read the words. Then have them add each word to the appropriate column on the chart. Monitor children's work.

Corrective feedback For corrective feedback, model the correct spelling and pronunciation. Read the words and have children echo you.

-ness	*-less*	*-able*	*-ible*
quickness	toothless	readable	forcible
lateness	flightless	teachable	collectible
stillness	shapeless	usable	sensible
soreness	speechless	enjoyable	convertible

Fluent Word Reading

MODEL Write *sweetness.* I recognize the base word *sweet* and the suffix *ness.* I put them together and read the word *sweetness*.

GUIDE PRACTICE Write the words below. Look for word parts you know. When I point to the word, we'll read it together. Allow one second per word part previewing time for the first reading.

rudeness	countless	likable	edible	fixable	loneliness

ON THEIR OWN Have children read the list above three or four times, until they can read one word per second.

Decode and Read

DECODE WORDS IN ISOLATION
Have children turn to page 243 in *Decodable Practice Readers* 2.2 and find the first list of words. Each word in this list ends with the suffix *-ness, -less, -able,* or *-ible*. Let's read these words. Be sure that children correctly read each word part. Next, have children read the high-frequency words.

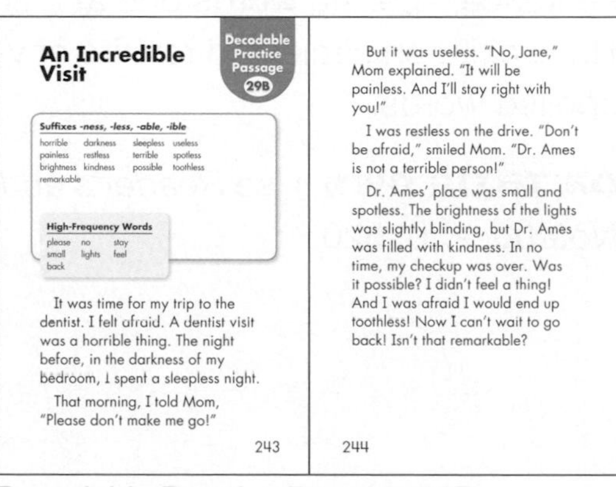
An Incredible Visit

Decodable Practice Passage 29B

Suffixes *-ness, -less, -able, -ible*

horrible	darkness	sleepless	useless
painless	restless	terrible	spotless
brightness	kindness	possible	toothless
remarkable			

High-Frequency Words

please	no	stay
small	lights	feel
back		

It was time for my trip to the dentist. I felt afraid. A dentist visit was a horrible thing. The night before, in the darkness of my bedroom, I spent a sleepless night.

That morning, I told Mom, "Please don't make me go!"

243

But it was useless. "No, Jane," Mom explained. "It will be painless. And I'll stay right with you!"

I was restless on the drive. "Don't be afraid," smiled Mom. "Dr. Ames is not a terrible person!"

Dr. Ames' place was small and spotless. The brightness of the lights was slightly blinding, but Dr. Ames was filled with kindness. In no time, my checkup was over. Was it possible? I didn't feel a thing! And I was afraid I would end up toothless! Now I can't wait to go back! Isn't that remarkable?

244

Decodable Practice Passage 29B

DECODE WORDS IN CONTEXT
Chorally read the story along with children. Have children identify words in the story that end in *-ness, -less, -able,* and *-ible.*

Team Talk Pair children and have them take turns reading the story aloud to each other. Monitor children as they read to check for proper pronunciation and appropriate pacing.

Access for All

SI Strategic Intervention

Support Reading List words with suffixes from the story and model reading them. Have children echo. Then have them find the words in the text. Have children chorally read the sentences.

A Advanced

Extend Reading Challenge children to add words with suffixes *-ness, -less, -able,* and *-ible* to the story. Have them read their new version to the class.

Cognates Students literate in Spanish may recognize the cognates *sensato/sensible* and *convertible/convertible.*

Common Core State Standards

Language 2. Demonstrate command of the conventions of standard English capitalization, punctuation, and spelling when writing. **Foundational Skills 4.b.** Read on-level text orally with accuracy, appropriate rate, and expression on successive readings.

Spelling Words

Suffixes *-ness, -less*

1. kindness	**7. sadness**
2. careless	**8. sickness**
3. goodness	**9. helpless**
4. useless	**10. thankless**
5. fearless	**11. fitness**
6. darkness	**12. weakness**

High-Frequency Words

13. machine	**14. wash**

Spelling

Suffixes *-ness, -less*

SPELL HIGH-FREQUENCY WORDS Write *machines* and *wash* and point them out on the Word Wall. Then write *machine* underneath *machines.* Review that *-s* was added to *machine* to show more than one. Have children say and spell *machine* and *wash* with you and then without you.

DICTATION Have children write these sentences. Say each sentence. Then repeat it slowly, one word at a time.

1. **I will not be careless when I wash the machine.**
2. **Good fitness helps prevent sickness and weakness.**
3. **Tim showed kindness and goodness to the helpless kitten.**

PROOFREAD AND CORRECT Write each sentence, spelling words one at a time. Have children circle and rewrite any misspelled words.

ON THEIR OWN Use *Reader's and Writer's Notebook,* p. 526.

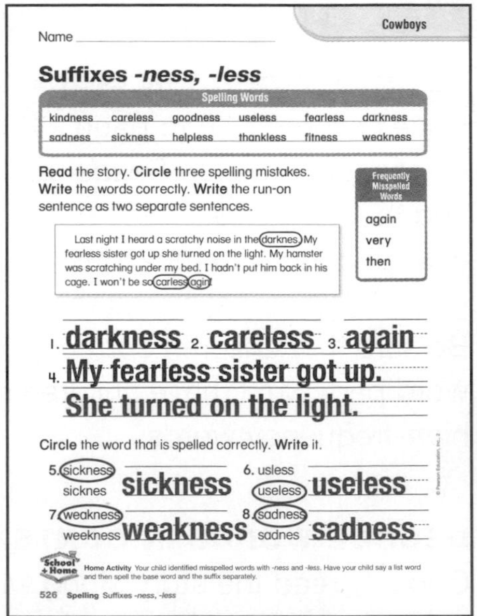

Name ____ Cowboys

Suffixes *-ness, -less*

Spelling Words					
kindness	careless	goodness	useless	fearless	darkness
sadness	sickness	helpless	thankless	fitness	weakness

Frequently Misspelled Words: again, very, then

Read the story. **Circle** three spelling mistakes. **Write** the words correctly. **Write** the run-on sentence as two separate sentences.

Last night I heard a scratchy noise in the darknes. My fearless sister got up she turned on the light. My hamster was scratching under my bed. I hadn't put him back in his cage. I won't be so carless agin.

1. darkness 2. careless 3. again
4. My fearless sister got up. She turned on the light.

Circle the word that is spelled correctly. **Write** it.

5. sickness / sicknes — sickness
6. usless / useless — useless
7. weakness / weekness — weakness
8. sadness / sadnes — sadness

Home Activity Your child identified misspelled words with -ness and -less. Have your child say a list word and then spell the base word and the suffix separately.

526 Spelling Suffixes -ness, -less

Reader's and Writer's Notebook, p. 526

If... children need more scaffolding and practice with reading the **Main Selection,**
then... use the ELL activities on p. DI•81 in the Teacher Resources section on SuccessNet.

Day 3 SMALL GROUP TIME • Differentiate Close Reading, p. SG•52

OL On-Level	SI Strategic Intervention	A Advanced
• **Reread** to Develop Vocabulary • **Reread** *Cowboys*	• **Reread** to Develop Vocabulary • **Reread** *Cowboys*	• **Reread** to Develop Vocabulary • **Reread** *Cowboys* • **Investigate** Inquiry Project

Fluency

Accuracy and Appropriate Rate

MODEL FLUENT READING Have children turn to Student Edition, page 468. Good readers read without making mistakes. They don't skip words. They read with accuracy. They also read at an appropriate rate—not too fast or too slow.

GUIDE PRACTICE Have children read the page with you. Then have them reread the page as a group without you until they read with no hesitation and no mistakes. Continue in the same way with page 469.

Corrective feedback	**If...** children have difficulty reading with accuracy and appropriate rate, **then...** prompt: • Are you reading too fast? • Are you skipping any words? • Try to read at a good pace, not too fast and not too slow.

Reread for Fluency

Routine Choral Reading

1. **Select a Passage** For *Cowboys,* use pp. 470–471.
2. **Model** First, have children track the print as you read.
3. **Guide Practice** Then have children read along with you.
4. **Corrective Feedback** Have the class read aloud without you. Monitor progress and provide feedback. For optimal fluency, children should reread three to four times.

Routines Flip Chart

CHECK COMPREHENSION Have children retell the passage in the correct sequence of events.

Access for All

Strategic Intervention

Base Words and Suffixes If children have trouble reading words with suffixes, have them cover the suffix with their finger and read the base word by itself. Then have them lift their finger and read the whole word.

Options for Oral Rereading

Use *Cowboys* or the Day 1 Decodable Practice Reader.

Preteach Phrases and Terms
Preteach certain phrases and terms from the story, such as "let it fly" and "wild and fast," that may be difficult for English learners.

Common Core State Standards

Informational Text 2. Identify the main topic of a multiparagraph text as well as the focus of specific paragraphs within the text. **Language 4.** Determine or clarify the meaning of unknown and multiple-meaning words and phrases based on grade 2 reading and content, choosing flexibly from an array of strategies. **Also Language 4.a.**

Selection Vocabulary

campfire an outdoor fire used for cooking or warmth

cattle cows, bulls, and steers that are raised for their milk, meat, or skins

cowboy a man who works on a cattle ranch or in rodeos

galloped ran fast (referring to a horse)

herd a group of the same kind of animals that are kept or fed together

railroad a road or track of two steel rails on which trains run

trails overland paths

Vocabulary

Selection Vocabulary

REVIEW SELECTION WORDS Display and review the selection words *cattle, trails, cowboy, herd, campfire, railroad,* and *galloped*. Have children read the words aloud.

Team Talk Have children work in pairs to write a sentence using each selection word and illustrate it on a separate sheet of paper. Have them assemble the pages to make a picture dictionary.

Unfamiliar Words

REVIEW UNFAMILIAR WORDS Tell children that they may come to a word they do not know in a selection. Explain that they can use context clues, or nearby words and sentences, to help them determine the relevant meaning of the unfamiliar word.

GUIDE PRACTICE Write *The cowboy's clothes were filthy after riding in the dust and dirt.* I think *filthy* means "dirty." The words *dust and dirt* give me clues. A cowboy who has been riding all day in dust and dirt would have dirty clothes.

Write the following sentences:

The cattle quietly grazed on the tall, green grass.

The cowboys following the herd rode in a dusty haze.

Have children read the sentences. Discuss the meanings of the underlined words. Have children tell the clues that helped them figure out each word.

grazed—ate; (clues) *tall, green grass*

haze—dust in the air; (clues) *following the herd, dusty*

Team Talk Have children review *Cowboys* to find two other unfamiliar words. Have them discuss the words, phrases, or surrounding sentences that helped them determine the relevant meaning of the unfamiliar words.

Text-Based Comprehension

Read Main Selection

REVIEW MAIN IDEA AND DETAILS Tell children that today they will read the selection again. Remind children that the **main idea** tells what a paragraph or selection is mainly about. **Details** are small pieces of information that can support the main idea. Identifying the main idea and its supporting details helps us recognize the most important ideas the author wants us to know about a topic. Have children turn to pages 474–475 in their Student Edition. Look at the details. Use them to decide what the main idea on these pages is. (Cowboys wore special clothing to protect themselves.) For additional practice with identifying main idea and details, see Let's Practice It!, p. 324 on the *Teacher Resources DVD-ROM.*

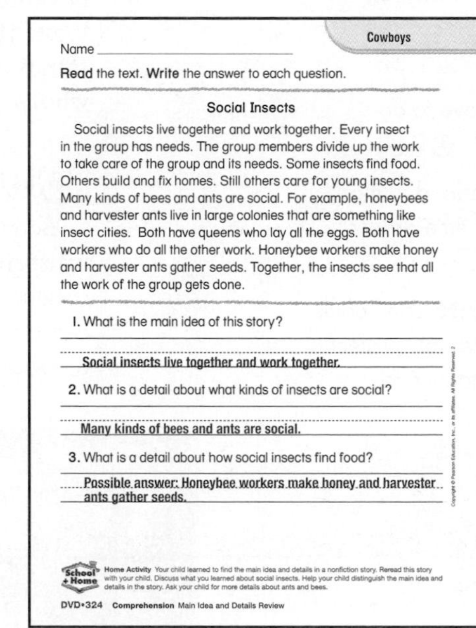

Cowboys

Name ______________

Read the text. **Write** the answer to each question.

Social Insects

Social insects live together and work together. Every insect in the group has needs. The group members divide up the work to take care of the group and its needs. Some insects find food. Others build and fix homes. Still others care for young insects. Many kinds of bees and ants are social. For example, honeybees and harvester ants live in large colonies that are something like insect cities. Both have queens who lay all the eggs. Both have workers who do all the other work. Honeybee workers make honey and harvester ants gather seeds. Together, the insects see that all the work of the group gets done.

1. What is the main idea of this story?
   Social insects live together and work together.
2. What is a detail about what kinds of insects are social?
   Many kinds of bees and ants are social.
3. What is a detail about how social insects find food?
   Possible answer: Honeybee workers make honey and harvester ants gather seeds.

School + Home **Home Activity** Your child learned to find the main idea and details in a nonfiction story. Reread this story with your child. Discuss what you learned about social insects. Help your child distinguish the main idea and details in the story. Ask your child for more details about ants and bees.

DVD•324 Comprehension Main Idea and Details Review

Let's Practice It! TR DVD•324

GENRE: INFORMATIONAL TEXT Remind children that informational text often gives facts about real people, places, and events that may reflect history or the traditions of communities. Have children recall facts from *Cowboys* that indicate this selection represents informational text. (It shares facts about the history of cattle drives and about how cowboys lived, worked, and dressed.)

READ Return to pages 466–487 and use the **2nd Read/Close Reading Notes** to reread *Cowboys.*

Routine Read for Understanding

Deepen understanding by reading the selection multiple times.

1. **First Read**—If children need support, use the **Access Text** notes to help them clarify understanding.
2. **Second Read**—Use the **Close Reading** notes to help children draw knowledge from the text.

Academic Vocabulary

main idea the big idea that tells what a paragraph or a selection is mainly about

details small pieces of information

Support Discussion To help children recall selection details that reflect the genre, use the Retelling Cards to provide visual support for the discussion.

Common Core State Standards
Informational Text 6. Identify the main purpose of a text, including what the author wants to answer, explain, or describe. **Also Informational Text 2., Writing 2.**

Envision It! Retell

READING STREET ONLINE
STORY SORT
www.ReadingStreet.com

Think Critically

1. In the text, cowboys took the cattle to market. How do you think today's cowboys get the cattle to market? Text to World
2. What does the author want you to know about the work cowboys did? Think Like an Author
3. What did cowboys have to do before the trail drive? Sequence
4. What events are described in the story? Are they put in time order? Text Structure
5. **Look Back and Write** Look back at page 474. How did hats protect cowboys? Provide evidence to support your answer.
   Key Ideas and Details • Text Evidence

488

Meet the Author and the Illustrator

LUCILLE RECHT PENNER

Lucille Recht Penner often writes about life long ago. She likes to write about cowboys. People were adventurous and brave in the Old West. They were willing to do hard things even when they didn't know what would happen to them.

Read more books written by Lucille Recht Penner or illustrated by Ben Carter.

Wilma Mankiller: Principal Chief of the Cherokee Nation

X Marks the Spot!

BEN CARTER

Ben Carter has been an artist since he graduated from college. He is of Native American descent, and his books often draw upon his heritage.

Reading Log
Use the *Reader's and Writer's Notebook* to record your independent reading.

489

Student Edition, pp. 488–489

Common Core State Standards

Informational Text 1. Ask and answer such questions as *who, what, where, when, why,* and *how* to demonstrate understanding of key details in a text. **Also Informational Text 2., 6. and Writing 2.**

Bridge to Common Core

KEY IDEAS AND DETAILS

By reading the text multiple times, children will make logical inferences from the text and cite textual evidence when writing or discussing the knowledge they have gained.

Use the Think Critically page to ensure a thorough understanding of *Cowboys.*

Think Critically

1. **TEXT TO WORLD** Cattle may get to market by trucks or trains.
2. **THINK LIKE AN AUTHOR** The author wants me to know that a cowboy's job was hard and even dangerous.
3. **SEQUENCE** Before a trail drive, cowboys had to round up the cattle.
4. **TEXT STRUCTURE** Events described are the roundup before the cattle drive, what happened along the drive, and what happened when the cowboys reached the market town. The events are in time order.
5. **LOOK BACK AND WRITE • TEXT EVIDENCE** For writing fluency, assign a five-minute time limit. As children finish, encourage them to reread their response and proofread for errors.

Scoring Rubric Look Back and Write

TOP-SCORE RESPONSE A top-score response uses details from the text and the picture to explain how hats protected cowboys.

A top-score response may include:
The wide brim of a cowboy hat kept the sun out of the cowboy's eyes. When it rained, the brim acted like an umbrella and kept the cowboy's face dry.

Retell

Have children work in pairs, retelling the selection to one another. Remind children that their partners should include the topic, main ideas, and what they learned from the reading. Have children use the retelling strip in the Student Edition or the Story Sort to retell the selection. Monitor children's retellings.

Scoring Rubric Expository Retelling

	4	3	2	1
Connections	Makes connections and generalizes beyond the text	Makes connections to other events, texts, or experiences	Makes a limited connection to another event, text, or experience	Makes no connection to another event, text, or experience
Author's Purpose	Elaborates on author's purpose	Tells author's purpose with some clarity	Makes some connection to author's purpose	Makes no connection to author's purpose
Topic	Describes the main topic	Identifies the main topic with some details early in retelling	Identifies the main topic	Retelling has no sense of topic
Important Ideas	Gives accurate information about ideas using key vocabulary	Gives accurate information about ideas with some key vocabulary	Gives limited or inaccurate information about ideas	Gives no information about ideas
Conclusions	Draws conclusions and makes inferences to generalize beyond the text	Draws conclusions about the text	Is able to tell some learnings about the text	Is unable to draw conclusions or make inferences about the text

Don't Wait Until Friday

MONITOR PROGRESS Check Retelling

If... children have difficulty retelling the selection,
then... use the Retelling Cards/Story Sort to scaffold their retelling.

Access for All

A Advanced

Look Back and Write Ask children who show proficiency with the writing prompt to explain what it was like to be a cowboy.

Strategy Response Log

Text Structure Have children revisit p. RR35 in their *Reader's and Writer's Notebook* to note the text characteristics they thought they might find in the selection. Which characteristics did they find? Were there characteristics they did not find? Were there characteristics they did not expect to find?

Plan to Assess Retelling

- ☐ **Week 1** Strategic Intervention
- ☐ **Week 2** Advanced
- ☐ **Week 3** Strategic Intervention
- ☑ **This Week** Assess On-Level children.
- ☐ **Week 5** Strategic Intervention
- ☐ **Week 6** Assess any children you have not yet checked during this unit.

Meet the Author and the Illustrator

Read aloud page 489 as children follow along. Discuss why Lucille Recht Penner likes writing about life long ago, especially cowboy life.

Read Independently

Have children enter their independent reading into their Reading Logs.

Common Core State Standards

Language 2. Demonstrate command of the conventions of standard English capitalization, punctuation, and spelling when writing. **Language 2.b.** Use commas in greetings and closings of letters. **Writing 2.** Write informative/explanatory texts in which they introduce a topic, use facts and definitions to develop points, and provide a concluding statement or section.

Daily Fix-It

5. How many cattel are in the herd. How many cattle are in the herd?
6. The Cowboy gallupped. The cowboy galloped.

Discuss the Daily Fix-It corrections with children. Review capitalization, question marks, and the spelling of *cattle* and *galloped.*

Conventions

Commas

REVIEW Remind children that commas are used in addresses, dates, and in the greeting and closing of a letter: *I will visit the dentist on Tuesday, November 1.*

GUIDE PRACTICE Write *April 18 2008, Greenwood CA, Dear Jen,* and *Your friend Cal.* Have children read each example aloud.

Where should we put a comma in each of these examples?

Team Talk Have partners work together to rewrite each example correctly. Have them identify if each example is a date, an address, a greeting, or a closing.

APPLY Have children orally complete each of the following sentence frames with a day and date. Ask children where a comma appears in each sentence.

1. **Today is ______.**
2. **Yesterday was ______.**
3. **Tomorrow will be ______.**

ON THEIR OWN Use Let's Practice It!, p. 327 on the *Teacher Resources DVD-ROM.*

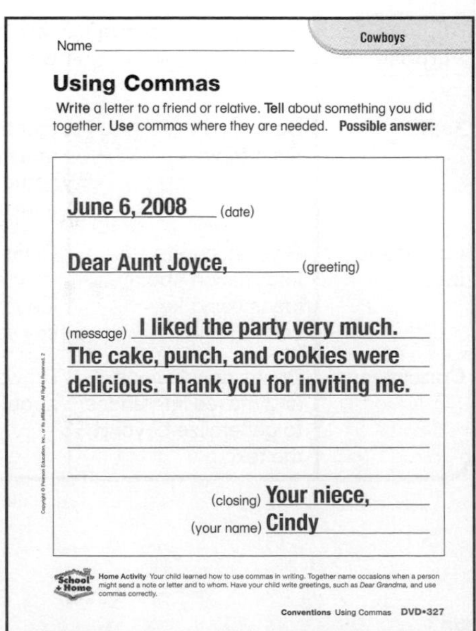
Name ______ Cowboys

Using Commas

Write a letter to a friend or relative. **Tell** about something you did together. **Use** commas where they are needed. **Possible answer:**

June 6, 2008 (date)

Dear Aunt Joyce, (greeting)

(message) I liked the party very much. The cake, punch, and cookies were delicious. Thank you for inviting me.

(closing) Your niece,

(your name) Cindy

Home Activity Your child learned how to use commas in writing. Together name occasions when a person might send a note or letter and to whom. Have your child write greetings, such as *Dear Grandma,* and use commas correctly.

Conventions Using Commas DVD•327

Let's Practice It! TR DVD•327

Common Core State Standards
Writing 8. Recall information from experiences or gather information from provided sources to answer a question. **Also Language 2.**

Let's Write It!

Key Features of a Compare-and-Contrast Text
- tells how two things are alike and how they are different
- uses clue words to show likenesses and differences

READING STREET ONLINE
GRAMMAR JAMMER
www.ReadingStreet.com

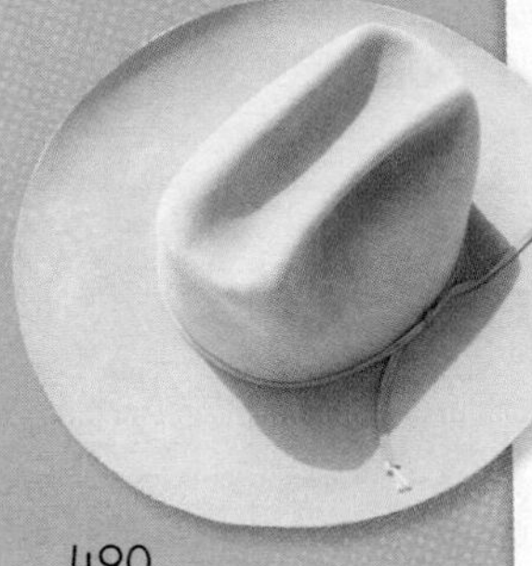

Expository

Compare-and-Contrast Text

A compare-and-contrast text tells how two things are alike and how they are different. Writers can use clue words to help them compare and contrast things. Some clue words are *both, and,* and *but.* The student model on the next page is an example of a compare-and-contrast text.

Writing Prompt Think about a job you do at home or at school. Think about tasks that cowboys did. Compare and contrast your job with a cowboy's job.

Writer's Checklist

Remember, you should ...
- ✓ tell how the tasks are alike and different.
- ✓ use clue words to help compare and contrast.
- ✓ focus on important ideas.
- ✓ use commas correctly.

490

Student Model

Caring for Animals

Both cowboys and I care for animals. Cowboys took care of cattle, and I take care of my fish. I have to feed my fish and help clean the tank. On a trail drive, cowboys had to get cattle food, water, and rest. Cowboys made sure the cattle stayed safe.

My job takes minutes. A cowboy's job took months. Mine is easy, but a cowboy's was hard. I do my job once a day, but a cowboy worked all day.

Writer uses **commas** correctly. They separate the items *food, water,* and *rest.*

Writing Trait Focus Writer focuses on likenesses and differences.

Genre This **compare-and-contrast text** tells how the jobs are alike and different.

Conventions

- **Commas**
  Remember Use **commas** to separate three or more items listed together in a sentence.
- Cowboys ate **beans, biscuits,** and **steak**.

491

Student Edition, pp. 490–491

Let's Write It!

WRITE A COMPARE-AND-CONTRAST TEXT Use pp. 490–491 in the Student Edition. Read aloud the Key Features of a Compare-and-Contrast Text and the definition. Read aloud the Writing Prompt and discuss the Writer's Checklist.

REVIEW THE STUDENT MODEL Read "Caring for Animals" on p. 491 aloud. Ask children to tell which jobs are being compared. Use the clue words *both, and,* and *but* to help children recognize how the jobs are alike and different. Then discuss the side notes about genre, the writing trait, and commas.

Scoring Rubric

TOP-SCORE RESPONSE Help children understand that a top-score response focuses on likeness and differences and uses clue words such as *both, like,* and *but.* For a complete rubric see Writing Rubric 29 from the *Teacher Resources DVD-ROM.*

CONNECT TO CONVENTIONS Read the Conventions note. Point out commas used to separate three or more items. (food, water, and rest)

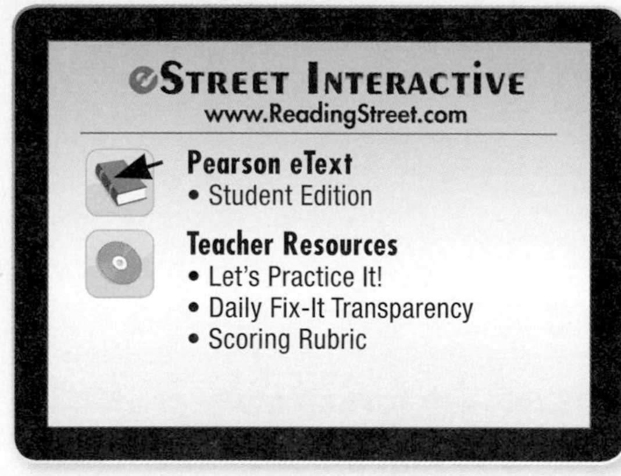

Write Guy *by Jeff Anderson*

Conferring Is Listening

Conferring about children's writing is more about teachers *listening* than teachers speaking. What is the child trying to say? What help does he need? We can ask questions to keep kids speaking. "What do you want your reader to know? Wow, how did you think of this vivid phrase?"

Common Core State Standards

Writing 2. Write informative/explanatory texts in which they introduce a topic, use facts and definitions to develop points, and provide a concluding statement or section. **Writing 7.** Participate in shared research and writing projects (e.g., read a number of books on a single topic to produce a report; record science observations). **Writing 8.** Recall information from experiences or gather information from provided sources to answer a question.

Writing

Compare-and-Contrast Text

Mini-Lesson Writer's Craft: Compare/Contrast Words

- **Introduce** Use the Venn diagram from yesterday and Writing Transparency 29A to model writing a compare-and-contrast text. I will use my Venn diagram to write. I said that my job of raking leaves was like a cowboy's round-up job. Both jobs round up scattered things. Reading *Cowboys* made me think a cowboy's job is hard. I do a hard job too, so I added those comments. I use clue words *like* and *both* to tell how the jobs are the same. In the diagram, I wrote I gather leaves, but the cowboy gathers cattle. I rake once during the year, but the cowboy rounds up cattle twice. Finally, I use a rake and bags, but a cowboy uses a horse, saddle, and rope. The clue word *but* helps me tell how the jobs are different. Read aloud the draft on the Transparency to model a compare-and-contrast text.

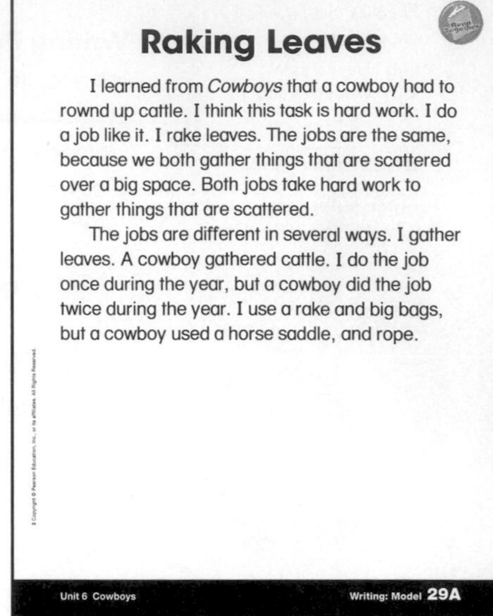

Raking Leaves

I learned from *Cowboys* that a cowboy had to rownd up cattle. I think this task is hard work. I do a job like it. I rake leaves. The jobs are the same, because we both gather things that are scattered over a big space. Both jobs take hard work to gather things that are scattered.

The jobs are different in several ways. I gather leaves. A cowboy gathered cattle. I do the job once during the year, but a cowboy did the job twice during the year. I use a rake and big bags, but a cowboy used a horse saddle, and rope.

Unit 6 Cowboys Writing: Model 29A

Writing Transparency 29A TR DVD

- Explain how children can use their diagram to draft a text. Remind them the goal is to write ideas. They can edit later.

GUIDE WRITING Now it is time to write your compare-and-contrast text. Use clue words to make the likenesses and differences clear. Have children use their Venn diagram, and guide them as they draft the text.

Routine Quick Write for Fluency

Team Talk

1. **Talk** Have partners take two minutes to talk about the school or home job they chose.
2. **Write** Each child writes sentences to compare the jobs.
3. **Share** Partners read aloud their sentences.

Routines Flip Chart

Research and Inquiry

Step 3 Gather and Record Information

TEACH Tell children that today they will gather information about routine cowboy tasks. Their goal is to find information that will help them make a schedule of a cowboy's routine. Review using appropriate sources for information.

Think Aloud **MODEL** Display the list of questions from Day 1. We asked the question *What would a cowboy do at the beginning of the day?* I can infer that he would wake up early and have breakfast, and from reading *Cowboys* I learned that one cowboy would start the cattle on the trail. Record the details in the chart.

GUIDE PRACTICE Have partners use what they have read in *Cowboys* and other relevant sources you provide to research a question. Have them take notes about the timing of each event. Tell them exact times will not be possible. Compile the information. Tell children that tomorrow they will review the topic to make sure their questions were answered.

ON THEIR OWN Use *Reader's and Writer's Notebook,* p. 525 to help children identify relevant sources.

Topic: Cowboy Routine

Question	Answer
What would a cowboy do at the beginning of the day?	wake up early, have breakfast, start the cattle on the trail

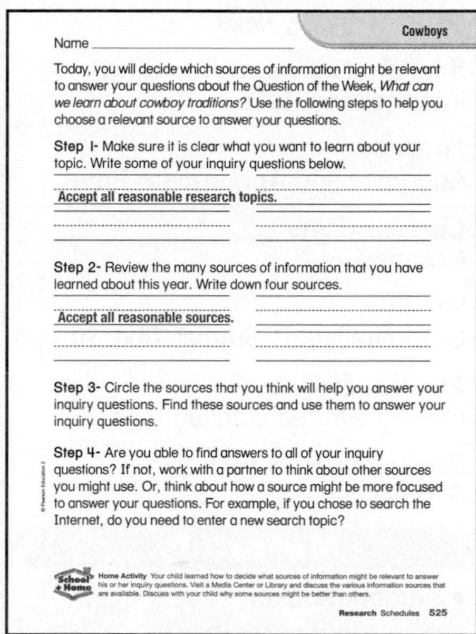
Cowboys

Name ____________

Today, you will decide which sources of information might be relevant to answer your questions about the Question of the Week, *What can we learn about cowboy traditions?* Use the following steps to help you choose a relevant source to answer your questions.

Step 1- Make sure it is clear what you want to learn about your topic. Write some of your inquiry questions below.

Accept all reasonable research topics.

Step 2- Review the many sources of information that you have learned about this year. Write down four sources.

Accept all reasonable sources.

Step 3- Circle the sources that you think will help you answer your inquiry questions. Find these sources and use them to answer your inquiry questions.

Step 4- Are you able to find answers to all of your inquiry questions? If not, work with a partner to think about other sources you might use. Or, think about how a source might be more focused to answer your questions. For example, if you chose to search the Internet, do you need to enter a new search topic?

School + Home **Home Activity** Your child learned how to decide what sources of information might be relevant to answer his or her inquiry questions. Visit a Media Center or Library and discuss the various information sources that are available. Discuss with your child why some sources might be better than others.

Research Schedules 525

Reader's and Writer's Notebook, p. 525

Wrap Up Your Day!

✔ **Sequence** What did cowboys do after they got paid for the cattle drive? (They took a bath.)

✔ **Text Structure** Have children tell how the details in *Cowboys* help them understand about cowboys.

Tell children that tomorrow they will read about the things cowboys use and wear.

DAY 4 at a Glance

Content Knowledge
Oral Vocabulary

Phonics
Review Final Syllables *-tion, -ture, -ion*

High-Frequency Words
Review

Spelling
Suffixes *-ness, -less*

Social Studies in Reading
Informational Text

Fluency
Accuracy and Appropriate Rate

Conventions
Commas

Writing
Compare-and-Contrast Text: Revise

Media Literacy
Identify Written Conventions

Research and Inquiry
Synthesize

Materials

- Student Edition
- Sing with Me Big Book
- Read Aloud Anthology
- Decodable Reader 29C
- Reader's and Writer's Notebook

Common Core State Standards

Speaking/Listening 2. Recount or describe key ideas or details from a text read aloud or information presented orally or through other media. **Language 6.** Use words and phrases acquired through conversations, reading and being read to, and responding to texts, including using adjectives and adverbs to describe (e.g., *When other kids are happy that makes me happy*).

Content Knowledge

Cowboys

EXPAND THE CONCEPT To reinforce concepts and to focus children's attention, have children sing "Occupation: Cowboy" from the *Sing with Me* Big Book. What kind of livestock does the song mention? (The song mentions cattle.)

REVIEW GENRE: INFORMATIONAL TEXT Have children tell the key features of informational text: it contains facts about real people, places, and events. It shares information about nature or society, such as culture and history. Explain that today you will read another selection about cowboy life, "Cowboy: An Album" by Linda Granfield.

"Cowboy: An Album"

MONITOR LISTENING COMPREHENSION Recall how cowboys lived and how they worked with cattle in the Old West. Have children listen to "Cowboy: An Album."

Team Talk **TALK ABOUT COWBOYS**
Read aloud the third paragraph on page 159 of the selection "Cowboy: An Album." Display it on a whiteboard if possible, and track the print as you read.

- Have pairs of children generate questions about what they visualize about modern cowboys when they hear this paragraph.
- Add words generated in the discussion to the concept map.

Build Oral Vocabulary

Amazing Words — Robust Vocabulary Routine

1. **Introduce the Word** Relate the word *legend* to the selection. Cowboys of the Old West are *legends.* Supply a child-friendly definition. A *legend* is a story that has been passed down through the years. *Legend* can also be used to refer to a famous person who had great talents. Have children say the word.

2. **Demonstrate** Provide examples to show meaning. There is a *legend* about a cowboy who could catch any wild horse. Davy Crockett is a *legend* in the history of the United States.

3. **Apply** Have children demonstrate their understanding. Which would be a *legend*—a story about a horse in the Old West or a story about your pet dog?

4. **Display the Word** Run your hand under the two syllables *leg-end* as you read the word. Point out /j/ spelled with the letter *g* as you read the word.

See p. OV•4 to teach *rawhide.*

Routines Flip Chart

ADD TO THE CONCEPT MAP Continue to discuss cowboy traditions.

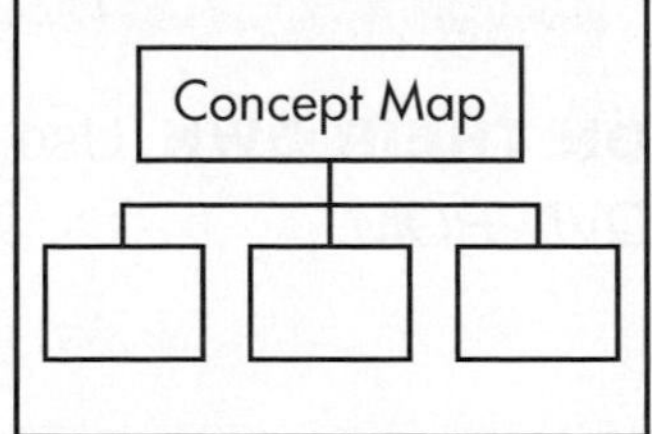

- What do we learn about cowboy traditions in "Cowboy: An Album"? (Some traditions have changed and some haven't.) Let's add this idea to our map.
- What are some things about cowboys that have changed? (Cowboys use different gear, such as computers. Cowboys may use machines instead of horses. Ranches are harder to run.) What are some things about cowboys that haven't changed? (Cowboys still work on ranches, work hard, and are proud of what they do.) Where can we add this information to our map?

Amazing Words

climate	drover
livestock	lariat
occupation	legend
buckaroo	rawhide

Access for All

A Advanced

Amazing Words Allow children who demonstrate an understanding of the word *legend* to retell a legend that they are familiar with.

ELL

Produce Oral Language Use the Day 4 instruction on ELL Poster 29 to extend and enrich language.

Preview Comprehension Use ELL Poster 29 before reading the selection to discuss what the open land of a ranch looks like and where a cowboy works.

Common Core State Standards

Foundational Skills 3. Know and apply grade-level phonics and word analysis skills in decoding words. **Foundational Skills 3.d.** Decode words with common prefixes and suffixes. **Foundational Skills 3.f.** Recognize and read grade-appropriate irregularly spelled words.

Vocabulary Support

You may wish to explain the meanings of these words.

fixture something that stays in one place

scallion a kind of small onion

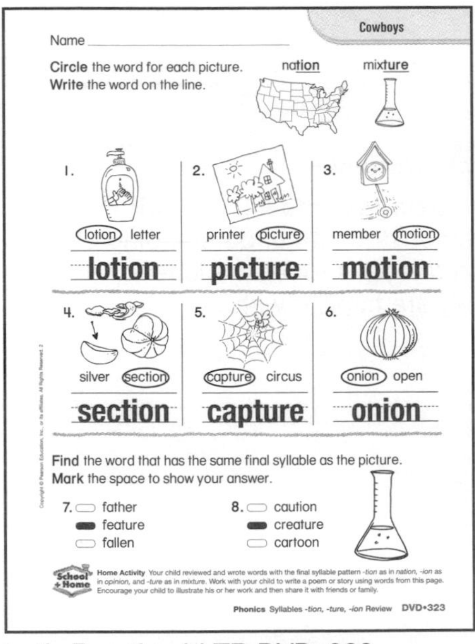
Cowboys

Name ________

Circle the word for each picture.
Write the word on the line.

nation mixture

1. lotion letter — lotion
2. printer picture — picture
3. member motion — motion
4. silver section — section
5. capture circus — capture
6. onion open — onion

Find the word that has the same final syllable as the picture.
Mark the space to show your answer.

7. father / feature / fallen
8. caution / creature / cartoon

School + Home **Home Activity** Your child reviewed and wrote words with the final syllable pattern *-tion* as in *nation*, *-ion* as in *opinion*, and *-ture* as in *mixture*. Work with your child to write a poem or story using words from this page. Encourage your child to illustrate his or her work and then share it with friends or family.

Phonics Syllables *-tion, -ture, -ion* Review DVD•323

Let's Practice It! TR DVD•323

Phonics

Review Final Syllables *-tion, -ture, -ion*

REVIEW FINAL SYLLABLES To review last week's phonics skill, write *station, mixture,* and *opinion.* You studied words like these last week. What do you know about the endings of these words? (The ending spelling patterns *-tion, -ture,* and *-ion* make up the final syllable in the words.)

Corrective feedback | If children are unable to answer the question about final syllables *-tion, -ture,* and *-ion,* refer them to Sound-Spelling Cards 135, 136, and 131.

GUIDE PRACTICE Write *-tion, -ture,* and *-ion* as heads in a three-column chart. I will write some words. Read each word in your head. Then hold up one finger if the word ends with *-tion.* Hold up two fingers if the word ends with *-ture.* Hold up three fingers if the word ends with *-ion.* Write *fixture, opinion, future, fiction, billion, motion, stallion, mention, furniture, solution, scallion,* and *adventure.* As children respond, write each word in the appropriate column. Then have children read the columns of words.

-tion	*-ture*	*-ion*
fiction	fixture	opinion
motion	future	billion
mention	furniture	stallion
solution	adventure	scallion

ON THEIR OWN Use Let's Practice It!, p. 323 on the *Teacher Resources DVD-ROM.*

Fluent Word Reading

Spiral Review

READ WORDS IN ISOLATION Display these words. Tell children that they can blend or chunk some words on this list and others are Word Wall words.

Have children read the list three or four times until they can read at the rate of two to three seconds per word.

buy	eagles	half	reversible	breathless
teaches	larger	many	horrible	meadow
hurried	their	sitting	reading	alone
tirelessly	darkness	gazing	youngest	enjoyable

Corrective feedback — **Word Reading**

If... children have difficulty reading whole words,
then... have them use sound-by-sound blending or combine meaningful word parts strategy for decodable words or have them say and spell high-frequency words.

If... children cannot read fluently at a rate of two to three seconds per word,
then... have pairs practice the list until they can read it fluently.

READ WORDS IN CONTEXT Display these sentences. Call on individuals to read a sentence. Then randomly point to review words and have children read them. To help you monitor word reading, high-frequency words are underlined and decodable words are italicized.

I *hurried* in the *darkness* feeling *horrible* and *breathless.*

<u>Their</u> <u>youngest</u> daughter *tirelessly teaches reading.*

Ron had an *enjoyable* day *sitting* <u>alone</u> in the *meadow gazing* at the <u>many</u> *eagles.*

I want to <u>buy</u> a *reversible* jacket that is a <u>half</u> size *larger.*

Corrective feedback — **Sentence Reading**

If... children are unable to read an underlined high-frequency word,
then... read the word and spell it, having them echo you.

If... children have difficulty reading an italicized decodable word,
then... guide them in blending or combining word parts.

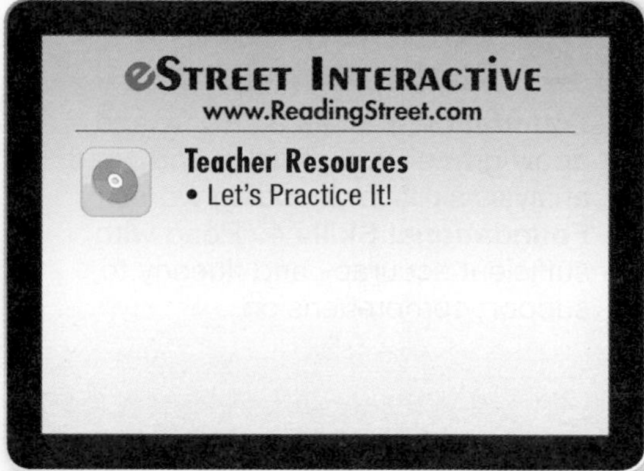

Spiral Review

These activities review

- your previously taught high-frequency words *alone, buy, half, many, their, youngest.*
- suffixes *-ness, -less, -able, -ible.*
- inflected endings.
- long and short *ea.*

Access for All

SI Strategic Intervention

Sounds of *ea* Write words with the *ea* spelling pattern having both the short and long *e* sounds, such as *leap, leave, bread, feast, feather,* and *weather.* Guide children to try both vowel sounds to decode each word. Have children use the words in sentences.

Fluent Word Reading Have children listen to a more fluent reader model the words or have pairs read the words together.

Common Core State Standards

Foundational Skills 3. Know and apply grade-level phonics and word analysis skills in decoding words. **Foundational Skills 4.** Read with sufficient accuracy and fluency to support comprehension.

Decodable Reader 29C

If children need help, then...

Read *In the Darkness*

DECODE WORDS IN ISOLATION Have children turn to page 245 in *Decodable Practice Readers* 2.2 and decode each word.

READ HIGH-FREQUENCY WORDS Have children identify and read the high-frequency words *power, no, lights, small, feel,* and *stay* on the first page.

PREVIEW Have children read the title and preview the story. Tell them they will read words with suffixes *-ness, -less, -able,* and *-ible.*

DECODE WORDS IN CONTEXT Pair children for reading and listen carefully as they decode. One child begins. Children read the entire story, switching readers after each page. Partners reread the story. This time the other child begins.

In the Darkness

Written by Joel Grand

Decodable Practice Reader 29C

Suffixes -ness, -less, -able, -ible

remarkable	useless	restless	darkness
dependable	brightness	helpless	readable
sleepless	kindness	edible	

High-Frequency Words

power	no	lights
small	feel	stay

245

Decodable Practice Reader 29C

There was a remarkable storm.
It knocked out our power.
We had no lights.
Many things in our house became useless.
246

We felt restless in the darkness.
We went to look for things to do.
We found something that helped us in the darkness.
247

Mom found a dependable flashlight.
The light was small, but its brightness made us feel brave.
Mom and I went to explore.
248

"We are not helpless," Mom added.
"We have light, and we have each other, so we're not lonely.
Let's find something readable."
249

When it was bedtime, Mom and I went to my room.
I was sleepless.
My nightlight did not glow.
Mom stayed with me.
250

Mom was still in my room when I woke.
"Why did you stay?" I asked.
"I didn't want you to be afraid," she said.
251

As I hugged Mom for her kindness, I saw that the clock blinked on and off. "Our power is on," Mom cried.
"No more staying in the darkness!
Let's find something edible!"
252

Corrective feedback	**If...** children have difficulty decoding a word, **then...** refer them to the Sound-Spelling Cards to identify sounds in a decodable word; prompt them to blend the word. If the word has the suffix *-ness, -less, -able,* or *-ible,* have them identify the word parts and read them together to say the word. • What is the new word? • Is the new word a word you know? • Does it make sense in the story?

CHECK DECODING AND COMPREHENSION Have children retell the story to include characters, setting, and events. Then have children find words that include suffixes *-ness, -less, -able,* and *-ible.* Children should supply the following words:

-ness: *darkness, brightness, kindness*

-less: *useless, restless, helpless, sleepless*

-able: *remarkable, dependable, readable*

-ible: *edible*

Reread for Fluency

REREAD DECODABLE READER Have children reread Decodable Practice Reader 29C to develop automaticity reading words with suffixes *-ness, -less, -able,* and *-ible.*

Routine Oral Rereading

1. **Read** Have children read the entire book orally.
2. **Reread** To achieve optimal fluency, children should reread the text three or four times.
3. **Corrective Feedback** Listen as children read. Provide corrective feedback regarding their fluency and decoding.

Routines Flip Chart

Decodable Reader

Beginning Preview *In the Darkness* with children. Identify the words *darkness* and *brightness* in pictures and print. Have children repeat them. Then have children draw a picture of something that shows darkness on one side of a sheet of paper and something that shows brightness on the other. Reread the story aloud. Have children hold up the corresponding picture when they hear *darkness* or *brightness.*

Intermediate After reading, write on the board *darkness, useless, brightness, sleepless, readable,* and *edible.* Have children read each word and identify the suffix. Then have each child use two of the words in a sentence about the story as he or she pages through the text.

Advanced After reading, have children find and read words with suffixes in the story. Then have them use the words to make up two sentences about the mom and boy in the story.

Common Core State Standards

Language 2. Demonstrate command of the conventions of standard English capitalization, punctuation, and spelling when writing. **Language 4.c.** Use a known root word as a clue to the meaning of an unknown word with the same root (e.g., *addition, additional*). **Informational Text 1.** Ask and answer such questions as *who, what, where, when, why,* and *how* to demonstrate understanding of key details in a text.

Spelling

Suffixes *-ness, -less*

PARTNER REVIEW Supply pairs of children with index cards on which the spelling words have been written. Have one child read a word while the other writes it. Then have children switch roles. Have them use the cards to check their spelling and correct any misspelled words.

ON THEIR OWN Have children identify each spelling word's meaning by using the known base word with the meaning of the suffix. For example, children would use their understanding of the base word *fear* and the meaning of the suffix *-less* to define *fearless* as "without fear."

Use Let's Practice It!, p. 326 on the *Teacher Resources DVD-ROM.*

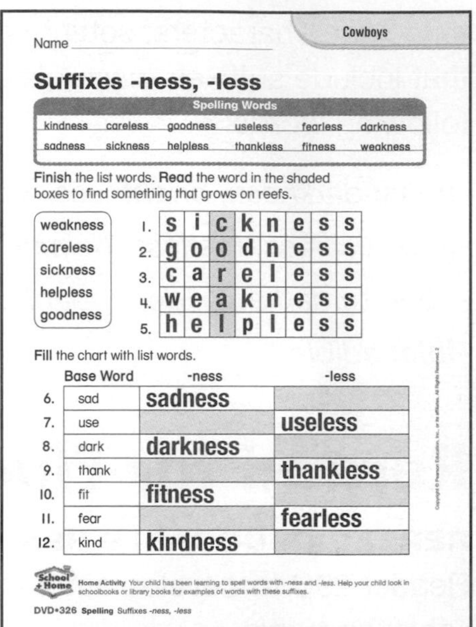

Name ______ Cowboys

Suffixes -ness, -less

Spelling Words

kindness	careless	goodness	useless	fearless	darkness
sadness	sickness	helpless	thankless	fitness	weakness

Finish the list words. **Read** the word in the shaded boxes to find something that grows on reefs.

weakness, careless, sickness, helpless, goodness

1. s i c k n e s s
2. g o o d n e s s
3. c a r e l e s s
4. w e a k n e s s
5. h e l p l e s s

Fill the chart with list words.

	Base Word	-ness	-less
6.	sad	sadness	
7.	use		useless
8.	dark	darkness	
9.	thank		thankless
10.	fit	fitness	
11.	fear		fearless
12.	kind	kindness	

School + Home **Home Activity** Your child has been learning to spell words with -ness and -less. Help your child look in schoolbooks or library books for examples of words with these suffixes.

DVD•326 Spelling Suffixes -ness, -less

Let's Practice It! TR DVD•326

ELL

If... children need more scaffolding and practice with **Amazing Words**, **then...** use the routine on pp. xxxvi–xxxvii in the *ELL Handbook.*

Day 4 SMALL GROUP TIME • Differentiate Vocabulary, p. SG•52

OL On-Level
- **Develop** Language Using Amazing Words
- **Read** *Reading Street Sleuth,* pp. 74–75

SI Strategic Intervention
- **Review/Discuss** Amazing Words
- **Read** *Reading Street Sleuth,* pp. 74–75

A Advanced
- **Extend** Amazing Words and Selection Vocabulary
- **Read** *Reading Street Sleuth,* pp. 74–75
- **Organize** Inquiry Project

Social Studies in Reading

Informational Text

ACTIVATE PRIOR KNOWLEDGE Ask children to recall what they learned from other texts this week about cowboys. (Cowboys lived and worked on ranches. They rode horses and drove cattle along trails to take them to market towns.)

PREVIEW AND PREDICT Read the title and the author's name of the selection on pages 492–493 of the Student Edition. Have children look through the selection and predict what they might learn. (They might learn about cowboys and what they wore.) Ask what clues helped them make their prediction. (the title, the subheads, and the picture)

READ INFORMATIONAL TEXT Tell children that they will read a selection that is an informational text. Review the key features of **informational text:** it gives facts about real people, places, and events that may reflect history or the traditions of communities. It often has headings and pictures that illustrate the text. Explain that this selection is informational text because it gives facts about real people—cowboys.

Genre

LET'S THINK ABOUT... As children read "Cowboy Gear," use Let's Think About in the Student Edition to help them focus on the features of informational text.

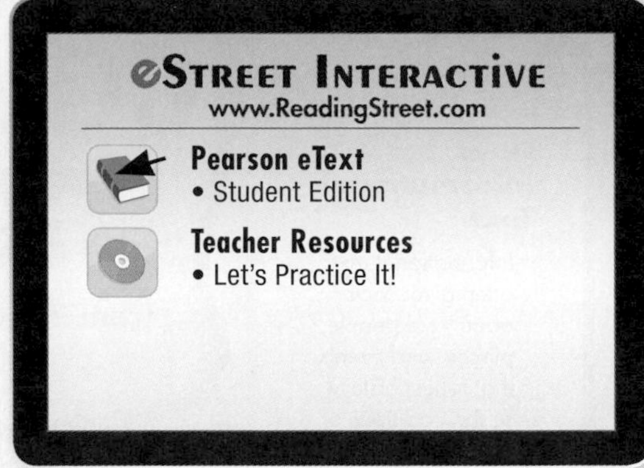

Academic Vocabulary

informational text gives facts about real people, places, and events that may reflect history or the traditions of communities

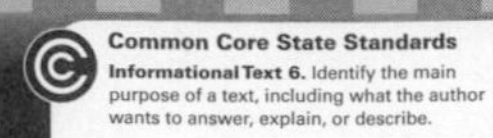

Common Core State Standards
Informational Text 6. Identify the main purpose of a text, including what the author wants to answer, explain, or describe.

Social Studies in Reading

Genre
Informational Text

- Informational text often gives facts about real people, places, and events that reflect history or the traditions of communities.
- Informational text may describe objects and their uses.
- Informational text may use pictures and headings.
- Read "Cowboy Gear." What is the topic, or the "big idea," of this text?

COWBOY GEAR

from *The Cowboy's Handbook*
★ by Tod Cody ★

A cowboy's clothes and equipment had to be hard-wearing. There was no room for luggage on the trail drive, and most cowboys wore the same thing for months. Mud-caked and smelly, these clothes were often burned at the end of the journey.

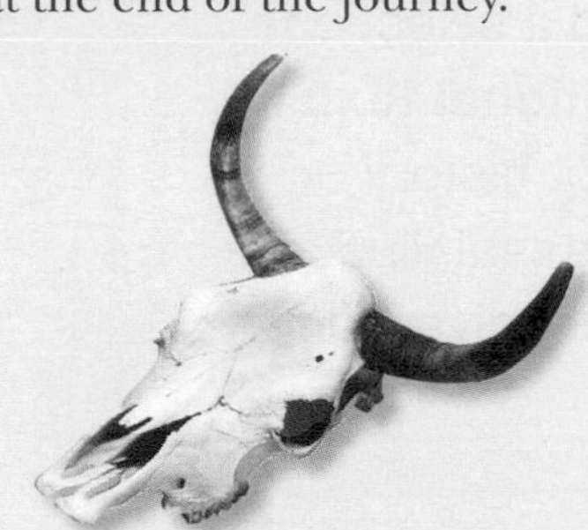

492

READY TO HIT THE TRAIL!

What to Wear When You're Riding the Range

HAT
You can use it to signal to other cowboys, beat trail dust off your clothes, and hold food for your horse. A true cowboy wears his hat when he's sleeping.

PANTS
Cowboys originally refused to wear jeans because they were worn by miners and farm laborers. Pants (trousers) made of thick woolen material are more comfortable to wear on horseback.

BOOTS
The pointed toes and high heels are designed for riding, not for walking. That's why cowboys in the movies walk the way they do!

BANDANNA
Soak it in water, roll it up into a wad, and place it under your hat to keep cool during a hot spell. You can also use it to filter muddy water and blindfold a "spooked" horse.

CHAPS
These thick leather leg-coverings will protect your legs from cow horns, rope burns, scrapes, and scratches. They also give a better grip to the saddle.

Let's Think About...

Why does the author tell what cowboys did with their clothing at the end of a trail drive? **Informational Text**

1

Let's Think About...

Reading Across Texts What information did each selection give about hats, bandannas, chaps, and boots?

Writing Across Texts Write a paragraph explaining which piece of gear you think cowboys needed most.

493

Student Edition, pp. 492–493

Common Core State Standards

Informational Text 5. Know and use various text features (e.g., captions, bold print, subheadings, glossaries, indexes, electronic menus, icons) to locate key facts or information in a text efficiently. **Informational Text 9.** Compare and contrast the most important points presented by two texts on the same topic. **Informational Text 10.** By the end of year, read and comprehend informational texts, including history/social studies, science, and technical texts, in the grades 2–3 text complexity band proficiently, with scaffolding as needed at the high end of the range.

Access Text

Think Aloud **TEXT STRUCTURE** Good readers look for the text structure, or how information is organized, as they read. I can see the small heads *Hat, Pants, Boots, Bandanna,* and *Chaps.* I know that the sentences following each head will give information about the item named in the head.

Think Aloud **FACT AND OPINION** Explain that informational text gives facts, but it can also contain opinions. When I read that you can use a hat to signal other cowboys, beat trail dust off your clothes, or hold food for your horse, I know those are facts because they can be checked by looking in a reference or asking a cowboy. When I read that a true cowboy wears his hat when he's sleeping, I know that's an opinion because it could not be checked. It is the author's belief of what a "true" cowboy does.

LET'S THINK ABOUT... features of informational text.

1 The author wanted to inform the reader about how hard the cowboys worked and how dirty their job was.

SEQUENCE What did cowboys usually do after wearing the same clothes for months on the trail? (They would burn their clothes at the end of the journey.)

TEXT STRUCTURE Where in the selection would you look if you wanted to learn whether cowboys have always worn jeans? Why? (I would look under the head *Pants* because that section would explain what kind of pants cowboys wore.)

Reading Across Texts

The two selections talk about basically the same things—hats, boots, bandannas, and chaps—but some of the information is different. For example, *Cowboys* says bandannas are good for keeping dust out of the nose. "Cowboy Gear" says you can use a bandanna to keep cool, filter muddy water, or blindfold a horse.

Writing Across Texts

Children should choose a particular item of clothing—hat, pants, boots, bandanna, or chaps—and support their opinion as to why it was needed most with information from the text.

Access Vocabulary Review that some words, such as *beginning* and *end,* tell when something happens. Have children locate the time phrase "at the end" in the selection. After they read the selection, ask children to explain what cowboys often did at the end of their journey on the trail and why. (Cowboys would often burn their clothes at the end of the journey because they were mud-caked and smelly.)

Common Core State Standards

Foundational Skills 4.b. Read on-level text orally with accuracy, appropriate rate, and expression on successive readings. **Language 2.** Demonstrate command of the conventions of standard English capitalization, punctuation, and spelling when writing. **Language 2.b.** Use commas in greetings and closings of letters.

Access for All

Advanced

Rate If children already read at 90 words correct per minute, have them read more challenging text.

Fluency Assessment Plan

Do a formal fluency assessment with eight to ten children every week. Assess four or five children on Day 4 and four or five children on Day 5. Use the reproducible fluency passage, Teacher's Edition, p. 495f.

Options for Oral Rereading

Use *Cowboys* or one of the week's Decodable Practice Readers.

Fluency

Accuracy and Appropriate Rate

- Have children turn to pp. 474–475 in *Cowboys.* Review that good readers read at an appropriate rate. I'll read these pages aloud at a good pace, not too fast and not too slow.
- Have children follow along as you read the pages accurately and at an appropriate rate.
- Have the class read the pages with you and then reread the pages as a group until they read with no hesitation and no mistakes. To provide additional fluency practice, pair nonfluent readers with fluent readers.

Routine Paired Reading

1. **Select a Passage** For *Cowboys,* use pp. 478–481.
2. **Model** First, have children track the print as you read.
3. **Guide Practice** Then have children read along with you.
4. **On Their Own** For optimal fluency, have partners reread three or four times.

Routines Flip Chart

Fluency Check

As children reread with a partner, monitor their progress toward their individual fluency goals. Current Goal: 80–90 words correct per minute. End-of-Year-Goal: 90 words correct per minute.

If... children cannot read fluently at a rate of 80–90 words correct per minute, **then...** have children practice with text at their independent level.

Conventions

Commas

TEST PRACTICE Use *Reader's* and *Writer's Notebook,* p. 528 to help children understand locating and placing commas in test items. Recall that commas are used in addresses, dates, and letters: *Juneau, Alaska.* Model identifying where to place commas in a sentence by writing this sentence on the board, reading it aloud, and underlining words that are separated by a comma.

The race took place on <u>Monday</u>, <u>July 9</u>, <u>2012</u>.

Then read the *Reader's* and *Writer's Notebook,* p. 528 directions. Guide children as they mark the answer for number 1.

ON THEIR OWN Use *Reader's* and *Writer's Notebook,* p. 528.

APPLY After children mark the answers to numbers 1–6, review the correct choices aloud, and have children read each sentence aloud and point out words that are separated by commas.

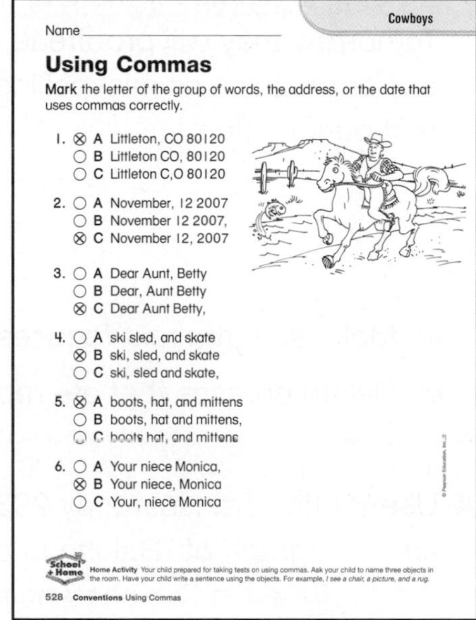

Name ______________ Cowboys

Using Commas

Mark the letter of the group of words, the address, or the date that uses commas correctly.

1. ⊗ A Littleton, CO 80120
   ○ B Littleton CO, 80120
   ○ C Littleton C,O 80120
2. ○ A November, 12 2007
   ○ B November 12 2007,
   ⊗ C November 12, 2007
3. ○ A Dear Aunt, Betty
   ○ B Dear, Aunt Betty
   ⊗ C Dear Aunt Betty,
4. ○ A ski sled, and skate
   ⊗ B ski, sled, and skate
   ○ C ski, sled and skate,
5. ⊗ A boots, hat, and mittens
   ○ B boots, hat and mittens,
   ○ C boots hat, and mittens
6. ○ A Your niece Monica,
   ⊗ B Your niece, Monica
   ○ C Your, niece Monica

© Pearson Education, Inc. 2

School + Home **Home Activity** Your child prepared for taking tests on using commas. Ask your child to name three objects in the room. Have your child write a sentence using the objects. For example, *I see a chair, a picture, and a rug.*

528 **Conventions** Using Commas

Reader's and Writer's Notebook, p. 528

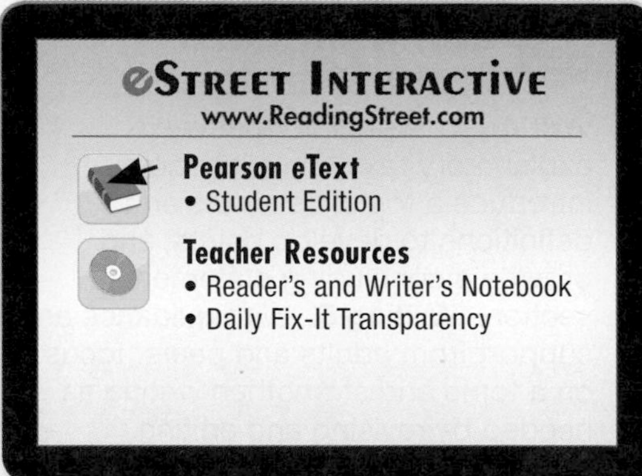

Bridge to Common Core

CONVENTIONS OF STANDARD ENGLISH

As children identify and use commas in letters and dates, they are gaining control of the conventions of standard English punctuation. Your guidance will help them use commas effectively as they write.

Daily Fix-It

7. We built a camp fire?
   We built a <u>campfire.</u>
8. did you see the herd of cattle
   <u>D</u>id you see the herd of cattle<u>?</u>

Discuss the Daily Fix-It corrections with children. Review punctuation, capitalization, and the spelling of *campfire.*

Conventions Support In some languages, the date precedes the month. Help English learners state the date as the day, month, date, and year, as in *Today is Tuesday, May 7, 2013.*

Common Core State Standards

Writing 2. Write informative/explanatory texts in which they introduce a topic, use facts and definitions to develop points, and provide a concluding statement or section. **Writing 5.** With guidance and support from adults and peers, focus on a topic and strengthen writing as needed by revising and editing.

Writing

Zoom in on

Compare-and-Contrast Text

Mini-Lesson Revise: Deleting Phrases

- Yesterday we wrote compare-and-contrast texts that told how a school or home job is the same as, and different from, a cowboy's job. Today we will revise to make the text clearer. We can review our sentences to find phrases that are repeated.

- Display the Revising Tips. Explain that revising is a time for making the text clear. Tomorrow they will proofread to correct any errors such as misspellings or incorrect punctuation.

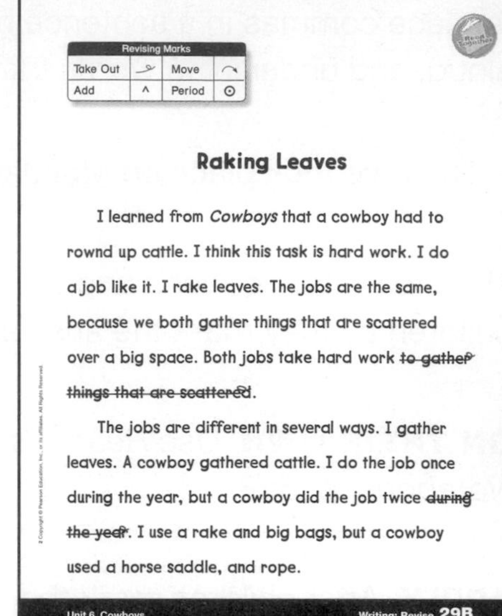

Revising Marks			
Take Out		Move	
Add	^	Period	⊙

Raking Leaves

I learned from *Cowboys* that a cowboy had to rownd up cattle. I think this task is hard work. I do a job like it. I rake leaves. The jobs are the same, because we both gather things that are scattered over a big space. Both jobs take hard work ~~to gather things that are scattered~~.

The jobs are different in several ways. I gather leaves. A cowboy gathered cattle. I do the job once during the year, but a cowboy did the job twice ~~during the year~~. I use a rake and big bags, but a cowboy used a horse saddle, and rope.

Unit 6 Cowboys Writing: Revise 29B

Writing Transparency 29B TR DVD

Revising Tips

✔ Make sure the text focuses on what is the same and what is different.

✔ Delete phrases that are repeated.

- Use Writing Transparency 29B to model deleting repeated phrases. In the first paragraph of "Raking Leaves," I have the phrase to *gather things that are scattered* in two sentences. Repeating words and phrases makes the text too wordy. I will remove these words from the second sentence. The phrase "during the year" is repeated in one sentence. I will delete the second phrase. Make the revision on the transparency.

  Tell children that they can delete words or phrases as they revise.

PEER CONFERENCING • PEER REVISION Pair children and tell partners to switch papers. Have readers comment if there are words or phrases that are repeated. Circulate to assist children planning to revise their texts. As appropriate, suggest deleting repeated phrases.

GUIDE PRACTICE Have children revise their drafts. For those who are not sure how to revise, have children refer to the Revising Tips or the Key Features of a compare-and-contrast text.

Corrective feedback	Circulate to monitor and confer with children as they write. Remind them that they will have time to proofread and edit tomorrow. Today they can make changes in compare-and-contrast details or make sentences clearer. Help them understand the benefits of deleting repeated phrases.

Routine Quick Write for Fluency

Team Talk

1. **Talk** Read these sentences aloud, and have children tell which words or phrases should be deleted to make the text clearer.
   Kim eats cereal, berries, and milk for breakfast each morning, but Lee eats a banana, oatmeal, and milk for breakfast each morning.
2. **Write** Have partners tell what they eat for breakfast. Then have each child write a compare or contrast sentence using the information.
3. **Share** Partners read the sentences to one another and discuss if the sentences are clear.

Routines Flip Chart

Access for All

A Advanced

Combining Sentences Have children review their text for short sentences. Help them combine sentences using conjunctions and commas.

Common Core State Standards

Speaking/Listening 2. Recount or describe key ideas or details from a text read aloud or information presented orally or through other media. **Informational Text 5.** Know and use various text features (e.g., captions, bold print, subheadings, glossaries, indexes, electronic menus, icons) to locate key facts or information in a text efficiently. **Writing 7.** Participate in shared research and writing projects (e.g., read a number of books on a single topic to produce a report; record science observations).

Bridge to Common Core

COMPREHENSION AND COLLABORATION

As children participate in viewing a classroom computer game, making lists of game phrases and their meanings, and summarizing information about playing games, they are evaluating information presented in the media.

Media Literacy

Identify Written Conventions

TEACH Tell children that we communicate through media. Explain that digital media includes information we can view on a computer screen:

- words
- graphics
- sounds
- moving pictures

Explain that video games are one form of digital media. Video games display words on the screen to help players know what to do. When we select one of these words or phrases, we make an action happen or bring up more information. Display these words and discuss the meaning of each one.

- How to Play
- Level
- Play (or Start)
- Help
- Pause
- Quit
- Play Again

Think Aloud

MODEL When I look at the opening screen of a video game, I first look for the title of the game and any pictures that show what the game is about. Next, I read about how to play the game. I select "How to Play" for instructions on what to do. I select "Level" to control how difficult the game will be to play. I select "Play" to start the game.

GUIDE PRACTICE Display a video game on a classroom computer. Read aloud the words that appear on the screen and ask children why you might select each one. Discuss what happens when you make each selection on the screen.

ON THEIR OWN Have children work in small groups to view a classroom computer game. Have them find words that tell them what to do or how to play. Direct them to make a list of words or phrases and the purpose of each one. Then have them work together to summarize how to play the game.

Research and Inquiry

Step 4 Synthesize

TEACH Tell children that the next step in their inquiry project is to review the topic to see if they have the information they set out to find or if their answers lead to a different topic.

MODEL We planned to find out more about a cowboy's routine. Display the list of inquiry questions and the answers recorded during research. The question I asked was *What would a cowboy do at the beginning of the day?* The answer was *wake up early, have breakfast, start the cattle on the trail.* That helps answer the topic, so it does not need to change.

GUIDE PRACTICE Read the remaining inquiry questions and answers. After each answer is read, have children discuss whether or not the answer provides information about a cowboy's routine. Note any new questions children have and revise the original topic if necessary. Finally, tell children that tomorrow they will organize all the information in order to share it with others.

Access for All

Strategic Intervention

Evaluate Relevance To help children review and evaluate relevant information about a cowboy's routine, have them ask themselves, "Did this activity usually happen?"

Wrap Up Your Day!

✔ **Phonics** Write the words *stillness, hopeless, readable,* and *collectible.* Have children read the words and identify the base words and suffixes. Then ask them to use the words in sentences.

✔ **Fluency** Display the sentence *A fearless cowboy had to show kindness to the valuable cattle no matter how impossible the cows behaved.* Have children read the sentence three or four times until they can do so fluently.

Preview DAY 5

Remind children that they heard about changing cowboy traditions. Tomorrow they will hear about changing traditions again.

DAY 5 at a Glance

Content Knowledge
Oral Vocabulary

Phonics/Spelling
Review Suffixes *-ness, -less, -able, -ible*

Text-Based Comprehension
Review Sequence

Selection Vocabulary
Review

Assessment
Phonics
Selection Vocabulary
Fluency
Comprehension

Conventions
Review Commas

Writing
Compare-and-Contrast Text: Proofread

Research and Inquiry
Communicate

Materials

- Student Edition
- Read Aloud Anthology
- Weekly Test

Bridge to Common Core

INTEGRATION OF KNOWLEDGE/IDEAS

This week children have integrated content presented in diverse formats and analyzed how different texts address similar topics. They have developed knowledge about cowboys to expand the unit concept of traditions.

Social Studies Knowledge Goals

Children have learned that cowboys

- worked hard
- had difficult working conditions
- wore protective clothing

Content Knowledge

Cowboys

REVIEW CONCEPT We have read and listened to stories about cowboy traditions. Today you will find out what is creeping into the cowboy's workplace. Read the selection.

- What is creeping into the cowboy's workplace? (Condominiums and subdivisions are creeping into the cowboy's workplace.)

"Cowboy: An Album"

Build Oral Language

REVIEW AMAZING WORDS Review this week's Amazing Words. Then display the concept map. Have children use Amazing Words and the concept map to answer the question, *What can we learn about cowboy traditions?*

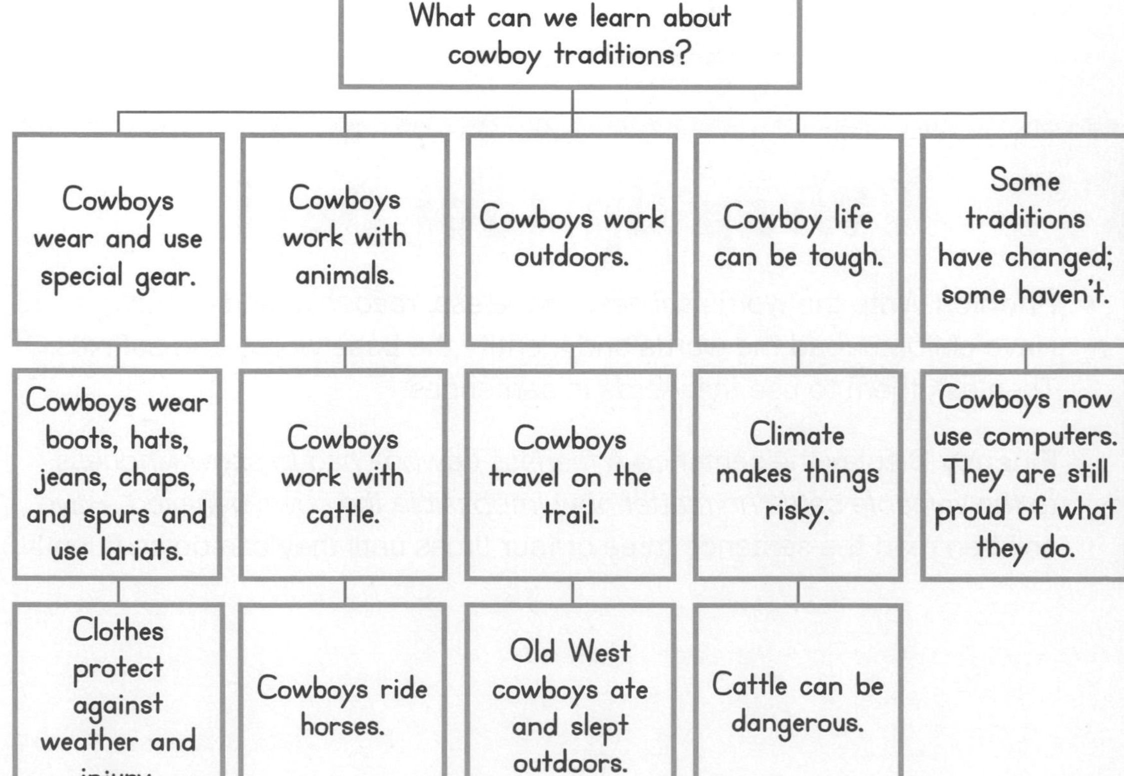

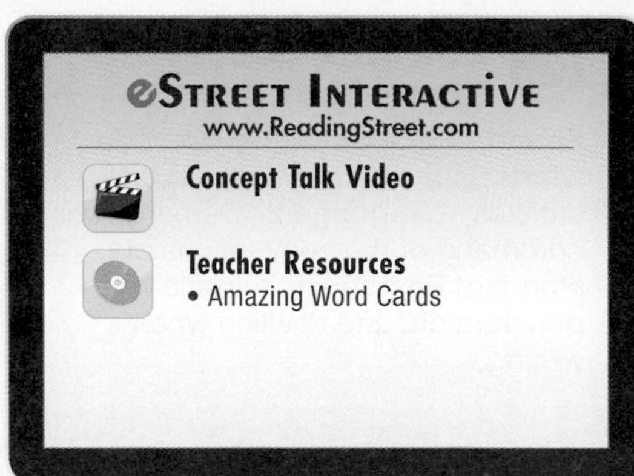

Build Oral Vocabulary

Team Talk **CONNECT TO AMAZING IDEAS** Pair children and have them discuss how the Question of the Week, *What can we learn about cowboy traditions?,* connects to the question of this unit of study: *Are traditions and celebrations important in our lives?* Tell children to use the concept map and what they've learned from this week's discussions and reading selections to form an Amazing Idea—a realization or "big idea" about **traditions.** Use the following ideas as prompts:

- How would you describe the work of a cowboy?
- How has being a cowboy changed over time? How is it the same?

Then ask each pair to share their Amazing Idea with the class. Encourage children to recall in which selection they learned their ideas.

Amazing Ideas might include these key concepts:

- Cowboys work hard and face many challenges.
- Cowboys are important to the past and the present.

Amazing Words

climate	drover
livestock	lariat
occupation	legend
buckaroo	rawhide

Check Oral Vocabulary

FORMATIVE ASSESSMENT Call on individuals to use this week's Amazing Words to talk about what we can learn about cowboy traditions. Prompt discussion with the questions below. Monitor children's ability to use the Amazing Words and note which words children are unable to use.

- **What different *climates* do cowboys work in?**
- **How does a cowboy's *occupation* involve *livestock?***
- **How are a *buckaroo* and *drover* alike?**
- **How could a cowboy become a *legend* with his *lariat?***
- **What can *rawhide* be turned into?**

If... children have difficulty using the Amazing Words,

then... reteach the unknown words using the Robust Vocabulary Routines, pp. 459a, 464b, 488b, 492b.

Check Concepts and Language Use the Day 5 instruction on ELL Poster 29 to monitor children's understanding of the lesson concept.

Amazing Words Rephrase the questions as needed so children have the opportunity to produce oral language.

Common Core State Standards

Foundational Skills 3.d. Decode words with common prefixes and suffixes. **Language 2.** Demonstrate command of the conventions of standard English capitalization, punctuation, and spelling when writing.

Phonics

Review Suffixes *-ness, -less, -able, -ible*

TARGET PHONICS SKILL Write the following sentences on the board. Have children read each one, first quietly to themselves and then aloud as you track the print.

1. **The lamp is not fixable, so it is useless.**
2. **Treat people with kindness, or you may be friendless.**
3. **Good fitness can make you feel ageless and tireless.**
4. **Some dolls are valuable, so they are collectible.**

Team Talk Have children discuss with a partner which words have suffixes, identifying the base word and suffix. Then call on individuals to share with the class.

Spelling Test

Suffixes *-ness, -less*

DICTATE SPELLING WORDS Say each word, read the sentence, repeat the word, and allow time for children to write the word.

1. helpless	I felt **helpless** when Bill scraped his knee.
2. thankless	Feeding my dog is never a **thankless** job!
3. darkness	**Darkness** falls after sunset.
4. useless	The broken vase is **useless.**
5. kindness	Thank you for your **kindness.**
6. fitness	The new **fitness** center is open.
7. fearless	A superhero is **fearless.**
8. careless	Don't be **careless** with your homework.
9. weakness	Eating too little food may cause **weakness.**
10. goodness	"My **goodness**, you've grown," said Mom.
11. sadness	Her **sadness** left when she found her dog.
12. sickness	**Sickness** means your body needs rest.

High-Frequency Words

13. wash	Will you help me **wash** the dishes?
14. machine	Please put soap in the washing **machine.**

Assess

- Spell words with suffixes *-ness, -less.*
- Spell high-frequency words.

Access for All

Check Spelling Say the spelling word. Guide children to identify the base word and suffix. Once children write the word, chunk the parts for them to review their spelling.

A Advanced

Extend Spelling Have children who have demonstrated proficiency in spelling individual words spell each word in a self-made sentence.

Day 5 SMALL GROUP TIME • Differentiate Reteaching, p. SG•52

OL On-Level

- **Develop** Commas
- **Reread** *Reading Street Sleuth,* pp. 74–75

SI Strategic Intervention

- **Review/Discuss** Commas
- **Reread** *Reading Street Sleuth,* pp. 74–75

- **Extend** Commas
- **Reread** *Reading Street Sleuth,* pp. 74–75
- **Communicate** Inquiry Project

If... children need more scaffolding and practice with **Conventions and Writing,**
then... use the Grammar Transition Lessons on pp. 310–385 in the *ELL Handbook.*

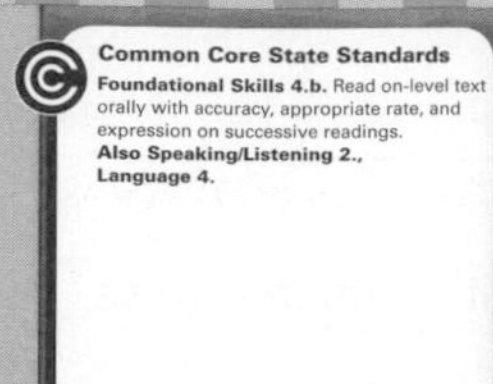

Common Core State Standards
Foundational Skills 4.b. Read on-level text orally with accuracy, appropriate rate, and expression on successive readings.
Also Speaking/Listening 2., Language 4.

READING STREET ONLINE
ONLINE STUDENT EDITION
www.ReadingStreet.com

Vocabulary

Unfamiliar Words

Context Clues Look at the context clues to help find the relevant meanings of unfamiliar words.

Practice It! Use context to determine the meaning of each bold word.

1. The **bashful** child would not say hello. She shyly covered her face as her dad held her.
2. The kids **searched** the room, hunting for the next clue. But they could not find it anywhere they looked.

Fluency

Accuracy and Appropriate Rate

When reading, read all the words. Do not add or leave out words. Read at an appropriate pace. Sometimes you will want to read a little faster, for example, when something exciting is happening.

Practice It! Read the text below to a partner.

I ran in the 300-meter race at school today. I was behind the lead runner, but then I had a spurt of energy. I crossed the finish line first! This is my first-place ribbon.

494

Media Literacy

Notice the words that programs use to guide you through the game.

Identify Written Conventions

Some video games have number games. Some video games have word games. Some games take players from one place to another. The games use words to help players know what to do. The game starts with a title, or the name of the game. Then you may see the words *start* or *begin*, or *click here to begin*. Other words such as *pause* or *stop* may let you stop the game for a while.

Practice It! Look at a classroom computer game. Like a video game, find words that tell you what to do and how to play. Describe the game to a friend. Give the title, and tell the friend how to begin playing the game.

Tips

- For the most fun, read and follow the directions that appear on the screen when playing a computer or video game.
- Identify the written conventions that are used for the game.

495

Student Edition, pp. 494–495

Common Core State Standards

Language 4. Determine or clarify the meaning of unknown and multiple-meaning words and phrases based on grade 2 reading and content, choosing flexibly from an array of strategies. **Language 4.a.** Use sentence-level context as a clue to the meaning of a word or phrase. **Foundational Skills 4.b.** Read on-level text orally with accuracy, appropriate rate, and expression on successive readings. **Speaking/Listening 2.** Recount or describe key ideas or details from a text read aloud or information presented orally or through other media.

Vocabulary

Unfamiliar Words

TEACH Read and discuss the Vocabulary lesson on page 494 of the Student Edition. Use the model below to explain that context—the words and sometimes pictures around a word we don't know—can help us figure out its meaning.

GUIDE PRACTICE Read the instructions for the Vocabulary Practice It! activity. Then read the sentences in item 1 aloud with children.

The context tells us that a bashful child would not say hello and shyly covered her face. What might *bashful* mean? (shy)

ON THEIR OWN Have pairs complete item 2.

Corrective feedback	Circulate around the room and listen as children infer the meaning of *searched* from context. Provide assistance as needed.

Fluency

Accuracy and Appropriate Rate

TEACH Read and discuss the Fluency instructions.

READ WORDS IN CONTEXT Give children a moment to look at the paragraph. Then have partners take turns reading it to each other with accuracy and at an appropriate rate.

Media Literacy

Identify Written Conventions

TEACH Read and discuss the Media Literacy lesson on page 495 in the Student Edition together. Explain that *conventions* means "the way things are usually done."

ANALYZE Explain to children that words such as *start* or *begin, pause, click here,* and *stop* are conventions of video game instructions. What happens when you click the pause button while playing a video game? (The screen freezes and stops the game.) Have children discuss what happens when the other conventions are followed during video game play.

INTRODUCE PROMPT Read the Practice It! prompt with the class. Remind children that they should use the key words that tell you what to do and how to play the game in their instructions.

Team Talk Have pairs take turns explaining game rules and listening to their partner. Remind children that good speakers give instructions clearly and slowly and use key words the listener might need to know. Good listeners pay close attention.

Identify Written Conventions

In addition to identifying key words to give instructions, children at Grade 3 should also be able to give oral instructions that involve a sequence of actions, explain and describe information in their own words, and employ an appropriate speaking rate to communicate ideas effectively.

Vocabulary Development For additional practice, after completing the Practice It! activity, have children use each unfamiliar word in another sentence of their own making.

Common Core State Standards

Literature 5. Describe the overall structure of a story, including describing how the beginning introduces the story and the ending concludes the action. **Informational Text 6.** Identify the main purpose of a text, including what the author wants to answer, explain, or describe. **Language 5.a.** Identify real-life connections between words and their use (e.g., describe foods that are *spicy* or *juicy*).

Text-Based Comprehension

Review Sequence

Remember that events in a selection happen in a certain order: first, next, and last. What is this order of events called? (sequence)

CHECK UNDERSTANDING Read aloud the following story and have children answer the questions that follow.

Tran and his mom worked together to make pancakes. First, Tran measured the pancake mix and poured it into a bowl. Next, he measured the water needed and added that to the bowl. Then he stirred the mix with a spoon until it was a moist batter. Tran's mother helped him drop the batter in a hot pan one spoonful at a time. He watched her flip the pancakes to cook both sides and then place them on his plate. Finally, Tran put berry topping on his pancakes and ate every one of them.

1. What is the first thing Tran did to make pancakes? (First, Tran measured the pancake mix and poured it into a bowl.)
2. What is something that Tran did in the middle? (With his mother's help, Tran dropped batter in a hot pan one spoonful at a time.)
3. What was the last thing Tran did with his pancakes? (He put berry topping on his pancakes and ate them all.)

Vocabulary

Review Selection Vocabulary

SELECTION WORDS Review this week's selection words: *cowboy, cattle, trails, herd, campfire, galloped,* and *railroad.* Say a riddle for one of the words for the class to solve, such as *People can follow one of these during a walk through the woods. (trails)* Encourage children to think of a riddle for one of the words to share with the class.

Corrective feedback	**If...** children cannot tell what the words mean, **then...** review the definitions on page 463a.

Genre

Review Informational Text

INFORMATIONAL TEXT Review with children that informational text gives facts about real people, places, and events that may reflect history or the traditions of communities.

TEACH An author writes an informational article because he or she has a message about those people, places, and events for the reader. The author has an idea or opinion about the topic and wants to share it with the reader. Let's see what the author of *The Stagecoach Driver* on page 463 is trying to tell us about stagecoach drivers and the time they lived in.

Think Aloud **MODEL** The author tells us that the stagecoach driver was responsible for the riders, their bags, the horses, and the coach. The author also explains how the routes were muddy and rocky and that both the driver and the horses were tired after the trip. I think the author wants us to know that a stagecoach driver had a hard, tiring job.

GUIDE PRACTICE Review *Cowboys* on pages 466–487 with children. Then ask the following questions to guide children in analyzing the **author's message** about cowboys and the time they lived in.

- What are some things the author tells us about the cowboy's job? (The author tells us what it was like to work as a cowboy more than a hundred years ago. She describes the tasks they had to do on the roundup and the dangers they faced on the trail drives, including rustlers and possible trouble with Indians. She also describes how they ate the same thing every day and slept outside in the cold.)
- What do you think the author wants us to know about cowboys and their time? (The author wants us to know it was not easy being a cowboy. The days were long, and the work was hard. The author also wants us to know that life was different back in the days of the trail drives.)

ON THEIR OWN Have small groups decide what the author's main message is in "Cowboy Gear" on pages 492–493. Have them share their ideas with the class.

Access for All

SI Strategic Intervention

Author's Message If children have difficulty determining the author's message, have them use the top two question boxes on Graphic Organizer 11 to help them collect their ideas about what information an author tells them and why the author tells them it.

Academic Vocabulary

author's message the underlying message the author wants to convey in a nonfiction text

Common Core State Standards

Foundational Skills 4.b. Read on-level text orally with accuracy, appropriate rate, and expression on successive readings.

Assess

- Suffixes *-ness, -less, -able, -ible*
- Fluency: Rate
- Sequence

Fluency Goals

Set individual fluency goals for children to enable them to reach the end-of-the-year goal.

- **Current Goal:** 80–90 WCPM
- **End-of-Year Goal:** 90 WCPM

Assessment

Monitor Progress

For a written assessment of suffixes *-ness, -less, -able, -ible* and sequence, use Weekly Test 29, pp. 169–174.

SENTENCE READING Use the following reproducible page to assess children's ability to read words in context. Call on children to read two sentences aloud. Start over with sentence one if necessary.

MONITOR PROGRESS Sentence Reading

If... children have trouble reading words with suffixes *-ness, -less, -able,* and *-ible,*
then... use the Reteach Lesson in *First Stop.*

FLUENCY Take a one-minute sample of children's oral reading. Have children read the fluency passage on p. 495f.

COMPREHENSION Have the child read the entire passage. (If the child has difficulty with the passage, you may read it aloud.) Then have the child retell the passage by stating the events in sequence.

MONITOR ACCURACY Have children monitor their accuracy by recording their scores using the Sentence Reading Chart and by recording the number of words read correctly per minute on their Fluency Progress Chart in *First Stop.*

MONITOR PROGRESS Fluency and Comprehension

If... a child does not achieve the fluency goal on the timed reading,
then... copy the passage and send it home with the child for additional fluency practice, or have the child practice with a fluent reader.

If... a child cannot retell the events in sequence,
then... use the Reteach Lesson in *First Stop.*

Name ____________________

Read the Sentences

1. The visible smaller trails were useless.

2. The lifeless railroad station was comfortable.

3. The cow's illness filled the cowboy with sadness.

4. The tasteless food cooked over the campfire was harmless.

5. The likeable man led the priceless cattle to the ranch.

6. The campfire made the cloudless night enjoyable.

7. The helpless herd of sheep was clueless about the flood.

8. The dirtless jogging trails have a springy softness.

9. It was impossible to escape the loudness of the railroad train.

10. The fearless horse galloped into the darkness.

MONITOR PROGRESS

- **Suffixes *-ness, -less, -able, -ible***
- **Selection Vocabulary**

Name ______________________________

Read the Story

Maggie's Wish

Maggie wished she had a dog. Her mom said she 10
couldn't have one because dogs were too much 18
trouble. Maggie knew it was useless to keep asking. 27

One rainy night, Maggie heard scratching at the 35
door. There in the darkness sat a little dog with big, 46
sad eyes. Maggie took the helpless dog into the 55
warm house. She dried off the dog because it was 65
soaking wet. 67

"May we keep the dog?" Maggie asked. "I think 76
it's homeless." 78

"You have to try to find its owner first," said Mom. 89

The little dog was quiet as it slept in a cozy corner 101
on a blanket. The next day, Maggie put an ad in the 113
paper. No one claimed the dog. 119

Maggie's mom let her keep the dog because 127
Maggie showed it such kindness. Maggie loved her 135
priceless little dog. 138

MONITOR PROGRESS

- **Check Fluency**
- **Sequence**

Conventions

Review Commas

REVIEW Remind children that commas appear after greetings and closings in letters. Commas also appear in addresses and dates. Have children give several examples of dates and identify where commas should be placed.

GUIDE PRACTICE Write the following letter. Have children identify where commas should be added. Have volunteers write in the missing commas.

July 14 2012

Dear Sonja

How are you? My family and I just took a summer trip. We went to Seattle Washington. It rained every day! I am glad to be back in Oakland California. School starts Monday September 4. How is your summer going? Write back soon!

Your friend

Anya

APPLY Call on a pair of children. Have children say a sentence for each place or date, for example: *Today is* _______. Ask children to snap their fingers when there should be a comma.

Tuesday, September 5

July 4, 1776

New York, New York

ON THEIR OWN Use Let's Practice It!, p. 328 on the *Teacher Resources DVD-ROM.*

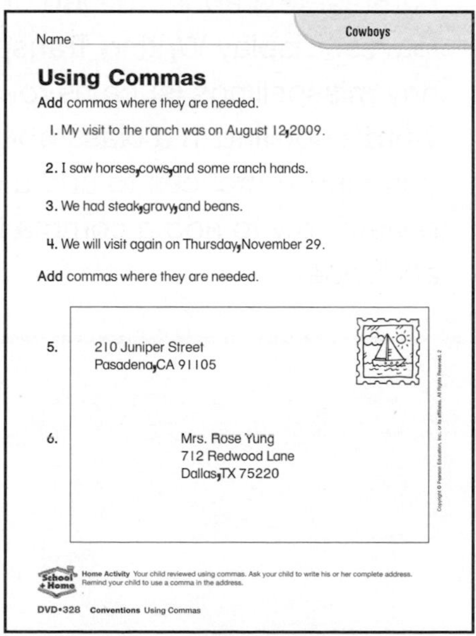
Name ____________ Cowboys

Using Commas

Add commas where they are needed.

1. My visit to the ranch was on August 12, 2009.
2. I saw horses, cows, and some ranch hands.
3. We had steak, gravy, and beans.
4. We will visit again on Thursday, November 29.

Add commas where they are needed.

5. 210 Juniper Street
Pasadena, CA 91105

6. Mrs. Rose Yung
712 Redwood Lane
Dallas, TX 75220

Copyright © Pearson Education, Inc., or its affiliates. All Rights Reserved. 2

Home Activity Your child reviewed using commas. Ask your child to write his or her complete address. Remind your child to use a comma in the address.

DVD•328 **Conventions** Using Commas

Let's Practice It! TR DVD•328

Common Core State Standards

Foundational Skills 4.a. Read on-level text with purpose and understanding. **Language 2.** Demonstrate command of the conventions of standard English capitalization, punctuation, and spelling when writing. **Language 2.b.** Use commas in greetings and closings of letters.

Daily Fix-It

9. Fore couboys sat around.
Four cowboys sat around.

10. The horses gallopped away
The horses galloped away.

Discuss the Daily Fix-It corrections with children. Review punctuation, homophones, diphthong *ow,* and adding *-ed.*

Common Core State Standards

Writing 2. Write informative/explanatory texts in which they introduce a topic, use facts and definitions to develop points, and provide a concluding statement or section. **Writing 5.** With guidance and support from adults and peers, focus on a topic and strengthen writing as needed by revising and editing. **Language 2.** Demonstrate command of the conventions of standard English capitalization, punctuation, and spelling when writing. **Language 2.e.** Consult reference materials, including beginning dictionaries, as needed to check and correct spellings.

Bridge to Common Core

PRODUCTION AND DISTRIBUTION OF WRITING

Children have developed and strengthened their drafts throughout the week. Their final well-structured drafts will reflect the changes they made to improve their compare-and-contrast texts. Children will present their compare-and-contrast texts by reading them aloud to an audience of classmates or by illustrating them and displaying them on a poster.

Writing Zoom in on

Compare-and-Contrast Text

REVIEW REVISING Remind children that yesterday they revised their compare-and-contrast texts. They may have deleted phrases that made the text wordy and hard to understand. Today they will proofread their texts.

Mini-Lesson Proofread

Proofread for Clue Words and Commas

- **Teach** If we spell words correctly, readers will know what words we mean. When we proofread, we check to make sure the words are correct. I can use our word lists or a dictionary to check them. Also, this text compares and contrasts two things, so I need to make sure I use clue words to help the reader understand the likenesses and differences. Finally, I will look at punctuation, especially commas in a list of three or more items.

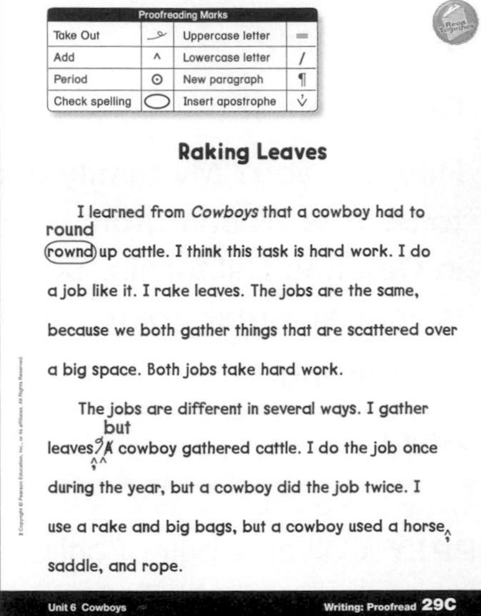

Proofreading Marks

Take Out		Uppercase letter	
Add	^	Lowercase letter	/
Period	⊙	New paragraph	¶
Check spelling	◯	Insert apostrophe	∨

Raking Leaves

I learned from *Cowboys* that a cowboy had to rownd (round) up cattle. I think this task is hard work. I do a job like it. I rake leaves. The jobs are the same, because we both gather things that are scattered over a big space. Both jobs take hard work.

The jobs are different in several ways. I gather leaves. A (but a) cowboy gathered cattle. I do the job once during the year, but a cowboy did the job twice. I use a rake and big bags, but a cowboy used a horse, saddle, and rope.

Unit 6 Cowboys — Writing: Proofread 29C

Writing Transparency 29C TR DVD

- **Model** Let us look at my compare-and-contrast text about the job of raking leaves. Display Writing Transparency 29C. Show how you would change any misspellings (such as *rownd* for *round*). Quickly show how to check a word's spelling in a classroom dictionary or word list. Model how you would combine sentences to add a compare-and-contrast clue word. Finally, review how to add a comma to a list of three or more items. *(horse, saddle, and rope)*

PROOFREAD Display the Proofreading Tips. Have children proofread their stories to correct any misspellings or errors with punctuation. Circulate to assist children with combining sentences using clue words.

Proofreading Tips

- ✔ Are my words spelled correctly? Check a dictionary.
- ✔ Do I use compare-and-contrast clue words to make the text clear?
- ✔ Do I use commas in a list of three or more things?
- ✔ Do all my sentences begin with a capital letter?

PRESENT Have children make a final draft of their texts, with their revisions and proofreading corrections. Help as appropriate.

Choose an option for children to present their writing.

They might prepare a poster with each job illustrated. They write the text on the poster.	They might read their texts out loud in small groups.

When children have finished writing their compare-and-contrast text, give them a copy of About My Writing, p. RR39 of the Reader's and Writer's Notebook. Then have children evaluate their writing by answering the questions on the page.

Routine Quick Write for Fluency

Team Talk

1. **Talk** Have partners describe their favorite school job.
2. **Write** Each child writes sentences telling how the jobs are alike and different.
3. **Share** Partners read the sentences aloud and identify clue words.

Routines Flip Chart

Support Editing For children to whom English sentence structure is unfamiliar, look for gradual improvement over the course of the year. Continue to help them understand simple sentence structures.

Common Core State Standards

Speaking/Listening 2. Recount or describe key ideas or details from a text read aloud or information presented orally or through other media. **Also Speaking/Listening 3.**

Research and Inquiry

Step 5 Communicate

TEACH Tell children that today they will organize the information they researched, create a schedule that displays the information, and share the information with the class.

Think Aloud **MODEL** Display the list of inquiry questions and the answers recorded during research. I was interested in the question *What would a cowboy do at the beginning of the day?* The answers I found were *wake up early, have breakfast, start the cattle on the trail.* On my schedule, I will include *Beginning of the Day* as a time period and list those three events beside it.

GUIDE PRACTICE Review the answers on the chart with children. Briefly discuss if children found the information they need to make a schedule.

ON THEIR OWN Have children make a schedule of a cowboy's routine. Remind children that the events on a schedule are sequenced. Have children share their schedules with a small group. Remind them how to be good speakers and listeners:

- Good speakers think about the ideas they want the audience to understand, so they choose their words carefully to express those ideas precisely.
- Good listeners face the speaker and show an interested expression. They raise their hands to ask a question if they do not understand something.

Topic: Cowboy Routine

Question	Answer	Evidence to Change Topic
What would a cowboy do at the beginning of the day?	wake up early, have breakfast, start the cattle on the trail	No change. The answer gives us information about the topic.

Wrap Up Your Week!

Cowboys

What can we learn about cowboy traditions?

Think Aloud This week, we explored cowboy traditions. In *Cowboys,* we learned that, in the Old West, *cowboys* rode horses on long dusty trails for months at a time to deliver cattle to market. In "Cowboy: An Album," we learned that today cowboys still use horses but they also use trucks and even helicopters to round up cattle!

Team Talk Have children work with partners to talk about their Amazing Ideas about cowboy traditions. Then have children use these ideas to help them demonstrate their understanding of the Question of the Week, *What can we learn about cowboy traditions?*

Amazing Words

You've learned 008 words this week!

You've learned 233 words this year!

Next Week's Concept

Celebrated and Shared Traditions

How are different traditions celebrated and shared?

ELL

Poster Preview Prepare children for next week by using Week 5, ELL Poster 30. Read the Poster Talk-Through to introduce the concept and vocabulary. Ask children to identify and describe objects and actions in the art.

Selection Summary Send home the summary of *Grace for President* in English and the child's home language if available. Children can read the summary with family members.

Preview Next Week

Tell children that next week they will read about more traditions and how people celebrate in different ways.

Assessment Checkpoints for the Week

Weekly Assessment

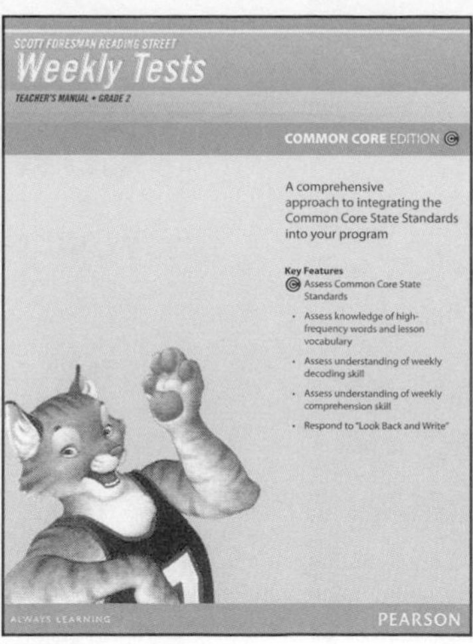

Weekly Tests

Use pp. 169–174 of *Weekly Tests* to check:

✔ **Phonics** Suffixes *-ness, -less, -able, -ible*

✔ **Comprehension** Sequence

✔ **Selection Vocabulary**

campfire	herd
cattle	railroad
cowboy	trails
galloped	

Differentiated Assessment

Fresh Reads for Fluency and Comprehension

Advanced

On-Level

Strategic Intervention

Use pp. 169–174 of *Fresh Reads for Fluency and Comprehension* to check:

✔ **Comprehension** Sequence

✔ **Review** **Comprehension** Main Idea and Details

✔ **Fluency** Words Correct Per Minute

Managing Assessment

Assessment Handbook

Use *Assessment Handbook* for:

✔ **Weekly Assessment Blackline Masters for Monitoring Progress**

✔ **Observation Checklists**

✔ **Record-Keeping Forms**

✔ **Portfolio Assessment**

DAY 1 Differentiate Phonics

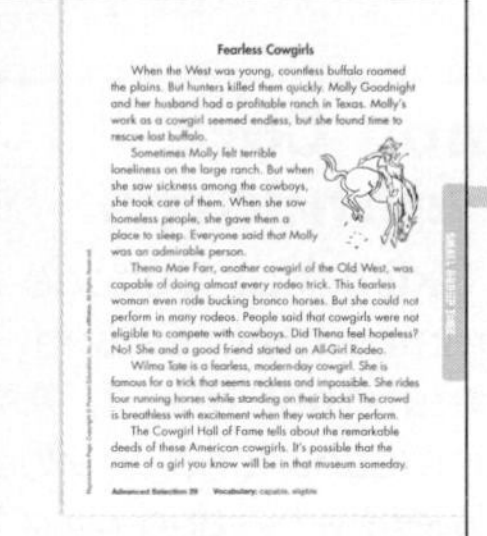

- Suffixes *-ness, -less, -able, -ible*
- Decodable Practice Reader
- Advanced Selection "Fearless Cowgirls"
- **Inquiry** Identify Questions

DAY 2 Differentiate Comprehension

- Selection Vocabulary
- **Access Text** Read *Cowboys*
- **Inquiry** Investigate

DAY 3 Differentiate Close Reading

- Develop Vocabulary
- **Close Reading** Reread *Cowboys*
- **Inquiry** Investigate

DAY 4 Differentiate Vocabulary

- Amazing Words
- **Read** "Curtis the Cowboy Cook" or Leveled Readers
- **Inquiry** Organize

"Curtis the Cowboy Cook," pp. 74–75

DAY 5 Differentiate Reteaching

- **Conventions** Commas
- **Read** "Curtis the Cowboy Cook" or Leveled Readers
- **Inquiry** Communicate

Teacher Guides and student pages can be found in the Leveled Reader Database.

Place English Language Learners in the groups that correspond to their reading abilities.
If... children need scaffolding and practice,
then... use the ELL notes on the instructional pages.

Independent Practice

Independent Practice Stations

See pp. 458h and 458i for Independent Stations.

Pearson Trade Book Library

See the Leveled Reader Database for Lesson Plans and student pages.

Reading Street Digital Path

Independent Practice Activities available in the Digital Path.

Independent Reading

See p. 458i for independent reading suggestions.

Common Core State Standards

Foundational Skills 3.d. Decode words with common prefixes and suffixes. **Informational Text 1.** Ask and answer such questions as *who, what, where, when, why,* and *how* to demonstrate understanding of key details in a text. **Informational Text 4.** Determine the meaning of words and phrases in a text relevant to a grade 2 topic or subject area.

On-Level

1 Build Word Knowledge

Practice Phonics

SUFFIXES *-ness, -less, -able, -ible* Write the following words and have children practice reading words with the suffixes *-ness, -less, -able,* and *-ible.*

happiness	thoughtless	reachable	flexible

Spelling

SUFFIXES *-ness, -less* Remind children that each spelling word ends with the suffix *-ness* or *-less.* Clarify the pronunciation and meaning of each word. For example, say: A fearless person is without fear. Have children spell each base word and then add the suffix to it.

2 Read

Decodable Reader 29A *Helpless Randy*

HIGH-FREQUENCY WORDS Have children read the decodable reader. Then have them reread the text to develop automaticity. Have children return to the text and find the previously taught high-frequency words. Help children demonstrate their understanding of the words. Provide sentence frames such as: I should never get on a boat _______ a life jacket. (without)

If... children need more scaffolding and practice with phonics,
then... use the Grammar Transition Lessons on pp. 213–309 in the *ELL Handbook.*

On-Level

SMALL GROUP TIME

1 Build Word Knowledge

Practice Selection Vocabulary

campfire	cattle	cowboy	galloped
herd	railroad	trails	

DEFINE IT Discuss the definition for the word *cowboy* with children. Ask: How would you describe a *cowboy* to a friend? (a man who rounds up cattle using a horse and rope) Continue with the remaining words.

Team Talk **TALK ABOUT IT** Have pairs use the selection words in sentences to internalize meaning. Ask: How can you pair the selection words together in a sentence? (Possible response: The cowboys led the herd of cattle to the ranch.) Allow time for children to play with the words and then share their sentences.

2 Read

Cowboys

If you read *Cowboys* during whole group time, then use the following instruction.

ACCESS TEXT Have children look at the picture on pp. 476–477. Reread both pages.

- What problem does the picture show? (A Longhorn is stuck in the mud, and the cowboys have to get it out.)
- What does *tramped* mean? (trodded, walked)
- What word gives you a clue to what *tramped* means? *(walked)*
- What was an important trait for a cow pony? (It needed to be fearless.)

If you are reading *Cowboys* during small group time, then return to pp. 465a–487a to guide the reading.

Independent Reading Options

Trade Book Library

eStreet Interactive
www.ReadingStreet.com

Teacher's Guides available on the Leveled Reader Database.

On-Level

Common Core State Standards

Language 5.a. Identify real-life connections between words and their use (e.g., describe foods that are *spicy* or *juicy*). **Informational Text 1.** Ask and answer such questions as *who, what, where, when, why,* and *how* to demonstrate understanding of key details in a text. **Informational Text 4.** Determine the meaning of words and phrases in a text relevant to a grade 2 topic or subject area.

1 Build Word Knowledge

Develop Vocabulary

REREAD FOR VOCABULARY Have children reread *Cowboys,* p. 482.

Read the following sentence and discuss words and phrases related to crossing a river. *(river, water)*

When the herd came to a big river, the cowboys in front galloped right into the water.

- What are some other words in this paragraph related to crossing a river? *(plunged, swam, under water)*
- What are some ways you can cross a river? (bridge, boat, swimming)

2 Read

Cowboys

If you read *Cowboys* during whole group time, then use the following instruction.

CLOSE READING Reread pp. 478–481. Have children summarize the ideas presented

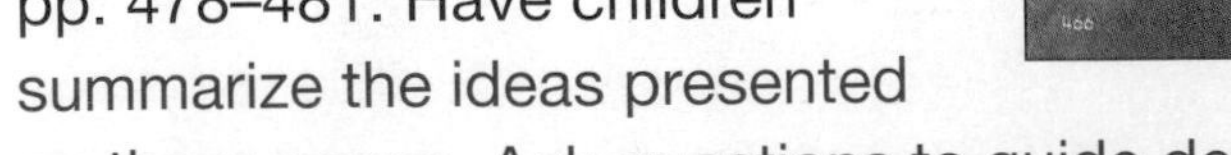

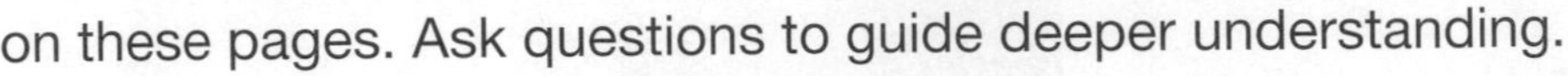

on these pages. Ask questions to guide deeper understanding.

- What made the chuckwagon different from other wagons? (It had different drawers for food and cooking utensils. It had a water barrel tied underneath.)
- What are some of the difficulties cowboys faced on the trail? (They had to eat the same thing every day. They had to sleep outside. They might have to deal with a stampede or with cattle rustlers.)
- What were some common comforts that cowboys lacked while driving cattle? (They had no tables and chairs to use when eating and no beds or pillows to use when sleeping.)

Have children look at the second sentence on p. 480. Have children add a prepositional phrase to the end of this sentence. (They were tired after a long day.)

If you are reading *Cowboys* during small group time, then return to pp. 465a–487a to guide the reading.

If... children need more scaffolding and practice with the main selection, **then...** use the activities on p. DI•81 on the Teacher Resources section on SuccessNet.

1 Build Word Knowledge

Practice Amazing Words

climate	livestock	occupation	buckaroo
drover	lariat	legend	rawhide

Team Talk **LANGUAGE DEVELOPMENT** Have children practice building complex sentences. Display a sentence starter and have children add an oral phrase or clause using the Amazing Words. For example: The occupation of a cowboy requires that he _______. (Possible response: The occupation of a cowboy requires that he work with livestock.)

2 Text-Based Comprehension

READ ALOUD "Curtis the Cowboy Cook" Lead children in a choral reading of "Curtis the Cowboy Cook" from *Reading Street Sleuth* on pp. 74–75. Then have partners take turns reading the paragraphs of the selection.

ACCESS TEXT Guide children as they work on the Be a Sleuth section.

Look for Clues Reread the story with children. Tell them to listen for clues that show how the cowboys felt about Curtis at the beginning and the end of the story. Then ask children to explain why the cowboys changed how they felt about Curtis.

Ask Questions Ask children to think about what cowboys did on cattle drives. Then have them ask questions about cowboys on a drive.

Make Your Case Ask children to identify some of Curtis's character traits and interests. What do we know about Curtis? Then have children identify kinds of work that might appeal to Curtis given what they know about him.

SMALL GROUP TIME

More Reading for Group Time

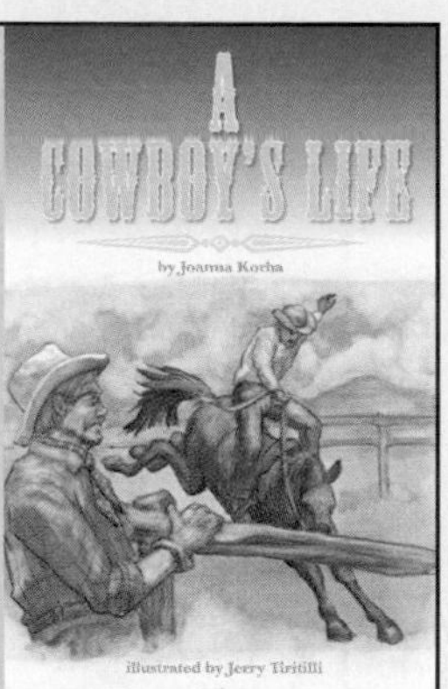

ON-LEVEL

Reviews
- Concept Vocabulary
- Sequence
- Text Structure

Use this suggested Leveled Reader or other text at children's instructional level.

eStreet Interactive
www.ReadingStreet.com

Use the Leveled Reader Database for lesson plans and student pages for *A Cowboy's Life.*

On-Level

Common Core State Standards

Foundational Skills 3.d. Decode words with common prefixes and suffixes. **Foundational Skills 4.** Read with sufficient accuracy and fluency to support comprehension. **Language 2.** Demonstrate command of the conventions of standard English capitalization, punctuation, and spelling when writing.

1 Build Word Knowledge

Practice Commas

REVIEW If needed, revisit the conventions lesson on p. 487c.

IDENTIFY COMMAS Have children turn to "Curtis the Cowboy Cook" to identify sentences with commas. Then discuss why the commas are used in each sentence.

2 Text-Based Comprehension

REREAD "Curtis the Cowboy Cook" Have partners reread "Curtis the Cowboy Cook."

EXTEND UNDERSTANDING Discuss supply and demand and their effect on price. Point out that cattle drives benefited both animal owners and buyers. In the 1860s, Texas had an enormous number of cattle, but other parts of the country had few cattle, so cattle that would sell for about two dollars in Texas could be sold in the northern part of the United States for about forty dollars.

PERFORMANCE TASK • Prove It! Children may be interested in finding out more about cowboy cooking. Help children do an Internet search to find examples of foods that cowboys ate and recipes they might have used. Have children select a recipe. They should list the ingredients and how to prepare the food.

COMMUNICATE Have children illustrate the recipes and compile them in a cookbook.

More Reading for Group Time

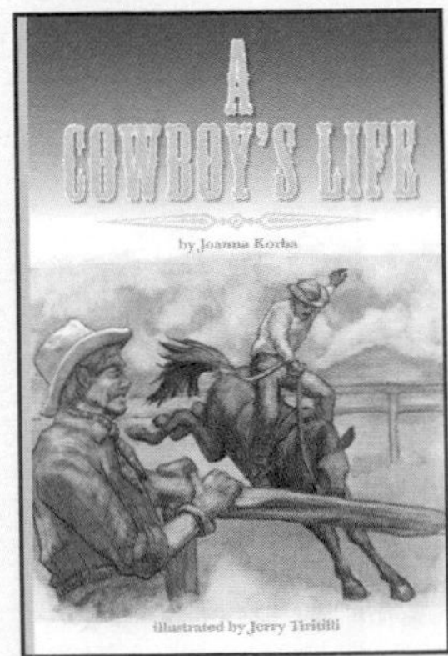

ON-LEVEL

Reviews

- Concept Vocabulary
- Sequence
- Text Structure

Use this suggested Leveled Reader or other text at children's instructional level.

eStreet Interactive
www.ReadingStreet.com

Use the Leveled Reader Database for lesson plans and student pages for *A Cowboy's Life.*

Strategic Intervention

1 Build Word Knowledge

Reteach Phonics

SUFFIXES *-ness, -less, -able, -ible* Reteach the lesson on p. 460a, Suffixes *-ness, -less, -able,* and *-ible.* Use these additional practice words.

pointless	correctable	gentleness	worthless	edible

Then have children sort the following words and circle the suffixes.

greatness	terrible	suitable	speechless
weakness	allowable	joyless	horrible

2 Read

Decodable Reader 29A *Helpless Randy*

DECODE WORDS Have children practice reading the words listed on p. 235.

Corrective feedback **If...** children have difficulty reading the words independently, **then...** reteach the words prior to reading Decodable Reader 29A.

READ IN CONTEXT Have children take turns reading a page in *Helpless Randy.* Have them reread the text several times to ensure accuracy.

Corrective feedback **If...** children have difficulty reading the selection independently, **then...** model reading a page and have children echo you.

3 Reread for Fluency

Have children reread the text to develop automaticity in their reading.

SMALL GROUP TIME

If... children need more scaffolding and practice with phonics, **then...** use the Grammar Transition Lessons on pp. 213–309 in the *ELL Handbook.*

Strategic Intervention

Common Core State Standards

Informational Text 1. Ask and answer such questions as *who, what, where, when, why,* and *how* to demonstrate understanding of key details in a text. **Informational Text 4.** Determine the meaning of words and phrases in a text relevant to a grade 2 topic or subject area.

1 Build Word Knowledge

Reteach Selection Vocabulary

campfire	cattle	cowboy	galloped
herd	railroad	trails	

DEFINE IT Describe *trails* to a friend. Restate the word in child-friendly terms. *Trails* are paths through the countryside. In the selection, cowboys follow trails to the big market towns to deliver the cattle.

Team Talk **TALK ABOUT IT** Where are some places you have walked on trails? Turn and talk to your partner about this. Allow time for children to discuss. Ask for examples. Rephrase their examples for usage when necessary or to correct misunderstandings. Continue with the remaining words.

Corrective feedback	**If...** children need more practice with selection vocabulary, **then...** use the *Envision It! Pictured Vocabulary Cards.*

2 Read

Cowboys

If you read *Cowboys* during whole group time, then use the instruction below.

ACCESS TEXT Have children look at the picture on pp. 474–475. Point to the cowboys in the picture. What else do you see in the picture? (horses, cattle, dust, hills, grass) Reread the text on these pages.

- Look at the cowboys' hats. What purpose did they serve? (They kept the sun out of their eyes and the brims made good umbrellas when it rained.)
- Point to a pair of boots. Why did cowboys wear boots? (They kept out dirt and pebbles.)

If you are reading *Cowboys* during small group time, then return to pp. 465a–487a to guide the reading.

Corrective feedback	**If...** children have difficulty understanding the section, **then...** read the section aloud using the Access Text Notes.

Independent Reading Options

Trade Book Library

eSTREET INTERACTIVE
www.ReadingStreet.com

Teacher's Guides available on the Leveled Reader Database.

1 Build Word Knowledge

Develop Vocabulary

REREAD FOR VOCABULARY Reread p. 468 of *Cowboys.* Let's read this page to find out what the word *bunkhouse* means. To help children understand the word *bunkhouse,* ask questions related to the context, such as: Who sleeps in a barn? (animals) Did each cowboy have his own house? (no)

Corrective feedback	**If...** children have difficulty understanding the word *bunkhouse,* **then...** guide children to use online sources to find more information.

2 Read

Cowboys

If you read *Cowboys* during whole group time, then use the instruction below.

CLOSE READING Reread pp. 470–471. Ask questions related to the context.

- What made the cattle dangerous? (They were wild and fast, and they had long, sharp horns.)
- How could cowboys and ranchers tell their cattle apart? (by brands)
- How would being athletic help you if you were a cowboy? (It was important to be quick enough to get out of the way of an angry longhorn. It also would help when trying to capture and lasso cattle.)

Corrective feedback	**If...** children have trouble answering questions, **then...** reread the page and have them fill in sentence frames to summarize the ideas. **Cowboys called the cattle ______ because of their long, dangerous horns. The cowboys and ranchers could tell who owned the cattle because of the ______ on their hide.**

If you are reading *Cowboys* during small group time, then return to pp. 465a–487a to guide the reading.

SMALL GROUP TIME

If... children need scaffolding and practice with the main selection, **then...** use the activities on p. DI•81 on the Teacher Resources section on SuccessNet.

Strategic Intervention

Common Core State Standards

Language 1. Demonstrate command of the conventions of standard English grammar and usage when writing or speaking. **Language 2.** Demonstrate command of the conventions of standard English capitalization, punctuation, and spelling when writing.

1 Build Word Knowledge

Review Amazing Words

climate	livestock	occupation	buckaroo
drover	lariat	legend	rawhide

Team Talk **LANGUAGE DEVELOPMENT** Help children practice building sentences. Display a sentence starter and have children add an oral phrase or clause using the Amazing Words. For example: If you're a cowboy, you must _______. (Possible response: If you're a cowboy, you must work with livestock.)

Corrective feedback | **If...** children have difficulty using Amazing Words orally, **then...** review the meaning of each of the words.

2 Text-Based Comprehension

READ ALOUD "Curtis the Cowboy Cook" Read aloud "Curtis the Cowboy Cook" from Reading Street Sleuth pp. 74–75 as children follow along. Then lead a choral reading of the selection.

ACCESS TEXT Guide children as they work on the Be a Sleuth section.

Look for Clues Reread the story aloud. Tell children to listen for clues that show how the cowboys felt about Curtis. How did the cowboys treat Curtis at the beginning of the story? How did they think about him at the end? What caused the change in the way the cowboys felt about Curtis?

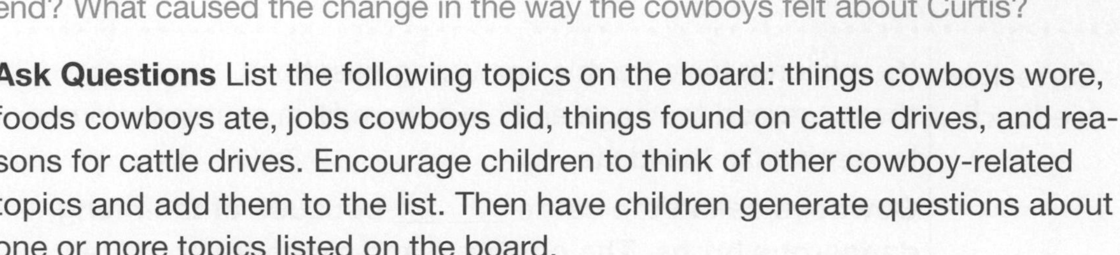

Ask Questions List the following topics on the board: things cowboys wore, foods cowboys ate, jobs cowboys did, things found on cattle drives, and reasons for cattle drives. Encourage children to think of other cowboy-related topics and add them to the list. Then have children generate questions about one or more topics listed on the board.

Make Your Case Help children identify Curtis's character traits and interests. We know Curtis hoped to work with cattle, could cook, and wanted an exciting job. What jobs might Curtis like to have today? Help children to think of jobs, offering suggestions such as forest ranger, astronaut, and firefighter, for children's consideration.

More Reading for Group Time

CONCEPT LITERACY

Practice
- Concept Words
- Selection Vocabulary

BELOW LEVEL

Review
- Sequence
- Text Structure
- Selection Vocabulary

Use these suggested Leveled Readers or other text at children's instructional level.

eSTREET INTERACTIVE
www.ReadingStreet.com

Use the Leveled Reader Database for lesson plans and student pages for *Cowboys* and *Down on the Ranch.*

Strategic Intervention

1 Build Word Knowledge

Review Commas

IDENTIFY Choral read the Conventions note at bottom of p. 491 with children to review using commas. Have children reread the model compare-and-contrast text on p. 491 to find examples of how the author used commas. Allow time for children to discuss the examples and correct any misunderstandings.

2 Text-Based Comprehension

REREAD "Curtis the Cowboy Cook" Have partners reread "Curtis the Cowboy Cook."

EXTEND UNDERSTANDING Discuss supply and demand and their effect on price. Explain that in the 1860s, Texas had an enormous number of cattle, but other parts of the country did not. As a result, cattle sold for very low prices in Texas but for very high prices in the northern parts of the United States.

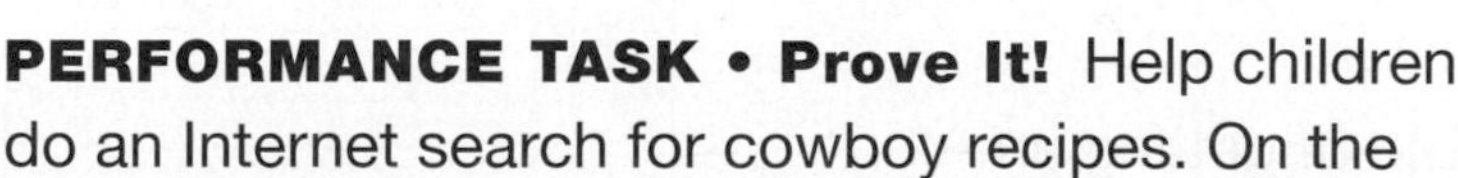

PERFORMANCE TASK • Prove It! Help children do an Internet search for cowboy recipes. On the board, write a list of foods that cowboys ate, such as pork and beans, biscuits, corn cakes, stew, jerky. Have each child choose a food to learn about. Then help children do an Internet search to find recipes or preparations for the foods.

COMMUNICATE Have children write their recipe and draw a picture of the food. Help them compile their recipes into a cowboy cookbook.

SMALL GROUP TIME

More Reading for Group Time

CONCEPT LITERACY

Practice
- Concept Words
- Selection Vocabulary

BELOW LEVEL

Review
- Sequence
- Text Structure
- Selection Vocabulary

Use these suggested Leveled Readers or other text at children's instructional level.

eStreet Interactive
www.ReadingStreet.com

Use the Leveled Reader Database for lesson plans and student pages for *Cowboys* and *Down on the Ranch.*

Advanced

Common Core State Standards

Foundational Skills 3.d. Decode words with common prefixes and suffixes. **Writing 8.** Recall information from experiences or gather information from provided sources to answer a question.

1 Build Word Knowledge

Extend Phonics

SUFFIXES *-ness, -less, -able, -ible* Have children practice with more complex words. Have them think of other words with these suffixes. Then have them use the words in sentences.

portable	craziness	regardless	cheapness
flexible	tasteless	harshness	effortless
manageable	gracefulness	heartless	collectible

2 Read

"Fearless Cowgirls"

TEACH VOCABULARY Before reading, introduce the selection words: *capable, eligible.* Help children determine the meaning of each word using these sentences:

1. We knew Ron was **capable** of getting an A on the test.
2. Being eighteen years old makes you **eligible** to vote.

Fearless Cowgirls

When the West was young, countless buffalo roamed the plains. But hunters killed them quickly. Molly Goodnight and her husband had a profitable ranch in Texas. Molly's work as a cowgirl seemed endless, but she found time to rescue lost buffalo.

Sometimes Molly felt terrible loneliness on the large ranch. But when she saw sickness among the cowboys, she took care of them. When she saw homeless people, she gave them a place to sleep. Everyone said that Molly was an admirable person.

Thena Mae Farr, another cowgirl of the Old West, was capable of doing almost every rodeo trick. This fearless woman even rode bucking bronco horses. But she could not perform in many rodeos. People said that cowgirls were not eligible to compete with cowboys. Did Thena feel hopeless? No! She and a good friend started an All-Girl Rodeo.

Wilma Tate is a fearless, modern-day cowgirl. She is famous for a trick that seems reckless and impossible. She rides four running horses while standing on their backs! The crowd is breathless with excitement when they watch her perform.

The Cowgirl Hall of Fame tells about the remarkable deeds of these American cowgirls. It's possible that the name of a girl you know will be in that museum someday.

Advanced Selection 29 **Vocabulary:** capable, eligible

SMALL GROUP TIME

Cowboys SG•64

READ Have children read "Fearless Cowgirls" silently. Then have children take turns reading aloud. After reading, have children recall the two most important ideas of the selection using details from the text.

3 Inquiry: Extend Concepts

IDENTIFY QUESTIONS Have children develop a play about the Old West. During the week, they should learn more about the Old West from reading, studying pictures, and talking with adults or older children. On Day 5 they will share their play. Guide children in brainstorming possible choices.

- Think about how the Old West used to be. How did people travel? What kind of jobs did they do?

If... children need practice with phonics,
then... use the Grammar Transition Lessons on pp. 213–309 in the *ELL Handbook.*

Fearless Cowgirls

When the West was young, countless buffalo roamed the plains. But hunters killed them quickly. Molly Goodnight and her husband had a profitable ranch in Texas. Molly's work as a cowgirl seemed endless, but she found time to rescue lost buffalo.

Sometimes Molly felt terrible loneliness on the large ranch. But when she saw sickness among the cowboys, she took care of them. When she saw homeless people, she gave them a place to sleep. Everyone said that Molly was an admirable person.

Thena Mae Farr, another cowgirl of the Old West, was capable of doing almost every rodeo trick. This fearless woman even rode bucking bronco horses. But she could not perform in many rodeos. People said that cowgirls were not eligible to compete with cowboys. Did Thena feel hopeless? No! She and a good friend started an All-Girl Rodeo.

Wilma Tate is a fearless, modern-day cowgirl. She is famous for a trick that seems reckless and impossible. She rides four running horses while standing on their backs! The crowd is breathless with excitement when they watch her perform.

The Cowgirl Hall of Fame tells about the remarkable deeds of these American cowgirls. It's possible that the name of a girl you know will be in that museum someday.

Advanced Selection 29 **Vocabulary:** capable, eligible

Advanced

Common Core State Standards

Informational Text 1. Ask and answer such questions as *who, what, where, when, why,* and *how* to demonstrate understanding of key details in a text. **Informational Text 2.** Identify the main topic of a multiparagraph text as well as the focus of specific paragraphs within the text. **Informational Text 4.** Determine the meaning of words and phrases in a text relevant to a grade 2 topic or subject area. **Language 5.a.** Identify real-life connections between words and their use (e.g., describe foods that are *spicy* or *juicy*).

1 Build Word Knowledge

Extend Selection Vocabulary

Team Talk Have partners use the selection words in sentences to internalize their meanings. Have children use as many of the words as they can while making sure the sentence is grammatically correct. (Possible response: We sat around the campfire and listened to the old cowboy tell tales of cattle drives.)

campfire	cattle	cowboy	galloped
herd	railroad	trails	

2 Read

Cowboys

If you read *Cowboys* during whole group time, then use the instruction below.

ACCESS TEXT Have children silently reread *Cowboys,* summarize the selection, and identify the main idea and details. (Main Idea: Being a cowboy in the Old West was a dangerous and difficult job. Details: Some trails from the ranches to the market were a thousand miles long. It was hot on the trail. Many things could go wrong on the trails, such as a stampede or cattle rustling.)

DISCUSS GENRE Discuss what makes *Cowboys* an informational text. Point out that the selection gives facts about real people, places, and events that reflect the history of a region.

If you are reading *Cowboys* during small group time, then return to pp. 465a–487a to guide the reading.

3 Inquiry: Extend Concepts

INVESTIGATE Guide children in choosing materials at their independent reading levels.

LOOK AHEAD Help children organize ideas and write the script for their play.

Independent Reading Options

Trade Book Library

eSTREET INTERACTIVE
www.ReadingStreet.com
Teacher's Guides available on the Leveled Reader Database.

Advanced

1 Build Word Knowledge

Develop Vocabulary

REREAD FOR VOCABULARY Have children reread *Cowboys* and make a two-column chart in which they list words associated with a cattle drive and tools or clothes cowboys used.

Cattle Drive Terms	Cowboy Tools and Clothes
ranch	rope
market	hats with wide brims
roundup	bandannas
trails	chaps
herd	boots
stampede	horse
rustlers	chuckwagon
	saddles
	six shooters

2 Read

Cowboys

If you read *Cowboys* during whole group time, then use the instruction below.

CLOSE READING Reread pp. 484–485 and look at the picture. Look at the picture. What shops do you think would be important in a market town? (a blacksmith shop, a general store, a hotel, a bank) Why do you think the cattle pens in market cities were located near the railroad tracks? (So the cattle could easily be shipped on the railroad.)

If you are reading *Cowboys* during small group time, then return to pp. 465a–487a to guide the reading.

3 Inquiry: Extend Concepts

INVESTIGATE Give children time to investigate their plays on the Old West by reading and studying pictures.

SMALL GROUP TIME

ELL

If... children need more scaffolding and practice with the main selection, **then...** use the activities on p. DI•81 on the Teacher Resources section on SuccessNet.

Advanced

Common Core State Standards

Writing 7. Participate in shared research and writing projects (e.g., read a number of books on a single topic to produce a report; record science observations). **Language 2.** Demonstrate command of the conventions of standard English capitalization, punctuation, and spelling when writing.

1 Build Word Knowledge

Extend Amazing Words and Selection Vocabulary

climate	drover
livestock	lariat
occupation	legend
buckaroo	rawhide

campfire	cattle
cowboy	galloped
herd	railroad
trails	

Team Talk Have children ask each other questions using the Amazing Words and the Selection Vocabulary, such as: Do you know of any cowboy legends from the Old West?

2 Text-Based Comprehension

READ ALOUD "Curtis the Cowboy Cook" Have partners take turns reading paragraphs of "Curtis the Cowboy Cook" from *Reading Street Sleuth* on pp. 74–75. Then have children read the selection independently.

ACCESS TEXT Guide children as they work on the Be a Sleuth section.

Look for Clues Tell children to reread the story. Have children focus on the last sentence of the selection. Ask them to explain the meaning of the phrase *was born to be ...*

Ask Questions Have children recall what they know about cowboys and cattle drives. Encourage them to ask questions about what else they would like to know about those topics.

Make Your Case Ask children to think about what they think Curtis's interests and ambitions are. Then have them try to match those interests and ambitions to a present-day career.

3 Inquiry: Extend Concepts

ORGANIZE INFORMATION Give children time to continue reading and preparing information. Provide any necessary materials, such as cardboard and art supplies to create props and paper costumes.

More Reading for Group Time

ADVANCED

- Extend Concept Vocabulary
- Review Target Skills

Use this suggested Leveled Reader or other text at children's instructional level.

eSTREET INTERACTIVE
www.ReadingStreet.com

Use the Leveled Reader Database for lesson plans and student pages for *Living on a Ranch.*

Advanced

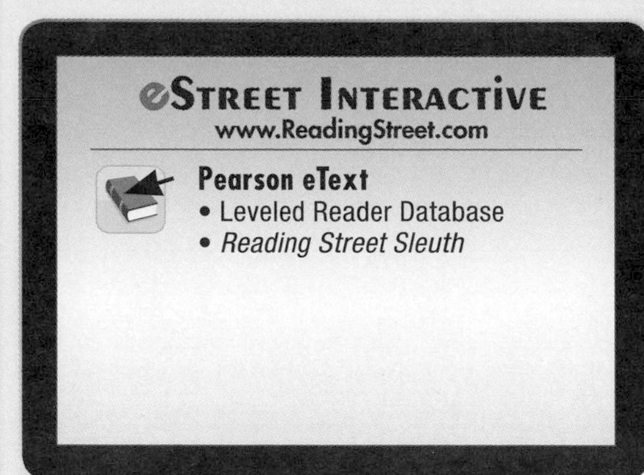

1 Build Word Knowledge

Commas

IDENTIFY COMMAS Have children identify each sentence in "Curtis the Cowboy Cook" that has commas and explain why the commas are used. Then direct them to use commas in a written sentence about the selection.

2 Text-Based Comprehension

REREAD "Curtis the Cowboy Cook" Have partners reread "Curtis the Cowboy Cook."

EXTEND UNDERSTANDING Discuss supply and demand and their effect on price. Point out that cattle drives benefited both animal owners and buyers. In the 1860s, Texas had an enormous number of cattle, but other parts of the country had few cattle, so cattle that would sell for about two dollars in Texas could be sold in the northern part of the United States for about forty dollars.

PERFORMANCE TASK • Prove It! Have children learn more about cowboy cooking by doing an Internet search to find examples of cowboy foods and recipes. Each child should select a food and write a recipe for it.

COMMUNICATE Have children illustrate their recipes and organize them into a cowboy cookbook. Suggest that they design a cover for the cookbook that includes the book's title and an illustration.

3 Inquiry: Extend Concepts

COMMUNICATE Have children rehearse and then perform their plays.

SMALL GROUP TIME

More Reading for Group Time

ADVANCED

- Extend Concept Vocabulary
- Review Target Skills

Use this suggested Leveled Reader or other text at children's instructional level.

eStreet Interactive
www.ReadingStreet.com

Use the Leveled Reader Database for lesson plans and student pages for *Living on a Ranch.*

TEACHER NOTES

Tennessee Common Core Edition 

This Week's Target Skills and Strategies

Target Skills and Strategies	Common Core State Standards for English Language Arts	Tennessee CUs and GLEs
Phonics and Spelling **Skill:** *Prefixes mis-, mid-, micro-, non-*	**CCSS Foundational Skills 3.d.** Decode words with common prefixes and suffixes. **(Also CCSS Language 2.)**	**TN CU 0201.1.11** Apply phonics generalizations in order to decode words.
Text-Based Comprehension **Skill:** Facts and Details	**CCSS Informational Text 1.** Ask and answer such questions as who, what, where, when, why, and how to demonstrate understanding of key details in a text.	**TN CU 0201.8.6** Derive meaning while reading by employing strategies.
Strategy: Predict and Set Purpose	**CCSS Informational Text 1.** Ask and answer such questions as who, what, where, when, why, and how to demonstrate understanding of key details in a text.	**TN CU 0201.8.6** Derive meaning while reading by employing strategies.
Vocabulary **Skill:** Multiple-Meaning Words **Strategy:** Dictionary/Glossary	**CCSS Language 4.** Determine or clarify the meaning of unknown and multiple-meaning words and phrases based on grade 2 reading and content, choosing flexibly from an array of strategies. **(Also CCSS Language 2.e., CCSS Language 4.c., CCS Language 4.e.)**	**TN CU 0201.1.9** Show evidence of expanding language through vocabulary growth. **(Also TN GLE 0201.1.2)**
Fluency **Skill:** Appropriate Phrasing	**CCSS Foundational Skills 4.a.** Read on-level text with purpose and understanding. **(Also CCSS Foundational Skills 4.b.)**	**TN CU 0201.8.6** Derive meaning while reading by employing strategies. **(Also TN CU 0201.8.1, TN CU 0201.8.8)**
Listening and Speaking Listen for Speaker's Purpose	**CCSS Speaking/Listening 2.** Recount or describe key ideas or details from a text read aloud or information presented orally or through other media.	**TN CU 0201.2.4** Summarize what has been heard using the logical sequence of events. **(Also TN CU 0201.2.9, TN CU 0201.7.1)**
Six-Trait Writing **Trait of the Week:** Word Choice	**CCSS Writing 1.** Write opinion pieces in which they introduce the topic or book they are writing about, state an opinion, supply reasons that support the opinion, use linking words (e.g., because, and, also) to connect opinion and reasons, and provide a concluding statement or section.	**TN CU 0201.3.7** Arrange events in a logical and sequential order when writing. **(Also TN GLE 0201.3.1, TN GLE 0201.3.3)**
Writing Persuasive Statement	**CCSS Writing 1.** Write opinion pieces in which they introduce the topic or book they are writing about, state an opinion, supply reasons that support the opinion, use linking words (e.g., because, and, also) to connect opinion and reasons, and provide a concluding statement or section.	**TN CU 0201.3.7** Arrange events in a logical and sequential order when writing. **(Also TN GLE 0201.3.1, TN GLE 0201.3.3)**
Conventions **Skill:** Commas in Compound Sentences	**CCSS Language 2.** Demonstrate command of the conventions of standard English capitalization, punctuation, and spelling when writing.	**TN GLE 0201.1.1** Demonstrate control of basic English usage, mechanics, spelling, and sentence structure.

Access for All to Differentiate Instruction

Reading Street Sleuth

A Few Words with a Big Effect
pp. 76–77

Follow the path to close reading using the Super Sleuth tips:

- Look for Clues
- Ask Questions
- Make Your Case
- Prove it!

This Week's Optional Tennessee Readers Provide Informational Text

Concept Literacy

CCSS Informational Text 1.; TN CU 0201.8.6

Below Level

CCSS Literature 1., CCSS Literature 5.; TN CU 0201.8.6, TN CU 0201.8.10

On Level

CCSS Literature 1., CCSS Literature 5.; TN CU 0201.8.6, TN CU 0201.8.10

Advanced

CCSS Literature 1., CCSS Literature 5.; TN CU 0201.8.6, TN CU 0201.8.10

ELL

CCSS Literature 1., CCSS Literature 5.; TN CU 0201.8.6, TN CU 0201.8.10

ELD

CCSS Literature 1., CCSS Literature 5.; TN CU 0201.8.6, TN CU 0201.8.10

ISBN-13: 978-0-328-73472-6 ISBN-10: 0-328-73472-1

Assessment

Tennessee Assessment Resources for Common Core Test Success

Tennessee Daily Formative Assessment in Your Teacher's Edition

Baseline Group Tests

CCSS Weekly Tests, pp. 175–180

CCSS Fresh Reads, pp. 175–180

Unit 6 CCSS Benchmark Test

CCSS Success Tracker, ExamView, and Online Lesson Planner

RTI

Response to Intervention Kits
Increase Instruction and Progress Monitoring

Intensive Intervention
My Sidewalks
Level B, Unit 6, pp. 226–241

Writing, Grammar, and Spelling

Six-Trait Writing

- Focus/Ideas
- Organization/Paragraphs
- Voice
- Word Choice
  Trait of the Week
  CCSS Writing 1.
  TN CU 0201.3.7
- Sentences
- Conventions

Resources for Six-Trait Writing, Grammar, and Spelling

Reader's and Writer's Notebook
- Practice Reading
- Practice Grammar
- Practice Spelling
- Practice Writing

Writing Rubrics and Anchor Papers

Digital Resources
- Online Journal
- Online Writing Transparencies
- Grammar Jammer

Teacher Resources DVD-ROM
- Reader's and Writer's Notebook
- Let's Practice It!
- Graphic Organizers
- Writing Transparencies

Grade 2 Skills Trace

Skills and Strategies	Looking Back	This Week's Selection	Looking Ahead
Phonics and Spelling **Skill:** *Prefixes mis-, mid-, micro-, non-*	**Unit 5** 224a, 224–225, 225a, 225c–225d, 228c	498a, 498–499, 499a, 499c–499d, 502c, 520c, 520d, 524d, 524e–524f, 528c, 529e	Grade 3 **Units 3, 4**
Text-Based Comprehension **Skill:** Facts and Details	**Unit 1** 175a, 178–179, 180–181 **Unit 2** 253a, 254h, 256–257	500a, 500–501, 504a, 508–509, 510–511, 512–513, 516–517, 521a, 529b, 529f	Skill not subsequently taught
Strategy: Predict and Set Purpose	**Unit 1** 156h, 160–161, 164–165 **Unit 3** 458h, 462–463, 466–467	500a, 500–501, 504a, 508–509, 510–511, 514–515, 516–517, 518–519, 521a, 529b, 529f	Grade 3 **Units 2, 3**
Vocabulary **Skill:** Multiple-Meaning Words **Strategy:** Dictionary/Glossary	**Unit 5** 228g, 228–229, 248g, 262g, 262–263	502g, 502–503, 506–507, 520g, 528–529	Grade 3 **Units 1, 3, 4, 6**
Fluency **Skill:** Appropriate Phrasing	**Unit 5** 348f, 355a, 357a **Unit 6** 448f, 455a, 457a	520f, 527a, 527f, 529a	Grade 3 **Units 1, 2, 3, 4, 5, 6**
Listening and Speaking Listen for Speaker's Purpose	Skill not previously taught	527e	Skill not subsequently taught
Six-Trait Writing **Trait of the Week:** Word Choice	**Unit 4** 75d–75e, 78–79, 79a, **Unit 4** 211d–211e, 214–215, 215a	501c–501d, 519c–519d, 522–523, 523a, 527c–527d	Grade 3 **Units 1, 2, 3, 4, 5, 6**
Writing Persuasive Statement	**Unit 4** 25c–25d, 41d–41e, 44–45, 45a, 51d–51e, 53h–53i	501c–501d, 519c–519d, 522–523, 523a, 527c–527d, 529h–529i	Grade 3 **Units 2, 4**
Conventions **Skill:** Commas in Compound Sentences	Skill not previously taught	501b, 519b, 522a, 522–523, 527b, 529g	Grade 3 **Unit 6**

Tennessee Social Studies Standards Taught During the Reading Lesson

TN 2.4.02.c Identify ways that public officials are selected, including election and appointment.

TN 2.4.04 Recognize the qualities of a contributing citizen in our participatory democracy.

Teaching the Common Core State Standards This Week

The Common Core State Standards for English Language Arts are divided into strands for **Reading** (including **Foundational Skills**), **Writing**, **Speaking and Listening**, and **Language**. The chart below shows some of the content you will teach this week, strand by strand. Turn to this week's 5-Day Planner on pages 496d–496e to see how this content is taught each day.

Reading Strand

- **Phonics:** Prefixes *mis-*, *mid-*, *micro-*, *non-*
- **Text-Based Comprehension:** Facts and Details; Predict and Set Purpose
- **Fluency:** Appropriate Phrasing
- **Literary Text:** Moral Lessons as Themes
- **Genre:** Main Selection: Realistic Fiction; Paired Selection: Informational Text

Common Core State Standards for English Language Arts

Writing Strand

- **Writing Mini-Lesson:** Persuasive Statement
- **Trait:** Word Choice
- **Look Back and Write:** Text Evidence

Speaking and Listening Strand

- **Content Knowledge:** Build Oral Language
- **Listening and Speaking:** Listen for Speaker's Purpose
- **Research and Inquiry**

Language Strand

- **Oral Vocabulary: Amazing Words** *ceremony*, *culture*, *festival*, *compliment*, *fidget*, *evergreen*, *multicolored*, *sash*
- **Vocabulary:** Multiple-Meaning Words; Dictionary/Glossary
- **Selection Vocabulary:** *assembly*, *election*, *microphone*, *rallies*, *slogan*, *speeches*
- **Academic Vocabulary:** *prefix, compound sentence, simple sentence, fact, persuade, interview, predict, source, compare, contrast, informational text, character*
- **Conventions:** Commas in Compound Sentences
- **Spelling:** Prefixes *mis-*, *mid-*, *micro-*, *non-*

Text-Based Comprehension

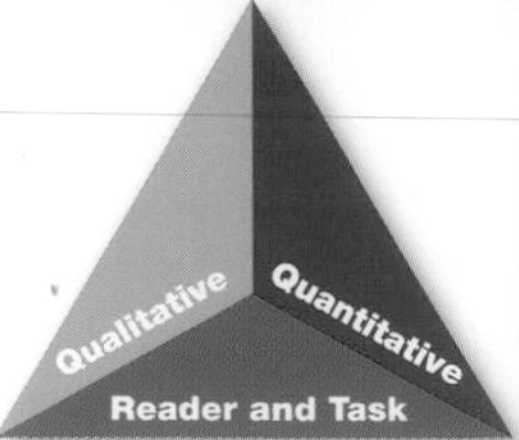

Text Complexity Measures

Use the rubric to familiarize yourself with the text complexity of ***Grace for President***.

Bridge to Complex Knowledge

Quantitative Measures	**Lexile**	570L
	Average Sentence Length	7.83
	Word Frequency	3.41

Qualitative Measures	**Levels of Meaning**	understand realistic fiction; understand Grace's motivation to become class president
	Structure	dialogue; multiple voices; multiple perspectives
	Language Conventionality and Clarity	close alignment between images and text
	Theme and Knowledge Demands	a basic knowledge of political elections and campaigns; simple theme

Reader and Task Suggestions

FORMATIVE ASSESSMENT Based on assessment results, use the **Reader and Task Suggestions** in Access Main Selection to scaffold the selection or support independence for children as they read ***Grace for President***.

READER AND TASK SUGGESTIONS	
Preparing to Read the Text	**Leveled Tasks**
• Review prefixes *mis-, mid-, non-,* and *micro-*. • Discuss the author's use of bold-faced words in all capital letters throughout the text. • Remind children that as they encounter unfamiliar words, they may need to read more slowly and think about context clues to better understand the text.	• **Structure** If children do not understand why some words are bold-faced, have them identify the words and discuss why the author chose to boldface them. • **Theme and Knowledge Demands** If children have difficulty understanding the sequence of campaigns and elections, have them list the events in order.

Recommended Placement Both the qualitative and quantitative measures suggest this text should be placed in the Grade 2–3 text complexity band, which is where both the Common Core State Standards and *Scott Foresman Reading Street* have placed it. Encourage children to access any unfamiliar vocabulary using the context clues and images.

Focus on Common Core State Standards

GRACE FOR PRESIDENT

by Kelly DiPucchio

illustrated by LeUyen Pham

Genre **Realistic Fiction** tells about made-up events that could happen in real life. Now read about a pretend election at a school.

Question of the Week
How are different traditions celebrated and shared?

504 505

Main Selection, pp. 504–519

Common Core State Standards Informational Text 6. Identify the main purpose of a text, including what the author wants to answer, explain, or describe. **Also Informational Text 2.**

Social Studies in Reading

Genre
Informational Text

- Informational text often gives facts about real people, places, and events that reflect history or the traditions of communities.
- Informational text usually has one topic.
- Informational text may have captions and pictures.
- Read "Home Sweet Home." Look for elements that make this an informational text.

Home Sweet Home

by Almira Astudillo Gilles

Long ago, there were no freeways or telephones, shopping malls or video games. Long ago, Native Americans were the only people in California.

Native Americans made many different kinds of homes, using materials that were easy to find. In the north, there were forests and plenty of wood for houses. The Miwok, a group that lived in Central California, had houses shaped like cones. Other houses, like those of the Chumash people of the south, were round. To build these round houses, poles made from branches were poked in the ground in a circle.

Chumash hut

These poles were bent at the top, and smaller branches were put around them. On the outside, pieces of bushes were added. A hole in the top let air inside. When it rained, the hole was covered with animal skin.

Inside a Native American house, you might see grass mats on the floor. You might see money made of sea snail shells. You might find moccasins and clothes of animal skins. You might find a bow and arrow for hunting. For children, there might be dolls or spinning tops made of acorns.

Families lived together in one village.

moccasins

What shape were the homes of the Miwok? **Informational Text** 1

Why does the author tell what may be inside a Native American house? **Informational Text** 2

524 525

Paired Selection, pp. 524–527

Text-Based Comprehension

Facts and Details
CCSS Informational Text 1.

Predict and Set Purpose
CCSS Informational Text 1.

Fluency

Appropriate Phrasing
CCSS Foundational Skills 4.a., CCSS Foundational Skills 4.b.

Writing and Conventions

Trait: Word Choice
CCSS Writing 1.

Writing Mini-Lesson: Writing for Tests: Persuasive Statements
CCSS Writing 1.

Conventions: Commas in Compound Sentences
CCSS Language 2.

Oral Vocabulary

Amazing Words

ceremony	**culture**
festival	**compliment**
fidget	**evergreen**
multicolored	**sash**

CCSS Language 6.

Selection Vocabulary

Multiple-Meaning Words
CCSS Language 4., CCSS Language 4.c.

Dictionary/Glossary
CCSS Language 2.e., CCSS Language 4.e.

assembly	**election**	**microphone**
rallies	**slogan**	**speeches**

Phonics and Spelling

Prefixes *mis-, mid-, micro-, non-*
CCSS Foundational Skills 3.d., CCSS Language 2.

midair	**misplace**	**mislead**
midway	**misprint**	**midday**
midweek	**misbehave**	**midyear**
mismatch	**misdeed**	**mistake**

Listening and Speaking

Listen for Speaker's Purpose
CCSS Speaking/Listening 2.

Preview Your Week

How are different traditions celebrated and shared?

Main Selection, pp. 504–519

Paired Selection, pp. 524–527

Genre: Realistic Fiction

Phonics: Prefixes *mis-, mid-, micro-, non-*

Text-Based Comprehension: Facts and Details

Vocabulary: Multiple-Meaning Words

Social Studies in Reading

Genre: Informational Text

Build Content Knowledge

KNOWLEDGE GOALS
Children will understand that traditions can be:

- shared and celebrated at special events
- brought from other lands
- learned at home and at school

THIS WEEK'S CONCEPT MAP
Develop a concept-related graphic organizer like the one below over the course of this week.

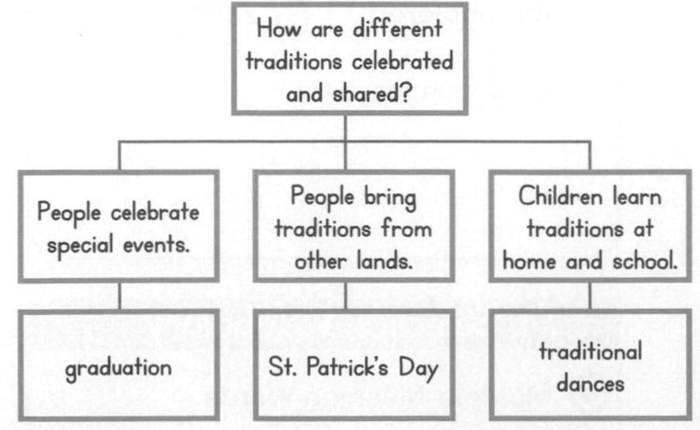

BUILD ORAL VOCABULARY
This week, children will acquire the following academic vocabulary/domain-specific words.

Amazing Words

ceremony	culture
festival	compliment
fidget	evergreen
multicolored	sash

OPTIONAL CONCEPT-BASED READING Use the Digital Path to access readers offering different levels of text complexity.

Concept Literacy

Below Level

On Level

Advanced

ELL

ELD

This Week's Digital Resources

eStreet Interactive
www.ReadingStreet.com

Get Ready to Read

Background Building Audio CD This audio CD provides valuable background information about celebrated and shared traditions to help children read and comprehend the weekly texts.

Concept Talk Video Use this video on the Digital Path to build momentum and introduce the weekly concept of celebrated and shared traditions.

Interactive Sing with Me Big Book "Festival Time" sung to the tune of "Do Your Ears Hang Low?," introduces the Amazing Words with a catchy, concept-related song.

Interactive Sound-Spelling Cards With these interactive cards on the Digital Path children see an image, hear the image name, and see the spelling for words with prefixes *mis-*, *mid-*, *micro-*, *non-*.

Pearson eText Use the eText for the Decodable Readers on the Leveled Reader Database for phonics and fluency support.

Letter Tile Drag and Drop Using this interactive tool on Pearson SuccessNet, children click and spell words to enhance their phonics skills.

Read and Comprehend

Envision It! Animations Use this colorful animation on the Digital Path to explain the target comprehension skill, Facts and Details.

Pearson eText Read the eText of the main selection, *Grace for President,* and the paired selection, "Home Sweet Home," with audio support on Pearson SuccessNet.

Story Sort Use the Story Sort Activity on the Digital Path after reading *Grace for President* to involve children in summarizing.

Journal: Word Bank Use the Word Bank on the Digital Path to have children write sentences using this week's selection words.

Vocabulary Activities A variety of interactive vocabulary activities on the Digital Path help children practice concept-related words.

Language Arts

Grammar Jammer Choose a whimsical animation on the Digital Path to provide an engaging grammar lesson that will capture children's attention.

Pearson eText Find the Student Edition eText of the Let's Write It! and Let's Learn It! pages with audio support on Pearson SuccessNet.

Additional Resources

Teacher Resources DVD-ROM Use the following resources on the TR DVD or on Pearson SuccessNet throughout the week:

- Amazing Word Cards
- Reader's and Writer's Notebook
- Writing Transparencies
- Daily Fix-It Transparencies
- Scoring Rubrics
- Grammar Transparencies
- Research Transparencies
- Let's Practice It!
- Graphic Organizers
- Vocabulary Cards
- Vocabulary Transparencies

This Week's Skills

Phonics
- Prefixes *mis-, mid-, micro-, non-*

Comprehension
- Facts and Details
- Predict and Set Purpose

Language
- **Vocabulary:** Multiple-Meaning Words
- **Conventions:** Commas in Compound Sentences

Fluency
Appropriate Phrasing

Writing
Persuasive Statements

5-Day Planner

DAY 1

Get Ready to Read

Content Knowledge 496j
Oral Vocabulary: *ceremony, culture, festival*

Phonics/Spelling 498a
- Prefixes *mis-, mid-, micro-, non-*
- Spelling Pretest
- **READ** Decodable Reader 30A
- Reread for Fluency

Monitor Progress
Check Word Reading

Read and Comprehend

Text-Based Comprehension 500a
- Facts and Details
- Predict and Set Purpose

Selection Vocabulary 501a
assembly, election, microphone, rallies, slogan, speeches

Language Arts

Conventions 501b
Commas in Compound Sentences

Writing 501c
Persuasive Statements

Research and Inquiry 501e
Identify and Focus Topic

DAY 2

Get Ready to Read

Content Knowledge 502a
Oral Vocabulary: *compliment*

Phonics/Spelling 502c
- Prefixes *mis-, mid-, micro-, non-*
- **Review** Suffixes *-ness, -less, -able, -ible*
- **Spelling:** Prefixes *mis-, mid-*

Read and Comprehend

Selection Vocabulary 502e
- **Review** Selection Words: *assembly, election, microphone, rallies, slogan, speeches*
- **Strategy:** Multiple-Meaning Words
- Reread for Fluency

Monitor Progress
Check Selection Words/
High-Frequency Words

Text-Based Comprehension 503a
READ *Grace for President*—1st Read

Literary Text 519a
Moral Lessons as Themes

Language Arts

Conventions 519b
Commas in Compound Sentences

Writing 519c
Persuasive Statements

Handwriting 519e
Cursive *L, D,* and *J*/Letter and Word Spacing

Research and Inquiry 519f
Research Skill: Interview and Natural Sources

DAY 3

Get Ready to Read

Content Knowledge 520a
Oral Vocabulary: *fidget*

Phonics/Spelling 520c
Build Words
Fluent Word Reading
Decode and Read
Spelling: Prefixes *mis-, mid-*

Read and Comprehend

Fluency 520f
Read with Appropriate Phrasing

Selection Vocabulary 520g
Selection Words: *assembly, election, microphone, rallies, slogan, speeches*
Multiple-Meaning Words

Text-Based Comprehension 520h
READ *Grace for President*—2nd Read
Monitor Progress Check Retelling

Language Arts

Conventions 522a
Commas in Compound Sentences

Writing 522–523
Persuasive Statements

Research and Inquiry 523b
Gather and Record Information

DAY 4

Get Ready to Read

Content Knowledge 524a
Oral Vocabulary: *evergreen, multicolored, sash*

Phonics/Spelling 524c
Review Suffixes *-ness, -less, -able, -ible*
Spiral Review Fluent Word Reading
READ Decodable Reader 30C
Spelling: Prefixes *mis-, mid-*

Read and Comprehend

Social Studies in Reading 524h
READ "Home Sweet Home" Paired Reading

Fluency 527a
Read with Appropriate Phrasing
Monitor Progress Fluency Check

Language Arts

Conventions 527b
Commas in Compound Sentences

Writing 527c
Persuasive Statements

Listening and Speaking 527e
Listen for Speaker's Purpose

Research and Inquiry 527f
Synthesize

DAY 5

Get Ready to Read

Content Knowledge 528a
Review Oral Vocabulary
Monitor Progress
Check Oral Vocabulary

Phonics/Spelling 528c
Review Prefixes *mis-, mid-, micro-, non-*
Spelling Test

Read and Comprehend

Vocabulary 528–529
Fluency 529a
Listening and Speaking 529a

Text-Based Comprehension 529b
Review Facts and Details

Vocabulary 529b
Review Selection Words: *assembly, election, microphone, rallies, slogan, speeches*

Genre 529c
Review Realistic Fiction

Assessment 529d
Monitor Progress
Sentence Reading; Fluency and Comprehension

Language Arts

Conventions 529g
Review Commas in Compound Sentences

Writing 529h
Persuasive Statements

Research and Inquiry 529j
Communicate

Wrap Up Your Week! 529k

Access for All

What do I do in group time?
It's as easy as 1-2-3!

1. TEACHER-LED SMALL GROUPS
2. INDEPENDENT PRACTICE STATIONS
3. INDEPENDENT READING

Small Group Time

Bridge to Common Core

SKILL DEVELOPMENT

- Prefixes *mis-, mid-, micro-, non-*
- Facts and Details
- Predict and Set Purpose
- Multiple-Meaning Words

DEEP UNDERSTANDING

This Week's Knowledge Goals

Children will understand that traditions can be:

- shared and celebrated at special events
- brought from other lands
- learned at home and at school

1 Small Group Lesson Plan

	DAY 1 — Differentiate Phonics	DAY 2 — Differentiate Comprehension
On-Level pp. SG•70–SG•74	**Practice Phonics** More Prefixes *mis-, mid-, micro-, non-* **Decodable Reader** Read *Hiking the Hard Way*	**Build Word Knowledge** Practice Selection Vocabulary **Access Text** Read *Grace for President*
Strategic Intervention pp. SG•75–SG•79	**Reteach Phonics** Blend Prefixes *mis-, mid-, micro-, non-* **Decodable Reader** Read *Hiking the Hard Way*	**Build Word Knowledge** Reteach Selection Vocabulary **Access Text** Read *Grace for President*
Advanced pp. SG•80–SG•85	**Extend Phonics** More Prefixes *mis-, mid-, micro-, non-* **Advanced Selection** Read "Midsummer Fun"	**Build Word Knowledge** Extend Selection Vocabulary **Access Text** Read *Grace for President*
Independent Inquiry Project	Introduce	Investigate
ELL If... children need more scaffolding and practice with...	**Phonics** **then...** use the ELL activities on pp. DI•100 in the Teacher Resources section on SuccessNet.	**Comprehension Skill** **then...** use the ELL activities on p. DI•101 in the Teacher Resources section on SuccessNet.

Reading Street Sleuth

- Provides access to grade-level text for all children
- Focuses on finding clues in text through close reading
- Builds capacity for complex text

Build Text-Based Comprehension

Grace for President

Optional Leveled Readers

Concept Literacy | Below Level | On Level | Advanced | ELL | ELD

DAY 3	DAY 4	DAY 5
Differentiate Close Reading	**Differentiate Vocabulary**	**Differentiate Reteaching**
Reread to Develop Vocabulary **Close Reading** Reread *Grace for President*	**Build Word Knowledge** Develop Language Using Amazing Words **Text-Based Comprehension** Read *Reading Street Sleuth,* pp. 76–77, or Leveled Readers	**Practice** Commas in Compound Sentences **Text-Based Comprehension** Reread *Reading Street Sleuth,* pp. 76–77, or Leveled Readers
Reread to Develop Vocabulary **Close Reading** Reread *Grace for President*	**Build Word Knowledge** Review/Discuss Amazing Words **Text-Based Comprehension** Read *Reading Street Sleuth,* pp. 76–77, or Leveled Readers	**Review** Commas in Compound Sentences **Text-Based Comprehension** Reread *Reading Street Sleuth,* pp. 76–77, or Leveled Readers
Reread to Develop Vocabulary **Close Reading** Reread *Grace for President* **Investigate**	**Build Word Knowledge** Extend Amazing Words and Selection Vocabulary **Text-Based Comprehension** Read *Reading Street Sleuth,* pp. 76–77, or Leveled Readers **Organize**	**Extend** Commas in Compound Sentences **Text-Based Comprehension** Reread *Reading Street Sleuth,* pp. 76–77, or Leveled Readers **Communicate**
Main Selection **then...** use the activities on p. DI•102 in the Teacher Resources section on SuccessNet.	**Amazing Words** **then...** use the routine on pp. xxxvi–xxxvii in the ELL Handbook.	**Conventions and Writing** **then...** use the activities on pp. DI•104–DI•105 in the Teacher Resources section on SuccessNet.

2 Independent Stations

Practice Last Week's Skills

Focus on these activities when time is limited.

ACCESS FOR ALL
- Below-Level Activities
- On-Level Activities
- Advanced Activities

WORD WISE

Spell words.

OBJECTIVES

- Spell words with suffixes *-less* and *-ness.*

MATERIALS

- *Word Wise* Flip Chart, Letter Tiles, paper, pencils

 **Interactive Sound-Spelling Cards**  **Letter Tile Drag and Drop**

● Children spell *kindness, careless, sickness,* and *fearless* using Letter Tiles. They say and write the words, circling the suffixes.

▲ Children spell *goodness, useless, helpless, fitness, weakness,* and *thankless* using Letter Tiles. They write a sentence for each word.

■ Children spell *awareness* and *wireless.* They write the words, circling the suffixes. They think of four more words for each suffix and write sentences for each.

WORD WORK

Identify suffixes.

OBJECTIVES

- Identify and use the suffixes *-less, -able, -ible,* and *-ness.*

MATERIALS

- *Word Work* Flip Chart; Teacher-made word cards: *kindness, careless, sensible, readable, fearless, darkness, fashionable, usable, helpless, fitness, forcible, convertible,* three-column charts headed *Root Word, Suffix,* and *Whole Word;* paper; pencils

 **Modeled Pronunciation Audio CD**  **Interactive Sound-Spelling Cards**

● Children pick a word card for each suffix. They write each word part in the correct column in the chart.

▲ Children pick two word cards for each suffix. They write each word part in the correct column and write a sentence for each word.

■ Children pick five word cards and write a paragraph, circling the different suffixes.

LET'S WRITE!

Write a compare-and-contrast text.

OBJECTIVES

- Focus on relevant qualities to compare and contrast two things.
- Write a compare-and-contrast text.

MATERIALS

- *Let's Write!* Flip Chart, compare-and-contrast graphic organizer, paper, pencils

 **Grammar Jammer**

● Children use the organizer to compare and contrast their chores and chores of pioneer children. They use their ideas to write a paragraph of at least three sentences.

▲ Children use the organizer to list their chores and chores of pioneer children. They write a compare-and-contrast paragraph of at least four sentences.

■ Children use the organizer to list their chores and chores of pioneer children. They write a paragraph comparing the chores.

WORDS TO KNOW

Use context clues.

OBJECTIVES

- Use context clues to find the relative meaning of unfamiliar words.

MATERIALS

- *Words to Know* Flip Chart, copies of sentences, paper, pencils, crayons

 **Vocabulary Activities**

● Children read the passage: "In Africa, Clio was our favorite lion in the **refuge.** We kept her safe there." They draw and label a picture showing the meaning of *refuge.*

▲ Children read the passage: "Sun Yi tried to **disguise** her heavy heart with a grin." They circle context words that tell the meaning of *disguise* and write a synonym.

■ Children read: "The men **donned** their hats and gloves and were ready to face the cold winter night." Write a paragraph about the men, including the word *donned.*

READ FOR MEANING

Use text-based comprehension tools.

OBJECTIVES

- Describe the order of events or ideas in sequence.

MATERIALS

- *Read for Meaning* Flip Chart, 2.6.4 Leveled Readers, time line graphic organizer, paper, note cards, pencils, crayons

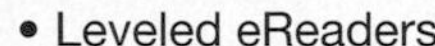
Pearson eText
- Leveled eReaders

Envision It! Animations

● Children read *Down on the Ranch.* They think about the main event and what happened first, next, and last. They illustrate the sequence of events in order.

▲ Children read *A Cowboy's Life.* On note cards labeled *1, 2, 3,* and *4,* they draw four key events in the story. They write a sentence to tell each event.

■ Children read *Living on a Ranch.* They use the time line to sequence eight to ten events and ideas from the text.

GET FLUENT

Practice fluent reading.

OBJECTIVES

- Read aloud with accuracy and at an appropriate rate.

MATERIALS

- *Get Fluent* Flip Chart, 2.6.4 Leveled Readers

Pearson eText
- Leveled Readers

● Children work with a partner to take turns reading from *Down on the Ranch.* They note punctuation and read with accuracy.

▲ Children work with a partner to take turns reading from *A Cowboy's Life.* They note punctuation and read with accuracy.

■ Children work with a partner to take turns reading from *Living on a Ranch.* They note punctuation and read with accuracy.

Manage the Stations

Use these management tools to set up and organize your Practice Stations:

Practice Station Flip Charts

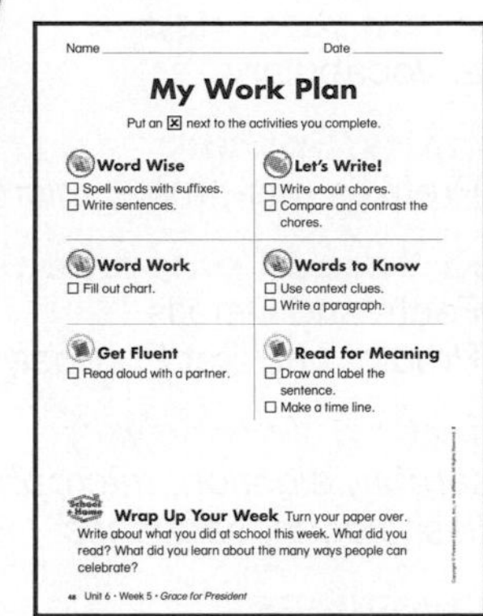
Name ______ Date ______

My Work Plan

Put an ☒ next to the activities you complete.

Word Wise
- ☐ Spell words with suffixes.
- ☐ Write sentences.

Let's Write!
- ☐ Write about chores.
- ☐ Compare and contrast the chores.

Word Work
- ☐ Fill out chart.

Words to Know
- ☐ Use context clues.
- ☐ Write a paragraph.

Get Fluent
- ☐ Read aloud with a partner.

Read for Meaning
- ☐ Draw and label the sentence.
- ☐ Make a time line.

Wrap Up Your Week Turn your paper over. Write about what you did at school this week. What did you read? What did you learn about the many ways people can celebrate?

48 Unit 6 • Week 5 • *Grace for President*

Classroom Management Handbook for Differentiated Instruction Practice Stations, p. 48

3 Independent Reading

Children should select appropriately complex texts to read and write about independently every day before, during, and after school.

Suggestions for this week's independent reading:

- Informational texts on last week's social studies topic: What can we learn about cowboy traditions?
- Nonfiction selections about what we can learn from cowboy traditions
- Nonfiction book by a favorite author

BOOK TALK Have partners discuss their independent reading for the week. Tell them to refer to their Reading Log and paraphrase what the selection was about. To focus the discussion, prompt them to talk about one or more of the following:

Key Ideas and Details
- Who is the author? Why did he or she write this piece?
- What did I learn from this text?

Craft and Structure
- How did the author show the order of events in the selection?
- How well did the author explain the topic?

Integration of Ideas
- How could I use the information in this work?
- Was this book like others I have read? How was it different?

Pearson eText
- Student Edition
- Decodable Readers
- Leveled Readers

Trade Book Library

Materials from School or Classroom Library

DAY 1 at a Glance

Content Knowledge
Oral Vocabulary

Phonics/Spelling
Prefixes *mis-, mid-, micro-, non-*

Text-Based Comprehension
Facts and Details
Predict and Set Purpose

Selection Vocabulary
assembly, election, microphone, rallies, slogan, speeches

Conventions
Commas in Compound Sentences

Writing
Persuasive Statement

Research and Inquiry
Identify and Focus Topic

Materials

- Student Edition
- Sing with Me Big Book
- Sound-Spelling Cards
- Decodable Reader 30A
- Reader's and Writer's Notebook

Bridge to Common Core

INTEGRATION OF KNOWLEDGE/IDEAS
This week children read, write, and talk about celebrated and shared traditions.

Texts This Week

- "Festival Time"
- "The White House"
- *Magda's Tortillas*
- "Marcus and Jin"
- *Grace for President*
- "Bringing the Light"
- "Home Sweet Home"

Social Studies Knowledge Goals
Children will understand that traditions can be

- shared and celebrated at special events
- brought from other lands
- learned at home and at school

Street Rhymes!

We will choose a President
By voting at the polls
For the one we're confident
Will carry out our goals.
We're looking for the candidate
The voters like the best.
The leader who is really great
–and better than the rest.

- To introduce this week's concept, read aloud the poem several times and ask children to join you.

Content Knowledge

Celebrated and Shared Traditions

CONCEPT TALK To help children gain knowledge and understanding, tell them that this week they will talk, sing, read, and write about sharing different traditions. Write the Question of the Week, *How are different traditions celebrated and shared?,* and track the print as you read it.

Build Oral Language

TALK ABOUT SHARING DIFFERENT TRADITIONS Have children turn to pages 496–497 in the Student Edition. Read the title and look at the photos to guide discussion and create a concept map.

- Look at the picture of the women in caps and gowns. What could they be celebrating? (the woman's graduation) Let's add *People celebrate special events* and the example *graduation* to our concept map.
- What are the girls wearing green shamrocks doing? (dancing in a St. Patrick's Day parade) The girls are celebrating a holiday their families brought from another country, Ireland. Let's add *People bring traditions from other lands* and the example *St. Patrick's Day* to the map.
- What do you see in the other small picture? (a Native American girl dancing) She learned this traditional dance in her community.

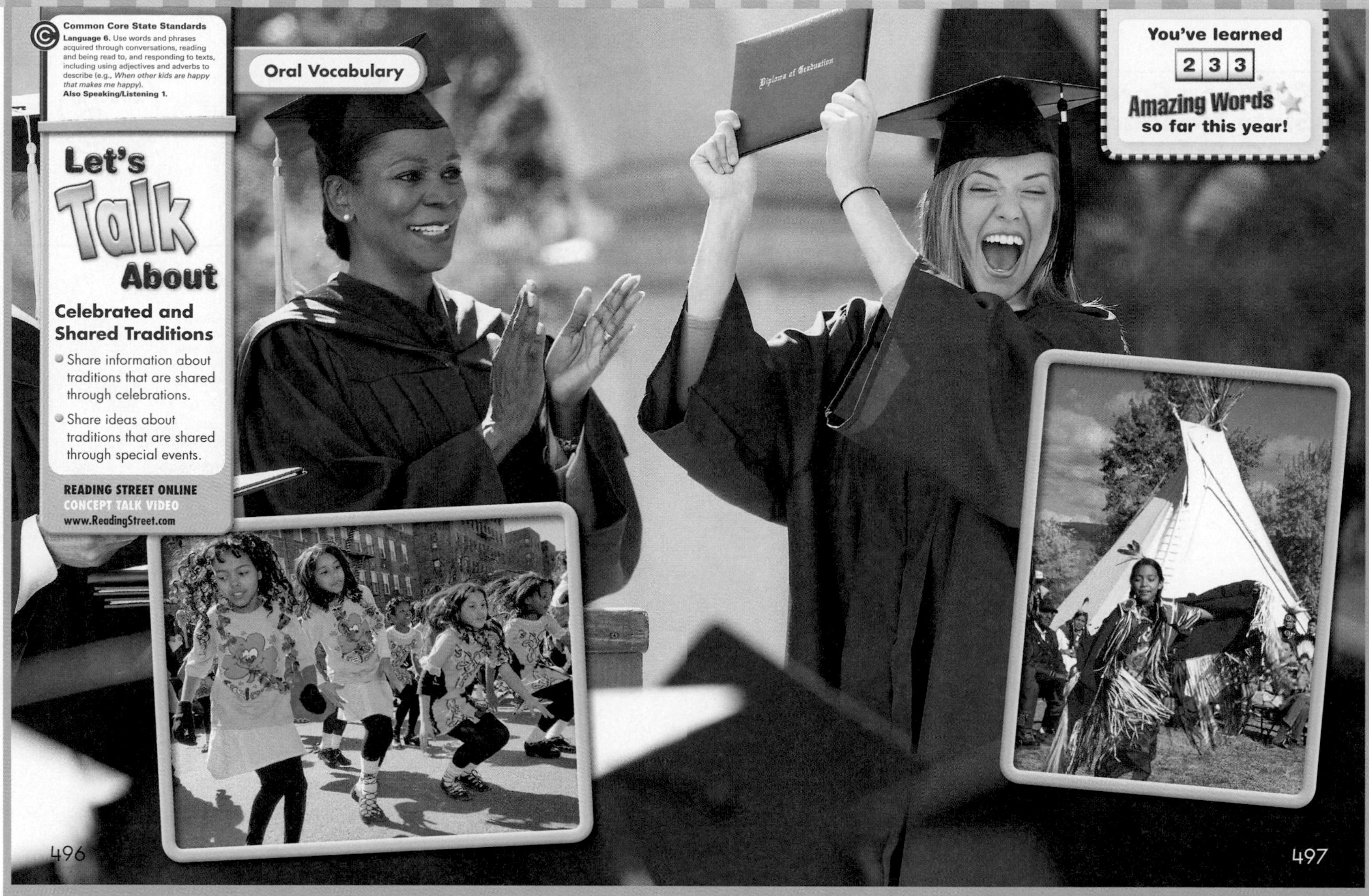

Common Core State Standards
Language 6. Use words and phrases acquired through conversations, reading and being read to, and responding to texts, including using adjectives and adverbs to describe (e.g., *When other kids are happy that makes me happy*).
Also Speaking/Listening 1.

Oral Vocabulary

Let's Talk About

Celebrated and Shared Traditions

- Share information about traditions that are shared through celebrations.
- Share ideas about traditions that are shared through special events.

READING STREET ONLINE
CONCEPT TALK VIDEO
www.ReadingStreet.com

You've learned 233 Amazing Words so far this year!

496 497

Student Edition, pp. 496–497

CONNECT TO READING Explain that this week, they will read about children learning an American tradition at school. Let's add *Children learn traditions at home and school* and the example *traditional dances* to our map.

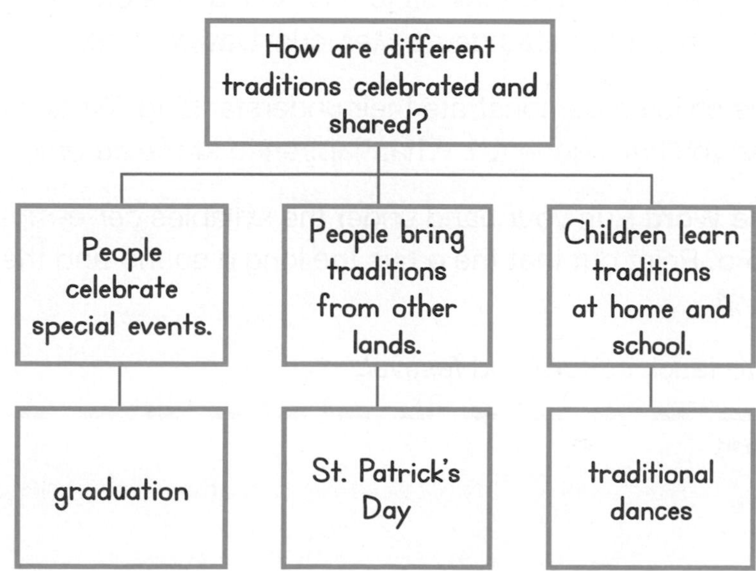

ELL

Preteach Concepts Use the Day 1 instruction on ELL Poster 30 to assess and build background knowledge, develop concepts, and build oral vocabulary.

ELL Support Additional support is provided in the *ELL Handbook* and in the ELL Support Lessons on the *Teacher Resources DVD-ROM.*

Common Core State Standards

Language 6. Use words and phrases acquired through conversations, reading and being read to, and responding to texts, including using adjectives and adverbs to describe (e.g., *When other kids are happy that makes me happy*).

Amazing Words

You've learned 233 words so far.

You'll learn 008 words this week!

ceremony	fidget
culture	evergreen
festival	multicolored
compliment	sash

Content Knowledge

Build Oral Vocabulary

INTRODUCE AMAZING WORDS Display page 30 of the *Sing with Me* Big Book. Tell children they are going to sing about a festival. Ask children to listen for the Amazing Words *festival, ceremony,* and *culture* as you sing. Sing the song again and have children join you.

Sing with Me Big Book, p. 30

Amazing Words — Robust Vocabulary Routine

1. **Introduce the Word** Relate the word *ceremony* to the song. People attend a *ceremony.* Supply a child-friendly definition. A *ceremony* is a special act done for a special occasion. Have children say the word.

2. **Demonstrate** Provide examples to show meaning. The school held a graduation *ceremony.* There were speakers and songs, and all the graduates marched to the front to get their diplomas. Tasha was part of her sister's wedding *ceremony.* We attended a Memorial Day *ceremony.*

3. **Apply** Have children demonstrate their understanding. What are some *ceremonies* you have gone to? What happened at the *ceremony*?

4. **Display the Word** Run your hand under the syllables *cer-e-mo-ny* as you say the word. Point out that the *o* has the long *o* sound and the *y* has the long *e* sound.

See p. OV•5 to teach *culture* and *festival.*

Routines Flip Chart

AMAZING WORDS AT WORK Have children look at the picture on page 30.

- Why do you think people are wearing a dragon costume? Use the word *festival* in your answer. (Possible response: The dragon costume is part of a festival.)
- Why are the boy and girl trying to hit a piñata? Use *culture* in your answer. (Possible response: They are trying to break it open to get candy. The piñata is part of the Mexican culture.)
- Why might the two girls be part of a *ceremony?* (Possible response: They are holding up lanterns, which is a special thing to do.)

APPLY AMAZING WORDS Have children demonstrate their understanding of the Amazing Words by completing these sentences orally.

My family attended a _______ **ceremony.**

The **festival** was _______.

_______ is important to my **culture.**

Corrective feedback	**If...** children have difficulty using the Amazing Words, **then...** remind them of the definitions and provide opportunities for children to use the words in sentences.

Pronunciation Speakers of some Asian languages may have difficulty pronouncing the sound /r/ in *ceremony.* If children say /l/ instead of /r/, say the word slowly, emphasizing that the tongue does not touch the roof of the mouth, and have children repeat.

Cognates The Amazing Words *ceremony* and *culture* have cognates that Spanish speakers may recognize: *ceremonia* and *cultura.* Point out how this prior knowledge can help children with learning new words.

Common Core State Standards

Foundational Skills 3. Know and apply grade-level phonics and word analysis skills in decoding words. **Foundational Skills 3.d.** Decode words with common prefixes and suffixes.

Skills Trace

Prefixes: *mis-, mid-, micro-, non-*

Introduce U6W5D1

Practice U6W5D2; U6W5D3; U6W5D4

Reteach/Review U6W5D5

Assess/Test Weekly Test U6W5
Benchmark Test Units 1–5

KEY: U=Unit W=Week D=Day

Phonics

Teach/Model

Prefixes *mis-, mid-, non-, micro-*

CONNECT Write *unzip.* Ask children what they know about the beginning of this word. (It begins with the prefix *un-.*) Explain that today they will learn about the prefixes *mis-, mid-, non-,* and *micro-.*

USE SOUND-SPELLING CARDS Display Card 157. Point to the prefix *mis-. Misplace* has the base word *place* and the prefix *mis-.* The prefix *mis-* means "not" or "wrong," so *misplace* means "to put in the wrong place." Repeat this procedure with Card 156 for *mid-* ("in the middle of"), Card 158 for *non-* ("not"), and Card 155 for *micro-* ("small").

Sound-Spelling Card 157

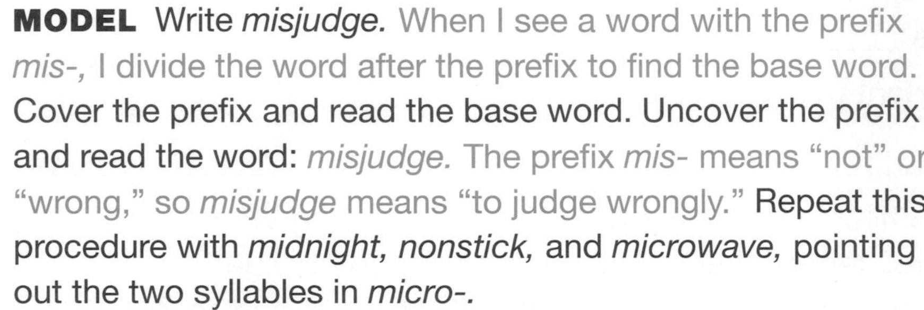

MODEL Write *misjudge.* When I see a word with the prefix *mis-,* I divide the word after the prefix to find the base word. Cover the prefix and read the base word. Uncover the prefix and read the word: *misjudge.* The prefix *mis-* means "not" or "wrong," so *misjudge* means "to judge wrongly." Repeat this procedure with *midnight, nonstick,* and *microwave,* pointing out the two syllables in *micro-.*

Write *midsection;* frame and identify the word parts: prefix *mid-* and parts *sec-* and *-tion* in the base word. Then blend the parts and read. *Midsection* means "the middle of a section." It often refers to the middle part of your body.

Sound-Spelling Card 156

GROUP PRACTICE Have children read all the words above with you. Write the words below. Have the group read the words with you. Then identify the base word and prefix in each word.

midway	**mistrust**	**nonskid**	**microfilm**	**midlife**
misprint	**microscope**	**misspelled**	**nonfiction**	**misunderstand**

REVIEW What do you know about reading words with prefixes? (A prefix forms a separate word part at the beginning of a word. Read the prefix, read the base word, and read the parts together.)

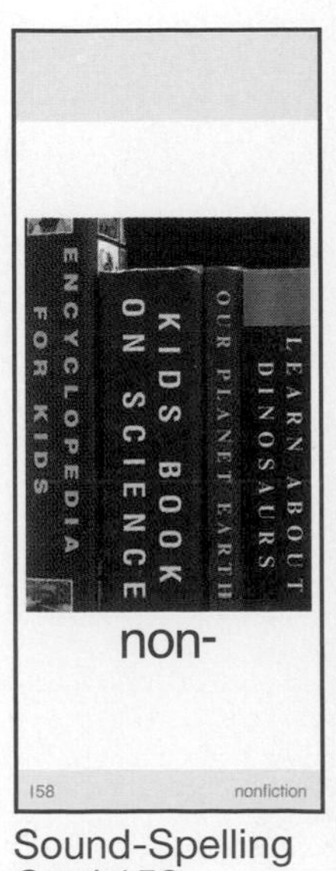

Sound-Spelling Card 158

Common Core State Standards
Foundational Skills 3.d. Decode words with common prefixes and suffixes.

Phonics

Prefixes *mis-, mid-, micro-, non-*

Words I Can Blend

micro**scope**

non**stop**

mid**day**

mis**place**

non**sense**

Sentences I Can Read

1. Beth looked into the new microscope for science class.
2. The flight left at midday and flew nonstop to New York.
3. Did he misplace his book that has nonsense verses?

498

Last night at midnight Jason woke up from a deep sleep. In his dream he was reading stories about himself in the midsection of the newspaper. These stories said that he was a local sports hero. Midway through the playoffs, he began scoring nonstop home runs. After each game, reporters with microphones always wanted to ask him questions.

Wait a second! Was that a misprint? Did he misread that? He told his friend Ben about that nonsense dream at their midday meal today. Ben was a nonbeliever.

You've learned

Prefixes *mis-, mid-, micro-, non-*

499

Student Edition, pp. 498–499

Guide Practice

BLEND WORDS Have children turn to page 498 in their Student Edition. Look at the pictures on this page. I see a child looking for something *misplaced,* a clock showing it's *midnight,* a book of *nonfiction,* and a *microphone.* Each word has a prefix and a base word. Point out these parts in each word: *mis-* and *place; mid-* and *night, non-* and *fiction, micro-* and *phone.*

GROUP PRACTICE For each word in "Words I Can Blend," ask children to say each word part. Make sure they identify the prefix and the base word. Then have children say the parts to read the whole word.

Corrective feedback	**If...** children have difficulty decoding a word, **then...** model sound-by-sound blending or the word parts strategy for decodable words.

Language Transfer The prefix *mid-* has cognates in the Spanish language. Invite children whose home language is Spanish to identify cognates with *medio-, (media-),* such as *medianoche/midnight* and *mediodía/midday.*

Common Core State Standards

Foundational Skills 3.d. Decode words with common prefixes and suffixes. **Foundational Skills 3.f.** Recognize and read grade-appropriate irregularly spelled words.

Academic Vocabulary 

prefix letters added to the beginning of a word that change the meaning of the word

Prefix Meanings

mis- bad, badly, wrongly

mid- in the middle of

micro- small

non- not

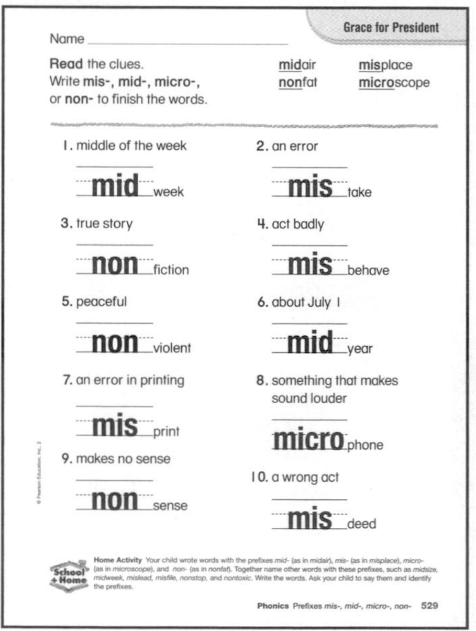

Grace for President

Name ____________

Read the clues.
Write **mis-**, **mid-**, **micro-**, or **non-** to finish the words.

midair misplace
nonfat microscope

1. middle of the week — **mid**week
2. an error — **mis**take
3. true story — **non**fiction
4. act badly — **mis**behave
5. peaceful — **non**violent
6. about July 1 — **mid**year
7. an error in printing — **mis**print
8. something that makes sound louder — **micro**phone
9. makes no sense — **non**sense
10. a wrong act — **mis**deed

© Pearson Education, Inc. 2

School + Home

Home Activity Your child wrote words with the prefixes *mid-* (as in *midair*), *mis-* (as in *misplace*), *micro-* (as in *microscope*), and *non-* (as in *nonfat*). Together name other words with these prefixes, such as *midsize*, *midweek*, *mislead*, *misfile*, *nonstop*, and *nontoxic*. Write the words. Ask your child to say them and identify the prefixes.

Phonics Prefixes *mis-*, *mid-*, *micro-*, *non-* 529

Reader's and Writer's Notebook, p. 529

Phonics

Apply

DECODE WORDS IN ISOLATION After children can successfully combine word parts to read the words on page 498 in their Student Edition, point to words in random order and ask children to read them naturally.

DECODE WORDS IN CONTEXT Have children read each of the sentences on page 498. Have them find words in the sentences that have the prefixes *mis-, mid-, non-,* and *micro-.*

Team Talk Pair children and have them take turns reading each of the sentences aloud.

Chorally read the "I Can Read!" passage on page 499 along with children. Then have them read the passage aloud to themselves.

ON THEIR OWN Use *Reader's and Writer's Notebook,* p. 529.

MONITOR PROGRESS *mis-, mid-, non-, micro-*

FORMATIVE ASSESSMENT Write the following words and have the class read them. Notice which words children miss during the group reading. Call on individuals to read some of the words.

midlife	**misstep**	**nonfiction**	**midway**	**microphone**	**Spiral Review**
miscopied	**nonliving**	**microwaved**	**misfiled**	**nonsmoking** ←	Row 2 reviews inflected endings.
midsection	**nonfiction**	**misdirection**	**misadventure**	←	Row 3 reviews final syllables *-tion, -ture.*

If... children cannot read words with these prefixes at this point,

then... use the Small Group Time Strategic Intervention lesson, p. SG•75, to reteach prefixes *mis-, mid-, non-,* and *micro-.* Continue to monitor children's progress using other instructional opportunities during the week. See the Skills Trace on p. 498a.

Spelling Pretest

Prefixes *mis-, mid-*

DICTATE SPELLING WORDS Dictate the spelling words and read the sentences. Have children write the words. If needed, break the words into meaningful word parts, clarify the pronunciations, and give meanings of words. Have children check their pretests and correct misspelled words.

1. midair	Noel caught the ball in **midair!**
2. misplace	I don't want to **misplace** my keys again.
3. mislead	Unclear directions can **mislead** us.
4. midway	We will stop **midway** between the cities.
5. misprint	There is a **misprint** in the newspaper.
6. midday	It is too hot to play in the **midday** sun.
7. midweek	Wednesday is **midweek** on a calendar.
8. misbehave	Do not **misbehave** in the classroom.
9. midyear	The teachers have a **midyear** meeting.
10. mismatch	I just saw that my socks are a **mismatch!**
11. misdeed	The little puppy was sorry for its **misdeed.**
12. mistake	Ron fixed a **mistake** in his math homework.

ON THEIR OWN Use Let's Practice It!, p. 335 on the *Teacher Resources DVD-ROM.*

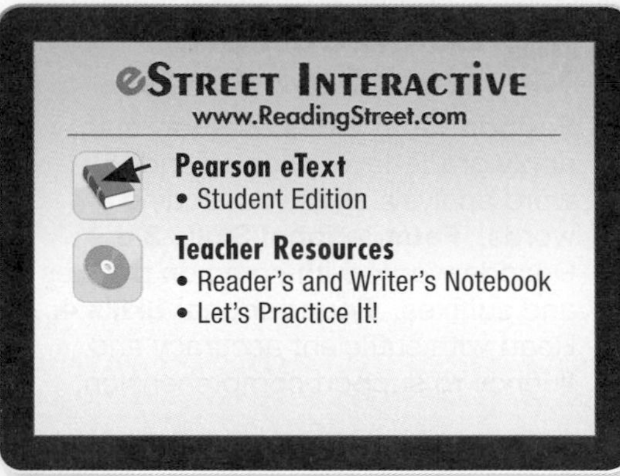

Phonics/Spelling Generalization

Each spelling word begins with the prefix *mis-* or the prefix *mid-*.

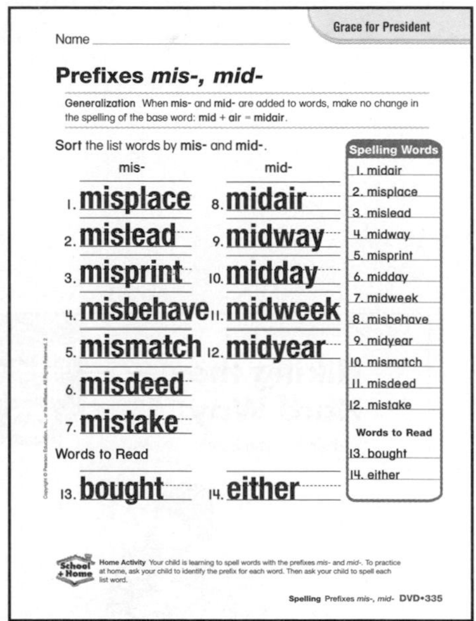

Name ______________ Grace for President

Prefixes *mis-, mid-*

Generalization When **mis-** and **mid-** are added to words, make no change in the spelling of the base word: **mid + air = midair**.

Sort the list words by **mis-** and **mid-**.

mis-	mid-
1. misplace	8. midair
2. mislead	9. midway
3. misprint	10. midday
4. misbehave	11. midweek
5. mismatch	12. midyear
6. misdeed	
7. mistake	

Words to Read

13. bought	14. either

Spelling Words: 1. midair 2. misplace 3. mislead 4. midway 5. misprint 6. midday 7. midweek 8. misbehave 9. midyear 10. mismatch 11. misdeed 12. mistake

Words to Read: 13. bought 14. either

Home Activity Your child is learning to spell words with the prefixes mis- and mid-. To practice at home, ask your child to identify the prefix for each word. Then ask your child to spell each list word.

Spelling Prefixes mis-, mid- DVD•335

Let's Practice It! TR DVD•335

Day 1 SMALL GROUP TIME • Differentiate Phonics, p. SG•69

OL On-Level	SI Strategic Intervention	A Advanced
• **Practice Phonics** Additional Words with Prefixes *mis-, mid-, non-, micro-* • **Read** Decodable Reader *Hiking the Hard Way*	• **Reteach Phonics** Blend Words with Prefixes *mis-, mid-, non-, micro-* • **Read** Decodable Reader *Hiking the Hard Way*	• **Extend Phonics** More Words with Prefixes *mis-, mid-, non-, micro-* • **Read** Advanced Selection for Words with Prefixes *mis-, mid-, non-, micro-* • **Introduce** Inquiry Project

If... children need more scaffolding and practice with **Phonics,** **then...** use the ELL activities on p. DI•100 in the Teacher Resources section on SuccessNet.

Common Core State Standards

Foundational Skills 3. Know and apply grade-level phonics and word analysis skills in decoding words. **Foundational Skills 3.d.** Decode words with common prefixes and suffixes. **Foundational Skills 4.** Read with sufficient accuracy and fluency to support comprehension.

Decodable Reader 30A

If children need help, then...

Read *Hiking the Hard Way*

DECODE WORDS IN ISOLATION Have children turn to page 253 in *Decodable Practice Readers* 2.2 and read each word.

REVIEW HIGH-FREQUENCY WORDS Have children identify and read the high-frequency words *right, start, stream, were,* and *wrong* on the first page.

PREVIEW DECODABLE READER Have children read the title and preview the story. Tell them they will decode words with prefixes *mis-, mid-, micro-,* and *non-.*

DECODE WORDS IN CONTEXT Pair children for reading and listen as they decode. One child begins. Children read the entire story, switching readers after each page. Partners reread the story. This time the other child begins.

Hiking the Hard Way

Written by Lynn South

Decodable Practice Reader 30A

Prefixes *micro-, mid-, mis-, non-*

mismatched	midway	mislaid
misstep	microscope	midstream
nonstop	midday	misplaced

High-Frequency Words

wrong	right	were
start	stream	

253

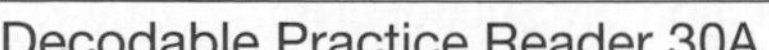
Decodable Practice Reader 30A

Danny was so excited!
His scout troop was going hiking.
He loaded his backpack.
But things started going wrong
right away.
254

Danny put on his boots
in the darkness.
When he got on the bus,
Danny looked down.
His boots were mismatched!
255

Midway through the bus trip,
Danny cried, "No, no!"
He had mislaid his water bottle.
It was not in his backpack.
"I have two bottles," Kim said.
256

At the start of that hike,
they crossed a stream.
Danny took a misstep
and slipped midstream.
Splash! Danny broke his microscope.
257

Danny dried off, and they hiked
nonstop.
The hikers stopped at midday for
lunch.
Danny was happy to stop.
258

He looked in his backpack
for his sack lunch.
"I misplaced my lunch!"
Danny cried.
"It must still be on our bus."
259

Kim gave him part of her lunch.
Then they hiked back.
"I like hiking," Danny said
when he was safe on the bus.
"But it seems that hiking doesn't
like me."
260

Corrective feedback	**If...** children have difficulty decoding a word, **then...** refer them to the Sound-Spelling Cards to identify the sounds in a decodable word; prompt them to blend the word. If the word has the prefix *mis-, mid-, micro-,* or *non-,* tell children to chunk the word and say the parts of the word, first separately and then together. • What is the new word? • Is the new word a word you know? • Does it make sense in the story?

CHECK DECODING AND COMPREHENSION Have children retell the story to include characters, setting, and events. Then have children find words with prefixes *mis-, mid-, micro-,* and *non-* in the story. Children should supply *mismatched, midway, mislaid, misstep, midstream, microscope, nonstop, midday,* and *misplaced.*

Reread for Fluency

REREAD DECODABLE READER Have children reread Decodable Practice Reader 30A to develop automaticity decoding words with prefixes *mis-, mid-, micro-,* and *non-.*

Routine Oral Rereading

1. **Read** Have children read the entire book orally.
2. **Reread** To achieve optimal fluency, children should reread the text three or four times.
3. **Corrective Feedback** Listen as children read. Provide corrective feedback regarding their fluency and decoding.

Routines Flip Chart

Words with Prefixes

Beginning Before reading, familiarize children with the words with prefixes on the first page of the story. Point out the word *mismatched* on p. 255 and illustrate its meaning by showing a pair of matched books and a pair of mismatched books. Have children raise their hand when they hear a word with the prefix *mis-.* Preview and read aloud the story.

Intermediate Preview the story. Point out the words with prefixes and have children repeat them. Provide definitions of the words and have children use picture clues to construct knowledge of the words. For example, explain that *mismatched* means "not matched." Have children use picture clues of the two different boots to confirm understanding.

Advanced After reading, have partners find words with prefixes in the story and say them aloud. Then have them make up sentences about Danny using those words.

Text-Based Comprehension

Facts and Details

Predict and Set Purpose

READ Remind children of the weekly concept—celebrated and shared traditions. Have children read "The White House" on page 501.

MODEL A CLOSE READ Before I read, I look at the title and picture. I think this selection will be about the White House. I can read the first paragraph to see if my prediction is correct. Have children follow along as you reread paragraph 1 aloud. I see my prediction was correct; the selection tells about the place where the President lives and works. This paragraph has facts and details about the White House. One detail is that it is a very big place; one fact is that it has 132 rooms. This fact can be proved true by checking in an encyclopedia or another book. It also supports the statement that the White House is big. The last two sentences give details about the White House: Some rooms are offices. Some rooms are for parties or dances.

INTRODUCE Have children read page 500. Explain that details are pieces of information that support main ideas. Facts are details that can be proved true. Show how the skill of facts and details and the strategy of predict and set purpose can be used to understand a text. Review the bulleted items and explanations on page 500. Then have children use a graphic organizer like the one shown to identify facts and details about the White House in the selection.

IDENTIFY TEXT EVIDENCE Have children reread "The White House," using the callouts as guides. Then ask volunteers to respond to the callouts, citing specific examples from the text to support their answers.

APPLY Use *Reader's and Writer's Notebook,* pp. 531 and 539 for additional practice with facts and details. Children may also turn to pp. EI•6 and EI•22 to review the skill and strategy if necessary.

Common Core State Standards

Informational Text 1. Ask and answer such questions as *who, what, where, when, why,* and *how* to demonstrate understanding of key details in a text.

Skills Trace

Facts and Details

Introduce U1W5D1; U2W3D1; U6W5D1

Practice U1W5D2; U1W5D3; U1W5D4; U2W3D2; U2W3D3; U2W3D4; U6W5D2; U6W5D3; U6W5D4

Reteach/Review U1W5D5; U2W2D3; U2W3D5; U4W3D3; U5W2D3; U6W5D5

Assess/Test Weekly Tests U1W5; U2W3; U6W5
Benchmark Test U6

KEY: U=Unit W=Week D=Day

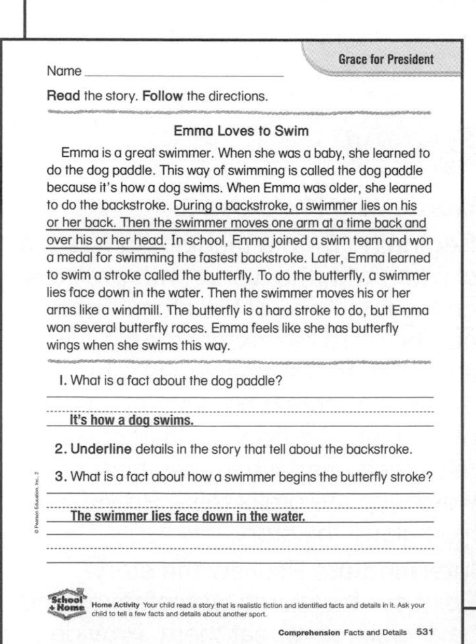

Grace for President

Name ______________

Read the story. **Follow** the directions.

Emma Loves to Swim

Emma is a great swimmer. When she was a baby, she learned to do the dog paddle. This way of swimming is called the dog paddle because it's how a dog swims. When Emma was older, she learned to do the backstroke. During a backstroke, a swimmer lies on his or her back. Then the swimmer moves one arm at a time back and over his or her head. In school, Emma joined a swim team and won a medal for swimming the fastest backstroke. Later, Emma learned to swim a stroke called the butterfly. To do the butterfly, a swimmer lies face down in the water. Then the swimmer moves his or her arms like a windmill. The butterfly is a hard stroke to do, but Emma won several butterfly races. Emma feels like she has butterfly wings when she swims this way.

1. What is a fact about the dog paddle?

   It's how a dog swims.

2. **Underline** details in the story that tell about the backstroke.

3. What is a fact about how a swimmer begins the butterfly stroke?

   The swimmer lies face down in the water.

School + Home **Home Activity** Your child read a story that is realistic fiction and identified facts and details in it. Ask your child to tell a few facts and details about another sport.

Comprehension Facts and Details 531

Reader's and Writer's Notebook, pp. 531 and 539

Common Core State Standards
Informational Text 1. Ask and answer such questions as *who, what, where, when, why,* and *how* to demonstrate understanding of key details in a text.

Envision It! Skill Strategy

Skill

Strategy

READING STREET ONLINE
ENVISION IT! ANIMATIONS
www.ReadingStreet.com

Comprehension Skill

Facts and Details

- Facts and details give information about a story.
- Facts are pieces of information that can be proven. Details can help you see what is taking place as you read.
- As you read "The White House," locate facts and details, and write them in a chart like this.

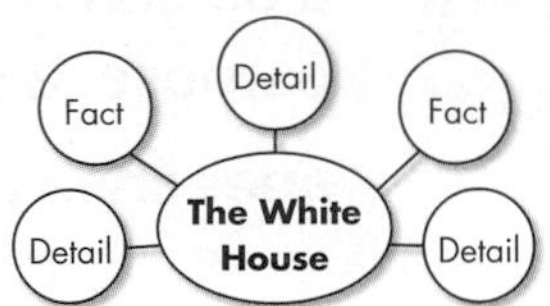

Comprehension Strategy

Predict and Set Purpose

Good readers think about what will happen next in a story. They then read to find out if they are right. This is called predicting and setting a purpose. You can use pictures, titles, and topic sentences to make a prediction. Then you can read to confirm your prediction.

500

THE WHITE HOUSE

Strategy Read the title. Look at the picture. What do you think this story will be about? Read to confirm your prediction.

The President lives and works in the White House in Washington, D.C. The White House is a very big place. It has 132 rooms. Some rooms are offices. Some rooms are for parties or dances.

The White House is a very busy working place. Many people work in offices there. Many people come to talk with the President. The President may have hundreds of visitors in one day!

The White House is also home to the President's family. The family lives on the top floor. Many would say the President's family is lucky! The White House has a swimming pool, so the family can swim at home. The White House also has a library, bowling lanes, and a movie theater. Even the President's doctor has an office in the White House!

Skill This paragraph has facts and details. Locate one fact and one detail about the White House.

Maybe some day you will visit the White House. It is a great place to visit!

Your Turn!

Need a Review? See the *Envision It! Handbook* for additional help with facts and details and predict and set purpose.

Ready to Try It? As you read *Grace for President*, use what you've learned to understand the text.

501

Student Edition, pp. 500–501

Model Fluent Reading

APPROPRIATE PHRASING Have children listen as you read paragraph 1 of "The White House" and model pausing for punctuation and grouping words in meaningful phrases.

Have children reread paragraphs 1 and 2 of "The White House."

Routine Paired Reading

1. **Reread** To achieve optimal fluency, partners should reread the text three or four times.
2. **Corrective Feedback** Listen as children read. Provide corrective feedback regarding their fluency and decoding.

eSTREET INTERACTIVE
www.ReadingStreet.com

Pearson eText
- Student Edition

Teacher Resources
- Reader's and Writer's Notebook

Skills/Strategies

Strategy The selection will probably be about the White House.

Skill Children might cite the following fact and detail: The White House is home to the President's family. The White House has a swimming pool.

Common Core State Standards

Language 1.f. Produce, expand, and rearrange complete simple and compound sentences (e.g., *The boy watched the movie; The little boy watched the movie; The action movie was watched by the little boy*). **Language 4.** Determine or clarify the meaning of unknown and multiple-meaning words and phrases based on grade 2 reading and content, choosing flexibly from an array of strategies.

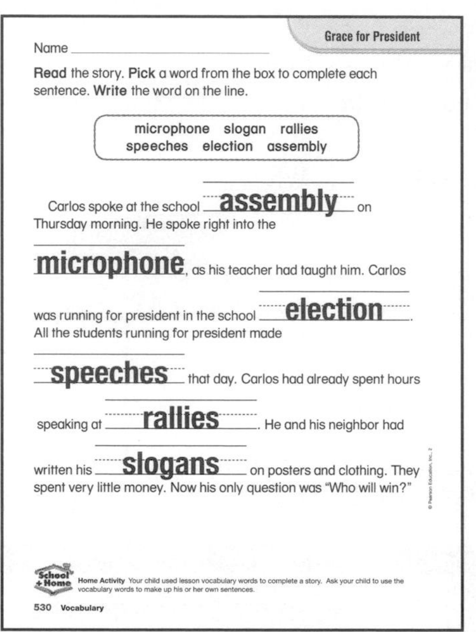

Grace for President

Name ______

Read the story. **Pick** a word from the box to complete each sentence. **Write** the word on the line.

microphone slogan rallies
speeches election assembly

Carlos spoke at the school **assembly** on Thursday morning. He spoke right into the **microphone**, as his teacher had taught him. Carlos was running for president in the school **election**. All the students running for president made **speeches** that day. Carlos had already spent hours speaking at **rallies**. He and his neighbor had written his **slogans** on posters and clothing. They spent very little money. Now his only question was "Who will win?"

School + Home **Home Activity** Your child used lesson vocabulary words to complete a story. Ask your child to use the vocabulary words to make up his or her own sentences.

530 **Vocabulary**

Reader's and Writer's Notebook, p. 530

Selection Vocabulary

Use the following routine to introduce this week's tested selection vocabulary.

assembly a group of people gathered for some purpose

election the act of choosing by vote

microphone an electrical device that makes sounds such as voices louder

rallies meetings of large crowds in support of something

slogan a word or phrase used by a person or group that states its purpose; a motto

speeches public talks

SEE IT/SAY IT Write *assembly.* Scan across the word with your finger as you say it: as-sem-bly.

HEAR IT Use the word in a sentence. The special assembly today is a puppet show.

DEFINE IT Elicit definitions from children. How would you tell another child what *assembly* means? Clarify or give a definition when necessary. It means "a gathering of people for information or entertainment." Restate the word in child-friendly terms. So an *assembly* is something an audience attends.

Team Talk When would the principal be most likely to have an assembly for all children? Turn and talk to your partner about this. Be prepared to explain your answer. Allow children time to discuss. Ask for examples. Rephrase their examples for usage when necessary or to correct misunderstandings.

MAKE CONNECTIONS Have children discuss the word. Would you rather attend an assembly to hear a speaker or watch a play? Turn and talk to your partner about this. Then be prepared to share. Have children share. Rephrase their ideas for usage when necessary or to correct misunderstandings.

RECORD Have children write the word and its meaning.

Continue this routine to introduce the remaining words in this manner.

ON THEIR OWN Use *Reader's and Writer's Notebook,* p. 530.

Corrective feedback	**If...** children are having difficulty understanding, **then...** review the definitions in small groups.

Conventions

Commas in Compound Sentences

MAKE CONNECTIONS Sometimes it makes sense to put two sentences together so we can show the connection between them: I love dogs, but some big dogs scare me.

TEACH Explain that a **simple sentence** has a subject and a verb. Tell children that when we join two simple sentences, we make a **compound sentence.** A compound sentence contains two sentences, and each sentence has a subject and verb: *Mr. Fields went* to the store, and *Mrs. Fields went* to work.

MODEL Display Grammar Transparency 30. Read the definition aloud. Model identifying the pair of simple sentences, and model the comma and connecting word in each compound sentence. Then read the directions and model number 1.

Commas in Compound Sentences

Sometimes two simple sentences have ideas that go together. These sentences can be combined using a comma and a conjunction or connecting word, such as **and** or **but.** The combined sentence is called a **compound sentence.**

Every year our school has an election. Everyone votes.
Every year our school has an election, and everyone votes.

We thought Thomas would win. Grace tried anyway.
We thought Thomas would win, but Grace tried anyway.

Use the word in ( ) and a comma to combine each pair of sentences. **Write** the new sentence on the lines.

1. Polls were taken. Voters made their choices. (and)
   Polls were taken, and voters made their choices.
2. Alabama voted for Thomas. Arizona voted for Grace. (but)
   Alabama voted for Thomas, but Arizona voted for Grace.
3. She won the election. I was glad that she did. (and)
   She won the election, and I was glad that she did.

Unit 6 Grace for President — Grammar 30

Grammar Transparency 30 TR DVD

GUIDE PRACTICE Continue with the next two examples, helping children to add a comma and the correct connecting word to form compound sentences.

APPLY Have children add to each sentence frame orally to make a compound sentence.

1. **Eva has two sisters, and ______.**
2. **Grandma can see a movie with Mom, or ______.**
3. **We went to the park, but ______.**

Team Talk Pair children and have them work together to identify the connecting word in each of the above examples. Have partners generate three new compound sentences with the connecting words *and, or,* and *but.*

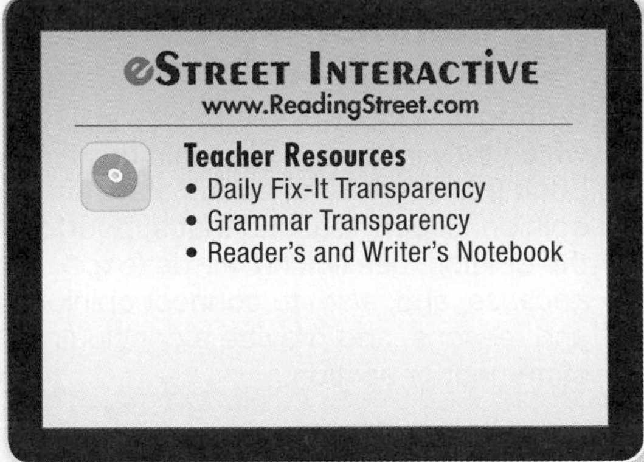

Academic Vocabulary 

compound sentence a sentence that contains two sentences joined by a comma and a word such as *and, but,* or *or*

simple sentence a sentence that expresses one complete thought. It has one subject and one predicate.

Daily Fix-It

1. May i borrow your bell.
   May I borrow your bell?
2. It is february," Matt said.
   "It is February," Matt said.

Discuss the Daily Fix-It corrections with children. Review end punctuation, quotation marks, and capitalization.

Options for Conventions Support
To provide children with practice with compound sentences use the conventions lesson on p. DI•104 in the Teacher Resources section on SuccessNet.

Common Core State Standards

Writing 1. Write opinion pieces in which they introduce the topic or book they are writing about, state an opinion, supply reasons that support the opinion, use linking words (e.g., *because, and, also*) to connect opinion and reasons, and provide a concluding statement or section.

Academic Vocabulary

fact piece of information that can be proved to be true

persuade convince someone to do or to believe something

Bridge to Common Core

TEXT TYPES AND PURPOSES

This week children write a persuasive statement as they practice writing for a test.

Opinion Writing

Through reading and discussion, children will gain a deeper understanding of celebrated and shared traditions. They will use the knowledge from the texts to write and support a persuasive statement.

Throughout the week, children will improve the range and content of their writing through daily mini-lessons.

5-Day Plan

DAY 1	Read Like a Writer
DAY 2	Supporting a Main Idea
DAY 3	Writing Trait: Word Choice
DAY 4	Using Vivid Words
DAY 5	Revise: Compound Sentences

Writing Zoom in on ©

Persuasive Statement

Mini-Lesson Writing for Tests: Read Like a Writer

- **Introduce** This week you will practice writing a persuasive statement for a test. A persuasive statement uses reasons, **facts,** or examples to **persuade,** or convince the reader to do or believe something.

Genre	Persuasive Statement
Trait	Word Choice
Mode	Opinion

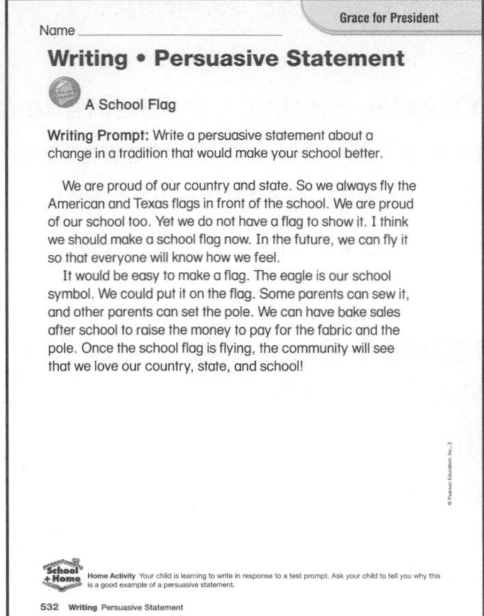

Name ____________ Grace for President

Writing • Persuasive Statement

A School Flag

Writing Prompt: Write a persuasive statement about a change in a tradition that would make your school better.

We are proud of our country and state. So we always fly the American and Texas flags in front of the school. We are proud of our school too. Yet we do not have a flag to show it. I think we should make a school flag now. In the future, we can fly it so that everyone will know how we feel.

It would be easy to make a flag. The eagle is our school symbol. We could put it on the flag. Some parents can sew it, and other parents can set the pole. We can have bake sales after school to raise the money to pay for the fabric and the pole. Once the school flag is flying, the community will see that we love our country, state, and school!

Home Activity Your child is learning to write in response to a test prompt. Ask your child to tell you why this is a good example of a persuasive statement.

532 Writing Persuasive Statement

Reader's and Writer's Notebook, p. 532

- **Examine Model Text** Let's listen to a persuasive statement that was written for a test. Track the print as you read aloud the test prompt and response on *Reader's and Writer's Notebook,* p. 532. Have children follow along.

- **Key Features** This test asks for a persuasive statement. Let's see how "A School Flag" is a good response to the test prompt. What does the writer want the readers to do? (make a school flag) Ask children to underline the sentence that states this idea. What reasons, facts, or examples does the writer give to support his or her idea? Help children find and circle these details. Discuss if the details support the writer's statement. Point out the word *proud.* Ask how the word might make the reader feel and could **persuade** the reader to take action.

This persuasive statement tells the opinion of the writer and what he or she wants the readers to do. The statement has reasons, facts, and examples that tell more about, or support, the writer's ideas. This evidence helps convince the reader that the writer's ideas are correct.

The writer carefully chooses words that make the reader feel a certain emotion or stress a point. The words persuade the reader to do or believe something.

Review Key Features

Review key features of a persuasive statement with children. You may want to post these key features in the classroom to allow children to refer to them as they work on their statements.

Key Features of a Persuasive Statement

- includes ideas to convince the reader
- has a main-idea sentence that asks the reader to do or believe something
- uses reasons, facts, and examples that support the main idea and the writer's opinion
- may use persuasive words to ask for action

Connect to Familiar Texts

Use an example from *Carl the Complainer* (Unit 5) or another selection familiar to children that includes persuasive features. In *Carl the Complainer,* Carl and his friends want to keep the park open later so they have a place to play. They start a petition and ask Mr. Henry to sign it. Carl uses the reason that Mr. Henry will not hear noise if the kids play in the park. Carl convinces Mr. Henry to sign the petition.

Routine Quick Write for Fluency

Team Talk

1. **Talk** Read the question below to children. Have partners take two to three minutes to discuss their ideas.
   What school tradition would you like to see changed?
2. **Write** Have children write a sentence stating how to change the school tradition and a detail to support the change.
3. **Share** Partners read their responses to one another and identify the action and supporting detail.

Routines Flip Chart

Write Guy *by Jeff Anderson*

What Do You Notice?
When children are examining the model text, ask, "What do you notice?" When you give children the responsibility of commenting on what they find effective in the text, they build self-confidence and often begin to notice features of the writing they might not have otherwise. Eventually they will start trying the features in their writing. Relish children's movement toward correctness and beauty.

 **Common Core State Standards**

Speaking/Listening 1. Participate in collaborative conversations with diverse partners about grade 2 topics and texts with peers and adults in small and larger groups.

Academic Vocabulary 

interview a conversation in which one person asks questions about a topic and the other person provides answers

21st Century Skills

Internet Guy *Don Leu*

Weekly Inquiry Project

STEP 1	Identify and Focus Topic
STEP 2	Research Skill
STEP 3	Gather and Record Information
STEP 4	Synthesize
STEP 5	Communicate

Research and Inquiry

Step 1 Identify and Focus Topic

TEACH Display and review the concept map that explores this week's question: *How are different traditions celebrated and shared?* What ideas about celebrating and sharing traditions would you like to learn more about? Ask children to share their interests. Help them identify favorite traditions and ways they are celebrated and shared.

MODEL We know that one way to learn about a topic is to interview someone who knows about it. During an **interview,** one person asks questions about a topic, and the other person provides the answers. For example, if I wanted to learn more about a tradition, I could ask someone who celebrates that tradition.

GUIDE PRACTICE Give children time to think about interview questions that, when answered, would help them learn more about traditions they celebrate and share. Record children's questions in a chart.

Topic: Traditions We Celebrate and Share

Question	Answer
How do you celebrate your favorite tradition?	

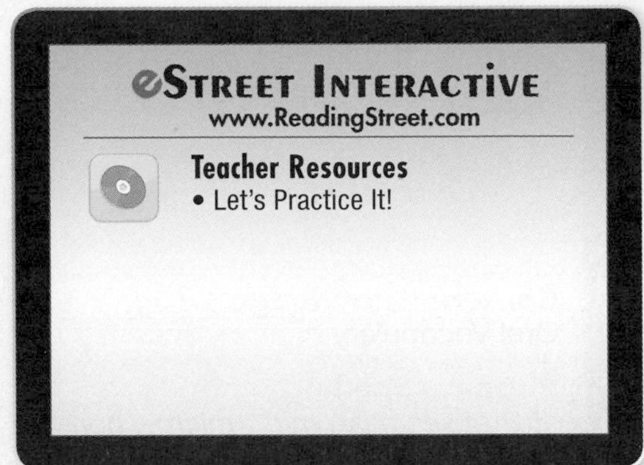

Wrap Up Your Day!

✔ **Phonics: Prefixes *mis-, mid-, micro-, non-*** Write *mishap,* and ask children to decode the word and identify the prefix. Continue with *midday, microwave,* and *nonsense.*

✔ **Spelling: Prefixes *mis-, mid-*** Have children add the prefix *mis-* to the words *fortune* and *judge.* Have them add the prefix *mid-* to *summer* and *point.*

✔ **Content Knowledge** Have children recall what happened in the *Sing with Me* song "Festival Time." What are some things you can do at a festival? (Possible response: We can attend a ceremony and learn about a culture.)

✔ **Homework** Send home this week's Family Times Newsletter from Let's Practice It!, pp. 331–332 on the *Teacher Resources DVD–ROM.*

Let's Practice It!
TR DVD•331–332

Tell children that tomorrow they will read a story about the tradition of voting in the United States.

DAY 2 at a Glance

Content Knowledge
Oral Vocabulary

Phonics/Spelling
Prefixes *mis-, mid-, micro-, non-*

Selection Vocabulary
assembly, election, microphone, rallies, slogan, speeches
Multiple-Meaning Words

Text-Based Comprehension
Facts and Details
Predict and Set Purpose

Conventions
Commas in Compound Sentences

Writing
Persuasive Statement

Handwriting
Cursive *L, D, J*/Letter and Word Spacing

Research and Inquiry
Research Skill: Interview and Natural Sources

Materials

- Student Edition
- Sing with Me Big Book
- Big Book
- Sound-Spelling Cards
- Reader's and Writer's Notebook

Common Core State Standards

Speaking/Listening 2. Recount or describe key ideas or details from a text read aloud or information presented orally or through other media. **Language 6.** Use words and phrases acquired through conversations, reading and being read to, and responding to texts, including using adjectives and adverbs to describe (e.g., *When other kids are happy that makes me happy*).

Content Knowledge

Celebrated and Shared Traditions

To reinforce concepts and to focus children's attention, have children sing "Festival Time" from the *Sing with Me* Big Book. In the song we sing about going to a festival. What can we learn about at a festival? (We can learn about a different culture at a festival.)

Build Oral Language

INTRODUCE AMAZING WORDS Display the Big Book *Magda's Tortillas.* Read the title and identify the author. Review that in this story, the author uses some Amazing Words. Have children listen for the word *compliment.*

Magda's Tortillas Big Book

TALK ABOUT SENTENCES AND WORDS Reread this sentence from the Big Book.

What an honor to hear such a compliment from her abuela, *who made such perfectly round tortillas!*

- Have children repeat the sentence with you. What does *What an honor to hear such a compliment* mean? (what a thrill to be praised)
- **Team Talk** What other words could we use in place of *compliment?* Have children share their suggestions.
- After children have tried other words, ask: Why do you think the author chose the word *compliment?* (It suggests good thoughts and praise.)
- **Team Talk** Turn to your partner and give him or her a compliment by saying something nice about your partner.

Build Oral Vocabulary

Amazing Words Robust Vocabulary Routine

1. **Introduce the Word** Relate the word *compliment* to the story. Magda's grandmother gives her a *compliment* on the tortillas she makes. Supply a child-friendly definition. A *compliment* is something nice that someone says about you. Have children say the word.

2. **Demonstrate** Provide examples to show meaning. I enjoy hearing *compliments* when I do something well. My mother always gets lots of *compliments* on her cooking.

3. **Apply** Have children demonstrate their understanding. Give the person sitting next to you a *compliment.*

4. **Display the Word** Run your hand under the word as you say each syllable: *com-pli-ment.*

Routines Flip Chart

ADD TO THE CONCEPT MAP Discuss different traditions and how they are shared.

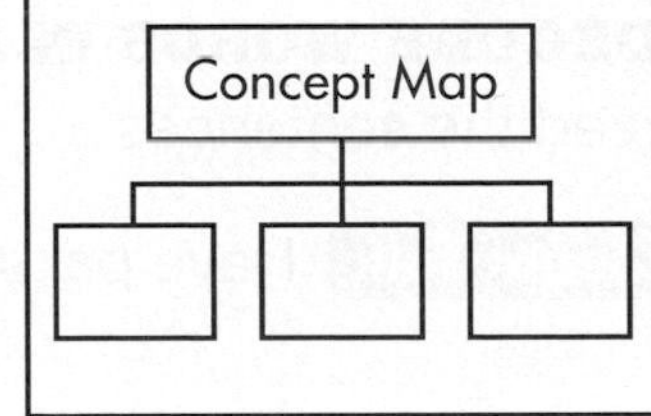

- Point to the picture that illustrates "Festival Time." What kind of special event do you see pictured? (Possible response: a Chinese parade) The Chinese New Year festival is one example of a cultural festival. We'll add *festivals* under *People celebrate special events* on our concept map.
- Where did the tradition of the piñata come from? (Possible response: From Mexico) That's one way traditions are shared. Let's add *Mexican piñata* under *People bring traditions from other lands.*
- In *Magda's Tortillas,* what does Magda learn on her seventh birthday? (Her grandmother teaches her to make tortillas.) Let's add *making special foods* under *Children learn traditions at home and school.*

Amazing Words

ceremony	fidget
culture	evergreen
festival	multicolored
compliment	sash

Access for All

 Advanced

Oral Report Interested children may want to research a cultural "borrowing," such as the piñata, and give an oral report on it to the class.

Reinforce Vocabulary Use the Day 2 instruction on ELL Poster 30 to teach selection vocabulary and discuss the lesson concept.

Common Core State Standards

Foundational Skills 3.d. Decode words with common prefixes and suffixes. **Language 2.** Demonstrate command of the conventions of standard English capitalization, punctuation, and spelling when writing. **Also Language 2.e.**

Phonics

Review Suffixes *-ness, -less, -able, -ible*

Prefixes *mis-, mid-, micro-, non-*

REVIEW SOUND-SPELLINGS Review reading words with suffixes *-ness, -less, -able,* and *-ible* using Sound-Spelling Cards 175, 172, 164, and 169 and prefixes *mis-, mid-, micro-,* and *non-* using Sound-Spelling Cards 157, 156, 155, and 158.

DECODE WORDS IN ISOLATION Display these words. Have the class combine meaningful word parts to read the words. Then point to the words in random order and ask children to read them quickly.

nonskid	**horrible**	**darkness**
happiness	**microchip**	**valuable**
miscopy	**midstream**	**harmless**

Corrective feedback | Model combining meaningful word parts to read the words and then ask children to combine and read them with you.

DECODE WORDS IN CONTEXT Display these sentences. Have the class read the sentences.

Team Talk Have pairs take turns reading the sentences naturally.

By **midday** the sun shone with **brightness** in the **cloudless** sky.

I was too **restless** to be **comfortable** on the **nonstop** flight.

John was **careless** and **misplaced** the **microphone.**

Spelling

Prefixes *mis-*, *mid-*

GUIDE PRACTICE Tell children you will break the spelling words into meaningful word parts. They should say the parts of each word aloud as they write them. Check the spelling of each word before saying the next word. Have children use resources such as a dictionary to find correct spellings.

1. mid air	**midair**	7. mid week	**midweek**
2. mis place	**misplace**	8. mis be have	**misbehave**
3. mis lead	**mislead**	9. mid year	**midyear**
4. mid way	**midway**	10. mis match	**mismatch**
5. mis print	**misprint**	11. mis deed	**misdeed**
6. mid day	**midday**	12. mis take	**mistake**

ON THEIR OWN Use *Reader's and Writer's Notebook,* p. 533.

Name ______

Grace for President

Prefixes *mis-*, *mid-*

Spelling Words					
midair	misplace	mislead	midway	misprint	midday
midweek	misbehave	midyear	mismatch	misdeed	mistake

Write a list word by adding **mis-** or **mid-** to each base word.

match 1. mismatch
print 2. misprint
week 3. midweek
air 4. midair
behave 5. misbehave
deed 6. misdeed
year 7. midyear
way 8. midway

Write the list word to complete each phrase.

9. misplace your keys
10. make a mistake
11. mislead people
12. midday nap

School + Home **Home Activity** Your child spelled words with the prefixes *mis-* and *mid-*. Take turns with your child using the words in sentences.

Spelling Prefixes *mis-*, *mid-* 533

Reader's and Writer's Notebook, p. 533

Access for All

 **Advanced**

Extend Phonics Write a list of the prefixes and suffixes children have learned, including *un-, re-, pre-, dis-, mis-, mid-, non-, -ly, -ful, -ness, -less, -ish, -able,* and *-ible.* Have children write words that have multiple prefixes and suffixes, such as *unenjoyable, unselfishness, disagreeable, unhopeful, misleadingly,* and *distrustful.*

Spelling Prefixes The writing systems of languages such as Arabic and Hebrew focus on consonants and long vowels. Short vowels are indicated with separate marks that are often optional. Speakers of these languages may need extra help in spelling words with *mis-* and *mid-*.

Common Core State Standards

Language 3. Use knowledge of language and its conventions when writing, speaking, reading, or listening. **Foundational Skills 3.** Know and apply grade-level phonics and word analysis skills in decoding words.

Selection Vocabulary

ACTIVATE PRIOR KNOWLEDGE Display the selection words and discuss what children already know about them.

Write incomplete sentences, such as those below. Have children identify the word that completes each sentence. Children may need to use the glossary.

- Speak into the ______ so the audience can hear you. (microphone)
- The governor will give two ______ to tell the people about her plans for the state. (speeches)
- Our school holds pep ______ for our sports teams. (rallies)
- Who will you vote for in the next ______? (election)
- The ______ for that toothpaste is "Don't Brush in a Rush!" (slogan)
- Students receive awards at the last ______ of the school year. (assembly)

REVIEW PLURALS Point out that children can use their knowledge of the ending *-es* to read and understand *speeches* and *rallies.*

Access for All

SI Strategic Intervention

Talk About It Lead a discussion in which children share personal experiences relating to selection vocabulary. For example, have children tell about assemblies they have attended this year, elections where they have voted for leaders of sports teams or groups, and product slogans they hear on the radio or television.

MONITOR PROGRESS Check Selection Vocabulary/ High-Frequency Words

FORMATIVE ASSESSMENT Write the following words and have the class read them. Listen for children who miss words during the reading. Call on those children to read some of the words individually.

slogan	assembly	rallies	microphone	**Spiral Review** Rows 3 and 4 review previously taught high-frequency words.
election	speeches			
hours	only	clothes	neighbor	←
question	taught	money		←

If... children cannot read these words,

then... use the Small Group Time Strategic Intervention lesson, p. SG•76, to reteach the words. Monitor children's fluency with these words during reading and provide additional practice.

Multilingual Vocabulary Lists
Children can apply knowledge of their home languages to acquire new English vocabulary by using the Multilingual Vocabulary Lists in the *ELL Handbook,* p. 440.

Common Core State Standards

Language 4.e. Use glossaries and beginning dictionaries, both print and digital, to determine or clarify the meaning of words and phrases. **Foundational Skills 4.a.** Read on-level text with purpose and understanding. **Foundational Skills 4.b.** Read on-level text orally with accuracy, appropriate rate, and expression on successive readings.

Selection Vocabulary

assembly a group of people gathered for some purpose

election the act of choosing by vote

microphone an electrical device that makes sounds such as voices louder

rallies meetings of large crowds in support of something

slogan a word or phrase used by a person or group that states its purpose; a motto

speeches public talks

Bridge to Common Core

VOCABULARY ACQUISITION AND USE

When children interact with this week's selection vocabulary, they are learning domain-specific words that they will encounter in school and beyond. Teaching the strategy of using the dictionary to determine the meaning of multiple-meaning words will help children gain independence as they encounter multiple-meaning words in other contexts.

Vocabulary Skill

Multiple-Meaning Words

READ Have children read "Marcus and Jin" on p. 503 with you. Use the vocabulary skill and strategy as tools to build comprehension.

TEACH Some words have more than one meaning. If you read a word and the meaning you know doesn't make sense in the sentence, the word could have another meaning. You can use a dictionary or a glossary to find out. Refer children to Words! on p. W•14 in the Student Edition for additional practice. Then read "Marcus and Jin" on page 503 with children.

Think Aloud Write on the board the sentence: *The assembly met in a large hall.* The word *assembly* can mean "putting together," as in "My father had no trouble with the assembly of my bike." But that meaning doesn't make sense in this sentence, so I'll look up the word in a dictionary. Demonstrate looking up the word, identifying the guide words on the page and then locating the entry *assembly.* I see that *assembly* has several meanings. One meaning is "a group of people gathered for some purpose." That's the meaning that fits the sentence.

GUIDE PRACTICE Write this sentence on the board: *The rallies for the President brought large, noisy crowds.* Have children use a dictionary to determine which meaning of the word *rallies* is being used in the sentence.

ON THEIR OWN Have children reread "Marcus and Jin" on page 503. Have them use a dictionary or glossary to determine meanings of words they do not know, including the other selection words. For additional practice, use *Reader's and Writer's Notebook,* p. 534.

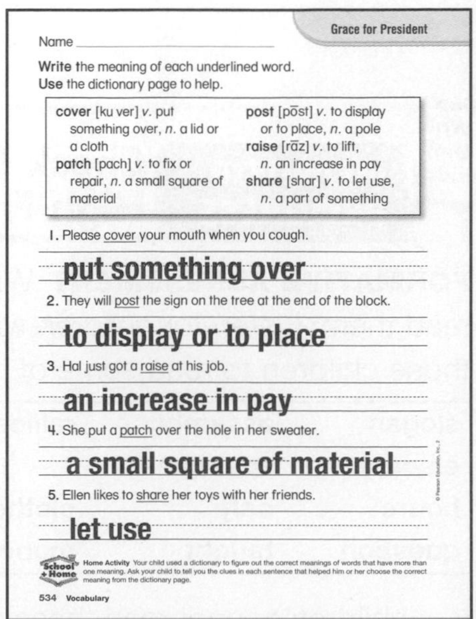
Grace for President

Name ____________

Write the meaning of each underlined word.
Use the dictionary page to help.

cover [ku ver] *v.* put something over, *n.* a lid or a cloth
patch [pach] *v.* to fix or repair, *n.* a small square of material
post [pōst] *v.* to display or to place, *n.* a pole
raise [rāz] *v.* to lift, *n.* an increase in pay
share [shar] *v.* to let use, *n.* a part of something

1. Please cover your mouth when you cough.
put something over
2. They will post the sign on the tree at the end of the block.
to display or to place
3. Hal just got a raise at his job.
an increase in pay
4. She put a patch over the hole in her sweater.
a small square of material
5. Ellen likes to share her toys with her friends.
let use

School + Home **Home Activity** Your child used a dictionary to figure out the correct meanings of words that have more than one meaning. Ask your child to tell you the clues in each sentence that helped him or her choose the correct meaning from the dictionary page.

534 Vocabulary

Reader's and Writer's Notebook, p. 534

Vocabulary Strategy for

Multiple-Meaning Words

Dictionary/Glossary When you read, you may see a word you know, but the meaning doesn't make sense in the sentence. The word may be a multiple-meaning word. You can look in a dictionary or a glossary to figure out the relevant meaning of the word.

1. Use the guide words at the top of each page to help you find the word.
2. Read the meanings given for the word.
3. Decide which meaning of the word makes sense in the sentence.

Read "Marcus and Jin." Use a dictionary or glossary to help you determine the meanings of multiple-meaning words.

Words to Write Reread "Marcus and Jin." Write at least three questions to Marcus about Washington, D.C. Use words from the *Words to Know* list.

502

Marcus and Jin

Marcus and Jin are friends. Marcus talked about his trip to Washington, D.C.

"It was fun," he said. "I got to see Capitol Hill. That's where members of Congress meet. It's an assembly."

Jin asked, "What do they do there?"

Marcus shrugged. "They make laws for our country," he said.

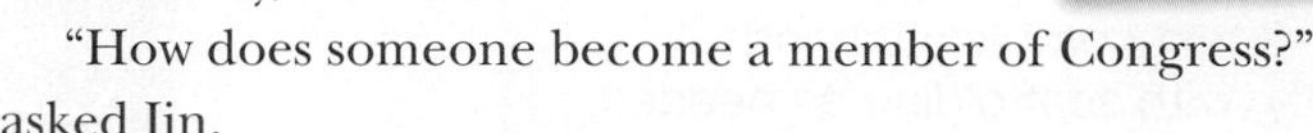

"How does someone become a member of Congress?" asked Jin.

"The country has an election. The people vote for who they want," said Marcus. "A person who wants to be in Congress has rallies. He or she gives speeches using a microphone so everyone can hear him or her talk. Then that person meets people and asks for everyone's vote. The person becomes a member if he or she gets enough votes. That person may use a slogan too."

"Why would that person use a slogan?" asked Jin.

"It helps people remember to vote for them," said Marcus.

"I wish I could visit Washington, D.C.," said Jin.

"I'm sure you will someday," said Marcus.

Your Turn!

Need a Review? For help with using a dictionary or glossary to find the meanings of multiple-meaning words, see *Words!* on p. W•14.

Ready to Try It? Read *Grace for President* on pp. 504–519.

503

Student Edition, pp. 502–503

Reread for Fluency

Have children reread the first five paragraphs of "Marcus and Jin."

Routine Paired Reading

1. **Reread** To achieve optimal fluency, have partners reread the text three or four times.
2. **Corrective Feedback** Listen as children read. Provide corrective feedback regarding their fluency and decoding.

Routines Flip Chart

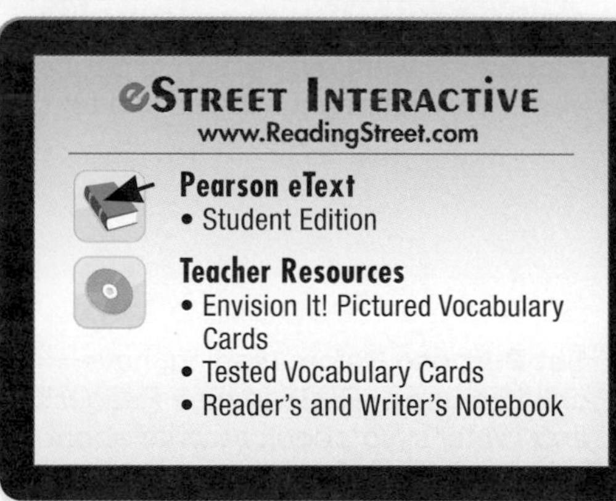

Cognates Point out the Spanish cognates in this week's selection vocabulary: *assembly/asamblea; microphone/micrófono;* and *slogan/eslogan.*

Preteach Words Have children describe the pictures illustrating *assembly, microphone,* and *rallies,* using the words.

Zoom in on 

Text-Based Comprehension

Introduce Main Selection

Student Edition, pp. 504–505

GENRE Realistic fiction tells about made-up events that could happen in real life. As they read *Grace for President,* children should look for events that could really happen.

PREVIEW AND PREDICT Have children identify the title of the story, the author, and the illustrator. Have children predict what might happen in the story.

PURPOSE By analyzing *Grace for President,* a realistic fiction story, children gain knowledge of sharing different traditions.

PREDICT AND SET PURPOSE Explain that as they read, good readers **predict** by thinking about what will happen next in a story. Thinking about what has already happened and looking at the illustrations and title help readers predict. Good readers also read for a purpose. Have children turn to page EI•22 in their Student Edition.

Student Edition, p. EI•22

Think Aloud Look at this picture. What prediction will the boys make about the movie? (They may predict it is about an elephant and monkey who are friends.) As I read *Grace for President,* I will stop and predict what will happen next. I'll also set a purpose for reading each section of the story.

Common Core State Standards

Literature 1. Ask and answer such questions as *who, what, where, when, why,* and *how* to demonstrate understanding of key details in a text. **Literature 10.** By the end of the year, read and comprehend literature, including stories and poetry, in the grades 2–3 text complexity band proficiently, with scaffolding as needed at the high end of the range.

Bridge to Common Core

CRAFT AND STRUCTURE

As children preview the selection and predict what it is about, they are determining how the purpose is connected to the content and style of realistic fiction. This sets the stage for children to see how different parts of realistic stories are connected to each other and the whole.

Academic Vocabulary 

predict tell what a selection might be about or what might happen in a text

Strategy Response Log

Set Purpose Before reading, have children use p. RR36 in their *Reader's and Writer's Notebook* to write about their own purpose for reading *Grace for President.*

Access Main Selection

READER AND TASK SUGGESTIONS	
Preparing to Read the Text	**Leveled Tasks**
• Review prefixes *mis-*, *mid-*, *non-*, and *micro-*. • Discuss the author's use of boldfaced words in all capital letters throughout the text. • Remind children that as they encounter unfamiliar words, they may need to read more slowly and think about context clues to better understand the text.	• **Structure** If children do not understand why some words are boldfaced, have them identify the words and discuss why the author chose to boldface them. • **Theme and Knowledge Demands** If children have difficulty understanding the sequence of campaigns and elections, have them list the events in order.

See Text Complexity Measures for *Grace for President* on the tab at the beginning of this week.

READ Tell children that today they will read *Grace for President* for the first time. Use the Read for Understanding routine.

Routine Read for Understanding

Deepen understanding by reading the selection multiple times.

1. **First Read**—If children need support, use the **Access Text** notes to help them clarify understanding.
2. **Second Read**—Use the **Close Reading** notes to help children draw knowledge from the text.

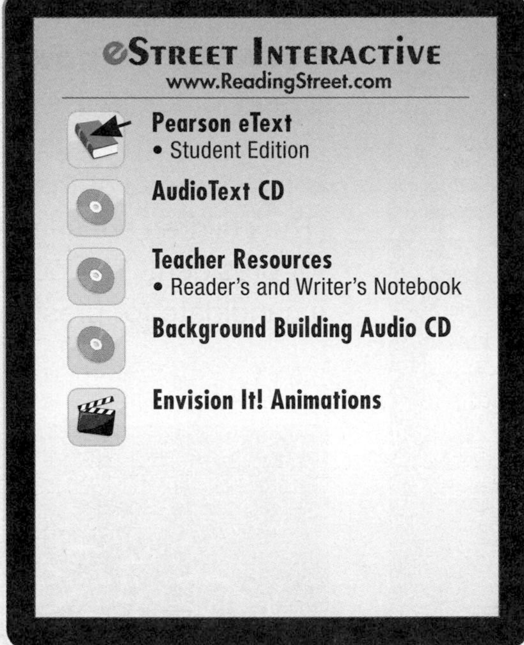

Preview Main Selection Ask children what they already know about elections using the pictures on pages 504–505. Then do a picture walk of the selection so children can talk about the candidates for president and the events in the election.

1ST READ

Access Text © If children need help, then...

CONNECT TO CONCEPT Look at the picture. Voting for leaders is an American tradition. What are the children in the large picture doing? What is the purpose of the posters shown on page 504? (The children are supporting Grace as a candidate for president. The posters are advertising Grace as a candidate for president.)

Student Edition, pp. 504–505

2ND READ

Close Reading ©

ANALYSIS • TEXT EVIDENCE Using details in the title and the pictures as clues, identify the candidate and tell what office she is running for. Tell which person in the large picture is the candidate. (Grace is the candidate, and she is running for class president. She is the person in the front middle of the large picture.)

FIND MEANING OF MULTIPLE-MEANING WORDS A dictionary can help you clarify the meaning of multiple-meaning words. Find the word *stewed* on page 507. The dictionary says this word means "cooked slowly in liquid" or "troubled and upset." Which meaning fits in the context of the sentence? ("troubled and upset")

Common Core State Standards

Language 4.e. Use glossaries and beginning dictionaries, both print and digital, to determine or clarify the meaning of words and phrases. **Literature 1.** Ask and answer such questions as *who, what, where, when, why,* and *how* to demonstrate understanding of key details in a text.

One morning in September, Mrs. Barrington rolled out a big poster with all of the Presidents' pictures on it. Grace Campbell could not believe her eyes.

"Where are the **GIRLS**?"

"That is a very good question!" said Mrs. Barrington.

"The truth is, our country has never had a woman President."

"**NO** girl President? **EVER**?" Grace asked.

"No, I'm afraid not," said Mrs. Barrington.

506

Grace sat at her desk and stewed. No girls? Who'd ever heard of such a crazy thing?

Finally, she raised her hand.

"Yes, Grace?"

"I've been thinking it over, and I'd like to be **PRESIDENT**!"

Several students in the class laughed.

"Well, I think that's a star-spangled idea, Grace!" said Mrs. Barrington.

"In fact, we can have our own election right here at Woodrow Wilson Elementary!"

507

Student Edition, pp. 506–507

ANALYSIS • TEXT EVIDENCE What question did Grace ask? What clues in Mrs. Barrington's response helped you figure out the question? (Grace asked if there had ever been a woman President in the United States. You know this because Mrs. Barrington says our country has never had a woman President.)

CONNECT TO SOCIAL STUDIES Every four years, U.S. citizens vote to elect the next President. The President leads the country, is commander in chief of the military, and works to carry out the laws passed by Congress.

1ST READ

Access Text If children need help, then...

FACTS AND DETAILS • REREAD CHALLENGING TEXT Reread page 508 to find facts about Thomas. How do these facts help explain Grace's reaction to the announcement of his candidacy? (Thomas is smart, successful, and good in spelling, science, and sports. He is also used to winning and being the best at whatever he does.)

PREDICT AND SET PURPOSE What predictions can you make about the election and the candidates? How might looking ahead at the illustrations help you make these predictions?

The snickering in the room stopped. Grace smiled.

"Would anyone else like to run for President?" Mrs. Barrington asked the class.

Nobody raised their hand.

Becoming President was going to be easy! Grace thought.

The next day, Mrs. Barrington made an announcement.

"In the name of **DEMOCRACY**, I have invited Mr. Waller's class to join our election.

Their class has nominated **THOMAS COBB** to be their presidential candidate!"

Grace's heart sank.

Thomas was the school spelling bee champion. His experiments always took a blue ribbon at the science fair. And he was captain of the soccer team.

508

Becoming President wasn't going to be so easy, after all, Grace thought.

The teachers put the names of all fifty states and the District of Columbia into a hat. Everyone except for Grace and Thomas got to choose a state.

"I'm Texas!" said Anthony.

"I'm New Hampshire!" said Rose.

"I'm Michigan," said Robbie. "What does the number 17 mean?"

"Each state is assigned a number of electoral votes. That number is determined by how many people live in that state," said Mrs. Barrington. "Each of you will be a representative for your state."

509

Student Edition, pp. 508–509

2ND READ

INFERENCE • TEXT EVIDENCE Reread the last paragraph on p. 509. Would you rather represent a state with a large or a small population? Why? (I would rather represent a state with a large population because it would mean I would have more electoral votes to cast in the election.)

FACTS AND DETAILS What facts and details help you understand how this election will be run? (Each student represents a state that is assigned a number of electoral votes based on population. On election day, each representative will cast these votes, and the candidate who gets 270 votes wins.)

Common Core State Standards

Literature 1. Ask and answer such questions as *who, what, where, when, why,* and *how* to demonstrate understanding of key details in a text. **Literature 3.** Describe how characters in a story respond to major events and challenges.

"Altogether, our country has 538 electoral votes," Mr. Waller explained. "On Election Day, the candidate who receives 270 electoral votes or more wins the election!"

"Why 270?" asked Rose.

"That's more than half of all the electoral votes," Mr. Waller said.

Becoming president REALLY wasn't going to be so easy, Grace thought.

Grace came up with a campaign slogan:

Thomas came up with his own campaign slogan:

510

Grace listened to what issues were important to the students, and she made a list of campaign promises:

Thomas made up his own list of promises:

511

Student Edition, pp. 510–511

ANALYSIS • TEXT EVIDENCE Look at the slogans on the posters on page 510. Slogans are meant to persuade voters and may contain a hidden message. What message does each candidate's slogan contain? (Grace wants to "Make History" by being the first girl to win. Thomas believes he is the "Best Man" because he is a boy.)

1ST READ

Access Text If children need help, then…

CHECK DECODING Have children check their reading of new words using these questions:

- Did I blend the sounds?
- Did it make sense?
- Did I look for word parts?

FACTS AND DETAILS What important fact explains why Thomas isn't worried about the campaign? (Thomas calculates that the boys have more electoral votes than the girls.)

Grace made campaign posters and buttons.

Thomas made posters and buttons too.

Each week, the teachers set aside time for the candidates to meet with their constituents.

Polls were taken. Voters were making their choices.

Grace continued to campaign.

At recess, she gave **SPEECHES**.

During lunch, she handed out free **CUPCAKES**.

After school, she held **RALLIES**.

512

MEANWHILE, Thomas wasn't worried.

He had cleverly calculated that the **BOYS** held slightly more electoral votes than the **GIRLS**.

At recess, Thomas studied his spelling words.

During lunch, he worked on his latest science experiment.

After school, he played soccer.

513

Student Edition, pp. 512–513

2ND READ

Close Reading

ANALYSIS • TEXT EVIDENCE Look at details in the story. How would you compare and contrast Grace's and Thomas's campaigns? (Both make posters and buttons. Only Grace continues to campaign. Thomas just continues his normal activities.)

EVALUATION Who do you think has been the better candidate up to this point in the election? Explain your thinking.

REVIEW SELECTION VOCABULARY Have children read page 514. Why would the representatives need to use a microphone during the assembly? (A microphone helps the audience at a large gathering hear the speakers.)

PREDICT AND SET PURPOSE Now that the campaign is over, who do you predict will win this election? On what information are you basing your prediction?

Common Core State Standards

Foundational Skills 3. Know and apply grade-level phonics and word analysis skills in decoding words. **Literature 3.** Describe how characters in a story respond to major events and challenges.

Even before the election, Grace made good on her promises. She joined the safety squad. She organized a school beautification committee, and she volunteered her time in the school cafeteria.

In early November, Woodrow Wilson Elementary hosted a special Election Day assembly. Grace and Thomas took their places onstage as the school band began to play.

Henry was the first representative to approach the microphone.

514

And so it went. State after state after state cast their electoral votes. The scoreboard in the gymnasium kept track of the totals.

515

Student Edition, pp. 514–515

SYNTHESIS • TEXT EVIDENCE What pattern is beginning to emerge as each representative casts his or her vote? (The boys are voting for Thomas and the girls are voting for Grace.)

1ST READ

Access Text If children need help, then...

Review **CAUSE AND EFFECT • REREAD CHALLENGING TEXT** Explain that children can reread to help them understand and explain events. Ask how many votes Thomas has and how many Grace has. (268; 267) Then ask why Sam's vote is so important. Have children reread pages 509 and 510 to help them answer the question. (Sam's vote will decide the election because a candidate must have at least 270 votes to win. Sam's vote will give either Thomas or Grace enough votes to win.)

The voting demonstration was quickly coming to an end.

Clara approached the podium.

"The Badger State of Wisconsin casts its 10 votes for my best friend, Grace Campbell!"

Grace looked at the scoreboard.

Thomas had 268 electoral votes. She had 267.

There was only one state still unaccounted for:

WYOMING.

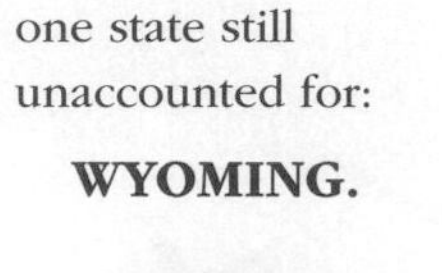

Thomas grinned.
Grace felt sick.

516

Sam walked up to the microphone.

He looked at Thomas.

He looked at Grace.

He looked down at Grace's handmade flag.

Sam didn't say a word.

"What are you waiting for?" Thomas whispered.

The band stopped playing.

All eyes were on Wyoming.

Finally, Sam cleared his throat.

"The Equality State of Wyoming casts its 3 electoral votes for . . .

GRACE CAMPBELL!!!"

517

Student Edition, pp. 516–517

2ND READ

Close Reading

ANALYSIS • TEXT EVIDENCE The word *equality* can mean "a condition where everyone has the same opportunities." What evidence can you find that Sam is aware of equality when he votes? (He examines both candidates and thinks before he votes. He uses the nickname Equality State for Wyoming when he votes.)

PREDICT AND SET PURPOSE Did you predict the winner? If you did, what clues did you use to predict correctly? If you did not predict the winner, what clues may have led you to predict incorrectly?

CROSS-TEXT EVALUATION

Use a Strategy to Self-Check How did the selection "Marcus and Jin" help you understand this selection?

Continue to DAY 2
Text-Based Comprehension p. 519a

Student Edition, pp. 518–519

ANALYSIS Why do you think Sam uses the word *person* in his response to Grace's question? (Sam wanted Grace to understand that he was not voting for a boy or a girl. Instead he was voting for the person he thought would do the best job as president.)

SYNTHESIS • TEXT EVIDENCE Using what you learned in this selection, tell how Grace's school shared the tradition of elections. Have children cite examples from the text.

Continue to DAY 3
Think Critically p. 520–521

Common Core State Standards

Literature 2. Recount stories, including fables and folktales from diverse cultures, and determine their central message, lesson, or moral. **Language 1.f.** Produce, expand, and rearrange complete simple and compound sentences (e.g., *The boy watched the movie; The little boy watched the movie; The action movie was watched by the little boy*).

ELL

If... children need more scaffolding and practice with the **Comprehension Skill,**
then... use the ELL activities on p. DI•101 in the Teacher Resources section on SuccessNet.

Text-Based Comprehension

Check Understanding

Have children discuss the question with a partner and share responses.

☑ **Realistic fiction** Do you think this story could happen in real life? (Yes, schools sometimes elect student presidents.)

Day 2 SMALL GROUP TIME • Differentiate Comprehension, p. SG•69

OL On-Level	SI Strategic Intervention	A Advanced
• **Practice** Selection Vocabulary	• **Reteach** Selection Vocabulary	• **Extend** Selection Vocabulary
• **Read** *Grace for President*	• **Read** *Grace for President*	• **Read** *Grace for President*
		• **Investigate** Inquiry Project

Literary Text

Moral Lessons as Themes

REVIEW Use *Grace for President* to identify the moral lesson that is the theme.

- The theme of a story may be a moral lesson about the right way to act.
- Who acted the right way? (Grace worked to improve the school and ran a good campaign.)
- Who was rewarded by getting what he or she wanted? (Grace)

GUIDE PRACTICE Together complete a chart to identify the moral lesson of *Grace for President.*

How Characters Acted	Who Was Rewarded?	Lesson Learned
Grace worked to improve the school. Thomas thought he would win all the boys' votes.	Grace won when one boy voted for her because she was the best person for the job.	Run a good campaign and you will be judged on what you do, not who you are.

ON THEIR OWN Have children work in small groups to identify the moral lesson of *Just Like Josh Gibson.*

Conventions

Commas in Compound Sentences

TEACH Write the following sentences: *Our class voted for class president. Trey got the most votes.* Point to each word as you read it. Ask children how they could combine the sentences. (Change the period to a comma and add a connecting word.) Two simple sentences can be combined with a comma and a connecting word, such as *and.* What do you call a sentence made up of two simple sentences put together with a comma and a connecting word? (a compound sentence)

GUIDE PRACTICE Write the following compound sentences on the board. Have children identify the two simple sentences that are connected by a comma and connecting word in each example.

1. **Jeff washes the dog, and Rose dries the dog.**
2. **I play soccer, but my sister plays baseball.**

APPLY Have children orally combine the following sentences into compound sentences using *and* or *but.*

1. **I like to play outside. It is raining today.**
2. **Sally claps her hands. Brett stamps his feet.**
3. **Mom rakes the leaves. Dad scoops leaves into bags.**

ON THEIR OWN Use *Reader's and Writer's Notebook,* p. 535.

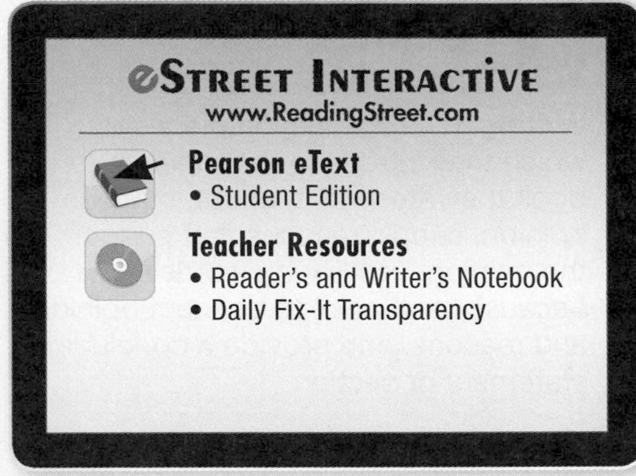

Daily Fix-It

3. Id like to borrw your drum.
   I'd like to borrow your drum.
4. Shake the sivler jingel bell.
   Shake the silver jingle bell.

Discuss the Daily Fix-It corrections with children. Review contractions, final syllable *-le,* and the spelling of *borrow, silver,* and *jingle.*

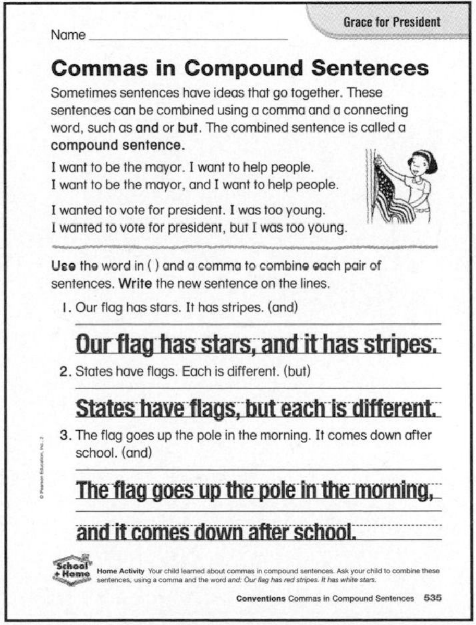

Name ______ Grace for President

Commas in Compound Sentences

Sometimes sentences have ideas that go together. These sentences can be combined using a comma and a connecting word, such as **and** or **but**. The combined sentence is called a **compound sentence.**

I want to be the mayor. I want to help people.
I want to be the mayor, and I want to help people.

I wanted to vote for president. I was too young.
I wanted to vote for president, but I was too young.

Use the word in ( ) and a comma to combine each pair of sentences. **Write** the new sentence on the lines.

1. Our flag has stars. It has stripes. (and)
   Our flag has stars, and it has stripes.
2. States have flags. Each is different. (but)
   States have flags, but each is different.
3. The flag goes up the pole in the morning. It comes down after school. (and)
   The flag goes up the pole in the morning, and it comes down after school.

Home Activity Your child learned about commas in compound sentences. Ask your child to combine these sentences, using a comma and the word and: Our flag has red stripes. It has white stars.

Conventions Commas in Compound Sentences 535

Reader's and Writer's Notebook, p. 535

Professional Development

Compound Predicates vs. Compound Sentences A compound sentence has two subjects, two verbs, a conjunction, and a comma: *The dog paced, and the cat glared.* A sentence with one subject, two verbs, a conjunction, and no comma is not a compound sentence: *The dog paced and glared.*

Common Core State Standards

Writing 1. Write opinion pieces in which they introduce the topic or book they are writing about, state an opinion, supply reasons that support the opinion, use linking words (e.g., *because, and, also*) to connect opinion and reasons, and provide a concluding statement or section.

Writing

Persuasive Statement

INTRODUCE THE PROMPT Review the key features of a persuasive statement using the example "A School Flag." Assure children that they can write a persuasive statement in test-taking situations. Explain that today children will write their own persuasive statement with convincing reasons, facts, or examples.

Read aloud the writing prompt. Tell children this is the kind of prompt they may get on a test.

Writing Prompt

Think about a tradition that you consider important. Share your opinion and write a statement to persuade people in your school or community to honor that tradition.

Mini-Lesson Writing for Tests: Supporting a Main Idea

- **Introduce** Model how to plan a main idea sentence for a persuasive statement in a test situation. The tradition I'll write about is that children who arrive before school play on the playground. On cold or rainy days, they sit in the lunchroom. My idea is to let children play in the gym on bad-weather days. To help me plan my statement, I'll write some notes. I'll write *I hope we can play in the gym on bad-weather days.* This is my main idea. Now I'll note reasons and facts to support my idea.
- **Model** One fact is that the gym is empty before school. I'll write this in my notes. Another fact is that there is lots of gym equipment, so the children will be busy. I'll write this detail. For a reason, I'll say that when children play outside, they are ready to sit and learn when school starts. If they sit in the lunchroom, it is hard to sit still in the classroom. I'll write this detail. Now plan your persuasive statement. Circulate to guide and assist children.

DISCUSS RUBRIC Have children look at the Scoring Rubric on *Reader's and Writer's Notebook,* p. 536. Explain that these points will be used to evaluate their writing this week. Discuss the traits they should include in their persuasive statements.

Name ____________ Grace for President

Scoring Rubric: Persuasive Statement

	4	3	2	1
Focus/Ideas	The statement is well-focused on an idea with three supporting facts, reasons, or examples.	The statement is focused on an idea with two supporting facts, reasons, or examples.	The statement is loosely focused on an idea with one supporting fact, reason, or example.	The statement is unfocused and lacks supporting facts, reasons, or examples.
Organization	Details are presented in a clearly organized way.	Details are presented in an organized way.	Some of the details are organized.	The details are not organized.
Voice	The writing uses a strong, persuasive tone and knowledge.	The writing uses a persuasive tone.	The writing sometimes uses a persuasive tone.	The writing does not use a persuasive tone.
Word Choice	The writer uses vivid and persuasive words.	The writer uses some persuasive words.	The writer uses few persuasive words.	The writer uses dull words.
Sentences	The sentences are complete and varied in length.	Most sentences are complete and varied in length.	Some sentences are complete and varied in length.	Few sentences are complete or varied in length.
Conventions	There are no spelling, capitalization, or punctuation errors.	There are few spelling, capitalization, or punctuation errors.	There are some spelling, capitalization, or punctuation errors.	There are many spelling, capitalization, or punctuation errors.

School + Home **Home Activity** Your child is learning to write a persuasive statement. Ask your child to explain the topic. Then have your child tell his or her main idea statement and supporting details. Your child's writing will be evaluated based on this four-point scoring rubric.

536 **Writing** Rubric

Reader's and Writer's Notebook, p. 536

SAMPLE TEST Explain that children will write persuasive statements just as they might do on a test. Have children get paper and pencil ready. Display the writing prompt, read it aloud, and allow children time to write a persuasive statement in response to the prompt. Remind them to take time after writing to reread what they've written and make changes or additions.

Routine Quick Write for Fluency

Team Talk

1. **Talk** Have children take two minutes to read their persuasive statements to a partner.
2. **Write** Each child briefly writes sentences to tell if the partner wrote a convincing persuasive statement, explaining why or why not.
3. **Share** Each child reads the response to the partner.

Routines Flip Chart

Support Main Idea

Beginning Children can draw a picture showing the tradition they think is important. Have children complete this sentence frame to state the main idea: *I think ________ is important.*

Intermediate Have children write one phrase that supports their main idea. Then have partners share their main idea and supporting details.

Advanced Have children write short sentences in their main idea charts. Then have them share the charts with a partner to discuss the details. Encourage them to focus on words that stress their point.

Common Core State Standards

Speaking/Listening 3. Ask and answer questions about what a speaker says in order to clarify comprehension, gather additional information, or deepen understanding of a topic or issue.

Handwriting

Cursive *L, D,* and *J*/Letter and Word Spacing

MODEL LETTER FORMATION Display uppercase cursive letters: *L, D,* and *J.* Use the stroke instructions pictured below to model proper letter formation. Have children write each letter several times and circle their best ones.

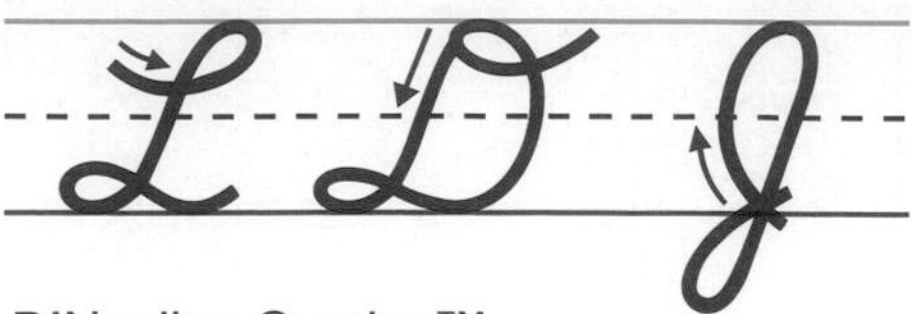

D'Nealian Cursive™

MODEL LETTER AND WORD SPACING Explain that when we write words in a sentence, the space between the letters in each word should be the same. The spaces between the words should be bigger. Write the sentence *Just send Luke and Dan* using correct spacing. When I write this sentence, I evenly space the letters within each word. I leave extra space between words to show where one word ends and another word begins. Write *Just send Luke and Dan* again, with uniform spacing between all the letters and between words. The spaces between words should not be the same as the spaces between letters. Write *Just send Luke and Dan* a third time, with varying amounts of space between each word. The spaces between words should not be big in some places and small in others. By correctly spacing letters within and between words, I make it easier for others to read what I write. Ask children which of the three writing examples is easiest to read, and have them explain why.

GUIDE PRACTICE Write the following sentence, spacing the words too far apart.

Lenny misplaced his hat.

Have children rewrite the sentence correctly.

Team Talk Have children work in pairs to discuss what was wrong with the sentence and how they corrected it. Have them share with the class.

Research and Inquiry

Step 2 Research Skill: Interview and Natural Sources

TEACH Review with children that an interview is a way to gather information by asking people questions and recording their answers. Remind children that such people are **sources** and they may be found inside their school. Review the steps for taking notes in an interview.

Think Aloud **MODEL** Before I interview, I think of questions to ask and write them down. During the interview, I listen carefully and take notes on the answers. To interview the principal about a graduation ceremony for the school, I would ask questions such as, *What happens at the graduation ceremony?* I would ask follow-up questions to clarify answers.

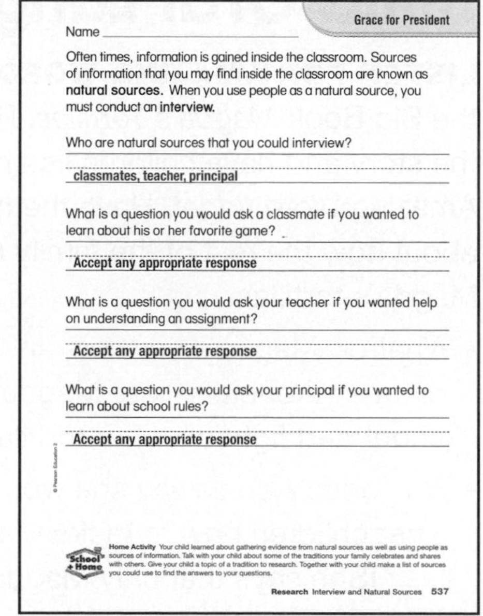

Grace for President

Name ______________________

Often times, information is gained inside the classroom. Sources of information that you may find inside the classroom are known as **natural sources.** When you use people as a natural source, you must conduct an **interview.**

Who are natural sources that you could interview?

classmates, teacher, principal

What is a question you would ask a classmate if you wanted to learn about his or her favorite game?

Accept any appropriate response

What is a question you would ask your teacher if you wanted help on understanding an assignment?

Accept any appropriate response

What is a question you would ask your principal if you wanted to learn about school rules?

Accept any appropriate response

© Pearson Education 2

School + Home **Home Activity** Your child learned about gathering evidence from natural sources as well as using people as sources of information. Talk with your child about some of the traditions your family celebrates and shares with others. Give your child a topic of a tradition to research. Together with your child make a list of sources you could use to find the answers to your questions.

Research Interview and Natural Sources 537

Reader's and Writer's Notebook, p. 537

GUIDE PRACTICE Have children use classmates as sources. Provide them with this interview question: *What do you like to do after school?* Then have children take turns interviewing each other.

ON THEIR OWN Use *Reader's and Writer's Notebook,* p. 537.

Academic Vocabulary 

source a person or thing that can give information

Bridge to Common Core

RESEARCH TO BUILD AND PRESENT KNOWLEDGE

Children will gather evidence from personal sources to use in answering questions for their research projects. They will also

- learn to conduct interviews
- learn to interview classmates as sources

Wrap Up Your Day!

✔ **Content Knowledge** Monitor children's use of oral vocabulary as they respond. Ask: What did Grace do on her campaign? (She wrote a slogan, gave speeches, and held rallies.) When did Grace learn the election results? (during an assembly)

Preview DAY 3

Tell children that tomorrow they will reread *Grace for President.*

DAY 3 at a Glance

Content Knowledge
Oral Vocabulary

Phonics/Spelling
Prefixes *mis-, mid-, micro-, non-*

Fluency
Appropriate Phrasing

Selection Vocabulary
assembly, election, microphone, rallies, slogan, speeches
Multiple-Meaning Words

Text-Based Comprehension
Review Compare and Contrast

Conventions
Commas in Compound Sentences

Writing
Persuasive Statement
Writing Trait: Word Choice

Research and Inquiry
Gather and Record Information

Materials

- Student Edition
- Sing with Me Big Book
- Big Book
- Decodable Reader 30B
- Reader's and Writer's Notebook
- Retelling Cards

Common Core State Standards

Speaking/Listening 2. Recount or describe key ideas or details from a text read aloud or information presented orally or through other media. **Language 6.** Use words and phrases acquired through conversations, reading and being read to, and responding to texts, including using adjectives and adverbs to describe (e.g., *When other kids are happy that makes me happy*).

Content Knowledge

Celebrated and Shared Traditions

EXPAND THE CONCEPT To reinforce concepts and to focus children's attention, have children sing "Festival Time" from the *Sing with Me* Big Book. What might you attend at a festival? (You might attend a ceremony.)

Build Oral Language

LISTEN FOR AMAZING WORDS Display the Big Book *Magda's Tortillas.* Read the story and have children listen for the Amazing Word *fidget.* Have them also think about how the rest of the family reacts to Magda's tortillas.

- What do Magda's brothers and cousins do when Abuela serves Magda's tortillas? (shout and fight over her tortillas)
- Why does Abuela say she won't teach the other children how to make Magda's tortillas? (She says that only Magda can teach them to make the shapes.)

Big Book

TALK ABOUT SENTENCES AND WORDS Write the following sentence from *Magda's Tortillas* on sentence strips or on the board.

Magda fidgeted with excitement.

- Ask children to read it with you as you track the print.
- Point to and read *Magda fidgeted.* What does this mean? (Magda squirmed.) Why did the author use the word *fidgeted* instead of *was nervous?* (It can be more easily visualized.) What other words could the author have used?
- **Team Talk** Now have children work with a partner to replace this key word in the sentence with simpler words or synonyms without changing the meaning. Use the following sentence frame.

Magda _______ with excitement.

Build Oral Vocabulary

Amazing Words — Robust Vocabulary Routine

1. **Introduce the Word** Relate the word *fidget* to the story. Magda *fidgets* with excitement. Supply a child-friendly definition. When you *fidget,* you can't sit still. You move around restlessly. Have children say the word.

2. **Demonstrate** Provide examples to show meaning. I *fidget* with my pencil before a test. The young girl *fidgets* as she waits for her grandmother to come.

3. **Apply** Have children demonstrate their understanding. What are some times when you are likely to *fidget?* Show me what it looks like to *fidget.*

4. **Display the Word** Point out that the *d* is silent and the *g* has the /j/ sound in *fidget.*

Routines Flip Chart

ADD TO THE CONCEPT MAP Discuss different traditions and how they are shared as you add to the concept map.

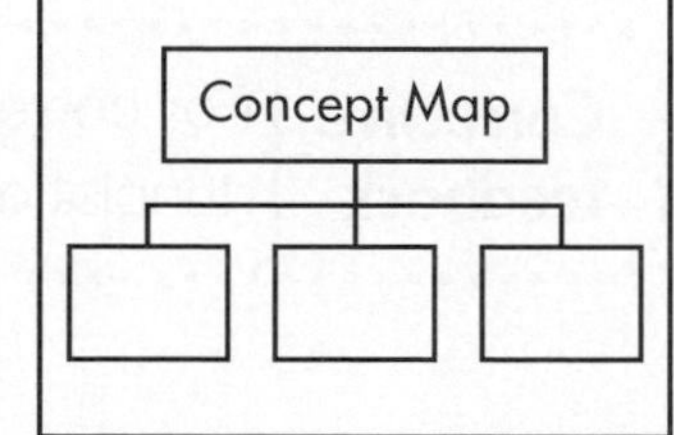

- What do Grace and the other children in school learn about in *Grace for President?* (They learn about the electoral college and how Presidents are elected.)
- What sorts of activities does Grace do during her campaign? (She has rallies and gives speeches.) These are part of our political traditions here in the United States. Children learn about them in school. We will write *political traditions* under *Children learn traditions at home and school.*

Amazing Words

ceremony	fidget
culture	evergreen
festival	multicolored
compliment	sash

Expand Vocabulary Use the Day 3 instruction on ELL Poster 30 to help children expand vocabulary.

Physical Response Demonstrate fidgeting and then have children do the same. Ask if they can describe how they are feeling when they fidget.

Common Core State Standards

Foundational Skills 3. Know and apply grade-level phonics and word analysis skills in decoding words. **Foundational Skills 3.d.** Decode words with common prefixes and suffixes.

Phonics

Build Words

MODEL WORD BUILDING Write *mis-, mid-, micro-,* and *non-* as labels on a four-column chart. Now we are going to build words with the prefixes *mis-, mid-, micro-,* and *non-.* Write *judge.* This word is *judge.* I will see which prefix I can add to *judge* to make a new word. Write *mis-* in front of *judge.* When I write the prefix *mis-* at the beginning of *judge,* I recognize the word *misjudge.* Model reading *misjudge.* Write *misjudge* on the chart under *mis-.*

GUIDE PRACTICE Write the remaining base words from the chart one at a time in random order. Have children add the appropriate prefix, read each word, and add the word to the appropriate column. Monitor children's work. When the chart is complete, have children read each column as you point to it.

mis-	*mid-*	*micro-*	*non-*
misjudge	midstream	microwave	nonstick
miscount	midpoint	microphone	nonliving
misfiled	midsized	microscope	nonpaying
mislabel	midlife	microcomputer	nonstandard

Corrective feedback For corrective feedback, model the correct spelling and pronunciation. Read the words and have children echo you.

Fluent Word Reading

MODEL Write *midmorning.* I recognize the prefix *mid-* and the base word *morning.* I put them together and read the word *midmorning.*

GUIDE PRACTICE Write the words below. Look for word parts you know. When I point to the word, we'll read it together. Allow one second per word part for the first reading.

misread mistrust microfilm nonsense misinform nonfiction

ON THEIR OWN Have children read the list above three or four times, until they can read one word per second.

Decode and Read

DECODE WORDS IN ISOLATION Have children turn to page 261 in *Decodable Practice Readers* 2.2 and find the first list of words. Each word in this list begins with the prefix *mis-, mid-, micro-,* or *non-.* Let's read these words. Be sure that children correctly read each word part.

Next, have children read the high-frequency words.

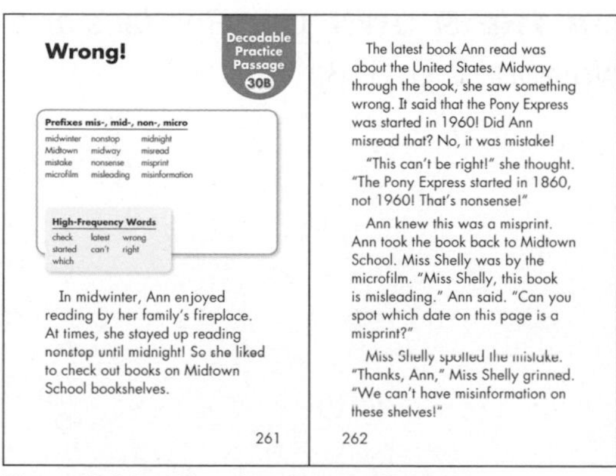

Wrong!

Decodable Practice Passage 30B

Prefixes mis-, mid-, non-, micro

midwinter	nonstop	midnight
Midtown	midway	misread
mistake	nonsense	misprint
microfilm	misleading	misinformation

High-Frequency Words

check	latest	wrong
started	can't	right
which		

In midwinter, Ann enjoyed reading by her family's fireplace. At times, she stayed up reading nonstop until midnight! So she liked to check out books on Midtown School bookshelves.

261

The latest book Ann read was about the United States. Midway through the book, she saw something wrong. It said that the Pony Express was started in 1960! Did Ann misread that? No, it was mistake!

"This can't be right!" she thought. "The Pony Express started in 1860, not 1960! That's nonsense!"

Ann knew this was a misprint. Ann took the book back to Midtown School. Miss Shelly was by the microfilm. "Miss Shelly, this book is misleading." Ann said. "Can you spot which date on this page is a misprint?"

Miss Shelly spotted the mistake. "Thanks, Ann," Miss Shelly grinned. "We can't have misinformation on these shelves!"

262

Decodable Practice Passage 30B

DECODE WORDS IN CONTEXT Chorally read the story along with children. Have children identify words in the story that begin with *mis-, mid-, micro-,* and *non-.*

Team Talk Pair children and have them take turns reading the story aloud to each other. Monitor children as they read to check for proper pronunciation and appropriate pacing.

ON THEIR OWN To further develop automaticity, have children reread the story.

Access for All

SI Strategic Intervention

Practice Prefixes Write the prefixes *mis-, mid-, micro-,* and *non-* and several base words such as *spell, trust, way, wave, stop, sense,* and *scope* on cards. Provide children with a prefix card and have children match it with a base word. Then have them read the prefix, the base word, and the combined prefix and base word.

Cognates Spanish speakers may recognize the cognates *micrófono* and *microphone.* Remind children that the *i* in *microphone* is pronounced differently than the *i* in *micrófono;* however, the *ph* in *microphone* is pronounced the same as the *f* in *micrófono.*

Common Core State Standards

Language 2. Demonstrate command of the conventions of standard English capitalization, punctuation, and spelling when writing. **Foundational Skills 3.f.** Recognize and read grade-appropriate irregularly spelled words. **Foundational Skills 4.b.** Read on-level text orally with accuracy, appropriate rate, and expression on successive readings.

Spelling Words

Prefixes *mis-*, *mid-*

1. midair	**7. midweek**
2. misplace	**8. misbehave**
3. mislead	**9. midyear**
4. midway	**10. mismatch**
5. misprint	**11. misdeed**
6. midday	**12. mistake**

High-Frequency Words

13. bought	**14. either**

Spelling

Prefixes *mis-*, *mid-*

SPELL HIGH-FREQUENCY WORDS Write *bought* and *either* and point them out on the Word Wall. Have children say and spell the words with you and then without you.

DICTATION Have children write these sentences. Say each sentence. Then repeat it slowly, one word at a time.

1. **I bought a poster that had a misprint midway down the page.**
2. **This misdeed is a huge mistake.**
3. **I will wash the clothes either at midday today or midweek.**

PROOFREAD AND CORRECT Write each sentence, spelling words one at a time. Have children circle and rewrite any misspelled words.

ON THEIR OWN Use *Reader's and Writer's Notebook,* p. 538.

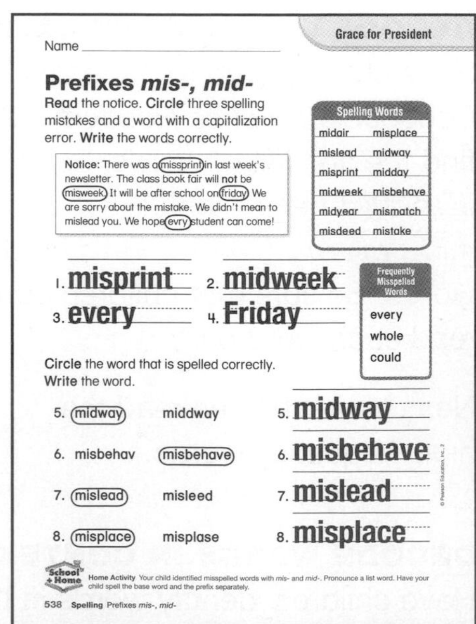

Grace for President

Name ____________

Prefixes *mis-*, *mid-*

Read the notice. **Circle** three spelling mistakes and a word with a capitalization error. **Write** the words correctly.

Notice: There was a missprint in last week's newsletter. The class book fair will **not** be misweek. It will be after school on friday. We are sorry about the mistake. We didn't mean to mislead you. We hope evry student can come!

Spelling Words	
midair	misplace
mislead	midway
misprint	midday
midweek	misbehave
midyear	mismatch
misdeed	mistake

1. misprint 2. midweek
3. every 4. Friday

Frequently Misspelled Words
every
whole
could

Circle the word that is spelled correctly. **Write** the word.

5. midway middway — 5. midway
6. misbehav misbehave — 6. misbehave
7. mislead misleed — 7. mislead
8. misplace misplase — 8. misplace

School + Home **Home Activity** Your child identified misspelled words with *mis-* and *mid-*. Pronounce a list word. Have your child spell the base word and the prefix separately.

538 **Spelling** Prefixes *mis-*, *mid-*

Reader's and Writer's Notebook, p. 538

ELL

If... children need more scaffolding and practice with reading the **Main Selection,**
then... use the ELL activities on p. DI•102 in the Teacher Resources section on SuccessNet.

Day 3 SMALL GROUP TIME • Differentiate Close Reading, p. SG•69

OL On-Level	SI Strategic Intervention	A Advanced
• **Reread** to Develop Vocabulary	• **Reread** to Develop Vocabulary	• **Reread** to Develop Vocabulary
• **Reread** *Grace for President*	• **Reread** *Grace for President*	• **Reread** *Grace for President*
		• **Investigate** Inquiry Project

Fluency

Read with Appropriate Phrasing

MODEL FLUENT READING Have children turn to Student Edition page 506. Follow along as I read pages 506–507. As I read, I will pause at punctuation, such as periods and commas, and I will group words into meaningful phrases and read these words together.

GUIDE PRACTICE Have children read the pages with you. Then have them reread the pages as a group without you until they read with appropriate phrasing. Continue in the same way with pages 508–509.

Corrective feedback	**If...** children have difficulty reading with appropriate phrasing, **then...** prompt: • Did you pause at periods and commas? • Did you read words in meaningful groups, such as phrases with prepositions?

Reread for Fluency

Routine Choral Reading

1. **Select a Passage** For *Grace for President,* use pages 510–511.
2. **Model** First, have children track the print as you read.
3. **Guide Practice** Then have children read along with you.
4. **Corrective Feedback** Have the class read aloud without you. Monitor progress and provide feedback. For optimal fluency, children should reread three to four times.

Routines Flip Chart

CHECK COMPREHENSION Why did Grace at first think that becoming president was going to be easy? (Nobody else in her class wanted to run for president. Grace thought she would be the only one running and would get all the votes.)

Access for All

 Strategic Intervention

Fluency Model for children running your finger under meaningful groups of words as you read. Have them repeat and then try a new page on their own.

Options for Oral Rereading

Use *Grace for President* or the Day 1 Decodable Practice Reader.

Common Core State Standards

Language 3. Use knowledge of language and its conventions when writing, speaking, reading, or listening. **Literature 10.** By the end of the year, read and comprehend literature, including stories and poetry, in the grades 2–3 text complexity band proficiently, with scaffolding as needed at the high end of the range.

Selection Vocabulary

assembly a group of people gathered for some purpose

election the act of choosing by vote

microphone an electrical device that makes sounds such as voices louder

rallies meetings of large crowds in support of something

slogan a word or phrase used by a person or group that states its purpose; a motto

speeches public talks

Vocabulary

Selection Vocabulary

REVIEW SELECTION WORDS Display and review the selection words *microphone, slogan, rallies, speeches, election,* and *assembly.* Have children read the words aloud.

Team Talk Have partners write fill-in-the-blank sentences with the selection vocabulary. Have them exchange sentences with another pair to complete the sentences.

Multiple-Meaning Words

REVIEW MULTIPLE-MEANING WORDS Explain that the selection word *rallies* can mean "meetings that people attend to show support"; *Grace held rallies after school to tell the children what she would do as president.* It can also mean "brings together and encourages"; *the coach rallies the players during a baseball game.* Model using context clues to determine the relevant meaning of a multiple-meaning word.

Write *play*. *Play* is a multiple-meaning word. It can mean "to have fun"; *Thomas likes to play soccer.* It can also mean "a show actors present on stage"; *my class is giving a play about the Presidents of the United States.*

GUIDE PRACTICE Write the following words. Record at least two meanings for each word. Have children use the word in sentences that show the relevant meaning.

band: a musical group; to gather in a group

track: to follow something by means of marks left behind by someone or something; a place where people run

state: to explain using words; an area of land where people follow a set of rules under a larger government

felt: touched; a soft cloth

Team Talk **ON THEIR OWN** Have children work in pairs to think of more multiple-meaning words. Have them choose one word and draw pictures to show the relevant meanings.

Text-Based Comprehension

Read Main Selection

REVIEW COMPARE AND CONTRAST Remind children that good readers often compare and contrast story events. When you tell how two or more things are alike, you **compare** them. What skill are you using when you tell how two or more things are different? (contrast) Yes, to **contrast** is to tell how things are different. Have children turn to pages 510–511 in their Student Edition. What things did Grace and Thomas both do? How was what they did different? (Both made up slogans and a list of campaign promises. Grace's slogan focused on making history by voting for a girl; Thomas's indicated he was the best man for the job. Grace's list of promises was based on information from voters. Thomas's list was based on things he could give others.) For more practice comparing and contrasting, see Let's Practice It!, p. 334 on the *Teacher Resources DVD-ROM.*

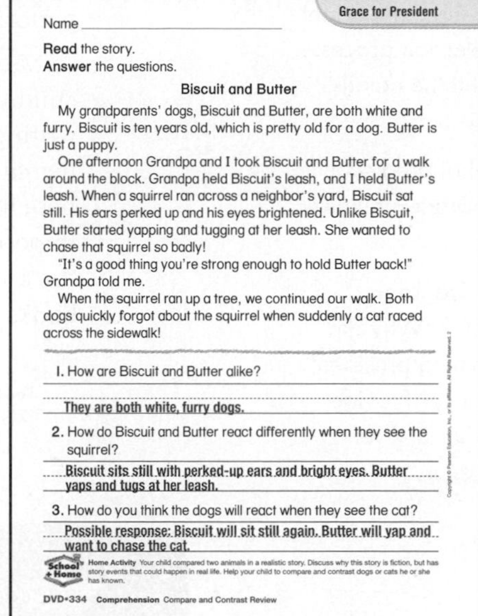
Grace for President

Name ______________________

Read the story.
Answer the questions.

Biscuit and Butter

My grandparents' dogs, Biscuit and Butter, are both white and furry. Biscuit is ten years old, which is pretty old for a dog. Butter is just a puppy.

One afternoon Grandpa and I took Biscuit and Butter for a walk around the block. Grandpa held Biscuit's leash, and I held Butter's leash. When a squirrel ran across a neighbor's yard, Biscuit sat still. His ears perked up and his eyes brightened. Unlike Biscuit, Butter started yapping and tugging at her leash. She wanted to chase that squirrel so badly!

"It's a good thing you're strong enough to hold Butter back!" Grandpa told me.

When the squirrel ran up a tree, we continued our walk. Both dogs quickly forgot about the squirrel when suddenly a cat raced across the sidewalk!

1. How are Biscuit and Butter alike?
   They are both white, furry dogs.
2. How do Biscuit and Butter react differently when they see the squirrel?
   Biscuit sits still with perked-up ears and bright eyes. Butter yaps and tugs at her leash.
3. How do you think the dogs will react when they see the cat?
   Possible response: Biscuit will sit still again. Butter will yap and want to chase the cat.

School + Home **Home Activity** Your child compared two animals in a realistic story. Discuss why this story is fiction, but has story events that could happen in real life. Help your child to compare and contrast dogs or cats he or she has known.

DVD•334 Comprehension Compare and Contrast Review

Let's Practice It! TR DVD • 334

GENRE: REALISTIC FICTION Remind children that realistic fiction tells about made-up events that could happen in real life. Have children recall some events in *Grace for President* that could really happen.

READ Return to pages 504–519 and use the **2nd Read/Close Reading Notes** to reread *Grace for President.*

Routine Read for Understanding

Deepen understanding by reading the selection multiple times.

1. **First Read**—If children need support, use the **Access Text** notes to help them clarify understanding.
2. **Second Read**—Use the **Close Reading** notes to help children draw knowledge from the text.

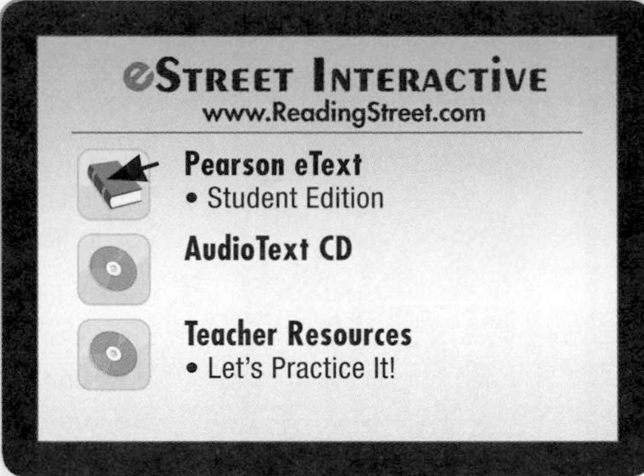

Access for All

Vocabulary Use the selection vocabulary in questions for children to answer. For example, *What speeches have you heard during an assembly? What happens when you speak through a microphone? Why do candidates have campaign slogans?*

Academic Vocabulary

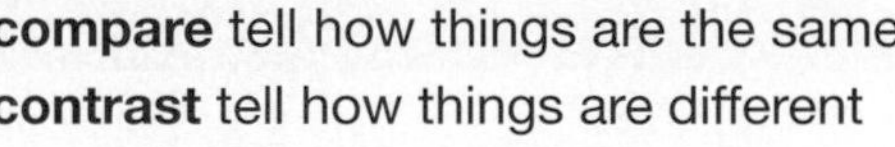

compare tell how things are the same
contrast tell how things are different

Support Discussion To help children recall selection details that reflect the genre, use the Retelling Cards to provide visual support for the discussion.

Common Core State Standards
Literature 1. Ask and answer such questions as *who, what, where, when, why,* and *how* to demonstrate understanding of key details in a text. **Also Writing 3.**

Envision It! Retell

READING STREET ONLINE
STORY SORT
www.ReadingStreet.com

Think Critically

1. In the story, Grace ran for president. Who is the President of the United States today? Text to World
2. What message does the author want you to know? Think Like an Author
3. Look back and locate three important details of America's election process. How can you find out if the details are true? Facts and Details
4. Based on the story, what prediction can you make about Grace's future? Predict and Set Purpose
5. **Look Back and Write** Look back at pages 508–509. Why did Grace think that becoming president was not going to be easy? Provide evidence to support your answer.

Key Ideas and Details • Text Evidence

520

Meet the Author

Kelly DiPucchio

Kelly DiPucchio has many talents. When growing up, she hoped to be a professional doodler or a musical performer. As an adult, she chose to become a writer.

Ms. DiPucchio has always enjoyed children's literature. She did not start writing her own stories until after her children were born. She says that her children taught her about the importance of humor. Kelly DiPucchio is the author of more than seven children's books and continues writing stories for children today.

Read more books by Kelly DiPucchio.

Bed Hogs

What's the Magic Word?

Reading Log — Use the *Reader's and Writer's Notebook* to record your independent reading.

521

Student Edition, pp. 520–521

Common Core State Standards

Literature 7. Use information gained from the illustrations and words in a print or digital text to demonstrate understanding of its characters, setting, or plot. **Also Literature 1., 2. and Writing 3.**

Think Critically

1. **TEXT TO WORLD** Children should name the current President.
2. **THINK LIKE AN AUTHOR** People can break with tradition and become what they want to be, including a girl becoming President.
3. **FACTS AND DETAILS** Each state has a set number of electoral votes. The country has 538 electoral votes total. The candidate who receives 270 or more electoral votes wins. These facts could be checked in an encyclopedia.
4. **PREDICT AND SET PURPOSE** Grace may run for President or some other government office when she grows up.
5. **LOOK BACK AND WRITE • TEXT EVIDENCE** For writing fluency, assign a five-minute time limit. As children finish, encourage them to reread their response and proofread for errors.

Bridge to Common Core

KEY IDEAS AND DETAILS

By reading the text multiple times, children will make logical inferences from the text and cite textual evidence when writing or discussing the knowledge they have gained.

Use the Think Critically page to ensure a thorough understanding of *Grace for President.*

Scoring Rubric Look Back and Write

TOP-SCORE RESPONSE A top-score response uses details from the text and the picture to explain why Grace thought that becoming president was not going to be easy.

A top-score response might include:
Grace thought becoming president was not going to be easy because Thomas was such a good student, and he was good at many things. Grace was worried that the other students would want to vote for him.

Retell

Have children use the retelling strip in the Student Edition or the Story Sort to retell the selection. Monitor children's retellings.

Scoring Rubric Narrative Retelling

	4	3	2	1
Connections	Makes connections and generalizes beyond the text	Makes connections to other events, stories, or experiences	Makes a limited connection to another event, story, or experience	Makes no connection to another event, story, or experience
Author's Purpose	Elaborates on author's purpose	Tells author's purpose with some clarity	Makes some connection to author's purpose	Makes no connection to author's purpose
Characters	Describes the main character(s) and any character development	Identifies the main character(s) and gives some information about them	Inaccurately identifies some characters or gives little information about them	Inaccurately identifies the characters or gives no information about them
Setting	Describes the time and location	Identifies the time and location	Omits details of time or location	Is unable to identify time or location
Plot	Describes the events in sequence using rich detail	Tells the plot with some errors in sequence that do not affect meaning	Tells parts of plot with gaps that affect meaning	Retelling has no sense of story

Don't Wait Until Friday

MONITOR PROGRESS Check Retelling

If... children have difficulty retelling the selection,

then... use Story Sequence Graphic Organizer 23 and the Retelling Cards/ Story Sort to scaffold their retelling.

Strategy Response Log

Predict and Set Purpose Have children revisit p. RR36 in their *Reader's and Writer's Notebook* to review the picture they drew or the purpose they set for reading. Have children either explain whether their purpose was met or add to their picture.

Plan to Assess Retelling

- ☐ **Week 1** Strategic Intervention
- ☐ **Week 2** Advanced
- ☐ **Week 3** Strategic Intervention
- ☐ **Week 4** On-Level
- ☑ **This Week** Assess Strategic Intervention children.
- ☐ **Week 6** Assess any children you have not yet checked during this unit.

Meet the Author

Read aloud page 521 as children follow along. Discuss what the author means when she says that her children taught her the importance of humor.

Read Independently

Have children enter their independent reading into their Reading Logs.

Common Core State Standards

Language 1.f. Produce, expand, and rearrange complete simple and compound sentences (e.g., *The boy watched the movie; The little boy watched the movie; The action movie was watched by the little boy*). **Language 2.** Demonstrate command of the conventions of standard English capitalization, punctuation, and spelling when writing. **Writing 1.** Write opinion pieces in which they introduce the topic or book they are writing about, state an opinion, supply reasons that support the opinion, use linking words (e.g., *because, and, also*) to connect opinion and reasons, and provide a concluding statement or section.

Conventions

Commas in Compound Sentences

REVIEW Remind children that two simple sentences can be combined with a comma and a connecting word, such as *and, or,* and *but,* to form a compound sentence: *The wind whistled, and the trees swayed.*

GUIDE PRACTICE Write these sentences on the board and have children read them aloud.

Raindrops splash the ground. Thunder fills the air.

Team Talk How could we combine these sentences to make a more interesting compound sentence? (Replace the first period with a comma, add *and,* and lowercase the *t* in *Thunder.*) Have partners work together to rewrite the example as a compound sentence. Have them circle each subject and verb, the comma, and the connecting word. Make the changes on the board and read the compound sentence aloud.

APPLY Have children orally answer the questions using compound sentences with *and, or,* or *but.*

1. **Do you like vegetables and fruit?**
2. **Can you ride a bike?**
3. **What do you do after school?**

ON THEIR OWN Use Let's Practice It!, p. 337 on the *Teacher Resources DVD-ROM.*

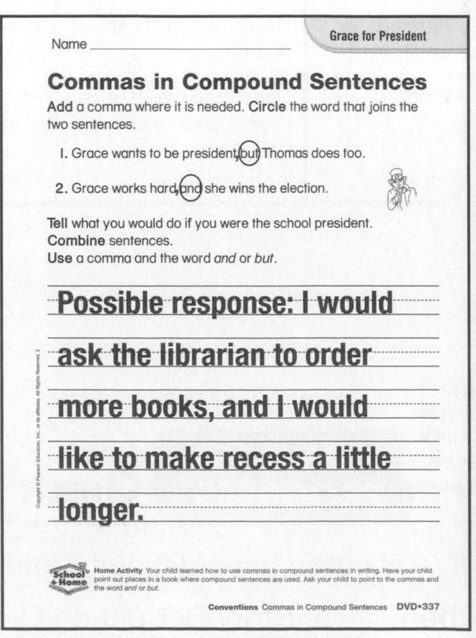
Name ______ Grace for President

Commas in Compound Sentences

Add a comma where it is needed. **Circle** the word that joins the two sentences.

1. Grace wants to be president, but Thomas does too.
2. Grace works hard, and she wins the election.

Tell what you would do if you were the school president. **Combine** sentences. **Use** a comma and the word *and* or *but.*

Possible response: I would ask the librarian to order more books, and I would like to make recess a little longer.

Home Activity Your child learned how to use commas in compound sentences in writing. Have your child point out places in a book where compound sentences are used. Ask your child to point to the commas and the word and or but.

Conventions Commas in Compound Sentences DVD•337

Let's Practice It! TR DVD•337

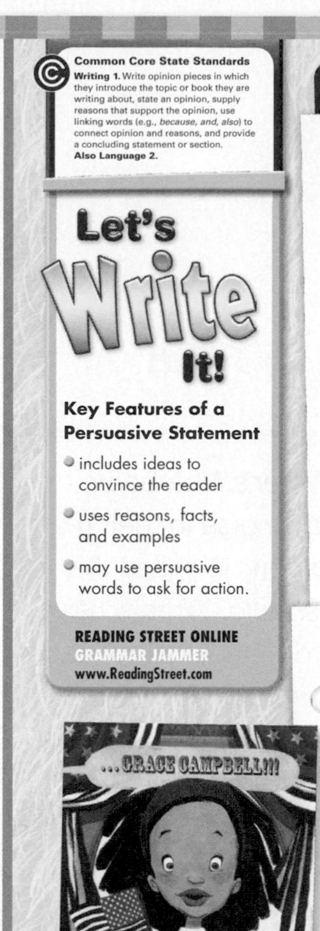

Persuasive

Persuasive Statement

A **persuasive statement** uses reasons, facts, or examples to convince the reader to do something or to think a certain way. The student model on the next page is an example of a persuasive statement.

Writing Prompt Think about a tradition that you consider important. Write a statement to persuade people in your school or community to honor that tradition.

Writer's Checklist

Remember, you should ...

- ✓ use reasons, facts, or examples to persuade.
- ✓ choose words to support your main idea.
- ✓ use commas correctly in compound sentences.

522

Student Model

Our Map of 50 States

We like our school's new map of our state. Now I hope we can make the USA playground map look new.

The USA map is fun. We can walk to all states, but they look dull now. We run on them, and the paint is old.

Students and grown-ups in our town can help paint. This will make our school bright. It will honor our red, white, and blue nation.

The writer uses **commas** correctly in compound sentences.

Genre This **persuasive statement** supports an idea with reasons and facts.

Writing Trait Word Choice The writer uses vivid words.

Conventions

Commas in Compound Sentences

Remember Two sentences with ideas that go together can be combined by using a comma and a word such as *and* or *but*. The combined sentence is called a **compound sentence.** It has one period at the end.

523

Student Edition, pp. 522–523

Let's Write It!

WRITE A PERSUASIVE STATEMENT Use pages 522–523 in the Student Edition. Read aloud the Key Features of a Persuasive Statement and the explanation. Read aloud the Writing Prompt and discuss the Writer's Checklist.

REVIEW THE STUDENT MODEL Then read "Our Map of 50 States" on page 523. Read aloud and briefly discuss the side notes about genre, the writing trait, and commas.

Scoring Rubric

TOP-SCORE RESPONSE Help children understand that a top-score response states what the reader should do or believe. It includes reasons, facts, examples, and persuasive words to convince the reader. For a complete rubric see Writing Rubric 30 from the *Teacher Resources DVD-ROM.*

CONNECT TO CONVENTIONS Read to children the Conventions note. Point out commas and compound sentences in the model.

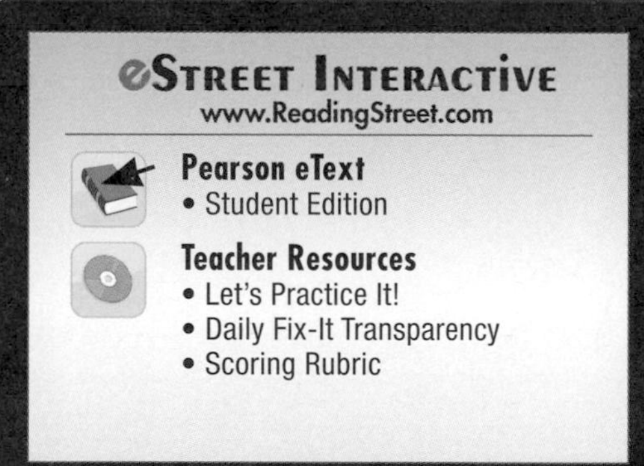

Daily Fix-It

5. The drumms were clatterin.
   The drums were clattering.
6. are the jingle bells sliver?
   Are the jingle bells silver?

Discuss the Daily Fix-It corrections with children. Review sentence capitalization and spelling patterns of inflected endings.

Common Core State Standards

Writing 1. Write opinion pieces in which they introduce the topic or book they are writing about, state an opinion, supply reasons that support the opinion, use linking words (e.g., *because, and, also*) to connect opinion and reasons, and provide a concluding statement or section. **Writing 8.** Recall information from experiences or gather information from provided sources to answer a question.

Writing

Persuasive Statement

Mini-Lesson: Writing for Tests: Writing Trait: Word Choice

- **Evaluate** Have children use the rubric on *Reader's and Writer's Notebook,* p. 536 to evaluate their writing. Have them focus on Word Choice in their main idea sentence. Write *I think we should make a school flag now.* We read this main idea sentence in the model "A School Flag." Circle *should.* Writers use the word *should* to persuade readers. It is a strong, clear word that asks the reader to do something. Other persuasive words include *must, need,* and *always.* If you choose persuasive words, they will often convince the reader to do something. Circle *now. Now* is a time-order transition word. It tells the time of the event so the reader can make sense of the order. Other transition words include *today, tomorrow,* and *yesterday.*

- Remind children that a statement may receive a good evaluation for each trait, or there may be traits they should improve, but that is all right. Differing scores can help them see their strengths and identify skills to improve.

Routine: Quick Write for Fluency

Team Talk

1. **Talk** Read these sentences. Have children identify the event order.
   Today we had an art class.
   Yesterday we had a music class.
2. **Write** Have children write two sentences that include time-order transition words.
3. **Share** Partners read the sentences, name the transition words, and identify the order of the sentences.

Routines Flip Chart

Research and Inquiry

Step 3 Gather and Record Information

TEACH Tell children that today they will conduct an interview in class. Their goal is to find out more about how traditions are celebrated and shared. Review and model the steps of how to conduct an interview.

Think Aloud **MODEL** Display the list of questions the class created on Day 1. Before the interview, we have to prepare a list of questions. We already have our list. I'm interested in learning more about how we celebrate traditions. So, I'll ask *How do you celebrate your favorite tradition?* Ask a child to answer the question. Record the answer next to the question.

GUIDE PRACTICE Have children choose one question and interview three classmates as school sources. Remind children to carefully record the answers and to then compile their information. Explain that tomorrow they will review their topic and make sure their question was answered.

Topic: Traditions We Celebrate and Share

Question	Answer
How do you celebrate your favorite tradition?	I celebrate Kwanzaa by lighting candles and giving gifts.

Access for All

A Advanced

Expand Sources Have children interview other school sources, such as the librarian and the principal.

Wrap Up Your Day!

✔ **Facts and Details** Who compliments Magda on her tortillas? (her grandmother)

✔ **Predict and Set Purpose** Have children tell why it is helpful to set a purpose for reading.

Preview DAY 4

Tell children that tomorrow they will read about Native American traditions.

DAY 4 at a Glance

Content Knowledge
Oral Vocabulary

Phonics
Review Suffixes *-ness, -less, -able, -ible*

High-Frequency Words
Review

Spelling
Prefixes *mis-, mid-*

Social Studies in Reading
Informational Text

Fluency
Appropriate Phrasing

Conventions
Commas in Compound Sentences

Writing
Persuasive Statement

Listening and Speaking
Listen for Speaker's Purpose

Research and Inquiry
Synthesize

Materials

- Student Edition
- Sing with Me Big Book
- Read Aloud Anthology
- Decodable Reader 30C
- Reader's and Writer's Notebook

Common Core State Standards

Speaking/Listening 2. Recount or describe key ideas or details from a text read aloud or information presented orally or through other media.

Content Knowledge

Celebrated and Shared Traditions

EXPAND THE CONCEPT To reinforce concepts and to focus children's attention, have children sing "Festival Time" from the *Sing with Me* Big Book. Why do people go to festivals? (to have fun; to learn about a culture)

Build Oral Language

REVIEW GENRE: REALISTIC FICTION
Have children tell the key features of realistic fiction: it tells about made-up people and events, but the characters seem real, and the events could happen in real life. Explain that today you will read a realistic story about a girl who moves from one culture to another in "Bringing the Light" by Elizabeth Gawlik.

"Bringing the Light"

MONITOR LISTENING COMPREHENSION
Recall how Grace wanted to break the tradition of no girl ever being president. Have children listen to find out what a girl named Karin does to try to carry on a tradition.

Team Talk **TALK ABOUT SHARING TRADITIONS** Read aloud the third paragraph of "Bringing the Light." Display it on a whiteboard if possible, and track the print as you read.

- Have pairs of children ask each other questions about Karin's Saint Lucia tradition based on what they heard in this paragraph.
- Add words and phrases generated to the concept map.

Build Oral Vocabulary

Amazing Words **Robust Vocabulary Routine**

1. **Introduce the Word** Relate the word *evergreen* to the story. Karin needs branches from an *evergreen.* Supply a child-friendly definition. An *evergreen* is a tree or bush that stays green all year. Have children say the word.
2. **Demonstrate** Provide examples to show meaning. A pine tree is an *evergreen.* Our *evergreen* gives off a fresh smell.
3. **Apply** Have children demonstrate their understanding. Why might an *evergreen* be a good place for a bird to build its nest? What does an *evergreen* look like in winter?
4. **Display** Point out the two smaller words in this compound word.

See p. OV•5 to teach *multicolored* and *sash.*

Routines Flip Chart

ADD TO THE CONCEPT MAP Discuss different traditions and how they are shared.

Concept Map

- What is the Saint Lucia tradition described in "Bringing the Light"? (The daughter in a family wears a white robe, a red sash, and a crown of evergreens with candles and brings treats on the morning of the celebration.) Where did Karin first practice the tradition, and where does she want to practice it now? (She first practiced it in Sweden, and now she lives in Peru.)
- Often when people move to another country, they bring their traditions with them. Let's add *Swedish St. Lucia ceremony* under *People bring traditions from other lands.*

Amazing Words

ceremony	fidget
culture	evergreen
festival	multicolored
compliment	sash

Access for All

Strategic Intervention

Word Structure Help children break apart the compound word *ever/green* to help them understand its meaning. Do the same for *multicolored,* explaining that the prefix *multi-* means "many."

Produce Oral Language Use the Day 4 instruction on ELL Poster 30 to extend and enrich language.

Common Core State Standards

Foundational Skills 3. Know and apply grade-level phonics and word analysis skills in decoding words. **Foundational Skills 3.d.** Decode words with common prefixes and suffixes. **Also Language 4.c.**

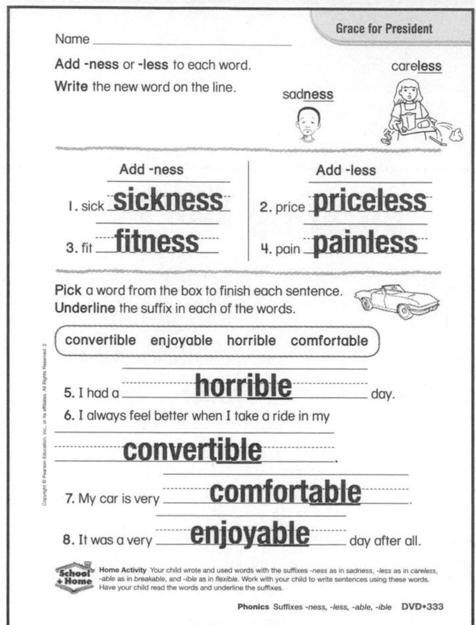

Grace for President

Name ____________

Add -ness or **-less** to each word.
Write the new word on the line.

sadness careless

Add -ness	Add -less
1. sick **sickness**	2. price **priceless**
3. fit **fitness**	4. pain **painless**

Pick a word from the box to finish each sentence.
Underline the suffix in each of the words.

convertible enjoyable horrible comfortable

5. I had a **horrible** day.
6. I always feel better when I take a ride in my **convertible**.
7. My car is very **comfortable**.
8. It was a very **enjoyable** day after all.

Home Activity Your child wrote and used words with the suffixes *-ness* as in *sadness*, *-less* as in *careless*, *-able* as in *breakable*, and *-ible* as in *flexible*. Work with your child to write sentences using these words. Have your child read the words and underline the suffixes.

Phonics Suffixes *-ness, -less, -able, -ible* **DVD•333**

Let's Practice It! TR DVD•333

Phonics

Review Suffixes *-ness, -less, -able, -ible*

REVIEW SUFFIXES To review last week's phonics skill, write *gentleness, joyless, huggable,* and *flexible.* You studied words like these last week. What do you know about their endings? (These words have the suffixes *-ness, -less, -able,* and *-ible.* To read a word with a suffix, read the base word and read the suffix. Then read the parts together.)

Corrective feedback If children are unable to answer the question about suffixes *-ness, -less, -able,* and *-ible,* refer them to Sound-Spelling Cards 175, 172, 164, and 169.

GUIDE PRACTICE Write *-ness, -less, -able,* and *-ible* as heads in a four-column chart. Now we are going to build words with the suffixes *-ness, -less, -able,* and *-ible.* Write *quick* in the *-ness* column. What's the word? *(quick)* What's the suffix? *(-ness)* Let's add *-ness* to the base word. Write *-ness.* What's the new word? *(quickness)* What does it mean? ("the state of being quick") Continue with *happy, silly, good, cord, color, spot, penny, reason, print, adore, like, sense, reverse, digest,* and *collect.* Then have children read the words in each column.

-ness	*-less*	*-able*	*-ible*
quickness	cordless	reasonable	sensible
happiness	colorless	printable	reversible
silliness	spotless	adorable	digestible
goodness	penniless	likable	collectible

ON THEIR OWN Use Let's Practice It!, p. 333 on the *Teacher Resources DVD-ROM.*

Fluent Word Reading

Spiral Review

READ WORDS IN ISOLATION Display these words. Tell children they can chunk some words and others are abbreviations or Word Wall words.

Have children read the list three or four times until they can read at the rate of two to three seconds per word.

only	**Mr.**	**hours**	**Ms.**	**sculptures**
auction	**taught**	**Ave.**	**clothes**	**microscope**
nonprofit	**vacation**	**question**	**misplaced**	**companion**
money	**location**	**action**	**neighbor**	**midsummer**

Corrective feedback **Word Reading**	**If...** children have difficulty reading whole words or abbreviations, **then...** have them chunk decodable words, work on identifying abbreviations, or say and spell high-frequency words. **If...** children cannot read fluently at a rate of two to three seconds per word, **then...** have pairs practice the list until they can read it fluently.

READ WORDS IN CONTEXT Display these sentences. Call on individuals to read a sentence. Then randomly point to review words for children to read. To help you monitor word reading, high-frequency words are underlined and decodable words are italicized.

I *misplaced* my map, so I have a question about the *location*.

My neighbor and her *companion* didn't make money selling their *sculptures* at the *nonprofit* art *auction* on Sunset *Ave*.

***Mr.* Lu taught us to use a *microscope* to see germs in *action*.**

***Ms.* Sands took only three hours to wash the clothes from her *midsummer vacation*.**

Corrective feedback **Sentence Reading**	**If...** children cannot read an underlined high-frequency word, **then...** read the word for them and spell it, having them echo you. **If...** children have difficulty reading an italicized decodable word, **then...** guide them in combining word parts or identifying abbreviations.

Access for All

Strategic Intervention

Word Matching Write the words on large self-stick notes. Then read the words, modeling how to divide them into syllables. Have children echo. Next, distribute the notes. Reread each sentence. Each child with a matching word places his or her note over the word and reads it. Have those at the board chorally read the whole sentence.

Spiral Review

These activities review
- your previously taught high-frequency words *clothes, hours, money, neighbor, only, question, taught.*
- prefixes *mis-, mid-, non-, micro-.*
- final syllables *-tion, -ture, -ion.*
- abbreviations.

Fluent Word Reading Have children listen to a more fluent reader model the words or have pairs read the words together.

Common Core State Standards

Foundational Skills 3. Know and apply grade-level phonics and word analysis skills in decoding words. **Foundational Skills 3.d.** Decode words with common prefixes and suffixes. **Foundational Skills 4.** Read with sufficient accuracy and fluency to support comprehension.

Decodable Reader 30C

If children need help, then...

Read *The Midtown Market Sale*

DECODE WORDS IN ISOLATION Have children turn to page 263 in *Decodable Practice Readers* 2.2 and decode each word.

READ HIGH-FREQUENCY WORDS Have children identify and read the high-frequency words *can't, check, late, shop,* and *which* on the first page.

PREVIEW Have children read the title and preview the story. Tell them they will read words with prefixes *mis-, mid-, micro-,* and *non-.*

DECODE WORDS IN CONTEXT Pair children for reading and listen as they decode. One child begins. Children read the entire story, switching readers after each page. Partners reread the story. This time the other child begins.

Decodable Practice Reader 30C

Corrective feedback	**If...** children have difficulty decoding a word, **then...** refer them to the Sound-Spelling Cards to identify the sounds in a decodable word; prompt them to blend the word. If the word has a prefix with *mis-, mid-, micro-,* or *non-,* tell children to chunk the word and say the parts of the word, first separately and then together. • What is the new word? • Is the new word a word you know? • Does it make sense in the story?

CHECK DECODING AND COMPREHENSION Have children retell the story to include characters, setting, and events. Then have children find words with prefixes *mis-, mid-, micro-,* and *non-* in the story. Children should supply *Midtown, midday, microwaves, nonsense, misprint, misleading, mid-year, midweek,* and *midnight.*

Reread for Fluency

REREAD DECODABLE READER Have children reread Decodable Practice Reader 30C to develop automaticity decoding words with prefixes *mis-, mid-, micro-,* and *non-.*

Routine Oral Rereading

1. **Read** Have children read the entire book orally.
2. **Reread** To achieve optimal fluency, children should reread the text three or four times.
3. **Corrective Feedback** Listen as children read. Provide corrective feedback regarding their fluency and decoding.

Routines Flip Chart

Decodable Practice Reader

Beginning Before reading, write the story words on cards using one color for prefixes and a second color for base words. Say each word, chunking it into parts as you point to it. Then say each word fluidly. Have children repeat it. Have children find each word in the story.

Intermediate Have one child choose a word with a prefix and say it aloud. Tell other children to find the word in the story and put their finger under the word. When all children have located the correct word, read it aloud together. Then read aloud the sentence in which it appears together.

Advanced Have partners find each word with a prefix in the story and read the sentence. Then have each child say a new sentence using the word.

Common Core State Standards

Foundational Skills 3.d. Decode words with common prefixes and suffixes. **Informational Text 6.** Identify the main purpose of a text, including what the author wants to answer, explain, or describe. **Also Language 2., Informational Text 10.**

Spelling

Prefixes *mis-, mid-*

PARTNER REVIEW Supply pairs of children with index cards on which the spelling words have been written. Have one child read a word while the other writes it. Then have children switch roles. Have them use the cards to check their spelling and correct any misspelled words.

ON THEIR OWN Use Let's Practice It!, p. 336 on the *Teacher Resources DVD-ROM*.

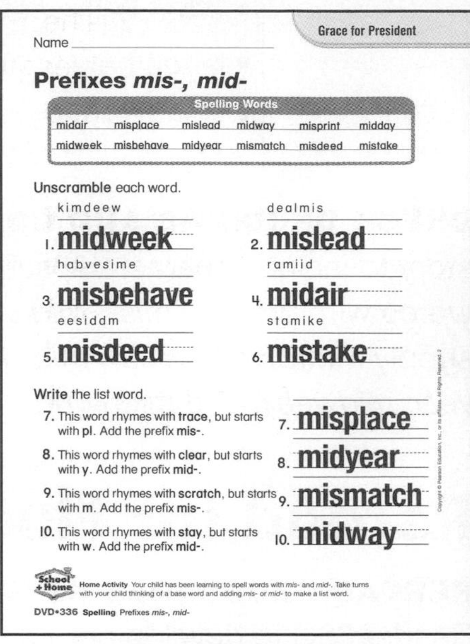

Name ____________ Grace for President

Prefixes *mis-, mid-*

Spelling Words					
midair	misplace	mislead	midway	misprint	midday
midweek	misbehave	midyear	mismatch	misdeed	mistake

Unscramble each word.

kimdeew 1. midweek
dealmis 2. mislead
habvesime 3. misbehave
ramiid 4. midair
eesiddm 5. misdeed
stamike 6. mistake

Write the list word.

7. This word rhymes with **trace**, but starts with **pl**. Add the prefix **mis-**. 7. misplace
8. This word rhymes with **clear**, but starts with **y**. Add the prefix **mid-**. 8. midyear
9. This word rhymes with **scratch**, but starts with **m**. Add the prefix **mis-**. 9. mismatch
10. This word rhymes with **stay**, but starts with **w**. Add the prefix **mid-**. 10. midway

School + Home **Home Activity** Your child has been learning to spell words with mis- and mid-. Take turns with your child thinking of a base word and adding mis- or mid- to make a list word.

DVD•336 Spelling Prefixes *mis-, mid-*

Let's Practice It! TR DVD•336

If... children need more scaffolding and practice with **Amazing Words, then...** use the routine on pp. xxxvi–xxxvii in the *ELL Handbook.*

Day 4 SMALL GROUP TIME • Differentiate Vocabulary, p. SG•69

OL On-Level
- **Develop** Language Using Amazing Words
- **Read** *Reading Street Sleuth,* pp. 76–77

SI Strategic Intervention
- **Review/Discuss** Amazing Words
- **Read** *Reading Street Sleuth,* pp. 76–77

A Advanced
- **Extend** Amazing Words and Selection Vocabulary
- **Read** *Reading Street Sleuth,* pp. 76–77
- **Organize** Inquiry Project

Informational Text

ACTIVATE PRIOR KNOWLEDGE Ask children what they learned from other texts this week about traditions of other cultures and groups of people.

PREVIEW AND PREDICT Read the title and the author's name on page 524 of the Student Edition. Have children look through the selection and predict what they might learn. (They might learn about the homes and lives of Native Americans.) Ask what clues helped them make their prediction. (the title, the illustrations, and the captions)

READ AN INFORMATIONAL TEXT Tell children that they will read informational text. **Informational text** gives facts about real people, places, and events that may reflect history or the traditions of communities. It is usually about one topic and often has captions and pictures that illustrate the text. Explain that this selection is informational text because it gives facts about Native Americans.

Genre

LET'S THINK ABOUT... As you read "Home Sweet Home" together, use Let's Think About in the Student Edition to help children focus on the features of informational text.

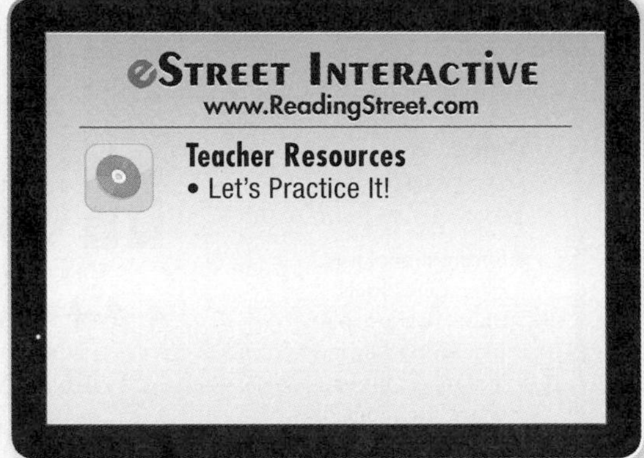

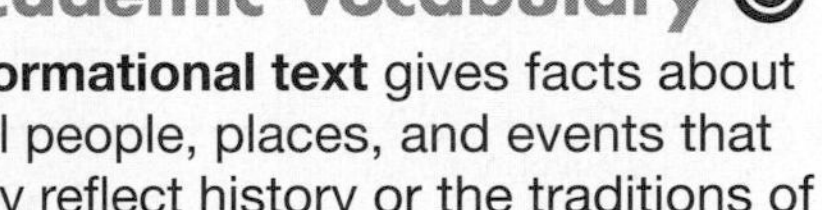

informational text gives facts about real people, places, and events that may reflect history or the traditions of communities

Common Core State Standards
Informational Text 6. Identify the main purpose of a text, including what the author wants to answer, explain, or describe. **Also Informational Text 2.**

Social Studies in Reading

Genre
Informational Text

- Informational text often gives facts about real people, places, and events that reflect history or the traditions of communities.
- Informational text usually has one topic.
- Informational text may have captions and pictures.
- Read "Home Sweet Home." Look for elements that make this an informational text.

Home Sweet Home

by Almira Astudillo Gilles

Long ago, there were no freeways or telephones, shopping malls or video games. Long ago, Native Americans were the only people in California.

Native Americans made many different kinds of homes, using materials that were easy to find. In the north, there were forests and plenty of wood for houses. The Miwok, a group that lived in Central California, had houses shaped like cones. Other houses, like those of the Chumash people of the south, were round. To build these round houses, poles made from branches were poked in the ground in a circle.

524

Chumash hut

These poles were bent at the top, and smaller branches were put around them. On the outside, pieces of bushes were added. A hole in the top let air inside. When it rained, the hole was covered with animal skin.

Inside a Native American house, you might see grass mats on the floor. You might see money made of sea snail shells. You might find moccasins and clothes of animal skins. You might find a bow and arrow for hunting. For children, there might be dolls or spinning tops made of acorns.

Families lived together in one village.

moccasins

Let's Think About...
What shape were the homes of the Miwok? **Informational Text** 1

Let's Think About...
Why does the author tell what may be inside a Native American house? **Informational Text** 2

525

Student Edition, pp. 524–525

Common Core State Standards
Informational Text 1. Ask and answer such questions as *who, what, where, when, why,* and *how* to demonstrate understanding of key details in a text.

Access Text

Think Aloud **INFERENCE** Good readers infer as they read. When I read about all the things that you might see in a Native American house, I think of the kinds of things I have in my own home. I can infer that in many ways people today and the Native Americans of long ago have similar homes.

Think Aloud **QUESTIONING** When I read, I think of questions I would like to have answered, and then I look for the answers to focus my reading. Some questions I had as I began to read were: *What were the different kinds of Native American homes like? How were they built?*

LET'S THINK ABOUT... features of informational text.

1. The homes of the Miwok were shaped like cones.
2. The author tells what may be inside the house to give facts and details about Native American traditions.

Grandparents, cousins, aunts, and uncles all lived nearby. Villages could be small, with just a few families, or large, with many families. Each village had a chief who could be a man or woman.

Many Native Americans in California used acorns for food. Some groups, like the Wiyot, lived far from the oak forests. They moved their homes into the forest when it was harvest time. Men shook the oak trees to make acorns fall. Women and children picked them up.

acorns

> **Let's Think About...**
> What is the topic, or the "big idea," of this paragraph? **Informational Text**

3 The most important thing about a Native American home was the family inside it. Just like today, a home was a place to rest and spend time together. These houses were one big room. Families played games. Elders told stories. Adults talked about important events in the village.

Native American men sometimes built a sweathouse. The sweathouse was a place men went to heal. Inside the sweathouse there was a fire pit with stones. With the fire burning, it became very hot inside. When the men became too sweaty, they ran outside and jumped into a cool creek.

A sweathouse is made this way:

Step 1. Make a frame out of long pieces of wood.

Step 2. Put branches across the frame.

Step 3. Put thick shrubs on top of the branches.

Step 4. Cover the roof with soil. The roof should be no more than five inches thick.

sweathouse

> **Let's Think About...**
> **Reading Across Texts** What do you learn about community leaders in both "Home Sweet Home" and *Grace for President?* Make a chart to record your ideas.
>
> **Writing Across Texts** Use your chart to write a short paragraph. Draw a conclusion about who can be leaders. Base your ideas on the selections.

526 527

Student Edition, pp. 526–527

FACTS AND DETAILS What were three Native American groups that lived in California? (the Miwok, the Chumash, and the Wiyot)

LET'S THINK ABOUT... features of informational text.

3 The topic of this paragraph is family life in Native American homes long ago in California.

Reading and Writing Across Texts

Have children make a chart with the heads Who Can Be a Leader? and What Makes a Good Leader? In column 1, they can name leaders in the two selections. In column 2, they can list leadership qualities demonstrated in the selections. Paragraphs should draw facts and details from the chart to support a conclusion about who can become a leader.

Social Studies Vocabulary

moccasins shoes with no heel made of soft leather pieces sewn together

Native Americans people whose ancestors first settled the Americas

sweathouse a structure where Native American men would go to heal and to pray

Common Core State Standards

Foundational Skills 4.b. Read on-level text orally with accuracy, appropriate rate, and expression on successive readings. **Language 1.f.** Produce, expand, and rearrange complete simple and compound sentences (e.g., *The boy watched the movie; The little boy watched the the movie; The action movie was watched by the little boy*).

Access for All

 Advanced

Rate If children already read at 90 words correct per minute, have them read more challenging text.

Fluency Assessment Plan

Do a formal fluency assessment with eight to ten children every week. Assess four or five children on Day 4 and four or five children on Day 5. Use the reproducible fluency passage, Teacher's Edition, p. 529f.

Options for Oral Rereading

Use *Grace for President* or one of this week's Decodable Practice Readers.

Fluency

Appropriate Phrasing

- Have children turn to pages 512–513 in *Grace for President.*
- Have children follow along as you read the pages with appropriate phrasing.
- Have the class read the pages with you and then reread the pages as a group until they read with appropriate phrasing. To provide additional fluency practice, pair nonfluent readers with fluent readers.

Routine Paired Reading

1. **Select a Passage** For *Grace for President,* use pages 514–515.
2. **Model** First, have children track the print as you read.
3. **Guide Practice** Then have children read along with you.
4. **On Their Own** For optimal fluency, have partners reread three or four times.

Routines Flip Chart

Fluency Check

As children reread, monitor their progress toward their individual fluency goals. Current Goal: 80–90 words correct per minute. End-of-Year-Goal: 90 words correct per minute.

If... children cannot read fluently at a rate of 80–90 words correct per minute,
then... have children practice with text at their independent level.

Conventions

Commas in Compound Sentences

TEST PRACTICE Use *Reader's and Writer's Notebook,* p. 540 to help children understand using commas in compound sentences. Recall that a comma and a connecting word are needed to combine two simple sentences into one compound sentence: *I wanted to stay up late, but Grandpa sent me to bed.* Write the following sentence on the board and model identifying the comma and connecting word in a compound sentence.

The driver honked his horn, and the man stopped at the curb.

ON THEIR OWN Then read the *Reader's and Writer's Notebook,* p. 540 directions. Guide children as they mark the answer for number 1.

APPLY After children mark the answers to numbers 1–4, review the correct choices aloud, and have children read each sentence and point out the comma and connecting word.

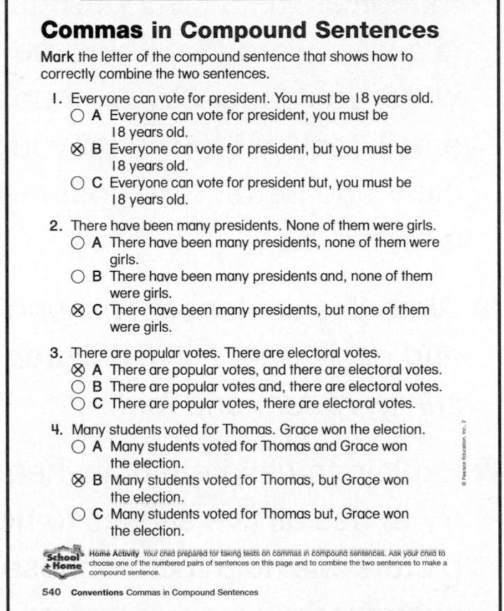
Grace for President

Name ____________

Commas in Compound Sentences

Mark the letter of the compound sentence that shows how to correctly combine the two sentences.

1. Everyone can vote for president. You must be 18 years old.
   - ○ A Everyone can vote for president, you must be 18 years old.
   - ⊗ B Everyone can vote for president, but you must be 18 years old.
   - ○ C Everyone can vote for president but, you must be 18 years old.
2. There have been many presidents. None of them were girls.
   - ○ A There have been many presidents, none of them were girls.
   - ○ B There have been many presidents and, none of them were girls.
   - ⊗ C There have been many presidents, but none of them were girls.
3. There are popular votes. There are electoral votes.
   - ⊗ A There are popular votes, and there are electoral votes.
   - ○ B There are popular votes and, there are electoral votes.
   - ○ C There are popular votes, there are electoral votes.
4. Many students voted for Thomas. Grace won the election.
   - ○ A Many students voted for Thomas and Grace won the election.
   - ⊗ B Many students voted for Thomas, but Grace won the election.
   - ○ C Many students voted for Thomas but, Grace won the election.

School + Home **Home Activity** Your child prepared for taking tests on commas in compound sentences. Ask your child to choose one of the numbered pairs of sentences on this page and to combine the two sentences to make a compound sentence.

540 **Conventions** Commas in Compound Sentences

Reader's and Writer's Notebook, p. 540

Bridge to Common Core

CONVENTIONS OF STANDARD ENGLISH

As children identify, form, and use compound sentences, they are gaining control of the conventions of standard English. Your guidance will help them use compound sentences effectively as they write.

Daily Fix-It

7. My voise craked last night.
   My voice cracked last night.
8. He playing the drom loudly.
   He played the drum loudly.

Discuss the Daily Fix-It corrections with children. Review *-ck* words, inflected endings, and the spelling of *voice* and *drum.*

Common Core State Standards

Writing 1. Write opinion pieces in which they introduce the topic or book they are writing about, state an opinion, supply reasons that support the opinion, use linking words (e.g., *because, and, also*) to connect opinion and reasons, and provide a concluding statement or section.

Writing

Persuasive Statement

Remind children that yesterday they learned about using persuasive words and time-order transition words in a persuasive statement. Explain that today children will write a persuasive statement in response to another prompt and have the opportunity to use these skills.

Mini-Lesson Writing for Tests: Using Vivid Words

- On the board, write *We can walk to all states, but they look dull now.* We read this sentence in the model "Our Map of 50 States." When sharing his or her opinion about the map, the writer chose the word *dull.* It is a word that gives me a clear description of what the playground map looks like. It is a vivid word that helps me see that the map is faded and dirty. When you write, you should try to choose vivid words that help the reader see, hear, smell, feel, or taste what you are sensing. Vivid words will make your ideas clear and better help your readers picture why you want them to think or act a certain way.
- Write this sentence: *The lunchroom garbage can smelled bad.* Read it aloud and circle *bad.* Have children name vivid words to replace *bad,* such as *stinky, rotten,* and *foul.*
- Explain to children that when they hear the new prompt, they should try to use all five senses to help them create a picture in their mind. The picture will help them choose vivid words as they write facts, reasons, and examples.

WRITE Tell children to prepare for writing for a test. Have them get paper and pencil ready. Display the Writing Prompt.

Writing Prompt

Write a paragraph to persuade someone at your home or school to try a traditional kind of food that you think is good.

Read the prompt to children and stress that they should choose a traditional food that is important to them. Briefly remind them of the key features of a persuasive statement.

- includes ideas that convince the reader
- has a main-idea sentence that asks the reader to do or believe something
- uses reasons, facts, or examples that support the main idea and the writer's opinion
- may use persuasive words to ask for action

Give children sufficient time to write their persuasive statement.

Routine Quick Write for Fluency

Team Talk

1. **Talk** Have partners take one minute to talk about their least favorite food.
2. **Write** Have each child write a sentence or two that uses vivid words to describe it.
3. **Share** Pair children and have them point out vivid words in the partner's sentence.

Routines Flip Chart

Access for All

 Strategic Intervention

Sense Words For children having difficulty understanding that words can relate to their senses, say the following words and have them tell which sense they would use. Then have children name vivid words they could use as a replacement.

See: *dirty—messy, grubby, muddy*

Hear: *yell—shout, scream, holler*

Taste: *sour—bitter, sharp, tart*

Smell: *odor—fragrance, scent, aroma*

Feel: *cold—frozen, icy, cool*

 Advanced

Extend Vivid Words Remind children that a thesaurus is a book that lists synonyms, words that have the same or similar meanings. Explain that it is a source they can use to find vivid words. Have partners use a thesaurus to find synonyms for these words: *hot, bumpy, loud, bright.*

Common Core State Standards

Speaking/Listening 2. Recount or describe key ideas or details from a text read aloud or information presented orally or through other media. **Writing 8.** Recall information from experiences or gather information from provided sources to answer a question.

Bridge to Common Core

PRESENTATION OF KNOWLEDGE/IDEAS

As children prepare for and deliver an oral report to a classmate, they are learning to organize and present their information in a style to task and audience, thus enabling listeners to follow the line of reasoning.

Listening and Speaking

Listen for Speaker's Purpose

TEACH Tell children that good listeners listen carefully to identify the speaker's purpose. As a listener, think carefully about what the speaker is saying. Ask yourself:

- What is the speaker trying to tell me?
- Is the speaker trying to explain something to me? persuade me to do something? tell a story?
- How well does the speaker achieve this purpose?

TEACH Tell children that good speakers make their purpose clear to their listeners. When you give an oral report:

- Stand tall with your head up and look your listeners in the eye.
- Speak loud enough, clearly, and at an appropriate pace so your listeners can hear you and understand your words.
- Let your listeners know what your report is about.
- Organize your information in a logical order so it is easy for your listeners to follow.

Think Aloud

MODEL I like all kinds of food, but my favorite is Chinese food. The rice is fluffy and soft, the vegetables are crunchy, and shrimp or chicken is always a choice. The sauces can be sweet and sour, hot and spicy, or anything in between. Perhaps what I like most about Chinese food is eating it with chopsticks. They can be tricky, but with a little practice, you can pick up the tiniest tidbit with them. If you haven't tried Chinese food with chopsticks yet, you don't know what you're missing!

GUIDE PRACTICE Discuss with children what your purpose as a speaker was in this report and whether you achieved this purpose.

ON THEIR OWN Have children give the oral reports about family traditions that they have worked on in this unit. Remind speakers that they will not just read aloud what they wrote; they should demonstrate the traits of good speakers. Encourage listeners to listen attentively, identify the speaker's purpose, and decide how well the speaker accomplished this purpose.

Research and Inquiry

Step 4 Synthesize

TEACH Tell children: The next step in the inquiry project is to review our topic to see if we have the information we set out to find or if our answers lead to a different topic.

MODEL We planned to find out more about ways that traditions are celebrated and shared. Display the list of inquiry questions and the answers recorded during research. The question I asked was *How do you celebrate your favorite tradition?* The answer was *I celebrate Kwanzaa by lighting candles and giving gifts.* So we have answered the topic, and it does not need to change.

GUIDE PRACTICE Read the remaining inquiry questions and answers. After each answer is read, have children discuss whether or not the answer provides information about ways that traditions are celebrated and shared. Note any new questions the children have and revise the original topic if necessary. Finally, tell children that tomorrow they will organize all the information so they can share it with others.

Access for All

 Advanced

Classify Answers Have children sort answers between ways traditions are celebrated and ways they are shared.

Wrap Up Your Day!

- ✔ **Phonics** Write the words *mislead, midday, microscope,* and *nonstick.* Have children read the words and identify the prefixes and base words. Then ask them to use the words in sentences.
- ✔ **Fluency** Display *Midway through the speech, the speaker misspoke into the microphone about the nonprofit group.* Have children read the sentence three or four times until they can do so fluently.

Preview DAY 5

Tell children that tomorrow they will hear about Karin and the tradition of St. Lucia again.

DAY 5 at a Glance

Content Knowledge
Oral Vocabulary

Phonics/Spelling
Review Prefixes *mis-, mid-, micro-, non-*

Text-Based Comprehension
Review Facts and Details

Selection Vocabulary
Review

Assessment
Phonics
Selection Vocabulary
Fluency
Comprehension

Conventions
Review Commas in Compound Sentences

Writing
Persuasive Statement: Revise

Research and Inquiry
Communicate

Materials

- Student Edition
- Read Aloud Anthology
- Weekly Test

Bridge to Common Core

INTEGRATION OF KNOWLEDGE/IDEAS

This week children have integrated content presented in diverse formats and analyzed how different texts address similar topics. They have developed knowledge about celebrated and shared traditions to expand the unit concept of traditions.

Social Studies Knowledge Goals

Children have learned that traditions can be

- shared and celebrated at special events
- brought from other lands
- learned at home and at school

Content Knowledge

Celebrated and Shared Traditions

REVIEW CONCEPT This week we have read and listened to selections about celebrating and sharing different traditions. Today you will listen again to "Bringing the Light." Read the story.

- How did Karin's father feel when she woke her parents in the morning as Saint Lucia? (He was surprised and pleased.)

"Bringing the Light"

Build Oral Language

REVIEW AMAZING WORDS Have children use this week's Amazing Words and the concept map to answer the question, *How are different traditions celebrated and shared?*

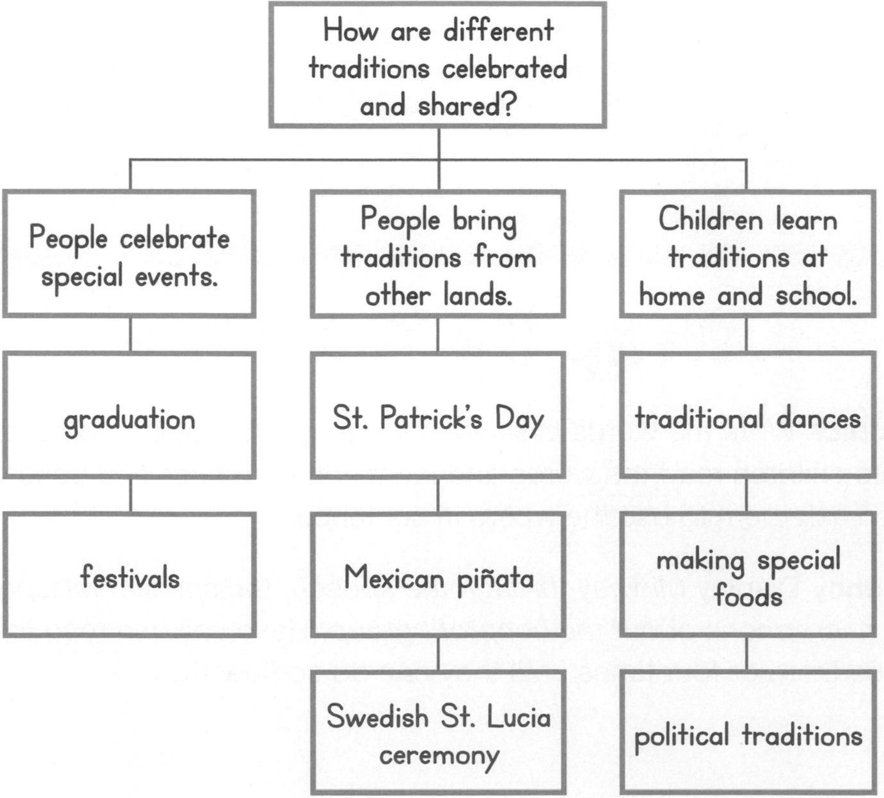

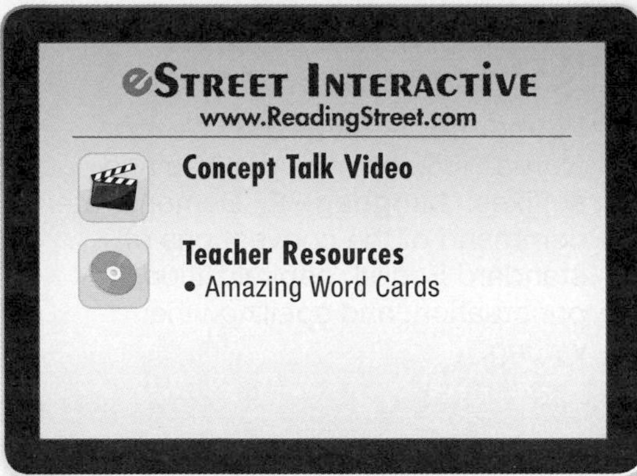

Build Oral Vocabulary

Team Talk **CONNECT TO AMAZING IDEAS** Pair children and have them discuss how the Question of the Week, *How are different traditions celebrated and shared?,* connects to the question of this unit of study, *Are traditions and celebrations important in our lives?* Tell children to use the concept map and what they've learned from this week's discussions and reading selections to form an Amazing Idea—a realization or "big idea" about **sharing different traditions.** Use the following ideas as prompts:

- What traditions have we read about? (St. Lucia, presidential elections, making tortillas)
- How did the characters feel about each tradition?

Then ask each pair to share their Amazing Idea with the class. Encourage children to recall in which selection they learned their ideas.

Amazing Ideas might include these key concepts:

- Many people who move to a new country still follow the traditions of their culture.
- One way of sharing a tradition is by teaching it to children.

Amazing Words

ceremony	fidget
culture	evergreen
festival	multicolored
compliment	sash

Check Oral Vocabulary

Call on individuals to use this week's Amazing Words to talk about different traditions. Prompt discussion with the questions below. Monitor children's ability to use the Amazing Words and note which words children are unable to use.

- Describe a ***ceremony*** you have been to.
- Why is it nice to give someone a ***compliment?***
- What would you do at a ***festival*** that celebrates another ***culture?***
- What would a ***multicolored sash*** look like?
- How is the ***evergreen*** used in some celebrations?
- Why might you ***fidget*** during a ceremony?

If... children have difficulty using the Amazing Words,

then... reteach the unknown words using the Robust Vocabulary Routines, pp. 497a, 502b, 520b, 524b.

Check Concepts and Language Use the Day 5 instruction on Poster 30 to monitor children's understanding of the lesson concept.

Amazing Words If children have trouble using complete sentences, write their answers on the board as sentences. Then read each sentence aloud, pointing to each word, and have children read along with you.

Common Core State Standards

Foundational Skills 3.d. Decode words with common prefixes and suffixes. **Language 2.** Demonstrate command of the conventions of standard English capitalization, punctuation, and spelling when writing.

Phonics

Review Prefixes *mis-, mid-, micro-, non-*

TARGET PHONICS SKILL Write the following sentences on the board. Have children read each one, first quietly to themselves and then aloud as you track the print.

1. **Did she misplace the nonstick pan midway through cooking dinner?**
2. **This nonfiction book is filled with mistakes and misprints.**
3. **We microwaved popcorn for a midmorning snack.**
4. **He misunderstood the rules about misbehaving in class.**

Team Talk Have children discuss with a partner which words have the prefixes *mis-, mid-, micro-,* and *non-.* Then call on individuals to share with the class.

Spelling Test

Prefixes *mis-, mid-*

DICTATE SPELLING WORDS Say each word, read the sentence, repeat the word, and allow time for children to write the word.

1. midyear	Our **midyear** break starts next week.
2. misplace	I hope I didn't **misplace** my homework.
3. misprint	The zip code on this letter is a **misprint.**
4. midway	We are **midway** through the year.
5. midday	Some people like to eat a **midday** snack.
6. mismatch	That shirt and pants are a **mismatch.**
7. misdeed	Jay's **misdeed** disappointed his parents.
8. mistake	Slow down so you don't make a **mistake.**
9. midweek	We will need to wash clothes **midweek.**
10. midair	The two kites crashed in **midair.**
11. mislead	Read carefully so it does not **mislead** you.
12. misbehave	If you **misbehave,** you can't come over.

High-Frequency Words

13. either	We can go to **either** the park or the beach.
14. bought	He **bought** flowers for five dollars.

Assess

- Spell words with prefixes *mis-, mid-.*
- Spell high-frequency words.

Access for All

Strategic Intervention

Check Spelling Have children choose the correct spelling of each word from three random spellings.

Advanced

Extend Spelling Have children who have demonstrated proficiency in spelling individual words make a word-find puzzle using the spelling words. Have partners exchange puzzles.

Day 5 SMALL GROUP TIME • Differentiate Reteaching, p. SG•69

OL On-Level

- **Develop** Commas in Compound Sentences
- **Reread** *Reading Street Sleuth,* pp. 76–77

SI Strategic Intervention

- **Review/Discuss** Commas in Compound Sentences
- **Reread** *Reading Street Sleuth,* pp. 76–77

A Advanced

- **Extend** Commas in Compound Sentences
- **Reread** *Reading Street Sleuth,* pp. 76–77
- **Communicate** Inquiry Project

If... children need more scaffolding and practice with **Conventions and Writing,**
then... use the activities on pp. DI•104–DI•105 in the Teacher Resources section on SuccessNet.

Vocabulary

Multiple-Meaning Words

Dictionary/Glossary You can look the word up in a dictionary or glossary to find its relevant meaning in a sentence.

Practice It! Read each sentence. Use a dictionary or glossary to find the relevant meaning for each bold word.

1. The firefighters in the fire engine will **lead** the parade.
2. The bank keeps money in a **safe**.
3. The water in that **spring** is fresh.

Fluency

Appropriate Phrasing

When you are reading, group words together. You can use commas and end punctuation to help you group words. Try to read the words in groups. Then you will understand the reading.

Practice It! Read the text aloud.

There are many different pieces in the game of chess. Each player gets one king and one queen. Each player gets two bishops, two rooks, two knights, and eight pawns.

528

Listening and Speaking

Listen for a speaker's purpose and decide if the speaker meets it.

Listen for Speaker's Purpose

When giving a report, you want to communicate with your listeners. Make sure to think about your listeners as you plan your report. Let listeners know why you are giving them the information. Listeners want to know your purpose. They may ask, "Why is the speaker telling me this?" Your report should help them identify the reason for listening.

For a report, do research on your topic. Look for facts to support your ideas. You might begin a report on dog tricks with this sentence: "Dogs can do many tricks." Then the listener will know what your report is about.

As a listener, think about what the speaker is saying. Do you know what the speaker's report is about? Does the speaker support ideas with facts? Does the speaker use details to make the report interesting?

Practice It! Write a short report on a topic that interests you. Give the report to the class. Speak clearly, at an appropriate pace, and use complete sentences. While listening, identify the speaker's purpose. Explain what the purpose is when the speaker is finished.

529

Student Edition, pp. 528–529

Common Core State Standards

Language 4.e. Use glossaries and beginning dictionaries, both print and digital, to determine or clarify the meaning of words and phrases. **Foundational Skills 4.a.** Read on-level text with purpose and understanding. **Foundational Skills 4.b.** Read on-level text orally with accuracy, appropriate rate, and expression on successive readings. **Also Speaking/Listening 6., Language 3.a.**

Vocabulary

Multiple-Meaning Words

TEACH Read and discuss the Vocabulary lesson on page 528. Remind children to use a dictionary or a glossary to decide which meaning of a word is being used.

GUIDE PRACTICE Read the instructions and the first sentence of the Vocabulary Practice It! activity. Let's look *lead* up in the dictionary. Read the definitions and have children choose the one that fits the context. ("be the first")

ON THEIR OWN Have small groups complete items 2 and 3.

Corrective feedback Circulate around the room and listen as children determine which meanings of *safe* and *spring* are used in the sentences. Provide assistance as needed.

Fluency

Appropriate Phrasing

TEACH Read and discuss the Fluency instructions.

READ WORDS IN CONTEXT Give children a moment to look at the paragraph. Then have partners take turns reading it to each other with appropriate phrasing.

Listening and Speaking

Listen for Speaker's Purpose

TEACH Read together the explanation of listening for a speaker's purpose on page 529 of the Student Edition. Remind children that good speakers make their purposes clear. Good listeners look for the speaker's purpose. They also ask themselves if the speaker met the purpose.

ANALYZE Explain to children that when giving a report, the speaker may begin the report with a sentence or two that tells the listener what the report is about. How could a speaker begin a report about the jaguar, which is an endangered species? (Possible response: The jaguar is an endangered species.)

INTRODUCE PROMPT Read the Practice It! prompt with the class. Remind children to speak in complete sentences when they give their reports and to make their purposes clear. Ask children to determine if the presentation requires them to use formal English and to explain why or why not.

Team Talk Have children give their reports before the class. Remind listeners to listen for each speaker's purpose. After each report, discuss what listeners thought the report was about.

Access for All

SI Strategic Intervention

Dictionary Use Use a multiple-meaning word in context for children. Have children read the dictionary definitions for the word one by one and explain why each is or is not the meaning of the word in the sentence.

Listen for Speaker's Purpose

In addition to listening for a speaker's purpose, children at Grade 3 should also be able to maintain attention when listening, determine both main and supporting ideas, and summarize what is heard.

Listening Comprehension
Have children demonstrate their comprehension of classmates' short oral reports by asking them to identify the topic and the main idea.

Text-Based Comprehension

Review Facts and Details

Remember that realistic fiction contains facts and details. Story facts are pieces of information. Story details, which provide more information about story characters, settings, and events, are also important. Read aloud the following story and have children answer the questions.

This year Laura was planning to make family birthday presents. Mom's birthday was in February, so Laura knew she'd better get started knitting a scarf. Holly's birthday wasn't until June, and so she had time to paint her dollhouse furniture. Grandpa's birthday came next. She planned to decorate a picture frame with shells for his birthday gift. Luckily, Dad's birthday wasn't until the end of November. She still wasn't sure what she'd make for him, but she had almost eleven months to figure it out.

1. Who is the main character? Where do you learn her name? (Laura; in the first sentence)
2. Whose birthday comes first, and what does Laura plan to make? (Mom's birthday; Laura plans to knit her a scarf.)
3. Whose birthday gift is still undecided? Why isn't Laura worried? (Dad's gift; she has almost eleven months to decide.)
4. Who will get painted dollhouse furniture? (Holly)

Vocabulary

Review Selection Vocabulary

SELECTION WORDS Review this week's selection vocabulary: *assembly, election, microphone, rallies, slogan,* and *speeches.* Provide a riddle using one of the words, such as: If you use this, even the largest crowd can hear you speak. (microphone)

Team Talk Pair children. Have partners take turns orally giving each other riddles to solve for the remaining five words.

Corrective feedback	**If...** children cannot tell what the words mean, **then...** review the definitions on p. 501a.

Common Core State Standards

Literature 1. Ask and answer such questions as *who, what, where, when, why,* and *how* to demonstrate understanding of key details in a text. **Literature 3.** Describe how characters in a story respond to major events and challenges. **Language 6.** Use words and phrases acquired through conversations, reading and being read to, and responding to texts, including using adjectives and adverbs to describe (e.g., *When other kids are happy that makes me happy*). **Also Literature 6.**

Genre

Review Realistic Fiction

REALISTIC FICTION Review with children that realistic fiction is a made-up story that seems real and could happen in real life. Realistic fiction has characters that talk and act like real people.

TEACH **Characters** are the people or animals in a story. We learn what characters are like by what they say and think and how they act. What have we learned about Grace?

Think Aloud **MODEL** In realistic fiction, characters talk and act like real people. In *Grace for President,* Grace learns that there has never been a woman President. She thinks that's crazy and declares that she wants to be President. From her thoughts and actions, I can tell that Grace is fair-minded and thinks girls can do anything boys can. She also has confidence in herself. These are qualities I have observed in real people around me.

GUIDE PRACTICE Ask the following questions to guide children in describing Grace and Thomas and inferring reasons for their actions.

- What does the way Grace runs her campaign tell you about her? (She is serious about wanting to be a good president. She is hardworking. She is enthusiastic.)
- Is the way Grace acts true-to-life? Explain why you think this. (Grace acts in a responsible and problem-solving way, as real leaders do.)
- What does the way Thomas runs his campaign tell you about him? (He doesn't think boys and girls are equal. He is clever to figure out that the boys' electoral votes favor him.)
- Thomas makes campaign promises such as free tutoring and free soccer lessons. How is this behavior like real life? (Some campaigners promise whatever they think will get them votes.)

ON THEIR OWN What does Sam do? Explain how his actions echo real-life behavior. Have children write a few sentences about Sam's character using story details and their own experiences to support their opinions.

Access for All

 Strategic Intervention

Inferring Character If children have difficulty analyzing a character, have them use Graphic Organizer 15 to create a character web. Ask them to write examples of how a character acts and what he or she says. Then ask them what kind of person would act that way.

Academic Vocabulary 

character a person or animal in a story

Common Core State Standards

Foundational Skills 3. Know and apply grade-level phonics and word analysis skills in decoding words. **Foundational Skills 3.d.** Decode words with common prefixes and suffixes. **Foundational Skills 4.a.** Read on-level text with purpose and understanding.

Assess

- Prefixes *mis-, mid-, micro-, non-*
- Fluency: Rate
- Facts and Details

Fluency Goals

Set individual fluency goals for children to enable them to reach the end-of-the-year goal.

- **Current Goal:** 80–90 WCPM
- **End-of-Year Goal:** 90 WCPM

Assessment

Monitor Progress

For a written assessment of prefixes *mis-, mid-, micro-,* and *non-* and facts and details, use Weekly Test 30, pp. 175–180.

SENTENCE READING Use the following reproducible page to assess children's ability to read words in context. Call on children to read two sentences aloud. Start over with sentence one if necessary.

MONITOR PROGRESS Sentence Reading

If... children have trouble reading words with prefixes *mis-, mid-, micro-,* and *non-,*

then... use the Reteach Lesson in *First Stop.*

FLUENCY Take a one-minute sample of children's oral reading. Have children read the fluency passage on p. 529f.

COMPREHENSION Have the child read the entire passage. (If the child has difficulty with the passage, you may read it aloud.) Then have the child sum up the passage by restating facts and details.

MONITOR ACCURACY Have children monitor their accuracy by recording their scores using the Sentence Reading Chart and by recording the number of words read correctly per minute on their Fluency Progress Chart in *First Stop.*

MONITOR PROGRESS Fluency and Comprehension

If... a child does not achieve the fluency goal on the timed reading,

then... copy the passage and send it home with the child for additional fluency practice, or have the child practice with a fluent reader.

If... a child cannot restate facts and details,

then... use the Reteach Lesson in *First Stop.*

Name ______________________________

Read the Sentences

1. I misspelled her name on a sign for the midyear election.
2. Chen misread the title of the nonfiction book over the microphone.
3. Dean wrote the slogan for the team, but Jean misplaced it midway through the game.
4. At the assembly, we will explain how you can use a microscope to view nonliving things.
5. Please do not misbehave or whisper nonstop during the speeches.
6. I misplaced the information about the rallies somewhere on the counter by the microwave.

MONITOR PROGRESS

- Prefixes *mis-*, *mid-*, *micro-*, *non-*
- Selection Vocabulary

Name ____________________________________

Read the Selection

The Layers of a Rain Forest

Most rain forests are found where it is hot and wet 11
all year. The hot, wet climate helps the trees grow very 22
tall. Because the trees are so tall, a rain forest has four 34
layers, or parts. Different animals live in each part. 43
The top part of a rain forest is the emergent layer. 54
The branches from the tallest trees reach for the 63
sunlight. Hawks and eagles build their nests here. 71
The second part is the canopy. The branches of 80
different trees spread out and touch each other. This 89
layer of the rain forest still gets sun. Most rain forest 100
animals, such as monkeys and parrots, live here. 108
The third part is the understory. The trees are 117
shorter because there isn't much sunlight. It is dark 126
and cool here. Frogs and spiders call this layer home. 136
The lowest part of the rain forest is the forest 146
floor. Bushes with flowers grow here. Larger 153
animals, like wild pigs and jaguars, hunt for food. 162

MONITOR PROGRESS

- **Check Fluency**
- **Facts and Details**

Conventions

Review Commas in Compound Sentences

REVIEW Remind children that a comma and a connecting word are used to combine two simple sentences into a compound sentence. Have children give several examples of compound sentences.

GUIDE PRACTICE Write the following sentences. Have children supply the missing commas in each sentence.

1. **Chris chopped carrots and Frank sliced bread.**
2. **The children can read or they can play outside.**
3. **The toy broke but Aunt Rita fixed it.**

APPLY Have children orally complete the following sentence frames.

1. **My brother plays the drums, but _______.**
2. **Our class put on a play, and _______.**
3. **She will choose the red dress, or _______.**

ON THEIR OWN Use Let's Practice It!, p. 338 on the *Teacher Resources DVD-ROM.*

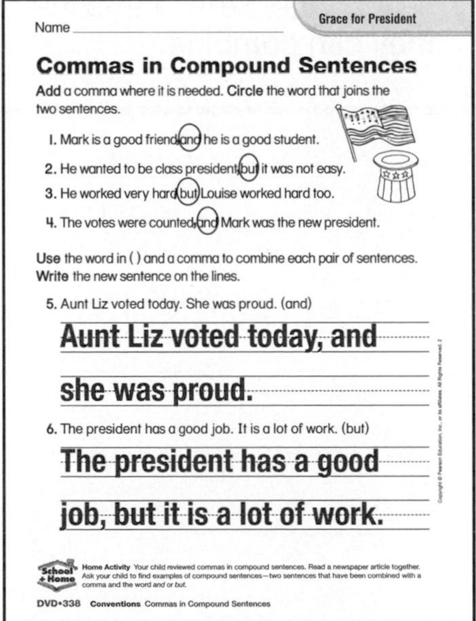
Name __________ Grace for President

Commas in Compound Sentences

Add a comma where it is needed. **Circle** the word that joins the two sentences.

1. Mark is a good friend, (and) he is a good student.
2. He wanted to be class president, (but) it was not easy.
3. He worked very hard, (but) Louise worked hard too.
4. The votes were counted, (and) Mark was the new president.

Use the word in ( ) and a comma to combine each pair of sentences. **Write** the new sentence on the lines.

5. Aunt Liz voted today. She was proud. (and)
   Aunt Liz voted today, and she was proud.
6. The president has a good job. It is a lot of work. (but)
   The president has a good job, but it is a lot of work.

Home Activity Your child reviewed commas in compound sentences. Read a newspaper article together. Ask your child to find examples of compound sentences—two sentences that have been combined with a comma and the word *and* or *but*.

DVD•338 **Conventions** Commas in Compound Sentences

Let's Practice It! TR DVD•338

Common Core State Standards

Foundational Skills 4.b. Read on-level text orally with accuracy, appropriate rate, and expression on successive readings. **Language 1.** Demonstrate command of the conventions of standard English grammar and usage when writing or speaking. **Language 1.f.** Produce, expand, and rearrange complete simple and compound sentences (e.g., *The boy watched the movie; The little boy watched the movie; The action movie was watched by the little boy*).

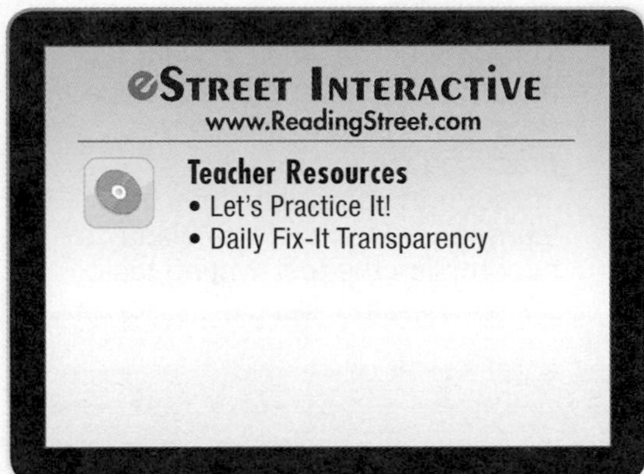

Daily Fix-It

9. I cant hear your voise.
   I can't hear your voice.
10. May i borro your silver ring?
    May I borrow your silver ring?

Discuss the Daily Fix-It corrections with children. Review contractions, sounds made by *c,* capitalization, and vowel pattern *ow.*

Common Core State Standards

Writing 5. With guidance and support from adults and peers, focus on a topic and strengthen writing as needed by revising and editing. **Language 2.** Demonstrate command of the conventions of standard English capitalization, punctuation, and spelling when writing.

PRODUCTION AND DISTRIBUTION OF WRITING

Throughout the week, children have developed and strengthened persuasive statements as they practiced writing for tests. Through the activities, they have learned to communicate clearly to accomplish the test-writing task.

Persuasive Statement

REVIEW REVISING Remind children that yesterday they learned about using vivid words in their persuasive statements and wrote a response to a second prompt. Tell children that today they will evaluate their writing from yesterday using the writing rubric.

Mini-Lesson Writing for Tests: Revise: Compound Sentences

- **Teach** In our persuasive statements, we want to use sentences that are a variety of lengths. Using long and short sentences makes the writing more interesting to read. When we revise, we can look for two simple sentences that have related ideas. We can combine them by using a comma and a connecting word, such as *and* or *but.* Then we begin the second sentence with a lowercase letter and end the sentence with a period.

- **Model** Write these sentences: *Broccoli is green. It looks like a tree.* Both of these sentences tell about broccoli. We can join them together to make one sentence. Show how you would add a comma and the connecting word *and* to make a compound sentence. Then have children review their sample test writing they completed on Day 4 to see if there are sentences they can combine.

EVALUATE Have children use the rubric on *Reader's and Writer's Notebook,* p. 536 to evaluate their writing. Guide them to read the paragraph once for focus and organization. Have them read it a second time for voice and word choice, and a third time for sentences and conventions.

Routine Quick Write for Fluency

1. **Talk** Have partners take one minute to review their persuasive statements and find a vivid word that tells about their traditional food.
2. **Write** Each child writes new sentences using the words.
3. **Share** Partners read their sentences aloud.

Routines Flip Chart

Common Core State Standards

Speaking/Listening 2. Recount or describe key ideas or details from a text read aloud or information presented orally or through other media. **Speaking/Listening 3.** Ask and answer questions about what a speaker says in order to clarify comprehension, gather additional information, or deepen understanding of a topic or issue.

Research and Inquiry

Step 5 Communicate

TEACH Tell children that today they will organize information they recorded in the interviews, create a chart that displays the information, and share the information with the class.

Think Aloud **MODEL** Display the list of inquiry questions and the answers recorded during research. I was interested in the question *How do you celebrate your favorite tradition?* One answer I found was *I celebrate Kwanzaa by lighting candles and giving gifts.* We are going to show our information on a chart. So on my chart one of the celebrations I will include is Kwanzaa, and I will include the details about how it is celebrated.

GUIDE PRACTICE Review the answers on the chart with children. Have them prompt you to circle the traditions that may be included on their charts.

ON THEIR OWN Have partners make a chart that shows ways traditions are celebrated and shared. Discuss how many columns and rows they will want on their charts. A sample T-chart is shown below. Have children share their charts in small groups. Remind them to be good speakers and listeners:

- Good speakers use good posture when they speak. They stand tall with their heads up and look the audience in the eye.
- Good listeners listen attentively and ask questions after a speaker is done to clear up misunderstandings or confusion.

Topic: We Celebrate Traditions

Tradition	Ways to Celebrate
Kwanzaa	People light candles and give gifts.

Wrap Up Your Week!

Celebrated and Shared Traditions

How are different traditions celebrated and shared?

Think Aloud This week we explored different traditions. In the selection *Grace for President,* we read about a girl who learned about political traditions of our country and then decided to one day break the history of "no girls" as President. In "Home Sweet Home," you learned about traditions of early Native Americans in California.

Team Talk Have children work with partners to talk about their Amazing Ideas about different traditions. Then have children use these ideas to help them demonstrate their understanding of the Question of the Week, *How are different traditions celebrated and shared?*

Amazing Words

You've learned 008 words this week!

You'll learn 241 words this year!

Assessment Checkpoints for the Week

Weekly Assessment

Use pp. 175–180 of *Weekly Tests* to check:

✔ **Phonics** Prefixes *mis-, mid-, micro-, non-*

✔ **Comprehension** Facts and Details

✔ **Selection Vocabulary**

assembly	**rallies**
election	**slogan**
microphone	**speeches**

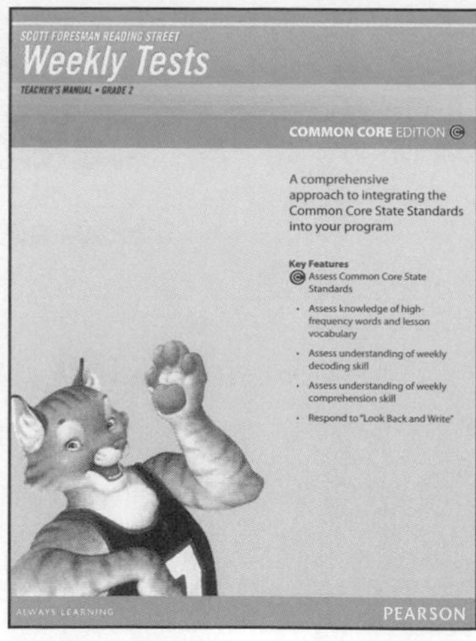

Weekly Tests

Differentiated Assessment

Advanced

On-Level

SI Strategic Intervention

Use pp. 175–180 of *Fresh Reads for Fluency and Comprehension* to check:

✔ **Comprehension** Facts and Details

✔ **Review** **Comprehension** Compare and Contrast

✔ **Fluency** Words Correct Per Minute

Fresh Reads for Fluency and Comprehension

Managing Assessment

Use *Assessment Handbook* for:

✔ **Weekly Assessment Blackline Masters for Monitoring Progress**

✔ **Observation Checklists**

✔ **Record-Keeping Forms**

✔ **Portfolio Assessment**

Assessment Handbook

DAY 1 Differentiate Phonics

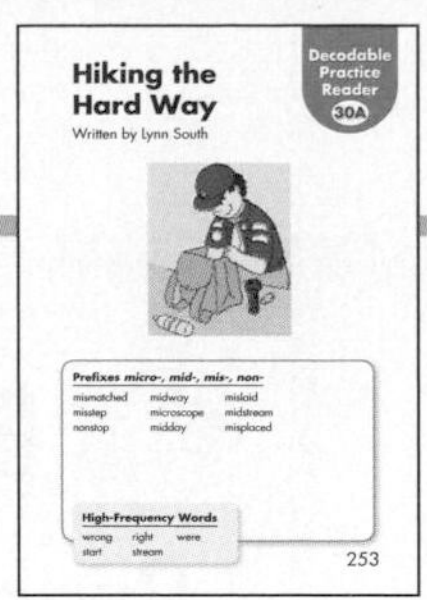

- Prefixes *mis-, mid-, micro-, non-*
- Decodable Practice Reader
- Advanced Selection “Midsummer Fun”
- **Inquiry** Identify Questions

DAY 2 Differentiate Comprehension

- Selection Vocabulary
- **Access Text** Read *Grace for President*
- **Inquiry** Investigate

DAY 3 Differentiate Close Reading

- Develop Vocabulary
- **Close Reading** Reread *Grace for President*
- **Inquiry** Investigate

“A Few Words with a Big Effect,” pp. 76–77

DAY 4 Differentiate Vocabulary

- Amazing Words
- **Read** “A Few Words with a Big Effect” or Leveled Readers
- **Inquiry** Organize

DAY 5 Differentiate Reteaching

- **Conventions** Contractions
- **Read** “A Few Words with a Big Effect” or Leveled Readers
- **Inquiry** Communicate

Teacher Guides and student pages can be found in the Leveled Reader Database.

Place English Language Learners in the groups that correspond to their reading abilities.
If... children need scaffolding and practice,
then... use the ELL notes on the instructional pages.

Independent Practice

Independent Practice Stations

See pp. 496h and 496i for Independent Stations.

Pearson Trade Book Library

See the Leveled Reader Database for Lesson Plans and student pages.

Reading Street Digital Path

Independent Practice Activities available in the Digital Path.

Independent Reading

See p. 496i for independent reading suggestions.

On-Level

Common Core State Standards

Foundational Skills 3.d. Decode words with common prefixes and suffixes. **Literature 1.** Ask and answer such questions as *who, what, where, when, why,* and *how* to demonstrate understanding of key details in a text. **Literature 7.** Use information gained from the illustrations and words in a print or digital text to demonstrate understanding of its characters, setting, or plot. **Also Literature 10. and Language 5.a.**

If... children need more scaffolding and practice with phonics,
then... use the activities on pp. DI•100 in the Teacher Resources section on SuccessNet.

1 Build Word Knowledge

Practice Phonics

PREFIXES *mis-, mid-, micro-, non-* Write the following words and have children practice reading words with the prefixes *mis-, mid-, micro-* and *non-.*

mislabel	midsummer	microchip	nonfiction

Spelling

PREFIXES *mis-, mid-* Remind children that each spelling word begins with the prefix *mis-* or *mid-.* Clarify the pronunciation and meaning of each word. For example, say: Something that happens midweek happens in the middle of the week. Have children spell each base word and then add the prefix.

2 Read

Decodable Reader 30A *Hiking the Hard Way*

HIGH-FREQUENCY WORDS Have children read the decodable reader. Then have them reread the text to develop automaticity. Have children return to the text and find the previously taught high-frequency words. Help children demonstrate their understanding of the words. Provide sentence frames such as: Small fish and toads made their home in the _______. (stream)

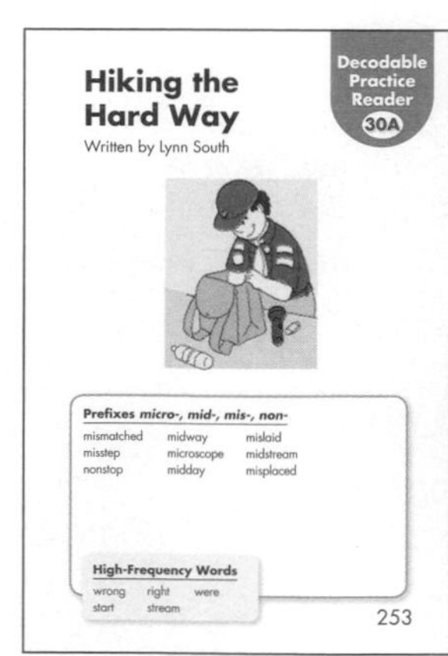
Hiking the Hard Way
Written by Lynn South
Decodable Practice Reader 30A

Prefixes *micro-, mid-, mis-, non-*

mismatched	midway	mislaid
misstep	microscope	midstream
nonstop	midday	misplaced

High-Frequency Words

wrong	right	were
start	stream	

253

On-Level

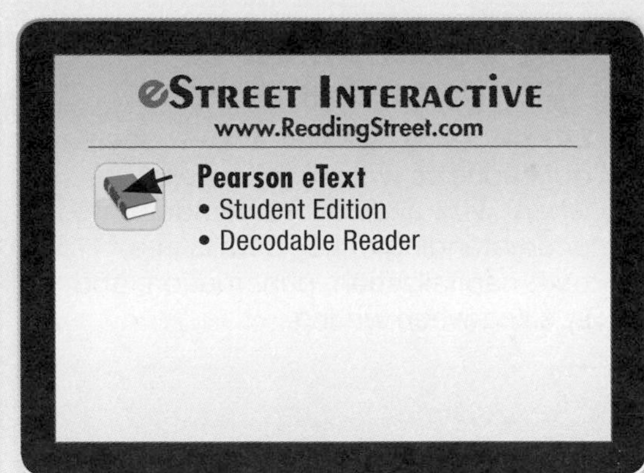

1 Build Word Knowledge

Practice Selection Vocabulary

assembly	election	microphone
rallies	slogan	speeches

DEFINE IT Discuss the definition for the word *assembly* with children. Ask: How would you describe an *assembly* to a friend? (It is a gathering of people for a special reason.) Continue with the remaining words.

Team Talk **TALK ABOUT IT** Have pairs use the selection words in sentences to internalize meaning. Ask: How can you pair the selection words together in a sentence? (Possible response: We listened to some important speeches at the assembly.) Allow time for children to play with the words and then share their sentences.

2 Read

Grace for President

If you read *Grace for President* during whole group time, then use the following instruction.

ACCESS TEXT Have children look at the pictures on pp. 510–511. Reread both pages.

- Look at the pictures on p. 511. Based on their signs, what issue do Grace and Thomas disagree on? (Grace wants to get rid of fish-stick tacos and Thomas wants more of them.)
- What is a *candidate?* (someone who runs for election)
- What other words on these pages let you know an election is taking place? *(votes, president, campaign, issues)*
- Grace's slogan on p. 510 says "Make History!" What history is she trying to make? (She wants to be the first woman president.)

If you are reading *Grace for President* during small group time, then return to pp. 503a–519a to guide the reading.

SMALL GROUP TIME

Independent Reading Options

Trade Book Library

eStreet Interactive
www.ReadingStreet.com
Teacher's Guides available on the Leveled Reader Database.

Common Core State Standards

Literature 1. Ask and answer such questions as *who, what, where, when, why,* and *how* to demonstrate understanding of key details in a text. capitalization, punctuation, and spelling when writing.

1 Build Word Knowledge

Develop Vocabulary

REREAD FOR VOCABULARY Have children reread *Grace for President,* p. 512.

Read the following sentence and discuss words and phrases related to elections. *(campaign, posters, buttons)*

Grace made campaign posters and buttons.

- What is a *campaign?* (a series of events used to convince voters to vote for someone)
- What are some events Grace held during her campaign? (She gave speeches, she handed out cupcakes, and she held rallies.)

2 Read

Grace for President

If you read *Grace for President* during whole group time, then use the following instruction.

CLOSE READING Look at the pictures on pp. 512–515 and reread the text. Have children summarize the ideas presented on these pages. Ask questions to guide deeper understanding.

- How can you tell Grace takes the election more seriously than Thomas? (Grace continues to campaign. Thomas works on his other school projects and activities.)
- Why does Thomas think he is going to win the election? (The boys have more electoral votes than the girls. He thinks all the boys will vote for him.)
- How does Grace prove she would be a good president before the election takes place? (She makes good on her promises. She joins clubs and volunteers.)

Remind children that pronouns take the place of nouns. Write the following sentence: *Grace looked at the scoreboard.* Ask children to rewrite the sentence, replacing *Grace* and *scoreboard* with pronouns. *(She* looked at *it.)*

If you are reading *Grace for President* during small group time, then return to pp. 503a–519a to guide the reading.

If... children need more scaffolding and practice with the main selection, **then...** use the activities on p. DI•102 in the Teacher Resources section on SuccessNet.

On-Level

1 Build Word Knowledge

Practice Amazing Words

ceremony	culture	festival	compliment
fidget	evergreen	multicolored	sash

Team Talk **LANGUAGE DEVELOPMENT** Have children practice building complex sentences. Display a sentence starter and have children add an oral phrase or clause using the Amazing Words. For example: The festival was a highlight of the year, with _______. (Possible response: The festival was a highlight of the year, with bright multicolored lights hanging around the park.)

2 Text-Based Comprehension

READ ALOUD "A Few Words with a Big Effect" Lead children in a choral reading of "A Few Words with a Big Effect" from *Reading Street Sleuth* on pp. 76–77. Then have partners take turns reading the paragraphs of the selection.

ACCESS TEXT Guide children as they work on the Be a Sleuth section.

Look for Clues Reread the campaign slogans in the selection and discuss their meanings. Then ask children to identify the purposes of the slogans.

Ask Questions Discuss the role of the President in the national government. Then ask children, What questions would you ask someone to find out if he or she would make a good President?

Make Your Case Ask, What should a slogan be about? Should slogans be about specific beliefs and ideas? Should they be catchy phrases that include the candidate's name? Should there be rules for the kinds of slogans candidates can use? Have children support their opinions with details.

SMALL GROUP TIME

More Reading for Group Time

ON-LEVEL

Reviews
- Concept Vocabulary
- Facts and Details
- Predict and Set Purpose

Use this suggested Leveled Reader or other text at children's instructional level.

eStreet Interactive
www.ReadingStreet.com

Use the Leveled Reader Database for lesson plans and student pages for *Voting Day.*

On-Level

Common Core State Standards

Foundational Skills 3.d. Decode words with common prefixes and suffixes. **Foundational Skills 4.** Read with sufficient accuracy and fluency to support comprehension. **Language 2.** Demonstrate command of the conventions of standard English capitalization, punctuation, and spelling when writing.

1 Build Word Knowledge

Practice Commas in Compound Sentences

REVIEW If needed, revisit the conventions lesson on p. 519b.

IDENTIFY COMMAS IN COMPOUND SENTENCES Have children turn to "A Few Words with a Big Effect" to identify the use of commas in the compound sentence in the second-to-last paragraph. Have them identify the two simple sentences that make up the compound sentence and the conjunction that joins them. Remind them that the comma is used to help separate the two sentences that make up the compound sentence.

2 Text-Based Comprehension

REREAD "A Few Words with a Big Effect" Have partners reread "A Few Words with a Big Effect."

EXTEND UNDERSTANDING Discuss the use of slogans for purposes other than elections. Point out that communities, organizations, and companies often use slogans to help people remember their products and services. If possible, display the motto or slogan used by your local community or an organization in the community. Discuss the meaning of the slogan.

PERFORMANCE TASK • Prove It! Tell children that slogans are also used to help gain support for causes other than elections. For example, a not-for-profit organization may have a slogan to help it raise awareness about a need in the community. Have pairs of children select a cause or an organization they would like to support. Have them develop a catchy slogan for their cause and create a poster with the slogan.

COMMUNICATE When the posters are completed, ask children to share their posters and explain why they think their slogans are good ones.

More Reading for Group Time

ON-LEVEL

Reviews

- Concept Vocabulary
- Facts and Details
- Predict and Set Purpose

Use this suggested Leveled Reader or other text at children's instructional level.

eSTREET INTERACTIVE
www.ReadingStreet.com

Use the Leveled Reader Database for lesson plans and student pages for *Voting Day.*

Strategic Intervention

1 Build Word Knowledge

Reteach Phonics

PREFIXES *mis-, mid-, micro-, non-* Reteach the lesson on p. 498a, Prefixes *mis-, mid-, micro-*, and *non-*. Use these additional practice words.

midday **misstep** **microscope** **nonsense**

Then have children sort the following *mis-, mid-, micro-*, and *non-* words and circle the prefixes.

midnight	**mislead**	**microwave**	**nontoxic**	**misspoke**
midline	**nonviolence**	**micromanage**	**mistreat**	**midway**

2 Read

Decodable Reader 30A *Hiking the Hard Way*

DECODE WORDS Have children practice reading the words listed on p. 253.

Corrective feedback	**If...** children have difficulty reading the words independently, **then...** reteach the words prior to reading Decodable Reader 30A.

READ IN CONTEXT Have children take turns reading a page in *Hiking the Hard Way.* Have them reread the text several times to ensure accuracy.

Corrective feedback	**If...** children have difficulty reading the selection independently, **then...** model reading a page and have children echo you.

3 Reread for Fluency

Have children reread the text to develop automaticity in their reading.

SMALL GROUP TIME

If... children need more scaffolding and practice with phonics, **then...** use the activities on p. DI•100 in the Teacher Resources section on SuccessNet.

Common Core State Standards

Literature 1. Ask and answer such questions as *who, what, where, when, why,* and *how* to demonstrate understanding of key details in a text. **Literature 3.** Describe how characters in a story respond to major events and challenges. **Language 4.a.** Use sentence-level context as a clue to the meaning of a word or phrase.

1 Build Word Knowledge

Reteach Selection Vocabulary

assembly	election	microphone
rallies	slogan	speeches

DEFINE IT Describe the word *slogan* to a friend. Restate the word in child-friendly terms. A *slogan* is a word or sentence that advertises an idea. In the selection, Grace used the slogan "Make History!"

Team Talk **TALK ABOUT IT** What is a famous slogan? What makes it memorable? Turn and talk to your partner about this. Allow time for children to discuss. Ask for examples. Rephrase their examples for usage when necessary or to correct misunderstandings. Continue with the remaining words.

Corrective feedback	**If...** children need more practice with selection vocabulary, **then...** use the *Envision It! Pictured Vocabulary Cards.*

2 Read

Grace for President

If you read *Grace for President* during whole group time, then use the instruction below.

ACCESS TEXT Have children look at the pictures on p. 515. Why are the children dressed in different costumes? (They are dressed up to represent their state.) Reread the text on pp. 514–515.

- Grace joined the safety squad and beautification committee and volunteered in the cafeteria. How does this show she would make a good president? (She follows through on her promises.)
- Would a beautification committee make the school look better or worse? (better)
- What root word do you recognize in the word *beautification?* (beauty)

If you are reading *Grace for President* during small group time, then return to pp. 503a–519a to guide the reading.

Corrective feedback	**If...** children have difficulty understanding the section, **then...** read the section aloud using the Access Text Notes.

Independent Reading Options

Trade Book Library

eStreet Interactive
www.ReadingStreet.com

Teacher's Guides available on the Leveled Reader Database.

1 Build Word Knowledge

Develop Vocabulary

REREAD FOR VOCABULARY Have children reread p. 518 of *Grace for President* and look at the picture. To help children understand the word *erupted,* ask questions related to the context, such as: Are people excited to hear the announcement of the winner? Are cheers and boos loud or quiet?

Corrective feedback	**If...** children have difficulty understanding the word *erupted,* **then...** guide children to use online sources to find more information.

2 Read

Grace for President

If you read *Grace for President* during whole group time, then use the instruction below.

CLOSE READING Reread pp. 508–509. Ask questions related to the context.

- Why does Grace first think becoming president is going to be easy? (No one else in Mrs. Barrington's class chooses to run for president.)
- What changes her mind? (Thomas Cobb from another class is running.)
- What clues tell you that Thomas Cobb will be tough for Grace to beat? (He is the school spelling bee champ, good at science, and captain of the soccer team. Also, in the picture, he has stars drawn all around him.)

Corrective feedback	**If...** children have trouble answering questions, **then...** reread the page and have them fill in sentence frames to summarize the ideas. **At first, Grace thinks becoming president will be ______, but then she finds out ______ is running.**

If you are reading *Grace for President* during small group time, then return to pp. 503a–519a to guide the reading.

SMALL GROUP TIME

ELL

If... children need scaffolding and practice with the main selection, **then...** use the activities on p. DI•102 in the Teacher Resources section on SuccessNet.

Strategic Intervention

Common Core State Standards

Language 1. Demonstrate command of the conventions of standard English grammar and usage when writing or speaking. **Language 2.** Demonstrate command of the conventions of standard English capitalization, punctuation, and spelling when writing.

1 Build Word Knowledge

Review Amazing Words

ceremony	culture	festival	compliment
fidget	evergreen	multicolored	sash

Team Talk **LANGUAGE DEVELOPMENT** Have children practice building more complex sentences. Display a sentence starter and have children add an oral phrase using the Amazing Words. For example: At the festival we saw ______. (Possible response: At the festival we saw multicolored lights.)

Corrective feedback | **If...** children have difficulty using Amazing Words orally, **then...** review the meaning of each of the words.

2 Text-Based Comprehension

READ ALOUD "A Few Words with a Big Effect" Read aloud "A Few Words with a Big Effect" from *Reading Street Sleuth* on pp. 76–77 as children follow along. Then lead a choral reading of the selection.

ACCESS TEXT Guide children as they work on the Be a Sleuth section.

Look for Clues Read the selection aloud. Write the three slogans used in the selection on the board: *Tippecanoe and Tyler too!, A chicken in every pot and a car in every garage.,* and *I like Ike.* Ask, Which presidential candidate used this slogan? What is the purpose of this slogan?

Ask Questions Tell children that the President is the head of the military, helps make sure laws are carried out, works with Congress, and appoints people to government jobs. What would you want to ask someone who is running for President? Then have children ask their questions.

Make Your Case Help children think of some reasons for restricting content of slogans. Ask, for example, Should a candidate be allowed to have a slogan that tells a lie? Record their opinions on the board and allow children to use the ideas as they answer the Make Your Case question.

More Reading for Group Time

CONCEPT LITERACY

Practice
- Concept Words
- Selection Vocabulary

BELOW LEVEL

Review
- Facts and Details
- Predict and Set Purpose
- Selection Vocabulary

Use these suggested Leveled Readers or other text at children's instructional level.

eSTREET INTERACTIVE
www.ReadingStreet.com

Use the Leveled Reader Database for lesson plans and student pages for *Election Day* and *Just Like Grandpa.*

1 Build Word Knowledge

Review Commas in Compound Sentences

IDENTIFY Choral read the Conventions note at the bottom of p. 523 with children to review using commas in compound sentences. Have children reread the model persuasive statement on p. 523 to find examples of how the author used commas in compound sentences. Allow time for children to discuss the examples and correct any misunderstandings.

2 Text-Based Comprehension

REREAD "A Few Words with a Big Effect" Have partners reread "A Few Words with a Big Effect."

EXTEND UNDERSTANDING Discuss the use of slogans for purposes other than elections. Point out that communities, organizations, and companies often use slogans to help people remember their products and services. If possible, display the motto or slogan used by your local community or an organization in the community. Discuss the meaning of the slogan.

PERFORMANCE TASK • Prove It! Name some well-known not-for-profit organizations, such as the Red Cross, the United Way, Boys and Girls Clubs, and UNICEF. Explain that a not-for-profit organization may have one or more slogans that tell about the organization and its work. Help small groups of children select a cause or organization they would like to support. Have group members work together to develop a catchy slogan for their cause and create a poster.

COMMUNICATE Have the groups present their posters and explain why they think their slogans are good ones.

SMALL GROUP TIME

More Reading for Group Time

CONCEPT LITERACY

Practice
- Concept Words
- Selection Vocabulary

BELOW LEVEL

Review
- Facts and Details
- Predict and Set Purpose
- Selection Vocabulary

Use these suggested Leveled Readers or other text at children's instructional level.

eSTREET INTERACTIVE
www.ReadingStreet.com

Use the Leveled Reader Database for lesson plans and student pages for *Election Day* and *Just Like Grandpa*.

Advanced

Common Core State Standards

Foundational Skills 3.d. Decode words with common prefixes and suffixes. **Writing 8.** Recall information from experiences or gather information from provided sources to answer a question.

1 Build Word Knowledge

Extend Phonics

PREFIXES *mis-, mid-, micro-, non-* Have children practice with more complex words. Have them write each word on two cards and play a matching game. Then have them use the words in sentences.

mistook	midterm	nonrefundable	miscount	microprocessor
midsummer	mischief	microscopic	nonbeliever	midsection

2 Read

"Midsummer Fun"

TEACH VOCABULARY Before reading, introduce the selection words: *solstice, mishaps.* Help children determine the meaning of each word using these sentences:

1. The summer **solstice** is the longest day of the year.
2. Despite our team's **mishaps,** we still managed to win the game.

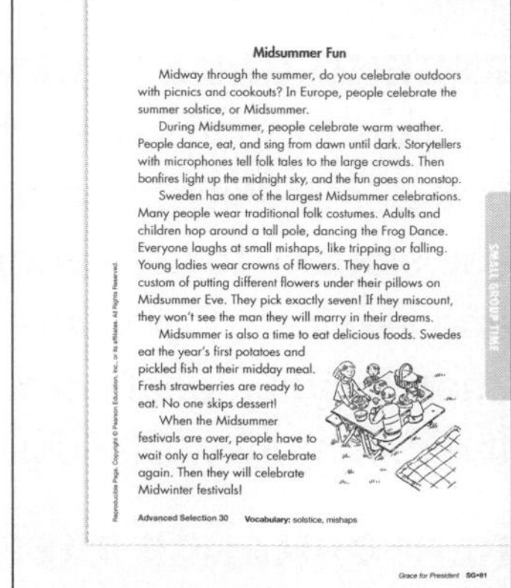
Midsummer Fun

Midway through the summer, do you celebrate outdoors with picnics and cookouts? In Europe, people celebrate the summer solstice, or Midsummer.

During Midsummer, people celebrate warm weather. People dance, eat, and sing from dawn until dark. Storytellers with microphones tell folk tales to the large crowds. Then bonfires light up the midnight sky, and the fun goes on nonstop.

Sweden has one of the largest Midsummer celebrations. Many people wear traditional folk costumes. Adults and children hop around a tall pole, dancing the Frog Dance. Everyone laughs at small mishaps, like tripping or falling. Young ladies wear crowns of flowers. They have a custom of putting different flowers under their pillows on Midsummer Eve. They pick exactly seven! If they miscount, they won't see the man they will marry in their dreams.

Midsummer is also a time to eat delicious foods. Swedes eat the year's first potatoes and pickled fish at their midday meal. Fresh strawberries are ready to eat. No one skips dessert!

When the Midsummer festivals are over, people have to wait only a half-year to celebrate again. Then they will celebrate Midwinter festivals!

Advanced Selection 30 Vocabulary: solstice, mishaps

Reproducible Page. Copyright © Pearson Education, Inc., or its affiliates. All Rights Reserved.

SMALL GROUP TIME

Grace for President SG•81

READ Have children read "Midsummer Fun" silently. Then have children take turns reading aloud. After reading, have children recall the two most important ideas of the selection using details from the text.

3 Inquiry: Extend Concepts

IDENTIFY QUESTIONS Tell children that music and musical instruments are an important part of many cultures. Then have children find out about instruments used in Native American music, such as the flute. During the week, they should learn more about the instruments from reading, studying pictures, listening to music, and talking with adults or older children. On Day 5 they will share what they learned. Guide children in brainstorming possible choices.

- Think about Native American music. What does a flute sound like? How is it made?

ELL

If... children need practice with phonics,
then... use the activities on p. DI•100 in the Teacher Resources section on SuccessNet.

Midsummer Fun

Midway through the summer, do you celebrate outdoors with picnics and cookouts? In Europe, people celebrate the summer solstice, or Midsummer.

During Midsummer, people celebrate warm weather. People dance, eat, and sing from dawn until dark. Storytellers with microphones tell folk tales to the large crowds. Then bonfires light up the midnight sky, and the fun goes on nonstop.

Sweden has one of the largest Midsummer celebrations. Many people wear traditional folk costumes. Adults and children hop around a tall pole, dancing the Frog Dance. Everyone laughs at small mishaps, like tripping or falling. Young ladies wear crowns of flowers. They have a custom of putting different flowers under their pillows on Midsummer Eve. They pick exactly seven! If they miscount, they won't see the man they will marry in their dreams.

Midsummer is also a time to eat delicious foods. Swedes eat the year's first potatoes and pickled fish at their midday meal. Fresh strawberries are ready to eat. No one skips dessert!

When the Midsummer festivals are over, people have to wait only a half-year to celebrate again. Then they will celebrate Midwinter festivals!

Advanced Selection 30 **Vocabulary:** solstice, mishaps

Advanced

Common Core State Standards

Literature 5. Describe the overall structure of a story, including describing how the beginning introduces the story and the ending concludes the action. **Literature 7.** Use information gained from the illustrations and words in a print or digital text to demonstrate understanding of its characters, setting, or plot. **Language 5.a.** Identify real-life connections between words and their use (e.g., describe foods that are *spicy* or *juicy*).

1 Build Word Knowledge

Extend Selection Vocabulary

assembly	election	microphone
rallies	slogan	speeches

Team Talk Have partners use the selection words in sentences to internalize their meanings. Have children use as many of the words as they can while making sure the sentence is grammatically correct. (Possible response: The mayor's supporters chanted his election slogan at the rallies.)

2 Read

Grace for President

If you read *Grace for President* during whole group time, then use the instruction below.

ACCESS TEXT Have children silently reread *Grace for President,* retell the selection and complete a plot map. (Beginning: Grace is shocked to find out no woman has ever been President of the United States. She decides to run for class president. Middle: Grace campaigns hard against Thomas Cobb. Thomas believes the boys' support will help him win. End: Grace wins the election.)

DISCUSS GENRE Discuss what makes *Grace for President* realistic fiction. Point out that the selection tells about made-up events that could happen in real life.

If you are reading *Grace for President* during small group time, then return to pp. 503a–519a to guide the reading.

3 Inquiry: Extend Concepts

INVESTIGATE Guide children in choosing materials at their independent reading levels.

LOOK AHEAD Help children choose formats to present their information, such as illustrated posters or audio samples.

Independent Reading Options

Trade Book Library

eStreet Interactive
www.ReadingStreet.com

Teacher's Guides available on the Leveled Reader Database.

Advanced

1 Build Word Knowledge

Develop Vocabulary

REREAD FOR VOCABULARY Have children reread *Grace for President* and make a two-column chart, listing words related to school and words related to an election.

School Vocabulary		Election Vocabulary	
desk	science fair	President	representative
students	teachers	democracy	campaign
class	studies	nominated	slogan
Elementary	gymnasium	candidate	issues
spelling bee		electoral votes	constituents

2 Read

Grace for President

If you read *Grace for President* during whole group time, then use the instruction below.

CLOSE READING Reread pp. 512–515 and look at the pictures. How were Thomas and Grace's campaigns similar? (They both made posters and buttons.) How were they different? (Grace campaigned hard. She gave speeches, handed out free cupcakes, and held rallies. Thomas continued to work on his other school projects and activities.) What important trait does Grace show the voters by joining the safety squad? (She follows through on her promises.)

If you are reading *Grace for President* during small group time, then return to pp. 503a–519a to guide the reading.

3 Inquiry: Extend Concepts

INVESTIGATE Give children time to investigate their projects on Native American musical instruments by reading, listening to music, and studying pictures. If necessary, help children make connections with instruments they have played or are familiar with and ones used by Native Americans.

SMALL GROUP TIME

If... children need more scaffolding and practice with the main selection, **then...** use the activities on p. DI•102 in the Teacher Resources section on SuccessNet.

Advanced

Common Core State Standards

Writing 7. Participate in shared research and writing projects (e.g., read a number of books on a single topic to produce a report; record science observations). **Speaking/ Listening 4.** Tell a story or recount an experience with appropriate facts and relevant, descriptive details, speaking audibly in coherent sentences. **Language 2.** Demonstrate command of the conventions of standard English capitalization, punctuation, and spelling when writing.

More Reading for Group Time

ADVANCED

- Extend Concept Vocabulary
- Review Target Skills

Use this suggested Leveled Reader or other text at children's instructional level.

eStreet Interactive
www.ReadingStreet.com

Use the Leveled Reader Database for lesson plans and student pages for *Happy New Year!*

1 Build Word Knowledge

Extend Amazing Words and Selection Vocabulary

ceremony	fidget
culture	evergreen
festival	multicolored
compliment	sash

assembly	election
microphone	rallies
slogan	speeches

Team Talk Have children ask each other questions using the Amazing Words and the Selection Vocabulary, such as: What are some ceremonies where people give speeches?

2 Text-Based Comprehension

READ ALOUD "A Few Words with a Big Effect" Have partners take turns reading paragraphs of "A Few Words with a Big Effect" from *Reading Street Sleuth* on pp. 76–77. Then have children read the selection independently.

ACCESS TEXT Guide children as they work on the Be a Sleuth section.

Look for Clues Have children make a three-column chart. Tell them to label the columns with the three purposes for slogans given in the story. Have children fill in the chart with slogans from the selection. Then identify other presidential slogans, such as Barack Obama's *Yes We Can!* or Ronald Reagan's *It's morning again in America,* and have children place them in the appropriate column.

Ask Questions Tell children to imagine they are a reporter working for the local newspaper. Have them write the questions they would ask a candidate for President.

Make Your Case Discuss slogans. What should a slogan be about? Is there anything candidates should not be able to say in slogans? Have children support their opinions with details.

3 Inquiry: Extend Concepts

ORGANIZE INFORMATION Give children time to continue reading and preparing information. Provide any necessary materials, such as poster board and art supplies.

Advanced

1 Build Word Knowledge

Commas in Compound Sentences

IDENTIFY COMMAS IN COMPOUND SENTENCES Have children identify the compound sentence in the selection "A Few Words with a Big Effect." Discuss the use of a comma and connecting words, such as *and, or,* and *but,* in compound sentences. Then have children combine two simple sentences from the selection or their own writing into a compound sentence.

2 Text-Based Comprehension

REREAD "A Few Words with a Big Effect" Have partners reread "A Few Words with a Big Effect."

EXTEND UNDERSTANDING Discuss the use of slogans for purposes other than elections. Point out that communities, organizations, and companies often use slogans to help people remember their products and services. If possible, display the motto or slogan used by your local community or an organization in the community. Discuss the meaning of the slogan.

PERFORMANCE TASK • Prove It! Remind children that slogans are also used to help gain support for causes other than elections. For example, a not-for-profit organization may have a slogan to help it raise awareness about a need in the community. Have pairs of children select a cause or an organization they would like to support. Tell them to write a short speech identifying the organization and its work. Have them develop a catchy slogan for their cause and create a poster with the slogan.

COMMUNICATE When the posters are completed, ask children to give their speeches and present their posters. Ask them to explain how they chose the slogans.

3 Inquiry: Extend Concepts

COMMUNICATE Have children share their inquiry projects about Native American musical instruments.

SMALL GROUP TIME

More Reading for Group Time

ADVANCED

- Extend Concept Vocabulary
- Review Target Skills

Use this suggested Leveled Reader or other text at children's instructional level.

eStreet Interactive
www.ReadingStreet.com

Use the Leveled Reader Database for lesson plans and student pages for *Happy New Year!*

TEACHER NOTES

Traditions

Are traditions and celebrations important in our lives?

During this week, you may wish to:

- ☑ Choose content to **review** based on progress monitoring
- ☑ Focus on **target skills** or use the **flexible plan** to adjust instruction
- ☑ Provide opportunities for interacting with texts by using **model text** in the *Reader's* and *Writer's Notebook*
- ☑ Develop children's understanding of genre and text structure using the **Strategy Response Log** in the *Reader's* and *Writer's Notebook*

DAY 1	DAY 2	DAY 3	DAY 4	DAY 5
REVIEW WEEK 1	REVIEW WEEK 2	REVIEW WEEK 3	REVIEW WEEK 4	REVIEW WEEK 5
Just Like Josh Gibson	*Red, White, and Blue: The Story of the American Flag*	*A Birthday Basket for Tía*	*Cowboys*	*Grace for President*
Why are sports traditions important in our country?	What traditions and celebrations involve our country's flag?	Why are family celebrations special?	What can we learn about cowboy traditions?	How are different traditions celebrated and shared?
• **Amazing Words** athlete, *challenge*, *effort*, *dainty*, *disguise*, *champion*, *professional*, *shortstop*	• **Amazing Words** *history*, *independence*, *symbol*, *patriotic*, *unfurl*, *frayed*, *allegiance*, *indivisible*	• **Amazing Words** *celebration*, *custom*, *tradition*, *create*, *inspect*, *angle*, *brilliant*, *snapshot*	• **Amazing Words** *climate*, *livestock*, *occupation*, *buckaroo*, *drover*, *lariat*, *legend*, *rawhide*	• **Amazing Words** *ceremony*, *culture*, *festival*, *compliment*, *fidget*, *evergreen*, *multicolored*, *sash*
Text-Based Comprehension Compare and Contrast; Monitor and Clarify	**Text-Based Comprehension** Author's Purpose; Summarize	**Text-Based Comprehension** Draw Conclusions; Questioning	**Text-Based Comprehension** Sequence; Text Structure	**Text-Based Comprehension** Facts and Details; Predict and Set Purpose
Phonics Inflected Endings	**Phonics** Abbreviations	**Phonics** Final Syllables *-tion*, *-ture*, *-ion*	**Phonics** Suffixes *-ness*, *-less*, *-able*, *-ible*	**Phonics** Prefixes *mis-*, *mid-*, *micro-*, *non-*
Vocabulary Homophones; Context Clues	**Vocabulary** Multiple-Meaning Words; Context Clues	**Vocabulary** Words from Other Languages; Context Clues	**Vocabulary** Unfamiliar Words; Context Clues	**Vocabulary** Multiple-Meaning Words; Dictionary/ Glossary
• **Fluency** Accuracy and Appropriate Rate	• **Fluency** Accuracy	• **Fluency** Appropriate Phrasing	• **Fluency** Accuracy and Appropriate Rate	• **Fluency** Appropriate Phrasing
• **Conventions** Using Capital Letters	• **Conventions** Quotation Marks	• **Conventions** Prepositions and Prepositional Phrases	• **Conventions** Commas	• **Conventions** Commas in Compound Sentences
• **Spelling** Inflected Endings	• **Spelling** Abbreviations	• **Spelling** Final Syllables *-tion*, *-ture*, *-ion*	• **Spelling** Suffixes *-ness*, *-less*, *-able*, *-ible*	• **Spelling** Prefixes *mis-*, *mid-*, *micro-*, *non-*

Preview Your Week

Are traditions and celebrations important in our lives?

DAY 1

Student Edition, pp. 368–369

Genre: Realistic Fiction
Phonics: Inflected Endings
Text-Based Comprehension: Compare and Contrast

DAY 2

Student Edition, pp. 400–401

Genre: Informational Text
Phonics: Abbreviations
Text-Based Comprehension: Author's Purpose

DAY 3

Student Edition, pp. 434–435

Genre: Realistic Fiction
Phonics: Final Syllables *-tion, -ture, -ion*
Text-Based Comprehension: Draw Conclusions

DAY 4

Student Edition, pp. 466–467

Genre: Informational Text
Phonics: Suffixes *-ness, -less, -able, -ible*
Text-Based Comprehension: Sequence

DAY 5

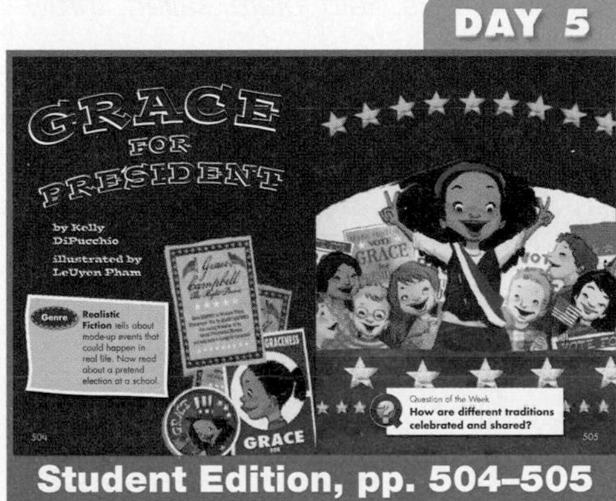

Student Edition, pp. 504–505

Genre: Realistic Fiction
Phonics: Prefixes *mis-, mid-, micro-, non-*
Text-Based Comprehension: Facts and Details

Reinforce Content Knowledge

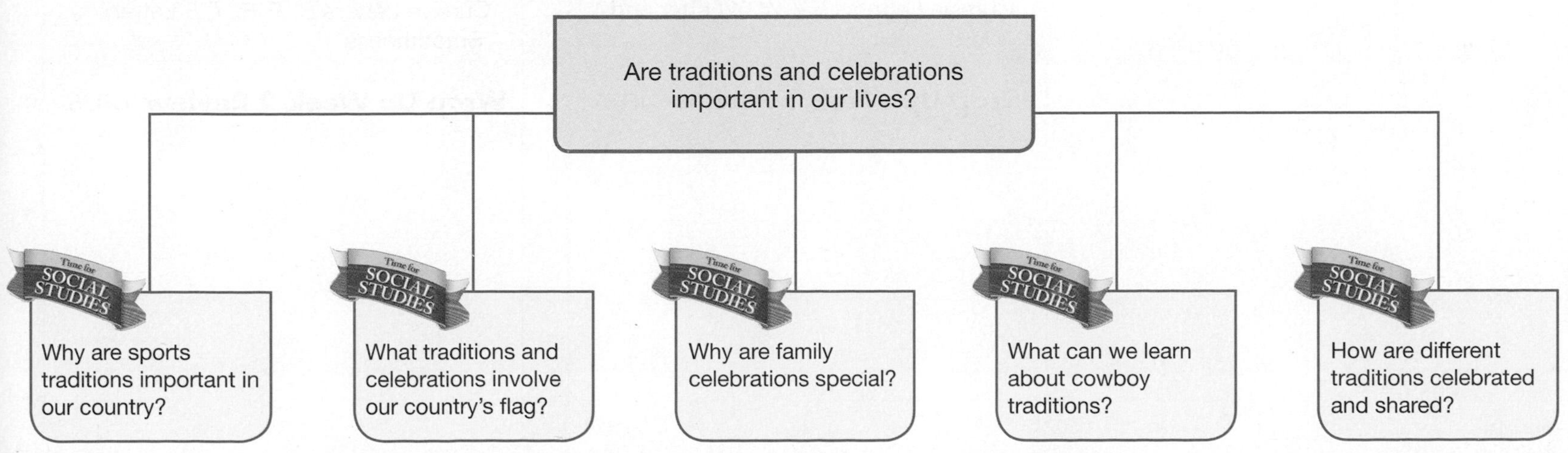

5-Day Planner

DAY 1 Review Week 1

Get Ready to Read

Content Knowledge UR6
Oral Vocabulary: *athlete, challenge, effort, dainty, disguise, champion, professional, shortstop*

Phonics UR8
Inflected Endings

Spelling UR9
Inflected Endings

Read and Comprehend

Selection Words UR10
bases, cheers, field, plate, sailed, threw

Vocabulary Skill UR10
Homophones

Text-Based Comprehension UR11–13
Compare and Contrast

Fluency UR13
Read with Accuracy and Appropriate Rate

Language Arts

Conventions UR14
Using Capital Letters

Handwriting UR14
Cursive Letters *U, V, W, Y*/Letter and Word Spacing

Wrap Up Week 1 Review UR15

DAY 2 Review Week 2

Get Ready to Read

Content Knowledge UR16
Oral Vocabulary: *history, independence, symbol, patriotic, unfurl, frayed, allegiance, indivisible*

Phonics UR18
Abbreviations

Spelling UR19
Abbreviations

Read and Comprehend

Selection Words UR20
America, birthday, flag, freedom, nicknames, stars, stripes

Vocabulary Skill UR20
Multiple-Meaning Words

Text-Based Comprehension UR21–23
Author's Purpose

Fluency UR23
Read with Accuracy

Language Arts

Conventions UR24
Quotation Marks

Handwriting UR24
Cursive Letters *B, P, R, T, F*/Letter Smoothness

Wrap Up Week 2 Review UR25

DAY 3 Review Week 3

Get Ready to Read

Content Knowledge UR26
Oral Vocabulary: *celebration, custom, tradition, create, inspect, angle, brilliant, snapshot*

Phonics UR28
Final Syllables *-tion, -ture, -ion*

Spelling UR29
Final Syllables *-tion, -ture*

Read and Comprehend

Selection Words UR30
aunt, bank, basket, collects, favorite, present

Vocabulary Skill UR30
Words from Other Languages

Text-Based Comprehension UR31–33
Draw Conclusions

Fluency UR33
Read with Appropriate Phrasing

Language Arts

Conventions UR34
Prepositions and Prepositional Phrases

Handwriting UR34
Cursive Letters *G, S, I*/Letter Size

Wrap Up Week 3 Review UR35

DAY 4 Review Week 4

Get Ready to Read

Content Knowledge UR36
Oral Vocabulary: *climate, livestock, occupation, buckaroo, drover, lariat, legend, rawhide*

Phonics UR38
Suffixes *-ness, -less, -able, -ible*

Spelling UR39
Suffixes *-ness, -less*

Read and Comprehend

Selection Words UR40
campfire, cattle, cowboy, galloped, herd, railroad, trails

Vocabulary Skill UR40
Unfamiliar Words

Text-Based Comprehension UR41–43
Sequence

Fluency UR43
Read with Accuracy and Appropriate Rate

Language Arts

Conventions UR44
Commas

Handwriting UR44
Cursive Letters *Z, Q, X*/Letter Slant

Wrap Up Week 4 Review UR45

DAY 5 Review Week 5

Get Ready to Read

Content Knowledge UR46
Oral Vocabulary: *ceremony, culture, festival, compliment, fidget, evergreen, multicolored, sash*

Phonics UR48
Prefixes *mis-, mid-, micro-, non-*

Spelling UR49
Prefixes *mis-, mid-*

Read and Comprehend

Selection Words UR50
assembly, election, microphone, rallies, slogan, speeches

Vocabulary Skill UR50
Multiple-Meaning Words

Text-Based Comprehension UR51–53
Facts and Details

Fluency UR53
Read with Appropriate Phrasing

Language Arts

Conventions UR54
Commas in Compound Sentences

Handwriting UR54
Cursive Letters *L, D, J*/Letter and Word Spacing

Wrap Up Week 5 Review UR55

Access for All

Small Group Lesson Plan

★ Focus on these activities when time is limited.

	DAY 1 Review Week 1	DAY 2 Review Week 2
	pages UR6–UR15	pages UR16–UR25
OL On-Level	**Review** ★ • Inflected Endings • Spelling • Homophones ★ • Compare and Contrast ★ • Monitor and Clarify ★ • Using Capital Letters	**Review** ★ • Abbreviations • Spelling • Multiple-Meaning Words ★ • Author's Purpose ★ • Summarize ★ • Quotation Marks
SI Strategic Intervention	**Reteach and Review** • Content Knowledge • Oral Vocabulary ★ • Inflected Endings • Spelling ★ • Selection Words • Homophones ★ • Compare and Contrast ★ • Monitor and Clarify • Read with Accuracy and Appropriate Rate ★ • Using Capital Letters • Cursive Letters *U, V, W, Y*/Letter and Word Spacing	**Reteach and Review** • Content Knowledge • Oral Vocabulary ★ • Abbreviations • Spelling ★ • Selection Words • Multiple-Meaning Words ★ • Author's Purpose ★ • Summarize • Read with Accuracy ★ • Quotation Marks • Cursive Letters *B, P, R, T, F*/Letter Smoothness
A Advanced	**Extend** ★ • Inflected Endings ★ • Compare and Contrast ★ • Monitor and Clarify	**Extend** ★ • Abbreviations ★ • Author's Purpose ★ • Summarize
ELL	**Reteach and Review** • Content Knowledge • Oral Vocabulary ★ • Inflected Endings ★ • Selection Words • Homophones ★ • Compare and Contrast ★ • Monitor and Clarify • Read with Accuracy and Appropriate Rate ★ • Using Capital Letters	**Reteach and Review** • Content Knowledge • Oral Vocabulary ★ • Abbreviations ★ • Selection Words • Multiple-Meaning Words ★ • Author's Purpose ★ • Summarize • Read with Accuracy ★ • Quotation Marks

DAY 3 Review Week 3	DAY 4 Review Week 4	DAY 5 Review Week 5
pages UR26–UR35	pages UR36–UR45	pages UR46–UR55
Review ★• Final Syllables *-tion, -ture, -ion* • Spelling • Words from Other Languages ★• Draw Conclusions ★• Questioning ★• Prepositions and Prepositional Phrases	**Review** ★• Suffixes *-ness, -less, -able, -ible* • Spelling • Unfamiliar Words ★• Sequence ★• Text Structure ★• Commas	**Review** ★• Prefixes *mis-, mid-, micro-, non-* • Spelling • Multiple-Meaning Words ★• Facts and Details ★• Predict and Set Purpose ★• Commas in Compound Sentences
Reteach and Review • Content Knowledge • Oral Vocabulary ★• Final Syllables *-tion, -ture, -ion* • Spelling ★• Selection Words • Words from Other Languages ★• Draw Conclusions ★• Questioning • Read with Appropriate Phrasing ★• Prepositions and Prepositional Phrases • Cursive Letters *G, S, I*/Letter Size	**Reteach and Review** • Content Knowledge • Oral Vocabulary ★• Suffixes *-ness, -less, -able, -ible* • Spelling ★• Selection Words • Unfamiliar Words ★• Sequence ★• Text Structure • Read with Accuracy and Appropriate Rate ★• Commas • Cursive Letters *Z, Q, X*/Letter Slant	**Reteach and Review** • Content Knowledge • Oral Vocabulary ★• Prefixes *mis-, mid-, micro-, non-* • Spelling ★• Selection Words • Multiple-Meaning Words ★• Facts and Details ★• Predict and Set Purpose • Read with Appropriate Phrasing ★• Commas in Compound Sentences • Cursive Letters *L, D, J*/Letter and Word Spacing
Extend ★• Final Syllables *-tion, -ture, -ion* ★• Draw Conclusions ★• Questioning	**Extend** ★• Suffixes *-ness, -less, -able, -ible* ★• Sequence ★• Text Structure	**Extend** ★• Prefixes *mis-, mid-, micro-, non-* ★• Facts and Details ★• Predict and Set Purpose
Reteach and Review • Content Knowledge • Oral Vocabulary ★• Final Syllables *-tion, -ture, -ion* ★• Selection Words • Words from Other Languages ★• Draw Conclusions ★• Questioning • Read with Appropriate Phrasing ★• Prepositions and Prepositional Phrases	**Reteach and Review** • Content Knowledge • Oral Vocabulary ★• Suffixes *-ness, -less, -able, -ible* ★• Selection Words • Unfamiliar Words ★• Sequence ★• Text Structure • Read with Accuracy and Appropriate Rate ★• Commas	**Reteach and Review** • Content Knowledge • Oral Vocabulary ★• Prefixes *mis-, mid-, micro-, non-* ★• Selection Words • Multiple-Meaning Words ★• Facts and Details ★• Predict and Set Purpose • Read with Appropriate Phrasing ★• Commas in Compound Sentences

Review Week 1

Content Knowledge
Review Oral Vocabulary

Phonics/Spelling
Review ◎ Inflected Endings

Selection Vocabulary
Review *bases, cheers, field, plate, sailed, threw*

Vocabulary
Review ◎ Homophones

Text-Based Comprehension
Review ◎ Compare and Contrast
Review ◎ Monitor and Clarify

Fluency
Read with Accuracy and Appropriate Rate

Conventions
Review Using Capital Letters

Handwriting
Review Cursive Letters/Letter and Word Spacing

Writing
Quick Write for Fluency

Materials

- Sing with Me Big Book
- Sound-Spelling Cards
- Reader's and Writer's Notebook

Common Core State Standards

Speaking/Listening 1. Participate in collaborative conversations with diverse partners about grade 2 topics and texts with peers and adults in small and larger groups. **Language 5.a.** Identify real-life connections between words and their use (e.g., describe foods that are *spicy* or *juicy*). **Also Language 6.**

Content Knowledge

Sports Traditions

REVISIT THE CONCEPT Today children will explore how the Question of the Week connects to *Just Like Josh Gibson.* Read the Question of the Week: *Why are sports traditions important in our country?* Remind children that *Just Like Josh Gibson* is realistic fiction about a young girl who wants to be like her sports hero, Josh Gibson.

Build Oral Language

TALK ABOUT SPORTS TRADITIONS Use these questions to connect the Week 1 question and selection to the Unit 6 Big Question, **Are traditions and celebrations important in our lives?**

- Why was the tradition of baseball important to Grandmama?
- What would you have done if you saw Grandmama watching you play?
- What sports traditions are important to you?

Build Oral Vocabulary

REVIEW AMAZING WORDS Remind children that they have learned some Amazing Words that they can use to answer the question *Why are sports traditions important in our country?* Display "An Athlete's Challenge" on p. 26 of the *Sing with Me* Big Book. Sing the song.

Go over all the Amazing Words from Week 1. Ask children to listen as you say them: *athlete, challenge, effort, dainty, disguise, champion, professional, shortstop.* Then say them again, and have children say each word after you.

- How would you describe a lace handkerchief—*dainty* or *professional?* (dainty)
- Which word is a position on a baseball team? (shortstop)
- What might you use as a *disguise?* (a mask, costume)

AMAZING WORDS AT WORK Have children demonstrate their understanding of Amazing Words by completing these sentences orally.

Amy has a **dainty** ______.

The **shortstop** made a great effort to catch the ______.

The ______ said he would **challenge** the **champion.**

Max wore a **disguise** to ______.

Molly is a ______ **athlete.**

Sam wants to be a **professional** ______ when he grows up.

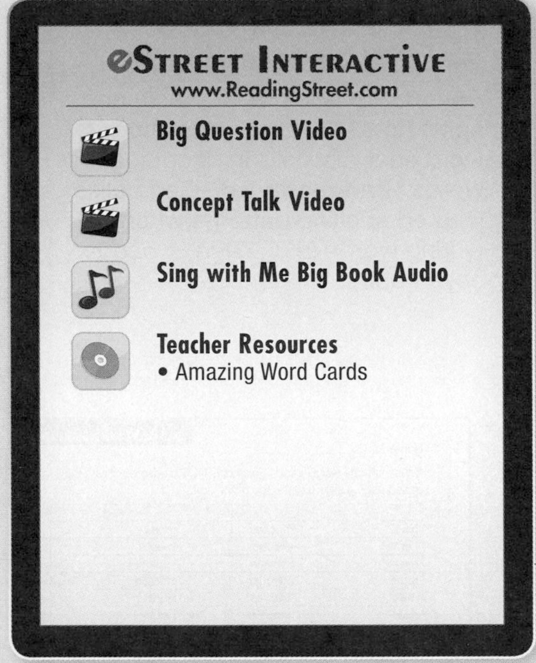

Amazing Words

athlete	disguise
challenge	champion
effort	professional
dainty	shortstop

Access for All

SI Strategic Intervention

Extend Amazing Words Before answering the questions about the Amazing Words, have children review the meaning of the words. Have children work in pairs or small groups to come up with a definition or example of each of the Amazing Words.

Reteach Concepts and Vocabulary Use the instruction on ELL Poster 26 to assess knowledge and concepts.

Common Core State Standards

Foundational Skills 3. Know and apply grade-level phonics and word analysis skills in decoding words. **Language 2.d.** Generalize learned spelling patterns when writing words (e.g., *cage* → *badge; boy* → *boil*).

Name ______ | Unit 6 Week 1 Interactive Review

Cross off any word in each box that is NOT a base word with the added ending shown at the top of the box.

-s	-es	-ed
~~his~~	reaches	~~red~~
hers	~~cheese~~	sailed
~~mess~~	presses	pointed
birds	punches	rested
walks	dresses	~~bed~~
~~does~~	~~lessons~~	~~cricket~~

-ing	-er	-est
talking	teacher	tallest
~~ring~~	~~another~~	~~west~~
~~string~~	shorter	fastest
ringing	~~banner~~	~~best~~
playing	lower	smartest
drinking	lighter	longest

Read the story.

The tallest boy in our class is David. He is also the smartest. One day David was playing in the schoolyard. He did not want to share the basketball. He just wanted to shoot baskets by himself. Then David tripped. He fell and scraped his knee. His pants were ripped. David didn't feel smarter than the rest of us then. We helped him up. We all played basketball. Sometimes it's better to have friends than to be the smartest one in school. Now David knows this too.

School + Home **Home Activity** Your child identified base words and endings -s, -es, -ing, -er, and -est. Have your child make up four sentences using the words talk, talks, talked, and talking. Check your child's work to make sure each word is used correctly in each sentence.

Phonics 541

Reader's and Writer's Notebook, p. 541

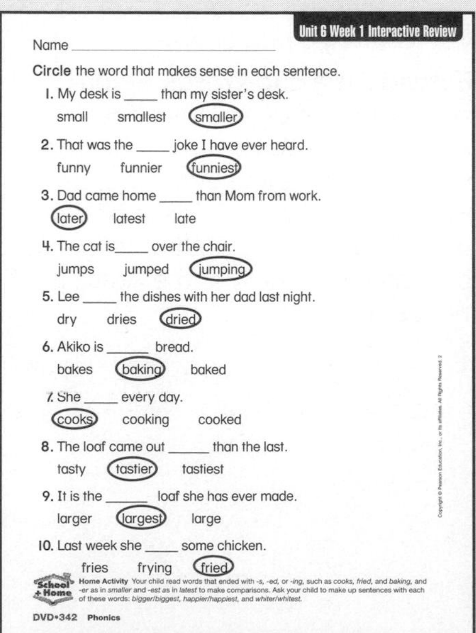
Name ______ | Unit 6 Week 1 Interactive Review

Circle the word that makes sense in each sentence.

1. My desk is ____ than my sister's desk.
   small smallest (smaller)
2. That was the ____ joke I have ever heard.
   funny funnier (funniest)
3. Dad came home ____ than Mom from work.
   (later) latest late
4. The cat is ____ over the chair.
   jumps jumped (jumping)
5. Lee ____ the dishes with her dad last night.
   dry dries (dried)
6. Akiko is ____ bread.
   bakes (baking) baked
7. She ____ every day.
   (cooks) cooking cooked
8. The loaf came out ____ than the last.
   tasty (tastier) tastiest
9. It is the ____ loaf she has ever made.
   larger (largest) large
10. Last week she ____ some chicken.
    fries frying (fried)

School + Home **Home Activity** Your child read words that ended with -s, -ed, or -ing, such as cooks, fried, and baking, and -er as in smaller and -est as in latest to make comparisons. Ask your child to make up sentences with each of these words: bigger/biggest, happier/happiest, and whiter/whitest.

DVD•342 Phonics

Let's Practice It! TR DVD•342

Phonics

Review Inflected Endings

TARGET PHONICS SKILLS Review inflected endings using Sound-Spelling Cards 118, 123, 124, 125, 126, and 129.

DECODE WORDS IN ISOLATION Use *Reader's and Writer's Notebook,* page 541. Point out that children know how to decode these words. Then tell children they will all read the words in each row together. Allow several seconds previewing time for the first reading.

Corrective feedback | **If...** children cannot decode all the words in a row consecutively without an error, **then...** return to the first word in the row, and have children reread all the words in the row. Repeat until children can read the words fluently.

DECODE WORDS IN CONTEXT Use the passage on *Reader's and Writer's Notebook,* page 541. Point out that there are many words with inflected endings in the passage that children already know how to decode. Have children read the passage together.

Corrective feedback | **If...** children have difficulty decoding words with inflected endings, **then...** guide them in chunking multisyllabic words and using sound-by-sound blending. Have children read each sentence. Repeat until children can read the sentences fluently.

ON THEIR OWN Use Let's Practice It!, p. 342 on the *Teacher Resources DVD-ROM.*

Spelling

Review Inflected Endings

SPELLING WORDS Write *tried, trying, planned, planning, liked, liking, heavier, heaviest, lighter,* and *lightest.* Point out that these words have inflected endings. Review the spelling changes made to some of the base words before the ending was added, such as changing *y* to *i,* doubling the final consonant, and dropping the final *e.* Remind children that they learned how to spell words with these inflected endings. Use Sound-Spelling Cards 118–123 and 125–128 to review words with inflected endings. Review the Week 1 spelling words.

Team Talk Have children review the spelling words using the index cards on which the words are written. Tell them to sort the words into the ones they know and the ones they need more practice with. Partners can quiz each other on the words in the second pile.

ON THEIR OWN Use *Reader's and Writer's Notebook,* p. 542.

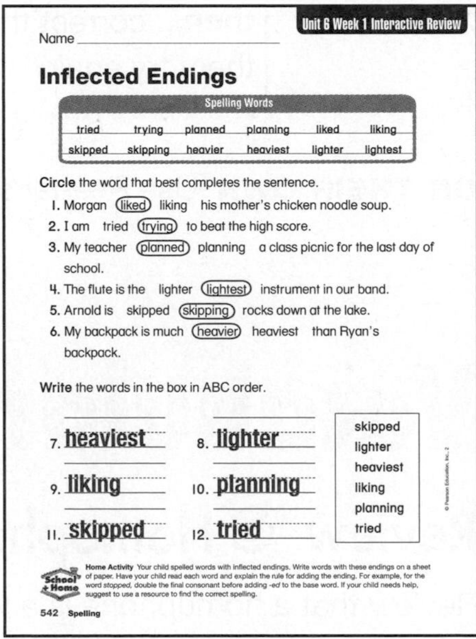

Unit 6 Week 1 Interactive Review

Name ____________

Inflected Endings

Spelling Words					
tried	trying	planned	planning	liked	liking
skipped	skipping	heavier	heaviest	lighter	lightest

Circle the word that best completes the sentence.

1. Morgan (liked) liking his mother's chicken noodle soup.
2. I am tried (trying) to beat the high score.
3. My teacher (planned) planning a class picnic for the last day of school.
4. The flute is the lighter (lightest) instrument in our band.
5. Arnold is skipped (skipping) rocks down at the lake.
6. My backpack is much (heavier) heaviest than Ryan's backpack.

Write the words in the box in ABC order.

7. heaviest 8. lighter
9. liking 10. planning
11. skipped 12. tried

skipped
lighter
heaviest
liking
planning
tried

School + Home **Home Activity** Your child spelled words with inflected endings. Write words with these endings on a sheet of paper. Have your child read each word and explain the rule for adding the ending. For example, for the word *stopped,* double the final consonant before adding *-ed* to the base word. If your child needs help, suggest to use a resource to find the correct spelling.

542 Spelling

Reader's and Writer's Notebook, p. 542

Unit 6 Week 1 Spelling Words

Inflected Endings

1. tried	7. skipped
2. trying	8. skipping
3. planned	9. heavier
4. planning	10. heaviest
5. liked	11. lighter
6. liking	12. lightest

Review Inflected Endings Remind children of the spelling-change patterns for words with inflected endings, including doubling consonants, dropping *e,* and changing *y* to *i.*

Beginning Write and read a list of words with inflected endings, such as *skipped, hiking, cried, braver,* and *hottest.* Circle the ending and discuss the spelling-change pattern. Write the base word underneath. Have children write the base words and the words with inflected endings. Have them read the word pairs with a partner.

Intermediate Have children sort words with inflected endings according to the spelling-change pattern. Then have them read the sorted words to a partner.

Advanced Have children name the spelling-change patterns for words with inflected endings. Have partners identify, write, and read at least three words containing each spelling-change pattern.

Common Core State Standards

Language 5. Demonstrate understanding of word relationships and nuances in word meanings. **Also Language 4.a.**

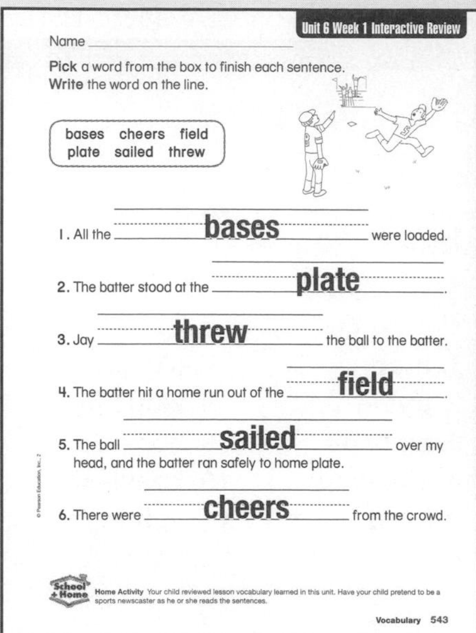

Unit 6 Week 1 Interactive Review

Name ______

Pick a word from the box to finish each sentence. **Write** the word on the line.

bases	cheers	field
plate	sailed	threw

1. All the **bases** were loaded.
2. The batter stood at the **plate**.
3. Jay **threw** the ball to the batter.
4. The batter hit a home run out of the **field**.
5. The ball **sailed** over my head, and the batter ran safely to home plate.
6. There were **cheers** from the crowd.

School + Home — Home Activity Your child reviewed lesson vocabulary learned in this unit. Have your child pretend to be a sports newscaster as he or she reads the sentences.

Vocabulary 543

Reader's and Writer's Notebook, p. 543

Selection Vocabulary

REVIEW READ WORDS IN ISOLATION Display the selection vocabulary. Have children read the words aloud with you. Review the definitions.

bases—places that are stations or goals in certain games, such as baseball
cheers—yells of encouragement
field—a piece of land used for some special purpose
plate—a hard rubber slab that a baseball player stands beside to bat
sailed—moved smoothly like a ship with sails
threw—sent something through the air by force of your arm

GUIDE PRACTICE Have children use each word in a sentence.

Corrective feedback	**If...** children do not use a word correctly, **then...** correct the sentence, model a sentence, and have them try again.

ON THEIR OWN Use *Reader's and Writer's Notebook,* page 543.

Vocabulary Skill

Review Homophones

Review that a homophone is a word that is pronounced the same as one or more other words but is different in meaning and spelling. An example of a pair of homophones is *hair* and *hare.*

- Which lesson vocabulary word has a homophone? *(threw)*
- What word is a homophone for *threw,* and what does it mean? (*through*—it means "among.")

Team Talk **GUIDE PRACTICE** Have children name and spell other homophones. Discuss the definitions. Have children work together to come up with a sentence that uses a pair of homophones.

Zoom in on

Text-Based Comprehension

REVIEW COMPARE AND CONTRAST Review that *compare* means "to explain how things are alike" and *contrast* means "to explain how things are different." Remind children that they know how to compare and contrast characters, settings, and plots. Recall that they compared and contrasted the characters and stories when they read *Just Like Josh Gibson* and *The Princesses Have a Ball.*

REVIEW MONITOR AND CLARIFY Remind children that good readers monitor their comprehension and clarify as they read. To monitor, check your understanding of words and ideas as you read. If you don't understand a word or an idea, look for ways to adjust your comprehension and clarify what you read. You might reread the part of the story that doesn't make sense. You also might look at the pictures.

REALISTIC FICTION Remind children that **realistic fiction** is a make-believe story that has made up characters and events but could happen in real life. In a realistic fiction story, the setting and characters seem real. It tells about problems people may have in real life.

PREVIEW AND PREDICT Have children read the title of the selection on p. 544 of *Reader's and Writer's Notebook.* Have children look through the selection and use the title to predict events that might happen in the story. Tell them this selection is realistic fiction.

SET A PURPOSE After we read "The Gift of Giving," we will compare and contrast characters and events in the story. Have children set a purpose for reading "The Gift of Giving."

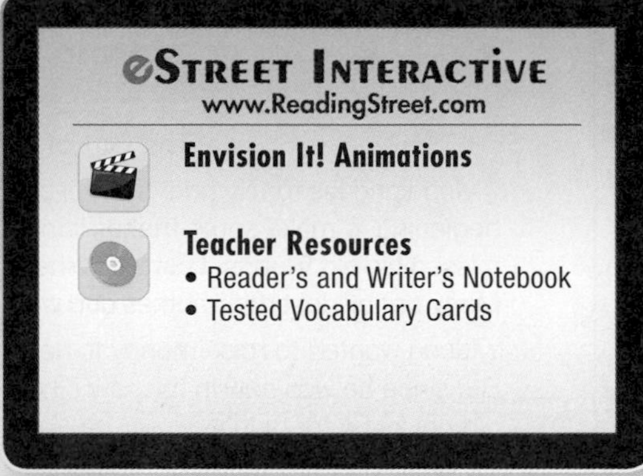

Access for All

 Advanced

Extend Compare/Contrast After reviewing the meanings of *compare* and *contrast,* have partners discuss how their favorite books are alike and different. Then have children record their thoughts using a Venn diagram.

Academic Vocabulary 

realistic fiction a story of imaginary people and events that could happen in real life.

Unit 6 Week 1 Interactive Review

Name ____________________

Read the story.
Answer the questions.

Help the Flood Victims

The Gift of Giving

Juan and his family had just moved to a new town. Juan was beginning to make some friends in his new neighborhood, but he missed his old friends. Last week there was a flood in his old town. Many people lost their homes and were living in tents in open fields.

Juan wanted to raise money to help the people in his old town. But since he was new in this town, he felt strange asking people he did not know for help.

"How can I ask them for money?" he asked his mother.

"It is not easy, but you will find that most people will want to help," she said. "First, you must make a plan. I will help you find a place where the money will do the most good."

Juan still felt strange, but he wanted to try to do something to help the flood victims. He and his sister Maria decided to go to stores in the neighborhood. The first stop was Flynn's Food Store.

"What can I do for you?" asked Mr. Flynn.

"Well, we're not here to buy anything, but we'd like to ask you something. Would you like to help the people that were hurt by the flood?" Juan asked. Then he explained to Mr. Flynn what his plan was.

"If a young man like yourself can do something like this, I want to do the same," Mr. Flynn exclaimed. "How about we work together?"

"Sure!" cheered Juan.

Home Activity Your child compared and contrasted characters in the story. Make a list with your child of ways people can help others in need. Compare and contrast the different ways.

544 **Comprehension**

Unit 6 Week 1 Interactive Review

Name ____________________

Mr. Flynn and Juan threw a party to raise money for the people in the flood area. Many of Mr. Flynn's customers offered money. Others offered clothing and canned food.

"I am so proud of you," Juan's mother cried. "I never told you, but when I was a little girl, a hurricane destroyed our home. We had nothing but the clothes we were wearing. We had nowhere to go, and little food and water. People around the world heard about the hurricane and sent food and medicine. So you see, many people help others without thinking about themselves. You have done just that!"

1. How are Juan and Mr. Flynn alike? **Possible answers:**

   They both want to help collect money for the people in the flood area.

2. How is what Juan is doing different than something his mother did when she was a child?

   Juan is collecting money to help people in a flood area. Juan's mother received help after a hurricane.

3. What is a way Juan's mother says people are alike?

   Many people like to help others in need.

Comprehension 545

Reader's and Writer's Notebook, pp. 544–545

Common Core State Standards

Literature 7. Use information gained from the illustrations and words in a print or digital text to demonstrate understanding of its characters, setting, or plot. **Foundational Skills 4.b.** Read on-level text orally with accuracy, appropriate rate, and expression on successive readings.

Access Text

Review Compare and Contrast

Have children read the story and respond to the questions.

Corrective feedback	**If...** children have difficulty responding to the questions, **then...** use the following to guide their responses.

1. Who is Juan and what does he want to do? Who is Mr. Flynn and how does he help Juan? Have children find the sentences that tell what Juan and Mr. Flynn both want to do.
2. What does Juan do to help the flood victims? What happened to Juan's mother when she was a girl? How was she helped? Have children find the sentences that tell what Juan is doing to help and how his mother was helped when she was a girl.
3. What does Juan's mother say about people who help? Have children find the sentence that tells what Juan's mother says many people do.

REVIEW MONITOR AND CLARIFY Discuss the comprehension tools that children used as they read "The Gift of Giving." What questions did you ask yourself as you read? Did you find answers to your questions in the story? Have children tell what questions they asked as they read, and whether they reread parts of the story to find answers.

Reread for Fluency

MODEL FLUENT READING Remind children that when they read, it is important to pay attention to each word, read with no mistakes, and read at an appropriate rate. Model reading the first two paragraphs of "The Gift of Giving" on *Reader's and Writer's Notebook,* page 544 with accuracy and at an appropriate rate. Have children track the print as you read.

GUIDE PRACTICE To provide additional fluency practice, pair children and have them read "The Gift of Giving."

Routine Paired Reading

1. **Reader 1 Begins** Children read the story, switching readers at the end of each paragraph.
2. **Reader 2 Begins** Have partners reread; this time the other partner begins.
3. **Reread** For optimal fluency, children should reread three or four times.
4. **Corrective Feedback** Listen to children read and provide corrective feedback regarding their oral reading and their use of the blending strategy.

Routines Flip Chart

Access for All

SI Strategic Intervention

Comprehension and Fluency Have children reread "The Gift of Giving" aloud. Have them think about how the characters are alike and different as they read. After children have read the story, have them tell about a time they helped other people.

Options for Oral Rereading

Use *Just Like Josh Gibson* or a leveled reader.

Common Core State Standards

Language 2. Demonstrate command of the conventions of standard English capitalization, punctuation, and spelling when writing. **Speaking/Listening 1.** Participate in collaborative conversations with diverse partners about grade 2 topics and texts with peers and adults in small and larger groups. **Also Language 2.a.**

Name

Unit 6 Week 1 Interactive Review

Using Capital Letters

Find the words that need capital letters. **Write** the words correctly on the line.

1. july and august are two summer months when baseball is played.

   July, August

2. Many games are played on saturday and sunday.

   Saturday, Sunday

3. dr. Shea and ms. Wallace took me to a Chicago Cubs game.

   Dr., Ms.

Underline the words that need capital letters. **Write** the words you underlined.

4. We went to the game on labor day. **Labor Day**
5. The game was on a monday. **Monday**
6. We saw mr. Ernie Banks there. **Mr.**

546 Conventions

Reader's and Writer's Notebook, p. 546

Name

Unit 6 Interactive Review

Day 1 Unit 6 Week 1 — Just Like Josh Gibson

Copy the sentences. Make sure your letters and words are spaced correctly.

We won't go to Vienna.

Check children's letters and words for correct spacing.

You don't know Uncle Will.

Day 2 Unit 6 Week 2 — Red, White, and Blue

Copy the sentences. Make sure your letters are written smoothly.

Beth and Pam like shopping.

Check children's letters for smoothness.

Rob hiked the Forest Trail.

Home Activity Your child practiced writing all cursive letters. Each day have your child copy a sentence from a favorite storybook using his or her best cursive handwriting.

Handwriting 547

Reader's and Writer's Notebook, pp. 547–548

Conventions

Review Using Capital Letters

Remind children that sentences begin with a capital letter. Say that certain words also start with a capital letter, including names, initials, holidays, days, months, titles (of people, books, poems, and songs), and the word *I*.

GUIDE PRACTICE Write the following sentences. Have children identify and correct the words that need a capital letter. Have them explain the reason for each capital letter.

> Last september uncle george and i went fishing on labor day.
> mr. sunomo is marcell's teacher at pleasant hill elementary school.
> on saturday, mike and i will play at simmons park.

Team Talk Have children write a sentence telling about an activity that happened during the day. Tell them to omit capital letters. Then pair children and have them exchange sentences for correction.

ON THEIR OWN Use *Reader's and Writer's Notebook,* page 546.

Handwriting

REVIEW CURSIVE LETTERS Demonstrate the proper formation of cursive letters *U, V, W,* and *Y.* Then review all lowercase letters. Have children write each capital letter several times and circle the best one. Then have them write each lowercase letter.

REVIEW LETTER AND WORD SPACING Remind children to insert the same amount of space between each letter in a word and to leave larger spaces between words.

GUIDE PRACTICE Write the following sentence. Have children copy it using appropriate letter spacing. Monitor children's spacing of words as they write. If children have not transitioned to cursive, have them write the words in manuscript.

> **We just visited Uncle Yogi, who lives in West Virginia.**

ON THEIR OWN Use the Day 1 section on *Reader's and Writer's Notebook,* pages 547–548.

Optional Unit Review

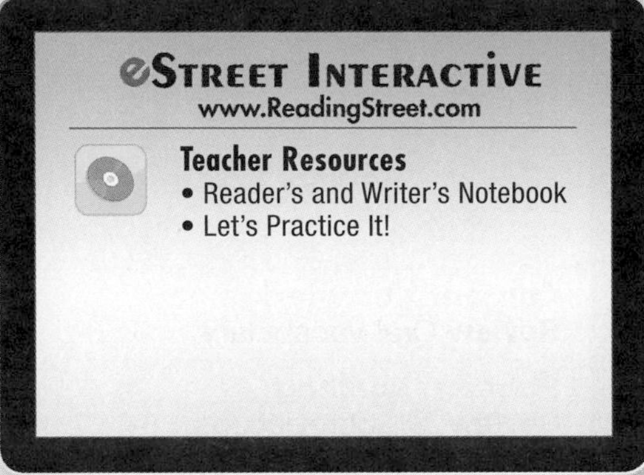

Routine Quick Write for Fluency

Team Talk

1. **Talk** Have pairs discuss what they learned about why sports traditions are important in our country.
2. **Write** Have children write a few sentences to summarize the discussion.
3. **Share** Partners can read their summaries to one another.

Routines Flip Chart

Writing Workshop

Use the writing process lesson on pages WP•1–WP•10 for this week's writing instruction.

ELL

Extend Amazing Words Tell children that the word *challenge* can mean "to test someone's abilities," such as *It is a challenge for a person to run twenty-six miles in a marathon race. Challenge* can also mean "to ask or take part in a contest."

Wrap Up Week 1 Review

- ✔ **Content Knowledge** Why do you think sports traditions are important? Which sports tradition is important to you? Why do you think so many Americans enjoy watching one team challenge another team?
- ✔ **Compare and Contrast** Look back at "The Gift of Giving." How are Juan and Mr. Flynn alike? How are they different? How are baseball and football alike? How are they different?
- ✔ **Homophones** What is a homophone? What are the definitions of *for* and *four?* Tell a sentence that uses these words. What are the definitions of *by* and *buy?* Tell a sentence that uses these words.
- ✔ **Homework** Send home this week's Family Times Newsletter on *Let's Practice It!*, pp. 283–284 on the *Teacher Resources DVD-ROM.*

Unit 6 Interactive Review
Name
Family Times
You are your child's first and best teacher!
This week we're
Reviewing Just Like Josh Gibson
Red, White, and Blue: The Story of the American Flag
A Birthday Basket for Tía
Cowboys
Grace for President
Talking About TRADITIONS
Are traditions and celebrations important in our lives?
1

Let's Practice It!
TR DVD•283–284

Tell children that tomorrow they will review more skills and read "Celebrating Hawaii."

Review
Week 2

Content Knowledge
Review Oral Vocabulary

Phonics/Spelling
Review Abbreviations

Selection Vocabulary
Review *America, birthday, flag, freedom, nicknames, stars, stripes*

Vocabulary
Review Multiple-Meaning Words

Text-Based Comprehension
Review Author's Purpose
Review Summarize

Fluency
Read with Accuracy

Conventions
Review Quotation Marks

Handwriting
Review Cursive Letters/Letter Smoothness

Writing
Quick Write for Fluency

Materials

- Sing with Me Big Book
- Sound-Spelling Cards
- Reader's and Writer's Notebook

Common Core State Standards

Speaking/Listening 1. Participate in collaborative conversations with diverse partners about grade 2 topics and texts with peers and adults in small and larger groups. **Language 5.a.** Identify real-life connections between words and their use (e.g., describe foods that are *spicy* or *juicy*). **Also Language 6.**

Content Knowledge

The American Flag

REVISIT THE CONCEPT Today children will explore how the Question of the Week connects to *Red, White, and Blue: The Story of the American Flag.* Read the Question of the Week: *What traditions and celebrations involve our country's flag?* Remind children that *Red, White, and Blue: The Story of the American Flag* is informational text about the history of the American flag.

Build Oral Language

TALK ABOUT THE AMERICAN FLAG Use these questions to connect the Week 2 question and selection to the Unit 6 Big Question, **Are traditions and celebrations important in our lives?**

- Why was an American flag needed?
- What nickname would you give the flag?
- How do you honor the tradition of the American flag?

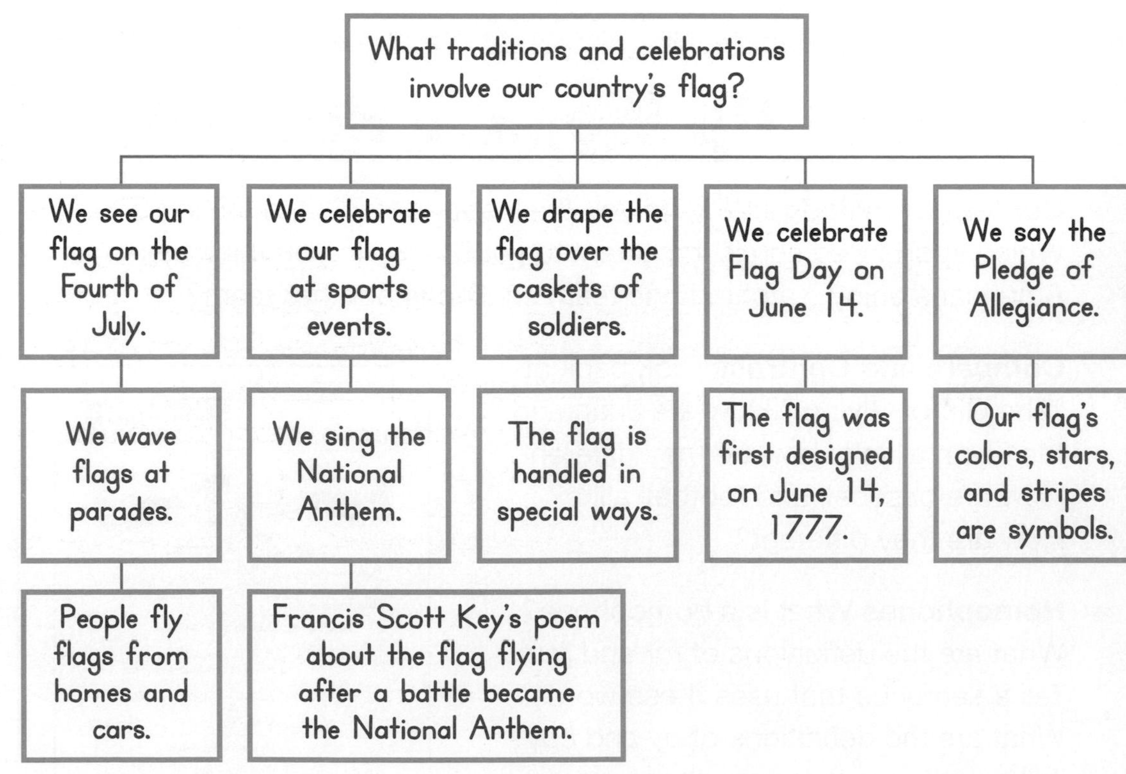

Build Oral Vocabulary

REVIEW AMAZING WORDS Remind children that they have learned some Amazing Words that they can use to answer the question *What celebrations and traditions involve our country's flag?* Display "Our Flag, Our Symbol" on page 27 of the *Sing with Me* Big Book. Sing the song.

Go over all the Amazing Words from Week 2. Ask children to listen as you say them: *history, independence, symbol, patriotic, unfurl, frayed, allegiance, indivisible.* Then say them again, and have children say each word after you.

- What is another word for *indivisible?* *(inseparable)*
- What can look *frayed*—a flag or a car? (flag)
- What is a *symbol* of our country? (the flag, Statue of Liberty, eagle)

AMAZING WORDS AT WORK Have children demonstrate their understanding of Amazing Words by completing these sentences orally.

Mia's _______ was beginning to looked **frayed.**
Our _______ is **indivisible.**
I feel **patriotic** when I pledge **allegiance** to the _______.
Mrs. Gray is teaching us the **history** of _______.
A _______ is a **symbol** of the United States.
Our teacher gave us **independence** to work on our _______.

Amazing Words

history	unfurl
independence	frayed
symbol	allegiance
patriotic	indivisible

Access for All

SI Strategic Intervention

Word Webs Work with children to create word webs for some of the Amazing Words. For example, write *independence* in the center of a web and have children supply synonyms as well as other related words, such as: *freedom, liberty, rights,* and *United States of America.*

Reteach Concepts and Vocabulary Use the instruction on ELL Poster 27 to assess knowledge and concepts.

Common Core State Standards

Foundational Skills 3. Know and apply grade-level phonics and word analysis skills in decoding words. **Foundational Skills 4.** Read with sufficient accuracy and fluency to support comprehension.

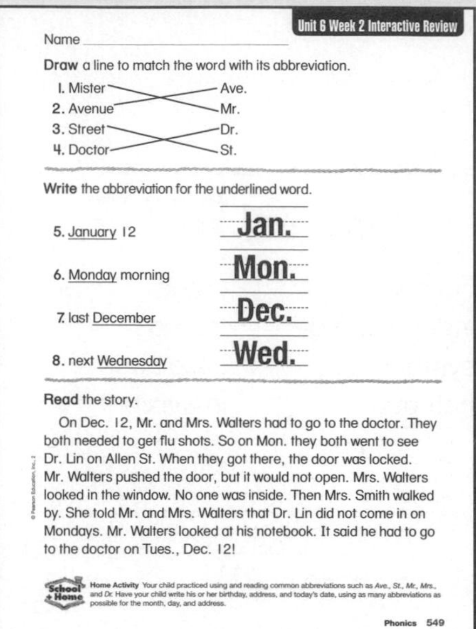

Unit 6 Week 2 Interactive Review

Name

Draw a line to match the word with its abbreviation.

1. Mister — Mr.
2. Avenue — Ave.
3. Street — St.
4. Doctor — Dr.

Write the abbreviation for the underlined word.

5. January 12 — Jan.
6. Monday morning — Mon.
7. last December — Dec.
8. next Wednesday — Wed.

Read the story.

On Dec. 12, Mr. and Mrs. Walters had to go to the doctor. They both needed to get flu shots. So on Mon. they both went to see Dr. Lin on Allen St. When they got there, the door was locked. Mr. Walters pushed the door, but it would not open. Mrs. Walters looked in the window. No one was inside. Then Mrs. Smith walked by. She told Mr. and Mrs. Walters that Dr. Lin did not come in on Mondays. Mr. Walters looked at his notebook. It said he had to go to the doctor on Tues., Dec. 12!

School + Home **Home Activity** Your child practiced using and reading common abbreviations such as *Ave.*, *St.*, *Mr.*, *Mrs.*, and *Dr.* Have your child write his or her birthday, address, and today's date, using as many abbreviations as possible for the month, day, and address.

Phonics 549

Reader's and Writer's Notebook, p. 549

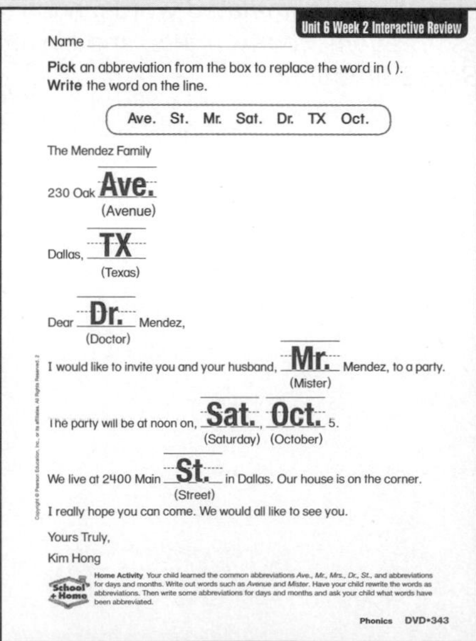

Unit 6 Week 2 Interactive Review

Name

Pick an abbreviation from the box to replace the word in ( ). **Write** the word on the line.

Ave. St. Mr. Sat. Dr. TX Oct.

The Mendez Family

230 Oak Ave. (Avenue)

Dallas, TX (Texas)

Dear Dr. (Doctor) Mendez,

I would like to invite you and your husband, Mr. (Mister) Mendez, to a party.

The party will be at noon on, Sat. (Saturday), Oct. (October) 5.

We live at 2400 Main St. (Street) in Dallas. Our house is on the corner.

I really hope you can come. We would all like to see you.

Yours Truly,

Kim Hong

School + Home **Home Activity** Your child learned the common abbreviations *Ave.*, *Mr.*, *Mrs.*, *Dr.*, *St.*, and abbreviations for days and months. Write out words such as *Avenue* and *Mister*. Have your child rewrite the words as abbreviations. Then write some abbreviations for days and months and ask your child what words have been abbreviated.

Phonics DVD•343

Let's Practice It! TR DVD•343

Phonics

Review Abbreviations

TARGET PHONICS SKILLS Review abbreviations using Sound-Spelling Card 107.

READ WORDS IN ISOLATION Use *Reader's and Writer's Notebook,* page 549. Point out that children know how to read these abbreviations. Then tell children they will all read the abbreviations. Allow several seconds previewing time for the first reading.

Corrective feedback

If... children cannot read all the abbreviations consecutively without an error,
then... return to the first abbreviation and have children reread all the abbreviations. Repeat until children can read the abbreviations fluently.

READ WORDS IN CONTEXT Use the passage on *Reader's and Writer's Notebook,* page 549. Point out that there are many abbreviations in the passage that children already know how to read. Have children read the passage together.

Corrective feedback

If... children have difficulty reading abbreviations,
then... guide them in reading abbreviations. Have children read each sentence. Repeat until children can read the sentences fluently.

ON THEIR OWN Use Let's Practice It!, p. 343 on the *Teacher Resources DVD-ROM.*

Spelling

Review Abbreviations

SPELLING WORDS Write *Mr., St.,* and *Jan.* Point out that these words are abbreviations. Remind children that they learned how to spell some abbreviations. Use Sound-Spelling Card 107 to review how to spell abbreviations. Review the Week 2 spelling words.

Team Talk Have children review the spelling words using index cards on which the abbreviations are written. Tell them to sort the words into the ones they know and the ones they need more practice with. Partners can quiz each other on the words in the second pile.

ON THEIR OWN Use *Reader's and Writer's Notebook,* page 550.

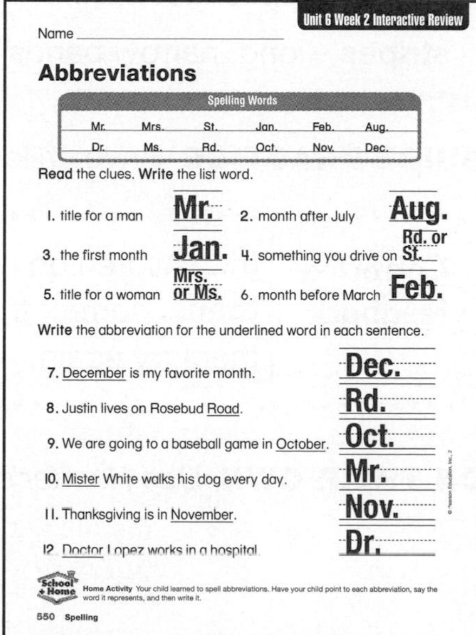

Name ____________ Unit 6 Week 2 Interactive Review

Abbreviations

Spelling Words

Mr.	Mrs.	St.	Jan.	Feb.	Aug.
Dr.	Ms.	Rd.	Oct.	Nov.	Dec.

Read the clues. Write the list word.

1. title for a man **Mr.**
2. month after July **Aug.**
3. the first month **Jan.**
4. something you drive on **Rd. or St.**
5. title for a woman **Mrs. or Ms.**
6. month before March **Feb.**

Write the abbreviation for the underlined word in each sentence.

7. December is my favorite month. **Dec.**
8. Justin lives on Rosebud Road. **Rd.**
9. We are going to a baseball game in October. **Oct.**
10. Mister White walks his dog every day. **Mr.**
11. Thanksgiving is in November. **Nov.**
12. Doctor Lopez works in a hospital. **Dr.**

School + Home Home Activity Your child learned to spell abbreviations. Have your child point to each abbreviation, say the word it represents, and then write it.

550 Spelling

Reader's and Writer's Notebook, p. 550

Unit 6 Week 2 Spelling Words

Abbreviations

1. **Mr.**
2. **Mrs.**
3. **St.**
4. **Jan.**
5. **Feb.**
6. **Aug.**
7. **Dr.**
8. **Ms.**
9. **Rd.**
10. **Oct.**
11. **Nov.**
12. **Dec.**

Review Abbreviations Remind children that an abbreviation is a shortened form of a word. It often begins with a capital letter and ends with a period. It is pronounced as if all the letters of the complete word are showing.

Beginning Write abbreviations and their corresponding words. Point to and say each abbreviation and word. Have children repeat. Discuss which letters are removed to spell the abbreviations. Have children write the abbreviations and read them with a partner.

Intermediate Write and say the following abbreviations and their corresponding words: *Dr., Dec., Mr., Mar., St., Sept.* Have partners write the abbreviations and words on separate cards. Then have them match the pairs and read them.

Advanced Write words that have abbreviations, such as *Tuesday* and *September.* Have children write the abbreviations in self-made sentences and read them aloud.

Common Core State Standards

Language 4. Determine or clarify the meaning of unknown and multiple-meaning words and phrases based on grade 2 reading and content, choosing flexibly from an array of strategies. **Language 4.a.** Use sentence-level context as a clue to the meaning of a word or phrase. **Also Foundational Skills 4.c.**

Unit 6 Week 2 Interactive Review

Name ________

Pick a word to match each clue. **Write** the word on the line.

birthday flag freedom
nicknames stars stripes America

1. The **flag** flies high on a pole.
2. I like to watch the **stars** sparkle and shine in the night sky.
3. Happy **birthday** to you!
4. Many people fought for the country's **freedom**.
5. A zebra has many **stripes**.
6. Fran has red hair. Fran's friends call her "Red." Leo loves to eat peanuts. Leo's dad calls him "Peanut." "Red" and "Peanut" are **nicknames**.
7. Another name for our country is **America**.

Write a nickname you might give a friendly white dog with black spots. **Possible answer: Spots**

Home Activity Your child reviewed lesson vocabulary learned in this unit. Ask your child to make up a poem about the U.S. flag using as many words in the box as possible. Your child can illustrate the poem with a picture.

Vocabulary 551

Reader's and Writer's Notebook, p. 551

Selection Vocabulary

REVIEW READ WORDS IN ISOLATION Display the selection vocabulary. Have children read the words aloud with you. Review the definitions.

America—the United States of America

birthday—the day something was born or something began, usually celebrated yearly

flag—a piece of cloth, usually with square corners, with a picture or pattern that stands for a country

freedom—the condition of not being under someone else's control

nicknames—names used instead of real names

stars—shapes that have five or more points

stripes—long, narrow bands of color

GUIDE PRACTICE Have children use each word in a sentence.

Corrective feedback	**If...** children do not use a word correctly, **then...** correct the sentence, model a sentence, and have them try again.

ON THEIR OWN Use *Reader's and Writer's Notebook,* page 551.

Vocabulary Skill

Review Multiple-Meaning Words

Review that a multiple-meaning word has two or more different meanings. Have children use context clues to determine the meaning of *stars* in these sentences.

- The *stars* twinkled brightly above me. (lights in the night sky made from burning gases)
- We saw many *stars* at the movie premiere. (talented or famous people)

Team Talk **GUIDE PRACTICE** Have children name and define other multiple-meaning words. Have partners use multiple-meaning words in sentences.

Zoom in on ©

Text-Based Comprehension

REVIEW ◎ AUTHOR'S PURPOSE Review that the author is the person who writes the story. Remind children that authors may write with the purpose of entertaining, informing, persuading, or stirring readers' emotions. Recall that they identified the **author's purpose,** or reason for writing, the informational text *Red, White, and Blue: The Story of the American Flag.*

REVIEW ◎ SUMMARIZE Remind children that good readers summarize as they read and after they read. To **summarize,** you find the most important ideas or events. Then you use that information to retell what the selection was mostly about in just a few sentences.

INFORMATIONAL TEXT Remind children that an informational text tells facts. **Informational text** often gives facts about real people, places, and events that may reflect history or the traditions of communities.

PREVIEW AND PREDICT Have children read the title of the selection on page 552 of *Reader's and Writer's Notebook.* Have children look through the selection and use the title to predict ideas or events that they will read about in the selection. Tell them this selection is an informational text.

SET A PURPOSE After we read "Celebrating Hawaii," we will identify the topic and talk about why the author wrote this selection. Have children set a purpose for reading "Celebrating Hawaii."

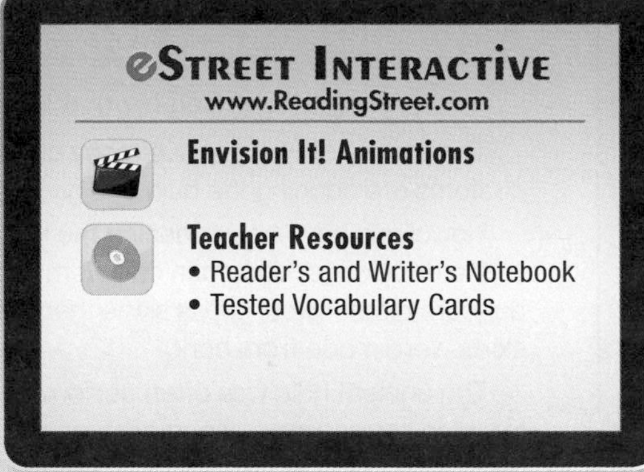

Access for All

A Advanced

Extend Author's Purpose and Summarizing After reviewing author's purpose and summarizing, have partners share the name and author of a favorite book. Have children summarize the selection and identify the author's reason for writing it.

Academic Vocabulary 

author's purpose the reason the author wrote the text

informational text writing that contains facts and information. Also called *expository text.*

summarize to retell the most important ideas of what was read

Unit 6 Week 2 Interactive Review

Name ______________________

Read the story. **Write** the answer to each question.

Celebrating Hawaii

The people of Hawaii have many ancient customs. Two of these customs are dancing the hula and giving leis.

Hawaiians have been dancing the hula for thousands of years. In the early days, both men and women danced the hula. The dancers did not wear grass skirts then. They did wear skirts, but the skirts were made from bark.

The ancient hula was often performed to chanting, called *mele*, in which sounds were repeated over and over. Sometimes the dancers danced to music played on ancient instruments. Hawaiians used coconuts, gourds, and small logs to make instruments that they would beat or shake.

A hula dancer's movements told a story. The dances would express the history, customs, and ceremonies of Hawaii. Sometimes the dancing gave thanks for the people's blessings. The ancient hula was a serious kind of dancing. Dance teachers taught young dancers the correct way to dance this hula.

Another important custom of the Hawaiian people is to make, wear, and give away leis. A lei is a necklace of flowers—real flowers. Beautiful flowers of bright colors grow all over Hawaii.

The people who make leis usually string flowers, but sometimes they string shiny green leaves. They may also make leis with shells, nuts, or feathers.

When visitors came to Hawaii in the 1900s, the Hawaiians gave them leis as a way to welcome them to the islands. They would place the lei around the visitor's neck. Today visitors to Hawaii are still welcomed with leis.

No one should refuse to accept and wear a lei. To do so would hurt the feelings of the person who gives it. Leis are so important to Hawaiians that May 1 is called Lei Day. It's a holiday.

Home Activity Your child read a nonfiction story and identified the author's purpose in writing it. Reread the story with your child. Ask your child why he or she thinks the author told readers about the ancient hula.

Unit 6 Week 2 Interactive Review

Name ______________________

1. What is the topic of this story?

two customs of Hawaii

2. What do you think was the author's purpose in writing this story? Underline the answer below.

to tell a funny story

to explain how to make something

<u>to give information</u>

3. Why do you think the author told the reader about chanting?

Possible answer: The author wanted readers to understand that the ancient hula was danced to repeated sounds as well as to music.

4. What facts about Hawaii did you learn as you read the story? Tell two things that you learned.

Possible answers: Dancers wore bark skirts when dancing the ancient hula. People visited Hawaii in the 1900s. May 1 is Lei Day.

Reader's and Writer's Notebook, pp. 552–553

Common Core State Standards

Informational Text 2. Identify the main topic of a multiparagraph text as well as the focus of specific paragraphs within the text. **Informational Text 6.** Identify the main purpose of a text, including what the author wants to answer, explain, or describe. **Also Foundational Skills 4.b.**

Access Text

Review Author's Purpose

Have children read the selection and respond to the questions.

Corrective feedback	**If...** children have difficulty responding to the questions, **then...** use the following to guide their responses.

1. What is the selection about? Help children find the sentence that tells what the topic is.

2. What information does the author give about the two customs of Hawaii? What is the author's purpose? Help children recognize that almost every sentence tells a fact about Hawaiian customs. Help them recognize that the author's purpose is to inform.

3. How have Hawaiians welcomed visitors since the 1900s? Have children find the sentences that tell how visitors are welcomed by Hawaiians.

REVIEW SUMMARIZE Discuss the comprehension tools that children used as they read "Celebrating Hawaii."

What did you do to remember important facts and details as you read? Did you stop to summarize important information? Have children tell how summarizing helped them check their understanding of what they read.

Reread for Fluency

MODEL FLUENT READING Remind children that when they read, it is important to pay attention to each word and to read without mistakes. Model reading the second paragraph of "Celebrating Hawaii" on *Reader's and Writer's Notebook,* page 552 with accuracy. Have children track the print as you read.

GUIDE PRACTICE To provide additional fluency practice, pair children and have them read "Celebrating Hawaii."

Routine Paired Reading

Team Talk

1. **Reader 1 Begins** Children read the selection, switching readers at the end of each paragraph.
2. **Reader 2 Begins** Have partners reread; this time the other partner begins.
3. **Reread** For optimal fluency, children should reread three or four times.
4. **Corrective Feedback** Listen to children read and provide corrective feedback regarding their oral reading and their use of the blending strategy.

Routines Flip Chart

Access for All

SI Strategic Intervention

Comprehension and Fluency
Have children reread "Celebrating Hawaii," using a whisper-level voice. As they read, have them think about the author's purpose. After children have read the selection, have them summarize the information they learned.

Options for Oral Rereading

Use *Red, White, and Blue: The Story of the American Flag* or a leveled reader.

Common Core State Standards

Language 2. Demonstrate command of the conventions of standard English capitalization, punctuation, and spelling when writing. **Speaking/Listening 1.** Participate in collaborative conversations with diverse partners about grade 2 topics and texts with peers and adults in small and larger groups.

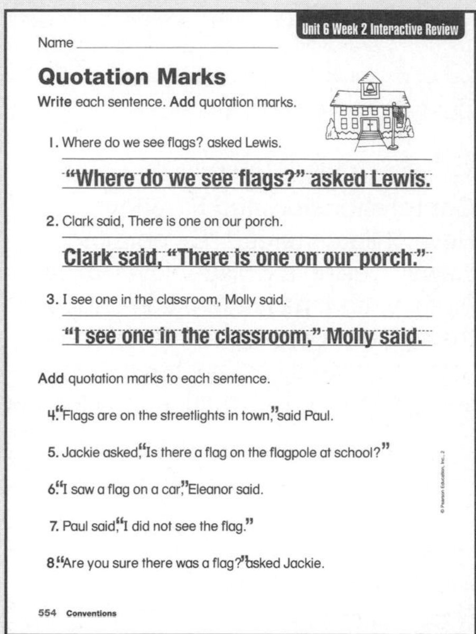

Unit 6 Week 2 Interactive Review

Name ____________

Quotation Marks

Write each sentence. Add quotation marks.

1. Where do we see flags? asked Lewis.
   "Where do we see flags?" asked Lewis.
2. Clark said, There is one on our porch.
   Clark said, "There is one on our porch."
3. I see one in the classroom, Molly said.
   "I see one in the classroom," Molly said.

Add quotation marks to each sentence.

4. "Flags are on the streetlights in town," said Paul.
5. Jackie asked, "Is there a flag on the flagpole at school?"
6. "I saw a flag on a car," Eleanor said.
7. Paul said, "I did not see the flag."
8. "Are you sure there was a flag?" asked Jackie.

554 Conventions

Reader's and Writer's Notebook, p. 554

Unit 6 Interactive Review

Name ____________

Day 1 Unit 6 Week 1 — Just Like Josh Gibson

Copy the sentences. Make sure your letters and words are spaced correctly.

We won't go to Vienna.

Check children's letters and words for correct spacing.

You don't know Uncle Will.

Day 2 Unit 6 Week 2 — Red, White, and Blue

Copy the sentences. Make sure your letters are written smoothly.

Beth and Pam like shopping.

Check children's letters for smoothness.

Rob hiked the Forest Trail.

School + Home **Home Activity** Your child practiced writing all cursive letters. Each day have your child copy a sentence from a favorite storybook using his or her best cursive handwriting.

Handwriting 547

Reader's and Writer's Notebook, pp. 547–548

Conventions

Review Quotation Marks

Remind children that the words a story character says are dialogue. Explain that quotation marks go before the first word a character says and after the punctuation of the character's sentence or sentences.

GUIDE PRACTICE Write the following dialogue without quotation marks. Have children add the quotation marks.

> The teacher said, "It is time for us to go to lunch."
> "May I get my lunchbox?" asked Matt.
> "Yes," said the teacher. "We will wait for you."

Team Talk Have each child write a statement or question in dialogue form using his or her own name. Tell children to omit the quotation marks. Have partners exchange papers, correct the sentence, and write a dialogue response. Continue the process several times.

ON THEIR OWN Use *Reader's and Writer's Notebook,* page 554.

Handwriting

REVIEW CURSIVE LETTERS Demonstrate the proper formation of cursive letters *B, P, R, T,* and *F.* Then review all lowercase letters. Have children write each capital letter several times and circle the best one. Then have them write each lowercase letter.

REVIEW LETTER SMOOTHNESS Review that letters should be formed and joined with smoothness.

GUIDE PRACTICE Write the following sentence. Have children copy it using appropriate letter smoothness. Monitor children's letters as they write. If children have not transitioned to cursive, have them write the words in manuscript.

> **Rita will be camping in Bastrop Park on Thursday and Friday.**

ON THEIR OWN Use the Day 2 section on *Reader's and Writer's Notebook,* pages 547–548.

Optional Unit Review

Routine Quick Write for Fluency

1. **Talk** Have pairs discuss what they learned about the traditions and celebrations that involve our country's flag.
2. **Write** Have children write a few sentences to summarize the discussion.
3. **Share** Partners can read their summaries to one another.

Routines Flip Chart

Writing Workshop

Use the writing process lesson on pages WP•1–WP•10 for this week's writing instruction.

ELL

Extend Amazing Words Write *symbol* and review its definition. Then write and say *cymbal.* Explain that *symbol* and *cymbal* are homophones. They are pronounced the same but have different spellings and meanings. Tell children that a *cymbal* is "a metal musical instrument that looks like a plate." Write and read these sentences: *A red, white, and blue flag is a symbol of The United States. Raul plays the cymbals in the marching band.*

Wrap Up Week 2 Review

✔ **Content Knowledge** What does the American Flag look like? In which places do you see American flags? Why do you think those places have flags? Why do people show American flags on Independence Day?

✔ **Author's Purpose** Look back at "Celebrating Hawaii." Why do you think the author gave so much information on Hawaii? What was the author's reason for writing *Red, White, and Blue: The Story of the American Flag?*

✔ **Multiple-Meaning Words** What are two meanings for the word *trip?* Use each meaning in a sentence. What are two meanings for the word *play?* Use each meaning in a sentence. What are some other multiple-meaning words?

Preview DAY 3

Tell children that tomorrow they will review more skills and read "The Family Tree."

Review Week 3

Content Knowledge
Review Oral Vocabulary

Phonics/Spelling
Review Final Syllables *-tion, -ture, -ion*

Selection Vocabulary
Review *aunt, bank, basket, collects, favorite, present*

Vocabulary
Review Words from Other Languages

Text-Based Comprehension
Review Draw Conclusions
Review Questioning

Fluency
Read with Appropriate Phrasing

Conventions
Review Prepositions

Handwriting
Review Cursive Letters/Letter Size

Writing
Quick Write for Fluency

Materials

- Sing with Me Big Book
- Sound-Spelling Cards
- Reader's and Writer's Notebook

Common Core State Standards

Speaking/Listening 1. Participate in collaborative conversations with diverse partners about grade 2 topics and texts with peers and adults in small and larger groups. **Language 5.a.** Identify real-life connections between words and their use (e.g., describe foods that are *spicy* or *juicy*). **Also Language 6.**

Content Knowledge

Family Celebrations

REVISIT THE CONCEPT Today children will explore how the Question of the Week connects to *A Birthday Basket for Tía.* Read the Question of the Week: *Why are family celebrations special?* Remind children that *A Birthday Basket for Tía* is realistic fiction about a special family celebration for an aunt's ninetieth birthday.

Build Oral Language

TALK ABOUT FAMILY CELEBRATIONS Use these questions to connect the Week 3 question and selection to the Unit 6 Big Question, **Are traditions and celebrations important in our lives?**

- How did Cecilia help make Tía's birthday special?
- What would you have done to make the celebration special?
- What special traditions does your family celebrate?

Why are family celebrations special?

We Celebrate Special Events	Family Members Get Together	We Do Special Activities
We celebrate the birth of a baby. We celebrate birthdays.	We dress up in special clothes. People share special foods. We enjoy the special qualities of our family.	We sometimes learn special things. We take photos to save memories. We share memories. We listen to music and play games.

Build Oral Vocabulary

REVIEW AMAZING WORDS Remind children that they have learned some Amazing Words that they can use to answer the question *Why are family celebrations special?* Display "Family Tradition" on page 28 of the *Sing with Me* Big Book. Sing the song.

Go over all the Amazing Words from Week 3. Ask children to listen as you say them: *celebration, custom, tradition, create, inspect, angle, brilliant, snapshot.* Then say them again, and have children say each word after you.

- Which word means "picture"? *(snapshot)*
- Name a *celebration* you share with your family. (birthday)
- What is another word for *brilliant*? *(bright, shiny, radiant)*

AMAZING WORDS AT WORK Have children demonstrate their understanding of Amazing Words by completing these sentences orally.

Mom took lots of **snapshots** at my ______ **celebration.**

The ______ was so **brilliant.**

My ______ has many **traditions** and **customs.**

Dad wanted the right **angle** before taking the ______.

The judges had to **inspect** each ______.

Our teacher said we had to **create** a ______ for our report.

Amazing Words

celebration	inspect
custom	angle
tradition	brilliant
create	snapshot

Access for All

SI Strategic Intervention

Related Words and Ideas Say an Amazing Word. Ask children to say other words and ideas that come to mind when they hear the word. For example, when you say *custom,* they might think of special clothing, food, or events; when you say *snapshot,* they might think of a vacation or picture day at school.

Reteach Concepts and Vocabulary Use the instruction on ELL Poster 28 to assess knowledge and concepts.

Common Core State Standards

Foundational Skills 3. Know and apply grade-level phonics and word analysis skills in decoding words.

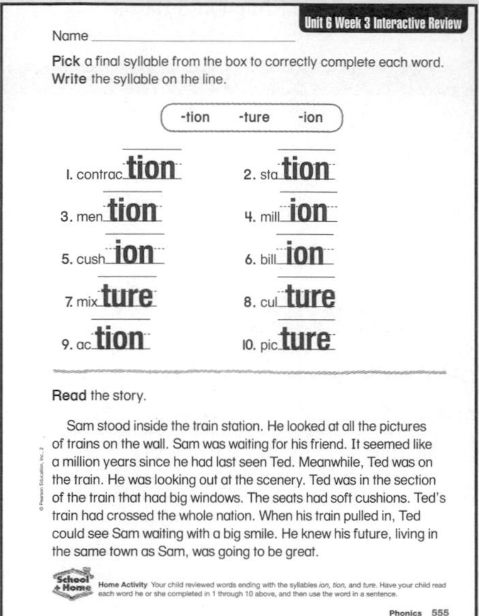
Unit 6 Week 3 Interactive Review

Name

Pick a final syllable from the box to correctly complete each word. **Write** the syllable on the line.

-tion -ture -ion

1. contrac tion
2. sta tion
3. men tion
4. mill ion
5. cush ion
6. bill ion
7. mix ture
8. cul ture
9. ac tion
10. pic ture

Read the story.

Sam stood inside the train station. He looked at all the pictures of trains on the wall. Sam was waiting for his friend. It seemed like a million years since he had last seen Ted. Meanwhile, Ted was on the train. He was looking out at the scenery. Ted was in the section of the train that had big windows. The seats had soft cushions. Ted's train had crossed the whole nation. When his train pulled in, Ted could see Sam waiting with a big smile. He knew his future, living in the same town as Sam, was going to be great.

Home Activity Your child reviewed words ending with the syllables *ion, tion,* and *ture*. Have your child read each word he or she completed in 1 through 10 above, and then use the word in a sentence.

Phonics 555

Reader's and Writer's Notebook, p. 555

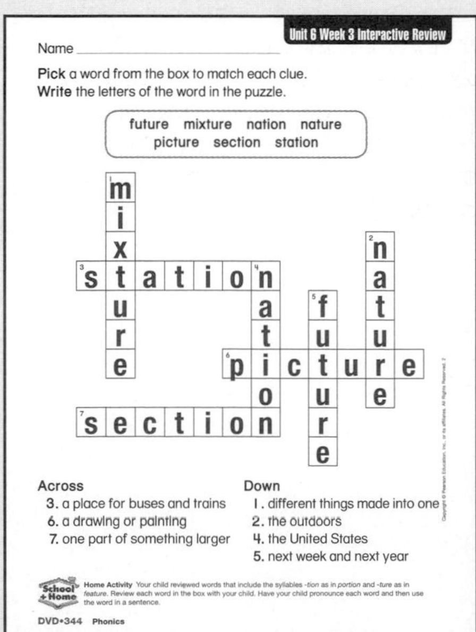
Unit 6 Week 3 Interactive Review

Name

Pick a word from the box to match each clue. **Write** the letters of the word in the puzzle.

future mixture nation nature picture section station

Across
3. a place for buses and trains
6. a drawing or painting
7. one part of something larger

Down
1. different things made into one
2. the outdoors
4. the United States
5. next week and next year

Home Activity Your child reviewed words that include the syllables *-tion* as in *portion* and *-ture* as in *feature*. Review each word in the box with your child. Have your child pronounce each word and then use the word in a sentence.

DVD•344 Phonics

Let's Practice It! TR DVD•344

Phonics

Review Final Syllables *-tion, -ture, -ion*

TARGET PHONICS SKILLS Review final syllables *-tion, -ture,* and *-ion* using Sound-Spelling Cards 131, 135, and 136.

DECODE WORDS IN ISOLATION Have children complete the top half of *Reader's and Writer's Notebook,* page 555 and review the correct answers as a group. Point out that children know how to decode these words. Then tell children they will all read the words in each row together. Allow several seconds previewing time for the first reading.

Corrective feedback

If... children cannot decode both words in a row without an error,
then... return to the first word in the row, and have children reread both words in the row. Repeat until children can read the words fluently.

DECODE WORDS IN CONTEXT Use the passage on *Reader's and Writer's Notebook,* page 555. Point out that there are many words with final syllables *tion, -ture,* and *-ion* in the passage that children already know how to decode. Have children read the passage together.

Corrective feedback

If... children have difficulty decoding words with final syllables *-tion, -ture,* and *-ion,*
then... guide them in chunking multisyllabic words and using sound-by-sound blending. Have children read each sentence. Repeat until children can read the sentences fluently.

ON THEIR OWN Use Let's Practice It!, p. 344 on the *Teacher Resources DVD-ROM.*

Spelling

Review Final Syllables *-tion, -ture*

SPELLING WORDS Write *station* and *picture.* Point out that these words have final syllables *-tion* and *-ture.* Remind children that they learned how to spell words with these final syllables. Use Sound-Spelling Cards 135 and 136 to review how to spell words with final syllables *-tion* and *-ture.* Review the Week 3 spelling words.

Team Talk Have children review the spelling words using index cards on which the words are written. Tell them to sort the words into the ones they know and the ones they need more practice with. Partners can quiz each other on the words in the second pile.

ON THEIR OWN Use *Reader's and Writer's Notebook,* p. 556.

Unit 6 Week 3 Interactive Review

Name ____________

Final Syllables *-tion, -ture*

Spelling Words					
mixture	nation	section	future	picture	action
caution	station	fixture	motion	nature	feature

Find two rhyming words in each box. **Circle** the words. **Write** the words.

(mixture)	future	action
feature	section	caution
nature	(fixture)	motion

future	section	nature
caution	picture	(nation)
(station)	motion	feature

1. mixture 2. fixture 3. nation 4. station

Write the missing letters to make a list word.

5. a division or slice s e c t i o n
6. a painting or photograph p i c t u r e
7. the process of doing something a c t i o n
8. what will be f u t u r e
9. movement m o t i o n
10. care to avoid danger c a u t i o n
11. everything on Earth not made by people n a t u r e
12. something that stands out f e a t u r e

© Pearson Education, Inc. 2

School + Home **Home Activity** Your child learned to spell words that end with *-tion* and *-ture*. Take turns thinking of other words with these letter combinations. Use a magazine or book if necessary.

556 Spelling

Reader's and Writer's Notebook, p. 556

Unit 6 Week 3 Spelling Words

Final Syllables *-tion, -ture*

1. mixture	**7. caution**
2. nation	**8. station**
3. section	**9. fixture**
4. future	**10. motion**
5. picture	**11. nature**
6. action	**12. feature**

Review Final Syllables *-tion, -ture,* and *-ion* Remind children that spelling patterns *-tion, -ture,* and *-ion* form their own syllables at the end of words.

Beginning Write and read a list of words with final syllables *-tion, -ture,* and *-ion.* Have children write the words and circle the final syllables. Have partners take turns reading the words.

Intermediate Have children sort words according to the final syllable. Then have them read the sorted words to a partner.

Advanced Have children write at least four sentences that contain one each of a *-tion, -ture,* and *-ion* word. Have children read their sentences to a partner.

Common Core State Standards

Language 4.a. Use sentence-level context as a clue to the meaning of a word or phrase. **Language 5.a.** Identify real-life connections between words and their use (e.g., describe foods that *are spicy* or *juicy*).

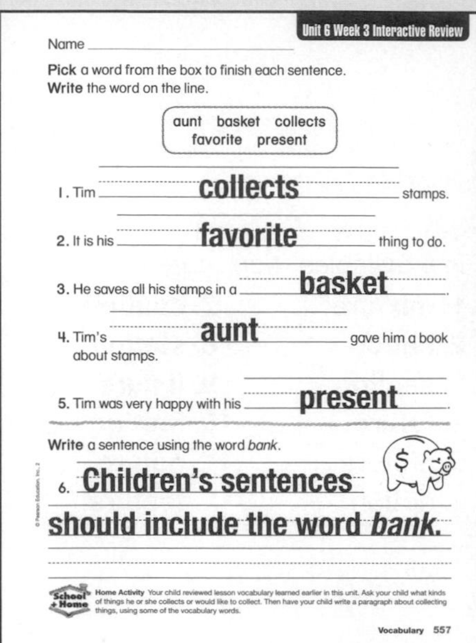
Unit 6 Week 3 Interactive Review

Name

Pick a word from the box to finish each sentence.
Write the word on the line.

aunt basket collects favorite present

1. Tim **collects** stamps.
2. It is his **favorite** thing to do.
3. He saves all his stamps in a **basket**
4. Tim's **aunt** gave him a book about stamps.
5. Tim was very happy with his **present**

Write a sentence using the word *bank*.

6. **Children's sentences should include the word *bank*.**

Vocabulary 557

Reader's and Writer's Notebook, p. 557

Selection Vocabulary

REVIEW READ WORDS IN ISOLATION Display the selection vocabulary. Have children read the words aloud with you. Review the definitions.

aunt—your father's sister, your mother's sister, or your uncle's wife

bank—a place where people keep their money

basket—a container made of twigs, grasses, or strips of wood woven together

collects—brings things together or gathers them together

favorite—the thing liked better than others

present—a gift; something given

GUIDE PRACTICE Have children use each word in a sentence.

Corrective feedback	**If...** children do not use a word correctly, **then...** correct the sentence, model a sentence, and have them try again.

ON THEIR OWN Use *Reader's and Writer's Notebook,* page 557.

Vocabulary Skill

Review Words from Other Languages

Review that English is a continuously growing and changing language. It sometimes borrows words from other languages. Explain that words from other languages may not follow familiar spelling or pronunciation patterns.

- The word *Tía* in *A Birthday Basket for Tía* is a word from another language. Which selection word has the same meaning? *(aunt)*
- Tía and Cecilia made *bizcochos.* What are *bizcochos?* (cookies)

Team Talk **GUIDE PRACTICE** Have partners review the text to find additional words from another language.

Zoom in on ©

Text-Based Comprehension

REVIEW ◎ DRAW CONCLUSIONS Review with children that readers can **draw conclusions** using their prior knowledge along with the text and illustrations. Recall that children drew conclusions when they read the story *A Birthday Basket for Tía.*

REVIEW ◎ QUESTIONING Remind children that good readers use **questioning** before, during, and after reading. They can use evidence in the text, prior knowledge, or a combination of both to answer questions and clarify meaning about information they don't understand. If you don't understand something you read, you can ask questions. Asking questions helps you look for details and bits of information to check your understanding of important words and ideas.

REALISTIC FICTION Remind children that a **realistic fiction** story is a make-believe story that has made up characters and events. In a realistic fiction story, the setting and characters seem real. It tells about events that could be real or problems people may have in real life.

PREVIEW AND PREDICT Have children read the title of the selection on page 558 of *Reader's and Writer's Notebook.* Have children look through the selection and use the title to predict events that might happen in the story. Tell them this selection is realistic fiction.

SET A PURPOSE After we read "The Family Tree," we will draw conclusions about the characters in the story. Have children set a purpose for reading "The Family Tree."

Access for All

Ⓐ Advanced

Extend Draw Conclusions After reviewing draw conclusions, have partners choose a picture or photograph. Have them discuss what they can conclude from it. Then have children share their thoughts with a partner.

Academic Vocabulary ©

draw conclusions arrive at decisions or opinions after thinking about facts and details and using prior knowledge

questioning a reading strategy in which readers use the text and prior knowledge to ask and answer questions about what they are reading

realistic fiction a story of imaginary people and events that could happen in real life

Unit 6 Week 3 Interactive Review

Name ____________________

Read the story. **Answer** the questions.

The Family Tree

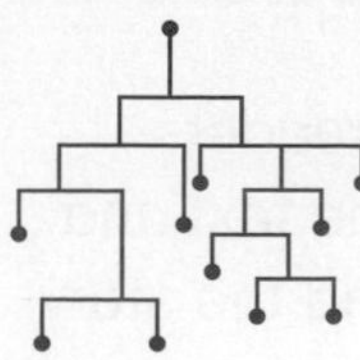

Every year the West family has a large family picnic. There are always baskets full of different foods. It is Mary West's favorite summer picnic. She gets to see her aunts and uncles and play with her cousins.

"This would be a good time to learn about our family tree," Mrs. West said.

"Where is the tree planted?" Mary asked.

"It's not the kind of tree that grows in the earth," Aunt Jill laughed. "It's a chart that shows a family's history."

"Like a real tree, it has branches. The branches show all the people in the family," explained Mr. West.

"I like to climb trees. Can I be on the top?" Mary asked.

"Sorry, the youngest family members are at the bottom of the tree," answered Mrs. West.

The West family began working on their family tree. Mary learned a lot about her family. The birthday present her grandmother always sent was handmade clothes. Mary learned that at one time, her grandmother owned a clothing store.

"Remember how Grandma always talked about her mother?" Mr. West asked. "She was a teacher in a one-room schoolhouse."

"The first West to go to college," Aunt Jill said proudly.

Home Activity Your child drew conclusions about characters in a story. Have your child tell if Mary has a big or small family and why he or she thinks so.

558 **Comprehension**

Unit 6 Week 3 Interactive Review

Name ____________________

The tree showed the people on both sides of Mary's family. The West family is her father's side. The Jacobs family is her mother's side. Mary discovered that the Jacobs family came to the United States from Russia.

"Do we have family in Russia?" asked Mary.

"My cousin Rachel is still in Russia," answered Mrs. West.

"Can we invite her to the picnic next year?" asked Mary excitedly.

"What a great idea!" said Mrs. West.

Mr. and Mrs. West collected all the information for the family tree.

"Can I keep adding branches to the tree?" asked Mary.

"Sure, and as time goes on, you won't be on the bottom anymore!" Mrs. West added.

1. How do you know Mary is interested in her family tree?

   Possible answer: She wants to add branches to the tree.

2. Why do you think the family is proud of their grandmother's mother?

   Possible answers: She was the first one in the family to go to college. She was a teacher.

3. How might Cousin Rachel get to the picnic next year?

   Possible answers: by plane or ship

Comprehension 559

Reader's and Writer's Notebook, pp. 558–559

Common Core State Standards

Literature 1. Ask and answer such questions as *who, what, where, when, why,* and *how* to demonstrate understanding of key details in a text. **Literature 5.** Describe the overall structure of a story, including describing how the beginning introduces the story and the ending concludes the action. **Also Foundational Skills 4.a.**

Access Text

Review Draw Conclusions

Have children read the story and respond to the questions.

Corrective feedback	**If...** children have difficulty responding to the questions, **then...** use the following to guide their responses.

1. What questions does Mary ask? Help children recognize that Mary asks questions about the family tree, which shows she is interested.
2. Who is at the bottom of a family tree? What happens as time goes on? Help children find the sentence that tells that the youngest family members are at the bottom of a family tree. Help children draw the conclusion that as time passes, Mary will get older and new children will be born, so she will no longer be at the bottom of the family tree.
3. Where does Rachel live? How do people travel from one country to another? Have children find the sentence that tells where Rachel lives. Help them draw the conclusion that Rachel might travel by plane or ship.

Optional Unit Review

REVIEW QUESTIONING Discuss the comprehension tools that children used as they read "The Family Tree." What questions did you ask yourself as you read? Did asking questions help you figure out what was happening in the story? Have children tell what questions they asked and whether their questions were answered in the story.

Reread for Fluency

MODEL FLUENT READING Remind children that when they read, it is important to read words that go together in a sentence in the way we normally speak. Model reading the first paragraph of "The Family Tree" on *Reader's and Writer's Notebook,* page 558 with appropriate phrasing. Have children track the print as you read.

GUIDE PRACTICE To provide additional fluency practice, pair children and have them read "The Family Tree."

Routine Paired Reading — Team Talk

1. **Reader 1 Begins** Children read the story, switching readers at the end of each paragraph.
2. **Reader 2 Begins** Have partners reread; this time the other partner begins.
3. **Reread** For optimal fluency, children should reread three or four times.
4. **Corrective Feedback** Listen to children read and provide corrective feedback regarding their oral reading and their use of the blending strategy.

Routines Flip Chart

Access for All

SI Strategic Intervention

Comprehension and Fluency Have children reread "The Family Tree" aloud with appropriate phrasing. As they read, have them think about Mary's curiosity about the family tree. After children have read the story, have them tell whether their family tree would be big, medium-sized, or small.

Options for Oral Rereading

Use *A Birthday Basket for Tía* or a leveled reader.

Common Core State Standards

Language 1. Demonstrate command of the conventions of standard English grammar and usage when writing or speaking. **Speaking/Listening 1.** Participate in collaborative conversations with diverse partners about grade 2 topics and texts with peers and adults in small and larger groups.

Unit 6 Week 3 Interactive Review

Name ______________

Prepositions and Prepositional Phrases

Underline the preposition in each sentence.

1. I went to the store.
2. I bought streamers for the party.
3. We will decorate in the morning.
4. I am getting help from my mom.

Write the prepositional phrase in each sentence. **Say** each sentence with a different prepositional phrase.

5. Tia is my aunt from Mexico.
   from Mexico
6. I visit her after school.
   after school
7. I like dancing with my family.
   with my family
8. I helped my mom in the kitchen.
   in the kitchen

560 Conventions

Reader's and Writer's Notebook, p. 560

Unit 6 Interactive Review

Name ______________

Day 1 Unit 6 Week 1 — Just Like Josh Gibson

Copy the sentences. Make sure your letters and words are spaced correctly.

We won't go to Vienna.

Check children's letters and words for correct spacing.

You don't know Uncle Will.

Day 2 Unit 6 Week 2 — Red, White, and Blue

Copy the sentences. Make sure your letters are written smoothly.

Beth and Pam like shopping.

Check children's letters for smoothness.

Rob hiked the Forest Trail.

Home Activity Your child practiced writing all cursive letters. Each day have your child copy a sentence from a favorite storybook using his or her best cursive handwriting.

Handwriting 547

Reader's and Writer's Notebook, pp. 547–548

Conventions

Review Prepositions and Prepositional Phrases

Remind children that a preposition shows the relationship between a noun or a pronoun and another word, such as a verb, adjective, or another noun. Prepositions often give information about place, direction, or time.

GUIDE PRACTICE Write the following sentences. Have children write appropriate prepositions to complete the prepositional phrases.

Set the book _______ the shelf _______ the paper. (on, by)

Dad is _______ the kitchen baking cookies _______ the bake sale. (in, for)

The bug crawled _______ the wall, _______ the floor, and _______ the table. (down, across, under)

Team Talk Have children silently choose an object in the classroom. Tell them to write directions telling how to find the object, starting from their desk. Pair children. Have them trade papers, circle the prepositions, and then follow the directions to identify the object.

ON THEIR OWN Use *Reader's and Writer's Notebook,* page 560.

Handwriting

REVIEW CURSIVE LETTERS Demonstrate the proper formation of cursive letters *G, S,* and *I.* Then review all lowercase letters. Have children write each capital letter several times and circle the best one. Then have them write each lowercase letter.

REVIEW LETTER SIZE Review that letters should be the correct size when compared.

GUIDE PRACTICE Write the following sentence. Have children copy it using the correct letter size. Monitor children's letters as they write. If children have not transitioned to cursive, have them write the words in manuscript.

Gail lives in a comfortable house on Inca Street.

ON THEIR OWN Use the Day 3 section on *Reader's and Writer's Notebook,* pages 547–548.

Optional Unit Review

Routine Quick Write for Fluency

Team Talk

Talk Have pairs discuss what they learned about why family celebrations are special.

Write Have children write a few sentences to summarize the discussion.

Share Partners can read their summaries to one another.

Routines Flip Chart

Writing Workshop

Use the writing process lesson on pages WP•1–WP•10 for this week's writing instruction.

Extend Amazing Words Tell children that the word *custom* can mean "the way that something is done again and again," such as *It is a custom in my family to sing "Happy Birthday" to the person having a birthday. Custom* can also mean "made to a specific request," such as *Tyler had a custom skateboard made with a special deck and wheels.* Tell children that the first definition applies to the Amazing Word for the week. Have children use the word in sentences to confirm understanding.

Wrap Up Week 3 Review

- ✔ **Content Knowledge** What does your family celebrate? What are some reasons why your family might have a special celebration? What special traditions does your family have?
- ✔ **Draw Conclusions** Look back at "The Family Tree." Why does Mary ask questions about her family tree? Do you think the family is proud of Mary's grandmother? Why? If a friend was smiling or laughing, what conclusions would you draw about your friend's feelings?
- ✔ **Words from Other Languages** Look back at *A Birthday Basket for Tía.* What words from other languages can you find in the story?

Preview DAY 4

Tell children that tomorrow they will review more skills and read "The Great Wheel."

Review Week 4

Content Knowledge
Review Oral Vocabulary

Phonics/Spelling
Review Suffixes *-ness, -less, -able, -ible*

Selection Vocabulary
Review *campfire, cattle, cowboy, galloped, herd, railroad, trails*

Vocabulary
Review Unfamiliar Words

Text-Based Comprehension
Review Sequence
Review Text Structure

Fluency
Read with Accuracy and Appropriate Rate

Conventions
Review Commas

Handwriting
Review Cursive Letters/Letter Slant

Writing
Quick Write for Fluency

Materials

- Sing with Me Big Book
- Sound-Spelling Cards
- Reader's and Writer's Notebook

Common Core State Standards

Speaking/Listening 1. Participate in collaborative conversations with diverse partners about grade 2 topics and texts with peers and adults in small and larger groups. **Language 5.a.** Identify real-life connections between words and their use (e.g., describe foods that are *spicy* or *juicy*). **Also Language 6.**

Content Knowledge

Cowboys

REVISIT THE CONCEPT Today children will explore how the Question of the Week connects to *Cowboys.* Read the Question of the Week: *What can we learn about cowboy traditions?* Remind children that *Cowboys* is an informational text about the traditions that cowboys had 100 years ago and how they worked and lived.

Build Oral Language

TALK ABOUT COWBOYS Use these questions to connect the Week 4 question and selection to the Unit 6 Big Question, **Are traditions and celebrations important in our lives?**

- What traditions did cowboys follow?
- Which cowboy tradition do you think you would like the most?
- What can you learn from the cowboy tradition of hard work?

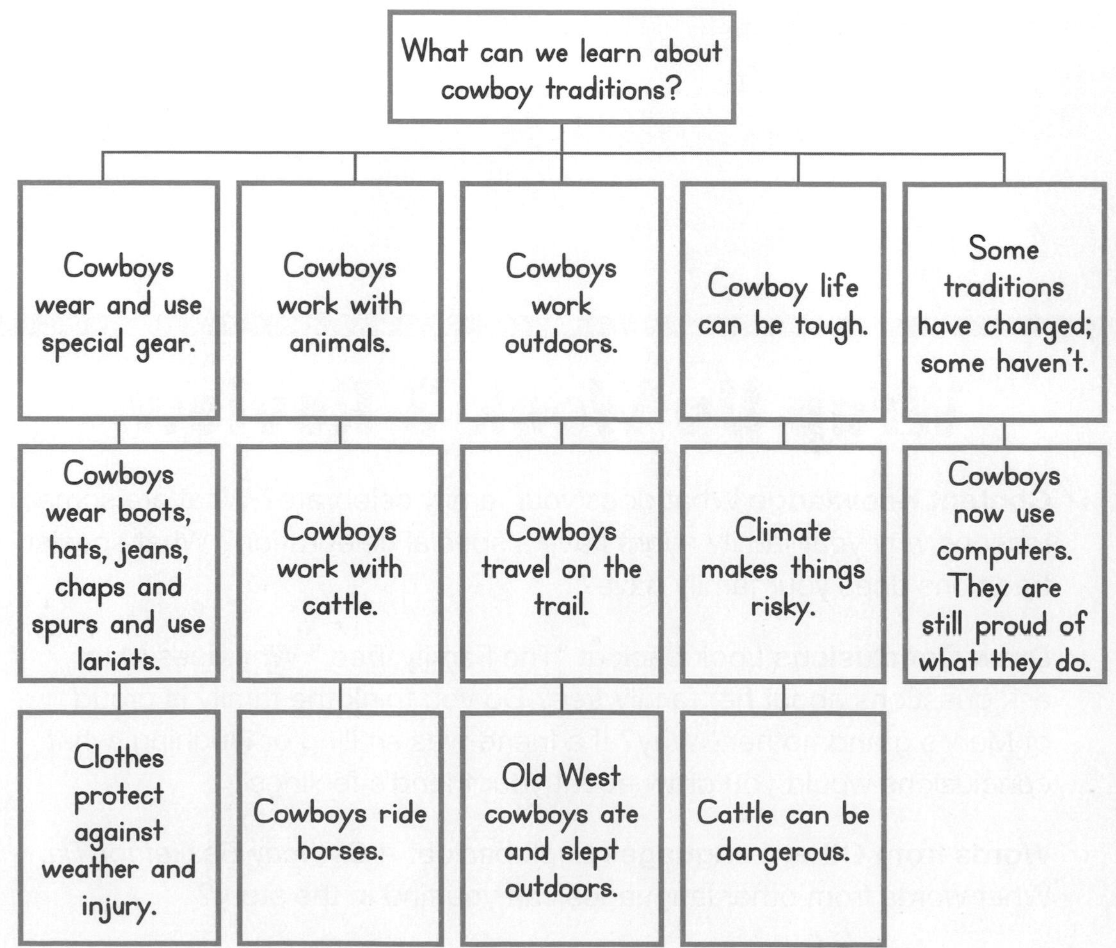

Build Oral Vocabulary

REVIEW AMAZING WORDS Remind children that they have learned some Amazing Words that they can use to answer the question *What can we learn about cowboy traditions?* Display "Occupation: Cowboy" on page 29 of the *Sing with Me* Big Book. Sing the song.

Go over all the Amazing Words from Week 4. Ask children to listen as you say them: *climate, livestock, occupation, buckaroo, drover, lariat, legend, rawhide.* Then say them again, and have children say each word after you.

- What is another word for *occupation?* *(job, career)*
- Which word has something to do with weather? *(climate)*
- Which word means "cowhand"? *(buckaroo)*

AMAZING WORDS AT WORK Have children demonstrate their understanding of Amazing Words by completing these sentences orally.

The **buckaroo's occupation** is to tame wild _______.
I _______ the **climate** where I live because it's _______.
The cowboy used the **lariat** on the _______.
The farmer's **livestock** includes cows and _______.
The **drover** moved the _______ to market.
_______ is a cowboy **legend.**
The _______ is made of **rawhide.**

Amazing Words

climate	drover
livestock	lariat
occupation	legend
buckaroo	rawhide

Access for All

A Advanced

Possible Sentences Have children write possible sentences to connect any two words. Then compare children's sentences that include a particular word, for example, *occupation.*

ELL

Reteach Concepts and Vocabulary Use the instruction on ELL Poster 29 to assess knowledge and concepts.

Common Core State Standards

Foundational Skills 3.d. Decode words with common prefixes and suffixes.

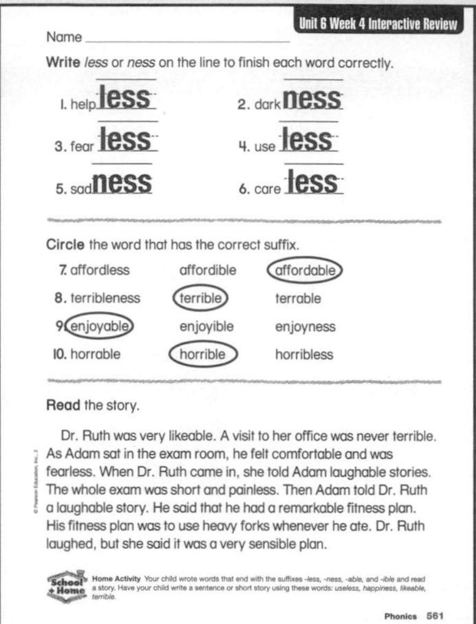
Unit 6 Week 4 Interactive Review

Name ____________

Write *less* or *ness* on the line to finish each word correctly.

1. help less
2. dark ness
3. fear less
4. use less
5. sad ness
6. care less

Circle the word that has the correct suffix.

7. affordless affordible affordable
8. terribleness terrible terrable
9. enjoyable enjoyible enjoyness
10. horrable horrible horribless

Read the story.

Dr. Ruth was very likeable. A visit to her office was never terrible. As Adam sat in the exam room, he felt comfortable and was fearless. When Dr. Ruth came in, she told Adam laughable stories. The whole exam was short and painless. Then Adam told Dr. Ruth a laughable story. He said that he had a remarkable fitness plan. His fitness plan was to use heavy forks whenever he ate. Dr. Ruth laughed, but she said it was a very sensible plan.

Home Activity Your child wrote words that end with the suffixes *-less, -ness, -able,* and *-ible* and read a story. Have your child write a sentence or short story using these words: *useless, happiness, likeable, terrible.*

Phonics 561

Reader's and Writer's Notebook, p. 561

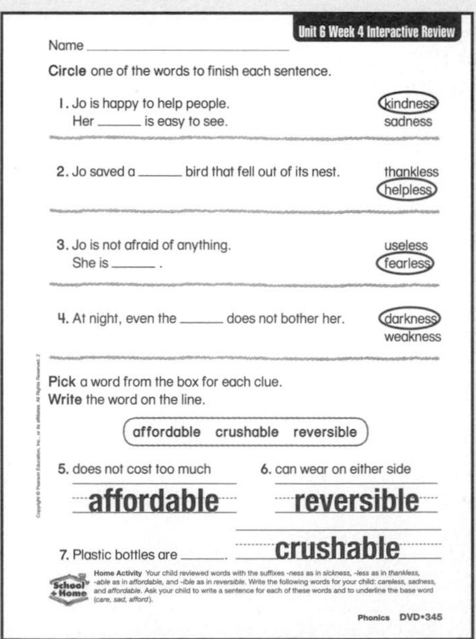
Unit 6 Week 4 Interactive Review

Name ____________

Circle one of the words to finish each sentence.

1. Jo is happy to help people. Her ______ is easy to see. kindness / sadness
2. Jo saved a ______ bird that fell out of its nest. thankless / helpless
3. Jo is not afraid of anything. She is ______ . useless / fearless
4. At night, even the ______ does not bother her. darkness / weakness

Pick a word from the box for each clue.
Write the word on the line.

affordable crushable reversible

5. does not cost too much affordable
6. can wear on either side reversible
7. Plastic bottles are ______. crushable

Home Activity Your child reviewed words with the suffixes *-ness* as in *sickness, -less* as in *thankless, -able* as in *affordable,* and *-ible* as in *reversible.* Write the following words for your child: *careless, sadness,* and *affordable.* Ask your child to write a sentence for each of these words and to underline the base word (*care, sad, afford*).

Phonics DVD•345

Let's Practice It! TR DVD•345

Phonics

Review Suffixes *-ness, -less, -able, -ible*

TARGET PHONICS SKILLS Review suffixes *-ness, -less, -able,* and *-ible* using Sound-Spelling Cards 164, 169, 172, and 175.

DECODE WORDS IN ISOLATION Have children complete the top third of *Reader's and Writer's Notebook,* page 561 and review the correct answers as a group. Point out that children know how to read these words. Then tell children they will all read the words in each row together. Allow several seconds previewing time for the first reading.

Corrective feedback	**If...** children cannot read both words in a row without an error, **then...** return to the first word in the row, and have children reread both words in the row. Repeat until children can read the words fluently.

DECODE WORDS IN CONTEXT Use the passage on *Reader's and Writer's Notebook*, page 561. Point out that there are many words with suffixes *-ness, -less, -able,* and *-ible* in the passage that children already know how to read. Have children read the passage together.

Corrective feedback	**If...** children have difficulty reading words with suffixes *-ness, -less, -able,* and *-ible,* **then...** guide them in chunking multisyllabic words and using sound-by-sound blending. Have children read each sentence. Repeat until children can read the sentences fluently.

ON THEIR OWN Use Let's Practice It!, p. 345 on the *Teacher Resources DVD-ROM.*

Spelling

Review Suffixes *-ness, -less*

SPELLING WORDS Write *darkness* and *useless.* Point out that these words have the suffixes *-ness* and *-less.* Remind children that they learned how to spell words with these suffixes. Use Sound-Spelling Cards 172 and 175 to review how to spell words with suffixes *-ness* and *-less.* Review the Week 4 spelling words.

Team Talk Have children review the spelling words using index cards on which the words are written. Tell them to sort the words into the ones they know and the ones they need more practice with. Partners can quiz each other on the words in the second pile.

ON THEIR OWN Use *Reader's and Writer's Notebook,* p. 562.

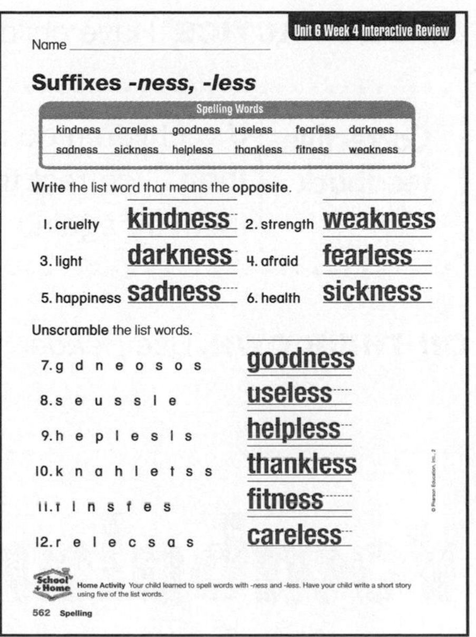

Unit 6 Week 4 Interactive Review

Name ______________

Suffixes *-ness, -less*

Spelling Words					
kindness	careless	goodness	useless	fearless	darkness
sadness	sickness	helpless	thankless	fitness	weakness

Write the list word that means the **opposite**.

1. cruelty **kindness**
2. strength **weakness**
3. light **darkness**
4. afraid **fearless**
5. happiness **sadness**
6. health **sickness**

Unscramble the list words.

7. g d n e o s o s **goodness**
8. s e u s l e **useless**
9. h e p l e s l s **helpless**
10. k n a h l e t s s **thankless**
11. t i n s f e s **fitness**
12. r e l e c s a s **careless**

School + Home **Home Activity** Your child learned to spell words with *-ness* and *-less*. Have your child write a short story using five of the list words.

562 Spelling

Reader's and Writer's Notebook, p. 562

Unit 6 Week 4 Spelling Words

Suffixes *-ness, -less*

1. kindness
2. careless
3. goodness
4. useless
5. fearless
6. darkness
7. sadness
8. sickness
9. helpless
10. thankless
11. fitness
12. weakness

Review Suffixes *-ness, -less, -able, -ible* Remind children that a suffix is added to the end of a word and changes the word's meaning.

Beginning Write and read a list of words with suffixes *-ness, -less, -able,* and *-ible.* Have children write the words and circle the suffix. Have partners take turns reading the words.

Intermediate Write sentences that contain words with suffixes *-ness, -less, -able,* and *-ible.* Read the sentences and have children repeat. Have children write the words with suffixes and identify the base word and suffix. Have partners read the words.

Advanced Have children identify, write, and read at least five words containing each target suffix.

Selection Vocabulary

REVIEW READ WORDS IN ISOLATION Display the selection vocabulary. Have children read the words aloud with you. Review the definitions.

campfire—an outdoor fire used for cooking or warmth
cattle—cows, bulls, and steers that are raised for their milk, meat, or skins
cowboy—a man who works on a cattle ranch or at rodeos
galloped—ran fast (referring to a horse)
herd—a group of the same kind of animals that are kept or fed together
railroad—a road or track of two steel rails on which trains run
trails—paths across a field or through the woods

GUIDE PRACTICE Have children use each word in a sentence.

Corrective feedback	**If...** children do not use a word correctly, **then...** correct the sentence, model a sentence, and have them try again.

ON THEIR OWN Use *Reader's and Writer's Notebook,* page 563.

Vocabulary Skill

Review Unfamiliar Words

Review that context clues are words in a sentence that help to determine the meaning of an unknown word.

- Which selection word tells how a horse ran? *(galloped)*
- Tell which words in the following sentences help you understand the meaning of *galloped. Cattle ran wildly in all directions. The horses with the bravest cowboys galloped to the front of the herd.* (ran wildly, front)

Team Talk **GUIDE PRACTICE** Have children tell which words help them understand the meaning of *herd.* Have partners review *Cowboys* to find unfamiliar words and context clues.

Common Core State Standards

Foundational Skills 4.c. Use context to confirm or self-correct word recognition and understanding, rereading as necessary. **Language 4.** Determine or clarify the meaning of unknown and multiple-meaning words and phrases based on grade 2 reading and content, choosing flexibly from an array of strategies. **Also Language 4.a.**

Unit 6 Week 4 Interactive Review

Name

Pick a word from the box to finish each sentence.
Write the word on the line.

campfire cattle cowboy galloped herd railroad trails

1. The **cowboy** rides a horse.
2. He cooks food over a **campfire**.
3. He takes the **cattle** across the plains.
4. There were no roads, only dusty **trails**.
5. Sometimes a **herd** of cattle would run off.
6. The cowboy **galloped** on his horse to get them back.
7. The cattle went in pens near the **railroad** tracks.

School + Home **Home Activity** Your child reviewed lesson vocabulary words learned earlier in this unit. Ask your child to write about a day in a cowboy's life using these vocabulary words.

Vocabulary 563

Reader's and Writer's Notebook, p. 563

Zoom in on

Text-Based Comprehension

REVIEW SEQUENCE Review that **sequence** is the order of events or ideas in a selection. Remind children that they know how to identify sequence using order and transition words such as *first, next, then,* and *finally.* Recall that they identified the sequence of events when they read the selection *Cowboys.*

REVIEW TEXT STRUCTURE Remind children that good readers look at text structure to help them understand the order of events and ideas in a selection. **Text structure** is the way a selection is organized. When writing, some authors put facts, events, or ideas in the order they happened in time. Using text structure helps you understand and remember the important ideas more easily.

INFORMATIONAL TEXT Remind children that an informational text tells facts. Informational text often gives facts about real people, places, and events that may reflect history or the traditions of communities.

PREVIEW AND PREDICT Have children read the title of the selection on page 564 of *Reader's and Writer's Notebook.* Have children look through the selection and use the title to predict events that might happen in the selection. Tell them this selection is informational text.

SET A PURPOSE After we read "The Great Wheel," we will identify the topic and talk about the sequence of events in this selection. Have children set a purpose for reading "The Great Wheel."

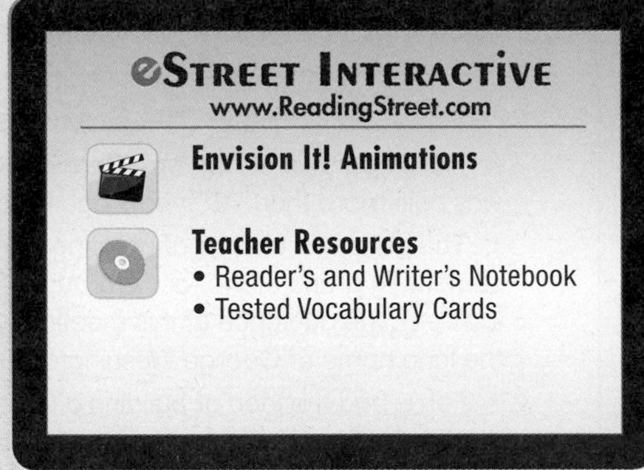

Access for All

A Advanced

Extend Sequence After reviewing sequence, have children write five or six sentences telling about a past event. Have them write each sentence on separate lines and cut the sentences apart into strips. Then have partners exchange sentences to sequence.

Academic Vocabulary

sequence the order of events or ideas in a selection

text structure the way a selection is organized

Unit 6 Week 4 Interactive Review

Name ____________________

Read the story. **Follow** the directions.

The Great Wheel

Have you ever ridden on a Ferris wheel? The first Ferris wheel was built more than 100 years ago for a World's Fair in Chicago.

The people in charge of creating the fair wanted to show off something grand at the fair. A group of men met to discuss their ideas. In the audience at this meeting was a young engineer with the long name of George Washington Gale Ferris.

Ferris had the idea of building a Great Wheel. You might think the Ferris wheels you've seen are big, but the wheel Ferris wanted to build was much bigger. It would be a GIANT wheel!

But first Ferris had to have his design approved. So in 1892, he took his plans to another meeting. Those at the meeting said Ferris was a fool. They told him his wheel would be impossible to build. But Ferris did not give up, and in the end, his idea was approved.

Then Ferris went to work immediately to build his wheel. Next, in June of 1893, Ferris arranged to test his finished wheel. He wanted to see if the enormous wheel would run before he hung cars on it. The wheel already weighed more than 2 million pounds! Would a wheel that heavy actually turn? Yes! The wheel passed the test easily.

So Ferris ordered 36 cars for his Great Wheel. The cars were huge. Each car weighed 26,000 pounds and was big enough to hold 60 passengers. Finally, Ferris hung the cars, and the wheel was ready.

Home Activity Your child identified the order of events in a story. Have your child tell you what happened in a movie he or she has seen recently. Ask your child to tell the events in the order in which they happened. Encourage your child to use time-order words.

564 Comprehension

Unit 6 Week 4 Interactive Review

Name ____________________

At last, in the fall of 1893, the World's Fair opened to the public. There was a grand ceremony on opening day with speakers, music, and crowds of visitors. The last speaker was George Washington Gale Ferris. After his speech, he blew a golden whistle to signal the start-up of the wheel. Everyone watched in awe and cheered excitedly as the magnificent wheel turned. The Great Wheel was a great success.

1. **Circle** the words in the story that give clues to the order in which the events happened.
2. **Write** the numbers 1, 2, 3, 4, 5, 6 to show the correct order of events.

2 Ferris goes to work to build his Great Wheel.

1 Ferris's idea is approved.

6 The World's Fair opens in 1893.

4 Ferris orders cars for his wheel.

3 Ferris tests his wheel to see if it will turn.

5 Ferris hangs cars on his wheel.

Comprehension 565

Reader's and Writer's Notebook, pp. 564–565

Common Core State Standards

Informational Text 1. Ask and answer such questions as *who, what, where, when, why,* and *how* to demonstrate understanding of key details in a text. **Informational Text 3.** Describe the connection between a series of historical events, scientific ideas or concepts, or steps in technical procedures in a text. **Also Foundational Skills 4.b.**

Access Text

Review Sequence

Have children read the selection and respond to the questions.

Corrective feedback | **If...** children have difficulty responding to the questions, **then...** use the following to guide their responses.

1. What did George Washington Gale Ferris have to do first before building the Great Wheel? Have children identify the sequence word *first* and find the sentence that tells what Ferris did first.
2. What did Ferris do after he built the wheel? Have children identify the sequence word *next,* and find the sentence that tells what Ferris did after he built the wheel.
3. What was the last thing Ferris had to do to get the Great Wheel ready? Have children identify the sequence word *finally,* and find the sentence that tells what Ferris did last.

REVIEW TEXT STRUCTURE Discuss the comprehension tools that children used as they read "The Great Wheel." Did you notice that the events in the selection were told in the order in which they happened? How did that help you understand the information? Have children tell how the organization of the selection helped them understand and remember the events.

Reread for Fluency

MODEL FLUENT READING Remind children that when they read, it is important to pay attention to each word, read without mistakes, and read at an appropriate rate. Model reading the first two paragraphs of "The Great Wheel" on *Reader's and Writer's Notebook,* page 564 with accuracy and at an appropriate rate. Have children track the print as you read.

GUIDE PRACTICE To provide additional fluency practice, pair children and have them read "The Great Wheel."

Routine — Paired Reading

Team Talk

1. **Reader 1 Begins** Children read the selection, switching readers at the end of each paragraph.
2. **Reader 2 Begins** Have partners reread; this time the other partner begins.
3. **Reread** For optimal fluency, children should reread three or four times.
4. **Corrective Feedback** Listen to children read and provide corrective feedback regarding their oral reading and their use of the blending strategy.

Routines Flip Chart

Access for All

SI Strategic Intervention

Comprehension and Fluency Have children reread "The Great Wheel" aloud. As they read, have them think about the sequence of events. After children have read the selection, have them describe the events that led to the first Ferris wheel.

Options for Oral Rereading

Use *Cowboys* or a leveled reader.

Common Core State Standards

Language 2. Demonstrate command of the conventions of standard English capitalization, punctuation, and spelling when writing. **Speaking/Listening 1.** Participate in collaborative conversations with diverse partners about grade 2 topics and texts with peers and adults in small and larger groups.

Unit 6 Week 4 Interactive Review

Name

Using Commas

Write parts of a letter. Use commas where they are needed.

1. Chicago IL 60616 — Chicago, IL 60616
2. March 18 2012 — March 18, 2012
3. Dear Pedro — Dear Pedro,

Write each sentence. Use commas where they are needed.

4. I visited the ranch on May 12 2012. — I visited the ranch on May 12, 2012.
5. We rode ate and played. — We rode, ate, and played.
6. I got back to the ranch on Monday July 2. — I got back to the ranch Monday, July 2.

566 Conventions

Reader's and Writer's Notebook, p. 566

Unit 6 Interactive Review

Name

Day 1 Unit 6 Week 1 — Just Like Josh Gibson

Copy the sentences. Make sure your letters and words are spaced correctly.

We won't go to Vienna.

Check children's letters and words for correct spacing.

You don't know Uncle Will.

Day 2 Unit 6 Week 2 — Red, White, and Blue

Copy the sentences. Make sure your letters are written smoothly.

Beth and Pam like shopping.

Check children's letters for smoothness.

Rob hiked the Forest Trail.

School+Home Home Activity Your child practiced writing all cursive letters. Each day have your child copy a sentence from a favorite storybook using his or her best cursive handwriting.

Handwriting 547

Reader's and Writer's Notebook, pp. 547–548

Conventions

Review Commas

Remind children that commas are used to separate words and phrases in writing. In an address, a comma is placed between the city and state. In a date, a comma is placed between the date and the year. A comma is used when listing three or more items, too.

GUIDE PRACTICE Write the following sentences without commas. Have children fill in the missing commas.

> Sanji lives in Cleveland, Ohio.
> School starts on Tuesday, September 5.
> My favorite foods are pizza, carrots, apples, and pretzels.
> On August 17, 2008, my family moved to Austin, Texas.

Team Talk Have partners dictate birth dates and a list of favorite foods to each other and tell where commas would be used.

ON THEIR OWN Use *Reader's and Writer's Notebook,* page 566.

Handwriting

REVIEW CURSIVE LETTERS Demonstrate the proper formation of cursive letters *Z, Q,* and *X.* Then review all lowercase letters. Have children write each capital letter several times and circle the best one. Then have them write each lowercase letter.

REVIEW LETTER SLANT Review that cursive letters should slant slightly to the right.

GUIDE PRACTICE Write the following sentence. Have children copy it using the correct letter slant. Monitor children's letters as they write. If children have not transitioned to cursive, have them write the words in manuscript.

> **Zane and Quentin canoed on the Xingu River in Brazil.**

ON THEIR OWN Use the Day 4 section on *Reader's and Writer's Notebook,* pages 547–548.

Optional Unit Review

Routine Quick Write for Fluency

Team Talk

1. **Talk** Have pairs discuss what they learned about cowboy traditions.
2. **Write** Have children write a few sentences to summarize the discussion.
3. **Share** Partners can read their summaries to one another.

Routines Flip Chart

Writing Workshop

Use the writing process lesson on pages WP•1–WP•10 for this week's writing instruction.

Extend Amazing Words Tell children that the word *legend* can mean "a story that has been passed down through the years," such as, *There is a legend of a cowboy who died saving a calf on a trail ride. Legend* can also mean "a person who is well-known for a special talent," such as *Fannie Steele is a cowgirl legend for her skill in bronco busting.* Have children tell how the words are alike.

Wrap Up Week 4 Review

✔ **Content Knowledge** What are some cowboy traditions? Why are they important? Do you think being a cowboy is a good occupation? Why or why not?

✔ **Sequence** Think back to yesterday. When you got home from school, what did you do first? What did you do next? What was the very last thing you did yesterday?

✔ **Unfamiliar Words** Look back at *Cowboys* and "The Great Wheel." What are some unfamiliar words in those selections? How did you find their meanings?

Preview DAY 5

Tell children that tomorrow they will review more skills and read "The Butterfly Place."

Review Week 5

Content Knowledge
Review Oral Vocabulary

Phonics/Spelling
Review Prefixes *mis-, mid-, micro-, non-*

Selection Vocabulary
Review *assembly, election, microphone, rallies, slogan, speeches*

Vocabulary
Review Multiple-Meaning Words

Text-Based Comprehension
Review Facts and Details
Review Predict and Set Purpose

Fluency
Read with Appropriate Phrasing

Conventions
Review Commas in Compound Sentences

Handwriting
Review Cursive Letters/Letter and Word Spacing

Writing
Quick Write for Fluency

Materials

- Sing with Me Big Book
- Sound-Spelling Cards
- Reader's and Writer's Notebook

Common Core State Standards

Speaking/Listening 1. Participate in collaborative conversations with diverse partners about grade 2 topics and texts with peers and adults in small and larger groups. **Language 5.a.** Identify real-life connections between words and their use (e.g., describe foods that are *spicy* or *juicy*). **Also Language 6.**

Content Knowledge

Celebrated and Shared Traditions

Today children will explore how the Question of the Week connects to *Grace for President.* Read the Question of the Week: *How are different traditions celebrated and shared?* Remind children that *Grace for President* is realistic fiction about how children in a school share in the tradition of voting for a president.

Build Oral Language

TALK ABOUT CELEBRATED AND SHARED TRADITIONS Use these questions to connect the Week 5 question and selection to the Unit 6 Big Question, **Are traditions and celebrations important in our lives?**

- How did Grace's school share in the voting tradition?
- How would you have shared in the tradition?
- How have you shared in voting traditions and celebrations?

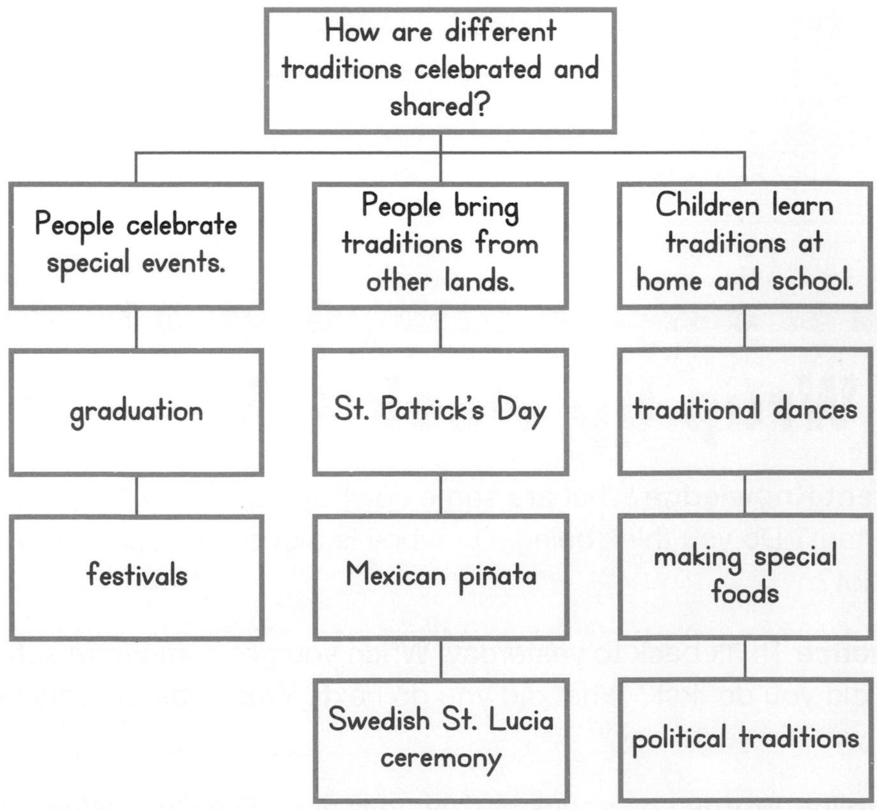

Build Oral Vocabulary

REVIEW AMAZING WORDS Remind children that they have learned some Amazing Words that they can use to answer the question *How are different traditions celebrated and shared?* Display the song on page 30 of the *Sing with Me* Big Book. Sing the song.

Go over all the Amazing Words from Week 5. Ask children to listen as you say them: *ceremony, culture, festival, compliment, fidget, evergreen, multicolored, sash.* Then say them again, and have children say each word after you.

- Is an *evergreen multicolored?* (no)
- Name a *ceremony* you have attended.
- If someone gives you a *compliment,* is he or she being nice or rude? (nice)

AMAZING WORDS AT WORK Have children demonstrate their understanding of Amazing Words by completing these sentences orally.

Joe gave Cara a **compliment** about her ______.

We attended the ______ **festival** this summer.

Maria wore a ______ with a sash to the **ceremony.**

The **multicolored** ______ on the **evergreen** were beautiful.

Mom told my ______ not to **fidget.**

______ is an example of **culture.**

Amazing Words

ceremony
culture
festival
compliment
fidget
evergreen
multicolored
sash

Access for All

SI Strategic Intervention

Describe a Ceremony Have partners describe a ceremony using as many of the Amazing Words as possible. For example: *The wedding ceremony was very beautiful. The bridesmaids wore green dresses with multicolored sashes. The bride received many compliments.* Have partners share their descriptions with the class.

Reteach Concepts and Vocabulary Use the instruction on ELL Poster 30 to assess knowledge and concepts.

Common Core State Standards

Foundational Skills 3.d. Decode words with common prefixes and suffixes.

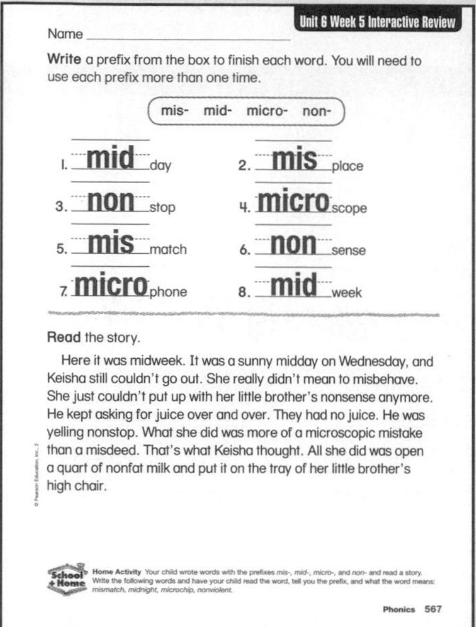
Unit 6 Week 5 Interactive Review

Name ______________

Write a prefix from the box to finish each word. You will need to use each prefix more than one time.

mis- mid- micro- non-

1. **mid**day
2. **mis**place
3. **non**stop
4. **micro**scope
5. **mis**match
6. **non**sense
7. **micro**phone
8. **mid**week

Read the story.

Here it was midweek. It was a sunny midday on Wednesday, and Keisha still couldn't go out. She really didn't mean to misbehave. She just couldn't put up with her little brother's nonsense anymore. He kept asking for juice over and over. They had no juice. He was yelling nonstop. What she did was more of a microscopic mistake than a misdeed. That's what Keisha thought. All she did was open a quart of nonfat milk and put it on the tray of her little brother's high chair.

Home Activity Your child wrote words with the prefixes *mis-*, *mid-*, *micro-*, and *non-* and read a story. Write the following words and have your child read the word, tell you the prefix, and what the word means: *mismatch, midnight, microchip, nonviolent.*

Phonics 567

Reader's and Writer's Notebook, p. 567

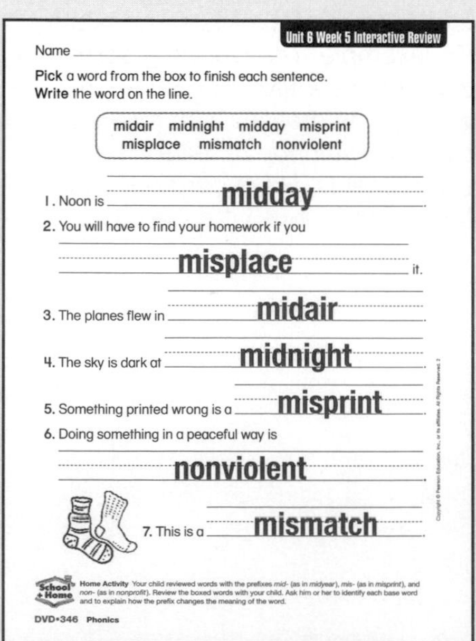
Unit 6 Week 5 Interactive Review

Name ______________

Pick a word from the box to finish each sentence.
Write the word on the line.

midair midnight midday misprint misplace mismatch nonviolent

1. Noon is **midday**.
2. You will have to find your homework if you **misplace** it.
3. The planes flew in **midair**.
4. The sky is dark at **midnight**.
5. Something printed wrong is a **misprint**.
6. Doing something in a peaceful way is **nonviolent**.
7. This is a **mismatch**.

Home Activity Your child reviewed words with the prefixes *mid-* (as in *midyear*), *mis-* (as in *misprint*), and *non-* (as in *nonprofit*). Review the boxed words with your child. Ask him or her to identify each base word and to explain how the prefix changes the meaning of the word.

DVD•346 Phonics

Let's Practice It! TR DVD•346

Phonics

Review ◎ Prefixes *mis-, mid-, micro-, non-*

TARGET PHONICS SKILLS Review prefixes *mis-*, *mid-*, *micro-*, and *non-* using Sound-Spelling Cards 155–158.

DECODE WORDS IN ISOLATION Have children complete the top half of *Reader's and Writer's Notebook,* page 567. Point out that children know how to read these words. Then tell children they will all read the words in each row together. Allow several seconds previewing time for the first reading.

Corrective feedback	**If...** children cannot read both words in a row without an error, **then...** return to the first word in the row, and have children reread both words in the row. Repeat until children can read the words fluently.

DECODE WORDS IN CONTEXT Use the passage on *Reader's and Writer's Notebook,* page 567. Point out that there are many words with prefixes *mis-*, *mid-*, *micro-*, and *non-* in the passage that children already know how to read. Have children read the passage together.

Corrective feedback	**If...** children have difficulty reading words with prefixes *mis-*, *mid-*, *micro-*, and *non-*, **then...** guide them in chunking multisyllabic words and using sound-by-sound blending. Have children read each sentence. Repeat until children can read the sentences fluently.

ON THEIR OWN Use Let's Practice It!, p. 346 on the *Teacher Resources DVD-ROM.*

Spelling

Review Prefixes *mis-, mid-*

Write *mislead* and *midway.* Point out that these words have the prefixes *mis-* and *mid-.* Remind children that they learned how to spell words with these prefixes. Use Sound-Spelling Cards 156 and 157 to review how to spell words with prefixes *mis-* and *mid-.* Review the Week 5 spelling words.

Team Talk Have children review the spelling words using index cards on which the words are written. Tell them to sort the words into the ones they know and the ones they need more practice with. Partners can quiz each other on the words in the second pile.

ON THEIR OWN Use *Reader's and Writer's Notebook,* p. 568.

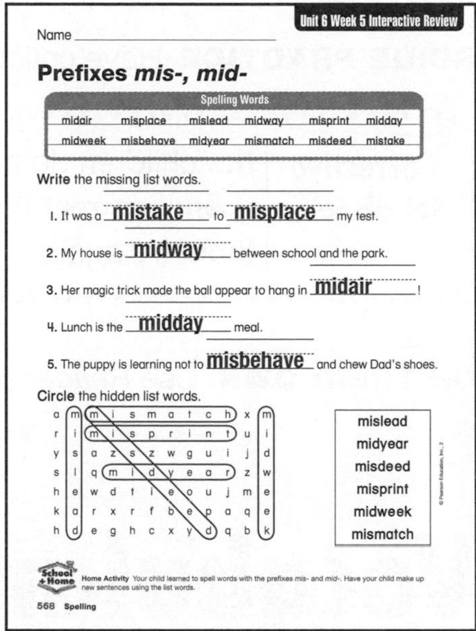
Unit 6 Week 5 Interactive Review

Name ______________________

Prefixes *mis-, mid-*

Spelling Words					
midair	misplace	mislead	midway	misprint	midday
midweek	misbehave	midyear	mismatch	misdeed	mistake

Write the missing list words.

1. It was a **mistake** to **misplace** my test.
2. My house is **midway** between school and the park.
3. Her magic trick made the ball appear to hang in **midair**!
4. Lunch is the **midday** meal.
5. The puppy is learning not to **misbehave** and chew Dad's shoes.

Circle the hidden list words.

a m m i s m a t c h x m
r i m i s p r i n t u i
y s a z s z w g u i j d
s l q m i d y e a r z w
h e w d t i e o u j m e
k a r x r f b e p a q e
h d e g h c x y d q b k

mislead
midyear
misdeed
misprint
midweek
mismatch

© Pearson Education, Inc., 2

School + Home **Home Activity** Your child learned to spell words with the prefixes *mis-* and *mid-*. Have your child make up new sentences using the list words.

568 Spelling

Reader's and Writer's Notebook, p. 568

Unit 6 Week 5 Spelling Words

Prefixes *mis-, mid-*

1. midair
2. misplace
3. mislead
4. midway
5. misprint
6. midday
7. midweek
8. misbehave
9. midyear
10. mismatch
11. misdeed
12. mistake

Review Prefixes *mis-, mid-, micro-, non-* Remind children that a prefix is added to the beginning of a word and changes the word's meaning.

Beginning Write and read a list of words with prefixes *mis-, mid-, micro-,* and *non-.* Have children write the words and circle the prefix. Have partners take turns reading the words.

Intermediate Write and read words with each target prefix. Have children draw a four-column chart and label the columns *mis-, mid-, micro-,* and *non-.* Have them write each word in the appropriate column and circle the prefix. Then have partners take turns reading the words.

Advanced Have children identify, write, and read at least five words containing each target prefix.

Common Core State Standards

Language 4. Determine or clarify the meaning of unknown and multiple-meaning words and phrases based on grade 2 reading and content, choosing flexibly from an array of strategies. **Language 4.a.** Use sentence-level context as a clue to the meaning of a word or phrase.

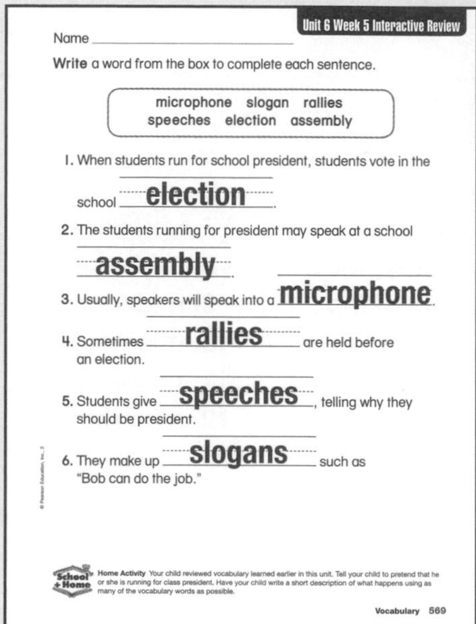

Unit 6 Week 5 Interactive Review

Name ____________

Write a word from the box to complete each sentence.

microphone slogan rallies
speeches election assembly

1. When students run for school president, students vote in the school election.
2. The students running for president may speak at a school assembly.
3. Usually, speakers will speak into a microphone.
4. Sometimes rallies are held before an election.
5. Students give speeches, telling why they should be president.
6. They make up slogans such as "Bob can do the job."

Home Activity Your child reviewed vocabulary learned earlier in this unit. Tell your child to pretend that he or she is running for class president. Have your child write a short description of what happens using as many of the vocabulary words as possible.

Vocabulary 569

Reader's and Writer's Notebook, p. 569

Selection Vocabulary

REVIEW READ WORDS IN ISOLATION Display the selection vocabulary. Have children read the words aloud with you. Review the definitions.

assembly—a gathering of the students in a school for a special purpose
election—the act of voting for a person to hold a position in a group
microphone—a machine that makes sound louder
rallies—meetings that people attend to show support
slogan—a word or short sentence used by a person or business that tells an idea
speeches—talks given to groups of people

GUIDE PRACTICE Have children use each word in a sentence.

Corrective feedback	**If...** children do not use a word correctly, **then...** correct the sentence, model a sentence, and have them try again.

ON THEIR OWN Use *Reader's and Writer's Notebook,* page 569.

Vocabulary Skill

Review Multiple-Meaning Words

Review that a multiple-meaning word has two or more different meanings. *Bug, pop,* and *run* are multiple-meaning words.

- Which selection word means "a gathering of the students in a school for a special purpose"? *(assembly)*
- Find another meaning in the dictionary for the word *assembly.*

Have children name and define other multiple-meaning words.

Team Talk **GUIDE PRACTICE** Have partners use multiple-meaning words in sentences.

Text-Based Comprehension

REVIEW FACTS AND DETAILS Review with children that **facts** are pieces of information that can be proved true and **details** are small pieces of information. Remind children that they know how to identify facts and details. Recall that children identified facts and details in *Grace for President.*

REVIEW PREDICT AND SET A PURPOSE Remind children that good readers make predictions, or tell what they think will happen next, before and during reading. As readers read on, they confirm or revise those predictions. You can learn a lot about a story if you page through it before reading. You can use the title and illustrations to learn what the story will be about. You can read the first sentence of different paragraphs, too. Once you have an idea of the topic of the story, you can set a reason to read to help you better focus on the story.

REALISTIC FICTION Remind children that **realistic fiction** is a make-believe story that has made up characters and events. In a realistic fiction story, the setting and characters seem real. It tells about problems people may have in real life.

PREVIEW AND PREDICT Have children read the title of the selection on page 570 of *Reader's and Writer's Notebook.* Have children look through the selection and use the title to predict events that might happen in the story. Tell them this selection is realistic fiction.

SET A PURPOSE After we read "The Butterfly Place," we will identify facts and details in the story. Have children set a purpose for reading "The Butterfly Place."

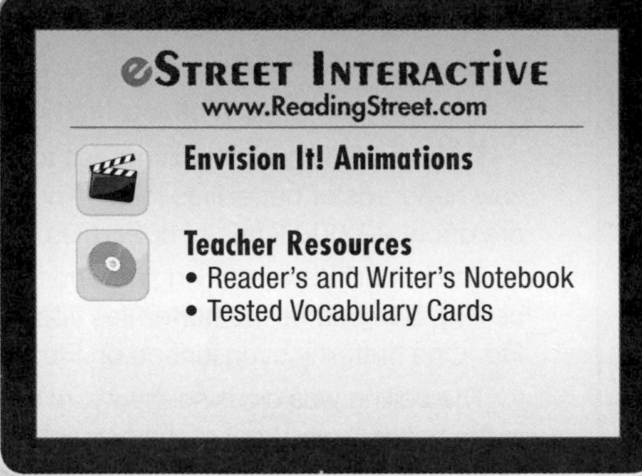

Access for All

 Advanced

Extend Facts and Details After reviewing facts and details, have partners give facts and details about a favorite sport. Then have children record their facts and details on a Web.

Academic Vocabulary

facts pieces of information that can be proved true

details small pieces of information

realistic fiction a story of imaginary people and events that could happen in real life

Unit 6 Week 5 Interactive Review

Name ____________________

Read the story. **Follow** the directions.

The Butterfly Place

Rich and Flo had an exciting visit to The Butterfly Place. They saw hundreds of butterflies there. The guide told them that there are about 28,000 kinds of butterflies.

The butterflies were flying around in a big building with a glass ceiling. Sometimes the butterflies floated very close to Rich and Flo. One butterfly even landed on Flo's head!

The ceiling was glass so the warm sun could shine in. The heat in the building was kept at the correct temperature for butterflies. Butterflies need warmth. If the temperature is lower than 86°F, butterflies cannot fly. That's why they're active in the day and sleep at night.

Rich and Flo learned that some butterflies are very small with a wingspan of only 1/8 inch. Others are large with a wingspan of almost 12 inches. Butterfly wings are covered with scales. These scales are beautiful colors and form interesting patterns. But the scales can be rubbed off the wings.

The guide explained that a butterfly does not grow once it comes out of its chrysalis. Rich and Flo were surprised to learn that most butterflies only live from two to four weeks.

As they were walking around, Rich wondered, "Can butterflies see?"

"They see three colors," the guide said, "red, yellow, and green."

Then Flo asked, "Do they make sounds?"

School + Home **Home Activity** Your child learned to identify facts and details from a story. Read part of a short biography written at your child's level. Work together to make a list of facts about the person.

Unit 6 Week 5 Interactive Review

Name ____________________

"Most butterflies make no sounds," the guide answered. "But a few will make loud clicks with their wings."

When it was time to leave, the visitors to The Butterfly Place thanked the guide for telling them about butterflies. As Rich and Flo walked out, they checked to make sure no butterflies were going along with them!

1. About how many kinds of butterflies are there?

   There are about 28,000 kinds of butterflies.

2. What is the correct temperature for butterflies?

   The correct temperature is 86°F or higher.

3. What is the wingspan of the smallest butterflies?

   The wingspan of the smallest butterflies is 1/8 inch.

4. How long do most butterflies live?

   Most butterflies live from two to four weeks.

5. **Underline** a fact about what butterflies see.

Reader's and Writer's Notebook, pp. 570–571

Common Core State Standards

Literature 1. Ask and answer such questions as *who, what, where, when, why,* and *how* to demonstrate understanding of key details in a text. **Literature 7.** Use information gained from the illustrations and words in a print or digital text to demonstrate understanding of its characters, setting, or plot. **Also Foundational Skills 4.a.**

Access Text

Review Facts and Details

Have children read the story and respond to the questions.

Corrective feedback	**If...** children have difficulty responding to the questions, **then...** use the following to guide their responses.

1. Identify a couple of details about butterfly wings. Have children find the sentences that tell about the scales on butterfly wings.
2. Why is it important that The Butterfly Place is warm? Have children find the sentences that tell about butterflies' needs for warmth, and that they cannot fly when the temperature is lower than 86°F.
3. How does the guide at The Butterfly Place answer Flo's question? Have children find the dialogue between the guide and the children to read how he responds to her.

REVIEW **PREDICT AND SET PURPOSE** Discuss the comprehension tools that children used as they read "The Butterfly Place."

What purpose did you set for reading? What predictions did you make as you read the story? What did you base your predictions on? Have children tell how setting a purpose and making predictions helped them focus their reading and better understand the characters and events in the story. Were your predictions correct? Have children tell how they confirmed their predictions.

Reread for Fluency

MODEL FLUENT READING Remind children that when they read, it is important to read words that go together in a sentence in the way we normally speak. Model reading the first paragraph of "The Butterfly Place" on *Reader's and Writer's Notebook,* page 570 with appropriate phrasing. Have children track the print as you read.

GUIDE PRACTICE To provide additional fluency practice, pair children and have them read "The Butterfly Place."

Routine Paired Reading — Team Talk

1. **Reader 1 Begins** Children read the story, switching readers at the end of each paragraph.
2. **Reader 2 Begins** Have partners reread; this time the other partner begins.
3. **Reread** For optimal fluency, children should reread three or four times.
4. **Corrective Feedback** Listen to children read and provide corrective feedback regarding their oral reading and their use of the blending strategy.

Routines Flip Chart

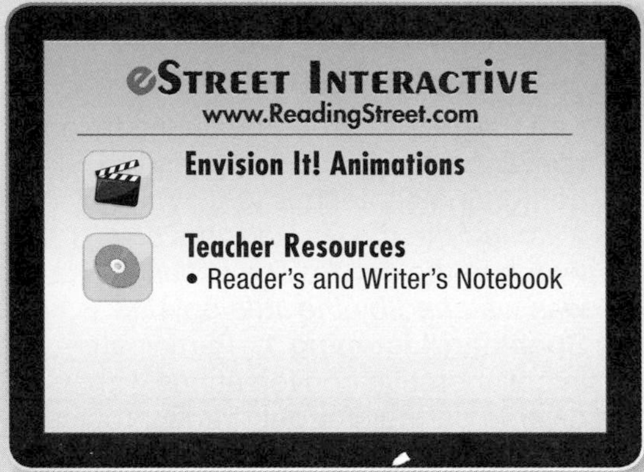

Access for All

SI Strategic Intervention

Comprehension and Fluency Have children reread "The Butterfly Place" aloud. As they read, have them think about the facts and details that are included in the story. After they have read the story, have them tell two facts they learned about butterflies.

Options for Oral Rereading

Use *Grace for President* or a leveled reader.

Common Core State Standards

Language 1.f. Produce, expand, and rearrange complete simple and compound sentences (e.g., *The boy watched the movie; The little boy watched the movie; The action movie was watched by the little boy*). **Speaking/Listening 1.** Participate in collaborative conversations with diverse partners about grade 2 topics and texts with peers and adults in small and larger groups.

Unit 6 Week 5 Interactive Review

Name

Commas in Compound Sentences

Use the word in ( ) and a comma to combine each pair of sentences. **Write** the new sentence on the lines.

1. The election is today. We will vote. (and)
   The election is today, and we will vote.
2. Sam wanted to vote. She has the flu. (but)
   Sam wanted to vote, but she has the flu.

Add a comma where it is needed. **Circle** the word that joins the two sentences.

3. Our teacher made a box, (and) we put our votes in.
4. Each vote was secret, (but) some tried to peek.
5. Mrs. Lee counted the votes, (and) she made a tally chart.
6. We will find out who won, (but) we must wait.

School + Home Home Activity Your child prepared for taking tests on compound sentences. Have your child tell you three compound sentences about his or her day.

572 Conventions

Reader's and Writer's Notebook, p. 572

Unit 6 Interactive Review

Name

Day 1 Unit 6 Week 1 Just Like Josh Gibson

Copy the sentences. Make sure your letters and words are spaced correctly.

We won't go to Vienna.

Check children's letters and words for correct spacing.

You don't know Uncle Will.

Day 2 Unit 6 Week 2 Red, White, and Blue

Copy the sentences. Make sure your letters are written smoothly.

Beth and Pam like shopping.

Check children's letters for smoothness.

Rob hiked the Forest Trail.

School + Home Home Activity Your child practiced writing all cursive letters. Each day have your child copy a sentence from a favorite storybook using his or her best cursive handwriting.

Handwriting 547

Reader's and Writer's Notebook, pp. 547–548

Conventions

Review Commas in Compound Sentences

Remind children that two simple sentences can be combined with a comma and a connecting word, such as *and* or *but,* to make a compound sentence.

GUIDE PRACTICE Write the following sentence pairs. Have children use a comma and a connecting word to make compound sentences.

I am a teacher. I love my job. (I am a teacher, and I love my job.)

Kim swims. She wants to dance. (Kim swims, but she wants to dance.)

Ann and Mary are twins. They are not identical. (Ann and Mary are twins, but they are not identical.)

Team Talk Have children write a simple sentence. Then have them trade papers with a partner. The partner writes another sentence to go along with the first. Have partners work together to make compound sentences.

ON THEIR OWN Use *Reader's and Writer's Notebook,* page 572.

Handwriting

REVIEW CURSIVE LETTERS Demonstrate the proper formation of cursive letters *L, D,* and *J.* Then review all lowercase letters. Have children write each capital letter several times and circle the best one. Then have them write each lowercase letter.

REVIEW LETTER AND WORD SPACING Remind children to insert the same amount of space between each letter in a word and to leave larger spaces between words.

GUIDE PRACTICE Write the following sentence. Have children copy it using proper letter and word spacing. Monitor children's spacing of letters and words. If children have not transitioned to cursive, have them write the words in manuscript.

Linda is taking a midnight flight to Dallas, Texas, in June.

ON THEIR OWN Use the Day 5 section on *Reader's and Writer's Notebook,* pages 547–548.

Optional Unit Review

Routine Quick Write for Fluency

Team Talk

1. **Talk** Have pairs discuss what they learned about voting traditions and other traditions and celebrations.
2. **Write** Have children write a few sentences to summarize the discussion.
3. **Share** Partners can read their summaries to one another.

Routines Flip Chart

Writing Workshop

Use the writing process lesson on pages WP•1–WP•10 for this week's writing instruction.

Wrap Up Week 5 Review

✔ **Content Knowledge** What are some traditions and celebrations in your culture? What kinds of multicolored objects might you see at a special celebration or festival? What are these objects used for?

✔ **Facts and Details** Look back at "The Butterfly Place." What are some facts from "The Butterfly Place?" What are some details? What is the largest wingspan of a butterfly in "The Butterfly Place"?

✔ **Multiple-Meaning Words** What is a multiple-meaning word? What is one meaning for the word *tire?* What is another meaning? Use both meanings in sentences. What is one meaning for the word *horn?* What is another meaning? Use both meanings in sentences.

Wrap Up Your Unit!

Discuss Content Knowledge Gained Through Reading

Are traditions and celebrations important in our lives?

WEEK 1

Why are sports traditions important to our country?

Children have learned that sports are:

- an important tradition in our culture
- enjoyed by players and spectators
- played by both boys and girls

WEEK 2

What traditions and celebrations involve our country's flag?

Children have learned some of the traditions that honor the flag:

- the Pledge of Allegiance
- the National Anthem
- the Fourth of July

WEEK 3

Why are family celebrations special?

Children have learned that family celebrations:

- involve cultural traditions
- include certain activities
- include special foods

What are the traditions and celebrations we have read about?

- baseball
- honoring our flag
- family celebrations
- cowboy traditions
- presidential elections

Discuss with children the selections they have explored surrounding the idea of traditions. Throughout discussions, children should support their comments and ideas with evidence from the texts.

How are traditions and celebrations important to people in the selections?

- *Just Like Josh Gibson:* The tradition of playing baseball was important to the little girl in this story.
- *Red, White, and Blue:* People value the flag as a symbol of our country.
- *A Birthday Basket for Tía:* Cecilia fills Tía's basket with reminders of good times.
- *Cowboys:* Cowboys are part of the American tradition of workers.
- *Grace for President:* The class participates in the tradition of a presidential election.

WEEK 4

What can we learn about cowboy traditions?

Children have learned that cowboys:

- worked hard
- had difficult working conditions
- wore protective clothing

WEEK 5

How are different traditions celebrated and shared?

Children have learned that traditions can be:

- shared and celebrated at special events
- brought from other lands
- learned at home and at school

Talk about traditions.

Think of a tradition or celebration you and your family share. What is it? Which tradition or celebration you read about is it most like? How does it differ? (Responses will vary.)

Team Talk Have children work in pairs to talk about the Amazing Ideas related to traditions that they discussed each week. Then have children use these ideas to help demonstrate their understanding of the question, *Are traditions and celebrations important in our lives?*

Amazing Words

You've learned 241 words this year!

You've learned 040 words this unit to use as you talk about traditions.

Assessment Checkpoints for the Week

Unit Assessment

Use Unit 6 *Benchmark Test* to check:

✔ **Passage Comprehension**

✔ **Writing Conventions**

✔ **Phonics**

✔ **Vocabulary**

✔ **Writing**

✔ **Fluency**

Unit and End-of-Year Benchmark Tests

Managing Assessment

Use *Assessment Handbook* for:

✔ **Weekly Assessment Blackline Masters for Monitoring Progress**

✔ **Observation Checklists**

✔ **Record-Keeping Forms**

✔ **Portfolio Assessment**

Assessment Handbook

Tennessee Writing on Reading Street

Process Writing and the Common Core State Standards, Tennessee CUs, and GLEs

This unit's Writing Process assignment will provide you with opportunities to instruct students in the steps of process writing: Plan and Prewrite, Draft, Revise, Edit, and Publish.

Process Writing Steps	Common Core State Standards	Tennessee CUs and GLEs
1 Plan and Prewrite	CCSS Writing 2., CCSS Writing 5., CCSS Writing 6., CCSS Writing 7., CCSS Writing 8.	TN CU 0201.3.1, TN CU 0201.3.3, TN CU 0201.3.11, TN CU 0201.4.7, TN GLE 0201.3.1, TN GLE 0201.3.3
2 Draft	CCSS Writing 2., CCSS Writing 7.	TN CU 0201.3.1, TN CU 0201.3.3, TN CU 0201.4.7, TN GLE 0201.3.1, TN GLE 0201.3.3
3 Revise	CCSS Writing 2., CCSS Writing 5.	TN CU 0201.3.1, TN GLE 0201.3.1, TN GLE 0201.3.3
4 Edit	CCSS Writing 5., CCSS Writing 6., CCSS Language 2.	TN CU 0201.3.11, TN GLE 0201.1.1
5 Publish and Present	CCSS Writing 6., CCSS Speaking and Listening 5.	TN CU 0201.7.4, TN GLE 0201.7.2

Writing Trait Skills Trace

All of the writing traits taught in Scott Foresman Reading Street are dimensions of good writing. The chart below shows you the writing traits taught each week of the unit. In the column on the right, the criteria to achieve the Tennessee Writing Scoring Rubric top score are identified. For a complete Tennessee Writing Scoring Rubric aligned to the unit writing process project, see the back of this page.

	Writing Trait of the Week/ Weekly Selection	Tennessee Writing Scoring Rubric Top Score Point Criteria Score of 6: A 6 paper is OUTSTANDING. An essay in this category:
Week 1	Organization **TN CU 0201.3.7** *Just Like Josh Gibson*	is well organized and coherently developed
Week 2	Voice **TN CU 0201.3.7** *Red, White, and Blue: The Story of the American Flag*	clearly displays facility in the use of language
Week 3	Sentences **TN CU 0201.1.6** *A Birthday Basket for Tía*	demonstrates syntactic variety; is generally free from errors in mechanics, usage, and sentence structure
Week 4	Focus/Ideas **TN CU 0201.3.1** *Cowboys*	clearly explains or illustrates key ideas
Week 5	Word Choice **TN CU 0201.3.7** *Grace for President*	clearly displays facility in the use of language

Tennessee Writing Resources

Use these resources to build writing skills during and after the teaching of Unit 6.

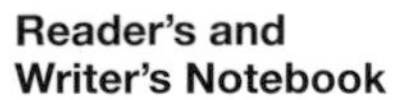

Reader's and Writer's Notebook

Writing Rubrics and Anchor Papers

Digital Resources
- Online Journal
- Online Writing Transparencies
- Grammar Jammer

Teacher Resources DVD-ROM
- Reader's and Writer's Notebook
- Let's Practice It!
- Graphic Organizers
- Writing Transparencies

ISBN-13: 978-0-328-73472-6 ISBN-10: 0-328-73472-1

Tennessee Research Report Rubric

The rubric below is a 6-point Tennessee Writing Scoring Rubric that has been modified to correspond with this unit's process writing project.

SCORE OF 6	A 6 PAPER IS OUTSTANDING.

It demonstrates a high degree of proficiency in response to the assignment but may have a few minor errors. A research report in this category:

- is well organized and coherently developed, giving complete, accurate information about a topic in an organized way
- clearly explains or illustrates key ideas using facts from several sources
- demonstrates syntactic variety
- clearly displays facility in the use of language
- is generally free from errors in mechanics, usage, and sentence structure

SCORE OF 5	A 5 PAPER IS STRONG.

It demonstrates clear proficiency in response to the assignment and may have minor errors. A research report in this category:

- is generally well organized and coherently developed, giving complete, accurate information about a topic in an organized way
- explains or illustrates key ideas using facts from several sources
- demonstrates some syntactic variety
- displays facility in the use of language
- is generally free from errors in mechanics, usage, and sentence structure

SCORE OF 4	A 4 PAPER IS COMPETENT.

It demonstrates proficiency in response to the assignment. A research report in this category:

- is adequately organized and developed, giving accurate information about a topic in an organized way
- explains or illustrates some of the key ideas using facts from several sources
- demonstrates adequate facility in the use of language
- may display some errors in mechanics, usage, or sentence structure

SCORE OF 3	A 3 PAPER IS LIMITED.

It demonstrates some degree of proficiency in response to the assignment, but it is clearly flawed. A research report in this category reveals one or more of the following weaknesses:

- inadequate organization or development, giving some information about a topic
- inadequate explanation or illustration of key ideas using facts from a few sources
- limited or inappropriate word choice
- a pattern or accumulation of errors in mechanics, usage, or sentence structure

SCORE OF 2	A 2 PAPER IS FLAWED.

It demonstrates limited proficiency in response to the assignment. A research report in this category reveals one or more of the following weaknesses:

- weak organization or very little development; the report may not give much, if any, information about a topic
- little or no relevant detail, with few or no facts
- serious errors in mechanics, usage, sentence structure, or word choice

SCORE OF 1	A 1 PAPER IS DEFICIENT.

It demonstrates fundamental deficiencies in writing skills. A research report in this category contains serious and persistent writing errors or is incoherent or is undeveloped.

SCORE OF 0	

A 0 paper could not be scored for one of the following reasons: blank or refusal, insufficient to score or illegible, off topic, written predominantly in another language.

Writing on Reading Street 

DAILY WRITING FOCUS

Quick Writes for Fluency

- Use the Quick Write routine for **writing on demand**.
- The Quick Write **prompt and routine** extend skills and strategies from daily writing lessons.
- Daily 10-minute **mini-lessons** focus instruction on the traits and craft of good writing.
- **Writing Traits** are focus/ideas, organization, voice, word choice, sentences, and conventions.
- **Craft** includes drafting strategies, revising strategies, and editing strategies.

WEEKLY WRITING FOCUS

Writing Forms and Patterns

- Instruction focuses on a different **product** each week.
- Mini-lessons and models help children learn key features and **organizational patterns**.
- Use **mentor text** every week as a model to exemplify the traits of good writing.
- **Grade 2 Products** include biography, personal narrative, realistic fiction, journal, expository nonfiction, thank-you note, and more.
- **Grade 2 Organizational Patterns** include cause and effect, beginning, middle, and end, main idea and details, letter, and more.

UNIT WRITING FOCUS

Writing Process

- Six **writing process** lessons provide structure to move children through the steps of the writing process.
- One-week and two-week pacing (see the back of this Tab) allows lessons to be used in **Writing Workshops**.
- The **steps of the writing process** are Plan and Prewrite, Draft, Revise, Edit, and Publish and Present.
- **Grade 2 Writing Process Products** include personal narrative, directions, compare and contrast essay, description, persuasive letter, and research report.

Research Report

PROCESS WRITING STEPS	COMMON CORE STATE STANDARDS FOR ENGLISH LANGUAGE ARTS	TIPS FOR UNIT 6 PROCESS WRITING
1 Plan and Prewrite	**Writing 2., Writing 5., Writing 6., Writing 7., Writing 8.**	As children prepare to **prewrite**, suggest that they look closely at each of their topics and think about whether it is the best topic for their report.
2 Draft	**Writing 2., Writing 7.**	As children **draft** their writing, show them how to use a KWL Chart to categorize and organize their ideas.
3 Revise	**Writing 2., Writing 5.**	As children **revise** their drafts, remind them to delete any words, phrases, or sentences that are not needed.
4 Edit	**Writing 5., Writing 6., Language 2.**	As children **edit** their writing, share with them editing strategies, such as checking for mistakes one kind at a time.
5 Publish and Present	**Writing 6., Speaking/Listening 5.**	When children are ready to **publish** their writing, have them use the Scoring Rubric to evaluate their own writing.

Alternate Pacing Plans for Unit Writing Projects

Sometimes you want to spend more time on writing – perhaps you do a **Writing Workshop.** Below you will find one- or two-week plans for the unit-level writing projects.

1-WEEK PLAN	Day 1	Day 2	Day 3	Day 4	Day 5
1 Plan and Prewrite					
2 Draft					
3 Revise					
4 Edit					
5 Publish and Present					

2-WEEK PLAN	Day 1	Day 2	Day 3	Day 4	Day 5	Day 6	Day 7	Day 8	Day 9	Day 10
1 Plan and Prewrite										
2 Draft										
3 Revise										
4 Edit										
5 Publish and Present										

Grade 2 Unit Writing Projects

UNIT WRITING PROCESS PROJECTS	
UNIT 1	Personal Narrative
UNIT 2	Directions
UNIT 3	Compare and Contrast Essay
UNIT 4	Description
UNIT 5	Persuasive Letter
UNIT 6	Research Report

UNIT 21ST CENTURY WRITING PROJECTS	
UNIT 1	Poetry Book
UNIT 2	Pen Pal E-mail
UNIT 3	Story Exchange
UNIT 4	E-Newsletter
UNIT 5	Interview
UNIT 6	Blog

You can find all of the Unit 21st Century Writing Projects in the Teacher Resources section on SuccessNet.

Research Report

Writing Prompt

Write about a tradition that is important to your school, community, or country. Find facts about your topic in books or magazines or on the Internet.

Purpose Inform

Audience People who can learn more about the tradition

INTRODUCE GENRE AND PROMPT Tell children that in this lesson they will learn about a kind of writing called a research report. A **research report** tells facts about a topic. When you write a research report, first you search for facts about a topic. Then you organize the facts and write about them.

INTRODUCE KEY FEATURES

Key Features of a Research Report

- gives information about a topic
- uses facts from several sources
- includes complete, accurate information
- presents information in an organized way

Academic Vocabulary

Research Report In a research report, the writer gathers, organizes, and writes about facts from several sources.

Introduce Genre Write the word *research* on the board. Remind children that research is searching for information about a topic. Point out that while a story can be made up, a research report contains facts. Facts are statements that can be proved to be true. Discuss with children the key features of a research report that appear on this page.

Common Core State Standards

Writing 2. Write informative/explanatory texts in which they introduce a topic, use facts and definitions to develop points, and provide a concluding statement or section. **Writing 5.** With guidance and support from adults and peers, focus on a topic and strengthen writing as needed by revising and editing. **Writing 6.** With guidance and support from adults, use a variety of digital tools to produce and publish writing, including in collaboration with peers. **Writing 7.** Participate in shared research and writing projects (e.g., read a number of books on a single topic to produce a report; record science observations). **Writing 8.** Recall information from experiences or gather information from provided sources to answer a question.

Academic Vocabulary

prewrite to think of and organize ideas for writing

Plan and Prewrite

Mini-Lesson Reading Like a Writer

■ **Examine Model Text** Let's look at an example of a research report. Display and read aloud to children "Martin Luther King, Jr., Day" on Writing Transparency WP31. Point out the three paragraphs and the indentation at the beginning of each paragraph. Note that each paragraph begins with a sentence that tells its main idea, which is followed by sentences that give details about the main idea. Encourage children to identify facts that the writer presents in the report. Remind them that accurate facts are important in a research report.

Martin Luther King, Jr., Day

Martin Luther King, Jr., was an important African American leader. He believed that all Americans should have the same rights. He made speeches, wrote books, and led peaceful marches. After King was killed in 1968, many people wanted a holiday to honor him.

In 1983, Congress said that Martin Luther King, Jr., Day would be celebrated on the third Monday in January. The first Martin Luther King, Jr., Day was on January 20, 1986.

A national holiday is a great honor. The birthdays of only two Americans have been made national holidays. King was the second person, but do you know who the first person was? It was George Washington. He was our first President.

Unit 6 Research Report • PLAN and PREWRITE Writing Process 31

Writing Transparency WP31, TR DVD

■ **Evaluate Model Text** Display "Traits of a Good Research Report" on Writing Transparency WP32. Discuss each trait with children. First read the name of the trait and remind them what it means. Then read aloud the statement, explaining any unfamiliar words. Finally, help children understand how the statement applies to the model research report.

Traits of a Good Research Report

Focus/Ideas	Report sticks to the topic and gives facts.
Organization	Writer organizes related facts into paragraphs and begins each paragraph with an important idea.
Voice	Report is interesting. Writer has learned about the topic.
Word Choice	Writer uses powerful words. (In the model report, they include *rights*, *peaceful*, and *honor*.)
Sentences	Writer uses short and long sentences.
Conventions	Writer uses good grammar, capitalization, and spelling.

Unit 6 Research Report • PLAN and PREWRITE Writing Process 32

Writing Transparency WP32, TR DVD

GENERATE IDEAS FOR WRITING Reread the writing prompt on page WP•1 to children. Explain that now is the time to **prewrite,** or generate, choose, and organize ideas for writing. The writing prompt asks you to write about a tradition that is important to your school, community, or country. A research report would be a good genre to choose for this. You can research your topic and use facts and information to write about it.

USE RANGE OF STRATEGIES Encourage children to generate ideas for their research reports using these strategies:

- ✔ In small groups, share traditions they have experienced and enjoyed.
- ✔ Look through books and magazines and search the Internet to find out about traditions they might use as their topics.
- ✔ Make a list of as many topics as possible. Circle their best ideas.

Follow school policies regarding Internet use. Direct children, in order to ensure safety.

Corrective feedback	**If...** children have difficulty thinking of a tradition to write about, **then...** provide books about traditions and encourage children to look through them for ideas.

NARROW TOPIC Now that you have thought of several topics, you need to choose one topic. Help children look closely at each of their topics and think about whether it is the best topic for their research report.

Tell children that during their search for information, they need to take careful notes and record their sources. Discuss the example note below. Point out that a book title is either underlined or put in italics, while a story title is put in quotation marks.

James Naismith was a PE teacher in Springfield, Massachusetts.	**Author:** Cordoba, Maria **Title:** <u>The Father of Basketball</u> **Publisher/Year:** Peppercorn Press, 2008 **Page:** 10

Write Guy *by Jeff Anderson*

Use Mentor Text

Ask children to look back at the unit selection *Red, White, and Blue: The Story of the American Flag.* Point out that before writing this book, the author had to find information about the flag. Invite children to find some of the facts the author included in the book. Explain that searching for information about a topic is called research. Tell children that they will search for information about a tradition before they write their research report.

Access for All

SI Strategic Intervention

Alternative Writing Prompt Think about a game you and your friends or family enjoy playing. Draw a picture showing you and others playing the game. Write a paragraph that describes what is happening in the picture.

A Advanced

Alternative Writing Prompt Write a research report about a tradition (food, celebration, game, clothing, music) in another country or culture that is new to you. Use three sources to find out about the tradition. Describe the tradition, tell about its history, and explain why people follow it.

Common Core State Standards

Writing 2. Write informative/explanatory texts in which they introduce a topic, use facts and definitions to develop points, and provide a concluding statement or section. **Writing 5.** With guidance and support from adults and peers, focus on a topic and strengthen writing as needed by revising and editing. **Writing 6.** With guidance and support from adults, use a variety of digital tools to produce and publish writing, including in collaboration with peers. **Writing 7.** Participate in shared research and writing projects (e.g., read a number of books on a single topic to produce a report; record science observations). **Writing 8.** Recall information from experiences or gather information from provided sources to answer a question.

1 Plan and Prewrite

Mini-Lesson Planning a First Draft

- **Use a K-W-L Chart** Display Writing Transparency WP33 and read it aloud to children.

  Think Aloud I wrote notes about basketball's early history on this chart. I wrote what I know about my topic in the K column. I wrote questions I wanted to answer in the W column. When I found and learned the answers, I wrote them in the L column. I wrote my notes in sentences. Now I can use them when I start to write the first draft of my research report.

- Have children use the K-W-L Chart graphic organizer *on Reader's and Writer's Notebook,* page 573 to help them sequence their ideas for their research report. Before you begin writing, decide what you know and what you want to know about your topic. Find and write the answers to your question. Use your notes to write sentences for your report.

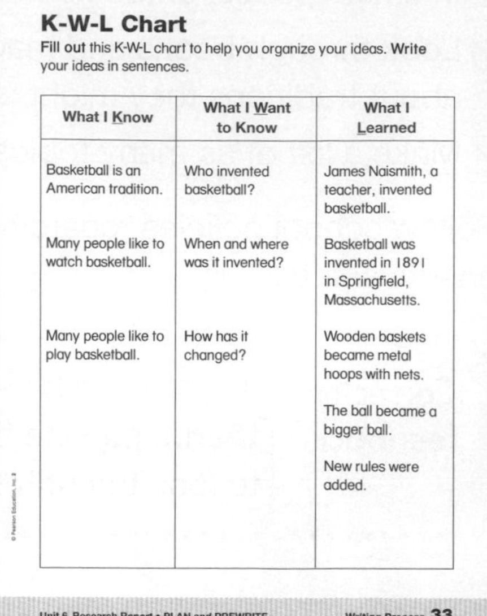

K-W-L Chart

Fill out this K-W-L chart to help you organize your ideas. **Write** your ideas in sentences.

What I Know	What I Want to Know	What I Learned
Basketball is an American tradition.	Who invented basketball?	James Naismith, a teacher, invented basketball.
Many people like to watch basketball.	When and where was it invented?	Basketball was invented in 1891 in Springfield, Massachusetts.
Many people like to play basketball.	How has it changed?	Wooden baskets became metal hoops with nets. The ball became a bigger ball. New rules were added.

Unit 6 Research Report • PLAN and PREWRITE Writing Process 33

Writing Transparency WP33, TR DVD

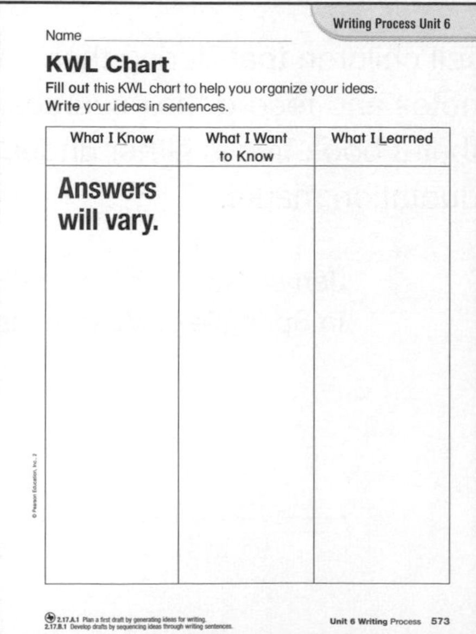

Writing Process Unit 6

Name ____________

KWL Chart

Fill out this KWL chart to help you organize your ideas. **Write** your ideas in sentences.

What I Know	What I Want to Know	What I Learned
Answers will vary.		

2.17.A.1 Plan a first draft by generating ideas for writing.
2.17.B.1 Develop drafts by sequencing ideas through writing sentences.

Unit 6 Writing Process 573

Reader's and Writer's Notebook, p. 573

Draft

DISPLAY RUBRIC Display Scoring Rubric WP6 from the *Teacher Resources DVD-ROM.* Read aloud and discuss with children the traits and criteria that you choose. Encourage children to think about these criteria as they develop drafts of their research reports. Tell them that rubrics such as this one are often used to evaluate and score writing.

Scoring Rubric Research Report

	4	3	2	1
Focus/Ideas	Reader learns many facts about the topic	Reader learns some facts about the topic	Reader learns few facts about the topic	Reader learns nothing about the topic
Organization	Ideas clearly grouped in paragraphs	Ideas grouped in paragraphs	Some ideas grouped in paragraphs	Ideas not organized; no paragraphs
Voice	Clearly shows that you know the topic	Shows a little that you know the topic	Does not show very well that you know the topic	Does not show that you know the topic
Word Choice	Uses transition words and phrases	Uses some transition words and phrases	Uses few transition words or phrases	No transition words or phrases
Sentences	Sentences clear, complete, not all alike; no run-ons	Sentences clear, complete; no run-ons	Some sentences not complete or clear; several run-ons	Sentences not complete or clear; many run-ons
Conventions	Uses good punctuation and grammar	Uses fair punctuation and grammar	Uses poor punctuation and grammar	Uses very poor punctuation and grammar

PREPARE TO DRAFT Have children look at the K-W-L charts they worked on earlier. Ask them whether they have found enough information to make an interesting report. If they have not, encourage children to look for more to add to their charts. Use your K-W-L chart as you **draft** your research report. You will have a chance to revise your draft later.

Corrective feedback **If...** children do not understand how the Scoring Rubric can be used to evaluate writing,
then... show them how you can use the Scoring Rubric to evaluate and score one or more traits of the model research report on Writing Transparency WP31.

Access for All

SI Strategic Intervention

Plan a First Draft Let children dictate to you what they want to say in their research reports. Take notes they can use for their reports. Circle words that could supply a focus for each paragraph.

Academic Vocabulary

draft to write a rough copy

Prepare to Draft As children gather information for their research reports, guide them to books, magazines, and possibly Web sites that offer comprehension support through features such as detailed photographs or illustrations, labeled diagrams, and strong picture/text correspondence.

Common Core State Standards

Writing 2. Write informative/explanatory texts in which they introduce a topic, use facts and definitions to develop points, and provide a concluding statement or section. **Writing 5.** With guidance and support from adults and peers, focus on a topic and strengthen writing as needed by revising and editing. **Writing 7.** Participate in shared research and writing projects (e.g., read a number of books on a single topic to produce a report; record science observations).

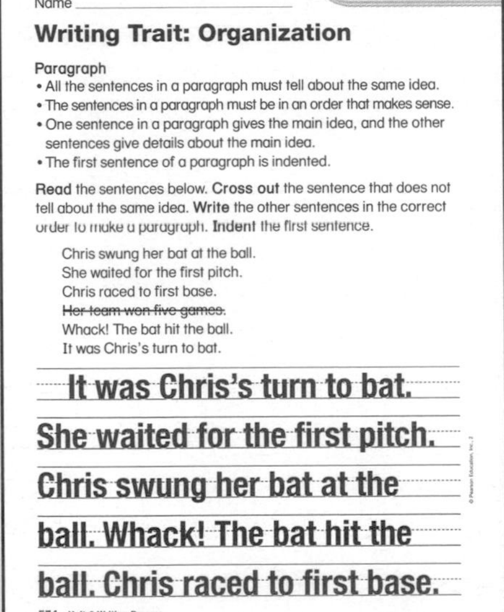

Writing Process Unit 6

Name

Writing Trait: Organization

Paragraph

- All the sentences in a paragraph must tell about the same idea.
- The sentences in a paragraph must be in an order that makes sense.
- One sentence in a paragraph gives the main idea, and the other sentences give details about the main idea.
- The first sentence of a paragraph is indented.

Read the sentences below. **Cross out** the sentence that does not tell about the same idea. **Write** the other sentences in the correct order to make a paragraph. **Indent** the first sentence.

Chris swung her bat at the ball.
She waited for the first pitch.
Chris raced to first base.
~~Her team won five games.~~
Whack! The bat hit the ball.
It was Chris's turn to bat.

It was Chris's turn to bat. She waited for the first pitch. Chris swung her bat at the ball. Whack! The bat hit the ball. Chris raced to first base.

574 Unit 6 Writing Process

Reader's and Writer's Notebook, p. 574

Draft

Mini-Lesson Writing Trait: Organization

- **Write Paragraphs** Tell children that the sentences in a paragraph must tell about the same idea and be in an order that makes sense. Write the following paragraph on the board. Read it aloud. Ask children what order the sentences should be in. (2, 4, 1, 3)

  He was killed in 1968. Dr. King was an African American leader. Today we celebrate his memory. He spent his life working for equal rights.

  Point out that the first sentence in a paragraph should be indented. This tells readers, "A new paragraph begins here."

- Have children use *Reader's and Writer's Notebook,* page 574 to work with sentences in a paragraph.

DEVELOP DRAFT Remind children that when they write their first drafts, they want to get their ideas down on paper. Suggest that they try these drafting strategies:

✔ Divide a sheet of paper into thirds and in each section write the facts that go together. Use the facts to write three paragraphs.

✔ Recognize that they will likely find more facts than they will use. Choose the best facts to include in their draft.

Have children write the research report. If possible, allow them to type their drafts in a word processing program.

Revise

Mini-Lesson Writer's Craft: Deleting Words, Phrases, or Sentences

- Explain to children that when writers **revise,** they may delete, or take out, words, phrases, or sentences. They delete words that have the same meaning as other words, phrases that are not needed, and sentences that are not about the topic. Discuss with children which sentence does not belong in this paragraph:

  Flutes belong in the woodwind family. Trumpets are in the brass family. I want to learn to play the trumpet. Drums are part of the percussion family. (third sentence)

- Have children use *Reader's and Writer's Notebook,* page 575 to practice deleting words, phrases, or sentences.

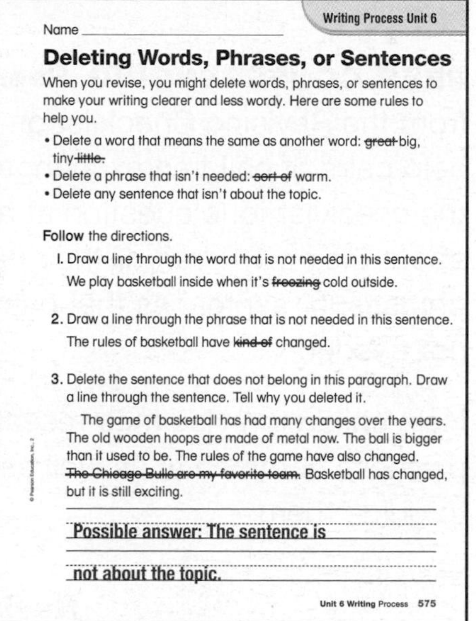

Writing Process Unit 6

Name ______

Deleting Words, Phrases, or Sentences

When you revise, you might delete words, phrases, or sentences to make your writing clearer and less wordy. Here are some rules to help you.

- Delete a word that means the same as another word: ~~great~~ big, tiny ~~little.~~
- Delete a phrase that isn't needed: ~~sort of~~ warm.
- Delete any sentence that isn't about the topic.

Follow the directions.

1. Draw a line through the word that is not needed in this sentence.
   We play basketball inside when it's ~~freezing~~ cold outside.
2. Draw a line through the phrase that is not needed in this sentence.
   The rules of basketball have ~~kind of~~ changed.
3. Delete the sentence that does not belong in this paragraph. Draw a line through the sentence. Tell why you deleted it.
   The game of basketball has had many changes over the years. The old wooden hoops are made of metal now. The ball is bigger than it used to be. The rules of the game have also changed. ~~The Chicago Bulls are my favorite team.~~ Basketball has changed, but it is still exciting.
   Possible answer: The sentence is not about the topic.

Unit 6 Writing Process 575

Reader's and Writer's Notebook, p. 575

REVISE MODEL Use Writing Transparency WP34 to model how to revise a research report. In the first paragraph, I deleted the third sentence because it wasn't about the topic. I combined three choppy sentences that began with the same word to make one longer, smoother-sounding sentence. In the second paragraph, I deleted the phrase *a lot of* because it wasn't needed. It made the sentence too wordy.

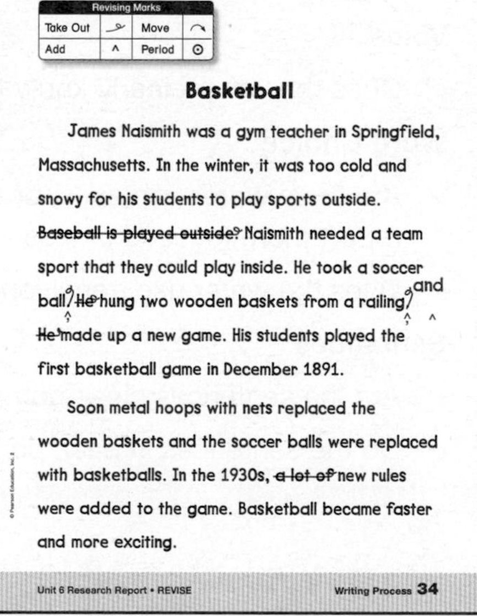

Revising Marks			
Take Out		Move	
Add	^	Period	⊙

Basketball

James Naismith was a gym teacher in Springfield, Massachusetts. In the winter, it was too cold and snowy for his students to play sports outside. ~~Baseball is played outside.~~ Naismith needed a team sport that they could play inside. He took a soccer ball, ~~He~~ hung two wooden baskets from a railing, and ~~He~~ made up a new game. His students played the first basketball game in December 1891.

Soon metal hoops with nets replaced the wooden baskets and the soccer balls were replaced with basketballs. In the 1930s, ~~a lot of~~ new rules were added to the game. Basketball became faster and more exciting.

Unit 6 Research Report • REVISE Writing Process 34

Writing Transparency WP34, TR DVD

Revising Tip

Suggest that children look for and fix these problems as they revise their draft: *run-on sentences* (make them into two separate sentences); *too many short, choppy sentences* (combine two that are related with a comma and a word such as *and, but,* or *or* to make a compound sentence); *weak connections between ideas or events* (add transition words and phrases such as *now, next, later, first,* and *after that*).

Academic Vocabulary

revise to change and improve a written work

ELL

Revise for Word Choice To help children find specific words to use in their reports, work with them to develop topical word webs that include vivid adjectives and strong verbs. Suggest that they look in bilingual or children's dictionaries for possible words.

Common Core State Standards

Writing 2. Write informative/explanatory texts in which they introduce a topic, use facts and definitions to develop points, and provide a concluding statement or section. **Writing 5.** With guidance and support from adults and peers, focus on a topic and strengthen writing as needed by revising and editing. **Writing 6.** With guidance and support from adults, use a variety of digital tools to produce and publish writing, including in collaboration with peers. **Language 2.** Demonstrate command of the conventions of standard English capitalization, punctuation, and spelling when writing.

Revise

REVISE DRAFT We have written first drafts of our research reports. Now we will revise our drafts. When we revise, we try to make our writing clearer and more interesting to read.

PEER CONFERENCING Peer Revision Write the questions that you choose from the Revising Checklist on the board. If you elect to use peer revision, help pairs of children exchange and read each other's drafts. Read aloud the checklist, one question at a time. Ask children to answer each question about their own draft or their partner's draft. Remind them to look for words, phrases, or sentences that can be deleted because they are not on topic or not needed.

Help children revise their research reports using their own ideas or their partner's comments, as well as what they have learned about research reports to guide them.

Revising Checklist

Focus/Ideas

✔ Does the research report stick to the topic?

✔ Are the facts complete and accurate?

Organization

✔ Does the writer organize the facts into paragraphs?

Voice

✔ Does the writer clearly know the topic?

Word Choice

✔ Are there words, phrases, or sentences the writer could delete to make the report more focused or less wordy?

✔ Does the writer use transition words and phrases?

Sentences

✔ Are the sentences clear, complete, and not all alike?

✔ Do the sentences in each paragraph tell about the same idea?

Edit

Mini-Lesson Editing Strategy: One Thing at a Time

■ Explain this editing strategy to children: **Proofread** for one kind of mistake at a time. First, look for spelling errors, then look for capitalization and punctuation errors, and last, look for grammar errors. Model this strategy using Writing Transparency WP35. If you elect to teach proofreading marks, explain what they mean and how they are used as you discuss the errors on the transparency. First, I look for spelling errors. *Thayd* should be the contraction *They'd.* Then I look for missing capital letters, but there are none. I look for incorrect or missing punctuation. The first sentence needs a comma because it is a compound sentence. There should be closing quotation marks after *Naismith* in the last sentence. Last, I look for grammar errors. *More faster* is incorrect; *more* should be deleted. I have one more correction. I should begin a new paragraph at the fourth sentence.

Proofreading Marks			
Take Out		Uppercase letter	≡
Add	^	Lowercase letter	/
Period	⊙	New paragraph	¶
Check spelling	◯	Insert apostrophe	✓

Soon metal hoops with nets replaced the wooden baskets, and the soccer balls were replaced with basketballs. In the 1930s, ~~a lot of~~ new rules were added to the game. Basketball became ~~more~~ faster and more exciting. ¶Today people around the world watch basketball or play it. ~~Thayd~~ They'd like to say, "Thank you, James Naismith."

Unit 6 Research Report • EDIT Writing Process 35

Writing Transparency WP35, TR DVD

■ Help children **edit** their own drafts. Provide a simple rubric to guide children. Have them check their spelling, grammar, punctuation, and capitalization. If children have used a word processing program to produce their drafts, have them print out and edit their drafts on paper and then make the edits to the draft in the program.

Technology Tips

Children who type their research reports on computers may find this tip useful as they edit:

✔ For reports that are longer than one page, use the header or footer feature to put in page numbers and other identifying information.

Access for All

A Advanced

Apply Revising Skills As they revise their work, children can consider ways to improve it.

- Avoid wordiness by using few words to say what they want to say.
- Make sure the sentences in each paragraph are in a logical order.
- Replace weak or vague words with strong verbs and vivid adjectives.

Academic Vocabulary

proofread to check writing for mistakes in grammar and conventions

edit to prepare for publishing by correcting errors and checking facts

Write Guy *by Jeff Anderson*

Let Me Check My Lists

By this point in the school year, children have probably been compiling lists of words for a variety of reasons. Encourage them to bring out and review their word lists when they are writing or revising their reports so that they can incorporate some of the words into their writing.

ELL

Support Editing When reviewing a child's draft, focus on ideas more than errors. If you find consistent spelling errors, choose one or two skills for attention during editing. Reinforce the skills with the appropriate lessons in the *ELL Handbook.*

Common Core State Standards

Writing 6. With guidance and support from adults, use a variety of digital tools to produce and publish writing, including in collaboration with peers. **Speaking/Listening 5.** Create audio recordings of stories or poems; add drawings or other visual displays to stories or recounts of experiences when appropriate to clarify ideas, thoughts, and feelings.

Academic Vocabulary

publish to prepare and share a final draft of writing with others

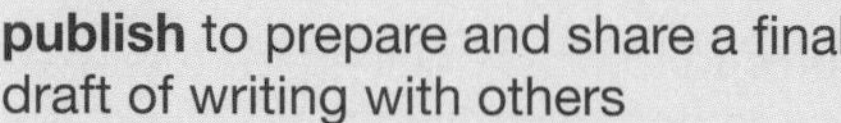

5 Publish and Present

OPTIONS FOR PRESENTING After children have revised and edited their research report, have them write a final draft. If children have produced their report in a word processing program, have them print out a copy. Offer them two ways to present, or **publish,** their work:

Add illustrations to support ideas in the report and make a class book to put in the reading center.	Read aloud their reports in small groups and explain why they chose their topics. Use illustrations to support the oral presentation.

Mini-Lesson Evaluating Writing

- Prepare children to fill out a Self-Evaluation Guide about their research report. Display and read aloud Writing Transparency WP36. Model the self-evaluation process.

  Think Aloud In my research report, I organized my facts in paragraphs. The sentences in my paragraphs are arranged in a logical order and are focused on the topic. I would mark *Yes* for numbers 1, 2, and 3. I like the sentence *Basketball became faster and more exciting.* If I could write the report again, I would tell what things made the game faster and more exciting.

- Have children complete the Self-Evaluation Guide on *Reader's and Writer's Notebook,* page 576 to evaluate their research reports. They can save their Self-Evaluation Guides and their work in a portfolio to monitor their development as writers. Encourage them to build on their skills and to note areas to improve.

Basketball

James Naismith was a gym teacher in Springfield, Massachusetts. In the winter, it was too cold and snowy for his students to play sports outside. Naismith needed a team sport that they could play inside. He took a soccer ball, hung two wooden baskets from a railing, and made up a new game. His students played the first basketball game in December 1891.

Soon metal hoops with nets replaced the wooden baskets, and the soccer balls were replaced with basketballs. In the 1930s, new rules were added to the game. Basketball became faster and more exciting.

Today people around the world watch basketball or play it. They'd like to say, "Thank you, James Naismith."

Unit 6 Research Report • PUBLISH Writing Process 36

Writing Transparency WP36, TR DVD

Writing Process Unit 6

Name ________________

Self-Evaluation Guide

Check **Yes** or **No** about paragraphs in your research report.

	Yes	No
1. I organized my facts in paragraphs.		
2. The sentences in my paragraphs are in an order that makes sense.		
3. The sentences in each paragraph tell about the same idea.		

Answer the questions.

4. What is the best part of your research report?

Answers will vary.

5. What is one thing you would change about this research report if you could write it again?

Answers will vary.

576 Unit 6 Writing Process • Evaluate the final writing product.

Reader's and Writer's Notebook, p. 576

Looking for Teacher Resources and other important information?

Go online to  Pearson SuccessNet

In the *First Stop* on Reading Street, you will find the following information.

- Research into Practice on Reading Street
- Guide to Reading Street
- Assessment on Reading Street
- Customize Writing on Reading Street
- Small Group Instruction on Reading Street
- ELL on Reading Street
- Customize Literacy on Reading Street
- 21st Century Skills on Reading Street
- Teacher Resources for Grade 2
- Index

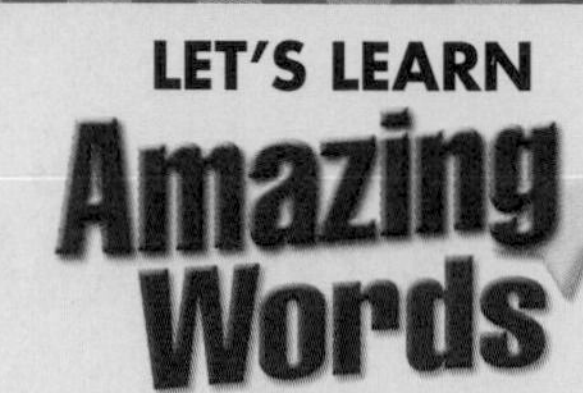

Oral Vocabulary for

Just Like Josh Gibson

Oral Vocabulary Routine

DAY 1		
challenge	1	**Introduce** A *challenge* is a task that is difficult to do.
	2	**Demonstrate** Learning to speak Spanish was a *challenge* for me. Skiing down the tallest mountain was a *challenge.*
	3	**Apply** What task would be a *challenge* for you?
	4	**Display the Word** Identify the sound-spelling for initial *ch*/ch/. Identify the sound-spelling for *g*/j/ in the second syllable.
effort	1	**Introduce** When you make an *effort* to do something, you are trying hard.
	2	**Demonstrate** Running a mile takes *effort.* Sounding out new words takes *effort.*
	3	**Apply** When have you made an *effort* to do something? Tell what you did. Use the word *effort* when you tell about it.
	4	**Display the Word** Identify the *r*-controlled vowel sound /ər/ spelled *or* in *effort.*

DAY 4		
professional	1	**Introduce** A person who has a *professional* job is being paid for his or her skill and training.
	2	**Demonstrate** Teaching school is a *professional* job. A newspaper reporter is a *professional* writer.
	3	**Apply** Would you prefer to have your hair cut by a *professional* haircutter or a friend? Why?
	4	**Display the Word** Run your hand under the four chunks, *pro-fes-sion-al,* as you read the word aloud.
shortstop	1	**Introduce** A *shortstop* is a baseball player who covers the field between second base and third base.
	2	**Demonstrate** The *shortstop* caught the ball and threw it to third base. The ball went over the head of the *shortstop.*
	3	**Apply** If a *shortstop* uses any of the things I name, say *shortstop:* a uniform, a football, a mitt, a cap, swim fins, an oar.
	4	**Display the Word** Point out the words *short* and *stop* that make up the compound word *shortstop.*

Oral Vocabulary for **Red, White, and Blue: The Story of the American Flag**

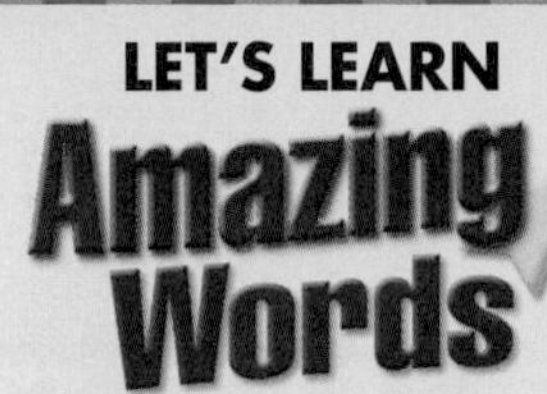

Oral Vocabulary Routine

DAY 1	independence	1 **Introduce** *Independence* means "freedom to make your own decisions." 2 **Demonstrate** The early settlers in America won *independence* from Great Britain. Americans celebrate their *independence* on the Fourth of July. 3 **Apply** Why would people feel that their *independence* is important? 4 **Display the Word** Run your hand under the four syllables, *in-de-pend-ence,* as you read the word aloud.
	symbol	1 **Introduce** A *symbol* is a sign, a mark, or an object that stands for something else. 2 **Demonstrate** The U.S. flag is a *symbol* for our country. We drew happy faces on a picture graph as *symbols* for people. 3 **Apply** What might a weather person use as a *symbol* for rainy weather? 4 **Display the Word** Point out the sound-spelling *y/i/* in the word's first syllable.
DAY 2	unfurl	1 **Introduce** When you *unfurl* something, you unroll it or spread it out. 2 **Demonstrate** I watched the man *unfurl* the sail on his boat. We *unfurled* the flag for the parade. 3 **Apply** Show me how to *unfurl* this folded piece of cloth. 4 **Display the Word** Have children decode *unfurl.*
DAY 4	indivisible	1 **Introduce** Something that is *indivisible* cannot be separated into parts. 2 **Demonstrate** The United States is an *indivisible* country. An *indivisible* country may have many states, but it is only one country. 3 **Apply** Is a jigsaw puzzle *indivisible?* Why or why not? 4 **Display the Word** Run your hand under the five syllables, *in-di-vis-i-ble,* as you read the word aloud.

LET'S LEARN Amazing Words

Oral Vocabulary for
A Birthday Basket for Tía

Oral Vocabulary Routine

DAY 1

custom

1. **Introduce** A *custom* is something people always do in a certain way or have done for a long time.
2. **Demonstrate** It is the *custom* of many Americans to eat turkey on Thanksgiving Day. It is a *custom* for some people to eat with chopsticks.
3. **Apply** What is an American *custom* you might see on the Fourth of July?
4. **Display the Word** Point out that the syllables of *custom* divide between the *s* and *t.*

tradition

1. **Introduce** A *tradition* is a custom or belief that is handed down from parents to children.
2. **Demonstrate** It is a *tradition* in my family for parents to name children after relatives. Singing holiday carols is a *tradition* in some families.
3. **Apply** Tell about something that is a *tradition* for your family. Use the word *tradition* when you tell about it.
4. **Display the Word** Identify the syllable *-tion* as you read the word aloud.

DAY 4

angle

1. **Introduce** The way you look at something is the *angle* from which you see it.
2. **Demonstrate** The seats were on the side of the theater at a bad *angle,* so we couldn't see the screen very well.
3. **Apply** What is the best *angle* in the classroom to see the board? Explain.
4. **Display the Word** Run your hand under the two word parts *an-gle* as you read the word aloud.

snapshot

1. **Introduce** A *snapshot* is a simple picture taken with a camera.
2. **Demonstrate** I looked surprised in the *snapshot* Dad took. Mom took a *snapshot* of the butterfly before it flew away.
3. **Apply** What is something you have seen in a *snapshot?*
4. **Display the Word** Point out the words *snap* and *shot* that make up the compound word *snapshot.*

Oral Vocabulary for Cowboys

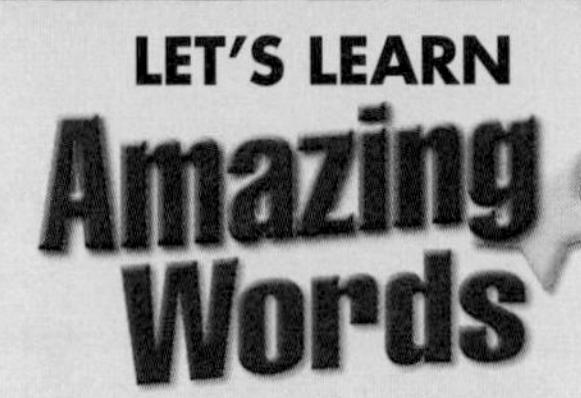

Oral Vocabulary Routine

DAY 1

livestock

1. **Introduce** Farm animals, such as cows or chickens, are called *livestock.*
2. **Demonstrate** Horses, pigs, and cows are *livestock.* Some farmers take their *livestock* to a county fair.
3. **Apply** If any of the animals I name are *livestock,* say *livestock:* deer, sheep, hens, wolves, cattle, goats, camels.
4. **Display the Word** Point out the words *live* and *stock* that make up the compound word *livestock.*

occupation

1. **Introduce** An *occupation* is the work or business a person does to earn a living.
2. **Demonstrate** Taking care of sick animals is a veterinarian's *occupation.* A waiter's *occupation* is serving meals.
3. **Apply** What is a detective's *occupation?*
4. **Display the Word** Point out the syllable *-tion* as you read the word aloud.

DAY 2

drover

1. **Introduce** A *drover* is a person who guides a large number of cattle along a trail.
2. **Demonstrate** A *drover* chased after the calf that ran away. A *drover* will herd cattle on horseback.
3. **Apply** Do you think a *drover* has an easy occupation or a difficult occupation? Explain.
4. **Display the Word** Identify the sound-spelling of the consonant blend *dr*/d//r/ and the long vowel *o* sound in *drover.*

DAY 4

rawhide

1. **Introduce** *Rawhide* is the animal hide that has not been made into leather.
2. **Demonstrate** The rancher hung the heavy bell on the porch with a strip of *rawhide.* Some dog toys are made of *rawhide.*
3. **Apply** Do you think *rawhide* is a strong material or a weak material? Explain.
4. **Display the Word** Point out the words *raw* and *hide* that make up the compound word *rawhide.*

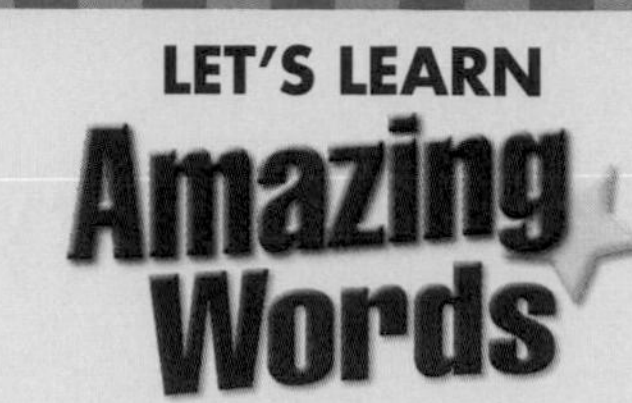

Oral Vocabulary for
Grace for President

Oral Vocabulary Routine

DAY 1	culture	1 **Introduce** The customs, arts, and ideas of a particular group of people are their *culture.* 2 **Demonstrate** In the *culture* of the Native American people called the Navajo, weaving rugs is important. The *culture* of Italy includes eating pasta and listening to opera music. 3 **Apply** Name three things that are part of American *culture.* 4 **Display the Word** Pronounce the word several times as you run your hand under its two syllables, *cul-ture.*
	festival	1 **Introduce** A *festival* is an entertaining celebration usually held every year. 2 **Demonstrate** We went to a music *festival* in the city. I enjoyed the dancing at a Greek *festival* in my neighborhood. 3 **Apply** Would you prefer to go to a *festival* or a museum? Why? 4 **Display the Word** Divide the word into syllables, *fes-ti-val,* emphasizing that the first and second syllables are divided bewteen the *s* and *t,* so the *s* and *t* do not form a consonant blend in the word.
DAY 4	multicolored	1 **Introduce** Something that is *multicolored* has many colors in it. 2 **Demonstrate** The man was wearing a *multicolored* necktie. My cat has *multicolored* fur. 3 **Apply** Name something in our classroom that is *multicolored.* 4 **Display the Word** Run your hand under the four syllables, *mul-ti-col-ored,* as you read the word aloud.
	sash	1 **Introduce** A *sash* is a long strip of cloth that a person wears. 2 **Demonstrate** The dancer wore a red *sash* around his waist. The woman wore a blue *sash* over a shoulder. 3 **Apply** Draw a quick picture of someone wearing a *sash.* 4 **Display the Word** Point out the consonant digraph *sh*/sh/ at the end of *sash.* Have children decode the word.

Teacher's Edition

Text

KWL Strategy: The KWL Interactive Reading Strategy was developed and is used by permission of Donna Ogle, National-Louis University, Skokie, Illinois, co-author of *Reading Today and Tomorrow,* Holt, Rinehart & Winston Publishers, 1988. (See also the *Reading Teacher,* February 1986, pp. 564–570.)

Photographs

Cover (C) ©Jupiterimages/Getty Images, (TR) ©Kim Karpeles/Alamy Images, (TC) ©lassendesignen/Fotolia, (TL) TongRo Image Stock, (BC) ©Benshot/Fotolia

Every effort has been made to secure permission and provide appropriate credit for photographic material. The publisher deeply regrets any omission and pledges to correct errors called to its attention in subsequent editions.

Unless otherwise acknowledged, all photographs are the property of Pearson Education, Inc.

Student Edition

Student Edition, p. 548

Student Edition, p. 549

TEACHER NOTES

TEACHER NOTES

TEACHER NOTES

TEACHER NOTES

TEACHER NOTES

TEACHER NOTES

TEACHER NOTES

Looking for Teacher Resources and other important information?

Go online to  Pearson SuccessNet

In the *First Stop* on Reading Street, you will find the following information.

- Research into Practice on Reading Street
- Guide to Reading Street
- Assessment on Reading Street
- Customize Writing on Reading Street
- Small Group Instruction on Reading Street
- ELL on Reading Street
- Customize Literacy on Reading Street
- 21st Century Skills on Reading Street
- Teacher Resources for Grade 2
- Index

Looking for Teacher Resources and other important information?

Go online to  Pearson SuccessNet

In the *First Stop* on Reading Street, you will find the following information.

- Research into Practice on Reading Street
- Guide to Reading Street
- Assessment on Reading Street
- Customize Writing on Reading Street
- Small Group Instruction on Reading Street
- ELL on Reading Street
- Customize Literacy on Reading Street
- 21st Century Skills on Reading Street
- Teacher Resources for Grade 2
- Index